U0920618

宁波2014统计年鉴

Ningbo Statistical YearBook

宁波市统计局 NINGBO MUNICIPAL STATISTICS BUREAU
国家统计局宁波调查队 STATE STATISTICAL BUREAU NINGBO INVESTIGATION TEAM 编

中国统计出版社
China Statistics Press

图书在版编目(CIP)数据

宁波统计年鉴. 2014 / 宁波市统计局, 国家统计局宁波调查队编. -- 北京 : 中国统计出版社, 2014.8
ISBN 978-7-5037-7154-5

Ⅰ. ①宁… Ⅱ. ①宁… ②国… Ⅲ. ①统计资料—宁波市—2014—年鉴 Ⅳ. ①C832.553-54

中国版本图书馆 CIP 数据核字(2014)第 172155 号

宁波统计年鉴-2014

作　　者/ 宁波市统计局 国家统计局宁波调查队
责任编辑/ 陈越月 徐霞欢 朱 惠
装帧设计/ 赵 阳
出版发行/ 中国统计出版社
通信地址/ 北京市丰台区西三环南路甲 6 号 邮政编码/100073
电　　话/ 邮购(010)63376909 书店(010)68783171
网　　址/ http://csp.stats.gov.cn
印　　刷/ 宁波银行印刷厂
经　　销/ 新华书店
开　　本/ 890mm×1240mm 1/16
字　　数/ 1013 千字
印　　张/ 29.6
版　　别/ 2014 年 8 月第 1 版
版　　次/ 2014 年 8 月第 1 次印刷
定　　价/ 368 元

本书附同版本 CD-ROM 一张，光盘内容以书面文字为准。
如有印装差错，由本社发行部调换。

编者说明

一、《宁波统计年鉴—2014》以大量统计数据，全面、系统地反映了2013年宁波经济、科技、社会各方面的发展情况，是一本信息密集的资料性年刊和工具书。本年鉴采用中英文排版方式。

二、《宁波统计年鉴—2014》在内容编排顺序上做了调整，本年鉴内容包括：

1.2013年宁波市国民经济和社会发展概况；2.综合；3.人口与劳动力；4.国民经济核算；5.财政、金融、保险、证券；6.物价指数、人民生活；7.农业；8.工业、能源消费和电力；9.固定资产投资和建筑业；10.港口、交通运输、邮电业；11.国内贸易、餐饮业；12.对外经济、旅游；13.文化、教育、卫生、体育、科学；14.市政、环保、民政、政法及其他；15.企业景气等十五个部分。为方便读者使用，各篇章前设有《主要统计指标》，篇末附有《主要统计指标解释》。

三、《宁波统计年鉴—2014》辑入的统计数据，以2013年年报为主，考虑到读者使用，年鉴中还列示了1978年改革开放以来历年的主要统计数据，这些统计数据已重新予以核实，凡以往发表过的统计数据与本年鉴有出入的，均以本年鉴为准。

四、《宁波统计年鉴—2014》在编辑中作如下规定，以使读者在使用时明了：

1、凡有注解均注在第一张表的下方。

2、"?"示之，表示有数据但不足计量单位中的最小数，故不再列数；凡在表内显示"空格"的，表示该项统计数据不详或无该项统计数据；显示"＃"表示其中的主要项。

五、《宁波统计年鉴—2014》辑入的统计数据，对来自非政府统计部门的，注明数据来源。

六、《宁波统计年鉴》出版以来，受到社会各界的关心、支持，不少读者对于年鉴的内容和编辑工作提出了许多宝贵的意见，对此，我们深表感谢。并欢迎读者一如既往地对年鉴的不足之处给予批评指正，以进一步提高编辑水平。

EDITOR'S NOTE

I. Ningbo Statistical Yearbook 2014 is an annual publication which provides comprehensive and systematic data covering the economic, technological and social development in Ningbo Municipality in 2013. This yearbook uses the Chinese and English mix typesetting the way.

II. This yearbook has made the adjustment in the content arrangement order. This yearbook is comprised of 15 parts including: 1.Brief Introduction of 2013 Ningbo National Economy and Social Development; 2.General Survey; 3.Population and labor force; 4.National Economic Accounting; 5.Finance, Banking, Insurance and Securities; 6.Price Index and People's Livelihood; 7.Agriculture; 8.Industry, Energy Consumption and Electricity; 9.Investment in Fixed Assets and Construction; 10.Port, Transportation, Post and Telecommunication; 11.Domestic Trade and Catering Trade; 12.Foreign Trade and Tourism; 13.Education, Culture, Public Health and Sports, Science and Technology; 14.Civil Facilities, Environmental Protection, Civil Affairs, Judicature and Others; 15.Prosperity Index on Enterprises. Major statistical indicators at the beginning of each chapter, Explanatory Notes on Main Statistical Indicators are provided at the end of each chapter.

III. The content of this yearbook are comprised of mainly the statistic of 2013 and statistical data of those key years after reform and opening to the outside world. The data in this yearbook have been already checked. If ever the readers find inconsistency of data here as compared with those in previous year books, please refer to this yearbook as accurate and final.

IV. This yearbook makes following stipulation in the edition, causes the reader to use is clear about. The footnotes are placed at the first page. Explanations on symbols used in this yearbook: "…"indicates that the data are not large enough to be rounded into the minimal unit; "space" indicates that the data is unknown or indicates the data not available; "#" indicates major item in a category.

V. In this yearbook, to come from the non- statistical department's statistical data, dedicates the data origin.

VI. Here we'd like to express our sincere thanks to the readers who have provided us so many invaluable suggestions on content selection and compilation of the yearbook. Our thanks also go to those friends in all circles of society who have shown their support and care to the publication of the yearbook. We welcome any suggestions and comments from readers at large so as to help us to further improve our work of compilation.

目 录
CONTENTS

第一篇 综 合 CHAPTER 1 GENERAL SURVEY

第二篇 人口与劳动力 CHAPTER 2 POPULATION AND LABOR FORCE

第三篇 国民经济核算 CHAPTER 3 NATIONAL ECONOMIC ACCOUNTING

第四篇 财政、金融、保险、证券 CHAPTER 4 FINANCE,BANKING,INSURANCE AND SECURITIES

第五篇 物价指数和人民生活 CHAPTER 5 PRICES INDEX AND PEOPLE'S LIVELIHOOD

第六篇 农 业 CHAPTER 6 AGRICULTURE

第七篇 工业、能源消费和电力 CHAPTER 7 INDUSTRY, ENERGY CONSUMPTION AND ELECTRICITY

第八篇 固定资产投资和建筑业 CHAPTER 8 INVESTMENT IN FIXED ASSETS AND CONSTRUCTION

第九篇 港口、交通、运输、邮电 CHAPTER 9 PORT,TRANSPORTATION,POST AND TELECOMMUNICATION SERVICE

第十篇 国内贸易、餐饮业 CHAPTER 10 DOMESTIC TRADE AND CATERING TRADE

第十一篇 对外经济、旅游 CHAPTER 11 FOREIGN TRADE AND TOURISM

第十二篇　文化、教育、卫生、体育、科学技术　CHAPTER 12 CULTURE, EDUCATION, PUBLIC HEALTH AND SPORTS, SCIENCE & TECHNOLOGY

第十三篇 市政、环保、民政、政法及其他 CHAPTER 13 CIVIL FACILITIES,ENVIRONMENT, CIVIL AFFAIRS,JUDICATURE AND OTHERS

第十四篇 企业景气指数 CHAPTER 14 PROSPERITY INDEX ON ENTERPRISES

2013 年宁波市国民经济和社会发展统计公报

宁波市统计局 国家统计局宁波调查队

2014 年 1 月 30 日

2013 年，面对国内外错综复杂的发展环境、频发的自然灾害特别是洪涝灾害的严重影响，全市上下牢牢把握“稳中求进、进中求好”的工作主基调，深入实施“六个加快”发展战略，着力稳增长、提效益、强创新、惠民生，经济运行总体保持了平稳增长态势，产业发展基本稳定，质量效益继续提高，创新驱动动力增强，民生福祉持续改善，为实现“两个基本”、建设“四好示范区”奠定了坚实基础。

一、综 合

地区生产总值。2013 年全市实现地区生产总值 7128.9 亿元，按可比价格计算，比上年增长 8.1%。其中，第一产业实现增加值 276.4 亿元，下降 1.2%；第二产业实现增加值 3741.7 亿元，增长 8.2%；第三产业实现增加值 3110.8 亿元，增长 8.8%。三次产业之比为 3.9 ∶ 52.5 ∶ 43.6，第三产业增加值占地区生产总值比重比上年提高 1.1 个百分点。按常住人口计算人均生产总值为 93176 元（按年平均汇率折算为 15046 美元）。

财政收支。2013 年全市完成公共财政预算收入 1651.2 亿元，比上年增长 7.5%，其中地方财政收入完成 792.8 亿元，增长 9.3%。在地方税收中，营业税、增值税、企业所得税、个人所得税分别增长 10.8%、3.0%、9.4%和 10.5%。全市完成公共财政预算支出 939.9 亿元，增长 13.5%。其中交通运输支出 71.0 亿元，增长 40.0%；节能环保支出 14.8 亿元，增长 25.2%；社会保障和就业支出 97.6 亿元，增长 23.5%；科学技术支出 37.6 亿元，增长 15.9%；农林水事务支出 80.4 亿元，增长 11.3%。认真落实中央八项规定和厉行节约反对浪费条例，大力压缩一般性支出，全年一般公共服务支出增长 4.4%，增速比上年下降 3.5 个百分点。

就业和再就业。2013 年全市新增就业人员 16.1 万，7.6 万名失业人员实现再就业，其中困难人员再就业 2.2 万。引导高校毕业生到企业、到基层就业创业，高校毕业生就业率达到 98%。职业教育校企合作公共服务平台“校企通”正式上线，全市 72 所院校加入服务平台，6100 家企业发布供求信息。积极应对洪涝灾害不利影响，及时出台扶持政策稳定就业，集中减征社保费 30 亿元，惠及企业 8.9 万家、职工 236 万人。组织农村劳动力培训 11 万人次，培训后转移就业 2.3 万人，全市已入库农村实用人才 13.5 万人，占农村劳动力总数的 4.6%。年末城镇登记失业率为 2.16%，处于历史低位水平。

市场价格。2013 年全市居民消费价格指数为 102.2%，比全国、全省平均水平分别低 0.4 和 0.1 个百分点，在全国 36 个大中城市中列第 34 位。八大类商品和服务项目价格同比涨跌呈“七升一降”格局：食品类上涨 2.6%，烟酒类上涨 0.8%，衣着类上涨 2.6%，家庭设备用品及维修服务类上涨 2.0%，医疗保健和个人用品类上涨 2.8%，娱乐教育文化用品及服务类上涨 1.9%，居住类上涨 3.5%；交通和通信类下降 0.6%。全年工业生产者购进价格指数为 96.34%，工业生产者出厂价格指数为 96.67%。12 月全市新建商品住宅销售价格环比上涨 0.5%，同比上涨 7.8%，同比涨幅居全国 70 个大中城市中第五十二位。

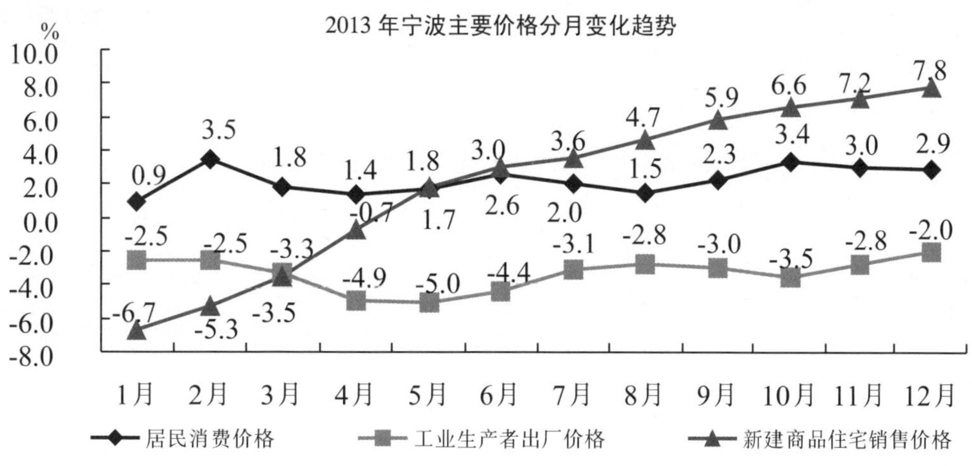

二、农业、农村

农业生产。2013年受H7N9禽流感疫情、极端高温干旱天气、“菲特”超强台风等一系列严重自然灾害的连续影响，农牧业生产损失较重，全市实现农林牧渔业总产值为429.9亿元，按可比价格计算，比上年减少1.5%。其中，完成农业产值202.3亿元，减少1.0%；林业产值11.5亿元，增长1.9%；牧业产值60.9亿元，减少9.4%；渔业产值149.0亿元，增长1.0%；农林牧渔服务业产值6.2亿元，增长3.4%。粮食作物播种面积222.9万亩，与上年持平，粮食总产量81.2万吨，同比减少6.2%。家禽生产形势依然严峻，家禽存栏、出栏同比分别减少10.4%和23.0%，禽肉总产量3.8万吨，减少24.2%。制定出台示范性家庭农场扶持办法，全年新增市级示范性家庭农场40家，全市家庭农场总数达到2754家，我市发展“家庭农场”的做法还被媒体称为全国“五大范本”之一。

新农村建设。2013年全市新增全面小康示范村46个，累计525个。加快推进农村生活垃圾和生活污水集中处理，全市农村垃圾集中处理率达到98%以上，新开展农村生活污水处理项目建设150个。全年农房“两改”共投入资金101亿元，开工改造建设农村住房10.5万户，新建成农村住房590万平方米，安置农户4.1万户。已累计实施和新启动农村集中住房建设项目185个。全年村庄整治建设共投入各类资金2.2亿元，实施项目594个，拆除危旧房22.8万平方米，外立面改造92.8万平方米，村内道路硬化29万平方米，村庄绿化19.4万平方米，60个村顺利通过验收。农家乐休闲旅游业的品牌影响力明显提升，全年农家乐休闲旅游业接待游客达到2234万人次，实现营业收入22.4亿元，同比分别增长30.6%和30.3%，带动采摘等农产品销售24亿元。

三、工业、建筑业

工业经济。2013年全市实现工业增加值3378亿元，按可比价计算，比上年增长8.4%。其中规模以上工业企业实现增加值2291.2亿元，增长8.0%。分行业看，在35个行业大类中，26个行业的全年增加值同比呈上升态势，行业发展普遍向好；占比前十位的行业共完成工业增加值1640.5亿元，占全部规模以上工业增加值的比重达71.6%，比上年提高0.8个百分点，其中电气机械和器材制造业完成增加值262.5亿元，居各行业之首；化学原料和化学制品制造业增长16.8%，增速居前十位行业之首。全年规模以上轻工业完成增加值802.1亿元，增长3.4%；重工业1489.1亿元，增长10.2%，轻重工业之比由上年的1 ∶ 1.77变化为1 ∶ 1.86。全年规模以上工业企业实现销售产值12381亿元，增长5%。其中，内销为9557.4亿元，增长6.9%；出口交货值为2823.6亿元，下降0.8%，内销增速高于出口7.7个百分点。全年规模以上工业企业实现利润664.6亿元，增长25.0%，实现利税总额1258.1亿元，增长17.2%。

工业创新转型。2013年规模以上工业企业科技活动经费支出173.9亿元，比上年增长10.7%，占主营业务收入的比重达到1.4%，同比提高0.1个百分点。实现新产品产值2940亿元，增长22.1%，快于规模以上工业总产值增速16.5个百分点，新产品产值率达23%，比上年提高3.1个百分点，创历史新高。“机器换人”成果初现，全年规模以上工业资产总计增长5.8%，而从业人员减少2.3%，劳动生产率达16.3万元/人，增长10.5%，人均创利税9万元，增长20%。

建筑业。2013年全市完成建筑业产值3148.6亿元，比上年增长25.5%。全年总承包及专业承包建筑业企业签订合同额5123.3亿元，增长了17.7%，省外业务不断拓展，全年完成省外建筑业产值1271.2亿元，增长29%。全年房屋建筑施工面积25136.1万平米，竣工面积7543.9万平米。

四、固定资产投资、城市建设

固定资产投资。2013年全市完成固定资产投资3423亿元，比上年增长18%。分产业看，第一产业完成投资21.2亿元，下降21.7%；第二产业完成投资1069.5亿元，增长30.5%；第三产业完成投资2332.3亿元，增长13.5%，三次产业投资比例为0.6 ∶ 31.3 ∶ 68.1。全年完成民间投资1735.6亿元，增长26.6%，民间投资占固定资产投资的比重十年以来首次突破50%，达50.7%，比上年提高3.5个百分点。全年完成工业投资1065.2亿元，增长30.3%，对固定资产投资增长的贡献率达47.5%，其中工业技改投资完成762.5亿元，增长35.1%，占工业投资的比重达71.6%，比上年提高2.6个百分点。全年完成房地产开发投资1123.4亿元，增长27%，商品房销售面积730.1万平方米，增长23.7%。

2013 年全市固定资产投资主要构成

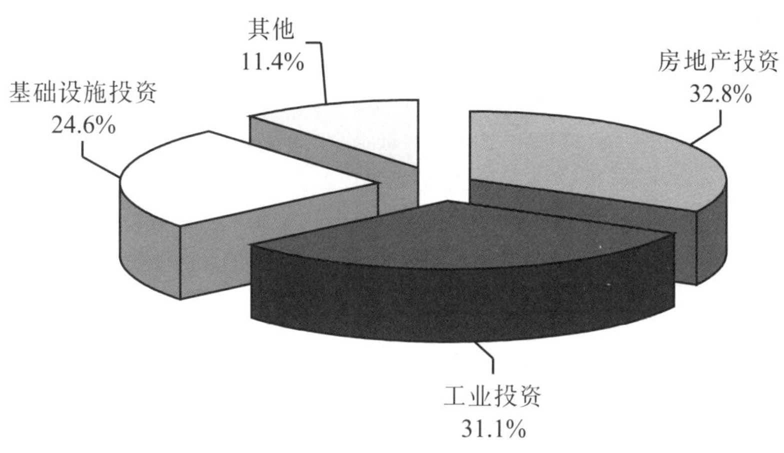

现代都市建设。深入实施现代都市"50100 工程","一核两翼多节点"现代都市格局进一步形成。"三江六岸"滨江休闲带工程启动段建成开放,16 条城市主要干道完成整治。深化道路清爽行动,中心城区道路机扫率突破 75%,长效保洁覆盖率达 100%,智慧城管辐射面从 137.6 平方公里增加至 208.7 平方公里,网格数达 2900 余个,平台基本实现全大市覆盖。历时 3 年的中心城区打通"断头路"行动圆满收官,59 条断头路如期打通。南北环快速路主线高架箱梁施工已基本完成,轨道交通 1 号线一期工程 20 个车站主体结构全部完成,地下段实现洞通、轨通、电通,2 号线一期工程 18 个地下车站结构全部封顶,第二轮建设规划获批。公共交通体系进一步优化,建成投用公交专用道(双向)30.4 公里,首创实施市区公交 1 小时优惠换乘及绕城高速浙 B 车辆半价优惠通行,累计共有 2420 万人次、超过 82.7 万车次受益。公共自行车系统正式投用,一期建成公共自行车网点 618 个,投用自行车 15035 辆。全面完成甬慈线公交化改造,城乡客运一体化率由 65%上升到 75%,成为国家公交都市创建示范城市。

五、贸易、旅游、会展

贸易业。2013 年全市商品销售总额 1.22 万亿元,比上年增长 15.4%。全年完成社会消费品零售总额 2635.7 亿元,增长 13.3%。分城乡看,城镇消费品零售额 2213.5 亿元,增长 13.3%;乡村消费品零售额 422.2 亿元,增长 13.8%。在限额以上企业销售的商品类值中,汽车类增长 10.6%,石油及制品类增长 16.3%,食品、饮料、烟酒类增长 7.7%,服装、鞋帽、针纺织品类增长 14.9%,金银珠宝类增长 32.1%。年末全市限额以上贸易企业达 2960 家,全年实现营业收入 7596.1 亿元,实现利润总额 70.0 亿元。

2008-2013 年社会消费品零售总额

单位:亿元

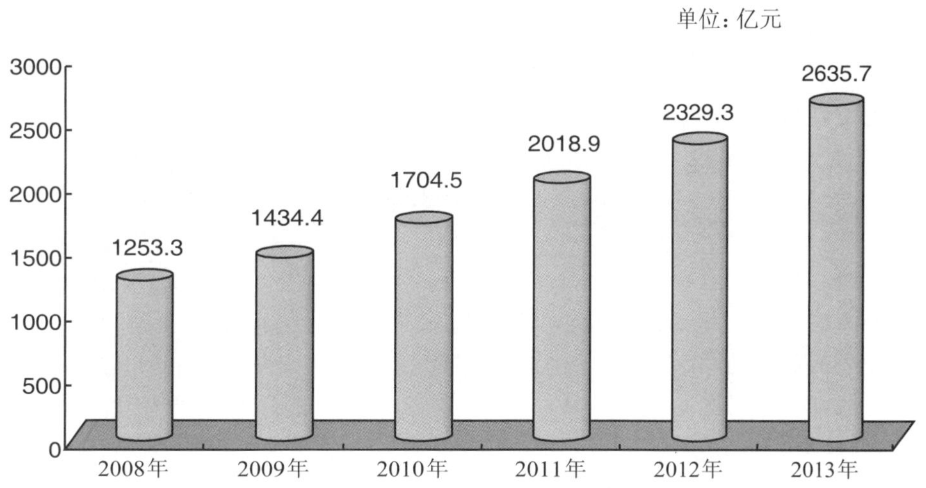

旅游业。2013 年全市实现旅游总收入 953.5 亿元，比上年增长 10.5%。接待入境旅游者 127.3 万人次，增长 9.3%；旅游外汇收入 7.96 亿美元，增长 8.2%；接待国内旅游者 6225.8 万人次，增长 8.3%；国内旅游收入 904.2 亿元，增长 10.8%。年末全市共有星级饭店 160 家，其中五星级 20 家，比上年新增 1 家；4A 级旅游景区 28 处，5A 级旅游景区 1 处。

会展业。2013 年全市会展业加快转型升级，量质并举发展取得了新成效，全年共举办会展项目 279 个。其中，举办展会 160 个，比上年增长 6%；展览总面积 186 万平方米，增长 4%；展览面积 2 万平方米以上的大型展会达 30 个。规范庆典、研讨会、论坛的举办，全年县域以上举办会议(论坛)68 个，比上年减少 12%；特色节庆 51 个，减少 7%。

六、对外经济、合作交流

对外贸易。2013 年全市实现口岸进出口总额 2119.0 亿美元，比上年增长 7.3%。外贸自营进出口总额首次突破 1000 亿美元，成为浙江首个、长三角地区第三个外贸总额超千亿美元的城市，全年自营进出口总额 1003.3 亿美元，增长 3.9%，其中出口 657.1 亿美元，增长 7.0%；进口 346.2 亿美元，下降 1.4%。全年新增对外贸易经营备案登记企业 2843 家，累计达 22500 家。有进出口实绩企业 13898 家。全年一般贸易出口占全市出口总额的比重为 81.0%，进口占全市进口总额的比重为 71.9%，比上年分别提高 1.0 和 2.1 个百分点。全年直接与我市开展贸易往来的国家和地区达 221 个，其中欧盟、美国、东盟、拉丁美洲贸易额占比分别为 20.1%、15.6%、8.2%和 7.8%。

2008-2013 年宁波自营进出口总额及增长速度

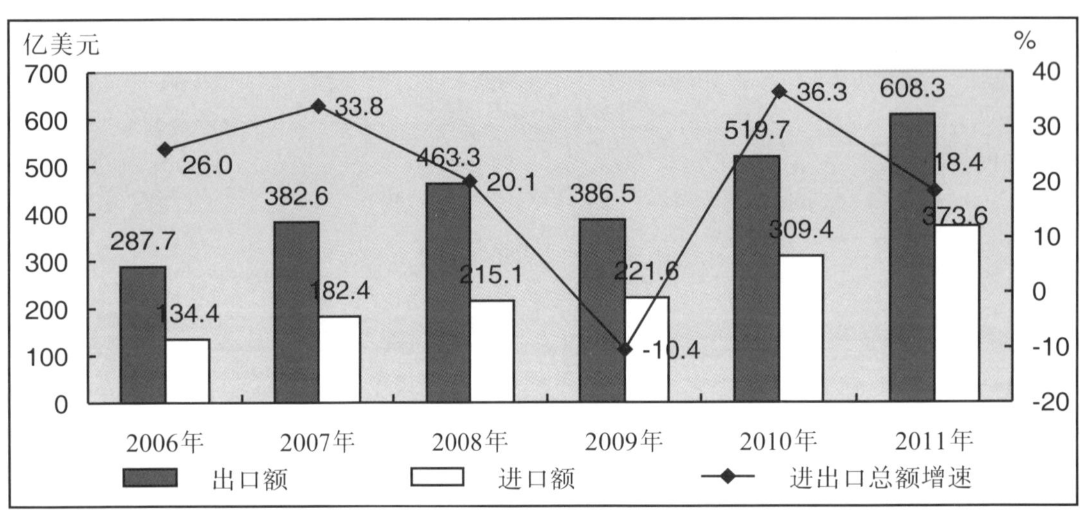

利用外资。2013 年全市合同利用外资 58.2 亿美元，比上年增长 9.6%，实际利用外资首次突破 30 亿美元，达 32.75 亿美元，增长 14.8%。第三产业新批项目 274 个，增长 26.9%；实际利用外资 18.5 亿美元，增长 20.7%。其中，房地产业实际利用外资 9.4 亿美元，增长 36.6%；交通运输、仓储和邮政业实际利用外资 2.9 亿美元，增长 963.9%。

对外合作。2013 年全市新批境外投资企业和机构 206 家，核准中方投资额 15.7 亿美元，比上年增长 20.2%，实际中方投资额 6.8 亿美元，增长 11.1%。完成境外承包工程劳务合作营业额 15.0 亿美元，增长 21.2%。

服务外包。2013 年全市完成服务外包合同额 144.0 亿元，比上年增长 25.7%；服务外包执行额 108.1 亿元，增长 27.7%；离岸服务外包合同额 7.7 亿美元，增长 44.1%；离岸服务外包执行额 6.0 亿美元，增长 47.1%。年末服务外包企业达 928 家，从业人员 3.6 万人。

国内合作。创新搭建各类招商引资载体，组织开展“2013 南京·宁波周”、重要客商“宁波行”、招商小分队“出宁波”等系列活动，国内招商引资和支持浙商创业创新工作取得明显成效，2013 年全市国内招商引资实际到位资金 658.7 亿元，比上年增长 17.1%，实现浙商甬商回归引进项目到位资金 506.1 亿元，增长 184.9%，分别为年度目标的 124.3%和 184.0%。全年引进 10 亿元以上内资项目 16 个，其中超过百亿元项目 3 个。全年实施山海协作产业合作项目 105 个，实际到位资金 29.8 亿元。全面启动新一轮对口帮扶贵州省黔西南州工作，全年在黔西南州实施了援助项目 70 个，帮扶资金 4496 万元，捐赠物资 1626 万元，援助万州三峡库区 6 个项目，资金 500 万元。积极帮助企业拓展国内市场，组织近 50 家企业先后参加了“西洽会”等国内重要展会，调查采集我市120家名特优产品企业和重点企业产品信息并录入浙货网。

七、港口、交通

港口生产。2013年宁波港货物吞吐量4.96亿吨，比上年增长9.5%，增幅比上年提高5.0个百分点，其中外贸货物吞吐量2.76亿吨，增长12.7%。三大主要货类增速“两高一低”，煤炭吞吐量7925.6万吨，增长19.5%，原油吞吐量6122.9万吨，增长11.1%，铁矿石吞吐量8812.8万吨，增长7.2%。全年集装箱吞吐量1677.4万标箱，增长7.0%，箱量排名保持大陆港口第三位、世界港口前六。集装箱航线总数达235条，其中远洋干线117条，近洋支线66条，内支线20条，内贸线32条，远洋干线占49.8%。共运作集装箱航班约16143班，月均航班约1345.3班。海铁联运业务进展快速，全年完成海铁联运箱量10.5万标箱，增长77%。

交通基础设施。2013年全市交通完成基本建设投资182.6亿元。穿山疏港高速公路建成通车，大大缓解北仑疏港压力。深入推进国省道提升工程，18个提升工程共改造里程164公里。年末全市公路总里程达到1.09万公里，公路网密度111公里/百平方公里，达到中等发达国家水平。其中高速公路495.8公里，一级公路1058.9公里，二级公路775.3公里，三级公路1533.1公里，四级公路6354.9公里。全年实施重大铁路项目4个，新增铁路里程65.5公里，杭甬客专建成通车，现代化铁路南站正式投用，货运北环线、北站迁建工程按计划推进。国际强港建设加快推进，建成万吨级码头泊位7个，梅山港区集装箱3-5#泊位水工工程交工验收，大榭港区中油燃料油30万吨级油码头通过竣工验收；穿山港区五期集装箱码头水工工程、陆域工程已完工；大榭信海油品仓储项目一期60万立方米原油、燃料油储罐建成投产。

综合运输。2013年完成全社会货运量3.54亿吨，比上年增长8.6%。其中，水路货运量1.54亿吨，货物周转量1905.3亿吨公里，分别增长9.4%和7.7%；公路货运量1.78亿吨，货物周转量325.5亿吨公里，分别增长7.4%和7.6%；铁路货物发送量2168.2万吨，增长13.6%；机场货邮吞吐量6.6万吨，增长7.3%。全社会客运量2.48亿人次，下降11.6%；铁路旅客发送量1273.1万人，增长12.9%；民航旅客吞吐量545.9万人次，增长3.7%。

八、银行、证券、保险

银行业。年末全市金融机构本外币存款余额1.32万亿元，比上年增长9.9%，其中人民币存款余额1.27万亿元，增长9.8%。年末金融机构本外币贷款余额1.33万亿元，增长11.3%，全年新增1326.5亿元，同比多增40.8亿元。年末小微企业贷款余额3941.7亿元，全年新增421.6亿元，同比多增107.5亿元，新增小微企业贷款占全部企业贷款增量的43.3%。年末全市银行业金融机构不良贷款率1.58%，比年初上升0.37个百分点，贷款风险整体可控。全年银行业金融机构实现税后利润244.2亿元，减少8.4%。年末全辖银行业金融机构达到63家，其中政策性银行3家，大型银行5家，股份制商业银行11家，城市商业银行12家，邮储银行1家，外资银行5家，农村合作金融机构9家，新型农村金融机构14家，非银行金融机构3家。

证券业。2013年全市证券成交总额2.16万亿元，比上年增长49.0%。其中股票和基金成交1.37万亿元，增长39.1%，证券客户交易结算资金余额66.2亿元，下降5.1%。期货代理交易量5297.4万手，代理交易额5.35万亿元，分别增长14.1%和27.4%。年末证券投资者开户98.4万户，增长5.6%。年内新增期货营业部4家，年末全市共有69家证券营业部，1家证券投资咨询公司，1家期货公司和35家期货营业部。年内境内上市公司实现融资18.6亿元；境内上市公司总数42家。

保险业。2013年全市保险业实现保费收入185.5亿元，比上年增长12.6%。其中，财产险保费收入96.8亿元，增长12.3%；人身险保费收入88.7亿元，增长13.0%。支出赔款和给付103.9亿元，增长61.7%。其中，财产险赔付支出89.5亿元，增长72.5%；人身险赔付支出14.4亿元，增长16.2%。共为3.7万家次企业、229.5万辆次机动车和1210.9万人次提供各类风险保障6.59万亿元。全年共为全市3361家次企业提供981.5亿元出口风险保障。全市政策性农险试点险种扩大到22个，累计向14.2万户次农户提供风险保障46.1亿元，支付赔款1.85亿元，增长76.2%。

九、科技、教育、人才

科技创新。创新能力显著提升，2013年全市省级科学技术奖33项，其中一、二等奖15项，“HP2-52C全自动电脑针织横机”列入国家战略性创新产品。全年专利授权量5.8万件，其中发明专利授权量2246件，比上年增长8.8%。全年认定省级高新技术企业研发中心45家，省级企业工程中心13家，市级企业工程(技术)中心116家。培育市创新型试点企业42家，新认定高新技术企业197家，市级科技型企业216家，省级创新型示范企业7家，省级创新型试点企业5家；培育认定市重点实验室10家、市企业研究院32家、省企业研究院11家，引进共建创新载体74家，组建产业技术创新联盟2家。农业科技创新支撑效果明显，培育农业新品种12项，有15个农业与社会发展领域科技项目被列为“863”计划、科技支撑计划等国家科技项目。年末限额以上科技服务业企业258家，全年实现营业收入131.0亿元，实现利润总额22.9亿元，比上年分别增长24.3%和23.5%。

教育事业。年末全市共有各级各类学校2097所，在校学生总数133.4万人。其中，高校16所，在校学生15.3万人；普通高中81所，在校学生9.7万人；中职学校55所，在校学生7.8万人；初中216所，在校学生18.9万人；小学465所，在校学生48.7万人；幼儿园1254所，在园幼儿27.6万人。完成列入市政府十方面实事项目的幼儿园新(改、扩)建88所。海曙、江东等7个县(市)区通过全国义务教育发展基本均衡督导检查。新增105所义务教育段标准化学校，我市义务教育段标准化学校达473所。推进普通高中特色化、多样化发展，全市申报省一级特色示范学校19所，省二级特色示范学校23所。全面开展国家级教育国际合作与交流综合改革试验区建设，成功举办了中美区域、宁波・奥克兰等教育合作交流会，签订了各类教育合作协议33项，在甬高校留学生规模达到2500人，比上年增长56%；推进“千校结好”行动计划，全市新增中小学姐妹学校78对。

人才开发。2013年全市新增各类人才18.2万人，年末全市人才总量达148.3万人，比上年增长12.2%。新增国家“千人计划”专家20人、省“千人计划”专家41人，新评审出市“3315计划”人才47名、高端创业创新团队21个，引进海外工程师225名、国家高端外国专家6名。新增院士工作站15家，累计达69家；新增国家级博士后工作站5家；博士、博士后总数近3800人。新建市级技能大师工作室11家、高技能人才公共实训基地3个，完成技能培训21.5万人次、技能鉴定13万人次，培养高技能人才2.4万人，高技能人才总量达23.4万人。

十、文化、卫生、体育

文化建设。2013年全市11个县(市)区全部成功创建浙江省文化先进县(市)区，鄞州区和慈溪市分别成功创建全国公共文化服务体系示范区和浙江省公共文化服务体系示范区。深入开展“万场电影千场戏剧进农村”活动，全年农村电影播放30000余场，演出戏剧6000多场次。创新形式推出“天然舞台”四大“演出季”等60场文化活动，参演人数达到8000余人，观众近50万人次。深化宁波市数字图书馆项目建设，全年文献传递176万余篇，文献下载1500余万篇。宁波文化百科大讲堂举办讲座512场，受众已逾10万人次，成为深受宁波社会各界欢迎的公共文化服务平台。大型原创歌剧《红帮裁缝》亮相国家大剧院，参加“2013年国家艺术院团演出季优秀剧目展演”；《竹儿青青》、《兵站故事》等七个作品获全国第十六届群星奖，占浙江获奖作品的一半，创历史新高。文化设施建设稳步推进，国内首创的大型获知型娱乐综合体——宁波文化广场正式对外开放。文化产业发展迅速，全市有9个企业和2个项目入围2013-2014年度国家级文化出口重点企业和重点项目，4家企业认定为国家动漫企业和动漫保护品牌，《少年阿凡提》被授予2013年国家动漫品牌。全年新增塔山遗址等9处国保单位，“国保”数量增至31处，继续位居全省第二，计划单列市第一。

卫生事业。城乡居民医疗卫生条件进一步改善，年末实有病床2.9万张，拥有专业卫生人员6.2万人，卫生技术人员5.2万人，其中执业医师(含助理)2.0万人，注册护士2.0万人。按户籍人口统计，每千人床位数、卫技人员数、执业医师(含助理)数和注册护士数分别达到5.0张、9.0人、3.4人和3.4人。市妇儿医院北部院区项目竣工，李惠利医院东部院区、市一院原医疗用房改扩建等基础设施建设项目顺利推进。年末全市共设置社区卫生服务中心(卫生院)152家，建成省级规范化社区卫生服务中心(卫生院)133家，创建率达87.5%，居全省前列；建成省级示范社区卫生服务中心28家，其中国家级社区卫生服务中心6家。新型农村合作医疗制度进一步巩固，参合人数为265.7万人，参合率达98.3%，人均筹资水平从2012年的565元增加到2013年的590元。全市甲乙类传染病报告总发病率为184.14/10万，适龄儿童免疫规划疫苗接种率98.4%，免疫预防服务质量保持全省先进水平。全年无偿献血7.1万人次，继续保持我市临床用血全部来自无偿献血的目标。

体育事业。体育公共服务有效提升，市直属场馆定期免费开放率达到100%，98%的城区公办中小学校体育设施向市民开放；建成各类球场173余个，更新健身路径530套，行政村体育健身路径拥有率达100%。江东区成功创建浙江省体育强区，宁海县、象山县顺利通过创强复评。群众体育活动丰富多彩，通过全民健身大讲堂等多种形式，指导市民科学健身，首次在东部新城举办了元旦万人长跑。在第十二届全运会上，共有 90 名甬籍运动员进入决赛，获得金牌 6 枚、银牌 8 枚、铜牌 13 枚，1 人 1 次超亚洲纪录，2 人 2 次破全国纪录，参赛人数、获得金牌数和奖牌数均创下宁波参加历届全运会之最，涌现了一批优秀年轻体育人才，“省队市办”结出丰硕成果。2013 年，我市运动员获得 2 个世界级比赛第三名；3 个亚洲级比赛第一名，1 个亚洲级比赛第二名，在全国赛事还获得 29 金 24 银 26 铜。体育事业与体育产业协调发展，全年共举办国家级以上赛事 50 项，鄞州和北仑分别被总局授予全国最佳赛区和全国优秀赛区；全年体育彩票销售额达 15.6 亿元，创历史新高。

十一、人口、居民生活、社会保障、社会组织

人口增长。年末全市户籍人口 580.1 万人，比上年增加 2.4 万人，其中市六区人口 227.6 万人。全市人口出生率 8.52‰、死亡率 6.13‰。全市计划生育率 95.9%，已婚育龄妇女综合避孕率 89.1%，适度低生育水平持续稳定。流动人口计划生育综合管理进一步加强，流入流出育龄妇女信息掌握率 97.5%。

居民收入。2013 年市区居民人均可支配收入 41729 元，比上年增长 10.1%，扣除价格因素，实际增长 7.7%；农村居民人均纯收入 20534 元，增长 11.1%，扣除价格因素，实际增长 8.8%。从收入来源看，工资性收入仍是居民收入增长的决定性因素，对城乡居民收入增长的贡献分别达 76.7%和 75.8%。城乡居民收入比由 2012 年的 2.05 ∶ 1 缩小为 2013 年的 2.03 ∶ 1，明显低于全国 3.03 ∶ 1 的平均水平。

社会保障体系。年末企业基本养老保险、职工基本医疗保险、失业保险、工伤保险、生育保险参保人数分别达 508.9 万人、346.3 万人、231.7 万人、283.4 万人和 245.5 万人，比上年末分别净增 34.6 万人、19.7 万人、15.5 万人、13.2 万人和 12.4 万人，社保卡持卡人数突破 330 万。年末外来务工人员参加五大社会保险人数为 213 万人. 参保人数净增 33.6 万人。年末被征地人员养老保险参保人数 51.2 万人，重点对象占比 88.9%。年末城乡居民社会养老保险参保人数 132.9 万人。社保待遇稳步提高，企业退休人员年人均养老金为 2083 元/月，增加 148 元/月；失业保险金发放标准增至 1103 元/月，增加 55 元/月；政策范围内城镇职工和居民住院及特殊病种报销比例达到 86.8%和 72.3%。

民生保障。2013 年市区城乡居民最低生活保障标准从月人均 525 元提高到 588 元，年末全市共有最低生活保障对象 5.5 万人，低保资金实际支出 2.3 亿元。医疗救助制度进一步完善，救助城乡患病困难群众 18.4 万人次，支出医疗救助资金 1.5 亿元。落实困难群众基本生活价格补贴联动机制，共支出资金 980.3 万元。养老服务社会参与有效扩大，全市共有民办养老机构 82 家，养老床位 26382 张；全年新(扩)建居家养老服务站点 183 个，居家养老服务覆盖 90%以上的城市社区和 50%以上的行政村。全年享受帮困助学政策学生达 90.6 万人次，受助金额累计 8 亿余元。

保障性安居工程。2013 年全市新开工各类保障性安居工程 160 万平方米，18301 套，竣工 134 万平方米、17427 套，新增解决户数 14069 户，超额完成省政府下达的目标任务。洪塘的和塘雅苑等一批公租房小区如期建成投用，配租工作顺利完成。

慈善事业。2013 年全市慈善总会募集善款 5.5 亿元，比上年增长 24.4%。全年救助支出 4.3 万元，增长 18.1%，受助的困难群众达 43.8 万人次。至 2013 年底，全市慈善总会累计募集已达 39.9 亿元。累计救助支出 27.6 亿元，受助 214.3 万人次。全年共开展各种志愿服务活动 1854 次，参加服务的义工 23341 人次，服务时间累计达 60035.5 小时。

社会组织。年末全市共有 6 个区、2 个县、3 个县级市、77 个镇、11 个乡、64 个街道办事处、663 个居民委员会和 2556 个村民委员会。

十二、生态建设、社会安全

生态建设。环境专项整治卓有成效，2013 年中心城区完成绕城高速以内 540 平方公里“禁燃区”建设，累计淘汰改造燃煤锅炉 1139 台；机动车排气防治工作实施高污染车辆限行，出台黄标车淘汰政策；继续深入开展电镀、印染、化工、造纸等十大重污染行业环境整治提升工作，投入市级环保专项资金 4600 万元，关停 830 家不合格企业；深入开展饮用水源保护区专项治理工作，保护区内 38 家污染企业实施挂牌督办。完成北仑电厂、宁海国华电厂、象山大唐乌沙山电厂等 10 台机组 720 万千瓦脱硫设施断旁路，8 台 350 万千瓦脱硝工程建设以及水泥行业脱硝工程；建设宁波市重点污染源刷卡排污系统，实施污染物总量控制管理，确保减排设施规范稳定运行。环境执法监管继续强化，出动执法人员近 50482 人次，检查企业 27642 多家次，立案查处违法案件 1245 件，下达处罚金额 5753 万元。监测监控能力不断提升，完成 10 个省控大气自动站监测设

备升级改造，建设全市大气复合污染监测网络，及时向公众发布空气质量和重污染天气预警信息。继续开展各类生态环保创建活动，北仑区通过省级生态区现场考核，宁海县和象山县分别通过国家级生态县验收。

“平安宁波”建设。2013年全市共发生各类生产安全事故2866起，死亡745人，受伤2855人，直接经济损失3007.9万元，比上年分别下降9.4%、3.1%、9.1%和9.8%，四项事故指标连续第九年实现下降。加大食品药品检验力度，全年完成食品检测47870批次，完成药品监督抽验2515批，分别占全年抽检任务的110.3%和100.6%，其中检出不合格188批，阳性检出率为7.5%；加强药品不良反应和医疗器械不良事件监测，全市共上报药品不良反应8124例，其中新的和严重的报告占46.7%。全年共出动执法人员14.1万次，共检查各类食品药品单位7.6万家次，药械、餐饮、保健品和化妆品共立案1532起，结案1419起，罚没款1627.3万元，没收物品货值金额共计161.4万元，移送公安案件23件。着力构建和谐稳定的劳动关系，企业劳动合同签订率和已建工会企业集体劳动合同签订率分别达到97%和92%；健全防范处置欠薪机制，为2.4万名劳动者追回被拖欠工资1.8亿元；提升劳动人事争议处理效能，全市受理劳动争议3.1万件，仲裁结案率达到93%，调解率达到73.6%。全年共受理群众信访35189件(人)次，下降3.6%，接待群众集体上访1327批17953人次，分别下降7.2%和7.4%。全年人民调解组织共调处各类民事纠纷11.8万件，调解成功11.6万件，成功率达98.4%，防止民间纠纷引起的自杀34件、34人次；防止民间纠纷转化为刑事案件155件、504人次。

注：(1)本公报所列各项数据均为初步统计数。

(2)全市生产总值、各产业增加值绝对数按当年价格计算，增长速度按可比价格计算。

(3)规模以上工业企业指年主营业务收入2000万元及以上企业。

限额以上批发、零售、住宿、餐饮企业指：

批发业：年主营业务收入2000万元及以上；

零售业：年主营业务收入500万元及以上；

住宿业：年主营业务收入200万元及以上；

餐饮业：年主营业务收入200万元及以上。

2013 Statistics Bulletin of National Economy and Social Development of Ningbo

Ningbo Municipal Statistics Bureau
State Statistical Bureau Ningbo Investigation Team
Jan. 30, 2014

In face of complex development environment at home and abroad and frequent occurrence of natural disasters, especially flood and waterlogging in 2013, Ningbo people stick to the keynote of "advancing in stability and then bettering in advancement" and strive to thoroughly implement the development strategy of "six accelerations", in order to implement relevant policies and strategies favorable to ensuring steady growth, improving economic performance, intensifying innovation and benefiting livelihood. With such actions taken, the overall economy has witnessed stable increase and improvement, the industry is under steady development, the quality and benefits have been improved continuously, the innovation and transformation have advanced effectively and people were well secured for well-being and better living standard, laying a solid foundation for the achievement of "two basic points" and the construction of "four demonstration zones".

I. Overview

Regional GDP: The GDP in Ningbo in 2013 amounted to ￥712.89 billion, up by 8.1% compared with that of last year if calculated by comparable price, among which, the added value of primary industry was ￥27.64 billion, down by 1.2%; the added value of secondary industry was ￥374.17 billion, up by 8.2%; and the added value of tertiary industry was ￥311.08 billion, up by 8.8%. The ratio of the increase of the three industries was 3.9:52.5:43.6. The proportion of increase of the tertiary industry in the regional GDP was 1.1% higher than that of last year. The GDP per capita was ￥93,176 if calculated by permanent resident population (converted to USD 15,046 according to annual average exchange rate).

Fiscal revenue and expenditure: The public fiscal budget revenue in Ningbo in 2013 was ￥165.12 billion, up by 7.5% compared with that of last year, among which, the local fiscal revenue was ￥79.28 billion, up by 9.3%. For local taxation, the growths for operation tax, VAT, enterprise income tax and individual were 10.8%, 3.0%, 9.4% and 10.5% respectively. The public fiscal budget expenditure was ￥93.99 billion, up by 13.5%, among which the transportation expenditure was ￥7.10 billion, up by 40.0%; the fiscal expenditure in energy conservation and environmental protection was ￥1.48 billion, up by 25.2%; the expenditure in social insurance and employment was ￥9.76 billion, up by 23.5% the expenditure in science and technology was ￥3.76 billion, up by 15.9%; the expenditure in agriculture, forestry and water was ￥8.04 billion, up by 11.3%. The "eight provisions" and regulation to ban official extravagance issued by the central government were conscientiously implemented, thus greatly reducing the general expenditures. The annual expenditure in general public services was increased by 4.4%, with the growth of 3.5% lower than the same period of last year.

Employment and re-employment: Employees newly created in urban areas and towns in Ningbo were 161,000 in 2013, and 76,000 laid-off workers were re-employed, 22,000 of which were the workers in trouble. The college graduates were instructed to work or establish a business in the enterprises and grassroots, with the employment rate of college graduates of 98%. The vocational education public service platform of "Xiaoqitong" under cooperation of colleges and enterprises was officially launched, which attracted 72 colleges and universities in Ningbo joining the service platform and 6,100 enterprises publishing the supply and demand information. Active measures were taken to cope with the unfavorable influence of flood disaster and supportive policies were issued in a timely manner to stabilize the employment. The total social insurance fee of ￥3.0 billion was reduced, benefiting 89,000 enterprises and 2.36 million employees. The rural labor forces of 110,000 were organized to accept trainings, 23,000 of which transferred their employment after trainings. The number of rural serviceable talents in Ningbo recorded reached 135,000, accounting for 4.6% of the total rural labor forces. The registered unemployment rate in urban areas and towns in Ningbo at the end of the year was 2.16%, which was historically low.

Market price: The consumer price index (CPI) in Ningbo was 102.2% in 2013, 0.4% and 0.1% respectively lower than those of national and provincial levels, ranking the 34th place in 36 large and medium-sized cities in China. The rises and falls of eight major goods and services items present a pattern of "seven rises and one fall": 2.6% increase for foods, 0.8% increase for alcohol and tobacco products, 2.6% increase for clothes, 2.0% increase for household facilities and articles, 2.8% increase for health care and personal products, 1.9% increase for entertainment, education and cultural articles and services, 3.5% increase for residential products, and 0.6% decrease for transportation and communication. The purchase price index and ex-factory price index for manufacturers were 96.34% and 96.67% respectively in 2013. The sales price of new commercial housing was up by 0.5% in December month on month and 7.8% year on year, with the increase ranking the 52nd place among 70 large and medium-sized cities in China.

2013 Fluctuation of Main Prices by Months in Ningbo

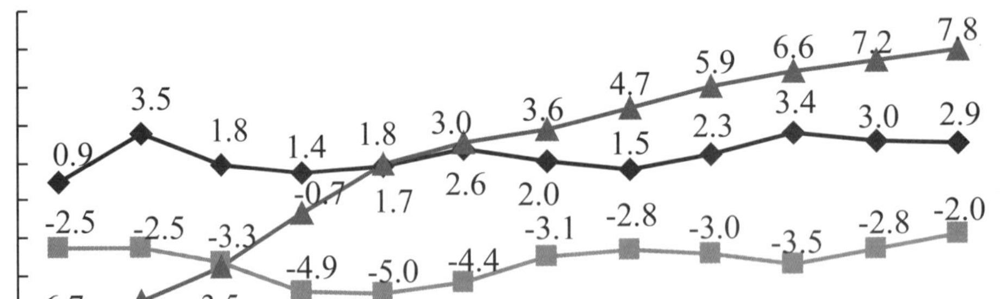

II. Agriculture and Rural Area

Agricultural production: Continuously affected by a series of serious natural disasters such as H7N9 avian-flu outbreak, extreme high-temperature and dry weather and Typhoon Fitow, the agricultural and animal husbandry production had witnessed serious losses. The gross output value of farming, forestry, husbandry and fishing in Ningbo has reached ￥42.99 billion in 2013, down by 1.5% than that of last year if calculated by comparable price. Among the gross value, the farming was ￥20.23 billion, down by 1.0%; the forestry ￥1.15 billion, up by 1.9%; the husbandry ￥6.09 billion, down by 9.4%; the fishing ￥14.90 billion, up by 1.0%; and the service of farming forestry, husbandry and fishing ￥0.62 billion, up by 3.4%. The sowing area of food crops reached 2.229 million mu, with the same number as last year. The total output of grains reached 812,000 tons, down by 6.2% when compared with that of last year. The situation of poultry production is still grim and the poultry stock and slaughter were decreased by 10.4% and 23.0% respectively when compared with that of last year; the total output of poultry reached 38,000 tons, down by 24.2%. The demonstrative family farm supportive measures were prepared. The new demonstrative family farms at municipal level were 40 in 2013 and the total number of family farms in Ningbo reached 2754. The development of "family farms" in Ningbo was also described by the media as one of the national "five models".

New countryside construction: 46 new all-round well-off villages were established in 2013, totaling 525 by far. Centralized treatment of rural household garbage and domestic sewage is accelerated and the centralized treatment rate of rural garbage in Ningbo reached more than 98% and 150 new rural living sewage treatment projects were established. A total amount of ￥10.1 billion was invested in "two reconstructions" for countryside houses in 2013, including 105,000 houses starting reconstruction, with a total area of 5.90 million square meters of rural houses constructed and a total number of 41,000 peasant household settled. 185 centralized housing construction projects were implemented and started. Various funds of ￥220 million were invested in the village renovation and construction in 2013 and 594 projects were constructed, with 228,000 m2 old and dilapidated houses removed, 928,000m2 of fa? ade renovated, 290,000 m2 of road hardening within countries conducted; 194,000 m2 village greening carried out and 60 villages passed the acceptance. The brand influence of rural leisure tourism was significantly improved and the number tourists in rural leisure tourism in 2013 reached 22.34 million and the total operating revenue reached ￥2.24 billion, up by 30.6% and 30.3% respectively year on year, with the agricultural marketing sales such as picking reaching ￥2.4 billion.

III. Industry and Construction

Industrial economy: The total industrial output value in Ningbo amounted to ￥337.8 billion in 2013, up by 8.4% compared with that of last year. Among which, the total increased industrial output value for industrial enterprise above designated size was ￥229.12 billion, up by 8.0%. From the perspective of industries, in the 35 industries, the total increased industrial output value of 26 of which was on the rise and enjoyed sound industrial development trend; the increased output value for top 10 industries above designated size was ￥164.05 billion, accounting for 71.6% of the total industrial output value above designated size and achieving 0.8% of increase compared with the same period of last year. The electric apparatus and equipment manufacturing industry have obtained ￥26.25 billion of total increased industrial output value, topping all industries; chemical raw materials and chemical products manufacturing have witnessed a growth of 16.8%, ranking first in growth among top ten industries. The gross output value of light industry in 2013 was ￥80.21 billion, up by 3.4%; and that for heavy industry was ￥148.91 billion, up by 10.2%. The ratio of light and heavy industries has changed from 1:1.77 last year to 1:1.86 in 2013. The sales value for industrial enterprises above designated value in 2013 was ￥1238.1 billion, up by 5.0%; among which, the sales value in domestic market was ￥955.74 billion, up by 6.9%; the value of export delivery was ￥282.36 billion, down by 0.8%, with the growth of sales in domestic market of 7.7% higher than that of export. The profits achieved by the industrial enterprises above the designated size was ￥66.46 billion, up by 25.0%; and taxation of profits achieved was ￥125.81 billion, up by 17.2%.

Industrial transformation and innovation: Expenditure in scientific and technological activities of industrial enterprises above designated size totaled ￥17.39 billion in 2013, up by 10.7% compared with that of last year and accounting for 1.4% of main business revenue (0.1% higher compared with the same period of last year). The output value of new products was ￥294.0 billion, up by 22.1%, 16.5% faster in growth than that of total industrial output value above designated size. The rate of output value of new products accounted for 23%, 3.1% higher compared with the same period last year, hitting a record high; the implementation effect of "replacement of labor force with machines" has been achieved and total growth of 5.8% of industrial assets above designated size was achieved; while the number of employees was decreased by 2.3%; the labor productivity reached ￥163,000/person, up by 10.5%; the per capita profit earnings and tax payment reached ￥90,000, up by 20%.

Construction industry: The output value of construction industry in Ningbo totaled ￥314.86 billion in 2013, up by 25.5% compared with that of last year. The annual total contracting and professional contracting construction enterprises have signed contracts valued at ￥512.33 billion, up by 17.7%; the businesses in other provinces were expanded continuously and the total output value of building industry in other provinces reached ￥127.12 billion, up by 29%. The construction area of house in 2013 was 251.361 million m2, and the completion area was 75.439 million m2.

IV. Investment in Fixed Asset and Urban Construction

Investment in fixed asset: Investment in fixed asset in Ningbo was ￥342.3 billion in 2013, up by 18% compared with that of last year. In perspective of industries, investment in primary industry was ￥2.12 billion, down by 21.7%; investment in secondary industry was ￥106.95 billion, up by 30.5%; investment in tertiary industry was ￥233.23 billion, up by 13.5%; the investment ratio of the three industries was 0.6:31.3:68.1. The private investment in 2013 reached ￥173.56 billion, up by 26.6%; the ratio of private investment in the investment of fixed assets exceeded 50% for the first time over the last decade, reaching 50.7%, up by 3.5% compared with that of last year. The total industrial investment in 2013 reached ￥106.52 billion, up by 30.3%; the contribution rate of the growth in fixed assets investment reached 47.5%, among which the investment in industrial technical transformation reached ￥76.25 billion, up by 35.1%, accounting for 71.6% of the industrial investment, up by 2.6% compared with that of last year. The total investment in real estate development in 2013 was ￥112.34 billion, up by 27%; the sales area of commercial residential building was 7.301 million m2, up by 23.7% compared with that of last year.

Main Structure of Investment in Ningbo Fixed Assets of 2013

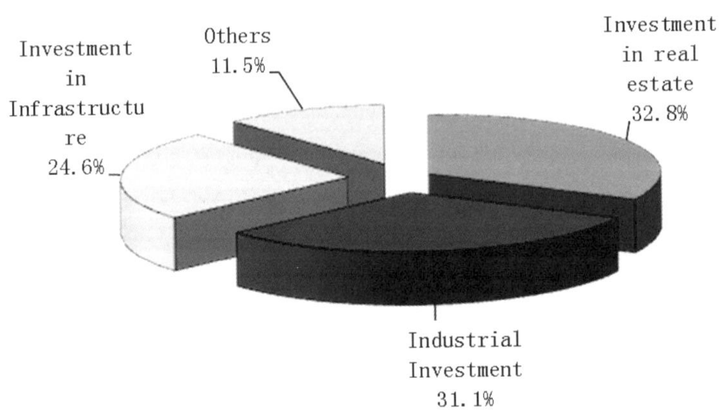

Modern urban construction: Modern metropolis of "50100 projects" is under thorough development and the modern metropolis pattern of "one core, two wings and multi-nodes" is further established. The leisure riverside belt project of "three rivers and six banks" was basically completed and 16 urban arterial roads were renovated. The cleaning action of roads was deepened; the machine cleaning rate of roads in central urban areas exceeded 75% and the coverage rate of long-acting clean keeping reached 100%; the radiating area of the intelligent city management was increased from 137.6 km2 to 208.7 km2, with the number of grids reaching more than 2900, thus the platform basically achieving 100% of coverage rate. The "unconnected roads" in central urban areas were finished within three years and 59 unconnected roads were constructed within scheduled period. The construction of elevated boxes in main line of south-north ring express way has been completed basically. The main structure of 20 stations in Phase I of rail transit No. 1 was finished completely and the underground sections achieved hole connection, rail connection and power connection; the structure construction of

18 underground stations of Phase I of rail transit No. 2 was completed and the second-round construction planning was approved. The public traffic system was further optimized, with 30.4 km public transportation lane being put into operation (two-way road). The city bus "one-hour" preferential transfer was implemented and the vehicles with the license plate number of "Z.B." in ring expressway were provided with half-price discount, benefiting a total number of 24.20 million person-time and 827,000 vehicle-time. The public bicycle system was officially put into use and 618 public bicycle networks of Phase I were constructed, with 15,035 bicycles being put into use. Ningbo-Cixi public transport transformation was finished completely and the integration rate of urban-rural passenger transport was increased from 65% to 75%, thus making Ningbo become the demonstration city of national transit metropolis.

V. Trade, Tourism and Exhibition

限额以上贸易企业达 2960 家,全年实现营业收入 7596.1 亿元,实现利润总额 70.0 亿元。Trade: The total sales volume of goods in Ningbo reached ￥1.22 trillion in 2013, up by 15.4% compared with that of last year. The total retail sales of consumer goods reached ￥263.57 billion, up by 13.3%. If viewed by countryside and town respectively, the total volume of consumer retail sales in towns was ￥221.35 billion, up by 13.3%, and total volume of consumer retail sales in countryside was ￥42.22 billion, up by 13.8%. In goods sales volume enterprises above designated size, automobile sales have been up by 10.6%; petroleum and related products 16.3%; foods, beverage, tobacco and liquor 7.7%; clothing, shoes and hats, and needle textile 14.9%; gold, silver and jewelry 32.1%. The number of trade companies above designated size in Ningbo has reached 2,960 at the end of 2013. The total operation revenue was ￥759.61 billion and profits of ￥7.00 billion.

Total Retail Sales of Consumer Goods from 2008 to 2013

Unit: ￥100 million

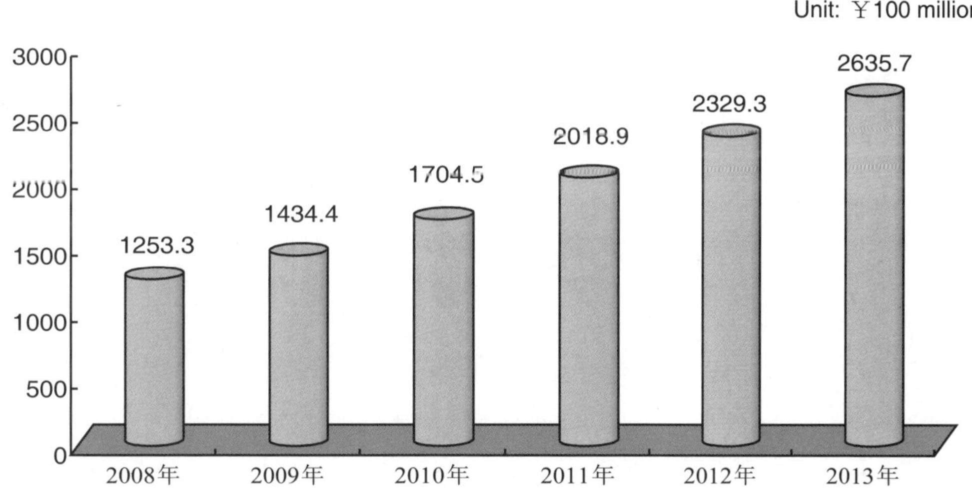

Tourism: Total revenue of tourism in Ningbo in 2013 was ￥95.35 billion, up by 10.5% compared with that of last year. The inbound tourists hit 1.273 million, up by 9.3%; foreign exchange earnings of tourism was USD 0.796 billion, up by 8.2%; domestic tourists in 2013 were 62.258 million, up by 8.3%; revenue from domestic tourists was ￥90.42 billion, up by 10.8%. There were 160 star-rated hotels in Ningbo in 2013, where 20 were five-star hotels (up by 1). There were 28 4A-class tourist attractions and 1 5A-class tourist attraction.

Exhibition: In 2013, the transformation and upgrading of conference and exhibition industry in Ningbo was accelerated and new achievements were made in the development of quality and quantity. 279 exhibition activities of various kinds were held in 2013 in Ningbo, of which 160 were exhibitions, up by 6% compared with that of last year, with a total exhibition area of 1.86 million m2, up by 4%. A total number of 30 large-scale exhibitions with more than 20,000 m2 of exhibition area were held. Ceremonies, seminar and forums were held up to standards. In 2013, 68 conferences (forums) and 51 festival activities above county level were held, which witnesses decreases of 12% and 7% respectively.

VI. Foreign Economy and Cooperation & Exchange

Foreign trade: The total volume of export and import in Ningbo reached USD 211.90 billion in 2013, up by 7.3% compared to that of last year. The total volume of self-support export exceeded USD 100 billion for the first time, thus making Ningbo become the first city in Zhejiang and the third city in Yangtze River Delta Region with the foreign trade volume of more than USD 100 billion. The total volume of self-support import and export in 2013 reached USD 100.33 billion, up by 3.9%, of which the total volume of export reached USD 65.71 billion, up by 7.0% and that of import reached USD 34.62 billion, down by 1.4%. The newly-increased enterprises for foreign trade registered in 2013 were 2843, totaling 22,500 by far, and the enterprises with actual export and import businesses were 13,898. The export volume of general trade accounted for 81.0%, among the total export volume, the import volume accounted for 71.9% of the total import volume, up by 1.0% and 2.1% respectively compared with those of last year. 221 nations and regions established direct trade relations with Ningbo in 2013, among which, the trade volume in EU, the United States, ASEAN and Latin America accounted for 20.1%, 15.6%, 8.2% and 7.8% respectively.

2008-2013 Self-support Import & Export Volume and Growth in Ningbo

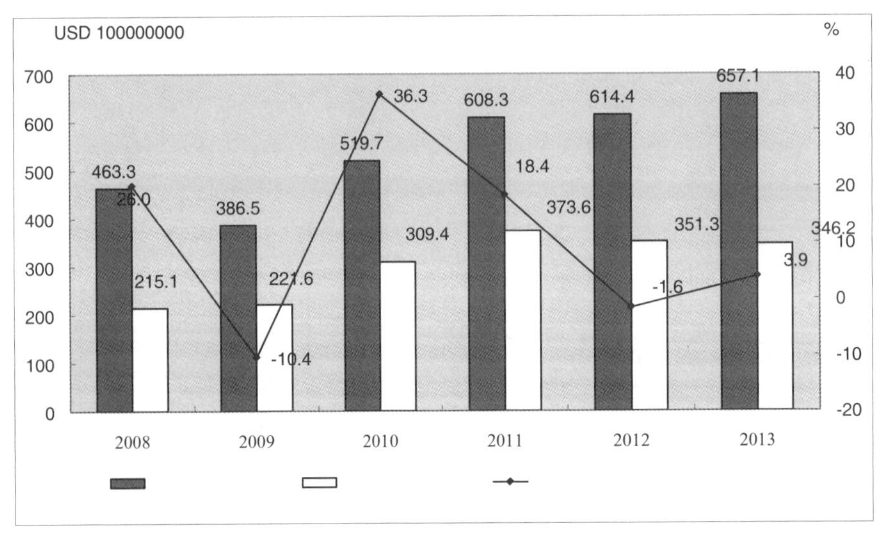

Foreign capital utilization: In 2013, foreign capital utilization by contract was USD 5.82 billion, up by 9.6% compared to that of last year; and actual utilization of foreign capital exceeded USD 3 billion for the first time and reached USD 3.275 billion, up by 14.8%. The total number of newly-approved projects in the tertiary industry reached 274, up by 26.9%; actual utilization of foreign capital reached USD 1.85 billion, up by 20.7%. Among the above, the actual utilization of foreign capital in real estate industry was USD 940 million, up by 36.6%; that in transportation, warehousing and postal service was USD 290 million, up by 963.9%.

Foreign cooperation: 206 overseas investment enterprises and organizations were approved in Ningbo in 2013, with Chinese investment approved up to USD 1.57 billion, up by 20.2% compared to that of last year, and the actual Chinese investment up to USD 680 million, up by 11.1%. The turnover of labor cooperation for overseas contracting projects was

USD 1.50 billion, up by 21.2%.

Outsourcing service: the contract volume of outsourced service completed in 2013 was ￥14.40 billion, up by 25.7% respectively; and the executed volume of outsourcing service was ￥ 10.81 billion, up by 27.7%; the contract volume of offshore outsourced service was USD 770 million and the executed volume of that was USD 600 million, up by 44.1% and 47.1% respectively. The enterprises specialized in outsourced services at the end of 2013 amounted to 928, with total employees of 36,000.

Domestic cooperation: various investment attraction and capital introduction carriers were innovatively established and series of activities such as "2013 Nanjing-Ningbo Week" and the "a visit to Ningbo" of important merchants and "go out of Ningbo" of merchants groups were successfully held. In 2013, the domestic investment attraction and capital introduction as well as innovation work supporting Zhejiang-born merchants' businesses witnessed significant result and actual attraction of domestic capital reached ￥65.87 billion, up by 17.1%, and the actual paid-in capital from merchants of Zhejiang Province reached ￥50.61 billion, up by 184.9%, accounting for 124.3% and 184.0% of the total annual goal respectively. 16 domestic capital projects that above 1 billion were brought in, 3 of which were over 10 billion for the whole year. A total number of 105 industrial cooperation projects of Nanshan District +Zhoushan Isles were fully implemented, with actual paid-in capital of ￥2.98 billion. A new round of assistance project for Qianxinan in Guizhou was started completely and 70 assistance projects were constructed in Qianxinan in 2013, with the assistance funds of ￥44.96 million and the donated goods and materials of ￥16.26 million. Six projects in Three Gorges Reservoir Region in Wanzhou District were assisted, with a fund of ￥5 million. Active assistance was provided for enterprises to expand the domestic market and nearly 50 enterprises were organized to take part in important domestic exhibitions such as "Investment and Trade Forum for Cooperation between East and West China". The information and materials about 120 enterprises with excellent products and products of key enterprises in Ningbo were investigated and input in Zhejiang Marketing Network.

VII. Port and Transportation

Port production: The cargo handling capacity of Ningbo Port in 2013 was 496 million tons, up by 9.5% compared with that of last year, with a growth of 5.0% higher than that of last year; and the handling capacity of foreign trade goods completed was 276 million tons, up by 12.7%. The rises and falls of three major cargoes: 79.256 million tons for coal, up by 19.5%; 61.229 million tons for crude oil, up by 11.1%; 88.128 million tons for iron ore, up by 7.2%. The container throughput in 2013 has exceeded 16.774 million TEU, up by 7.0%, ranking third among ports in China mainland, and sixth among the worldwide ports. The total container marine lines have totaled 235, where the ocean-going lines were 117, near marine lines were 66, domestic container feeder lines were 20, and domestic trade lines were 32, among which the ocean-going lines accounted for 49.8%. The total container navigation times were 16,143 and monthly average navigation times were about 1,345.3. The marine-railway combined transportation business was developed rapidly and total containers through marine and railway in 2013 amounted to 105,000 TEU, up by 77%.

Transportation infrastructure: The investment in the transportation infrastructure in Ningbo was ￥18.26 billion in 2013. The Chuanshan Port Evacuation Highway has been completed, which can greatly relieve the pressure of evacuation of Beilun Harbor. The national highway and provincial highway promotion projects were constructed further and 18 promotion projects were constructed, with mileage of 164km completed. At the end of 2013, the total mileage of roads has reached 10,900 km, and the highway density was 111 km per 100 km2, equaling the level of that in moderately developed countries. The length of expressway was 495.8 km, first-class road 1058.9 km, secondary 775.3 km, tertiary 1533.1 km, and forth-class 6354.9 km. Four major railway projects were constructed in 2013 and a mileage of 65.5 km was increased. Hangzhou-Ningbo passenger transport lines were put into use and modern railway of south station was officially put into operation. The replacement of north goods ring lines and north station carried forward in 2013 as scheduled. The construction of a internationally-competitive port was accelerated. Construction of seven 10,000-ton berths was completed; the container berth 3-5# water works in Meishan Port were completed and accepted; the oil fuel 300,000-ton oil wharf in Daxie Port passed the acceptance; the container wharf water works and land works in Phase V in Chuanshan Port were completed; Daxie Xinhai oil products storage project of crude oil and fuel oil tank of 600,000 m3 in Phase I was completed and put into operation.

Integrated transportation: The social cargo transportation volume in 2013 was 354 million tons, up by 8.6%, where, the water cargo transportation volume was 154 million tons with turnover volume of 190.53 billion tons, increased respectively by 9.4% and 7.7%; and road cargo transportation volume was 178 million tons with turnover volume of 32.55 billion tons, increased respectively by 7.4% and 7.6%; railway transportation volume was 21.682 million tons, up by 13.6%; airport cargo transportation volume was 66,000 tons, up by 7.3%. The total passenger volume was 248 million person-time, down by 11.6%; railway passenger transportation volume was 12.731 million person-time, up by 12.9%; and the passenger transportation volume by civil aviation was 5.459 million person-time, up by 3.7%.

VIII. Banking, Securities and Insurance

Banking: The deposit of domestic and foreign currency in the financial institutions in Ningbo has reached ￥1.32 trillion at the end of 2013, up by 9.9% compared with that of last year. Among which, the RMB deposit balance of was ￥1.27 trillion, up by 9.8%; the loan balance of domestic and foreign currency in financial institutional at the end of 2013 was ￥1.33 trillion, up by 11.3%. The newly-increased deposit balance reached ￥132.65 billion, up by ￥4.08 billion. The loan balance of small and micro businesses at the end of the year was 394.17, up by ￥10.75 billion compared with that of last year. The newly-increased small and micro enterprise loan accounted for 43.3% of the total increased enterprise loan. The non-performing loan ratio in financial institutions in Ningbo at the end of 2013 was 1.58%, up by 0.37% compared with that at the beginning of 2013, indicating that the overall loan risk is controllable. The net profits of financial institutions in 2013 were ￥24.42 billion, down by 8.4%. The number of financial institutions at the end of 2013 has totaled 63, including 3 policy banks, 5 large-scale banks, 11 joint-stock commercial banks, 12 city commercial banks, 1 postal savings bank, 5 foreign banks, 9 rural cooperative financial institutions, 14 new-type rural financial institutions and 3 non-bank financial institutions.

Securities: The total transaction volume of securities in Ningbo in 2013 has reached ￥2.16 trillion, up by 49.0%, where, the transaction volume of share and funds was ￥1.37 trillion, up by 39.1%. The settlement amount of securities transaction was ￥6.62 billion, decreased by 5.1%. The transaction volume of futures agent was 52.974 million and agent transaction amount of ￥5.35 trillion, increased respectively by 14.1% and 27.4%. The new clients of securities at the end of 2013 were 984,000, up by 5.6%. The new operation offices of futures were 4 within 2013. By the end of 2013, there were 69 securities operation offices, 1 securities investment and consultation company, 1 futures company and 35 futures operation offices. The domestic listing companies in 2013 achieved IPO of ￥1.86 billion, totaling 42 public companies by far.

Insurance: The premium income of insurance industry in Ningbo in 2013 was ￥18.55 billion, up by 12.6% compared with that of last year. Among the above, ￥9.68 billion was for property insurance, up by 12.3%; ￥8.87 billion was for life insurance, up by 13.0%. The accumulative compensation and payment in insurance industry was ￥10.39 billion, up by 61.7%. Among the above, ￥8.95 billion was for property insurance, up by 72.5%; and ￥1.44 billion for life insurance, up by 16.2%. Various risk guarantee of￥6.59 trillion was provided for 37,000 enterprises, 2.295 million vehicles and 12.109 million people. Annual export risk guarantee of ￥98.15 billion was provided for 3,361 enterprises in Ningbo. The pilot insurance types of policy-oriented agricultural insurance were increased to 22 and an accumulative risk guarantee of ￥4.61 billion was provided to 142,000 farmers, with total indemnity of ￥185 million paid, up by 76.2%.

IX. Science & Technology, Education and Talents

Scientific and technical innovation: the innovation ability is improved significantly. In 2013, 33 provincial science and technology awards in Ningbo were granted, including 15 first prizes and second prices. "HP2-52C full automatic computerized flat knitter" was listed as the national strategic innovation product. The number of patents awarded was 58,000 and the number of patents for innovation awarded was 2246, up by 8.8% compared with that of last year. The 45 R&D centers of provincial high-tech technical enterprises, 13 engineering centers of provincial enterprises and 116 engineering (technical) centers of municipal enterprises were evaluated and identified by Ningbo city. The 42 high-tech enterprises in Ningbo were newly-developed, with 197 high-tech enterprises, 216 municipal science and technology enterprises, 7 provincial innovation and demonstration enterprises and 5 provincial innovation and pilot enterprises being newly identified. The 10 municipal key labs, 32 municipal enterprise research institutes, 11 provincial enterprise research institutes were developed and identified; 74 innovation carriers were introduced and co-constructed and 2 industrial technology innovation unions were constructed. The support effect of agricultural technological innovation was obvious: 12 new agricultural varieties were cultivated and 15 scientific and technological projects in agricultural and social development field were listed as national scientific and technological projects such as "863" plan and science and technology support program. There were 258 technical service enterprises above designed size at the end of 2013, achieving annual turnover revenue of ￥13.10 billion and total profits of ￥2.29 billion, increased respectively by 24.3% and 23.5%.

Education: There were 2,097 schools at different levels and varieties in Ningbo at the end of 2013, with students enrolled of 1.334 million, among which there were 16 colleges and universities, with students enrolled of 153,000; 81 ordinary high schools, with students enrolled of 97,000; 55 secondary vocational schools, with students enrolled of 78,000; 216 middle schools, with students enrolled of 189,000; 465 primary schools, with students enrolled of 487,000; 1,254 kindergartens, with students enrolled of 276,000. There were 88 new (renovated and expanded) kindergartens listed in Ningbo ten practical projects. Seven counties (cities) such as Haishu County and Jiangdong County have passed the supervision and inspection of basic balanced development of national compulsory education. There were 105 compulsory education standardized schools increased and the number of compulsory education standardized schools in Ningbo reached 473. The characteristic and diversified development of ordinary high schools was promoted: 19 provincial Grade-1 characteristic model schools in Ningbo and 23 provincial Grade-2 characteristic model schools in Ningbo were declared. The national education international cooperation, communication and comprehensive reform pilot area were constructed; the education cooperation and communication conferences in China, the United States, Ningbo and Auckland have been successfully held and 33 education cooperation agreements were signed. The number of overseas students in Ningbo colleges and universities reached 2500, up by 56% compared with that of last year; "friendly communication between colleges and universities" action plan was implemented and the number of new sister middle and primary schools reached 78.

Talent cultivation: The number of talents of different industries was up by 182,000 in 2013, and the total talents in Ningbo at the end of 2013 amounted to 1.483 million, up by 12.2%. There were 20 new experts from national "Program of Overseas Talent Introduction", 41 new experts from provincial "Program of Overseas Talent Introduction", 47 talents newly evaluated from "3315 plan", 21 high-end entrepreneurial innovation teams, 225 overseas engineers introduced and 6 high-end foreign experts. There were 15 new academician research stations, totaling 69 stations; there were 5 national postdoctoral research workstations, with the total number of doctors and post doctors being about 3,800. There were 11 new municipal technicians studios and 3 public practical training bases for high-skilled talents, in which 215,000 talents accepted the skill trainings and 130,000 talents accepted the skill appraisal and 24,000 high-skilled talents were cultivated, with the total number of high-skill talents reaching 234,000.

X. Culture, Health and Sports

Cultural construction: In 2013, 11 counties (cities) in Ningbo successfully established Zhejiang advanced cultural counties (cities) and Yinzhou District and Cixi City separately established the national public cultural service system demonstration zone and Zhejiang public cultural service system demonstration zone. The activity of "introduction of 10,000 movies and 1,000 dramas into country" was carried out in a deep-going way, with more than 30,000 rural movies played and more than 6000 dramas performed. The innovative "natural stage" was launched for 60 cultural activities such as four major "performance seasons", with the total number of actors reaching more than 8000 and the number of audiences reaching about 500,000. Ningbo digital library project was constructed in a deep-going way and more than 1.76 million references and literatures were displayed and more than 15 million literatures were downloaded. There were 512 lectures held in Ningbo Cultural Lecture Hall, with the audience of more than 100,000 attended, thus making the Hall become the most popular public cultural service platform in Ningbo. The large-scale original opera "Hongbang Tailor" was performed in National Grand Theatre and was listed as one of the performances in "2013 Excellent Performances of National Arts Group"; seven works such as "Green Bamboo" and "Story of Army Service Station" were awarded "the National 16th Galaxy Award", accounting for half of the total awarded works in Zhejiang, hitting a historical high. The cultural facilities were under stable construction and the domestic first large-scale knowledge imparting-oriented entertainment complex-Ningbo Cultural Plaza was officially opened. The cultural industry is under rapid development. There were 9 enterprises and 2 projects in Ningbo were shortlisted as 2013-2014 national key cultural export enterprises and key projects and 4 enterprises were identified as national animation enterprises and animation protection brands; "Yong Effendi" was awarded the 2013 national animation brand. In 2013, nine national protection units such as Tashan Historic Site were newly identified and the number of national protection units was increased to 31, ranking the second place in Zhejiang Province and ranking the first place in municipalities within independent planning status.

Medical and health services: The medical treatment and public health conditions of urban and rural residents have been further improved. At the end of 2013, Ningbo owned 29,000 hospital beds, 62,000 health workers and 52,000 health workers, including 20,000 medical practitioners (assistants included) and 20,000 registered nurses. According to the statistics of registered population, the number of hospital beds, health workers, medical practitioners (assistants included) and registered nurses per thousand people reached 5.0, 9.0, 3.4 and 3.4 respectively. The northern project of Ningbo Women's & Children's Hospital was completed, and the infrastructures construction project such as the eastern project of Lihuili Hospital and original medical building reconstruction and expansion of Ningbo First People's Hospital were under smooth construction. By the end of 2013, there have been 152 community health service centers (health center) in total, 133 of which satisfied the provincial level, at a rate of 87.5%, ranking the first in Zhejiang Province. In addition, 28 demonstration community health service centers at provincial level have been established, 6 of which meet national standard. New rural co-operative medical system was further consolidated, benefiting 2.657 million people, accounting for 98.3% of the rural population. Per capita funding level has increased from ￥565 of last year to ￥590 in 2013. The total reported morbidity of Class A and B infectious diseases was 184.14/100,000; the vaccine inoculation rate of children at school age was 98.4%. The immunoprophylaxis service quality stood out around the whole province. The work of blood donation without payment was under steady development with 71,000 person-time donation around the year, maintaining our target that all blood for clinical use was from voluntary blood donation.

Sports: The public sports service was effectively improved and the rate of free and regular opening of municipal venues reached 100%. About 98% of the sports facilities of public middle and primary schools in the urban areas were open to citizens; more than 173 stadiums were constructed and 530 sets of fitness paths were updated; the owning rate of administrative sports fitness paths reached 100%. Jiangdong District successfully established a powerful sports area in Zhejiang Province. Ninghai County and Xiangshan County successfully passed the re-evaluation of excellence counties. The mass sports were abundant and colorful; with various forms of national fitness lecture halls established, the citizens were instructed to do exercises in a scientific manner. New Year 10,000 Long-distance Run was held in East New City for the first time. In the 12th National Games, 90 Ningbo-born athletes reached the final and won 6 gold medals, 8 silver medals and 13 bronze medals, 1 of which broke the Asian record once and 2 of which broke the national records for twice. The number of athletes, gold medals and other medals hit a historical high since Ningbo City jointed the National Games, with a large number of excellent young sports talents developed and “provincial and municipal sports teams” made rich achievements. In 2013, Ningbo athletes won the third price of two world-class competitions, the first price of three Asian competitions, second price of one Asian competition and 29 gold medals, 24 silver medals and 26 bronze medals in national games. The sports undertakings and sport industry were under harmonious development. We have held 50 games of national level or above; Yinzhou District and Beilun District were awarded the national best competition area and national excellent competition area respectively by State General Administration of Sports; and the sales of sports lottery tickets have witnessed a new breakthrough, reaching ￥1.56 billion and becoming a historically high.

XI. Population, Livelihood, Social Insurance and Social Organization

Population increase: The registered population in Ningbo was 5.801 million in 2013, up by 24,000, including 2.276 million urban population. The birth rate and death rate were 8.52‰ and 6.13‰ respectively. The proportion of planned birth was 95.9% and comprehensive contraception rate of married women of reproductive age was 89.1%, with moderately low birth rate remaining stable. The integrated management of family planning of floating population was further enhanced, with the controlled information rate of floating reproductive aged women being 97.5%.

Resident income: The disposable income per urban resident was ￥41,729 in 2013, up by 10.1% (actual growth of 7.7% if the price element counted); the net income per rural resident was ￥20,534, up by 11.1% (actual growth of 8.8% if the price element counted). From the perspective of income source, wage remained the decisive element for the income increase of residents, which contributed to the income increase for urban and rural residents at 76.7% and 75.8% respectively. The ratio of income of urban and rural residents was reduced from 2.05:1 in 2012 to 2.03:1 in 2013, which was remarkably lower than the national average level (3.03:1). In 2013, the per capita consumption expenditure of urban residents was ￥24,685, up by 6.0% compared with that of last year; the per capita consumption expenditure of rural residents was ￥13,915, up by 9.6%.

Social security system: At the end of 2013, the number of people purchasing basic retirement insurance in enterprises, basic medical insurance of employees, unemployment insurance, work-related injury insurance and maternity insurance was 5.089 million, 3.463 million, 2.317 million, 2.834 million and 2.455 million respectively, with a net increase of 346,000 people, 197,000 people, 155,000 people, 132,000 people and 124,000 people respectively compared with that of last year. The number of card holders reached more than 3.30 million. By the end of 2013, the number of migrant workers purchasing five social insurances has reached 2.13 million and the net increased number of people purchasing such insurances during the whole year has been 336,000. At the end of 2013, the number of people purchasing retirement insurance for land-deprived persons was 512,000, with the proportion of key objects of 88.9%. At the end of 2013, the number of people purchasing urban and rural resident endowment insurance was 1.329 million. The social security benefits were gradually improved and the per capita pension of enterprise retirees was ￥2083/month, with an increase of ￥148/month; the distribution standard of unemployment insurance benefits was increased to ￥1103/month, with an increase of ￥55/month; and the ratio for reimbursement of hospitalization expenses and special disease expenses within the policy area of urban employees and residents has risen to 86.8% and 72.3% respectively.

People' s livelihood security: In 2013, the minimum living standard of urban and rural residents in Ningbo was increased from ￥525/month to ￥588/month. At the end of 2013, the total number of people receiving basic cost of living allowances was 55,000 and the actual cost of minimum living allowances reached ￥230 million. The medical assistance system was further improved, with the number of people in illness and difficulties in living of 184,000 and the expenditure of medical assistance funds of ￥150 million. The linkage mechanism of basic living price subsidies of people in straitened circumstances was implemented and a total amount of funds of ￥9.803 million was spent. Social endowment coverage was effectively expanded and 82 private retirement organizations were established in Ningbo, with the number of beds for the aged of 26,382; 183 home-based care services stations were newly established or expanded in 2013 and the home-based care service covered more than 90% of the urban communities and more than 50% of the administrative villages. In 2013, the number of students accepting hardship-aid policies was 906,000, with the accumulative aid funds reaching ￥800 million.

Government-subsidized housing project: In 2013, the area and number of government-subsidized housing projects newly constructed in the city was 1.6 millionm2 and 18,301 sets. The number of completed government-subsidized housing projects was 1.34 millionm2 and 17,427 sets. The number of people solved the living problems was 14,069 and tasks specified by provincial government have been outperformed The public rental housing communities such as Hongtang and Tangyayuan were constructed and put into operation as scheduled and the rental services were successfully completed.

Charity: In 2013, city and county level charitable organizations have raised a donation of ￥550 million, up by 24.4% compared with that of last year and paid ￥43,000 for aid work, up by 18.1%. The number of people in straitened circumstances and receiving help from such charitable organizations was 438,000. By the end of 2013, the accumulated funds raised by charitable organizations in the city have reached ￥3.99 billion and accumulated funds paid for aid work have been ￥2.76 billion. The number of people in straitened circumstances and receiving help from such charitable organizations was 2.143 million. Over 1,854 various voluntary service activities have been conducted and more than 23,341 volunteers have participated in providing the service all the year around. The accumulated service time was 60,035.5 hours.

Social organization: By the end of 2013, there were 6 districts, 2 counties, 3 county-level cities, 77 towns, 11 villages, 64 sub-district offices, 663 neighborhood committees and 2,556 villages committees in the whole city.

XII. Ecological Construction and Social Safety

Ecological construction: Special environmental rectification has proved highly successful. In 2013, the construction of "no burning zone" that is 540 km2 away from the ring expressway in central urban area was completed, with the accumulative sets of obsolete and transformed coal-fired boilers reaching 1,139; prevention and control of motor vehicle exhaust was implemented to limit the transportation of high-pollution vehicles and the elimination policy of yellow label car was issued; environmental improvement was continuously carried out in a deep-going way in top 10 heavy pollution industries such as electroplating, printing and dyeing, chemical engineering and paper making and a total amount of ￥46 million special funds were invested in municipal environmental protection projects; 830 unqualified enterprises were closed; special treatment of drinking water source protection areas was conducted and 38 polluting enterprises within the protection areas were listed for supervision. Ten sets of units such as Beilun Power Plant, Ninghai Guohua Power Plant and Xiangshan Datang Wushashan Power Plant with 7.2 million kilowatts of desulfurization facilities, open circuits and bypasses and 8 sets of 3.5 million kilowatts denitrification construction and cement industry denitrification projects were completed; Ningbo key pollution source card swiping and sewage system was constructed and control management of total quantity of pollutants was implemented in order to ensure stable and standard operation of emission reduction facilities. Environmental law enforcement and supervision were strengthened continuously and nearly 50,482 law enforcement officers were deployed to inspect more than 27,642 companies. A total number of 1245 illegal cases were filed, with the amount of ￥57.53 million penalties reached. Monitoring and control capabilities were improved continuously; monitoring equipment of 10 provincial-controlled atmospheric automatic stations was upgraded and reconstructed, Ningbo monitoring network of atmospheric combined pollution was constructed to ensure timely release of air quality and heavy pollution weather warning information to the public. Various eco-environment protection activities were carried out continuously; Beilun District passed site assessment of provincial ecological zone, while Ninghai County and Xiangshan County passed national ecological county acceptance respectively.

“Peaceful Ningbo” construction: In 2013, there were 2,866 work safety accidents occurred in Ningbo, which resulted in 745 deaths, 2,855 injuries and direct economic losses of ￥30.079 million. Such figures have dropped by 9.4%, 3.1%, 9.1% and 9.8% respectively when compared with those of last year. The four indicators of safety production have been lowered in the 9th consecutive year when compared with that of last year. The inspection of food and drugs was enhanced. In 2013, 47,870 batches of food have been subject to quantitative inspection and 2,515 batches of drugs have been subject to supervision and casual inspection, accounting for 110.3% and 100.6% of the total task load of the whole year respectively; among which, 188 batches were inspected to be unqualified and positive rate was 7.5%; the monitoring of adverse drug reaction and medical device administration events was enhanced. A total number of 8124 cases of adverse drug reaction were reported, among which the number of new and serious adverse drug reaction accounted for 46.7%. In 2013, a total number of 141,000 law enforcement officers attended the enforcement actions and inspected 76,000 food and drugs units; 1,532 cases about medical instrument and catering were put on record. Among these cases, 1419 cases were settled. The fine and confiscated amount was 16.273 million while the value for confiscated articles totaled 1.614 million, and 23 cases were handed over to public security organ. Establishment of stable and harmonious labor relationship was enhanced and the rate of signed enterprise labor contracts and rate of signed collective labor contracts of established unions and enterprises reached 97% and 92% respectively; prevention and treatment of back-salary mechanism was established, based which a total amount of ￥180 million unpaid salary was recovered for 24,000 employees; the labor dispute processing efficiency was improved and 31,000 cases of labor disputes were accepted, with the settlement rate of arbitration and mediation being 93% and 73.6% respectively. In 2013, 35,189 letters and visits of the masses had been accepted, down by 3.6% and 1327 times (17,953 people) of collective appeals from the masses had been received, down by 7.2% and 7.4% respectively. People's compromise organizations have mediated 118,000 civil disputes during the whole year. Among these disputes, 116,000 disputes have been successfully settled through mediation with success rate of 98.4%. The 34 suicides committed by 34 people because of civil disputes have been prevented; 155 civil disputes involving 504 people have been prevented from developing into criminal cases.

Note: (1) All figures in this Bulletin are preliminary statistics.

(2) Figures in value terms on gross municipal product and value-added quoted in this Bulletin are at current prices,

whereas growth rates are calculated at comparable prices.

(3) Industrial enterprises above designated size refer to those enterprises with annual main business income equal to more than ￥20 million.

Wholesale, retail, accommodation and catering enterprises above the limit refer to:

Wholesale industry: wholesale enterprises with annual main business income equal to or more than ￥20 million;

Retail industry: retail enterprises with annual main business income equal to or more than ￥5 million;

Accommodation industry: enterprises with annual main business income equal to or more than ￥2 million;

Catering industry: catering enterprises with annual main business income equal to or more than ￥2 million.

CHAPTER 1

NINGBO 2014 Statistical YearBook

第一篇

综合

GENERAL SURVEY

综合
General Survey

宁波的经济发展
Economic Development of Ningbo

		2013	比上年增长(%) Increase Over Last Year
国内生产总值(亿元)	Gross Domestic Product(100 million yuan)	7128.87	8.1
第一产业	Primary Industry	276.35	−1.2
第二产业	Secondary Industry	3741.72	8.2
第三产业	Tertiary Industry	3110.80	8.4
规模以上工业总产值	Gross Output Value of Above Designated Sized Industry	13010.09	7.0
固定资产投资	Investemnt in Fixed Assets	3422.95	18.0
社会消费品零售总额	Total Retail Sales of Consumer Goods	2635.71	13.2
公共财政预算收入	Public Fiscal Budget Revenue	1651.18	7.5
港口货物吞吐量(万吨)	Ports Cargo Handling Capacity(10000 tons)	49591.71	9.5
集装箱吞吐量(万标箱)	Container Handled at Ports(10000 TEU)	1677.37	7.0
自营进出口额(亿美元)	Directive Import and Export(USD 100 million)	1003.29	3.9
出口额(亿美元)	Export(USD 100 million)	657.10	7.0
实际利用外资	Amount of Foreign Capital Actually Used	32.75	14.8

宁波的一天
One Day in Ningbo

国内生产总值	Gross Domestic Product	195311	万元	10000 yuan
农业增加值	Value−added of Agriculture	7531	万元	10000 yuan
工业增加值	Value−added of Industry	92547	万元	10000 yuan
第三产业增加值	Value−added of Tertiary Industry	85227	万元	10000 yuan
固定资产投资	Investment in Fixed Assets	93780	万元	10000 yuan
社会消费品零售额	Retail Sales of Consumer Goods	72211	万元	10000 yuan
公共财政预算收入	Public Fiscal Budget Revenue	45238	万元	10000 yuan
港口货物吞吐量	Ports Cargo Handling Capacity	135.87	万吨	10000 tons
集装箱吞吐量	Container Handled at Ports	45955	标箱	TEU
自营出口额	Directive Export	18003	万美元	USD 10000
全社会用电量	Electricity Consumption	15326	万千瓦时	10000 kwh

表 1－1 行政区划和陆域面积(2013) Administrative Division and Land Area

单位:个(unit)

地区	Region	镇 Town	乡 Township	街道办事处 Subdistrict Offices	居民委员会 Neighborhood Committee	村民委员会 Villages Committee	陆域面积(平方公里) Land Area (sq. km)
全市	**Whole Municipality**	**77**	**11**	**64**	**663**	**2556**	**9816**
市区	**Urban Area**	**22**	**2**	**41**	**407**	**786**	**2461**
海曙	Haishu			8	76		29
江东	Jiangdong			8	79		34
江北	Jiangbei	1		7	68	93	208
北仑	Beilun	2	1	7	48	204	599
镇海	Zhenhai	2		4	31	60	246
鄞州	Yinzhou	17	1	7	105	429	1345
县级市	**County**	**55**	**9**	**23**	**256**	**1770**	**7355**
余姚	Yuyao	14	1	6	56	265	1501
慈溪	Cixi	14		5	78	297	1361
奉化	Fenghua	6		5	37	355	1268
象山	Xiangshan	10	5	3	45	490	1382
宁海	Ninghai	11	3	4	40	363	1843

表 1－2 各月主要气象指标(2013) Main Climate Indicators

时间 Item		平均气温(℃) Average Temperature (℃)	降水量(毫米) Precipitation (millimeters)	相对湿度(%) Relative Humidity (%)	日照时数(小时) Sunshine Hours (hours)
1月	Jan.	4.8	34.1	74.0	122.8
2月	Feb.	7.9	89.2	80.0	46.0
3月	Mar.	12.1	114.5	69.0	171.0
4月	Apr.	16.4	112.5	60.0	192.8
5月	May	22.2	73.6	74.0	192.4
6月	June	24.9	324.2	82.0	100.6
7月	July	31.2	69.3	63.0	338.3
8月	Aug.	30.7	251.6	67.0	263.1
9月	Sept.	25.5	32.9	71.0	223.8
10月	Oct.	19.9	424.0	73.0	161.3
11月	Nov.	13.8	42.6	67.0	178.3
12月	Dec.	6.6	114.3	64.0	173.1

注:本表数据来自宁波市气象局。

Note:Data in this table are obtained from Ningbo Meteorological Bureau.

表1—3 部分年份国民经济主要指标 Main Indicators of National Economy in Partial Years

指标	单位	Indicators	Unit
人口		**Population**	
年末总人口	万人	Year—end Population	10000 persons
#非农业人口	万人	Non—Agriculture Population	10000 persons
地区生产总值	**亿元**	**Gross Domestic Product**	**100 million yuan**
第一产业增加值	亿元	Added Value of Primary Industry	100 million yuan
第二产业增加值	亿元	Added Value of Secondary Industry	100 million yuan
第三产业增加值	亿元	Added Value of Tertiary Industry	100 million yuan
人均生产总值(户籍人口)	**元**	**Per Capital GDP(by Registered Population)**	**yuan**
人均生产总值(常住人口)	**元**	**Per Capital GDP(by Permanent Population)**	**yuan**
农业		**Agriculture**	
农村实有劳动力	万人	Rural Labor force	10000 persons
粮食产量	万吨	Yield of Grain Crops	10000 tons
工业		**Industry**	
全部工业增加值	亿元	Added Value of Industry	100 million yuan
运输、邮电和通信		**Transportation, Post and Telecommunications Services**	
港口货物吞吐量	万吨	Cargo Handled at Ports	10000 tons
集装箱吞吐量	万标箱	Container Handled at Ports	10000 TEU
旅客运输量	万人	Passenger Traffic	10000 persons
货物运输量	万吨	Freight Traffic	10000 tons
固定电话用户	万户	Number of Local Telephone Subscribers	10000 subscribers
移动电话用户	万户	Number of Subscribers of Mobile Telephone	10000 subscribers
全社会用电量	**亿千瓦时**	**Total Consumption of Electricity**	**100 million kwh**
#工业用电	亿千瓦时	Electricity Consumption for Industry Use	100 million kwh
生活用电	亿千瓦时	Electricity Consumption for Urban and Rural Residents	100 million kwh
固定资产投资	**亿元**	**Investment in Fixed Assets**	**100 million yuan**
#房地产开发投资	亿元	Real Estate Development	100 million yuan

注:本表价值量指标按当年价格计算,发展速度按可比价格计算。

Note:Figures in value terms are calculated at current prices,While the indices and growth rates are calculated at comparable prices.

1978	1990	2000	2010	2011	2012	2013	指数(2013 为以下各年%) Index(2013As Percentage of the Following Years)			年平均增长(%) Average Annual Growth Rate(%)	
							1978	2000	2010	1978—2013	2000—2013
457.70	510.76	540.94	574.08	576.40	577.71	580.15	126.8	107.2	101.1	0.7	0.5
63.42	102.98	142.03	205.23	208.18	211.45	214.35	338.0	150.9	104.4	3.5	3.2
20.17	**141.40**	**1144.57**	**5163.00**	**6059.24**	**6582.21**	**7128.87**	**9238.3**	**429.3**	**128.2**	**13.8**	**11.9**
6.52	29.35	94.24	219.13	255.23	268.52	276.35	458.5	154.9	103.7	4.4	3.4
9.69	80.31	635.83	2870.69	3349.53	3516.84	3741.72	16056.2	431.0	125.8	15.6	11.9
3.96	31.74	414.50	2073.18	2454.48	2796.85	3110.80	11597.9	489.1	134.1	14.5	13.0
437	**2777**	**21208**	**90175**	**105333**	**114065**	**123139**	**6745.2**	**392.8**	**126.7**	**12.8**	**11.1**
			69368	**79524**	**86228**	**93176**			**124.6**		
195.42	254.12	257.44	306.32	306.36	293.79	312.07	159.7	121.2	101.9	1.3	1.5
180.51	189.06	132.51	87.13	90.14	86.57	81.25	45.0	61.3	93.3	−2.3	−3.7
8.62	72.12	578.30	2586.17	3019.00	3170.07	3377.97	20838.1	442.8	126.7	16.5	12.1
214	2554	11547	41217	43339	45303	49592	23173.8	429.5	120.3	16.8	11.0
	2.21	90.20	1300.35	1451.24	1567.14	1677.37		1859.6	129.0		25.2
2966	7378	22736	33911	28745	28053	24793	835.9	109.0	73.1	6.3	0.7
1385	4763	10819	30553	31228	32616	35409	2556.6	327.3	115.9	9.7	9.5
1.07	6.19	130.15	317.39	312.45	308	298	27850.5	229.0	93.9	17.4	6.6
		117.92	845.50	1029.46	1088	1228		1041.4	145.2		19.8
7.09	**31.49**	**113.48**	**459.04**	**505.30**	**514.09**	**559.39**	**7889.9**	**492.9**	**121.9**	**13.3**	**13.1**
4.37	23.38	84.01	354.27	388.62	384.59	414.98	9496.1	494.0	117.1	13.9	13.1
0.43	4.30	15.13	49.83	53.59	59.31	66.13	15378.5	437.1	132.7	15.5	12.0
5.02	**39.28**	**360.75**	**2193.28**	**2385.50**	**2901.43**	**3422.95**	**68186.3**	**948.8**	**156.1**	**20.5**	**18.9**
	2.49	59.71	557.27	754.94	884.35	1123.14		1881.0	201.5		25.3

表 1—3 续表 Continued

指标	单位	Indicators	Unit
财政金融		**Finance and Banking**	
财政总收入	亿元	Financial Budgetary Revenue	100 million yuan
财政支出	亿元	Financial Expenditure	100 million yuan
年末金融机构存款余额	亿元	Balance of Deposits of Financial Institutions	100 million yuan
#城乡居民储蓄存款	亿元	Saving Deposits of Urban and Rural Residents	100 million yuan
年末金融机构贷款余额	亿元	Balance of Loans of Financial Institutions	100 million yuan
社会消费品零售总额	**亿元**	**Total Retail Sales of Consumer Goods**	**100 million yuan**
对外经济		**Foreign Trade**	
进出口总额	亿美元	Total Exports and Imports Value	USD 100 million
#出口总额	亿美元	Total Exports Value	USD 100 million
进口总额	亿美元	Total Imports Value	USD 100 million
合同利用外资	亿美元	Foreign Investment Contracted	USD 100 million
实际利用外资	亿美元	Foreign Investments Actually Use	USD 100 million
城乡居民生活		**Living Standard**	
市区居民人均可支配收入	元	Per Capital Disposable Income of Urban Households	yuan
市区居民人均消费性支出	元	Per Capital Annual Expenditure for Consumption of Urban Households	yuan
农村居民人均纯收入	元	Per Capital Annual Net Income of Rural Housholds	yuan
农村居民人均生活消费支出	元	Per Capita Annual Living Expenditure of Rural Residents	yuan
教育		**Education**	
高等学校在校学生数	万人	Students Enrollment in Institutions of Higher Education	10000 persons
中等专业学校在校学生数	万人	Students Enrollment in Specializad Secondary Schools	10000 persons
中学在校学生数	万人	Students Enrollment in Secondary Schools	10000 persons
小学在校学生数	万人	Students Enrollment in Primary Schools	10000 persons
专任教师数	万人	Number of Full—times Teachers	10000 persons
卫生事业		**Health Care**	
卫生技术人员数	万人	Number of Medical Technical Personnel	10000 persons
#医生	万人	Doctor	10000 persons
卫生机构床位数	张	Number of Beds in Health Institutions	bed

1978	1990	2000	2010	2011	2012	2013	指数(2013 为以下各年%) Index(2013As Percentage of the Following Years)			年平均增长(%) Average Annual Growth Rate(%)	
							1978	2000	2010	1978—2013	2000—2013
4.97	15.89	148.01	2068.62	2271.95	2206.04	2666.26	53647.1	1801.4	128.9	19.7	24.9
1.12	9.71	89.23	1452.17	1596.78	1516.16	1971.44	176021.3	2209.4	135.8	23.8	26.9
4.84	90.13	1172.94	9552.03	10435.92	11602.32	12740.52	263233.9	1086.2	133.4	25.2	20.1
1.52	46.12	586.06	3282.26	3666.23	4175.96	4562.36	300155.5	778.5	139.0	25.7	17.1
6.50	97.44	883.12	9000.62	10209.99	11300.32	12493.28	192204.2	1414.7	138.8	24.1	22.6
7.07	**54.98**	**389.29**	**1704.51**	**2018.86**	**2329.26**	**2635.71**	**37280.2**	**677.1**	**154.6**	**18.4**	**15.8**
	2.98	75.41	829.04	981.87	965.73	1003.29		1330.4	121.0		22.0
	2.80	51.68	519.67	608.32	614.45	657.10		1271.5	126.4		21.6
	0.18	23.73	309.37	373.55	351.27	346.19		1458.9	111.9		22.9
	0.56	9.52	40.46	50.15	53.13	58.20		611.4	143.9		14.9
	0.22	6.22	23.23	28.09	28.53	32.75		526.5	141.0		13.6
306	1963	10921	30166	34058	37902	41729	13636.9	382.1	138.3	15.1	10.9
299	1628	7997	19420	21779	23288	24685	8255.9	308.7	127.1	13.4	9.1
	1254	5069	14261	16518	18475	20534		405.1	144.0		11.4
	1166	3929	9794	11253	12699	13915		354.2	142.1		10.2
0.10	0.49	2.59	14.08	14.44	14.54	14.90	14895.4	575.1	105.8	15.4	14.4
0.29	0.90	2.51	8.07	8.28	8.03	7.83	2701.6	312.1	97.1	9.9	9.2
27.16	19.65	27.98	32.54	30.86	29.52	28.59	105.3	102.2	87.9	0.1	0.2
59.11	42.70	42.40	46.19	47.61	47.88	48.70	82.4	114.9	105.4	−0.6	1.1
3.55	3.34	5.17	7.29	7.70	7.63	7.82	220.2	151.2	107.2	2.3	3.2
0.93	1.58	1.92	4.31	4.67	4.92	5.15	553.9	268.3	119.5	5.0	7.9
0.36	0.75	0.95	1.72	1.84	1.91	1.99	554.1	210.0	116.0	5.0	5.9
5989	11449	14535	26097	27127	28290	29356	490.2	202.0	112.5	4.6	5.6

表1—4 各县(市)社会经济基本情况(2013)
Main Indicators of Society and Economy by Region

指标	单位	Indicators	Unit
人口、劳动力及土地面积		**Population, Employment and Land Areas**	
年末总人口	万人	Year—end Population	10000 persons
年平均人口	万人	Annual Average Population	10000 persons
常住人口	万人	Permanent Population	10000 persons
年末总户数	万户	Total Households of Year—end	10000 households
全社会从业人员	万人	Total Employment Personnel	10000 persons
第一产业	万人	Primary Industry	10000 persons
第二产业	万人	Secondary Industry	10000 persons
第三产业	万人	Tertiary Industry	10000 persons
年末城镇集体以上从业人员数	万人	Employed Personnel in Urban Collective—owned Units and Above Level	10000 persons
第一产业	万人	Primary Industry	10000 persons
第二产业	万人	Secondary Industry	10000 persons
第三产业	万人	Tertiary Industry	10000 persons
城镇私营和个体从业人员	万人	Employed Persons Individuals and Private Enterprises in Urban Areas	10000 persons
年末城镇登记失业人员数	人	Unemployed Persons in Urban Areas at Year—end	person
行政区域土地面积	平方公里	Land Area of Districts	sq. km
#建成区面积	平方公里	Developed Areas	sq. km
综合经济		**General Economy**	
生产总值(当年价格)	万元	Gross Domestic Product(at Current Price)	10000 yuan
第一产业增加值	万元	Value—added of Primary Industry	10000 yuan
第二产业增加值	万元	Value—added of Secondary Industry	10000 yuan
#工业增加值	万元	Value—added of Industry	10000 yuan
第三产业增加值	万元	Value—added of Tertiary Industry	10000 yuan
人均生产总值(常住)	元	Per Capital GDP(by Permanent Population)	yuan
人均生产总值(户籍)	元	Per Capital GDP(by Registered Population)	yuan
生产总值增长率	%	Increase Rate of GDP Over 2011	%
地方财政收入	万元	Local Financial Revenue	10000 yuan
公共财政预算支出	万元	Public Fiscal Budget Revenue	10000 yuan
#一般性公共服务支出	万元	Expenditure for General Public Services	10000 yuan
科学技术支出	万元	Expenditure for Science and Technology Promotion	10000 yuan
教育支出	万元	Expenditure for Education	10000 yuan
文化体育与传媒支出	万元	Expenditure for Culture, Sports & Media Services	10000 yuan
医疗卫生支出	万元	Expenditure for Medical and Health	10000 yuan
节能保护支出	万元	Expenditure for Energy Saving and Environmental Protection	10000 yuan
城乡社区事务支出	万元	Expenditure for Urban and Rural Community Services	10000 yuan
交通运输支出	万元	Expenditure for Transportation	10000 yuan
社会保障和就业支出	万元	Expenditure for Social Security & Employment	10000 yuan
住房保障支出	万元	Expenditure for Housing Security	10000 yuan
农林水事务支出	万元	Expenditure for Farming, Forestry and Fishery Service	10000 yuan

注:本表非年报数据。
Note: Data in this table was not reported data.

全市 Total	市区 Urban District	#鄞州 Yinzhou	余姚 Yuyao	慈溪 Cixi	奉化 Fenghua	象山 Xiangshan	宁海 Ninghai
580.15	227.59	84.01	83.51	104.36	48.37	54.38	61.93
578.93	226.85	83.57	83.48	104.28	48.36	54.21	61.75
766.30	352.08	136.98	101.61	147.14	49.52	50.99	64.96
223.56	90.57	33.82	30.89	42.26	18.20	18.62	23.01
503.36	234.97	96.61	65.74	83.20	35.36	36.29	47.80
28.85		5.56	7.33	10.20	6.39	8.12	8.30
274.07	133.98	57.61	32.63	49.60	18.19	17.07	22.60
200.44	112.48	33.44	25.78	23.40	10.78	11.10	16.90
171.35	99.55	25.29	15.30	14.07	5.87	29.27	7.28
0.06	0.02	0.00	0.01	0.02	0.00	0.00	0.01
112.05	57.86	17.62	11.12	9.03	3.56	26.51	3.99
59.24	41.68	7.67	4.18	5.02	2.32	2.77	3.28
1704800	1251700	383600	80400	65000	100300	69400	138000
69230	56100	13917	3544	3116	2259	3046	1165
9816.23	2461.76	1345.54	1500.80	1360.63	1267.60	1382.18	1843.26
468.39	294.95		49.24	43.30	18.75	28.45	33.70
71288672	43094609	11776776	7496274	10310947	2903589	3638457	3844796
2763456	613391	400543	400600	492980	283532	579680	393273
37417195	21947242	7148237	4444737	5935659	1340238	1664999	2084320
33779655	19869387	6838486	4135167	5520098	1157510	1223610	1873883
31108021	20533976	4227996	2650937	3882308	1279819	1393778	1367203
93176	12260						
123139	189967	140926	89799	98882	60037	67121	62262
8.1	8.0	9.5	7.3	9.0	6.7	8.0	9.1
7928080	5507299	1532853	596390	920508	265662	306867	331354
9398939	6201396	1594212	745919	983925	455230	545353	467116
1048949	679903	156539	90190	109389	54853	52712	61902
375758	255258	73013	29708	49516	15224	13998	12054
1484777	867080	251581	134426	206843	93087	90969	92372
139095	96371	24646	14240	11191	4469	6045	6779
622133	352781	100791	75188	78038	32765	38023	45338
148078	98645	24214	12144	22369	4872	3956	6092
892401	786111	103205	26287	40418	12755	16757	10073
709516	562141	74874	35040	23967	27146	23431	37791
975644	600511	182082	119714	113544	36738	46605	58532
204488	153484	48668	8232	18485	6440	7386	10461
803773	260109	119623	84778	105769	110732	180587	61798

表 1—4 续 1 Continued

指标	单位	Indicators	Unit
年末金融机构存款余额	万元	Balance of Deposits of Financial Institutions	10000 yuan
#城乡居民储蓄年末余额	万元	Saving Deposits of Urban and Rural Residents	10000 yuan
年末金融机构各项贷款余额	万元	Balance of Loans of Financial Institutions	10000 yuan
保险		**Insurance**	
保费收入	万元	Insurance Income	10000 yuan
#财产险	万元	Property Insurance	10000 yuan
人身险	万元	Life Insurance	10000 yuan
赔款、给付	万元	Insurance Paid	10000 yuan
规模以上工业企业		**Industry Enterprises Above Designated Size**	
工业企业数	个	Number of Industrial Enterprises	unit
从业人员年平均人数	万人	Annual Average Employees	10000 persons
工业总产值(当年价)	万元	Gross Output Value of Indutry (at current price)	10000 yuan
主营业务收入	万元	Prime Operating Revenue	10000 yuan
本年应交增值税	万元	Value—added Taxes Payable in This Year	10000 yuan
利润总额	万元	Total Profits	10000 yuan
交通运输、邮电通信、能源电力		**Transport, Post & Telecommunications, Energy and Electricity**	
铁路客运量	万人	Railway Passenger Traffic	10000 persons
铁路货运量	万吨	Railway Freight Traffic	10000 tons
公路客运量	万人	Highways Passenger Traffic	10000 persons
公路货运量	万吨	Highways Freight Traffic	10000 tons
水运客运量	万人	Waterways Passenger Traffic	10000 persons
水运货运量	万吨	Waterways Freight Traffic	10000 tons
民用航空客运量	万人	Civil Aviation Passenger Traffic	10000 persons
民用航空货邮运量	万吨	Civil Aviation Freight Traffic	10000 ton
民用汽车拥有量	辆	Number of Civil Motor Vehicles	unit
#私人汽车拥有量	辆	Number of Private Car	unit
公路里程	公里	Length of Highways	km
邮政业务收入	万元	Business Value of Post	10000 yuan
电信业务收入	万元	Business Value of Telecommunications	10000 yuan
本地电话用户数	万户	Number of Subscribers of Local Telephone	10000 subscribers
年末移动电话用户数	万户	Number of Mobile Telephone Subscribers at Year—end	10000 subscribers
#3G 移动电话用户	万户	User of 3G Mobile Phone	10000 subscribers
国际互联网用户数	万户	User of International Computer Network	10000 subscribers
能源消费量	万吨标准煤	Total Volume of Energy Consumptions	10000 tons SCE
全年用电量	万千瓦时	Electricity Consumption	10000 kwh
国内贸易、对外经济		**Domestic Trade, Foreign Trade**	
社会消费品零售额	万元	Total Retail Sales of Consumer Goods	10000 yuan

全市 Total	市区 Urban District	#鄞州 Yinzhou	余姚 Yuyao	慈溪 Cixi	奉化 Fenghua	象山 Xiangshan	宁海 Ninghai
127405215	86815636	16657723	11542406	16686320	4061054	3816476	4111581
45623634	25915297	7400637	5652270	8234248	2196342	1721342	1875645
124932759	82045757	14288927	11609849	15787998	4677353	5444641	5137047
1854926							
968425							
886501							
1039131							
7167	3379	1689	1184	1268	437	430	469
147.50	75.02	31.15	20.18	27.24	8.64	7.07	9.35
130100892	85985775	21623686	12376426	17448888	3692926	4823726	5773151
125942442	84440119	20972989	11895625	16046908	3510517	4609019	5440254
3376861	2191453	489154	280827	437471	88143	158627	220342
7016804	4842992	1332701	517936	740702	98403	305552	511219
2834.09	2201.89		455.03		34.40		142.77
2904.60	2727.53	25.95	118.67	58.40			
22850	11060	3595	2450	2640	2260	2020	2420
17790	12260	3850	1470	1450	1110	720	780
124.00	7.79	7.79	0.29			84.18	31.74
15441	11566	820	40	12	342	2548	933
545.93	545.93	545.93					
94856.60	94856.60	94856.60					
1420578	777972	252390	182756	224926	79578	75699	79647
10892	3307	1924	1896	1554	1287	1301	1547
1060489	557604	182194	141243	178402	60142	61825	61273
95951	46124		12023	21892	5973	4016	5923
1225466	690047	189000	133369	204986	63850	65057	68156
298.00	158.94	48.82	36.27	47.08	20.11	20.18	15.42
1228.00	573.85	183.02	163.53	260.51	66.26	84.32	79.53
441.51							
250.00	131.48	41.85	30.49	43.42	14.46	15.75	14.41
2380.25	1875.71	170.35	143.28	180.43	39.86	57.93	83.03
5593943	3081224	765887	707855	1105005	261108	186261	252490
26357078	14077290	3562755	3412918	4448640	1238141	1698925	1481165

表 1—4 续 2 Continued

指标	单位	Indicators	Unit
当年新签合同项目数	个	New Signed Constract	unit
当年实际使用外资金额	万美元	Amount of Foreign Capital Actually Used	USD 10000
进口额	万美元	Total Import	USD 10000
出口额	万美元	Total Export	USD 10000
固定资产投资		**Investemnt in Fixed Assets**	
固定资产投资	万元	Investment in Fixed Assets	10000 yuan
#房地产开发投资完成额	万元	Real Estate Development	10000 yuan
#住宅	万元	Residential Buildings	10000 yuan
全年新增固定资产	万元	Newly Increase Fixed Assets in This Year	10000 yuan
商品房屋销售面积	万平方米	Floor Space of Building Sold	10000 sq. m
#住宅	万平方米	Residential Buildings	10000 sq. m
商品房屋销售额	万元	Total Actually Sales of Commercial Buildings	10000 yuan
#住宅	万元	Residential Buildings	10000 yuan
待售面积	万平方米	Floor Space of Sale Building	10000 sq. m
文教、卫生、科技		**Culture, Education, Public Health, Science**	
全日制学校数	所	Number of Full—time Schools	unit
各类学校专任教师数	人	Teachers	person
各类学校在校学生数	人	Students in School	person
专利申请受理量	项	Number of Patent Appliactions	piece
专利申请授权量	项	Number of Patent Certified	piece
#发明专利	项	Inventions	piece
体育场馆数	个	Number of Public Stadiums and Gymnasiums	unit
剧场、影剧院数	个	Number of Cinemas and Theatres	unit
公共图书馆图书藏量	千册、件	Collection of Public Libraries	1000 copies
医院、卫生院数	个	Number of Health Institutions	unit
卫生机构床位数	张	Number of Beds in Health Institutions	bed
医生数	人	Number of Doctors	person
注册护士	人	Number of Register Nurses	person
人民生活		**People's Livelihood**	
在岗职工平均人数	万人	Number of Full Employed Staff and Workers	10000 persons
在岗职工工资总额	万元	Total Wage of Full Employed Staff and Workers	10000 yuan
城镇居民人均可支配收入	元	Per Capital Annual Disposable Income of Urban Residents	yuan
城镇居民人均消费支出	元	Per Capital Annual Expenditure for Consumption of Urban Residents	yuan
农村居民人均纯收入	元	Per Capital Annual Net Income of Rural Residents	yuan
农村居民人均消费性支出	元	Per Capital Annual Expenditure for Consumption of Rural Residents	yuan
居民消费价格指数(上年=100)	%	Consumer Price Index (Preceding Year=100)	%

全市 Total	市区 Urban District	#鄞州 Yinzhou	余姚 Yuyao	慈溪 Cixi	奉化 Fenghua	象山 Xiangshan	宁海 Ninghai
442	297	88	42	49	8	21	25
327483	222459	46560	37011	41293	7108	9011	10601
3461875	2995576	358322	182381	189940	41330	29757	22891
6571020	4382176	1098340	650015	879116	246363	208159	205191
34229529	19320211	5050840	4400581	5449750	1540246	1611571	1907170
11231401	6687711	1988960	1330347	1749189	536220	526725	401209
6423263	3577483	1193453	716459	1084328	389331	381180	274482
22966367	15671565	3142710	2467468	2272283	960815	1055945	538291
730.09	429.34	136.04	79.40	128.15	20.87	30.61	41.72
581.95	328.68	102.31	61.52	110.45	18.93	29.05	33.32
8104011	5069095	1774042	919136	1224419	218575	327262	345524
6637387	4183544	1452711	630536	1019178	200881	307356	295892
491.45	302.51	99.04	60.09	71.95	16.64	17.88	22.39
831	336	144	141	142	56	60	82
78176	40017	11735	8768	13233	4707	5389	6062
1175467	596486	172704	143487	190508	72664	75360	96962
83334	42190	23926	17860	15422	2418	2513	2931
58406	28308	15131	12507	11443	2198	1854	2096
2246	1595	653	183	282	63	46	77
122	56	22	19	24	7	2	14
48	26	12	10	4	2	3	3
6678	4564	1160	533	617	210	408	347
219	84	29	21	32	30	23	29
28053	16930	3491	2501	3245	2154	1634	1589
19949	11025	2772	2031	3030	1257	1180	1426
19668	11292	2488	2087	2815	1086	1098	1290
144.48	86.92	23.65	14.10	13.14	5.45	18.60	6.26
9124123	5899934	1465496	767580	772455	318250	988040	377864
—	41729	44742	40938	41254	39414	40175	39942
—	24685	27482	23594	24973	22968	18429	18256
20534	22605	23156	19864	22702	19442	18127	18431
13915	16849	14921	12632	14700	10295	11168	12480
102.2	102.2	102.2	102.5	102.1	102.2	100.9	101.1

表 1—4 续 3 Continued

指标	单位	Indicators	Unit
基本养老保险参保人数	人	Number of Personnel Engaged Basic Endowment Insurance	person
基本医疗保险参保人数	人	Number of Personnel Engaged Basic Medical Insurance	person
失业保险参保人数	人	Number of Personnel Engaged Unemployment Insurance	person
社会福利院床位数	张	Number of Beds in Social Welfare Institutions	bed
社区服务设施数	个	Volunm of Service Establishment in Community	unit
城镇居民最低生活保障人数	人	Number Personnel Below Minimum Standard of Living	person
社会治安		**Social Security**	
交通事故死亡人数	人	Death of Traffic Accidents	person
交通事故损失额	万元	Losses Converted into Cash of Traffic Accidents	10000 yuan
刑事案件立案数	件	Number of Criminal Cases Registered	case
犯罪人数	人	Number of People of the Crime	person
市政公用事业		**Civil Facilities, Environment Protection**	
城市维护建设资金支出	万元	Expenditure on Urban Construction and Maintenance	10000 yuan
年末实有城市道路面积	万平方米	Area of City Roads(Year—end)	10000 sq. m
排水管道总长度	公里	Length of Sewage Pipes	km
供水综合生产能力(含自备水源)	万吨/日	General Productive Capacity of Tap Water Supply	10000 tons/day
全年售水总量	万吨	Annuall Volume of Tap Water Sale	10000 tons
#居民家庭用水量	万吨	Water Consumption for Residents Use	10000 tons
用水人口	万人	Population with Access Tap Water	10000 persons
液化石油气供气总量	吨	Total Volume of Liquefied Petroleum Gas	ton
#家庭用量	吨	For Residents Use	ton
用液化气人口	万人	Population with Access Liquefied Petroleum Gas	10000 persons
年末实有公共汽(电)车营运车辆数	辆	Number of Public Transportations Vehicles under Operation	unit
全年公共汽(电)车客运总量	万人次	Number of Passengers Carried with Public Transportations Vehicles	10000 person—times
年末实有出租汽车数	辆	Operating Taxes at Year—end	unit
绿地面积	公顷	Green Areas	hectare
#公园绿地面积	公顷	Public Green Areas	hectare
建成区绿化覆盖面积	公顷	Coverage Area of Green Area in Developed Area	hectare
环境保护		**Environment Protect**	
工业废水排放量	万吨	Valume of Industrial Waste Water Discharged	10000 tons
工业二氧化硫产生量	吨	Volume of Industrial sulfur dioxide production	ton
工业二氧化硫排放量	吨	Volume of Industrial Sulphur Dioxide Emission	ton
工业烟(粉)尘去除量	吨	Volume of Dispeled Industrial Soot	ton
工业烟(粉)尘排放量	吨	Volume of Industrial Soot Emission	ton
一般工业固体废物综合利用率	%	Rate of General Industrial Solid Waste Treated and Utilized	%
污水处理厂集中处理率	%	Rate of Disposal Living Waste Water in Sewage Treatment Plant	%
生活垃圾无害化处理率	%	Rate of Living Garbage Harmless Treatment	%

全市 Total	市区 Urban District	#鄞州 Yinzhou	余姚 Yuyao	慈溪 Cixi	奉化 Fenghua	象山 Xiangshan	宁海 Ninghai
5089401	3069162	902472	595111	751364	225271	216751	231742
4505108	2968572	783550	531783	379173	244524	179945	201111
2317404	1598860	450016	189231	229832	93873	102746	102862
37934	19267	9228	5228	4178	2073	3658	3530
2459	982	66	582	374	29	472	20
8625	5868	688	804	562	605	486	300
655	275	97	117	129	48	35	51
724.97	320.56	86.02	77.33	61.86	120.00	78.80	66.42
13013	6045	1829	1867	2253	1236	810	802
17769	8375	2248	2412	3331	1572	1047	1032
1228021	757265	30260	69008	275154	12404	101824	12366
7277	2869	337	1053	1715	422	727	491
7762	4492	285	719	1277	199	522	553
366	225	44	33	44	20	22	23
62540	40608		4339	9136	2882	3056	2518
23354	14606		2103	2596	1487	1174	1388
354.18	182.22		44.70	51.74	33.25	23.80	18.47
194218	133323		4753	29179	6487	11954	8522
105255	54050		3451	27051	5618	8582	6503
163.94	21.52		27.88	41.52	33.25	23.80	15.97
6349	4454	1465	633	623	211	211	217
64230	47759	11431	6177	4096	1725	2510	1963
6360	4627	1609	440	605	200	210	278
17640	10905		1761	1890	973	852	1259
3986	1927		459	673	400	284	243
17907	11290		1989	1722	762	787	1357
19666	12725	1880	1535	1828	1244	1714	620
576750	397748	9279	6908	11862	2650	55376	102206
134630	95849	4458	5268	8548	2393	7368	15204
6796256	4109995	49447	426657	63992	4077	1022609	1168926
25275	14620	1751	2922	2240	545	2832	2115
90	89	81	91	54	86	91	99
77	73		85	85	85	81	87
100.00	100.00	100.00	100.00	100.00	100.00	100.00	100.00

表1—5 部分年份经济社会结构指标
Structural Indicators of Society and Economy in Partial Years

单位:%

指标	Indicators	2000	2010	2011	2012	2003
生产总值产业结构	**Industrial Structure of GDP**					
第一产业	Primary Industry	8.2	4.2	4.2	4.1	3.9
第二产业	Secondary Industry	55.6	55.6	55.3	53.4	52.5
第三产业	Tertiary Industry	36.2	40.2	40.5	42.5	43.6
农林牧渔业产值结构	**Structure of Agricultural Gross Output Value**					
农业	Farming	48.2	49.3	48.2	47.9	47.2
林业	Forestry	3.1	2.9	2.7	2.7	2.7
牧业	Animal Husbandry	13.8	15.2	15.7	15.4	14.1
渔业	Fishery	34.9	31.1	32.1	32.6	34.6
农林牧渔服务业	Services		1.4	1.3	1.4	1.4
规模以上工业总产值比例	**Structure of Gross Industrial Output Value**					
轻工业	Light Industry	46.6	31.4	28.8	28.0	28.0
重工业	Heavy Industry	53.4	75.4	71.2	72.0	72.0
全社会固定资产投资产业结构	**Industrial Structure of Fixed Assets Investment**					
第一产业	Primary Industry	2.5	0.5	0.8	0.9	0.6
第二产业	Secondary Industry	41.1	31.8	28.0	28.3	31.2
第三产业	Tertiary Industry	56.3	67.7	71.2	70.8	68.2
自营进出口结构	**Structure of Directive Import and Export**					
出口	Exports	68.5	62.7	62.0	63.6	65.5
进口	Imports	31.5	37.3	38.0	36.4	34.5
社会消费品零售额结构	**Structure of Retail Sales of Consumer Goods**					
批发和零售贸易业	Wholesale and Retail Sale Trades	76.2	90.7	90.9	90.8	91.2
餐饮业	Catering Trade	9.7	9.3	9.1	9.2	8.8
其他	Others	14.1				
农业人口与非农业人口比例	**Structure of Population by Agriculture and Non—argiculture**					
农业人口	Agriculture	70.6	64.3	63.9	63.4	63.1
非农业人口	Non—Agriculture	29.4	35.7	36.1	36.6	36.9

表 1－6 部分年份平均每天主要社会经济活动
Indicators on Average Daily Social and Economic Activities in Partial Years

指标	单位	Indicators	unit	2000	2010	2011	2012	2013
平均每天创造财富		**Daily Production**						
生产总值	万元	Gross Domestic Product	10000 yuan	31358	140433	166007	179842	195311
第一产业	万元	Primary Industry	10000 yuan	2582	6004	6993	7337	7571
第二产业	万元	Secondary Industry	10000 yuan	17420	78649	91768	96088	102513
＃工业增加值	万元	Added－value of Industry	10000 yuan	15844	70400	82712	86614	92547
第三产业	万元	Tertiary Industry	10000 yuan	11356	56415	67246	76417	85227
公共财政预算收入	万元	Public Fiscal Budget Revenue	10000 yuan	3922	32103	39226	41981	45238
每天其他经济活动		**Other Daily Economic Activities**						
固定资产投资额	万元	Invesment in Fixed Assets	10000 yuan	9884	60452	65356	79274	93780
社会消费品零售总额	万元	Total Retail Sales of Consumer Goods	10000 yuan	10666	46699	55311	63641	72211
港口货物吞吐量	万吨	Cargo Throughput	10000 tons	31.64	112.92	118.74	123.78	135.87
集装箱吞吐量	标箱	Container Throughput	TEU	2471	35627	39760	42818	45955
全社会用电量	万千瓦时	Total Electricity Consumption	10000 kwh	3109	12577	13844	14046	15326
＃工业用电量	万千瓦时	Industrial Electricity Consumption	10000 kwh	2302	9706	10647	10508	11369
客运量	万人	Passenger Traffic	10000 persons	62.29	92.91	78.75	76.65	67.93
货运量	万吨	Freight Traffic	10000 tons	29.64	83.71	85.56	89.11	97.01
进出口总额	万美元	Total Imports and Exports	USD 10000	2066	22713	26900	26386	27487
＃出口	万美元	Exports	USD 10000	1416	14238	16666	16788	18003
实际利用外资	万美元	Foreign Capital Actually Used	USD 10000	170	637	770	779	897
人口变动和婚姻		**Population Changes and Marriages**						
出生	人	Births	person	137	134	126	137	135
死亡	人	Deaths	person	92	97	95	104	97
结婚	对	Marriages	couple	111	146	136	147	147
离婚	对	Divorces	couple	10	38	38	41	45

注：本表价值量指标按当年价格计算。

Note: The data in value terms in the table are calculated at current prices.

表1—7 部分年份国民经济主要指标人均水平
Main Per Capita Indicators of National Economy in Partial Years

单位:元(yuan)

指标	Indicators	2000	2010	2011	2012	2013
经济活动	**Economical Indicators**					
生产总值(户籍)	Gross Domestic Products(by Registered Population)	21208	90175	105334	114065	123139
农业总产值	Gross Agritural Output Value	2749	5931	6918	7275	7405
固定资产投资额	Investment in Fixed Assets	6685	38307	41470	50279	59125
社会消费品零售总额	Total Retail Sales of Consumer Goods	7213	29769	35096	40364	45527
自营进出口额(美元)	Directive Exports and Imports(USD)	1397	14480	17069	16735	17330
#出口(美元)	Export(USD)	958	9076	10575	10648	11350
实际利用外资(美元)	Foreign Capital Actually Used(USD)	115	406	488	494	566
公共财政预算收入	Public Fiscal Budget Revenue	2653	20465	24890	26627	28521
公共财政预算支出	Public Fiscal Budget Expenditure	1653	10492	13051	14356	16235
人民生活	**People's Livelihood**					
城镇集体以上在岗职工工资	Avergae Wage of Working Staff and Workers in Urban Collective—owned Units andAbove	14823	43476	49755	56257	63152
市区居民人均可支配收入	Annual Disposable Income of Urban Residents	9193	30166	34058	37902	41729
市区居民人均消费性支出	Annual Living Expenditures of Urban Residents	7912	19420	21779	23288	24685
农村居民人均纯收入	Annual Net Income of Rural Residents	4697	14261	16518	18475	20534
农村居民生活消费支出	Annual Living Expenditure of Rural Residents	3929	9794	11253	12699	13915
城乡居民储蓄存款余额	Balance of Saving Deposits of Urban and Rural Households	10859	57850	63734	72366	78807
人均生活用电量(千瓦时)	Residential Electricity Consumption(kwh)	280	870	932	1028	1142
社会事业	**Society Indicators**					
人均拥有道路面积(平方米)	Per Capita Area of Roads (sq. m)	13.85	19.65	20.44	20.53	20.54
人均公园绿地面积(平方米)	Per Capita Public Green Area (sq. m)	7.32	10.62	10.80	10.97	11.25

表1—8　部分年份社会经济发展相对指标
Relative Indicators on Social and Economic Development in Partial Yeats

指标	Indicators	2000	2010	2011	2012	2013
人口与劳动力	**Population and Labor**					
出生率(‰)	Birth Rate(‰)	9.3	8.5	8.0	8.7	8.5
死亡率(‰)	Death Rate(‰)	6.2	6.2	6.1	6.6	6.1
自然增长率(‰)	Natural Growth Rate(‰)	3.1	2.3	2.0	2.1	2.4
人口净迁移率(‰)	Migration Rate(‰)	2.3	3.4	2.4	1.4	2.0
全社会从业人员结构（%）	Structure of Total Employment Personnel（%）					
第一产业比重	Perentage of Primary Industry	31.0	6.8	6.6	5.9	5.7
第二产业比重	Perentage of Secondary Industry	43.1	55.9	55.4	54.9	54.4
第三产业比重	Perentage of Tertiary Industry	25.9	37.3	38.0	39.2	39.8
国民经济	**Domestic Economic**					
第三产业占 GDP 比重（%）	Perentage of Tertiary Industry as GDP（%）	36.2	40.2	40.5	42.5	43.6
固定资产投资占 GDP 比重(%)	Perentage of Investment in Fixed Assets as GDP（%）	31.5	42.5	39.4	44.1	48.0
社会消费品零售额占 GDP 比重(%)	Perentage of Total Retail Sales of Cunsumer Goods as GDP（%）	34.0	33.0	33.3	35.4	37.0
财政总收入占 GDP 比重(%)	Total Fiscal Revenue as Percentage of GDP（%）	12.9	40.1	37.5	33.5	37.4
进出口总额占 GDP 比重(%)	Total Value of Imports and Exports as Perentage of GDP（%）	54.6	108.7	104.7	92.6	87.2
出口总额占 GDP 比重(%)	Total Value of Exports as Perentage of GDP（%）	37.4	68.1	64.8	58.9	57.1
研究与实验发展经费占 GDP 比重（%）	R&D Expenditure as Percentage of GDP（%）		1.60	1.89	2.04	2.21
外资项目平均利用合同外资（万美元）	Contractual Foreign Investment on Per Project（USD 10000）	173.0	817.4	1220.1	1215.7	1316.8
金融机构贷款占存款比重（%）	Loans as Percentage of Deposits in Financial Institutions（%）	75.3	96.5	100.2	99.8	98.1

注：在进出口、出口总额占 GDP 比重中，美元汇率按当年平均汇率计算。

Note: Total Value of Imports and Exports as Perentage of GDP, Exchange rate of USD are calculated according to in those years.

表 1—8 续表 Continued

指标	Indicators	2000	2010	2011	2012	2013
每公顷播种面积农产品产量(公斤)	Output of Farm Crops Per Hectare of Sowning Area (kg)					
粮食	Grain	5369	5765	5972	5828	5469
油料	Oil Plants	2023	2438	2512	2497	2518
蔬菜	Vegetables	29662	31790	32764	32355	31079
城乡居民收入比例	Ratio of Annual Disposable Income of Urban Resident to Rural's	2.15	2.12	2.06	2.05	2.03
社会发展	**Social Development**					
日均接待境外旅游者人数(人)	Number of Oversea Tourists Average Daily (person)	339	2608	2943	3175	3489
日均旅客周转量(万人公里)	Turnover Volume of Passengers Average Daily (10000 persons—km)	2192	3732	3789	3912	3405
日均货物周转量(万吨公里)	Turnover Volume of Freight Traffic Average Daily (10000 tons—km)	6486	43160	57270	56586	61115
每万人拥有在校大学生数(人)	Students Enrollment of Higher Education Per 10000 Persons (person)	48.0	245.3	245.7	251.9	257.3
初中毕业生升学率(%)	Enrollment Rate of Junior Middle School Graduates (%)	82.4	99.0	99.1	99.1	99.0
每万人拥有移动电话数	Subscribers of Mobile Telephone Per 10000 Persons (subscriber)	2185	14728	17860	18833	21212
每万人拥有医生数(人)	Number of Doctors Per 10000 Persons (Person)	17.0	30.0	31.8	33.0	34.4
每万人拥有病床数(张)	Total Beds of Per 10000 Persons(bed)	26.93	45.46	47.06	48.97	50.60
每万人拥有公共图书馆藏书量(册)	Number of Publice Libraries Collection Book Per 10000 persons (volume)	3280	12786	12712	12683	11535
每万人拥有公共交通车辆(辆)	Number of Buses Per 10000 Persons (vehicle)		6.5	7.0	8.1	12.3
每十万人拥有律师数(人)	Number of Lawyer Per 100,000 Persons (persons)	9.9	21.4	24.1	25.9	29.9
建成区绿化覆盖率(%)	Coverage Rate of Green Area in Developed Area (%)	28.44	37.52	37.82	38.21	38.23
污水处理率(%)	Percentage of Sewage Disposed (%)	35.92	82.81	84.16	85.75	88.42
计划生育率(%)	Rate of Famili Planning	99.22	95.50	96.15	93.30	95.92

表 1—9 "六五"以来各计划时期社会经济主要指标
Major Social and Economic Indicators of Each Period since "Sixth Five—Year Plan" Period

单位:亿元(100 million yuan)

时期	Period	生产总值 Gross Domestic Product	其中 of Which 第一产业 Primary Industyr	第二产业 Secondary Industyr	第三产业 Tertiary Industry	工业增加值 Value—added of Industry
"六五"时期	"Sixth Five—Year Plan" Period	234.77	61.74	128.16	44.87	118.28
"七五"时期	"Seventh Five—Year Plan" Period	573.48	128.31	322.89	122.28	292.77
"八五"时期	"Eighth Five—Year Plan" Period	1777.40	258.70	1015.70	503.00	893.52
"九五"时期	"Ninth Five—Year Plan" Period	4777.61	450.59	2671.33	1655.69	2412.79
"十五"时期	"Tenth Five—Year Plan" Period	9040.12	564.70	4946.76	3528.66	4403.76
"十一五"时期	"11th Five—Year Plan" Period	19765.80	860.64	10912.17	7992.99	9838.51
"十二五"时期	"12th Five—Year Plan" Period	19770.32	800.10	10608.09	8362.13	9567.04
2013	2013	7128.87	276.35	3741.72	3110.80	3377.97

表 1—9 续 1 Continued

单位:单位:亿元(100 million yuan)

时期	Period	固定资产投资 Investment in Fixed Assets	社会消费品零售总额 Retail Sale of Consumer Goods	自营出口总额(亿美元) Value of Direct Exports (100 million USD)	公共财政预算收入 Public Fiscal Budgetary Revenue	财政支出 Fiscal Expenditure
"六五"时期	"Sixth Five—Year Plan" Period	51.68	86.81	0.04	40.23	10.83
"七五"时期	"Seventh Five—Year Plan" Period	159.35	222.77	5.88	66.07	34.75
"八五"时期	"Eighth Five—Year Plan" Period	705.73	651.23	63.86	161.00	101.10
"九五"时期	"Ninth Five—Year Plan" Period	1600.03	1596.17	168.72	475.78	328.22
"十五"时期	"Tenth Five—Year Plan" Period	4347.56	2825.19	654.04	1641.17	1007.84
"十一五"时期	"11th Five—Year Plan" Period	9026.05	6325.15	2039.70	4233.99	4264.53
"十二五"时期	"12th Five—Year Plan" Period	8709.88	6983.83	1879.87	4619.45	5084.38
2013	2013	3422.95	2635.71	657.10	1651.18	1971.44

表 1—9 续表 2 Continued

时期	Period	港口货物吞吐量(万吨) Cargo of Ports Throughput (10000 tons)	集装箱吞吐量(万标箱) Container Throughput (10000 TEU)	全社会用电量(亿千瓦时) Total Electricity Consumption (100 million Kwh)	粮食产量(万吨) Yield of Grain (10000 tons)	人口自然增长(人) Population NaturalIncrease (person)
"六五"时期	"Sixth Five—Year Plan" Period	2840		74.52	913.51	191824
"七五"时期	"Seventh Five—Year Plan" Period	10502	2.2	135.67	936.76	203889
"八五"时期	"Eighth Five—Year Plan" Period	25781	45.3	244.06	907.96	128862
"九五"时期	"Ninth Five—Year Plan" Period	45772	231.5	423.77	850.60	102695
"十五"时期	"Tenth Five—Year Plan" Period	96260	1505.7	955.17	446.52	49734
"十一五"时期	"11th Five—Year Plan" Period	181275	5069.1	1924.91	417.94	60064
"十二五"时期	"12th Five—Year Plan" Period	138233	4695.8	1578.79	257.96	37185
2013	2013	49592	1677.4	559.39	81.25	13807

注:2006 年粮食产量根据农普数据调整。
Note: Yield of grain crops of the year 2006 has been amended according to the last census of agriculture.

表 1—10 “六五”以来各计划时期社会经济主要指标平均增长率
Growth Rate of Major Social and Economic Indicators of Each Period since "Sixth Five—Year Plan" Period

单位：%

时期	Period	生产总值 Gross Domestic Product	其中 of Which 第一产业 Primary Industyr	第二产业 Secondary Industyr	第三产业 Tertiary Industry	工业增加值 Value—added of Industry
“六五”时期	"Sixth Five—Year Plan" Period	17.2	8.5	21.0	17.4	21.7
“七五”时期	"Seventh Five—Year Plan" Period	8.8	0.9	10.9	8.5	11.0
“八五”时期	"Eighth Five—Year Plan" Period	21.0	7.7	23.4	23.9	28.5
“九五”时期	"Ninth Five—Year Plan" Period	13.0	3.6	13.9	14.2	14.7
“十五”时期	"Tenth Five—Year Plan" Period	13.8	3.9	14.4	14.5	14.0
“十一五”时期	"11th Five—Year Plan" Period	12.0	4.3	11.8	13.1	12.6
“十二五”时期	"12th Five—Year Plan" Period	8.6	1.2	8.0	10.3	8.2
2013	2013	8.1	−1.2	8.2	8.8	8.4

表 1—10 续 1 Continued

单位：%

时期	Period	固定资产投资 Investment in Fixed Assets	社会消费品零售总额 Retail Sale of Consumer Goods	自营出口总额 Value of Direct Exports	公共财政预算收入 Public Fiscal Budgetary Revenue	财政支出 Fiscal Expenditure
“六五”时期	"Sixth Five—Year Plan" Period	15.9	17.8		10.1	17.1
“七五”时期	"Seventh Five—Year Plan" Period	19.5	16.8	135.1	11.7	22.9
“八五”时期	"Eighth Five—Year Plan" Period	46.2	32.8	52.0	27.3	29.5
“九五”时期	"Ninth Five—Year Plan" Period	6.5	11.4	17.9	21.9	20.3
“十五”时期	"Tenth Five—Year Plan" Period	30.9	11.8	33.9	26.7	29.6
“十一五”时期	"11th Five—Year Plan" Period	10.4	17.5	18.5	20.2	34.8
“十二五”时期	"12th Five—Year Plan" Period	19.1	15.7	8.2	12.1	10.7
2013	2013	18.0	13.2	7.0	7.5	30.0

表 1—10 续表 2 Continued

单位：%

时期	Period	港口货物吞吐量 Cargo of Ports Throughput	集装箱吞吐量 Container Throughput	全社会用电量 Total Electricity Consumption	粮食产量 Yield of Grain	人口自然增率（‰） Natural Growth Rate
“六五”时期	"Sixth Five—Year Plan" Period	26.1		11.7	1.9	8.0
“七五”时期	"Seventh Five—Year Plan" Period	19.7		11.2	0.1	8.2
“八五”时期	"Eighth Five—Year Plan" Period	21.8	48.7	14.5	−1.8	5.1
“九五”时期	"Ninth Five—Year Plan" Period	11.0	41.3	12.9	−5.2	3.9
“十五”时期	"Tenth Five—Year Plan" Period	18.4	42.0	18.8	−9.6	1.8
“十一五”时期	"11th Five—Year Plan" Period	8.9	20.1	11.3	1.7	3.0
“十二五”时期	"12th Five—Year Plan" Period	6.4	8.9	6.8	−2.3	2.1
2013	2013	9.5	7.0	8.8	−6.2	2.4

表1－11 国民经济主要指标比上年增长(1978－2013)
Growth Rate of Major National Economic Indicators Increase Precding Year

单位：%

年份 Year	生产总值 Gross Domestic Product	#第二产业 Secondary Industry	第三产业 Tertiary Industry	工业增加值 Value－added of Industry	固定资产投资 Investment in Fixed Assets	社会消费品零售总额 Retail Sales of Consumer Goods	公共财政预算收入 Public Fiscal Budgetary Revenue
1978	22.5	33.2	6.7		54.9	15.1	22.7
1979	13.4	16.4	19.2	14.1	15.3	24.0	－1.7
1980	17.7	28.4	4.9	38.7	12.3	27.6	15.2
1981	9.3	16.4	11.4	20.3	－1.7	16.4	16.2
1982	13.7	5.5	16.1	4.0	34.1	7.4	9.3
1983	17.7	24.8	15.0	21.3	－10.3	12.2	12.9
1984	18.0	19.5	19.1	25.0	42.4	19.7	15.5
1985	28.1	41.4	25.7	40.7	65.1	34.8	－2.2
1986	9.0	8.0	16.9	7.4	21.7	20.2	12.1
1987	14.1	18.2	11.1	18.6	33.8	16.5	10.8
1988	11.1	16.2	6.8	19.2	21.6	38.3	17.7
1989	4.5	8.8	－4.6	7.2	－8.4	7.7	14.5
1990	5.7	4.0	13.6	3.7	19.8	4.1	4.0
1991	24.9	18.2	52.0	24.0	30.9	15.3	11.9
1992	17.9	26.2	15.6	29.4	48.3	25.3	11.5
1993	20.8	26.4	14.8	37.4	69.5	48.9	42.4
1994	21.1	22.6	25.1	21.4	42.8	38.2	48.8
1995	20.5	24.0	15.5	24.4	43.1	38.8	26.4
1996	17.2	18.5	17.9	18.3	17.3	14.3	24.2
1997	13.7	16.4	15.4	19.4	－3.0	11.3	13.8
1998	11.1	11.5	12.1	12.0	3.1	8.6	16.8
1999	11.0	10.7	12.7	11.2	2.9	10.3	18.7
2000	12.0	12.6	13.2	12.7	13.1	12.6	37.6
2001	12.1	13.0	12.4	12.9	30.4	6.4	32.9
2002	13.2	15.0	12.4	15.0	27.9	11.8	35.8
2003	15.6	16.9	15.9	15.7	39.0	12.7	25.8
2004	15.5	16.6	15.7	16.0	32.1	14.2	－11.3
2005	12.6	10.8	16.3	10.9	21.1	14.0	16.4
2006	13.6	12.7	16.2	13.9	12.5	16.1	20.3
2007	14.9	15.1	15.8	16.4	6.3	17.3	29.0
2008	10.1	10.0	11.0	9.9	8.2	19.6	12.0
2009	8.9	8.3	10.4	8.5	16.0	15.9	19.2
2010	12.5	13.4	12.2	14.3	9.4	19.2	21.3
2011	10.0	9.7	11.1	10.3	17.6	18.4	22.2
2012	7.8	6.0	10.9	6.0	21.6	15.4	7.3
2013	8.1	8.2	8.8	8.4	18.0	13.2	7.5

表 1—11 续表 Continued　　　　单位：%

年份 Year	自营进出口总额 Value of Direct Exports and Imports	#出口 Export	实际利用外资 Foreign Capital Actually Used	港口货物吞吐量 Cargo at Throughput Ports	集装箱吞吐量 Container Throughput	市区居民人均可支配收入 Per Capital Annual Disposable Income of Urban Residents
1978						
1979				10.3		11.1
1980				38.1		26.2
1981				7.1		12.1
1982				6.3		5.8
1983				30.2		4.1
1984				23.6		21.3
1985			1609.5	74.2		38.3
1986	102.0	38.8	39.3	72.8		24.9
1987	−0.9	46.5	−14.2	8.0		7.4
1988	616.4	1348.5	60.6	3.2		27.3
1989	49.2	57.1	155.2	10.3		14.8
1990	35.5	55.3	25.0	15.6		12.7
1991	92.2	70.0	22.0	32.7	63.6	11.2
1992	72.8	64.9	329.0	28.8	47.2	22.5
1993	71.0	41.4	199.7	21.8	49.1	49.0
1994	48.4	57.9	3.9	9.9	58.2	50.8
1995	53.2	29.6	11.4	17.1	28.0	21.1
1996	8.6	2.7	25.7	11.5	26.3	14.8
1997	10.1	25.9	10.5	7.6	27.2	8.6
1998	−8.6	1.0	−9.2	5.9	37.4	1.4
1999	18.9	17.3	3.4	10.9	70.3	3.3
2000	50.5	48.6	19.5	19.5	50.1	15.1
2001	17.9	20.8	40.6	11.3	34.5	9.8
2002	38.0	30.7	42.6	19.8	53.3	8.2
2003	53.3	47.9	38.5	20.4	49.1	10.1
2004	38.8	38.2	21.8	21.8	44.5	11.2
2005	28.5	33.2	9.9	19.0	30.0	9.6
2006	26.0	29.4	5.2	15.2	35.7	13.0
2007	33.8	33.0	3.1	11.5	32.3	13.4
2008	20.1	21.1	1.3	4.8	16.0	13.4
2009	−10.4	−16.6	−13.1	6.1	−3.9	9.2
2010	36.3	34.5	5.3	7.4	24.8	10.2
2011	18.4	17.1	20.9	5.1	11.6	12.9
2012	−1.6	1.0	1.5	4.5	8.0	11.3
2013	3.9	7.0	14.8	9.5	7.0	10.1

主要统计指标解释

【行政区划】 指国家对行政区域的划分。根据宪法规定，我国的行政区域划分如下：⑴全国分为省、自治区、直辖市；⑵省、自治区分为自治州、县、自治县、市；⑶自治州分为县、自治县、市；⑷县、自治县分为乡、民族乡、镇；⑸直辖市和较大的市分为区、县；⑹国家在必要时设立的特别行政区。

【气温】 指空气的温度，我国一般以摄氏度(℃)为单位表示。气象观测的温度表是放在离地面约 1.5 米处通风良好的百叶箱里测量的，因此，通常说的气温指的是离地面 1.5 米处百叶箱中的温度。其统计计算方法为：

月平均气温是将全月各日的平均气温相加，除以该月的天数而得。

年平均气温是将 12 个月的月平均气温累加后除以 12 而得。

【相对湿度】 指空气中实际水气压与当时气温下的饱合水气压之比。其统计方法与气温相同。

【降水量】 指从天空降落到地面的液态或固态(经融化后)水，未经蒸发、渗透、流失而在地面上积聚的深度。其统计计算方法为：

月降水量是将全月各日的降水量累加而得。

年降水量是将 12 个月的月降水量累加而得。

【日照时数】 指太阳实际照射地面的时间。其统计方法与降水量相同。

【可比价格】 指计算各种总量指标所采用的扣除了价格变动因素的价格，可进行不同时期总量指标的对比。按可比价格计算总量指标有两种方法：一种是直接用产品产量乘某一年的不变价格计算；另一种是用价格指数进行缩减。

【不变价格】 指以同类产品某年的平均价格作为固定价格，用于计算各年的产品价值。按不变价格计算的产品价值消除了价格变动因素，不同时期对比可以反映生产的发展速度。新中国成立后，随着工农业产品价格水平的变化，国家统计局先后五次制定了全国统一的工业产品不变价格和农业产品不变价格。从 1952 年到 1957 年使用 1952 年工(农)业产品不变价格，从 1957 年到 1970 年使用 1957 年不变价格，从 1971 年到 1980 年使用 1970 年不变价格，从 1981 年到 1990 年使用 1980 年不变价格，从 1991 年开始使用 1990 年不变价格。

【平均增长速度】 我国计算平均增长速度有两种方法：一种是习惯上经常使用的"水平法"，又称几何平均法，是以间隔期最后一年的水平同基期水平对比来计算平均每年增长(或下降)速度；另一种是"累计法"，又称代数平均法或方程法，是以间隔期内各年水平的总和同基期水平对比来计算平均每年增长(或下降)速度。在一般正常情况下，两种方法计算的平均每年增长速度比较接近；但在经济发展不平衡、出现大起大落时，两种方法计算的结果差别较大。

本《年鉴》内所列的平均增长速度，除固定资产投资用"累计法"计算外，其余均用"水平法"计算。从某年到某年平均增长速度的年份，均不包括基期年在内。

Explanatory Notes on Main Statistical Indicators

【Administrative Division】 refers to the division of administrative areas by the state. The Constitution of the People's Republic of China stipulates that the administrative areas in China are divided as: 1) The whole country is divided into provinces, autonomous regions and municipalities directly under the central government; 2) Provinces and autonomous regions are divided into autonomous prefectures, counties, autonomous counties and cities; 3) Autonomous prefectures are divided into counties, autonomous counties and cities; 4) Counties and autonomous counties are divided into townships, nationality townships and towns; 5) Municipalities and large cities are divided into districts and counties, 6) The state shall, when necessary, establish special administrative regions.

【Temperature】 refers to the air temperature. China uses centigrade as the unit. The thermometry used for weather observation is put in a breezy shutter, which is 1. 5 meters high from the ground. Therefore, the commonly used temperature refers to the temperature in the breezy shutter 1. 5 meters away from the ground. The calculation method is as follows:

Monthly average temperature is the summation of average daily temperature of one month divided by the actual days of that particular month.

Annual average temperature is the summation of monthly average of a year divided by 12 months.

【Relative Humidity】 refers to the ratio of actual water vapor pressure to the saturation water vapor density under the current temperature. The statistical method is the same as that of temperature.

【Volume of Precipitation】 refers to the deepness of liquid state or solid state (thawed) water falling from the sky to the ground that has not been evaporated, infiltrated or run off. The calculation method is as follows:

Monthly precipitation is the summation of daily precipitation of a month.

Annual precipitation is the summation of 12 months precipitation of a year.

【Sunshine Hours】 refer to the actual hours of sun irradiating the earth. The calculation method is the same as that of the precipitation.

【Comparable Prices】 refer to prices that are used to remove the factors of price change in calculating economic aggregates, so as to facilitate comparison of aggregates over time. Two methods are used for calculating economic aggregates at comparable prices: 1. Multiplying the output of products by their constant prices of certain year; 2. Deflation of data at current prices by relevant price index.

【Constant Price】 refers to the average price of a given product in certain year, which is used for comparison of output value over time. As the output value at constant prices removes the factor of price changes, it reflects the trend of production development over time. Since 1949, with the changes in general price level, National Bureau of Statistics has issued nationally unified constant prices five times: the 1952 constant prices for 1949—1957; the 1957 constant prices for 1957—1971; the 1970 constant prices for 1971—1981; the 1980 constant prices for 1981—1990; and the 1990 constant prices have been used since 1991.

【Average Annual Growth Rate】 Two methods for calculating average annual growth rate are applied in China, one is often called "level approach", or the method of calculating geometric average, which is derived by comparing the level of the last year of the interval with that of the beginning year; the other is called "accumulative approach" or algebraic average or equation method, which is derived by the summation of the actual figure of each year in the interval divided by the figure in the base year.

Usually the results calculated by the two methods are fairly close, but they differed sharply when uneven economic development occurred with striking fluctuations in growth.

The average annual growth rates listed in this statistical yearbook are calculated by "level approach" except for the growth rate of investment in fixed assets. The base years are not listed when the years are listed for average annual growth rates.

CHAPTER 2

NINGBO 2014

Statistical YearBook

第二篇

人口与劳动力

POPULATION AND LABOR FORCE

人口和劳动力
Population and Labour Force

主要统计指标
Major Statistics Indicators

2013 年末户籍人口数	2013 Year—end Registred Populations	580.15	万人	10000 persons
其中：非农业人口	Non—agriculture	214.35	万人	10000 persons
其中：市区	Urban Districts	277.59	万人	10000 persons
2013 年出生人口	Birth Population	49321	人	persons
2013 年死亡人口	Death Population	35514	人	persons
2013 年人口自然增长率	Natural Growth Rate	2.38	‰	
2013 年人口净迁移率	Migration Rate	2.05	‰	
2013 年末人口密度	Density of Population	590	人/平方公里	person/sq. km
2013 年计划生育率	Rate of Family Planning	95.92	%	
2013 年末全社会从业人员数	Total Employmed Personnel at The Year—end	503.36	万人	10000 persons
2013 年城镇从业人员数	Number of Employed Personnel at The Year—end Above Town Level	171.38	万人	10000 persons
2013 年城镇在岗职工数	Number of Staff and Workers at Work Above Town Level	146.60	万人	10000 persons
2013 年城镇集体以上在岗职工平均工资	Average Wage of Staff and Workers at Work Above Town Level	63152	元	yuan
2013 城镇集体以上在岗职工大专以上人数	Number of Junior College and Above at Worker at Work Above Toen Level	58.80	万人	10000 persons
2013 年末城镇登记失业人员数	Number of Registered Urban Unemployment at the Year—end	69230	人	persons
2013 年末城镇登记失业率	Registered Urban Unemployed Rate	2.16	%	

表 2—1 历年总户数和总人口 Households and Population Over the Years

单位:万户,万人(10000 households,10000 persons)

年份 Year	总户数 Total Households	总人口 Total Population	其中 of Which			
			按性别分 By Sex		按农业和非农业分 By Agriculture &Non—agriculture	
			男性 Male	女性 Female	农业人口 Agriculture	非农业人口 Non—agriculture
1978	123.30	457.70	234.18	223.52	394.28	63.42
1979	124.48	462.07	235.78	226.29	394.31	67.76
1980	128.57	465.99	237.98	228.01	393.13	72.86
1981	136.86	471.76	240.95	230.81	394.39	70.37
1982	140.56	478.33	244.20	234.13	396.40	81.93
1983	143.27	481.46	245.79	235.67	397.68	83.78
1984	147.57	484.18	247.26	236.92	398.64	85.54
1985	153.57	487.74	249.24	238.50	394.50	93.24
1986	158.53	491.89	251.56	240.33	394.69	97.20
1987	164.78	498.15	254.80	243.35	399.48	98.67
1988	170.92	503.06	257.19	245.89	402.81	100.25
1989	175.12	507.64	259.75	247.89	406.08	101.56
1990	176.06	510.76	260.99	249.77	407.78	102.98
1991	179.22	514.16	262.68	251.48	409.61	104.55
1992	180.89	516.72	264.09	252.63	409.90	106.82
1993	182.80	519.85	265.72	254.26	410.17	109.81
1994	184.38	522.85	267.24	255.61	410.17	112.68
1995	186.26	526.20	268.72	257.48	410.94	115.29
1996	186.82	530.08	270.30	259.78	410.57	119.51
1997	188.83	533.31	271.89	261.42	409.81	123.50
1998	190.39	535.27	272.40	262.87	404.79	130.48
1999	192.52	538.41	273.65	264.76	401.29	137.12
2000	193.99	540.94	274.50	266.44	398.91	142.03
2001	196.10	543.34	275.50	267.84	392.48	150.86
2002	198.94	546.19	276.60	269.60	383.76	162.43
2003	203.47	549.07	277.64	271.44	380.26	168.81
2004	207.01	552.69	278.84	273.85	376.50	176.19
2005	211.17	556.70	280.35	276.35	374.09	182.61
2006	215.03	560.45	281.71	278.74	371.47	188.98
2007	218.77	564.56	283.42	281.14	370.35	194.21
2008	221.48	568.09	284.84	283.25	369.60	198.49
2009	222.46	571.02	285.96	285.05	368.98	202.04
2010	222.98	574.08	287.15	286.93	368.86	205.23
2011	223.79	576.40	287.90	288.50	368.23	208.18
2012	223.46	577.71	288.30	289.41	366.26	211.45
2013	223.56	580.15	289.15	290.99	365.80	214.35

表 2—2 历年人口自然变动情况
Population Natural Changes Over the Years

单位：人，‰（persons，‰）

年份 Year	出生 Birth		死亡 Death		自然增长 Natural Growth	
	人数 Population	出生率 Birth Rate	人数 Population	死亡率 Death Rate	人数 Population	自然增长率 Natural Growth Rate
1978	75180	15.06	26150	5.74	49030	9.32
1979	71642	15.58	27393	5.96	44249	9.62
1980	57417	12.37	27989	6.03	29428	6.34
1981	78132	16.66	28557	6.09	49575	10.57
1982	84905	17.87	28258	5.95	56647	11.92
1983	69668	14.52	30875	6.43	38793	8.09
1984	51040	10.57	28114	5.82	22926	4.75
1985	53366	10.98	29483	6.07	23883	4.91
1986	62535	12.77	28738	5.87	33797	6.90
1987	83541	16.88	30239	6.11	53302	10.77
1988	69248	13.83	30171	6.03	39077	7.80
1989	71283	14.11	30364	6.01	40919	8.10
1990	67464	13.25	30670	6.02	36794	7.23
1991	60140	11.74	29329	5.75	30811	6.01
1992	50700	10.22	30573	5.93	20127	4.29
1993	55242	10.66	29169	5.63	26073	5.03
1994	54990	10.55	30050	5.76	24940	4.78
1995	59600	11.36	32689	6.23	26911	5.13
1996	58282	11.04	30652	5.80	27630	5.24
1997	55231	10.39	31417	5.91	23814	4.48
1998	47116	8.82	32902	6.16	14214	2.66
1999	51544	9.57	31237	5.80	20307	3.77
2000	50168	9.30	33438	6.20	16730	3.10
2001	39867	7.35	30632	5.65	9235	1.70
2002	41404	7.60	32361	5.94	9043	1.66
2003	42445	7.80	35173	6.40	7272	1.30
2004	49192	8.93	36558	6.64	12634	2.29
2005	45185	8.15	33635	6.06	11550	2.08
2006	41749	7.47	31380	5.62	10369	1.86
2007	46830	8.33	33737	6.00	13093	2.33
2008	46155	8.15	33804	5.97	12351	2.18
2009	45114	7.92	34277	6.02	10837	1.90
2010	48837	8.53	35423	6.19	13414	2.34
2011	46103	8.01	34816	6.05	11287	1.96
2012	49998	8.66	37907	6.57	12091	2.10
2013	49321	8.53	35514	6.15	13807	2.38

表 2—3 历年人口迁移情况 Bacis Statistics on Migration Over the Years

单位：人，‰(person，‰)

年份 Year	迁入 inflows	其中 of Which 省内迁入 From Zhejiang	其中 of Which 省外迁入 Form Other Province	迁出 Outflows	其中 of Which 迁往省内 Outflow to Zhejiang	其中 of Which 迁往省外 Outflow to Other Province	净迁移率 Migration Rate
1990	43055	34763	8292	43996	35646	8350	−0.18
1991	35526	27628	7898	32260	25142	7118	0.64
1992	54895	46773	8122	49969	43721	6248	0.96
1993	51257	41921	9336	43716	36697	7019	1.45
1994	55877	46390	9487	49826	42731	7095	1.16
1995	61832	50483	11349	52873	45598	7275	1.71
1996	66392	53141	13251	55103	47097	8006	2.14
1997	64083	51097	12986	53669	45306	8363	1.96
1998	73735	59605	14130	67191	58068	9123	1.22
1999	99809	82531	17278	89491	79170	10321	1.92
2000	85277	66946	18331	73024	60774	12250	2.27
2001	112559	91837	20722	95907	82261	13646	3.07
2002	105609	77127	28482	85498	71518	13980	3.69
2003	105057	76140	28917	80102	65019	15083	4.56
2004	104523	72455	32068	74307	59665	14642	5.49
2005	93433	64157	29276	62900	48874	14026	5.50
2006	90684	60320	30364	59694	46742	12952	5.55
2007	85199	55378	29821	54649	44955	9694	5.43
2008	77022	46195	30827	52036	40749	11287	4.41
2009	69949	40163	29786	48037	37595	10442	3.85
2010	67588	40093	27495	47814	37584	10230	3.45
2011	56088	31626	24462	42543	31859	10684	2.35
2012	47704	25619	22085	39715	28056	11659	1.38
2013	46493	24467	22026	34645	22518	12127	2.05

表 2—4 部分年份各县(市)人口密度 Density of Population by Region in Partial Years

单位：人/平方公里(person/sq. km)

地区	Region	2007	2008	2009	2010	2011	2012	2013
全市	**Total**	**575**	**579**	**582**	**585**	**587**	**588**	**590**
市区	Urban Districts	886	894	901	907	913	916	922
#鄞州	Yinzhou	587	592	597	604	611	614	621
余姚	Yuyao	552	553	554	556	556	556	556
慈溪	Cixi	755	758	761	764	765	766	766
奉化	Fenghua	379	380	380	381	382	382	382
象山	Xiangshan	385	387	389	391	392	391	392
宁海	Ninghai	323	326	328	331	334	334	335

表 2—5 各县(市)、区人口、户口情况(2013 年底)
Basic Statistics on Population and Households by Region(End of 2013)

指标	单位	Indiators	Unit	全市 Total	市区 Urban District	海曙 Haishu
总户数	户	**Total Households**	**household**	**2235581**	**905726**	**112937**
总人口	人	**Total Population**	**person**	**5801464**	**2275941**	**298667**
男性	人	Male	person	2891546	1122801	146532
女性	人	Female	person	2909918	1153140	152135
非农业人口	人	Non—agriculture Population	person	2143489	1434139	298658
未落常住户口的	人	Non—registered Residence	person	1189	26	4
平均人口	人	Average Population	person	5789295	2268529	298755
出生人数	人	**Birth Population**	**person**	**49321**	**18438**	**2348**
男性	人	Male	person	25554	9500	1245
女性	人	Female	person	23767	8938	1103
出生率	‰	Birth Rate	‰	8. 53	8. 12	7. 86
死亡人数	人	**Death Population**	**person**	**35514**	**12247**	**1391**
男性	人	Male	person	19916	6754	784
女性	人	Female	person	15598	5493	607
死亡率	‰	Death Rate	‰	6. 15	5. 40	4. 66
本年自然增加人数	人	**Natural Growth Population**	**person**	**13807**	**6191**	**957**
人口自然增长率	‰	Natural Growth Rate	‰	2. 38	2. 72	3. 20
迁入人数	人	**Number of the Persons Moved in**	**person**	**46493**	**22418**	**2980**
省内迁入	人	From Zhejiang Province	person	24467	8524	1439
省外迁入	人	From Other Province	person	22026	13894	1541
迁出人数	人	**Number of the Persons Moved Out**	**person**	**34645**	**13371**	**2144**
迁往省内	人	To Zhejiang Province	person	22518	6490	1172
迁往省外	人	To Other Province	person	12127	6881	972

注:本表数据来自宁波市公安局。

Note:Data in this table are obtained from Bureau of Public Security of Ningbo Municipality.

各区 by Districts									
江东 Jiangdong	江北 Jiangbei	北仑 Beilun	镇海 Zhenhai	鄞州 Yinzhou	余姚 Yuyao	慈溪 Cixi	奉化 Fenghua	象山 Xiangshan	宁海 Ninghai
106858	**101013**	**154327**	**92404**	**338187**	**308894**	**422646**	**182013**	**186169**	**230133**
280322	**241802**	**385983**	**229059**	**840108**	**835068**	**1043609**	**483723**	**543825**	**619298**
138046	118739	190688	115028	413768	413428	513762	243953	276757	320845
142276	123063	195295	114031	426340	421640	529847	239770	267068	298453
280322	159523	221079	169533	305024	190017	194232	109534	115245	100322
		1		21	90	1073			
279807	241454	384509	228335	835670	834781	1042757	483636	542074	617520
2417	**2160**	**3113**	**1366**	**7034**	**6503**	**8338**	**3416**	**6171**	**6455**
1278	1089	1598	686	3604	3316	4286	1770	3210	3472
1139	1071	1515	680	3430	3187	4052	1646	2961	2983
8.64	8.95	8.10	5.98	8.42	7.79	8.00	7.06	11.38	10.45
1161	**1257**	**2232**	**1145**	**5061**	**6333**	**6986**	**3097**	**3331**	**3520**
626	712	1232	657	2743	3524	3891	1775	1927	2045
535	545	1000	488	2318	2809	3095	1322	1404	1475
4.15	5.21	5.80	5.01	6.06	7.59	6.70	6.40	6.14	5.70
1256	**903**	**881**	**221**	**2243**	**170**	**1352**	**319**	**2840**	**2935**
4.49	3.74	2.30	0.97	2.36	0.20	1.30	0.66	5.24	4.75
2882	**2927**	**4323**	**2206**	**7100**	**6741**	**6024**	**3035**	**3422**	**4853**
1316	999	876	677	3217	4939	4029	1961	1443	3571
1566	1928	3447	1529	3883	1802	1995	1074	1979	1282
1641	**2514**	**1899**	**1077**	**4096**	**6202**	**5274**	**3079**	**2574**	**4145**
861	1230	709	438	2080	5134	3996	2419	1063	3416
780	1284	1190	639	2016	1068	1278	660	1511	729

表 2－6 部分年份各县(市)、区总户数与总人口
HousehoLes and Population by Region in Partial Years

单位：人(person)

指标	Indicators	2009	2010	2011	2012	2013
总户数(户)	**Total Households(Household)**	**2224625**	**2229770**	**2237911**	**2234602**	**2235581**
海曙区	Haishu	113416	112893	112571	112502	112937
江东区	Jiangdong	104732	105321	105832	106262	106858
江北区	Jiangbei	98149	99171	99999	100458	101013
北仑区	Beilun	152988	153297	153468	153703	154327
镇海区	Zhenhai	92201	91962	91916	92107	92404
鄞州区	Yinzhou	326621	329992	334318	335535	338187
余姚市	Yuyao	311421	311793	311331	310127	308894
慈溪市	Cixi	427496	425462	427423	425201	422646
奉化市	Fenghua	182701	183049	182987	182404	182013
象山县	Xiangshan	190806	190604	189901	188281	186169
宁海县	Ninghai	224094	226226	228165	228022	230133
总人口	**Total Population**	**5710172**	**5740836**	**5764042**	**5777125**	**5801464**
海曙区	Haishu	304633	302384	300047	298843	298667
江东区	Jiangdong	276341	277701	278472	279291	280322
江北区	Jiangbei	236691	238867	240498	241105	241802
北仑区	Beilun	373171	377206	380081	383034	385983
镇海区	Zhenhai	224642	225227	226140	227611	229059
鄞州区	Yinzhou	802785	812068	822140	831232	840108
余姚市	Yuyao	832456	833837	834611	834493	835068
慈溪市	Cixi	1035224	1038847	1041503	1041904	1043609
奉化市	Fenghua	482137	483455	483937	483548	483723
象山县	Xiangshan	537135	540330	541688	540322	543825
宁海县	Ninghai	604957	610914	614925	615742	619298
男性人数	**Number of Male**	**2859646**	**2871526**	**2878994**	**2882985**	**2891546**
海曙区	Haishu	150503	149091	147710	146903	146532
江东区	Jiangdong	137082	137400	137566	137711	138046
江北区	Jiangbei	117192	117948	118508	118564	118739
北仑区	Beilun	185672	187357	188416	189500	190688
镇海区	Zhenhai	113593	113711	113959	114615	115028

表 2—6 续表 Continued　　　　单位：人(person)

指标	Indicators	2009	2010	2011	2012	2013
鄞州区	Yinzhou	396134	400771	405477	409748	413768
余姚市	Yuyao	414701	414593	414333	413670	413428
慈溪市	Cixi	511745	513088	513813	513540	513762
奉化市	Fenghua	244512	244773	244708	244207	243953
象山县	Xiangshan	274378	275805	275688	275230	276757
宁海县	Ninghai	314134	316989	318816	319297	320845
女性人数	**Number of Female**	**2850526**	**2869310**	**2885048**	**2894140**	**2909918**
海曙区	Haishu	154130	153293	152337	151940	152135
江东区	Jiangdong	139259	140301	140906	141580	142276
江北区	Jiangbei	119499	120919	121990	122541	123063
北仑区	Beilun	187499	189849	191665	193534	195295
镇海区	Zhenhai	111049	111516	112181	112996	114031
鄞州区	Yinzhou	406651	411297	416663	421484	426340
余姚市	Yuyao	417755	419244	420278	420823	421640
慈溪市	Cixi	523479	525759	527690	528364	529847
奉化市	Fenghua	237625	238682	239229	239341	239770
象山县	Xiangshan	262757	264525	266000	265092	267068
宁海县	Ninghai	290823	293925	296109	296445	298453
非农业人口	**Number of Non—agriculture**	**2020381**	**2052283**	**2081751**	**2114509**	**2143489**
海曙区	Haishu	304573	302362	300036	298834	298658
江东区	Jiangdong	276341	277701	278472	279291	280322
江北区	Jiangbei	151146	153572	155843	158246	159523
北仑区	Beilun	191911	199283	206123	214948	221079
镇海区	Zhenhai	161257	162701	164720	167357	169533
鄞州区	Yinzhou	258966	269344	281656	294546	305024
余姚市	Yuyao	181755	184515	186617	188594	190017
慈溪市	Cixi	182770	186892	189741	192089	194232
奉化市	Fenghua	106534	107531	108168	108814	109534
象山县	Xiangshan	111333	111861	112558	113391	115245
宁海县	Ninghai	93795	96521	97817	98399	100322

表 2-7　部分年份各县(市)、区人口自然变动情况
Natural Changes of Population by Region in Partial Years

单位：人(person)

指标	Indicators	2009	2010	2011	2012	2013
出生人口	**Birth**	**45114**	**48837**	**46103**	**49998**	**49321**
海曙区	Haishu	2282	2397	2390	2622	2348
江东区	Jiangdong	2491	2688	2465	2780	2417
江北区	Jiangbei	1866	2035	2228	2431	2160
北仑区	Beilun	3009	3248	3125	3516	3113
镇海区	Zhenhai	1070	1105	1229	1428	1366
鄞州区	Yinzhou	6024	6306	6766	7485	7034
余姚市	Yuyao	5396	5624	5396	6035	6503
慈溪市	Cixi	7967	7797	7349	7723	8338
奉化市	Fenghua	3506	4013	3285	3490	3416
象山县	Xiangshan	4727	5497	5031	5741	6171
宁海县	Ninghai	6776	8127	6839	6747	6455
死亡人口	**Death**	**34277**	**35423**	**34816**	**37907**	**35514**
海曙区	Haishu	1131	1404	1432	1487	1391
江东区	Jiangdong	1106	1165	1123	1430	1161
江北区	Jiangbei	1219	1250	1187	1442	1257
北仑区	Beilun	2216	2098	2192	2188	2232
镇海区	Zhenhai	1051	1159	1169	1248	1145
鄞州区	Yinzhou	4692	4995	4719	5025	5061
余姚市	Yuyao	6059	6023	6233	6421	6333
慈溪市	Cixi	6670	7011	6803	7386	6986
奉化市	Fenghua	3345	3293	3129	3440	3097
象山县	Xiangshan	3269	3352	3265	3497	3331
宁海县	Ninghai	3519	3673	3564	4343	3520

表 2－7 续表 Continued　　单位：人(person)

指标	Indicators	2009	2010	2011	2012	2013
自然增长	**Natural Growth**	**10837**	**13414**	**11287**	**12091**	**13807**
海曙区	Haishu	1151	993	958	1135	957
江东区	Jiangdong	1385	1523	1342	1350	1256
江北区	Jiangbei	647	785	1041	989	903
北仑区	Beilun	793	1150	933	1328	881
镇海区	Zhenhai	19	－54	60	180	221
鄞州区	Yinzhou	1332	1311	2047	2460	2243
余姚市	Yuyao	－663	－399	－837	－386	170
慈溪市	Cixi	1297	786	546	337	1352
奉化市	Fenghua	161	720	156	50	319
象山县	Xiangshan	1458	2145	1766	2244	2840
宁海县	Ninghai	3257	4454	3275	2404	2935
自然增长率(‰)	**Natural Growth Rate(‰)**	**1.90**	**2.34**	**1.96**	**2.10**	**2.38**
海曙区	Haishu	3.77	3.27	3.18	3.79	3.20
江东区	Jiangdong	5.05	5.50	4.83	4.84	4.49
江北区	Jiangbei	2.75	3.30	4.34	4.11	3.74
北仑区	Beilun	2.14	3.07	2.46	3.48	2.30
镇海区	Zhenhai	0.08	－0.24	0.27	0.79	0.97
鄞州区	Yinzhou	1.67	1.62	2.51	2.98	2.36
余姚市	Yuyao	－0.80	－0.48	－1.00	－0.46	0.20
慈溪市	Cixi	1.26	0.76	0.52	0.32	1.30
奉化市	Fenghua	0.33	1.49	0.32	0.10	0.66
象山县	Xiangshan	2.72	3.98	3.26	4.15	5.24
宁海县	Ninghai	5.40	7.33	5.34	3.91	4.75

表 2—8　部分年份各县(市)、区人口迁移情况
Migration of Population by Region in Partial Years

单位:人(person)

指标	Indicators	2009	2010	2011	2012	2013
迁入人口	**Population Inflows**	**69949**	**67588**	**56088**	**47704**	**46493**
海曙区	Haishu	4648	3203	2815	2759	2980
江东区	Jiangdong	4239	3384	2995	2854	2882
江北区	Jiangbei	5370	4477	3758	3171	2927
北仑区	Beilun	6489	5099	4355	4061	4323
镇海区	Zhenhai	3020	2723	2413	2461	2206
鄞州区	Yinzhou	10912	9934	8631	7263	7100
余姚市	Yuyao	10522	13589	9498	8289	6741
慈溪市	Cixi	10554	9728	7517	6735	6024
奉化市	Fenghua	4174	4222	3596	3336	3035
象山县	Xiangshan	4625	5176	5939	2575	3422
宁海县	Ninghai	5396	6053	4571	4200	4853
其中:省内迁入	**of Which:From Zhejiang**	**40163**	**40093**	**31626**	**25619**	**24467**
海曙区	Haishu	2184	1482	1259	1231	1439
江东区	Jiangdong	2018	1577	1339	1384	1316
江北区	Jiangbei	2028	1610	1267	1132	999
北仑区	Beilun	1532	1188	1077	904	876
镇海区	Zhenhai	912	866	732	722	677
鄞州区	Yinzhou	5477	4682	3763	3336	3217
余姚市	Yuyao	8283	10964	7134	6063	4939
慈溪市	Cixi	7787	6947	4961	4483	4029
奉化市	Fenghua	2896	2796	2352	2201	1961
象山县	Xiangshan	3375	3851	4703	1357	1443
宁海县	Ninghai	3671	4130	3039	2806	3571

表 2-8 续表 Continued　　　　单位：人(person)

指标	Indicators	2009	2010	2011	2012	2013
迁出人口	**Population Outflows**	**48037**	**47814**	**42543**	**39715**	**34645**
海曙区	Haishu	3373	2587	2478	2453	2144
江东区	Jiangdong	1550	1668	1620	1694	1641
江北区	Jiangbei	3806	3495	3166	2899	2514
北仑区	Beilun	1896	2019	2244	2154	1899
镇海区	Zhenhai	1683	1263	1200	1045	1077
鄞州区	Yinzhou	8201	6401	5403	4807	4096
余姚市	Yuyao	8414	11648	7823	7284	6202
慈溪市	Cixi	7410	6560	5353	5868	5274
奉化市	Fenghua	3606	3564	3195	3428	3079
象山县	Xiangshan	3947	4122	6358	4366	2574
宁海县	Ninghai	4151	4487	3703	3717	4145
其中：迁往省内	**Of Which: To Zhejiang**	**37595**	**37584**	**31859**	**28056**	**22518**
海曙区	Haishu	2475	1777	1571	1444	1172
江东区	Jiangdong	790	885	833	841	861
江北区	Jiangbei	2755	2332	1840	1596	1230
北仑区	Beilun	999	933	891	787	709
镇海区	Zhenhai	1109	702	572	468	438
鄞州区	Yinzhou	6752	4782	3749	2987	2080
余姚市	Yuyao	7161	10522	6723	6108	5134
慈溪市	Cixi	6031	5473	4312	4659	3996
奉化市	Fenghua	2986	2825	2614	2538	2419
象山县	Xiangshan	3229	3587	5677	3531	1063
宁海县	Ninghai	3308	3766	3077	3097	3416

表 2—9 各县(市)计划生育情况(2013)
Basic Statistics on Family Planning by Region

指标	单位	Indicators	Unit
计划生育率	%	Rate of Family Planning	%
年内出生人数	人	Number of Birth in This Year	person
#女	人	Female	person
1. 一孩人数	人	One—Child	person
#计划内	人	Under Control	person
2. 两孩人数	人	Two—Child	person
#计划内	人	Under Control	person
3. 多孩人数	人	Over Two Child	person
#政策性	人	Policy	person
计划内出生人数	人	Number of Birth Under Control	person
计划外出生人数	人	Number of Birth Out of Control	person
1. 一孩人数	人	One—Child	person
2. 两孩人数	人	Two—Child	person
3. 多孩人数	人	Over Two Child	person
育龄妇女人数	万人	Number of Women at Child—Bearing Age	10000 persons
已婚育龄妇女人数	万人	Number of Marriged Women at Child—Bearing Age	10000 persons
#已有一孩	万人	1st Birth	10000 persons
#已领独生证	万人	With One—Child Certificate	10000 persons
#已婚育龄妇女一孩率	%	Rate of 1st Birth of Marriged Women at Child—Bearing Age	%
#已婚育龄妇女领独生证率	%	Rate of One—Child Certificate	%
初婚妇女人数	人	Number of First Marrige for Women	10000 persons
已婚育龄妇女节育率	%	Rate of Controlling—Birth for Marriged Women at Child—Bearing Age	%
采取节育措施人数	万人	Number of Controlling—Birth Method	10000 persons
年内节育手术例数	例	Number of Controlling—Birth Surgery in This Year	case
年内取环例数	例	Number of Remove Contraceptive	case
出生率	‰	Brith Rate	‰
死亡率	‰	Death Rate	‰

注：本表数据来自宁波市计划生育委员会。

Note: Data in this table are obtained from Ningbo Family Planning Committee.

全市 Total	市区 Urban District	#鄞州 Yinzhou	余姚 Yuyao	慈溪 Cixi	奉化 Fenghua	象山 Xiangshan	宁海 Ninghai
95.92	97.15	96.90	97.08	95.26	96.03	92.89	93.86
42948	17215	6518	5889	7526	2975	4373	4970
20710	8357	3159	2825	3630	1431	2136	2331
33640	14577	5347	4634	5906	2219	3058	3246
33558	14558	5339	4624	5888	2215	3049	3224
9063	2583	1146	1233	1579	739	1267	1662
7550	2143	971	1084	1264	635	1004	1420
245	55	25	22	41	17	48	62
87	24	6	9	17	7	9	21
41195	16725	6316	5717	7169	2857	4062	4665
1753	490	202	172	357	118	311	305
82	19	8	10	18	4	9	22
1513	440	175	149	315	104	263	242
158	31	19	13	24	10	39	41
147.98	57.20	22.13	21.32	26.43	12.33	14.58	16.12
113.73	44.83	17.33	15.86	19.72	9.49	11.10	12.73
88.02	37.39	14.29	12.63	14.99	7.37	7.72	7.92
45.53	22.37	8.61	6.96	8.60	3.81	2.21	1.57
77.40	83.42	82.46	79.67	75.99	77.67	69.53	62.20
40.03	49.91	49.67	43.91	43.60	40.12	19.95	12.37
36418	13816	4959	5935	7173	2376	3505	3613
91.68	90.02	90.96	94.56	94.54	90.39	91.78	90.39
104.27	40.35	15.77	15.00	18.64	8.58	10.19	11.51
38613	10465	5690	2936	5447	3451	6259	10055
10997	4256	2249	1286	1464	1034	1348	1609
8.54	8.98	8.84	6.88	7.03	7.16	9.75	11.73
6.57	5.69	6.00	7.69	7.09	7.11	6.46	7.06

表 2—10 各县(市)婚姻状况(2013) Basic Statistics on Marrige by Region

指标	单位	Indicators	Unit	全市 Total
准予登记结婚数	对	**Registering Marrige Permitted**	**couple**	**53742**
#涉外婚姻	人	Chinese—Foreign Marrige	person	326
(1)国内公民	人	Demestic Citizen	person	160
#女性	人	Female	person	113
(2)港澳台同胞	人	Chinese of Hong Kong, Macao and Taiwan	person	58
(3)华侨	人	Overseas Chinese	person	5
(4)外国人	人	Foreigner	person	103
1. 初婚人数	人	First Marriage	person	71166
2. 再婚人数	人	Remarriage	person	14968
#再婚中恢复结婚	对	Resume Marriage	couple	6998
准予离婚数	对	**Divorce Approved**	**couple**	**16414**

注：本表数据由市民政局提供。

Note: Data in this table are obtained from Ningbo Municipal Bureau of Civil Affairs.

表 2—11 主要年份婚姻状况 Marriage Statistics in Main Years

年份 Year	准予登记结婚(对) Marriage Registration Permitted (Couple)	初婚(人) First Marriage (person)	再婚(人) Remarriage (person)	再婚中恢复结婚(对) Resume Marriage (Couple)	准予离婚数(对) Divorce Approved (couple)
1990	51349	96680	3312		1378
1991	46429	88283	4373	85	1508
1992	47504	91636	3372	152	1543
1993	43522	83451	3593	224	1815
1994	48029	92611	3447	209	2201
1995	45950	88406	3494	160	2501
1996	47197	89369	5025	169	2870
1997	40432	75369	5495	228	3689
1998	44559	83403	5715	466	3623
1999	39616	72299	6531	269	3881
2000	40505	74415	6125	242	3781
2001	38813	70658	6326	288	4206
2002	46931	85892	7572	371	4444
2003	42075	75735	8097	394	5538
2004	48214	86584	9518	743	7570
2005	39445	68699	9835	525	8570
2006	51725	90762	12688	736	9687
2007	41954	73877	10031	840	10232
2008	51956	90228	13684	509	11376
2009	46181	77918	14444	961	12698
2010	52508	87780	17236	1333	13754
2011	49710	83624	15796	2291	13911
2012	53721	92191	15251	2787	14893
2013	53742	71166	14968	6998	16414

市区 Urban District	#鄞州 Yinzhou	余姚 Yuyao	慈溪 Cixi	奉化 Fenghua	象山 Xiangshan	宁海 Ninghai
22763	**7487**	**7669**	**9241**	**3378**	**5261**	**5430**
326						
160						
113						
58						
5						
103						
32300	12963	7821	10243	5169	7076	8557
7328	1153	1679	1785	1091	1494	1591
3648	950	618	726	538	780	688
7698	**2335**	**1736**	**1766**	**1367**	**2010**	**1837**

涉外婚姻（对） Chinese—Foreign Marriage (couple)	其中:of Which				
	国内公民（人） Chinese Citizens (person)	#女性 Female	港澳台同胞（人） Cninese of HongKong, Macao, Taiwan(person)	华侨（人） Overseas Chinese (person)	外国人（人） Foreigner (person)
85	85	80	69	11	5
101	101	95	88	8	5
133	133	127	114	9	10
157	157	150	128	20	9
119	119	112	93	20	6
127	127	121	70	27	30
160	160	154	105	23	32
144	144	144	84	16	44
142	142	134	82	16	44
201	201	188	144	14	43
235	235	229	177	7	51
321	321	313	249	10	62
199	199	189	137	10	52
159	159	152	106	8	45
163	163	154	88	14	61
178	178	166	96	9	73
181	178	162	100	13	71
170	170	154	78	10	82
172	168	148	60	17	99
162	160	133	63	7	94
138	136	114	44	8	88
306	153	127	69	4	80
284	142	113	45	9	88
326	160	113	58	5	103

表 2—12 城乡劳动力资源配置情况(2013 年底)
Sources and Distribution of Urban and Rural Labor Force(End of 2013)

单位:万人(10000 persons)

项目	Item	城乡合计 Total	其中 of Which 城镇 Urban	乡村 Rural
年末人口数	**Total Population at The Year—end**	**766.30**	**445.20**	**321.10**
年末 16 岁以上全部人口数	Total Population Above 16 Ages at the Year—end	670.10	388.70	281.40
#不计入劳动力资源的人数	Non labor Force Resource	25.90	10.40	15.50
年末劳动力资源总数	**Total Labor Force Resource at The Year—end**	**644.20**	**378.30**	**265.90**
经济活动人口	**Economically Activity Population**	**510.28**	**348.84**	**161.44**
从业人员数	Number of Employmed Person	503.36	341.92	161.44
按就业身份分组	Group by Employment Identity			
城镇集体以上单位从业人员	Urban Collective—Owned Level and Above	171.38	171.38	
私营业主	Private Owner	34..32	22.24	12.08
个体户主	Self—employed Worker	36.98	17.12	19.86
私营企业和个体从业人员	Employed Persons in Private and Individual Units	235.58	131.18	104.50
乡镇企业从业人员	Employed Persons in Township Enterprises			
乡村农业劳动力	Rural Labor Force	25.00		25.00
其他	Others			
按登记注册类型分组	Group by Registered Type			
国有单位	State—Owned Units	30.34	30.34	
集体单位	Collective—Owned Units	27.90	2.90	25.00
股份合作单位	Share—holding Cooperative Units	1.24	1.24	
联营单位	Joint Ownership Units	0.10	0.10	
有限责任公司	Limited Liability Corporations	34.90	34.90	
股份有限公司	Share—holding Coporations Ltd.	35.09	35.09	
私营单位	Private Enterprises	224.39	132.90	91.49
其他	Others	1.88	1.88	
港、澳、台商投资单位	HongKong,Macao and Taiwan Funded	36.05	36.05	
外商投资单位	Foreign Funded Units	28.94	28.94	
个体	Self—employed Individual	82.53	37.58	44.95

表 2—12 续表 Continued　　单位:万人(10000 persons)

项目	Item	城乡合计 Total	其中 of Which 城镇 Urban	乡村 Rural
按国民经济行业分组	Group by Sector			
农、林、牧、渔业	Framing,Forestry,Animal Husbandry and Fishery	28.85	1.23	27.62
采矿业	Mining and Quarrying	0.16	0.04	0.12
制造业	Manufacuring	230.71	141.17	89.54
电力、燃气及水的生产和供应业	Electric Power,Gas and Water Production and Supply	2.03	1.95	0.08
建筑业	Construction	41.17	37.25	2.92
交通运输、仓储和邮政业	Transportation,Storage and Post	15.58	12.33	4.25
信息传输、计算机服务和软件业	Information Transmission,Computer Service and Software	4.59	3.95	0.64
批发和零售业	Wholesale and Retail Trade	89.62	63.82	25.80
住宿和餐饮业	Hotel and Catering Services	9.36	7.15	2.21
金融业	Financial Industries	7.64	7.40	0.24
房地产业	Real Estate Industries	5.77	4.79	0.98
租赁和商务服务业	Leasing and Business Service Industries	17.80	16.42	1.38
科学研究、技术服务和地质勘查业	Scientific Research,Technical Service and Geologic Prospecting	9.86	8.07	1.79
水利、环境和公共设施管理业	Water Conservancy,Environment and Public Facility Management	2.01	1.85	0.16
居民服务和其他服务业	Resident Service and Other Service Industries	10.96	8.06	2.90
教育	Education	9.04	8.98	0.06
卫生、社会保障和社会福利业	Health Care,Social Security and Social Welfare	6.09	5.99	0.10
文化、体育和娱乐业	Culture,Sports and Entertainment	3.06	2.41	0.65
公共管理和社会组织	Public Management and Social Organizations	9.06	9.06	
国际组织	International Organizations			
城镇登记失业人员数	**Number of Registered Unemployed Persons in Urban**	**6.92**	**6.92**	
非经济活动人口	**Non Economically Activity Population**	**133.92**	**29.46**	**104.46**
#16 岁以上在上在校学生	Student Enrollment Above 16 Ages	25.70	16.30	9.40
家务劳动者	House Work Labourer	72.20	7.20	65.00

表 2—13 部分年份按就业者身份和经济类型分组的从业人员
Employees Grouped by Identity and Registered Type in Partail Years

单位：万人(10000 persons)

指标	Indicators	2011	2012	2013
从业人员数	**Number of Employmed Person**	**493.83**	**501.58**	**503.36**
按就业身份分组	**Group by Employment Identity**			
城镇集体以上单位从业人员	Urban Collective—Owned and Above	151.79	174.22	171.38
私营业主	Private Owner	28.23	30.91	34.32
个体户主	Self—employed Worker	33.04	35.99	36.98
私营企业和个体从业人员	Employed in Private and Individual Units	230.77	233.46	235.58
乡镇企业从业人员	Employed in Township Enterprises	20.00		
乡村农业劳动力	Rural Labor Force	30.00	27.00	25.00
其他	Others			
按登记注册类型分组	**Group by Registered Type**			
国有单位	State—Owned Units	31.83	31.18	30.34
集体单位	Collective—Owned Units	53.43	30.23	27.90
股份合作单位	Share—holding Cooperative Units	1.30	1.63	1.24
联营单位	Joint Ownership Units	0.13	0.13	0.10
有限责任公司	Limited Liability Corporations	22.90	30.03	34.90
股份有限公司	Share—holding Coporations Ltd.	29.15	36.70	35.09
私营单位	Private Enterprises	192.13	198.80	224.39
其他	Others	0.72	1.71	1.88
港、澳、台商投资单位	HongKong,Macao and Taiwan Funded	31.16	38.20	36.05
外商投资单位	Foreign Funded Units	31.17	31.41	28.94
个体	Self—employed Individual	99.91	101.56	82.53

表 2—14 部分年份按国民经济行业分组的从业人员数 Employees Grouped by Sectors in Partail Years

单位：万人(10000 persons)

指标	Indicators	2011	2012	2013
从业人员数	**Number of Employmed Person**	**493.83**	**501.58**	**503.36**
按国民经济行业分组	**Group by Sector**			
农、林、牧、渔业	Framing, Forestry, Animal Husbandry and Fishery	32.54	29.74	28.85
采矿业	Mining and Quarrying	0.18	0.12	0.16
制造业	Manufacuring	230.21	231.55	230.71
电力、燃气及水的生产和供应业	Electric Power, Gas and Water Production and Supply	2.27	2.03	2.03
建筑业	Construction	41.00	41.57	41.17
交通运输、仓储和邮政业	Transportation, Storage and Post	15.36	15.87	15.58
信息传输、计算机服务和软件业	Information Transmission, Computer Service and Software	4.68	4.80	4.59
批发和零售业	Wholesale and Retail Trade	88.65	89.48	89.62
住宿和餐饮业	Hotel and Catering Services	9.96	10.36	9.36
金融业	Financial Industries	6.35	7.06	7.64
房地产业	Real Estate Industries	5.08	5.14	5.77
租赁和商务服务业	Leasing and Business Service Industries	15.12	17.66	17.80
科学研究、技术服务和地质勘查业	Scientific Research, Technical Service and Geologic Prospecting	6.94	8.43	9.86
水利、环境和公共设施管理业	Water Conservancy, Environment and Public Facility Management	1.88	1.95	2.01
居民服务和其他服务业	Resident Service and Other Service Industries	10.01	10.46	10.96
教育	Education	7.91	8.54	9.04
卫生、社会保障和社会福利业	Health Care, Social Security and Social Welfare	5.44	5.72	6.09
文化、体育和娱乐业	Culture, Sports and Entertainment	2.29	2.39	3.06
公共管理和社会组织	Public Management and Social Organizations	7.96	8.71	9.06
国际组织	International Organizations			

表 2—15　全市城镇集体以上从业人员和劳动报酬情况(2013)
Employed Personnel and Remuneration Payment in Urban Collective—owned Units and Above Level

指标	Indicators
总计	**Total**
按企、事业和机关分组	**Grouped by Enterprises, Institutions and Agencies**
企业	Enterprises
事业	Institutions
机关	Agencies
按国民经济行业分组	**Grouped by Sector**
农、林、牧、渔业	Framing, Forestry, Animal Husbandry and Fishery
采矿业	Mining and Quarrying
制造业	Manufacuring
电力、燃气及水的生产和供应业	Electric Power, Gas and Water Production and Supply
建筑业	Construction
交通运输、仓储和邮政业	Transport, Storage and Post
信息传输、计算机服务和软件业	Information Transmission, Computer Service and Software
批发与零售业	Wholesale and Retail Trade
住宿与餐饮业	Hotels and Catering Trade
金融业	Financial Industries
房地产业	Real Estate Trade
租赁与商务服务业	Leasing and Business Services
科学研究、技术服务与地质勘查业	Scientific Research, Technical Service and Geologic Prospecting
水利环境和公共设施管理业	Water Conservancy, Environment and Public Facility Management
居民服务和其他服务业	Resident Service and Other Service Industries
教育	Education
卫生、社会保障和社会福利业	Health Care, Sports and Social Welfare
文化、体育和娱乐业	Culture, Sports and Entertainment
公共管理与社会组织	Public Management and Social Organizations
按经济类型分	**Group by Type of Ownership**
国有单位	State—Owned Units
城镇集体单位	Collective Owned Units
其他单位	Others Units

单位从业人员年末人数(人) Number of Employees at the Year－end (person)	其中 of Which		职工平均工资(元) Average Wage of Staff and Workers (yuan)
	女性 Female	在岗职工合计 Working Staff and Workers	
1713472	**666211**	**1465639**	**63152**
1444251	532372	1229141	56718
183736	105939	164947	94279
74334	21562	62487	108444
581	169	562	60061
51	8	45	48766
787853	366792	737851	47924
19042	4178	13766	114530
313553	28819	209225	53123
58106	14170	48302	75085
11748	5129	8722	102259
64120	37514	56781	56078
18203	9189	17291	39706
71827	41082	48281	160763
25006	8479	22475	66543
56903	10727	50348	60618
19406	5799	16186	97540
15656	5748	14876	54267
4987	1341	4175	41888
89132	56135	78585	94346
57653	39895	52424	99262
8979	3963	8347	89868
90666	27074	77397	102931
297262	129739	255541	98291
28687	15618	25736	70763
1387523	520854	1184362	55413

表 2—16 城镇集体以上从业人员文化程度情况(2013) Educational Level of Working Staff and Workers in Urban Collective—owned Units and Above Level

指标	Indicators	单位从业人员 Working Staff and Workers
总计	**Total**	**1713472**
按企、事业和机关分组	Grouped by Enterprises,Institutions and Agencies	
企业	Enterprises	1444251
事业	Institutions	183736
机关	Agencies	74334
按国民经济行业分组	**Grouped by Sector**	
农、林、牧、渔业	Framing,Forestry,Animal Husbandry and Fishery	581
采矿业	Mining and Quarrying	51
制造业	Manufacuring	787853
电力、燃气及水的生产和供应业	Electric Power,Gas and Water Production and Supply	19042
建筑业	Construction	313553
交通运输、仓储和邮政业	Transport,Storage and Post	58106
信息传输、计算机服务和软件业	Information Transmission,Computer Service and Software	11748
批发与零售业	Wholesale and Retail Trade	64120
住宿与餐饮业	Hotels and Catering Trade	18203
金融业	Financial Industries	71827
房地产业	Real Estate Trade	25006
租赁与商务服务业	Leasing and Business Services	56903
科学研究、技术服务与地质勘查业	Scientific Research,Technical Service and Geologic Prospecting	19406
水利环境和公共设施管理业	Water Conservancy,Environment and Public Facility Management	15656
居民服务和其他服务业	Resident Service and Other Service Industries	4987
教育	Education	89132
卫生、社会保障和社会福利业	Health Care,Sports and Social Welfare	57653
文化、体育和娱乐业	Culture,Sports and Entertainment	8979
公共管理与社会组织	Public Management and Social Organizations	90666
按经济类型分	**Group by Type of Ownership**	
国有单位	State—Owned Units	297262
城镇集体单位	Collective Owned nits	28687
其他单位	Others Units	1387523

单位:人(person)

单位从业人员按文化程度分 Group by Educational Background of Personnel				单位从业人员人才资源 Number of Trained Personnel Resources	单位从业人员专业技术人员 Specialized Technical Personnel
大学本科及以上 Regular Collage and Higher Level	大专 Junior College	中专及高中 Specialized Secondary Schools & Senior Secondary Schools	初中及以下 Junior Secondary Schools and Below Level		
312443	**276129**	**475208**	**649692**	**1088583**	**366544**
165616	218511	440138	619986	863278	234246
101775	36630	21961	23370	151547	12321
41973	18145	10625	3591	66985	6827
97	54	141	289	227	110
4	11	25	11	39	
57497	105100	245926	379330	445726	81090
5847	5303	4338	3554	16672	5042
23136	38685	102071	149661	221282	69633
8490	13277	18319	18020	34150	7703
4854	4384	1954	556	7281	4698
10447	14620	20567	18486	19905	5242
922	3303	6768	7210	4116	990
37369	18816	13135	2507	55687	39602
4969	4476	5830	9731	11258	4954
6888	7528	17429	25058	36413	8342
10346	3973	2806	2271	15296	11407
1674	1759	2247	9976	6806	2149
310	549	1526	2602	1477	262
59714	14304	6851	8263	76632	65361
27568	15898	10156	4031	53354	47191
3506	2294	1791	1388	6361	3742
48805	21795	13328	6738	75901	9386
148777	63740	43980	40765	244975	127171
9084	6475	5658	7470	20461	15169
154582	205914	425570	601457	823147	224204

表2—17 部分年份按行业分组的城镇集体以上在岗职工平均工资
Avergae Wage of Working Staff and Workers in Urban Collective—owned Units and Above Grouped by Sectors in Partial Years

单位:元(yuan)

项目	Item	2011	2012	2013
总计	**Total**	**49755**	**56257**	**63152**
按企业、事业、机关分组	**Grouped by Enterprises, Institutions and Agencies**			
企业	Enterprises	44365	50372	56718
事业	Institutions	77432	86337	94279
机关	Agencies	93382	99162	108444
按国民经济行业分组	**Grouped by Sector**			
农、林、牧、渔业	Framing, Forestry, Animal Husbandry and Fishery	52700	52338	60061
采矿业	Mining and Quarrying	29580	46143	48766
制造业	Manufacuring	37517	42850	47924
电力、燃气及水的生产和供应业	Electric Power, Gas and Water Production and Supply	95079	104106	114530
建筑业	Construction	39312	46214	53123
交通运输、仓储和邮政业	Transport, Storage and Post	67080	67595	75085
信息传输、计算机服务和软件业	Information Transmission, Computer Service and Software	95633	94701	102259
批发与零售业	Wholesale and Retail Trade	49168	52335	56078
住宿与餐饮业	Hotel and Catering Services	31197	35872	39706
金融业	Financial Industries	148732	152892	160763
房地产业	Real Estate Industries	51451	57260	66543
租赁与商务服务业	Leasing and Business Service	48240	55313	60618
科学研究、技术服务与地质勘查业	Scientific Research, Technical Service and Geologic Prospecting	82877	90803	97540
水利环境和公共设施管理业	Water Conservancy, Environment and Public Facility Management	43296	46023	54267
居民服务和其他服务业	Resident Service and Other Service	33050	40808	41888
教育	Education	80484	86924	94346
卫生、社会保障和社会福利业	Health Care, Social Security and Social Welfare	79702	90517	99262
文化、体育和娱乐业	Culture, Sports and Entertainment	74244	81832	89868
公共管理与社会组织	Public Management and Social Organizations	89850	94610	102931
按经济类型分组	**Group by Type of Ownership**			
国有单位	State—Owned Units	81725	88219	98291
城镇集体单位	Collective Owned Units	50052	61678	70763
其他单位	Others Units	42493	48895	55413

表 2—18 部分年份城镇登记失业人数和城镇登记失业率
Number of Registered Urban Unemployed and Registered Urban Unemployed Rate in Partial Years

单位：人(person)

指标	Indicators	2009	2010	2011	2012	2013
失业人员总数	Total Unemployment	121246	56642	127192	102409	69230
#新增失业人员	Newly Added Unemployment	63210	64116	70550	14965	67404
#女性	Female	28667	32451	35591	7765	34997
失业人员转就业人数	Unemployed to Reemployed	62063	66657	62673	20331	80252
#女性	Female	28691	31226	31019	9115	39738
城镇登记失业人员数	Registered Urban Unemployment	59183	56642	64519	82078	69230
#女性	Female	26797	27475	30763	38891	34150
#长期失业者	Long—term Unemployment	7599	6680	6955	8577	762
城镇登记失业率(%)	Registered Urban Unemployed Rate(%)	3.16	3.03	3.44	2.55	2.16

注：本表至 2—21 表数据来自宁波市劳动和社会保障局。

Note: Dara from Tables 2—18 to 2—21 are obtained from Ningbo Municipal Bureau of Labor and Social Security.

表 2—19 部分年份社会保险基本情况
Basic Statistics on Social Insurance in Partial Years

单位：万人(10000 persons)

指标	Indicators	2009	2010	2011	2012	2013
企业养老保险参保人数	Number of Staff and Worker Participated in Basic Pension Insurance at the year—end	344.28	383.50	434.44	474.30	508.94
企业养老保险实际缴费人数	Number of Factial Pay Participated in Basic Pension Insurance at the year—end	216.05	241.27	261.22	277.02	291.95
基本医疗保险参保人数	Population Particaipated Medical Insurance at the year—end	251.84	281.28	304.98	326.56	346.28
失业保险参保人数	Population Particaipated Unemployment Insurance at the year—end	173.21	186.25	200.62	216.22	231.74
工伤保险参保人数	Population Particaipated Work Injury Insurance at the year—end	214.90	238.14	253.36	270.22	283.38
生育保险参保人数	Population Particaipated Maternity Insurance at the year—end	177.63	201.46	214.71	233.09	245.54
被征地人员养老保障参保人数	Number of Taken Over Land Farmers Participated in Rural Social Old—aged Security	55.69	56.78	56.61	55.85	51.20

表 2—20 各县(市)城镇登记失业人员基本情况(2013)
Basic Statistics On Unemployed Persons in Urban Areas by Region

指标	Indicators	全市 Total
总计	**Total**	**69230**
按年龄和性别分	**Group by Age and Sex**	
16—25 周岁	Between 15 to 25 Years Old	3038
#女性	Female	1624
26 岁及以上	26 Years Old and Above	66192
#女性	Female	32526
按失业时间分	**Group by Unemployment Time**	
六个月以下	Below 6 Months	68468
#女性	Female	34009
六个月以上	6 Months and Above	762
#女性	Female	141
按文化程度分	**Group by Education Background**	
大专及以上	Junior College Degree and Above	8146
#女性	Female	4183
中专和高中	Special Secondary school and Senior Secondary Schools Degree	25411
#女性	Female	12009
初中及以下	Junior Secondary Schools Degree and Below	35673
#女性	Female	17958

注:失业时间以办理失业登记时间开始计算。

Note:Unemployment time begins to calculate with the time of applying for unemployment registration.

表 2—21 各县(市)城镇就业和失业人员变化情况(2013 年底)
Number of Being Employed and Being Unemployed by Region (End of 2013)

指标	Indicators	全市 Total
上期末结转的失业人数	**From the Previous Year**	**82078**
本期增加的失业人员	**Newly Added in this Year**	**67404**
#女性	Female	34997
由就业转失业	Reemployed to Unemployed	52201
本期失业人员就业人数	**Unemployed to Reemployed at This Year**	**80252**
#女性	Female	39738
期末实有登记失业人数	**Registered Unemployment at the Year—end**	**69230**
#女性	Female	34150
长期失业者	Long—term Unemployment	762
本期末从业人员总数	**Total Employed Persons at the Year—end**	**1713472**
城镇登记失业率(%)	**Registered Urban Unemployed Rate (%)**	**2.16**

单位：人(person)

市区 Urban District	#鄞州 Yinzhou	余姚 Yuyao	慈溪 Cixi	奉化 Fenghua	象山 Xiangshan	宁海 Ninghai
56100	**13917**	**3544**	**3116**	**2259**	**3046**	**1165**
1877	40	53	13	348	446	301
972	22	28	5	171	302	146
54223	13877	3491	3103	1911	2600	864
26887	6858	1769	1396	759	1280	435
55488	13723	3515	3035	2256	3041	1133
27749	6845	1790	1387	929	1579	575
612	194	29	81	3	5	32
110	35	7	14	1	3	6
7011	1814	394	399	28	53	261
3725	1050	115	179	16	29	119
19853	4109	1396	781	1211	1489	681
9336	2038	697	351	502	778	345
29236	7994	1754	1936	1020	1504	223
14798	3792	985	871	412	775	117

单位：人(person)

市区 Urban District	#鄞州 Yinzhou	余姚 Yuyao	慈溪 Cixi	奉化 Fenghua	象山 Xiangshan	宁海 Ninghai
64320	**4940**	**4607**	**5584**	**2599**	**3435**	**1533**
42696	**16631**	**2113**	**3089**	**5280**	**3296**	**10930**
22586	8705	1057	1236	2872	1877	5369
33952	12314	1537	3088	3744	2447	7433
50916	**7654**	**3176**	**5557**	**5620**	**3685**	**11298**
25625	4426	1534	2297	2776	2109	5397
56100	**13917**	**3544**	**3116**	**2259**	**3046**	**1165**
27859	6880	1797	1401	930	1582	581
612	194	29	81	3	5	32
	252851	**153034**	**140712**	**58735**	**292722**	**72797**
2.22	**2.22**	**1.76**	**2.39**	**2.56**	**2.83**	**2.1**

主要统计指标解释

【出生率(又称粗出生率)】 指在一定时期内(通常为一年)平均每千人所出生的人数的比率,一般用千分率表示。计算公式为:

出生率=年出生人数/年平均人数×1000‰

式中:出生人数指活产婴儿,即胎儿脱离母体时(不管怀孕月数),有过呼吸或其他生命现象。年平均人数指年初、年底人口数的平均数,也可用年中人口数代替。

【死亡率(又称粗死亡率)】 指在一定时期内(通常为一年)一定地区的死亡人数与同期平均人数(或期中人数)之比,一般用千分率表示。计算公式为:

死亡率=年死亡人数/年平均人数×1000‰

【人口自然增长率】 指在一定时期内(通常为一年)人口自然增加数(出生人数减死亡人数)与该时期内平均人数(或期中人数)之比,一般用千分率表示。计算公式为:

人口自然增长率=(本年出生人数-本年死亡人数)/年平均人数×1000‰=人口出生率-人口死亡率

【经济活动人口】 指在16岁以上,有劳动能力,参加或要求参加社会经济活动的人口;包括从业人员和失业人员。

【单位从业人员】 各单位的从业人员是指在各级国家机关、政党机关、社会团体及企业、事业单位中工作,并取得劳动报酬的全部人员。包括:在岗职工、再就业的离退休人员、民办教师以及在各单位中工作的外方人员和港澳台方人员、兼职人员、聘用的外单位下岗人员、借用的外单位人员和第二职业者。不包括离开本单位仍保留劳动关系的职工。

【在岗职工】 指在本单位工作并由单位支付劳动报酬的职工。包括由单位派出学习、劳务及病伤产假且仍由单位支付劳动报酬的人员。

【职工平均工资】 指企业、事业、机关单位的职工在一定时期内平均每人所得的货币工资额。它表明一定时期职工工资收入的高低程度,是反映职工工资水平的主要指标。计算公式为:

职工平均工资=报告期实际支付的全部职工工资总额/报告期全部职工平均人数

【专业技术人员】 指从事专业技术和从事专业技术管理工作的人员。统计对象为事业、企业单位中已经聘任专业技术职务从事专业技术工作的人员,以及未聘任专业技术职务,现在专业技术岗位上工作的具有中专以上学历的人员。

【城镇登记失业人员】 指有非农业户口,在一定的劳动年龄内,有劳动能力,无业而要求就业,并在当地就业服务机构进行求职登记的人员。

【城镇登记失业率】 指城镇登记失业人数同城镇从业人数与城镇登记失业人数之和的比。计算公式为:

城镇登记失业率=城镇登记失业人数/(城镇从业人数+城镇登记失业人数)×100%

Explanatory Notes on Main Statistical Indicators

【Birth Rate or (Crude Birth Rate)】 refers to the ratio of the number of births to the average population (or mid—period population) during a certain period of time (usually a year) which is often expressed in ‰. Birth rate in the chapter refers to annual birth rate. The following formula is used:

Birth Rate = Number of Births/Average Number of Population×1000‰

Number of births refers to live births i. e. the births when babies had showed any vital phenomena regardless of the length of pregnancy. Annual Average Number of Population is the average of the number of population at the beginning of the year and that at the end of the year. Sometimes it is substituted for with the mid year population.

【Death Rate (or Crude Death Rate)】 refers to the ratio of the number of deaths to the average population (or mid—period population) during a certain period of time (usually a year) which is often expressed in ‰. Death rate in the chapter refers to annual death rate. The following formula is used:

Death Rate= Number of Deaths/Annual Average Number of Population×1000‰

【Natural Growth Rate of Population】 refers to the ratio of natural increase in population (number of births minus number of deaths) in a certain period of time (usually a year) to the average population (or mid—period population) of the same period which is often expressed in ‰. The following formulas are applied:

Natural Growth of Population = (Number of Births—Number of Deaths)/Average Number of Population×1000‰

Natural Growth Rate of Population = Birth Rate—Death Rate

【Economically Active Population】 refers to the population aged 16 and over who are capable to work, are participating in or willing to participate in economic activities, including employed persons and unemployed persons.

【Employees of the Unit】 refers to the personnel who work in the government offices, political parties, social communities, enterprises and public undertakings and get paid. Including: on—the—job employees, reemployed retirees, teachers in schools run by the local people, personnel from abroad or HK, Macao, TW who work in the unit, persons on part time, laid—off personnel from other units, hands borrow ed from other units and concurrent employees. Employees who had left their units but still retain labor contracts with them are excluded.

【Full Employed Staff and Workers】 refers to the employees who work for the unit and get paid by it, including those who are leave because of illness, injuries and pregnancies.

【Average Wage of Staff and Workers】 refers to the average wage in money terms per person during a certain period of time for staff and workers in enterprises, institutions, and government agencies, which reflects the general level of wage income during a certain period of time and is calculated as follows:

Average Wage of Staff and Workers = Total Wages of Staff and Workers in Reference Period/Average Number of Staff and Workers in Reference Period.

【Specialized Technical Personnel】 refer to the professional technology and administrative personnel. Its statistical targets include personnel who had been employed and given professional posts by the enterprises and pubic under takings, and the personnel who work in the unit have degrees higher than polytechnic school, but not given professional posts.

【Registered Urban Unemployed Persons】 The registered unemployed persons in urban areas refer to the persons who are registered as permanent residents in the urban areas engaged in non—agricultural activities, aged within the range of working age, capable to labor, unemployed but desirous to be employed and have been registered at the local employment service agencies to apply for a job.

【Registered Urban Unemployment Rate】 Registered unemployment rate in urban areas refers to the ratio of the number of the registered unemployed persons to the sum of the number of employed persons and the registered unemployed persons . The formula is as follows:

Registered urban unemployment rate = number of registered urban unemployed persons÷(number of urban employed persons + number of registered urban unemployed persons) × 100%.

CHAPTER 3

NINGBO 2014 Statistical YearBook

第三篇

国民经济核算

NATIONAL ECONOMIC ACCOUNTING

国民经济核算
National Economic Accounting

主要统计指标
Major Statistics Indicators

		总量 Total	比上年增长(%) Increase Over Last Year
宁波市生产总值(亿元)	Gross Domestic Product (100 million yuan)	7128.87	8.1
第一产业	Primary Industry	276.35	−1.2
第二产业	Secondary Industry	3741.72	8.2
工业增加值	Value−added of Industry	3377.97	8.4
第三产业	Tertiary Industry	3110.80	8.8
			比上年增减(百分点) Increase Over Last Year(percent)
产业结构(%)	Structure of Gross Domestic Product		
总计	Total		
第一产业	Primary Industry	3.88	−0.2
第二产业	Secondary Industry	52.49	−0.94
第三产业	Tertiary Industry	43.63	1.14
最终消费构成(%)	Compositon of Final Consumption		
总计	Total		
居民消费	Resident Consumption	49.6	−1.4
农村居民	Rural Resident	23.6	−0.2
城镇居民	Urban Resident	26.0	−1.2
政府消费	Government Consumption	50.4	1.4

表 3－1　历年生产总值
Gross Domestic Product Over the Years

单位：亿元、元(100 million yuan、yuan)

年份 Year	生产总值 Gross Domestic Product	其中 of Which 第一产业 Primary Industry	第二产业 Secondary Industry	#工业 Industry	第三产业 Tertiary Industry	人均生产总值 (按户籍人口) Per Capita GDP (by Registered Population)	人均生产总值 (按常住人口) Per Capita GDP (by Permanent Population)
1978	20.17	6.52	9.69	8.62	3.96	437	
1979	24.15	7.99	11.43	10.11	4.73	522	
1980	29.53	8.69	15.54	14.21	5.30	634	
1981	31.99	7.85	18.11	16.82	6.03	680	
1982	36.88	11.20	18.79	17.26	6.89	776	
1983	41.68	10.91	22.63	21.22	8.14	864	
1984	53.17	14.93	28.23	26.02	10.01	1096	
1985	71.05	16.85	40.40	36.96	13.80	1455	
1986	80.22	18.61	44.47	40.59	17.14	1626	
1987	95.99	22.11	53.99	48.76	19.89	1928	
1988	118.62	27.11	66.43	60.28	25.08	2356	
1989	137.25	31.13	77.69	71.02	28.43	2702	
1990	141.40	29.35	80.31	72.12	31.74	2777	
1991	169.87	32.75	98.39	88.22	38.73	3315	
1992	213.05	35.32	128.70	116.20	49.03	4516	
1993	315.11	46.09	189.12	165.61	79.90	6079	
1994	459.66	63.48	260.97	227.59	135.21	8815	
1995	602.65	81.11	338.99	295.90	182.55	12024	
1996	784.07	92.21	442.64	390.74	249.22	14846	
1997	879.10	84.53	500.06	452.24	294.51	16534	
1998	952.79	87.76	528.73	478.67	336.30	17832	
1999	1017.08	91.85	564.07	512.84	361.16	18946	
2000	1144.57	94.24	635.83	578.30	414.50	21208	
2001	1278.75	98.53	690.81	624.92	489.41	23587	
2002	1453.34	103.60	793.01	715.24	556.73	26678	
2003	1749.27	109.77	954.04	847.79	685.46	31943	
2004	2109.45	120.54	1167.44	1027.26	821.47	38292	
2005	2447.32	132.25	1341.87	1184.21	973.20	44120	36824
2006	2874.42	139.31	1580.70	1412.87	1154.41	51459	42299
2007	3418.57	150.92	1894.14	1703.20	1373.51	60774	49142
2008	3946.52	166.85	2190.78	1957.42	1588.89	69687	55616
2009	4329.30	183.53	2362.14	2110.82	1783.63	76012	60000
2010	5163.00	219.13	2870.69	2586.17	2073.18	90175	69368
2011	6059.24	255.23	3349.53	3019.00	2454.48	105333	79524
2012	6582.21	268.52	3516.84	3170.07	2796.85	114065	86228
2013	7128.87	276.35	3741.72	3377.97	3110.80	123139	93176

表 3－2 历年生产总值指数(以 1978 年为 100)
Index of Gross Domestic Product Over the Years(1978＝100)

年份 Year	生产总值 Gross Domestic Product	其中 of Which 第一产业 Primary Industry	第二产业 Secondary Industry	♯工业 Industry	第三产业 Tertiary Industry	人均生产总值(按户籍人口) Per Capita GDP (by Registered Population)
1978	100.0	100.0	100.0	100.0	100.0	100.0
1979	113.4	106.4	116.4	114.1	119.2	113.6
1980	133.5	108.8	156.0	158.3	125.0	132.7
1981	145.9	103.1	181.6	190.5	139.2	143.6
1982	165.9	134.7	191.5	198.2	161.6	161.1
1983	195.2	143.1	239.0	240.4	185.8	187.5
1984	230.4	162.8	285.7	300.5	221.3	219.9
1985	295.1	163.6	403.9	422.8	278.2	279.8
1986	321.7	171.5	436.2	454.0	325.2	302.4
1987	367.0	177.3	515.6	538.5	361.3	341.4
1988	407.8	170.2	599.2	641.9	385.9	374.9
1989	426.1	163.6	651.9	688.1	368.1	388.0
1990	450.4	171.1	678.0	713.5	418.2	407.0
1991	562.5	188.7	801.3	884.8	635.6	479.9
1992	663.2	184.0	1011.3	1144.9	734.8	566.8
1993	801.2	203.0	1278.3	1573.1	843.5	664.9
1994	970.2	217.2	1567.2	1909.8	1055.2	803.1
1995	1169.1	247.6	1943.3	2373.8	1218.8	960.5
1996	1370.2	269.1	2302.8	2808.3	1436.9	1118.0
1997	1558.0	252.2	2680.5	3353.1	1658.2	1261.1
1998	1730.9	265.0	2988.7	3755.4	1858.9	1394.8
1999	1921.3	286.5	3308.5	4176.0	2094.9	1541.3
2000	2151.9	296.0	3725.4	4706.4	2371.5	1717.0
2001	2412.3	310.8	4209.7	5313.5	2665.5	1916.2
2002	2730.7	322.6	4841.2	6110.5	2996.1	2161.5
2003	3156.7	334.2	5659.4	7069.8	3472.4	2485.7
2004	3646.0	350.9	6598.9	8201.0	4017.6	2853.6
2005	4094.5	357.6	7311.6	9094.9	4672.5	3121.4
2006	4651.3	374.8	8230.6	10362.1	5429.9	3521.3
2007	5332.8	395.0	9474.3	12059.2	6254.1	4009.1
2008	5880.5	411.0	10394.0	13259.0	6986.9	4391.0
2009	6405.6	426.6	11251.6	14389.4	7710.4	4756.0
2010	7207.1	442.3	12762.8	16450.6	8651.3	5323.1
2011	7928.1	459.3	13999.5	18142.5	9610.4	5828.2
2012	8546.1	464.1	14839.4	19223.3	10659.8	6262.7
2013	9238.3	458.5	16056.2	20838.1	11597.9	6745.2

表 3—3 历年生产总值比上年增长
Growth Rate of Gross Domestic Product Raised Preceding Year Over the Years

单位：%

年份 Year	生产总值 Gross Domestic Product	其中 of Which 第一产业 Primary Industry	第二产业 Secondary Industry	#工业 Industry	第三产业 Tertiary Industry	人均生产总值（按户籍人口）Per Capita GDP (by Registered Population)	人均生产总值（按常住人口）Per Capita GDP (by Permanent Population)
1978	22.5	19.8	33.2		6.7	21.4	
1979	13.4	6.4	16.4	14.1	19.2	13.6	
1980	17.7	2.3	34.0	38.7	4.9	16.8	
1981	9.3	−5.2	16.4	20.3	11.4	8.2	
1982	13.7	30.6	5.5	4.0	16.1	12.2	
1983	17.7	6.2	24.8	21.3	15.0	16.4	
1984	18.0	13.8	19.5	25.0	19.1	17.3	
1985	28.1	0.5	41.4	40.7	25.7	27.2	
1986	9.0	4.8	8.0	7.4	16.9	8.1	
1987	14.1	3.4	18.2	18.6	11.1	12.9	
1988	11.1	−4.0	16.2	19.2	6.8	9.8	
1989	4.5	−3.9	8.8	7.2	−4.6	3.5	
1990	5.7	4.6	4.0	3.7	13.6	4.9	
1991	24.9	10.3	18.2	24.0	52.0	17.9	
1992	17.9	−2.5	26.2	29.4	15.6	18.1	
1993	20.8	10.3	26.4	37.4	14.8	17.3	
1994	21.1	7.0	22.6	21.4	25.1	20.8	
1995	20.5	14.0	24.0	24.4	15.5	19.6	
1996	17.2	8.7	18.5	18.3	17.9	16.4	
1997	13.7	−6.3	16.4	19.4	15.4	12.8	
1998	11.1	5.1	11.5	12.0	12.1	10.6	
1999	11.0	8.1	10.7	11.2	12.7	10.5	
2000	12.0	3.3	12.6	12.7	13.2	11.4	
2001	12.1	5.0	13.0	12.9	12.4	11.6	
2002	13.2	3.8	15.0	15.0	12.4	12.8	
2003	15.6	3.6	16.9	15.7	15.9	15.0	
2004	15.5	5.0	16.6	16.0	15.7	14.8	
2005	12.3	1.9	10.8	10.9	16.3	9.4	
2006	13.6	4.8	12.6	13.9	16.2	12.8	11.1
2007	14.7	5.4	15.1	16.4	15.2	13.9	12.0
2008	10.3	4.1	9.7	9.9	11.7	9.5	8.1
2009	8.9	3.8	8.3	8.5	10.4	8.3	7.1
2010	12.5	3.7	13.4	14.3	12.2	11.9	9.1
2011	10.0	3.8	9.7	10.3	11.1	9.5	7.5
2012	7.8	1.0	6.0	6.0	10.9	7.5	7.6
2013	8.1	−1.2	8.2	8.4	8.8	7.7	7.8

表 3—4 历年生产总值构成
Strucure of Gross Domestic Productoin Over the Years

单位:%

年份 Year	生产总值 Gross Domestic Product	其中 of Which			
		第一产业 Primary Industry	第二产业 Secondary Industry	#工业 Industry	第三产业 Tertiary Industry
1978	100.00	32.33	48.04	42.74	19.63
1979	100.00	33.08	47.33	41.86	19.59
1980	100.00	29.43	52.62	48.12	17.95
1981	100.00	24.54	56.61	52.58	18.85
1982	100.00	30.37	50.95	46.80	18.68
1983	100.00	26.18	54.29	50.91	19.53
1984	100.00	28.08	53.09	48.94	18.83
1985	100.00	23.72	56.86	52.02	19.42
1986	100.00	23.20	55.43	50.60	21.37
1987	100.00	23.03	56.25	50.80	20.72
1988	100.00	22.85	56.00	50.82	21.15
1989	100.00	22.68	56.60	51.74	20.71
1990	100.00	20.76	56.80	51.00	22.45
1991	100.00	19.28	57.92	51.93	22.80
1992	100.00	16.58	60.41	54.54	23.01
1993	100.00	14.63	60.02	52.56	25.35
1994	100.00	13.81	56.77	49.51	29.42
1995	100.00	13.46	56.25	49.10	30.29
1996	100.00	11.76	56.45	49.83	31.79
1997	100.00	9.62	56.88	51.44	33.50
1998	100.00	9.21	55.49	50.24	35.30
1999	100.00	9.03	55.46	50.42	35.51
2000	100.00	8.23	55.55	50.53	36.22
2001	100.00	7.71	54.02	48.87	38.27
2002	100.00	7.13	54.56	49.21	38.31
2003	100.00	6.28	54.54	48.47	39.18
2004	100.00	5.71	55.34	48.70	38.95
2005	100.00	5.40	54.83	48.39	39.77
2006	100.00	4.85	54.99	49.15	40.16
2007	100.00	4.41	55.41	49.82	40.18
2008	100.00	4.23	55.51	49.60	40.26
2009	100.00	4.24	54.56	48.76	41.20
2010	100.00	4.24	55.60	50.09	40.16
2011	100.00	4.21	55.28	49.82	40.51
2012	100.00	4.08	53.43	48.16	42.49
2013	100.00	3.88	52.49	47.40	43.63

表 3－5 按产业划分的生产总值(2012－2013)
Gross Domestic Product Classified by Industries

单位:万元(10000 yuan)

指标	Indicators	2012	2013	发展速度(%) Growth Rate over 2012(%)
宁波市生产总值	**Gross Domestic Product**	**65822064**	**71288672**	**108.1**
第一产业	Primary Industry	2685159	2763456	98.8
第二产业	Secondary Industry	35168381	37417195	108.2
工业	Industry	31700695	33779655	108.4
建筑业	Constructions	3467686	3637540	105.4
第三产业	Tertiary Industry	27968524	31108021	108.8
交通运输、仓储和邮政业	Transportation,Storage and Post	2971215	3090878	105.0
信息传输、计算机服务和软件业	Information Transmission,Computer Service and Soltware Industries	914560	941552	102.6
批发和零售业	Retail and Wholesale Industries	6784344	7414578	108.2
住宿和餐饮业	Hoteling and Catering	1491370	1648525	107.5
金融业	Financial Industry	4506628	4964365	108.9
房地产业	Real Estate Industry	3697576	4564829	117.0
租赁和商务服务业	Leasehold and Busniess Service	1480442		
科学研究、技术服务和地质勘查业	Scientific Research,Technology Service and Geological Prospecting	661922		
水利、环境和公共设施管理业	Water Conservancy,Environment and Public Facility Management	190212		
居民服务和其他服务业	Resident Service and Other Service Industries	726544		
教育	Education	1368208		
卫生、社会保障和社会福利业	Health,Social Security and Welfare Industries	1003991		
文化、体育和娱乐业	Culture,Sports and Entertainment	300217		
公共管理和社会组织	Public Administration and Social Organizations	1871295		

表 3－6 生产总值项目构成(1993－2013)
Structure of Gross Domestic Product

单位:万元(10000 yuan)

年份	增加值 Value－Added	其中 of Which			
		劳动者报酬 Compensation of Employees	生产税净额 Net Taxes on Production	固定资产折旧 Depreciation of Fixed Assets	营业盈余 Operating Surplus
总计 Gross Domestic Product					
1993	3151137	1506857	499355	311430	833495
1994	4596645	2480140	699264	432964	984277
1995	6026524	3092917	953362	589020	1391225
1996	7840727	4197455	1297978	761269	1584025
1997	8791042	4760824	1466876	1000186	1563156
1998	9527859	4405743	1756795	1329018	2036303
1999	10170826	4858140	1765615	1485977	2061094
2000	11445653	5197257	1898185	1503767	2846444
2001	12787531	6129433	1872390	1619514	3166194
2002	14533421	6574217	2288833	1702915	3967456
2003	17492728	7522559	2888138	1983778	5098253
2004	21094461	8252916	3428099	2584132	6829314
2005	24473219	9538821	3773843	3121554	8039001
2006	28744210	11332844	4850566	3698732	8862068
2007	34185710	12843300	5480230	4593868	11268312
2008	39465245	16647075	6572526	5614314	10631330
2009	43293025	15876983	8602395	5178915	13634732
2010	51630017	19567241	9972959	5500116	16589701
2011	60592409	24455961	12282823	6803754	17049871
2012	65822064	28475509	13437771	8097017	15811767
2013	71288672				
第一产业 Primary Industry					
1993	460932	362995	6022	12583	79332
1994	634751	497816	11730	16599	108606
1995	811080	642492	17182	24416	126990
1996	922101	715773	17978	29039	159311
1997	845307	665351	21563	32441	125952
1998	877645	691633	15435	34769	135808
1999	918527	722231	15389	38032	142875
2000	942353	737186	14797	39345	151025
2001	985257	770231	15638	41004	158384
2002	1035968	812679	16182	43465	163642
2003	1097567	861928	10418	46163	179058
2004	1205371	1156158	10467	38746	
2005	1322475	1250993	14513	56969	
2006	1393123	1338826	－9413	63710	
2007	1509165	1473464	－33840	69541	
2008	1668464	1651964	－61244	77744	
2009	1835355	1785501	－42707	92561	
2010	2191327	2143132	－60191	108386	
2011	2552270	2498175	－70923	125018	
2012	2685159	2627034	－75549	133674	
2013	2763456				

表 3－6 续 Continued　　单位：万元(10000 yuan)

年份	增加值 Value－Added	其中 of Which 劳动者报酬 Compensation of Employees	生产税净额 Net Taxes on Production	固定资产折旧 Depreciation of Fixed Assets	营业盈余 Operating Surplus
第二产业 Secondary Industry					
1993	1891201	822727	360007	189250	519217
1994	2609752	1307376	541991	254130	506255
1995	3389919	1499859	728377	342581	819102
1996	4426403	2279485	966565	422195	758158
1997	5000559	2709675	1035314	520105	735465
1998	5287306	2080907	1265643	708150	1232606
1999	5640654	2355823	1271128	809524	1204179
2000	6358306	2462503	1378338	794615	1722850
2001	6908111	2768675	1404624	806206	1928606
2002	7930119	3381081	1752335	730237	2066466
2003	9540385	4030508	1808864	912346	2788667
2004	11674425	4360196	2305394	1266901	3741934
2005	13418692	4952203	2504702	1602800	4358987
2006	15806994	6113649	3285801	2129942	4277602
2007	18941412	7005672	3824969	2450357	5660414
2008	21907835	9744814	3606886	3451214	5104921
2009	23621397	8139761	5196507	2887974	7397155
2010	28706872	10178369	5778262	2894652	9855589
2011	33495283	12960405	7164265	3817708	9552905
2012	35168381	14852736	7641880	4253104	8420661
2013	37417195				
第三产业 Tertiary Industry					
1993	799004	321135	133326	109597	234946
1994	1352142	674948	145543	162235	369416
1995	1825525	950566	207803	222023	445133
1996	2492223	1202197	313435	310035	666556
1997	2945176	1385798	409999	447640	701739
1998	3362908	1633203	475717	586099	667889
1999	3611645	1780086	479098	638421	714040
2000	4144994	1997568	505050	669807	972569
2001	4894163	2590527	452128	772304	1079204
2002	5567334	2380457	520316	929213	1737348
2003	6854776	2630123	1068856	1025269	2130528
2004	8214665	2736562	1112238	1278485	3087380
2005	9732052	3335625	1254628	1461785	3680014
2006	11544093	3880369	1574178	1505080	4584466
2007	13735133	4364164	1689101	2073970	5607898
2008	15888946	5250297	3026884	2085356	5526409
2009	17836273	5951721	3448595	2198380	6237577
2010	20731818	7245740	4254888	2497078	6734112
2011	24544856	8997381	5189481	2861028	7496966
2012	27968524	10995739	5871440	3710239	7391106
2013	31108021				

表 3－7 部分年份按支出法计算的生产总值
Gross Domestic Product Calculated with Expenditure Approach in Partial Years

单位：亿元(100 million yuan)

指标	Indicators	2009	2010	2011	2012	2013
支出法生产总值	**Gross Domestic Product**	**4334.45**	**5167.47**	**6065.97**	**6592.60**	**7141.76**
最终消费	Final Consumption	1658.29	1834.85	2187.58	2404.79	2658.14
居民消费	Resident Consumption	938.19	980.16	1119.22	1225.32	1319.44
农村居民	Rural Resident	443.37	443.36	509.42	572.33	627.27
城镇居民	Urban Resident	494.82	536.80	609.80	652.99	692.17
政府消费	Government Consumption	720.10	854.69	1068.36	1179.47	1338.70
资本形成总额	Total Capital Formation	2068.74	2523.96	2771.37	2912.88	3666.57
固定资本形成总额	Fixed Capital Formation	2004.22	2193.28	2385.51	2901.42	3422.95
库存增加	Stock Increased	64.52	330.68	385.86	11.46	243.62
货物和服务净流出	Net Outflows of Goods and Services	607.42	808.66	1107.02	1274.93	817.05
流出	Outfloe	2650.87	3518.19	4074.41	4384.94	4306.64
流入	Inflows	2043.45	2709.53	2967.39	3110.01	3489.59
统计误差	Statistical Error	－5.15	－4.47	－6.73	－10.39	－12.89

表 3－8 部分年份按支出法计算的生产总值指数(以上年为 100)
Index of Gross Domestic Product Calculated with Expenditure Approach in Partial Years(Preceding Year＝100)

指标	Indicators	2009	2010	2011	2012	2013
支出法生产总值	**Gross Domestic Product**	**109.6**	**113.8**	**110.4**	**107.7**	**108.0**
最终消费	Final Consumption	113.4	106.4	113.2	108.1	108.2
居民消费	Resident Consumption	110.7	100.5	108.4	107.6	105.4
农村居民	Rural Resident	107.2	96.2	109.1	110.5	107.2
城镇居民	Urban Resident	114.0	104.3	107.9	105.3	103.7
政府消费	Government Consumption	117.1	114.1	118.7	108.6	111.1
资本形成总额	Total Capital Formation	113.0	115.6	108.4	105.2	127.6
固定资本形成总额	Fixed Capital Formation	116.7	104.2	108.1	121.7	119.4
库存增加	Stock Increased	57.0	470.2	110.2	2.9	2198.3
货物和服务净流出	Net Outflows of Goods and Services	92.2	128.0	110.6	113.2	62.7
流出	Outfloe	90.8	127.6	105.9	105.8	96.1
流入	Inflows	90.4	127.5	104.5	103.1	109.8

表 3-9 部分年份按行业划分的资本形成总额
Gross Capital Formation by Sector in Partial Years

单位:亿元(100 million yuan)

指标	Indicators	2009	2010	2011	2012	2013
资本形成总额	**Gross Capital Formation**	**2068.74**	**2523.96**	**2771.37**	**2912.88**	**3666.57**
固定资本形成总额	Fixed Assets Formation	2004.22	2193.28	2385.51	2901.42	3422.95
第一产业	Primary Industry	4.80	10.42	18.39	27.02	21.17
第二产业	Secondary Industry	800.11	831.28	672.79	819.86	1066.23
工业	Industry	778.95	819.50	668.36	817.24	1061.89
建筑业	Construction	21.16	11.78	4.43	2.62	4.34
第三产业	Tertiary Industry	1199.30	1351.58	1694.33	2054.54	2335.55
交通运输邮电通讯业	Transportation, Storage, Post and Telecommunications	300.01	297.21	336.26	351.35	288.93
批发和零售贸易、餐饮业	Wholesale, Retail Trade and Catering Services	55.28	72.58	64.24	89.52	84.26
金融保险业	Banking and Insurance	15.16	22.83	6.52	5.98	13.96
房地产业	Real Estate	455.33	533.84	919.92	1143.46	1408.72
其他行业	Others	373.52	425.12	367.39	464.23	539.68
库存增加	Stock Change	64.52	330.68	385.86	11.46	243.62
第一产业	Primary Industry	0.26	0.35	0.47	0.59	0.68
第二产业	Secondary Industry	39.40	297.86	347.71	55.44	86.03
工业	Industry	33.99	290.74	338.14	43.27	68.45
建筑业	Construction	5.41	7.12	9.57	12.17	17.58
第三产业	Tertiary Industry	24.86	32.47	37.68	−44.57	156.91
交通运输邮电通讯业	Transportation, Storage, Post and Telecommunications	0.36	0.51	0.63	0.85	1.65
批发和零售贸易、餐饮业	Wholesale, Retail Trade and Catering Services	6.52	8.59	10.46	−79.89	76.14
其他行业	Others	17.98	23.37	26.59	34.47	79.12

表 3－10 最终消费情况（2012－2013）
Final Consumption

单位：亿元（100 millon yuan）

指标	Indicators	2012	2013
最终消费支出	**Final Consumption Expenditure**	**2404.79**	**2658.14**
一、居民消费支出	**Household Consumption Expenditures**	**1225.32**	**1319.44**
（一）农村居民	Rural Household	572.33	627.27
1. 食品类支出	Food	199.39	207.37
2. 衣着类支出	Garments	33.01	34.13
3. 居住类支出	Residence	122.29	112.63
4. 家庭设备、用品及服务类支出	Houshold Facilities Articles and Services	19.25	16.89
5. 医疗保健类支出	Medical and Hygiencic Expenditure	32.44	37.47
6. 公共医疗消费支出	Public Health	0.69	0.81
7. 交通和通信类支出	Traffic and Telecommunications	50.71	88.39
8. 文教娱乐用品及服务类支出	Recreation, Education and Cultural Services	53.09	54.63
9. 金融中介服务虚拟支出	Imaginary Expenditure of Middle Finance Services	3.57	4.29
10. 金融机构实际服务消费支出	Fact Expenditure of Finance Services	6.51	7.85
11. 保险服务消费支出	Expenditure of Insurance Services	8.47	10.21
12. 自有住房服务虚拟支出	Imaginary Expenditure of Freeform Resident Services	27.63	33.31
13. 其它商品和服务类支出	Other Goods and Services	15.28	19.29
（二）城镇居民	Urban Household	652.99	692.17
1. 食品类支出	Food	157.87	151.56
2. 衣着类支出	Garments	51.68	55.81
3. 居住类支出	Residence	94.89	119.28
4. 家庭设备、用品及服务类支出	Houshold Facilities Articles and Services	26.29	24.09
5. 医疗保健类支出	Medical and Hygiencic Expenditure	15.29	15.89
6. 公共医疗消费支出	Public Health	2.73	2.84
7. 交通和通信类支出	Traffic and Telecommunications	83.58	81.82
8. 文教娱乐用品及服务类支出	Recreation, Education and Cultural Services	75.19	76.92
9. 金融中介服务虚拟支出	Imaginary Expenditure of Middle Finance Services	4.11	4.41
10. 金融机构实际服务消费支出	Fact Expenditure of Finance Services	6.17	6.62
11. 保险服务消费支出	Expenditure of Insurance Services	11.42	12.25
12. 自有住房服务虚拟支出	Imaginary Expenditure of Freeform Resident Services	92.53	99.28
13. 实物消费支出	Reality Consumption	16.27	17.45
14. 其它商品和服务类支出	Other Goods and Services	14.97	23.95
二、政府消费支出	**Government Consumption Expenditures**	**1179.47**	**1338.70**

表 3－11 部分年份居民总消费水平 Resident Consumption Level in Partial Years

单位：元/人(yuan/person)

指标	Indicators	2009	2010	2011	2012	2013
当年价居民消费水平	**Resident Consumption Level at Current Price**	**16473**	**17119**	**19457**	**21234**	**22791**
农村居民	Rural Resident	12006	12018	13823	15586	17137
城镇居民	Urban Resident	24709	26361	29502	31123	32512
可比价居民消费水平	**Resident Consumption Level at Comparable Price**	**16572**	**16508**	**18477**	**20879**	**22300**
农村居民	Rural Resident	12078	11589	13127	15324	16768
城镇居民	Urban Resident	24858	25420	28017	30602	31812
居民年平均人口(人)	**Annual Average Population(person)**	**5695523**	**5725504**	**5752421**	**5770584**	**5789295**
农村居民	Rural Resident	3692896	3689172	3685395	3672454	3660296
城镇居民	Urban Resident	2002627	2036332	2067026	2098130	2128999

表 3－12 部分年份居民消费指数(以上年为 100) Index of Resident Consumption in Partial Years(Preceding Year＝100)

指标	Indicators	2009	2010	2011	2012	2013
当年价居民消费水平	**Resident Consumption Level at Current Price**	**109.4**	**103.9**	**113.7**	**109.1**	**107.3**
农村居民	Rural Resident	106.7	100.1	115.0	112.8	110.0
城镇居民	Urban Resident	111.1	106.7	111.9	105.5	104.5
可比价居民消费水平	**Resident Consumption Level at Comparable Price**	**110.0**	**100.2**	**107.9**	**107.3**	**105.0**
农村居民	Rural Resident	107.3	96.5	109.2	110.9	107.6
城镇居民	Urban Resident	111.8	102.9	106.3	103.7	102.2
居民年平均人口(人)	**Annual Average Population(person)**	**100.6**	**100.5**	**100.5**	**100.3**	**100.3**
农村居民	Rural Resident	99.8	99.9	99.9	99.6	99.7
城镇居民	Urban Resident	102.0	101.7	101.5	101.5	101.5

表 3－13 各县(市)按产业划分的生产总值(2013)
Gross Domestic Product Classified by Industries and by Region

指标	Indicators	全市 Total
地区生产总值	**Gross Domestic Product**	**71288672**
第一产业	Primary Industry	2763456
第二产业	Secondary Industry	37417195
工业	Industry	33779655
建筑业	Constructions	3637540
第三产业	Tertiary Industry	31108021
交通运输、仓储和邮政业	Transportation, Storage and Post	3090878
信息传输、计算机服务和软件业	Information Transmission, Computer Service and Soltware Industries	
批发和零售业	Retail and Wholesale Industries	7414578
住宿和餐饮业	Hoteling and Catering	1648525
金融业	Financial Industry	4964365
房地产业	Real Estate Industry	4564829
租赁和商务服务业	Leasehold and Busniess Service	
科学研究、技术服务和地质勘查业	Scientific Research, Technology Service and Geological Prospecting	
水利、环境和公共设施管理业	Water Conservancy, Environment and Public Facility Management	
居民服务和其他服务业	Resident Service and Other Service Industries	
教育	Education	
卫生、社会保障和社会福利业	Health, Social Security and Welfare Industries	
文化、体育和娱乐业	Culture, Sports and Entertainment	
公共管理和社会组织	Public Administration and Social Organizations	

单位:万元(10000 yuan)

市区 Urban Districts	#鄞州 Yinzhou	余姚 Yuyao	慈溪 Cixi	奉化 Fenghua	象山 Xiangshan	宁海 Ninghai
43094609	**11776776**	**7496274**	**10310947**	**2903589**	**3638457**	**3844796**
613391	400543	400600	492980	283532	579680	393273
21947242	7148237	4444737	5935659	1340238	1664999	2084320
19869387	6838486	4135167	5520098	1157510	1223610	1873883
2077855	309751	309570	415561	182728	441389	210437
20533976	4227996	2650937	3882308	1279818	1393778	1367203
2338833	177973	139489	239843	112771	114678	145263
4401740	1028732	771608	1248159	287563	333087	372420
1006789	134398	137204	221718	89510	113471	79833
3584362	725947	411305	473195	166071	183083	146349
3208262	867261	327027	642347	99563	162892	124738

表 3－14 各县(市)生产总值结构及增长速度(2013) Structure and Grawth Rate of Gross Domestic Product by Region

单位:%

地区	Region	生产总值 Gross Domestic Product	其中 of Which 第一产业 Primary Industry	第二产业 Secondary Industry	#工业 Industry	第三产业 Tertiary Industry
产业结构	**Structure**					
全市	Ningbo	100.0	3.9	52.5	47.4	43.6
市区	Urban Districts	100.0	1.4	50.9	46.1	47.7
#鄞州	Yinzhou	100.0	3.4	60.7	58.1	35.9
余姚	Yuyao	100.0	5.3	59.3	55.2	35.4
慈溪	Cixi	100.0	4.8	57.6	53.5	37.6
奉化	Fenghua	100.0	9.8	46.1	39.9	44.1
象山	Xiangshan	100.0	15.9	45.8	33.6	38.3
宁海	Ninghai	100.0	10.2	54.2	48.7	35.6
增长速度	**Grawth Rate**					
全市	Ningbo	8.1	−1.2	8.2	8.4	8.8
市区	Urban Districts	8.0	−1.9	7.7	8.2	8.6
#鄞州	Yinzhou	9.5	0.5	8.6	8.7	12.3
余姚	Yuyao	7.3	−10.0	8.7	8.6	7.6
慈溪	Cixi	9.0	1.9	9.5	9.5	9.0
奉化	Fenghua	6.7	−0.9	6.2	7.1	9.0
象山	Xiangshan	8.0	1.4	8.3	8.2	10.1
宁海	Ninghai	9.1	2.1	8.8	8.5	11.6

主要统计指标解释

【国内生产总值(GDP)】 指一个国家(或地区)所有常住单位在一定时期内生产活动的最终成果。国内生产总值有三种表现形态,即价值形态、收入形态和产品形态。从价值形态看,它是所有常住单位在一定时期内生产的全部货物和服务价值超过同期中间投入的全部非固定资产货物和服务价值的差额,即所有常住单位的增加值之和;从收入形态看,它是所有常住单位在一定时期内创造并分配给常住单位和非常住单位的初次收入分配之和;从产品形态看,它是所有常住单位在一定时期内最终使用的货物和服务价值与货物和服务净出口价值之和。在实际核算中,国内生产总值有三种计算方法,即生产法、收入法和支出法。三种方法分别从不同的方面反映国内生产总值及其构成。

【三次产业】 根据社会生产活动历史发展的顺序对产业结构的划分,产品直接取自自然界的部门为第一产业;对初级产品进行再加工的部门称为第二产业;为生产和消费提供服务的部门称为第三产业。它是世界上通用的产业结构分类,但各国的划分不尽一致。我国的三次产业划分为:

第一产业:农业(包括种植业、林业、牧业、渔业、农林牧渔服务业)。

第二产业:工业(包括采掘业、制造业、电力、燃气及水的生产和供应业)和建筑业。

第三产业:除第一、第二产业以外的其他各业。

【劳动者报酬】 指劳动者因从事生产活动所获得的全部报酬。包括劳动者获得的各种形式的工资、奖金和津贴,既包括货币形式的,也包括实物形式的;还包括劳动者所享受的公费医疗和医药卫生费、上下班交通补贴和单位支付的社会保险费等。

【生产税净额】 指生产税减生产补贴后的余额。生产税指政府对生产单位生产、销售和从事经营活动以及因从事生产活动使用某些生产要素(如固定资产、土地、劳动力)所征收的各种税、附加费和规费。生产补贴与生产税相反,指政府对生产单位的单方面收入转移,因此视为负生产税,包括政策亏损补贴、粮食系统价格补贴、外贸企业出口退税收入等。

【固定资产折旧】 指一定时期内为弥补固定资产损耗按照核定的固定资产折旧率提取的固定资产折旧,或按国民经济核算统一规定的折旧率虚拟计算的固定资产折旧。它反映了固定资产在当期生产中的转移价值。各类企业和企业化管理的事业单位的固定资产折旧是指实际计提并计入成本费中的折旧费;不计提折旧的政府机关、非企业化管理的事业单位和居民住房的固定资产折旧是按照统一规定的折旧率和固定资产原值计算的虚拟折旧。原则上,固定资产折旧应按固定资产的重置价值计算,但是目前我国尚不具备对全社会固定资产进行重估价的基础,所以暂时只能采用上述办法。

【营业盈余】 指常住单位创造的增加值扣除劳动者报酬、生产税净额和固定资产折旧后的余额。它相当于企业的营业利润加上生产补贴,但要扣除从利润中开支的工资和福利等。

【支出法国内生产总值】 指一个国家(或地区)所有常住单位在一定时期内用于最终消费、资本形成总额,以及货物和服务的净出口总额,它反映本期生产的国内生产总值的使用及构成。

【最终消费】 指常住单位在一定时期内对于货物和服务的全部最终消费支出,也就是常住单位为满足物质、文化和精神生活的需要,从本国经济领土和国外购买的货物和服务的支出;不包括非常住单位在本国经济领土内的消费支出。最终消费分为居民消费和政府消费。

【资本形成总额】 指常住单位在一定时期内获得的减去处置的固定资产加存货的变动,包括固定资本形成总额和存货增加。

Explanatory Notes on Main Statistical Indicators

【Gross Domestic Product (GDP)】 refers to the final products of all resident units in a country (or a region) during a certain period of time. Gross domestic product is expressed in three different forms, i. e. value, income, and products respectively. The form of value refers to the total value of all products and services produced by all resident units during a certain period of time ,minus total value of intimidate input of materials and services of the nature of non—fixed assets or the summation of the value—added of all resident units; the form of income includes all the income created by all resident units and distributed primarily to all resident and non—resident units; the form of products refers to the value of all final goods and services for final use by all resident units plus the value of net exports of goods and services during a given period of time. In the practice of national accounting, gross domestic product is calculated with three approaches, i. e. production approach, income approach, and expenditure approach, which reflect gross domestic product and its composition from different aspects.

【Three Industries Industry】 structure has been classified according to the historical sequence of development. Primary industry refers to extraction of natural resources; secondary industry involves processing of primary products; and tertiary industry provides services of various kinds for production and consumption. The above classification is universal although it various to some extent from country to country. Industry in China comprises;

Primary Industry: agriculture (including farming, forestry, animal husbandry,fishery and services).

Secondary Industry: industry (including mining and quarrying, manufacturing, electric power,Gas and water production and supply) and construction.

Tertiary Industry: all other industries not included in primary or secondary industries.

【Laborers' Remuneration】 refers to the whole payment of various forms earned by the laborers from the productive activities they are engaged in. It includes wages, bonuses and allowances the laborers earned in monetary form and in kind. It also includes the free medical services provided to the laborers and the medicine expenses, traffic subsidies and social insurance fee paid by the laborers' working units for them.

【Net Taxes on Production】 refers to the residual of the taxes on production minus the subsidies on production. The taxes on production refers to the various taxes, extra charges and fees levied on the production units on their production, sale and business activities as well as on some factors of production, such as fixed assets, land and labor force, used in the production activities they are engaged in. In contrast to the taxes on production, the subsidies on production refer to the unilateral transfer of part of the government's revenue to the production units and is therefore regarded as negative taxes on production. They include subsidies on the loss due to implementation of government policies, price subsidies to the grain institutions, foreign trade corporations receipts from drawback, etc.

【Depreciation of Fixed Assets】 refers to the depreciation of fixed assets of a given period, drawn in accordance with the stipulated depreciation rate for the purpose of compensating the wear loss of the fixed assets or the depreciation of fixed assets calculated in a fictitious way in accordance with the stipulated unified depreciation rate in the national economic accounting system. It reflects the value of transfer of the fixed assets in the production of the current period. The depreciation of fixed assets in various enterprises and institutions managed as enterprises refers to the depreciation expenses actually drawn and calculated as part of the cost. In government agencies and institutions not managed as enterprises which do not draw the depreciation expenses, as well as for the houses of residents, the depreciation of fixed assets is the imputed depreciation, which is calculated in accordance with the stipulated unified depreciation rate. In principle, the depreciation of fixed assets should be calculated on the basis of the re—purchased value of the fixed assets. However, there is no actual condition to re—evaluate all the fixed assets in China. Therefore, the above—mentioned methods are temporarily adopted at present.

【Operating Surplus】 refers to the balance of the value added created by the resident units deducting the laborers' remuneration, net taxes on production and the depreciation of fixed assets. It is equivalent to the business profit of the enterprises plus subsidies on production, but the wages and welfare expenses paid from the profits should be deducted.

【GDP Calculated with Expenditure Approach】 refers to total expenditure on final consumption, total capital formation and net export of goods and services by resident units of a country in a certain period of time. It reflects the composition of GDP by its use.

【Final Consumption】 refers to the total expenditure of resident units on final consumption of goods and services in a certain period, namely the expenditure of the resident units for purchases of goods and services from domestic economic territory and abroad to meet the requirements of material, cultural and spiritual life. It excludes the expenditure of non—resident units on consumption in the economic territory of the country. The final consumption is classified into household consumption and government consumption.

【Total Capital Formation】 refers to the fixed assets acquired minus those disposed and the change in inventory, including the total fixed assets formation and the increase in inventory.

CHAPTER 4

NINGBO 2014 Statistical YearBook

第四篇

财政、金融、保险、证券

FINANCE, BANKING INSURANCE AND SECURITIES

财政、金融、保险、证券
Finance, Banking, Insurancen and Securities

主要统计指标
Major Statistics Indicators

2013年全市财政总收入	Total Financial Revenue	2666.26	亿元	100 million yuan
比上年增长	Increase Over Last Year	20.9	%	
2013年全市公共财政预算收入	Public Fiscal Budget Revenue	1651.18	亿元	100 million yuan
比上年增长	Increase Over Last Year	7.5	%	
2013年地方财政收入	Local Financial Revenue	792.81	亿元	100 million yuan
比上年增长	Increase Over Last Year	9.3	%	
2013年财政支出	Total Financial Expenditure	1971.44	亿元	100 million yuan
比上年增长	Increase Over Last Year	30.0	%	
2013年公共财政预算支出	Public Fiscal Budget Expenditure	939.89	亿元	100 million yuan
比上年增长	Increase Over Last Year	13.5	%	
2013年金融机构人民币存款余额	Deposits of Financial Institutions at Year－end	12740.52	亿元	100 million yuan
比上年增长	Increase Over Last Year	9.8	%	
2013年城乡居民储蓄存款余额	Urban and Rural Residents SavingBalance at Year－end	4562.36	亿元	100 million yuan
比上年增长	Increase Over Last Year	9.3	%	
2013年金融机构人民币贷款余额	Loans Balance of Financial Institutions at Year－end	12493.28	亿元	100 million yuan
比上年增长	Increase Over Last Year	10.6	%	

表 4—1 历年公共财政预算收入及支出情况 The Public Fiscal Budget Revenue and Expenditure Over Years

单位:万元(10000 yuan)

年份 Year	公共财政预算收入 Public Fiscal Budget Revenue		财政支出 Financial Expenditure	
	全市 Total	市区 Urban District	全市 Total	市区 Urban District
1978	49697	29662	11176	4672
1979	48860	29536	11803	4252
1980	56290	34924	15712	6956
1981	65432	41157	14585	5812
1982	71546	44574	14689	5331
1983	80801	49130	18873	7747
1984	93318	58817	25544	12148
1985	91237	46963	34610	17449
1986	102264	50872	48978	27413
1987	113351	55227	41655	19490
1988	133395	66580	70336	38395
1989	152751	74892	89355	50141
1990	158910	75725	97133	54389
1991	177875	86733	106961	58704
1992	198354	96918	119133	62758
1993	282429	137495	180622	92931
1994	420202	244253	250553	145946
1995	531135	328458	353700	231321
1996	659529	424052	453292	306509
1997	750412	485289	549989	364757
1998	876351	572222	646080	417522
1999	1039976	679852	740516	477550
2000	1431511	937655	892345	566103
2001	1903064	1209606	1219330	759071
2002	2583984	1869395	1501556	1039828
2003	3250078	2287641	1870929	1268421
2004	4009592	2896291	2223509	1535768
2005	4664968	3294643	3263061	2323203
2006	5611702	3922945	3903046	2678424
2007	7239222	5124685	5691897	3878062
2008	8109020	5698607	7838113	5116301
2009	9662496	7109554	10690545	7038194
2010	11717470	8758532	14521735	9766602
2011	14317563	10691006	15967831	9732235
2012	15365101	11311780	15161555	9387493
2013	16511797	12181059	19714388	13236177

表 4－2　各县（市）财政收入情况（2013）
Basic Statistics on Financial Revenue by Region

指标	Indicators	全市 Total	市区 Urban District
财政收入	**Financial Revenue**	**26662597**	**19269345**
一、公共财政预算收入	Budgetary Revenue	16511797	12181059
（一）中央财政收入	Revenue of Central Government	8583717	6673760
＃消费税	Consumption Tax	2170419	2118740
（二）地方财政收入	Local Financial Revenue	7928080	5507299
1. 税收收入小计	**Total Tax Revenue**	**7337175**	**5107689**
增值税	Value－added Tax	1521674	1069706
＃成品油价税费改革增值税划出	Refined Oil Prices to Draw	－44910	－44909
改征增值税	VAT	227087	200595
营业税	Business Tax	1887297	1247384
企业所得税	Enterprises Income Tax	1266624	990582
个人所得税	Individual Income Tax	398790	276315
城市维护建设税	Tax on Urban Construction and Maintenance	545373	412650
＃成品油价税费改革城市维护建设税划出	Refined Oil Prices to Draw	－86458	－86457
耕地占用税	Tax on the Use of Cultivated Land	122625	54439
契税	Contract Tax	529447	370590
2. 非税收收入小计	**Total non－Tax Revenue**	**590905**	**399610**
专项收入	Special Projects Income	276737	193397
＃教育费附加	Additional Education Tax	253377	177327
＃成品油价税费改革教育费附加收入划出	Refined Oil Prices to Draw	－37152	－37151
排污费	Sewage Tax	16316	13359
行政事业性收费收入	Administrative Fees and Charges Income	127787	88860
罚没收入	Penally and Confiscatory Income	123794	69126
国有资本经营收收入	State－owned Capital Management Income	－154297	－92335
＃国有企业计划亏损补贴	Subsidies to Loss of State－owned Enterprises	－154613	－92335
二、基金收入	Fund Revenue	10150800	7088286
＃政府性基金收入	Government Fund Revenue	7477232	5323293
社会保险基金收入	Social Insurance Fund Revenue	2673568	1764993

单位:万元(10000 yuan)

海曙 Haishu	江东 Jiangdong	江北 Jiangbei	北仑 Beilun	镇海 Zhenhai	鄞州 Yinzhou	余姚 Yuyao	慈溪 Cixi	奉化 Fenghua	象山 Xiangshan	宁海 Ninghai
1051742	**859327**	**1290026**	**3982254**	**1242548**	**5053245**	**1763093**	**2724782**	**887100**	**1020091**	**998186**
780796	656177	664979	3172018	825098	2586276	1063402	1645257	511778	506226	604075
243822	190367	245932	1789935	375442	1053423	467012	724749	246116	199359	272721
3643	441	249	233298	−4769	5483	1204	22625	25162	28	2660
536974	465810	419047	1382083	449656	1532853	596390	920508	265662	306867	331354
516661	**431088**	**400024**	**1280743**	**419961**	**1429578**	**572825**	**861690**	**241373**	**275551**	**278047**
54977	46397	76356	375987	99737	238216	112901	171383	55909	45701	66074
			−7902	178	−8	−1				
24891	22710	32252	50402	13262	32733	5910	9584	2819	3862	4317
217671	181220	102821	227119	115408	371814	170707	238817	70132	85077	75180
66114	50830	54608	307301	61328	190962	62887	105021	30301	37120	40713
33493	27566	20360	63387	20555	97905	36272	42898	11946	13993	17366
24808	19237	23663	109832	32357	88808	29723	50897	19097	13490	19516
			−15144	341	−15	−1				
214	130	2581	18048	5258	28208	12253	21166	6989	19692	8086
41987	59994	56450	41589	25380	145190	49565	55529	14007	22707	17049
20313	**34722**	**19023**	**101340**	**29695**	**103275**	**23565**	**58818**	**24289**	**31316**	**53307**
10355	8239	10271	55982	17879	39926	20074	28481	10391	10392	14002
10355	8239	10241	47728	13811	38116	18549	27893	9036	8792	11780
			−6586	148	−6	−1				
			7836	3960	896	301	314	281	900	1161
6593	2798	10580	19901	2143	19413	3953	7187	2469	5090	20228
3064	1762	1634	8582	6035	17358	9628	18763	6127	10971	9179
	−3435	−10000	−2200	−8000	−20200	−29184	−30200			−2578
	−3435	−10000	−2200	−8000	−20200	−29500	−30200			−2578
270946	203150	625047	810236	417450	2466969	699691	1079525	375322	513865	394111
22297	18021	466222	477160	258688	1935575	396638	878560	238216	394900	245625
248649	185129	158825	333076	158762	531394	303053	200965	137106	118965	148486

表 4－3　各县(市)财政支出情况(2013) Basic Statistics on Financial Expenditure by Region

指标	Indicators	全市 Total	市区 Urban District
财政支出	**Financial Expenditure**	**19714388**	**13236177**
公共财政预算支出	**Public Fiscal Budget Expenditure**	**9398939**	**6201396**
一般公共服务	General Public Service	1048949	679903
公共安全	Public Safety	626630	400394
教育	Education	1484777	867080
科学技术	Science and Technology	375758	255258
文化体育与传媒	Culture,Sports and Media	139095	96371
社会保障和就业	Social Security and Reemployment	975644	600511
医疗卫生	Health Care	622133	352781
节能环保	Energy Saving and Environmental Protection	148078	98645
城乡社区服务	Community Service in Urban and Rural Areas	892401	786111
农林水事务	Affairs Such as Agriculture, Forestry, Water Conservancy,etc.	803773	260109
交通运输	Communications and Transportation	709516	562141
资源勘探电力信息等事务	Resource exploration and Power Information	604181	461258
商业服务业等事务	Business services and Other Services	303388	248707
粮油物资储备管理事务	Grain Material Reserve Management Services	12940	8310
基金支出	**Fund Expenditure**	**10315449**	**7034781**
政府性基金	Government Funds	7641882	5269789
社会保险基金	Social Insurance Funds	2673567	1764992

单位:万元(10000 yuan)

海曙 Haishu	江东 Jiangdong	江北 Jiangbei	北仑 Beilun	镇海 Zhenhai	鄞州 Yinzhou	余姚 Yuyao	慈溪 Cixi	奉化 Fenghua	象山 Xiangshan	宁海 Ninghai
412656	**612580**	**972524**	**1789114**	**690304**	**3578416**	**1509755**	**2167657**	**874242**	**1069348**	**857209**
258462	**302087**	**349283**	**1308206**	**418686**	**1594212**	**745919**	**983925**	**455230**	**545353**	**467116**
41679	36746	57527	146338	52412	156539	90190	109389	54853	52712	61902
25999	24640	32984	42714	30930	75372	51882	80906	27219	29271	36958
45778	43643	52583	153210	73340	251581	134426	206843	93087	90969	92372
12066	17404	15086	61615	20981	73013	29708	49516	15224	13998	12054
1513	3341	4253	11879	8119	24646	14240	11191	4469	6045	6779
32723	37288	20857	83764	43702	182082	119714	113544	36738	46605	58532
15053	17842	22713	55105	29923	100791	75188	78038	32765	38023	45338
770	1817	2415	48185	8195	24214	12144	22369	4872	3956	6092
39189	56801	30927	228745	64871	103205	26287	40418	12755	16757	10073
1147	977	30530	23999	17552	119623	84778	105769	110732	180587	61798
391	177	31820	60648	21439	74874	35040	23967	27146	23431	37791
16818	4183	22462	216472	21462	159272	21330	91218	7756	11277	11342
6400	25682	9793	102703	9835	62082	13075	21590	5538	6801	7677
			1259	288	194	1814		201	2613	2
154194	**310493**	**623241**	**480908**	**271618**	**1984204**	**763836**	**1183732**	**419012**	**523995**	**390093**
154194	310493	623241	480908	271618	1984204	460783	982767	281906	405030	241607
						303053	200965	137106	118965	148486

表 4—4　历年金融机构人民币存贷款与现金收支情况
Savings Deposits and Loans Balances of Financial Institutions & Cash Revenue and Expenditures Over the Years(RMB)

单位:万元(10000 yuan)

年份 Year	存款余额 Deposits Balance	#城乡居民储蓄 Urban and Rural Savings Deposits	贷款余额 Loans Balance	现金收入 Cash Income	现金支出 Cash Expenditure	货币投放(+) 回笼(—) Currency Issues (+) or Cash Withdrawal(—)
1978	50194	14997	68843	92387	101326	8939
1979	64379	20612	78939	119923	130544	10621
1980	90536	28781	107339	159955	174339	14384
1981	107253	34418	114394	187306	198061	10755
1982	130697	46298	130617	216530	227547	11017
1983	154150	60536	146636	277321	288711	11390
1984	207363	81558	242546	356422	392814	36392
1985	266510	109853	304823	522442	562304	39862
1986	354390	149451	414921	640814	679516	38702
1987	445081	199524	522160	860563	926247	65684
1988	522116	215357	643234	1212594	1328827	116233
1989	639228	317572	765704	1344442	1415310	70868
1990	899295	461220	973946	1044032	1102545	58513
1991	1180588	605796	1227009	1321446	1401416	79970
1992	1605229	792466	1603689	1957225	2099612	142387
1993	2012813	979740	2116122	3295921	3441608	145687
1994	2972601	1468634	2671174	4949086	5199010	249924
1995	4546806	2094162	3892271	7121855	7452530	330675
1996	5981440	2846051	5240845	9312625	9789622	476997
1997	7172242	3644769	5747533	12202712	12646470	443758
1998	8552754	4596343	6700817	19733593	20136905	403312
1999	10080232	5296350	7734820	24090235	24591240	501005
2000	11729400	5860592	8831213	30467325	31088353	621028
2001	14445304	6994639	10515601	36286694	37062049	775355
2002	19062375	8623909	14794722	49240318	50379541	1139223
2003	26290346	10596339	21027772	68390220	69703625	1313405
2004	30917954	12089813	24836090	90446530	91895140	1448610
2005	37919362	14588012	29597759	100679426	102368573	1689147
2006	45734811	17520388	37274957	121414154	123296128	1881974
2007	51772379	18274856	47359146	153033733	155234259	2200526
2008	62164580	23670651	56727416	155387621	157911068	2523447
2009	80839363	28695587	74248698	143230611	145798647	2568037
2010	95520308	32822564	90006170	158421425	161613115	3191690
2011	104359176	36662324	102099855			
2012	116023188	41759634	113003187			
2013	127405215	45623634	124932759			

注:本表至4—8表数据来自中国人民银行宁波中心支行。2011年现金收支统计制度取消。

Note:Data from Tables 4—4 to 4—8 are obtained from Central Subbranch of Ningbo of The People's Bank of China. Cancel the cash income and expenditure statistics system in 2011.

表4－5 金融机构人民币信贷资金来源主要指标(2013) Main Indicators of Credit Funds of Financial Institutions－Sources of Funds

(年末余额)单位:万元(year－end)(10000 yuan)

指标	Indicators	2013
资金来源总计	**Funds Sources**	**165571790**
一、各项存款	Total Deposits	127405215
1.单位存款	Unit Deposits	70680442
其中按产品	By Product	
活期存款	Demand Deposits	21673660
定期存款	Time Deposits	19941315
通知存款	Call Deposits	1538312
保证金存款	Margin Deposits	13273766
其中按交易对手	By Counterparty	
企业存款	Deposits by Enterprises	52225070
机关团体存款	Deposits by Government Departments & Organizations	11175319
社保基金存款	Social Security Fund Deposits	5784221
部队存款	Force Deposits	693090
住房公积金存款	Housing Provident Fund Deposits	785362
非居民存款	Nonresisdent Deposits	12011
2.个人存款	Individual Deposits	47817321
储蓄存款	Household Savings Deposits	45623634
保证金存款	Margin Deposits	56255
结构性存款	Structured Deposits	2137432
3.财政性存款	Fiscal Deposits	2421120
4.临时性存款	Temporary Deposits	172321
5.委托存款	Commissiom Deposits	541396
6.其他存款	Other Deposits	5772615
二、金融债券	Financial Bond	2111211
三、中长期借款	Medium&Long－Term Deposits	
四、应付及暂收款	Account Payable and Collecting of Money for the Time Being	4008993
其中:应付利息	Interest Payable	2021077
五、同业往来(来源方)	Inter－bnak Credits	1400881
六、系统内资金往来(来源方)	Inter－system Credit	19508736
七、外汇买卖(来源方)	Foreign Exchange	18914041
其中:结售汇	Exchange Settlement and Sales	16318765
八、各项准备	Provisions	2706298
其中:贷款损失准备金	Loan Loss Provisions	2655501
九、所有者权益	Creditors Equity	7513748
其中:实收资本	Capital Obtained	2003485
十、其他	Others	－17997333

注:金融机构包括人民银行、政策性银行、国有商业银行、邮政储蓄银行、股份制商业银行、城市商业银行、农村合作银行、农村信用社、城市信用社、外资银行、村镇银行、信托投资公司、租赁公司、财务公司等。

Note:Financial institutions including the people's Bank of China, policy banks,state－owned commercial banks, postal savings banks, joint－stock commercial banks, city commercial banks, rural cooperative banks, rural credit cooperatives, city credit cooperatives, rural banks, foreign banks, Trust Investment Company, financial leasing companies etc.

表 4—6　金融机构人民币信贷资金运用主要指标(2013)
Main Indicators of Credit Funds of Financial Institutions—Use of Funds (RMB)

(年末余额)单位:万元(year—end)(10000　yuan)

指标	Indicators	2013
资金运用总计	**Funds Uses**	**165571790**
一、各项贷款	Total Loans	124932759
(一)境内贷款	Domestic Loans	124920587
1. 短期贷款	Short—term Loans	68736442
(1)个人贷款及透支	Individual Loans and Overdrafts	14150323
其中:个人消费贷款	Individual Consumption Loans	6367700
其中:住房贷款	Housing Mortgage	58840
(2)单位普通贷款及透支	Unit Loans and Overdrafts	50951192
其中:经营贷款	Business Loans	50505856
固定资产贷款	Fixed Asset Loans	443799
(3)普通并购贷款	Ordinary Aquasition Loans	
(4)银团贷款	Syndicated Loans	5000
(5)贸易融资	Trade Loans	3629928
(6)境外筹资转贷款	Overseas Financing Transiferred Loans	
2. 中长期贷款	Medium&Long—Term Loans	52907541
(1)个人贷款	Individual Loans	15601197
其中:个人消费贷款	Individual Consumption Loans	13870581
其中:住房贷款	Housing Mortgage	12080924
(2)单位普通贷款	Unit Loans	31412506
其中:经营贷款	Business Loans	3368947
固定资产贷款	Fixed Asset Loans	28043559
(3)普通并购贷款	Ordinary Aquasition Loans	147700
(4)银团贷款	Syndicated Loans	5088631
(5)贸易融资	Trade Loans	657507
(6)境外筹资转贷款	Overseas Financing Transiferred Loans	
3. 融资租赁	Financial and Leasehold	514547
4. 票据融资	Bill Financing	2434459
其中:贴现	Discount	2434459
5. 各项垫款	Advances	327598
(二)境外贷款	Foreign Loans	12172
二、有价证券	Securities	6481982
三、股权及其他投资	Euqities and Other Investment	11771804
四、应收及预付款	Receivables and Prepayments	1954814
其中:应收利息	Interest Receivable	904015
五、同业往来(运用方)	Inter—Bank Trasactions/use	1456317
六、系统内资金往来(运用方)	Inter—systmen Trasacton/use	
七、金银占款	Gold and Silver	
八、外汇买卖(运用方)	Foreign Exchange	16547229
其中:结售汇	Exchange Settlement and Sales	13183407
九、固定资产	Fixed Asset	1644440
十、库存现金	Cashes	774348
十一、投资性房地产	Investment Real Estate	8098

表 4－7 各县(市)金融机构人民币存贷款情况(2013)
Savings Deposits and Loans Balances of Financial Institutions by Region(RMB)

单位:万元(10000 yuan)

地区	Region	存款余额 Deposits	其中 of Which 单位存款 Unit Deposits	企业存款 by Enterprise	个人存款 Individual Deposits	储蓄存款 Savings Deposits	贷款余额 Loans	其中 of Which 短期贷款 Short－term Loans	中长期贷款 Medium and Long－term Loans
全市	**Total**	**127405215**	**70680442**	**52225070**	**47817321**	**45623634**	**124932759**	**68736442**	**52907541**
市区	Urban Districts	87187378	51121512	37960274	27522888	25943786	82275871	40543996	38938156
＃鄞州	Yinzhou	16657723	8556941	6993563	7724050	7400637	14288927	9814232	3831780
余姚	Yuyao	11542406	5622091	4308039	5862492	5652270	11609849	7778626	3651312
慈溪	Cixi	16686320	7941843	6238222	8484452	8234248	15787998	11426053	4143125
奉化	Fenghua	4061054	1782079	945899	2263725	2196342	4677353	2885462	1778731
象山	Xiangshan	3816476	2048894	1555651	1755965	1721342	5444641	3315172	2106669
宁海	Ninghai	4111581	2164024	1216986	1927798	1875645	5137047	2787132	2289549

表 4－8 部分年份金融机构本外币存贷款情况
Savings Deposits and Loans Balances of Financial Institutions in Partial Years(in RMB and Foreign Currency)

单位:万元(10000 yuan)

指标	Indicators	2010	2011	2012	2013
本外币存款余额	**Total Deposits in RMB and Foreign Currency**	**97555158**	**106592654**	**119804984**	**131646045**
＃人民币	RMB	95520308	104359176	116023188	127405215
外币	Foreign Currency	2034850	2233478	3781795	4240830
＃本外币储蓄存款	Household Savings Deposits in RMB and Foreign Currency	33121737	36962819	42088122	45964728
本外币贷款余额	**Total Loans in RMB and Foreign Currency**	**94141982**	**106768424**	**119610158**	**133140166**
＃人民币	RMB	90006170	102099855	113003187	124932759
外币	Foreign Currency	4135812	4668569	6606972	8207408

表 4－9　保险公司业务经济技术指标(2013)
Economic and Technical Indicators of Insurance Companies

单位：万元(10000 yuan)

指标	Indicators	保费收入 Premiums		赔付支出 Claim and Payment	
		绝对量 Total	同比增长(%) Growth Rate(%)	绝对量 Total	同比增长(%) Growth Rate(%)
合计	**Total**	**1854981**	**12.6**	**1039131**	**61.7**
财产险	Property Insurance	968425	12.3	895443	72.5
＃机动车辆保险	Motor Vehicle Insurance	704733	13.1	588173	55.1
人身险	Life Insurance	886556	13.0	143688	16.2
人身意外伤害险	Personal Accident Insurance	46611	16.1	7508	3.4
健康险	Health insurance	58860	13.0	24714	27.9
寿险	Life insurance	781030	12.8	111466	14.8
按公司类别分	**Of Which**				
财产保险公司	**Property Insurance Companies**	**1001895**	**12.2**	**907785**	**71.9**
财产险	Property Insurance	968425	12.3	895443	72.5
＃机动车辆保险	Motor Vehicle Insurance	704733	13.1	588173	55.1
人身险	Life Insurance	33470	10.1	12342	34.9
人身意外伤害险	Personal Accident Insurance	21439	14.7	3665	－2.6
健康险	Health insurance	12031	2.8	8677	61.1
寿险	Life insurance				
人寿保险公司	**Property Insurance Companies**	**853087**	**13.1**	**131348**	**14.7**
财产险	Property Insurance				
＃机动车辆保险	Motor Vehicle Insurance				
人身险	Life Insurance	853087	13.1	131348	14.7
人身意外伤害险	Personal Accident Insurance	25183	17.3	3844	9.8
健康险	Health insurance	46873	16.1	16038	15.0
寿险	Life insurance	781030	12.8	111466	14.8

注：本表数据来自于中国保险监督管理委员会宁波监管局。

Note: Data in this table are obtained from China Insurance Regulatory Commission Ningbo Burean.

表4－10 部分年份保险业务情况 Conditions of Insurance Business in Partial Years

单位：亿元(100 million yuan)

指标	Indicators	2007	2008	2009	2010	2011	2012	2013
保费收入	**Premiums**	**72.22**	**87.11**	**107.44**	**144.06**	**148.60**	**164.71**	**185.50**
财产险	Property Insurance	34.43	40.34	51.08	66.20	77.29	86.23	96.84
人身险	Life Insurance	37.80	46.76	56.37	77.86	71.31	78.48	88.66
赔付支出	**Claim and Payment**	**26.28**	**37.90**	**36.29**	**38.14**	**48.19**	**64.27**	**103.91**
财产险	Property Insurance	18.08	24.54	25.44	27.45	37.47	51.91	89.54
人身险	Life Insurance	8.21	13.37	10.85	10.69	10.72	12.37	14.37

注：2011年起，保险业采用新会计准则二号解释的新口径进行计算。

Note：From 2011，the insurance industry in accordance with the new accounting standards new dianeter calculation.

表4－11 证券市场基本情况(2013) Basic Statistics on Securities Markets

指标	单位	Indicators	unit	绝对量 Total	比上年增长(%) Growth Rate(%)
上市公司总家数	家	Total Listed Companies (A Share and H Share)	Unit	55	0.0
＃A股上市公司	家	A Share	Unit	42	0.0
A股上市公司总股本	亿股	Total Issued Capital of Listed Companies (A Share)	100 million shares	345.92	1.7
A股上市公司总市值	亿元	Total Market Capitalization of Listed Companies(A Share)	100 million yuan	2037.20	0.1
境内证券市场融资额	亿元	Total Financing on Securities Markets in Mainland	100 million yuan	18.58	－67.5
证券成交总额	亿元	Total Negotiable Securities Turnover	100 million yuan	21597.64	49.0
＃股票和基金	亿元	Stock and Fund	100 million yuan	13713.14	39.1
证券客户交易结算资金余额	亿元	Total Exchange and Settlement Capital of Securities Customer	100 million yuan	66.17	－5.1
指定与托管证券市值	亿元	Securities Market Capitalization of Appointment and Trusteeship	100 million yuan	1288.12	12.9
证券投资者股票账户数	万户	Total Stock Investors	10000 accounts	98.44	5.6
证券营业部利润总额	亿元	Total Profits of Stock Exchange	100 million yuan	5.51	92.0
期货代理交易量	万手	Agency's Trading Volume of Futures	10000 pieces	5297.44	－14.1
期货代理交易额	亿元	Agent's Turnover of Futures	100 million yuan	53479.29	27.4
期货保证金余额	万元	Balance Cover Cost	10000 yuan	317500	6.5
期货投资者开户数	户	Total Future Investors	account	20639	7.8

注：本表数据来自于中国证券监督管理委员会宁波监管局。

Note：Data in this table are obtained from China Securities Regulatory Commission Ningbo Burean.

表 4—12　银行业分支机构及人员数(2013)
Branches and Personnel of the Banking Sector

单位:家,人(Unit,person)

行列名称		法人 corporation	分行(分公司) Branch	支行 Subbranch	分理处(储蓄所) Saving Branch	机构小计 Total	人员数 Employee
全市	**Total**	**29**	**36**	**1314**	**756**	**2135**	**44044**
政策性银行合计	**Policy Bank**		**3**	**8**		**11**	**425**
国家开发银行	China Development Bank		1			1	180
进出口银行	Export—Import Bank		1			1	59
农业发展银行	Agricultural Development Bank of China		1	8		9	186
大型银行合计	**State—owned Commercial Bank**		**7**	**616**	**93**	**716**	**16708**
工商银行	Industrial and Commercial Bank of China		1	174	6	181	4224
农业银行	Agricultural Bank of China		1	154	44	199	4304
中国银行	Bank of China		3	129	1	133	3416
建设银行	China Constuction Bank		1	119	42	162	3650
交通银行	Bank of Communications		1	40		41	1114
股份制商业银行合计	**Joint—stock Commercial Bank**		**11**	**145**		**156**	**7330**
中信银行	China CITIC Bank		1	21		22	875
光大银行	China Everbright Bank Co., Ltd.		1	16		17	787
华夏银行	Huaxia Bank		1	7		8	416
广发银行	China Guangfa Bank		1	14		15	521
平安银行	Ping An Bank Co.,Ltd		1	12		13	729
招商银行	China Merchants Bank		1	18		19	945
浦东发展	Shanghai Pudong Development Bank		1	20		21	935
兴业银行	Industrial Bank Co., Ltd.		1	12		13	764
民生银行	China Minsheng Banking Co., Ltd.		1	17		18	836
浙商银行	China Zheshang Bank Co., Ltd.		1	8		9	404
恒丰银行	EverGrowing Bank Co.,Ltd		1			1	118

表4－12 续表 单位：家，人(Unit，person)

行列名称		法人 corporation	分行(分公司) Branch	支行 Subbranch	分理处(储蓄所) Saving Branch	机构小计 Total	人员数 Employee
城市商业银行合计	**City Commercial Bank**	**3**	**9**	**209**		**221**	**8041**
宁波银行(宁波地区)	Bank of Ningbo (Ningbo Area)	1		150		151	4626
宁波通商银行	Ningbo commerce Bank	1		2		3	298
宁波东海银行	Ningbo Donghai Bank	1		9		10	225
上海银行	Shanghai Bank		1	8		9	473
包商银行	Baoshang Bank		1	4		5	232
温州银行	Wenzhou Bank		1	4		5	177
泰隆银行	Zhejiang Tailong Commercial Bank		1	12		13	567
临商银行	Linshang Bank		1	6		7	376
杭州银行	Bank of Wenzhou		1	6		7	331
民泰银行	Zhejiang Mintai Commercial Bank		1	6		7	412
稠州银行	Zhejiang Chouzhou Commercial Bank		1	2		3	190
台州银行	Taizhou Bank		1			1	134
邮储银行	**Postal Savings Bank of China**		**1**	**148**	**164**	**313**	**2736**
农村中小金融机构	**Rural Small and Medium Financial Institutions**	**23**		**185**	**499**	**707**	**8498**
农村合作金融机构	Rural Cooperative Financial Institutions	9		168	498	675	7899
新型农村金融机构	New－type Rural Financial Institutions	14		17	1	32	599
非银行金融机构合计	**Non－bank Financial Institutions**	**2**	**1**			**3**	**105**
信托投资公司	Trust and Investment Corporation	1				1	56
财务公司	Finance Company	1				1	29
租赁公司	Leasing Company		1			1	20
外资银行合计	**Foreign Bank**	**1**	**4**	**3**		**8**	**201**
协和银行	Union Bank	1				1	14
恒生银行(中国)	Hang Seng Bank(China)		1			1	32
汇丰银行(中国)	HSBC Bank (China)		1	1		2	48
渣打银行(中国)	Standard Chartered Bank (China)		1	2		3	76
东亚银行(中国)	The Bank of East Asia Limited		1			1	31

注：本表数据来自于中国银行业监督管理委员会宁波监管局。

Note：Data in this table are obtained from China Banking Regulatory Commission Ningbo Burean.

主要统计指标解释

【财政收入】 国家财政参与社会产品分配所取得收入，是实现国家职能的财力保证。财政收入包括的内容几经变化，目前主要包括：

(1)各项税收 包括增值税、营业税、消费税、土地增值税、城市维护建设税、资源税、城市土地使用税、印花税、固定资产投资方向调节税、个人所得税、企业所得税、关税、农牧业税和耕地占用税等。

(2)专项收入 包括征收排污费、征收城市水资源费收入，教育费附加收入等。

(3)其他收入 包括基本建设贷款归还收入、国家能源交通重点建设基金收入、国家预算调节基金等。

(4)国有企业计划亏损补贴 这项为负收入，冲减财政收入。

【财政支出】 国家财政将筹集起来的资金进行分配使用，以满足经济建设和各项事业的需要，主要包括(2007年支出项目作过调整)：

(1)基本建设支出

(2)企业挖潜改造资金

(3)地质勘探费用

(4)科技三项费用

(5)支援农村生产支出

(6)农林水利气象等部门的事业费用

(7)工业交通商业等部门的事业费

(8)文教科学卫生事业费

(9)抚恤和社会福利救济费

(10)国防支出

(11)行政管理费

(12)价格补贴支出

【存款】 企业、机关、团体或居民根据可以收回的原则，把货币资金存入银行或其他信用机构保管并取得一定利息的一种信用活动形式。根据存款对象的不同可划分为企业存款、财政存款、机关团体存款、基本建设存款、城镇储蓄存款、农村存款等科目。它是银行信贷资金的主要来源。

【贷款】 银行或其他信用机构根据必须归还的原则，按一定利率，为企业、个人等提供资金的一种信用活动形式。我国银行贷款分为流动资金贷款、固定资产贷款、城乡个体工商户贷款以农业贷款等科目。

【承保额】 又叫保险金额。它是保险人员对被保险人负提损失补偿或约定给付的金额。它是保险合同上的最高责任额，也是计算保费的依据。

【保费】 又叫保险费。是保险人根据保险合同的有关规定，为被保险人取得因约定危险事故发生所造成的经济损失补偿(或给付)权利，付给保险人的代价。包括财产险和人身险储金收入。

【赔款】 保险事故发生后，经查证确属保险责任范围以内的保险标的损失，保险人根据保险合同的规定履行赔偿义务，给与被保险人的款项叫做赔款。赔款可以分为已决赔款和未决赔款两种。

Explanatory Notes on Main Statistical Indicators

【Government Revenue】 refers to the revenue of government finance by means of participating the distribution of the social products, which is the financial resources for ensuring the government to function. The contents of government revenue have been changed several times. Now it includes the following main items:

(1) Various tax revenue, including value added tax, business tax, consumption tax, land value added tax, tax on city maintenance and construction, resources tax, tax on the urban land, stamp tax, tax on the adjustment of orientation of investment in the fixed assets, personal income tax, tariff, tax on agriculture and animal husbandry and tax on occupation of cultivated land, etc.

(2) Special revenues, including revenue collected from imposing fee on sewage treatment, revenue collected from imposing fee on urban water resources, and extra—charges for educations, etc.

(3) Other revenues, including revenue from the re—payment of capital construction loan, the funds for the state key construction projects in energy industry and transportation, and the funds for state budget adjustment, etc.

(4) Planned subsidies for the losses of the state——owned enterprises. This is an item of negative revenue, used to eat up part of the government revenue.

【Government Expenditure】 refers to the distribution and use of the funds the government finance has raised, so as to meet the need s of economic construction and various causes. It included the following main items(The items has changed from the year of 2007):

(1) Expenditure for capital construction

(2) Innovation funds of the enterprises(3) Geological prospecting expenses

(4) Expenditures for science and technology promotion

(5) Expenditure for supporting rural production

(6) Operating Expenses of departments of farming, forestry, water conservancy and meteorology etc.

(7) Operating expenses of departments of industry, transport and commerce

(8) Operating expenses of departments of culture, education, science and public health

(9) Pension for the disabled or the families of the bereaved and relief funds for social welfare

(10) Expenditures for national defense

(11) Administrative expenses:

(12) Expenditure for price subsidies

【Deposit】 is a form a of credit by which enterprises, institutions, organizations or residents can put money into banks and other credit institutions for safekeeping and interest earning under the principle of free withdrawal. According to different depositors, deposits are divided into enterprise deposits, deposits of government agencies and institutions, capital construction deposits, urban savings deposits, rural deposits and other deposits. Deposits are major sources of the credit funds of banks.

【Loan】 is a form a of credit by which banks and other institutions provide funds at a certain interest rate to enterprise sand individuals in light of the principle of unconditional re—payment. Loans from Chinese banks include circulating capital loans, fixed assets loans, loans to urban and rural individuals engaged in industrial and commercial business and agricultural loans.

【Amount Insured】 refers to the amount of compensation for loss or agreed sum of money to be paid by the insurer to the insurant. It is the maximum amount of liabilities written in the insurance contract and is also used as a basis to calculate the premium.

【Premium】 is the fee paid by the insurant based on a proportion of the benefit he or she may get from the insurance plus the insurance value. It includes the income from the deposit of property insurance and personal insurance.

【Settled Claim】 is the compensation paid by the insurer to the insurant in accordance with the insurance contract for the loss which has been checked and found to be in the range of liability of insurance after an accident has happened to the insured property or to a person who has insured for his life. It is further divided into settled and unsettled claim.

CHAPTER 5

NINGBO 2014 Statistical YearBook

第五篇

物价指数和人民生活

PRICES INDEX AND PEOPLE'S LIVELIHOOD

物价指数和人民生活
Price Index and People's Livelihood

主要统计指标
Major Statistics Indicators

以上年价格为100	The Price of Preceding Year is Taken as 100			
2013年市区居民消费价格总指数	General Consumer Price Index of Urban Residents	102.2		
2013年市区商品零售价价格指数	General Retail Price Index of Commodities in Urban Area	101.0		
2013年全部工业品出厂价格指数	Total Industrial Products Producer Price Index	96.67		
2013年全部原材料购进价格指数	Purchase Price Indices of Raw Mater,Fuels and Power	96.34		
2013年市区居民人均可支配收入	Per Capital Disposable Income of Urban Resident	41729	元	yuan
2013年市区居民人均消费支出	Per Capita Living Expenditure for Consumption of Urban Area	24685	元	yuan
2013年农村居民人均纯收入	Per Capital Net Income of Rural Resident	20534	元	yuan
2013年农村居民生活消费性支出	Per Capita Living Expenditures for Consumption of Rural Resident	13915	元	yuan

表 5—1 市区居民消费价格指数及商品零售价格指数(以上年价格为 100)
Consumer Price Indices and Retail Price Indices in Urban Area(Preceding Year=100)

年份 Year	各年以上年价格为 100 (The Price of Preceding Year is Taken as 100)		
	居民消费价格总指数 General Consumer Price Index	#服务项目 Service	商品零售价格总指数 General Retail Price Index of Commodities
1978	100.0	104.4	99.3
1985	116.6	113.6	116.9
1986	106.4	106.0	106.4
1987	110.6	105.2	111.1
1988	124.2	123.9	124.2
1989	116.7	111.6	117.1
1990	104.0	113.7	103.2
1991	106.8	111.5	106.4
1992	112.2	119.5	111.4
1993	126.0	149.5	122.8
1994	123.5	129.8	118.0
1995	119.1	129.8	112.6
1996	110.4	122.0	106.3
1997	103.9	119.5	100.8
1998	99.8	108.4	97.6
1999	100.1	117.8	97.3
2000	100.3	114.0	98.3
2001	99.3	105.4	94.8
2002	99.2	100.6	98.6
2003	101.2	101.3	101.6
2004	102.7	101.9	102.0
2005	102.0	101.7	101.1
2006	101.9	101.2	101.8
2007	103.9	100.6	103.3
2008	105.0	98.2	107.1
2009	99.4	97.7	98.8
2010	103.7	102.0	103.9
2011	105.3	101.8	105.7
2012	101.7	99.5	101.8
2013	102.2	103.8	101.0

表 5—2 市区居民消费价格指数及商品零售价格指数(以 1952 年为 100)
Residents Consumer Price Indices and Retail Price Indices in Urban Area(1952=100)

年份 Year	以 1952 年为 100 (1952=100) 居民消费价格总指数 General Consumer Price Index	#服务项目 Service	商品零售价格总指数 General Retail Price Index of Commodities
1953	106.8	100.0	106.1
1957	110.7	113.6	108.8
1965	117.2	114.2	116.4
1975	116.5	105.2	116.5
1978	116.3	109.8	115.4
1980	135.4	109.8	124.6
1985	171.6	137.4	158.2
1989	292.7	211.8	272.1
1990	304.4	240.9	280.8
1991	325.1	268.5	298.7
1992	364.7	320.9	332.8
1993	459.6	479.8	408.7
1994	567.6	622.7	482.2
1995	676.0	808.3	543.0
1996	746.3	986.1	577.2
1997	775.4	1178.4	581.8
1998	773.8	1277.4	567.8
1999	774.6	1504.8	552.5
2000	776.9	1715.5	543.1
2001	771.5	1808.1	514.9
2002	765.3	1819.0	507.7
2003	774.5	1842.6	515.8
2004	795.4	1877.6	526.1
2005	811.3	1909.6	531.9
2006	826.8	1932.5	541.5
2007	859.0	1944.1	559.3
2008	901.9	1909.1	599.1
2009	896.5	1865.2	591.9
2010	929.7	1902.5	614.9
2011	979.0	1936.7	650.0
2012	995.6	1927.0	661.7
2013	1017.5	2000.3	668.3

表 5—3　城市及农村居民消费价格分类指数(2013)
Residents Consumer Price Indices by Category and by Urban and Rural

(以上年价格为 100 The Price of Preceding Year is Taken as 100)

指标	Indicators	城市 Urban	农村 Rural
居民消费价格总指数	**General Consumer Price Index**	**102.2**	**101.8**
服务项目价格指数	**Price Index for Service**	**103.8**	**103.1**
一、食品	Food	102.6	103.6
1.粮食	Grain	101.9	104.4
2.肉禽及其制品	Meat,Poultry and Related Products	104.8	106.1
3.蛋	Eggs	101.3	106.9
4.水产品	Aquatic Products	102.7	103.0
5.蔬菜	Vegetables	101.3	105.6
#鲜菜	Fresh Vegetables	100.1	105.4
6.在外用膳食品	Eating Outside	101.0	101.0
二、烟酒	Tobacco and Liquor	100.8	101.0
三、衣着	Garments	102.6	102.8
四、家庭设备用品及维修服务	Houshold Facilities Articles and Maintenance Services	102.0	101.3
#耐用消费品	Durable Consumer Goods	100.7	100.7
五、医疗保健和个人用品	Medicine,Medical Articles and Personal Goods	102.8	100.4
#医疗保健	Medicine and medical Articles	102.7	100.4
六、交通和通信	Transportation and Communication	99.4	99.3
1.交通	Transportation	99.2	99.1
2.通信	Communication	99.8	99.6
七、娱乐教育文化用品及服务	Recreation. Education. Culture Articles and Services	101.9	100.8
#文娱用耐用消费品及服务	Durable Consumer Goods for Recreational Use	99.1	99.1
教育	Education	103.0	102.1
八、居住	Residence	103.5	101.6

表5—4 市区商品零售价格分类指数(2013)
Urban Retail Price Index by Category of Commodities

(以上年同期价格为100 The Price of Preceding Years is Taken as 100)

指标	Indicators	城市 Urban
商品零售价格总指数	General Retail Price Index	101.0
一、食品	Food	102.6
1.粮食	Grain	101.9
2.油脂	Oil or Fat	96.3
3.肉禽及其制品	Meat,Poultry and Eggs	105.4
4.水产品	Aquatic Products	102.7
5.蔬菜	Vegetables	101.3
#鲜菜	Fresh Vegetables	100.1
6.在外用膳食品	Eating Outside	100.9
二、饮料、烟酒	Beverages,Tobacco and Liguor	101.4
三、服装、鞋帽	Garments,Shoes and Hats	102.5
四、纺织品	Textiles	101.9
五、家用电器及音像器材	Household Appliance and Audio—video Apparatus	99.9
六、文化办公用品	Stationery and Office Goods	99.1
七、日用品	Daily Use Articles	100.9
八、体育娱乐用品	Sports and Recreation Articles	100.3
九、交通、通信用品	Transportation and Communication Articles	99.1
十、家具	Furniture	101.3
十一、化妆品	Cosmetics	101.5
十二、金银珠宝	Gold,silvrt and Jewelry	90.9
十三、中西药品及医疗保健用品	Traditional Chinese and Western Medicines, Medical Treatment & Health Proterction Articles	103.1
十四、书报杂志及电子出版物	Book,Newspapers,Magazines and Electronic Publication	100.0
十五、燃料	Fuels	98.9
十六、建筑材料及五金电料	Building,Hardware and Electrical Equipment Materials	99.6

表 5—5 部分年份工业生产者出厂价格指数 Industrial Producers Ex—factory Price Index in Partial Years

指标	Indicators	各年以上年价格为 100 (The Price of Preceding Years is Taken as 100)				
		2009	2010	2011	2012	2013
总指数	**Combined Index**	**94.04**	**108.89**	**105.86**	**97.05**	**96.67**
轻工业	Light Industry	96.57	104.66	104.92	98.46	97.54
以农产品为原料	Using Farm Products as Raw Materials	97.15	106.04	106.93	98.39	97.29
以非农产品为原料	Using Non Farm Products as Raw Materials	96.21	103.98	103.11	98.52	97.76
重工业	Heavy Industry	91.46	113.13	106.36	96.31	96.21
采掘	Mining and Quarrying Industry	85.58	127.80	100.00	100.00	100.00
原料	Raw Material Industry	91.26	119.57	110.77	98.18	97.32
加工	Manufacturing Industry	91.62	108.00	104.19	95.41	95.64
生产资料	Production Goods	91.95	111.61	106.31	95.73	96.04
采掘	Mining and Quarrying Industry	85.58	127.80	100.00	100.0	100.00
原料	Raw Material Industry	90.61	119.94	110.08	97.36	96.96
加工	Manufacturing Industry	92.63	107.43	104.54	94.98	95.58
生活资料	Means of Subsistence	98.32	101.83	104.67	100.55	98.27
食品	Food	97.57	107.58	108.09	101.97	96.84
衣着	Garments	99.07	102.43	106.05	100.85	98.44
一般日用品	Articles for Daily Use	97.99	100.53	104.09	101.51	99.46
耐用消费品	Durable Consumer Goods	98.55	100.53	102.55	98.32	97.05

表 5－6　部分年份工业生产者购进价格指数 Purchase Price Index of Industrial Producers in Partial Years

指标	Indicators	各年以上年价格为 100 (The Price of Preceding Years is Taken as 100)				
		2009	2010	2011	2012	2013
总指数	**Combined Index**	**88.99**	**113.10**	**108.56**	**97.05**	**96.34**
燃料动力类	Fuels and Energy	83.47	124.81	113.15	100.53	93.94
黑色金属材料类	Ferrous Metals	83.49	110.95	108.10	91.46	94.18
有色金属材料及电线类	Nonferrous Metal and Electric Wire	81.72	137.74	112.68	90.48	95.37
化工原料类	Chemical Raw Materials	87.22	115.82	111.94	93.15	97.36
木材及纸浆类	Wood and Paper Pulps	95.12	122.53	101.35	95.02	96.31
建筑材料及非金属矿类	Building Materials and Nonmetal Minerals	98.46	106.97	118.75	93.65	98.35
其它工业原材料及半成品类	Other Industrial Raw and Processed Materials	95.26	101.39	102.33	98.52	97.85
农副产品类	Farm and Sideline Products	93.85	122.45	124.93	101.73	99.75
纺织原料类	Textile Raw Materials	95.55	112.08	110.02	92.57	97.49

表 5—7 住宅销售价格指数(2013) Residential Building Sales Price Index

(以上年同期价格为 100 The Price of Preceding Years is Taken as 100)

月份	Mouth	新建住宅 New Residential Buildings	新建商品住房 New Commodity Housing	按套型分 By House Size 90 平方及以下 90 Sq. m and Below	90—144 平方米 90—144 Sq. m	144 平方米以上 More than 144 Sq. m	二手住宅 Second—hand Residential Buildings	按套型分 By House Size 90 平方及以下 90 Sq. m and Below	90—144 平方米 90—144 Sq. m	144 平方米以上 More than 144 Sq. m
一月份	January	93.7	93.3	92.3	91.8	94.9	96.0	96.9	96.1	92.9
二月份	February	95.0	94.7	94.2	93.3	96.0	98.1	99.3	97.4	95.1
三月份	March	96.7	96.5	96.2	96.9	96.3	98.7	99.8	98.1	95.8
四月份	April	99.4	99.3	99.5	99.4	99.3	99.8	101.0	98.8	97.4
五月份	May	101.7	101.8	103.0	102.8	100.7	101.2	102.3	100.3	99.3
六月份	June	102.9	103.0	104.0	104.0	101.9	101.3	101.8	101.0	99.7
七月份	July	103.4	103.6	104.4	104.2	102.7	101.9	102.7	101.1	100.7
八月份	August	104.5	104.7	105.2	105.3	104.1	102.3	103.1	101.2	101.6
九月份	September	105.6	105.9	106.5	106.7	105.1	102.6	103.4	101.3	102.6
十月份	October	106.3	106.6	107.0	107.5	105.8	103.1	103.6	102.0	103.6
十一月份	November	106.8	107.2	107.4	107.3	107.0	103.8	104.2	102.6	105.2
十二月份	December	107.3	107.8	107.5	107.8	107.8	104.4	104.5	103.5	105.4

注:由于 2011 年房地产价格专业制度全方面改革,故指标分类有所变化。且只计算月度数据,没有季度和年度汇总数据。

Note: Due to the reform of the professional system of 2011 real estate prices, so the index classification are subject to change. And only monthly data, there is no summary of quarterly and annual data.

表 5—8 房地产其他价格指数(2013) Other Price Index of Real Estate

(以上年同期价格为 100 The Price of Preceding Years is Taken as 100)

指标	Indicators	一季度 1. Quarter	二季度 2. Quarter	三季度 3. Quarter	四季度 4. Quarter
住宅租赁价格指数	Real Estate Rent and Leasing Price Index	105.1	102.2	103.3	103.6
住宅物业服务价格指数	Residential property service price index	100.0	100.1	100.1	100.1
土地交易价格指数	Land Transcation Price Index	104.2	106.5	107.2	105.9

表 5—9 市区城市住户基本情况(2013)
Basic Statistics on Urban Districts Households

指标	Indicators	单位	Unit	合计 Total
现住房总建筑面积	**Total Floor Space of Buildings**	**平方米**	**sq. m**	**33.58**
住宅配套率	**Rate of Housing Complete Unit**	**%**	**%**	**96.01**
房屋产权(合计)	**Housing Property Right (Total)**	**%**	**%**	**100.00**
租赁公房	Leasing of State—owned Housing	%	%	3.35
租赁私房	Leasing of Private Housing	%	%	16.05
原有私房	Private Housing existed	%	%	8.60
房改私房	Private Housing through Housing Reforming	%	%	17.04
商品房	Commercial Housing	%	%	53.35
其他	Other	%	%	1.61
住宅建筑式样(合计)	**Construction Model of Building (Total)**	**%**	**%**	**100.00**
单栋住宅	Single Housing	%	%	5.31
四居室	With Four Rooms	%	%	3.61
三居室	With Three Rooms	%	%	34.53
二居室	With Two Rooms	%	%	43.73
一居室	Only One Rooms	%	%	8.83
普通楼房	Common Building	%	%	1.03
平房及其他	One—Story Housing and Other	%	%	2.96
饮水情况(合计)	**Drink (Total)**	**%**	**%**	**100.00**
自来水	Tap Water	%	%	98.92
矿泉水	Mineral Water	%	%	
纯净水	Clean Water	%	%	
井、河水	Well—Water,River Water	%	%	
其他	Other	%	%	1.08

表 5—9 续表

指标	Indicators	单位	Unit	合计 Total
用水情况(合计)	**Consumption of Water (Total)**	%	%	**100.00**
独用自来水	Separate Using Tap Water	%	%	100.00
公用自来水	Public Using Tap Water	%	%	
井、河水	Well and River Water	%	%	
卫生设备(合计)	**Sanitary Equipment**	%	%	**100.00**
无卫生设备	Non—sanitary Equipment	%	%	2.18
有厕所浴室	With Toilet	%	%	90.14
有厕所无浴室	Non—toilet	%	%	2.71
公用	Public Using Tap Water	%	%	4.97
炊用燃料使用情况(合计)	**Consumption of Fuil (Total)**	%	%	**100.00**
煤炭	Coal	%	%	
罐装液化石油气	Liquefied Petroleum By Gas Cylinders	%	%	25.46
管道液化石油气	Liquefied Petroleum By Pipeline	%	%	7.79
管道煤气	Gas By Pipeline	%	%	0.23
管道天然气	Piped Natural Gas	%	%	63.74
柴油	Diesel Fuel	%	%	
其他燃料	Other Fuel	%	%	2.78

表 5—10 市区居民家庭生活基本情况(2013)
Basic Living Statistics on Urban Districts Households

指标	Indicators	单位	Unit
调查家庭所占比重	**Weight of Surveyed Households**	**%**	**%**
人均房屋总建筑面积	Per Capita General Usable Floor Area of Housing	平方米	sq. m
平均每户家庭人口数	**Average Household Size**	**人**	**person**
#平均每户就业人数	Average Number of Employed Persons Per Household	人	person
负担系数	Persons Supported By Each Employee	人	person
全年人均总收入	**Per Capita Annual Total Income**	**元**	**yuan**
#可支配收入	fx Per Capita Disposable Income	元	yuan
全年人均总支出	**Per Capita Annual Total Expenditure**	**元**	**yuan**
消费支出	Per Capita Annual Living Expenditure	元	yuan
恩格尔系数	Engel Coeffcient	%	%
1. 食品	Food	元	yuan
2. 衣着	Garments	元	yuan
3. 家庭设备用品及服务	Houshold Facilities Articles and Services	元	yuan
4. 医疗保健	Medicine and medical Articles	元	yuan
5. 交通和通信	Transportation and Communication	元	yuan
6. 教育文化娱乐服务	fx Recreation, Education and Cultural Services	元	yuan
7. 居住	Residence	元	yuan
8. 杂项商品和服务	Miscellaneous Commodities and Service	元	yuan

按可支配收入分组 Group by Disposable Income					
合计 Income Total	低收入户 Low Income Households	较低收入户 Relatively Low Income Households	中间收入户 Medium Income Households	较高收入户 Medium—high Income Households	高收入户 high Households
100	**20**	**20**	**20**	**20**	**20**
33.58	25.64	30.11	33.96	38.34	46.40
2.50	**2.75**	**2.47**	**2.44**	**2.33**	**2.27**
1.43	1.50	1.42	1.25	1.38	1.35
1.75	1.83	1.74	1.95	1.69	1.68
46474	**23507**	**32604**	**40334**	**52151**	**90037**
41729	20387	29007	36112	47722	80516
33654	**18855**	**24848**	**32430**	**40277**	**58971**
24685	14580	18885	21619	28953	42446
34.30	41.27	39.31	40.69	33.40	27.23
8466	6017	7424	8796	9671	11560
2593	1543	1873	2003	2906	4862
1400	611	1253	1195	1647	2592
990	579	736	898	1470	1561
4619	2425	2925	3494	5285	8476
3741	1889	2549	2787	3800	8520
1628	1112	1298	1390	2612	2025
1248	404	827	1056	1562	2850

表 5—11 部分年份市区每百户居民家庭主要耐用消费品拥有量 Per 100 Urban Households Annual Average Possession of Durable Consumer Goods in Partial Years

指标	Indicators	单位	Unit	2009	2010	2011	2012	2013
摩托车	Motorcycles	辆	unit	5.38	5.57	4.24	4.39	4.37
助力车	Electric Bicycles	辆	unit	46.90	52.78	53.64	57.35	61.42
家用汽车	Homeuse Car	辆	unit	22.10	25.13	33.15	37.01	41.89
洗衣机	Washing Machines	台	unit	93.78	94.54	95.54	96.24	95.49
电冰箱	Refrigerators	台	unit	97.56	99.07	100.26	100.08	99.80
彩色电视机	Color TV Sets	台	unit	174.50	184.78	193.36	197.27	191.83
家用电脑	Micro—Computers	台	unit	82.43	92.87	102.52	107.69	105.39
组合音响	Music Centers	套	set	28.86	30.64	30.38	30.44	30.13
摄像机	Video Camera	架	unit	10.21	10.30	9.19	10.00	10.21
照相机	Cameras	架	unit	49.57	53.73	52.82	55.69	54.03
钢琴	Pianos	架	unit	3.02	3.96	3.65	3.85	3.82
微波炉	Microwave Ovens	台	unit	73.63	75.12	78.80	79.61	77.98
空调器	Air—conditioners	台	unit	185.36	197.00	213.50	214.63	208.30
淋浴热水器	Shower Heaters	台	unit	97.82	100.96	102.69	103.90	104.55
消毒碗柜	Disinfecting Case	台	unit	16.70	20.05	18.69	18.23	17.65
洗碗机	Dishwasher	台	unit	1.85	1.15	0.65	0.78	1.21
健身器材	Training Equipment	套	set	5.13	6.10	5.07	6.05	5.53
普通电话	common Telephone	部	set	89.51	88.38	87.53	87.39	87.71
移动电话	Handy	部	set	182.45	194.79	202.86	211.55	203.07

表 5—12 历年城乡居民人均收支及住房情况
Per Capita Annual Income and Living Expenditures and Housing Conditions of Urban and Rural Residents Over the Years

单位:元,平方米(yuan,sq. m)

年份 Year	市区居民人均可支配收入 Per Capita Annual Disposable Income of Urban Districts Residents	市区居民人均消费性支出 Per Capita Annual Expenditure for Consumption of Urban Districts Residents	农村居民人均纯收入 Per Capita Annual Net Income of Rural Residents	农村居民人均生活消费支出 Per Capita Annual Living Expenditure of Rural Residents	市区居民人均建筑面积 Per Capita Floor Space of Urban Districts Residents	农村居民人均住房面积 Per Capita Floor Space of Rural Residents
1978	306	299				
1979	340	332				
1980	429	419	222	183		
1981	481	490	217	274		
1982	509	492	353	338		
1983	530	502	340	375	12.62	
1984	643	561	483	428	12.84	
1985	889	862	627	564	12.94	21.30
1986	1110	1057	735	673	12.92	22.80
1987	1192	1076	871	762	13.44	24.50
1988	1518	1469	1066	964	14.49	26.00
1989	1742	1543	1199	1051	15.32	27.30
1990	1963	1628	1254	1166	15.56	27.70
1991	2182	1854	1441	1221	15.93	29.90
1992	2674	2204	1624	1368	16.00	31.00
1993	3983	3139	2060	1599	16.08	30.20
1994	6008	4442	2685	2215	17.25	33.60
1995	7275	5566	3484	2432	17.41	31.30
1996	8354	6545	4267	3283	17.09	30.75
1997	9069	7189	4568	3483	17.42	39.95
1998	9193	7912	4697	3589	18.21	37.58
1999	9492	7493	4798	3591	19.40	39.78
2000	10921	7997	5069	3929	20.34	41.57
2001	11991	9463	5362	4383	21.53	43.14
2002	12970	9396	5764	4508	21.86	45.74
2003	14277	10463	6221	4194	23.22	46.86
2004	15882	11283	7018	6102	23.85	49.90
2005	17408	11758	7810	6623	24.92	50.44
2006	19674	12666	8847	7378	24.91	51.88
2007	22307	13921	10051	8062	26.09	53.24
2008	25304	16739	11450	9174	28.85	55.86
2009	27368	18203	12641	9789	29.72	55.88
2010	30166	19420	14261	9794	30.22	56.00
2011	34058	21779	16518	11253	32.88	57.22
2012	37902	23288	18475	12699	32.55	58.29
2013	41729	24685	20534	13915	33.58	58.87

表5—13 部分年份农村居民人均总收入和纯收入
Per Capita Annual Total Income and Net Income of Rural Households in Partial Years

单位:元(yuan)

指标	Indicators	2009	2010	2011	2012	2013
全年人均总收入	**Per Capital Annual Total Income**	**15090**	**17160**	**18393**	**20220**	**22203**
工资性收入	Wages Incomes	7373	8125	9667	11023	12583
家庭经营收入	Household Business Income	5551	6790	5621	5661	5922
农业收入	Planting	1241	1384	1225	1295	1493
林业收入	Forestry	90	110	119	92	192
牧业收入	Animal Husbandry	818	1090	440	240	157
渔业收入	Fishery	716	883	790	588	632
工业收入	Industry	607	899	774	1030	865
建筑业收入	Construction	575	624	701	756	680
交通运输邮电业收入	Transport,Post & Communications	601	628	471	518	534
批零贸易和餐饮业收入	Wholesale. Retail Sale & Catering Services	445	597	633	561	678
服务业收入	Social Service Trade	214	252	338	460	369
其他家庭经营收入	Others	244	323	130	121	322
转移性收入	Per Capital Annual Transfer Income	1144	1259	2216	2530	2477
财产性收入	Per Capital Annual Property Income	1023	986	888	1007	1221
全年人均纯收入	**Per Capital Annual Net Income**	**12641**	**14261**	**16518**	**18475**	**20534**
恩格尔系数(%)	**Engel Coeffcient(%)**	**38.7**	**41.3**	**43.6**	**41.7**	**39.5**

注:本表至5—18表为农村住户抽样调查资料。

Note:Data from Tables 5—13 to 5—18 are obtained from the sample surveys on rural households.

表 5－14 按收入等级分组的农村居民人均收入(2013)
Per Capita Annual Income of Rural Households Grouped by Level of Income

单位:元(yuan)

指标	Indicators	按人均纯收入等级分组 Grouped by Level of Net Income				
		低 20% 收入户 Lower Income Households (20%)	次低 20% 收入户 Low Income Households (20%)	中等 20% 收入户 Middle Income Households (20%)	次高 20% 收入户 High Income Households (20%)	高 20% 收入户 Higher Income Households (20%)
全年人均总收入	**Per Capital Annual Total Income**	**10048.68**	**15472.90**	**19467.00**	**24902.22**	**40287.56**
工资性收入	Per Capital Annual Wages Income	3208.29	7826.35	12214.34	16516.06	21246.51
家庭经营收入	Household Business Income	4354.51	5348.21	4773.03	5331.97	12044.33
农业收入	Agriculture	648.72	1052.88	924.34	1403.14	3808.09
林业收入	Forestry	65.49	60.78	90.09	100.16	1173.00
牧业收入	Animal Husbandy	81.69	273.76	209.53	23.03	321.76
渔业收入	Fishery	1829.84	758.00	251.23	178.95	1773.43
工业收入	Industry	541.74	523.92	767.92	829.16	1089.31
建筑业收入	Construction	215.95	910.46	548.40	1090.83	954.42
交通运输和邮电业收入	Transport, Posts & Telecommunication	443.84	463.36	746.51	623.17	439.57
批零贸易、餐饮收入	Wholesale. Retail Sale & Catering Services	313.32	712.56	642.24	772.85	1184.84
社会服务业收入	Social Services	174.18	496.13	540.20	227.47	390.72
文教卫生业收入	Culture. Education and Health Care					
其他家庭经营收入	Others	39.75	96.36	52.56	83.22	909.18
财产性收入	Per Capital Annual Property Income	363.36	717.50	918.64	1017.33	2627.08
转移性收入	Per Capital Annual Transfer Income	2122.52	1580.83	1560.99	2036.86	4369.64
全年人均纯收入	**Per Capital Annual Net Income**	**8705.00**	**13450.77**	**18398.70**	**23822.74**	**38008.58**

表 5－15 各县(市)农村住户收入与支出情况(2013)
Per Capita Annual Income and Per Capita Annual Expenditure of Rural Households by Region

指标	Indicators	全市 Total
全年人均总收入	**Per Capita Annual Total Revenue**	**22203**
工资性收入	Wages Income	12583
家庭经营收入	Income from Households Business Operation	5922
财产性收入	Porperty Income	1221
转移性收入	Transfer Income	2477
全年人均总支出	Per Capita Annual Total Expenditures	16967
家庭经营费用支出	Expenditure for Households Business	1056
购置生产性固定资产支出	Purchasing Productive Fixed Assets	83
生产性固定资产折旧	Depreciation of Productive Fixed Assets	551
税费支出	Expenditure for Tax and Public Expense	
生活消费支出	Living Expenditures for Consumption	13915
财产性支出	Prorerty Expenditure	8
转移性支出	Transfer Expenditure	1905
全年人均纯收入	**Per Capita Annual Net Income**	**20534**
工资性收入	Wages Income	12583
家庭经营纯收入	Income from Households Business Operation	4314
非经营性纯收入	Income from Non－business Operation	3637

单位：元(yuan)

市区 Urban District	余姚 Yuyao	慈溪 Cixi	奉化 Fenghua	象山 Xiangshan	宁海 Ninghai
23080					
13974					
3265					
2248					
3592					
20201	13786	12570	14609	16701	16093
281	151	528	935	2720	2541
7	53	9	633	26	8
183	548	624	115	619	1117
16849	12632	14700	10295	11168	12480
1					
3063					
22605	**19864**	**22702**	**19442**	**18127**	**18431**
13974	13354	13086	9988	9046	10453
2802	3970	6063	6657	6122	5963
5829	2540	3553	2797	2959	2015

表 5—16 部分年份农村居民人均支出情况
Per Capita Annual Expenditure of Rural Households in Partial Years

单位:元(yuan)

指标	Indicators	2008	2010	2011	2012	2013
全年人均总支出	**Per Capita Annual Total Expenditure**	**13086**	**13266**	**13935**	**15583**	**16967**
家庭经营费用支出	Expenditure for Household Business	1757	2160	1288	1091	1056
农业生产支出	Framing	322	337	306	282	360
林业生产支出	Forestry	7	24	29	25	19
牧业生产支出	Animal Husbandry	758	997	271	175	69
渔业生产支出	Fishery	335	433	403	134	419
工业生产支出	Industry	149	138	78	277	24
建筑业支出	Construction	36	64	69	47	66
交通运输邮电业支出	Transport,Post and Communications	105	78	62	37	41
批零售贸易餐饮业支出	Wholesale. Retail Sale and Catering Trade	17	34	22	51	24
服务业支出	Social Service Trade	10	12	43	61	11
其他经营支出	Others	18	42	5	2	6
生活消费支出	Living Expenditure for Consumption	9789	9794	11253	12699	13915
食品	Food	3788	4049	4905	5293	5503
衣着	Clothing	662	774	888	918	946
居住	Residence	1868	1305	1404	2228	2051
家庭设备、用品及服务	Household Facilities. Articles and Services	381	398	578	702	616
交通和通讯	Transportations and Communications	1167	1407	1244	1328	2315
文教娱乐服务	Cultural. Edcational and Recreational Services	1037	939	960	1026	1056
医疗保健	Medicines and Medical Services	657	694	998	858	991
其他商品和服务	Other Commodities and Services	229	228	276	346	438
购置生产用固定资产	PurchasingProductive Fixed Assets	309	113	64	154	83
税费支出	Expenditure for Taxes and Expenses	9	21	2	2	
财产性支出	Prorerty Expenditure	37	57	14	4	8
转移性支出	Transfer Expenditure	1185	1122	1314	1631	1905
生产用固定资产折旧	**Depreciation of Productive Fixed Assets**	**418**	**476**	**417**	**471**	**551**

表 5—17 按收入等级分组的农村居民人均支出(2013)
Per Capita Annual Expenditure of Rural Households Grouped by Level of Net Income

单位:元(yuan)

指标	Indicators	按人均纯收入等级分组 Grouped by Level of Net Income				
		低 20% 收入户 Lower Income Households (20%)	次低 20% 收入户 Low Income Households (20%)	中等 20% 收入户 Middle Income Households (20%)	次高 20% 收入户 High Income Households (20%)	高 20% 收入户 Higher Income Households (20%)
全年人均总支出	Per Capita Annual Total Expenditure	**13631.92**	**13059.12**	**15263.15**	**17981.42**	**25315.09**
生活消费支出	Per Capita Annual Living Expenditure	9481.64	10154.18	12931.24	15324.11	21001.95
食品	Food	3760.70	4677.24	5596.77	5702.08	7151.26
衣着	Clothing	409.75	688.99	983.70	1128.45	1483.79
居住	Residence	2062.02	1219.31	1520.73	2472.34	3419.64
家庭设备、用品及服务	Household Facilities. Articles and Services	342.80	401.12	578.65	649.76	1116.41
交通和通迅	Transportation and Communications	918.77	1070.78	1891.48	2805.45	4448.98
文教娱乐用品及服务	Cultural. Educational and Recreational Articles and Services	557.92	890.95	1101.58	1130.54	1441.93
医疗保健	Medicines and Medical Services	1256.28	912.76	917.35	875.77	1195.24
其他商品和服务	Other Commodities and Services	173.41	293.02	340.97	559.72	744.70
家庭经营费用支出	Expenditure for Household Business	2602.84	1448.89	607.38	638.90	1536.92
农业生产支出	Agriculture	352.58	371.75	135.67	391.43	808.28
林业生产支出	Forestry	3.05	7.11	22.29	66.53	15.36
牧业生产支出	Animal Husbandry	13.58	148.15	140.41	4.83	103.16
渔业生产支出	Fishery	2010.90	557.19	140.66	10.13	516.23
工业生产支出	Industry	12.87	20.62	44.67	18.54	27.36
财产性支出	Prorerty Expenditure	6.78	0.74	5.91	9.40	23.80
转移性支出	Transfer Expenditure	1124.36	1425.94	1701.26	2001.97	2640.23
生产费用现金支出	Productive Expenditure Pay for Cash	3014.81	1472.71	622.83	644.30	1644.65
生活消费现金支出	Living Expenditure Pay for Cash	9296.60	10014.73	12800.00	15136.30	20730.29
食品	Food	3591.93	4549.67	5478.64	5543.57	6938.95
衣着	Clothing	409.49	688.99	983.70	1127.47	1482.88
居住	Residence	2057.21	1218.29	1518.84	2456.16	3395.68
家庭设备、用品及服务	Household Facilities. Articles and Services	333.48	394.31	570.46	639.81	1100.63
交通和通讯	Transportation and Communications	918.77	1070.63	1891.41	2805.30	4444.60
文教娱乐用品及服务	Cultural. Educational and Recreational Articles and Services	557.51	890.16	1101.23	1130.39	1433.61
医疗保健	Medicines and Medical Services	1256.22	912.76	917.35	875.77	1193.45
其他商品和服务	Others	171.99	289.91	338.36	557.83	740.51

表 5－18　部分年份农村居民家庭平均每百户耐用消费品拥有量
Per 100 Rual Huoseholds Annual Averger Possession of Durable Consumer Goods in Partial Years

指标	Indicators	2008	2009	2010	2011	2012	2013
洗衣机（台）	Washing Machine (unti)	71	73	74	71	74	77
电冰箱	Refrigerator	95	96	99	95	96	96
空调机	Air Conditioner	87	93	99	105	109	130
抽油烟机	Range Hoods	80	82	83	76	77	77
微波炉	Micro－wave Oven	27	28	30	37	38	36
热水器	Shower Heaters	61	65	67	72	74	77
摩托车(辆)	Motorcycle	49	47	48	28	27	25
汽车(生活用)	Homeuse Car	4	6	7	9	10	12
电话机（部）	Telephone (set)	98	99	98	87	86	78
移动电话	Mobile Phone	170	179	186	175	180	191
彩色电视机（台）	Color TV Set (unit)	175	180	181	172	174	179
摄像机	Pickup Camera	2	2	2	2	2	2
影碟机	Video CD　Sets	43	43	43	22	22	22
照相机（架）	Cameras (unit)	16	17	17	17	18	17
家用计算机（台）	Micro－Computers	40	44	49	46	47	52
中高档乐器（件）	Medium and High Grade Musical Instruments	1	1	2	2	2	1

主要统计指标解释

【居民消费价格指数】 居民消费价格，是指城乡居民支付生活消费品和服务项目消费的价格，是社会产品和服务项目的最终价格。居民消费价格指数，就是反映一定时期内居民消费价格变动趋势和变动程度的相对数。利用居民消费价格指数，可以全面观察居民消费价格变动对居民生活的影响。居民消费价格指数还是反映通货膨胀程度的重要指标。

【商品零售价格指数】 商品的零售价格是商品在流通过程中的最后一个环节的价格，是工业、商业、餐饮业和其他零售企业向城乡居民、机关团体出售生活消费品和办公用品的价格。因此，商品零售价格指数是全面反映市场零售物价总水平变动趋势和程度的相对数。其目的在于掌握零售商品的价格变动状况，为国家制定经济政策、研究城乡市场流通和为国民经济核算提供科学依据。

【工业品出厂价格指数】 工业品出厂价格，是指工业企业向商业(物资)部门或商业企业、其他生产单位、个人出售的或调拨产品的价格，亦称工业生产者价格。它是工业品进入流通领域的最初价格。工业品出厂价格指数是指反映一定时期内工业品出厂价格水平变动趋势及变动程度的相对数，是国民经济核算和计算工业发展速度的一个重要参考指标。

【原材料、燃料和动力购进价格指数】 是反映工业企业作为生产投入，而从物资交易市场和能源、原材料生产企业购买原材料、燃料、动力产品时，所支付的价格水平变动趋势和程度的统计指标，是扣除工业企业物质消耗成本中价格变动影响的重要依据。

【房屋销售价格指数】 房屋销售价格是指房产所有权转移时买卖双方实际成交的价格。它包括商品房销售、旧房交易和公有住房出售三部分。房屋销售价格指数，就是反映一定时期内房屋销售价格变动趋势和变动程度的相对数。

【城镇居民家庭就业人口】 指城镇居民从事社会劳动并取得劳动报酬或经营收入的人口。就业人口包括国家统筹规划和指导由劳动部门介绍就业，自愿组织起来就业合自谋职业等方式，在国有制、集体所有制、中外合资、中外合作、外商在华独资的企事业单位或私营企业单位工作或从事个体劳动又固定性职业或临时性职业的人口。被聘用或留用的离退休人员也计入就业人口。本指标可以反映出城镇人口的就业情况，是计算就业面、负担系数的资料。

【城镇居民家庭全部收入】 指调查户中生活在一起的所有家庭成员在调查期得到的工薪收入、经营净收入、财产性收入、转移性收入的总和，不包括出售财物和借贷收入。收入的统计标准以实际发生的数额为准，无论收入是补发还是预发，只要是调查期得到的都如实计算，不作分摊。

【城镇居民家庭可支配收入】 指调查户可用于最终消费支出和其它非义务性支出以及储蓄的总和，即居民家庭可以用来自由支配的收入。它是家庭总收入扣除交纳的所得税、个人交纳的社会保障费以及调查户的记帐补贴后的收入。

【城镇居民家庭消费性支出】 指被调查的居民家庭用于满足家庭日常生活消费需要的全部支出，包括食品、衣着、家庭设备用品及服务、医疗保健、交通与通讯、娱乐教育文化服务、居住、杂项商品及服务支出等八大类。包括用于赠送的商品和劳务，不包括罚没、丢失款和缴纳的各种税款(如个人所得税、牌照税、房产税等)，也不包括个体劳动者生产经营过程中发生的各项费用。

【农村住户纯收入】 是总收入扣除各项费用性支出后，归农民所有的收入。它是用于生产、非生产投资，改善物质文化生活，以及用于再分配和结余的收入。这个指标用来观察农民实际收入水平，以及农民扩大再生产和改善生活的能力。

纯收入＝总收入－家庭经营费用支出－生产用固定资产折旧－税收

【农村住户生活消费支出】 是指农村住户年内用于物质生活和精神生生活方面的支出，直接反映出农民的生活水平、研究农民消费结构的基本指标。生活消费支出包括食品、衣着、家庭设备用品及服务、医疗保险、交通与通讯、文教娱乐服务、其他商品和服务等消费支出。

【恩格尔系数】 恩格尔(E. ENGEL)是十九世纪德国的统计学家。他根据经验统计资料，对消费结构的变化提出这样一个看法：一个家庭收入越少，家庭收入中或家庭总支出中用来购买食物的支出所占的比例就越大；一个国家越穷，每个国民的平均收入或平均支出中用来购买食物的费用所占比例就越大；随着家庭收入的增加，家庭收入中或家庭支出中用来购买食物的比例将会下降。这就是恩格尔定律。恩格尔系数是根据恩格尔定律而得出的比例数。即：

恩格尔系数＝食物支出金额/总消费支出金额×100％

国际上常常用恩格尔系数来衡量一个国家和地区人民生活水平的状况。根据联合国粮农组织提出的标准，恩格尔系数在60％以上为贫困、50％－60％为温饱、40％－50％为小康、低于40％以下为富裕。

Explanatory Notes on Main Statistical Indicators

【Consumer Price Index】 refers to the consumption price for living necessities and services by people in urban and rural areas. It is the ultimate price of consumer goods and services. Thus it reflects the relative change in prices of consumer goods and services purchased by urban and rural families and can be used to observe and analyse the impact of price changes in consumer goods and services on living expenditure and actual charge in urban and rural households. The index also serves as a key norm in inflation.

【Retail Price Index】 refers to the last price of goods in the circulation. It is the price that industry, commerce, catering trade and other retail enterprises sell consumer goods and appliances to urban and rural residents, institutions and social organizations. The index thus reflects the relative change of the price in retail markets and as a result the index provides basis for the government on the policymaking, studies of market circulation in urban and rural areas, and national economy accounting.

【Ex—factory Price Index of Industrial Products】 It means that the industrial enterprises sell, allocate and transfer the products price from the commercial (or goods and material) departments or commercial enterprises, other manufactures and individuals, it is also called as industrial producers price. It is the initial price that the industrial products enter into circulate domain. The industrial products Ex—factory price index means that it reflects the ex—factory price level alteration trend and the change degree comparative figure for the industrial products within a certain period of time. It is an important reference target for the national economy accounting and calculation industry development speed as well.

【Price Index of the Purchased Materials, Fuel and Power】 refers to the statistical index of the trend and extent of the price fluctuation which industrial enterprises paid in purchasing the raw materials, fuel and power from goods exchange markets and fuel, material manufacturing enterprises for their own production needs. It is an important basis for the industrial enterprises in deducting fluctuant affections of the price from the material consumption cost.

【Price Index of Houses Selling】 houses selling price refers to the actual price paid in the deal between buyer and seller when the proprietary of houses transfers. Include commodity houses sales, second—hand houses transactions and the public—owned houses sales. The price index of house selling reflects the relative figures which indicate the trend and extent of house price fluctuations within a certain period.

【Employment Population in Urban Households】 refers to urban residents engaged in certain work and receiving payment for their labor or income from their business operation, including those who work in state—owned or collective units, joint ventures, foreign—owned units and private with permanent or temporary jobs. The self—employed individuals and re—employed retirees are also included. This indicator reflects the situation of urban employment and is the basic data for calculating employment rate and dependency ratio.

【Total Income of Urban Households】 It means the summation of the salary income, business net income, property income and transferring income obtained from all the family members lived together who were investigated during the period of investigation, it does not include property sale and the income of the debit and credit. The income statistical standard is subjected to the actual occurred amount no matter what complementary or advanced income. So long as the amount obtained during the period of investigation, it should be calculated as what it is, not be calculated by apportionment.

【Disposable Income of Urban Households】 It means that the investigated family can use final consumed expenditure and the other non—obligation expenditure as well as the saving deposit summation that is the income disposed freely by the resident family. It is the income after the paid income tax, individual paid social security fee and billing allowance of which are deducted from the family total income.

【Expenditure for Consumption of Urban Households】 refers to total expenditure of the sample households for consumption in daily life, including expenditure for various commodities and expenses for non—commodity items such as culture and service, etc., but excluding fines and confiscation, loss, tax payments (such as income tax, license tax, real estates tax, etc.)and various expenses by individual laborers for business purposes.

【Net income of Rural Households】 refers to the income owned by peasants after the deduction of various expenses from total income. It's used for productive and non—productive investment, for improvement of material and cultural life, for expenditure and balance in redistribution. This indicator is used to observe the actual income level of peasants, and the peasants' capacity of expanding reproduction and improving livelihood.

Net income = total income—expenditure of household operational expenses—depreciation of fixed assets from production—tax—payment for collective units for contracted tasks—collective reserve and apportion—subsidy from survey.

【Expenditure of Rural Households for Consumption】 refer to total expenditure of rural households on daily life, including expenses on food, clothing, housing, fuel, articles for daily use, and expenditures on daily life and services. This indicator is used to show the actual consumption level of peasants.

【Engel Coefficient】 Mr. E. Engel is a German Statistician at the nineteenth century. According to his experience for statistic information, he pointed out such an opinion for the variation of the consumption structure: the lower a family's income is, the higher ratio is for the expenditure used to buy food from the family total expenditure. The poorer the country is, the higher ratio is for the expenditure used to buy food from every civil average income or average expenditure. Along with the family income increasing, the ratio for the expenditure used to buy food from family income or family expenditure will be decreased. This is called as Engel Law. Engel coefficient is the proportion figure obtained according to the Engel Law. That is: Engel coefficient = food expenditures amount / overall consumption expenditures amount X 100 %.

Internationally, Engel coefficient is frequently used for evaluating the people's living standard in a country or area. According to the Standard by the Food and Agricultural Organization's of the United Nation, Engel coefficient above 60% deems as poverty, 50%—60% deems as subsistence level, 40%—50% deems as fairly well—off level, less than 40% deems as well—riched level.

CHAPTER 6

NINGBO 2014 Statistical YearBook

第六篇

农业

AGRICULTURE

农业
Agriculture

主要统计指标
Major Statistics Indicators

2013年农村劳动力	Rural Laborers in this Year	312.07	万人	10000 persons
比上年增长	Increase Over Last Year	6.2	%	
2013年农业总产值	Total Output Value of Agriculture	428.72	亿元	million yuan
比上年增长	Increase Over Last Year	2.12	%	
2013年粮食总产量	Total Yield of Grain Grops	812458	吨	ton
比上年增长	Increase Over Last Year	—6.15	%	
2013年油料总产量	Yield of Oil—bearing Crops	35798	吨	ton
比上年增长	Increase Over Last Year	—2.36	%	
2013年肉类产量	Output of Meat	195034	吨	ton
比上年增长	Increase Over Last Year	—8.19	%	
2013年水产品总产量	Total Aquatic Products	992050	吨	ton
比上年增长	Increase Over Last Year	0.05	%	
2013农业机械总动力	Total Power of Agricultural Machinery	3236960	千瓦	kw
比上年增长	Increase Over Last Year	—5.12	%	

表 6－1 部分年份农村基本情况
Basic Statistics on Rural Areas in Partial Years

项目	Item	2010	2011	2012	2013
农村基层组织	**Rural Grass Roots Units**				
乡镇政府(个)	Township and Town Governments (unit)	89	89	89	88
#镇政府(个)	Town Governments	78	78	78	77
乡政府(个)	Township Governments	11	11	11	11
农村街道办事处(个)	Subdistrict Offices(unit)	40	39	40	39
农村居民委员会(个)	Neighbourhood Committees(unit)				
农村社区居委会(个)	Neighbourhood Committees of community(unit)	80	70	41	32
村民委员会(个)	Villages Committees(unit)	2578	2559	2558	2555
村民小组(万个)	Villages Groups(10000 units)	3.21	3.17	3.17	3.15
农村住户数、人口	**Rural Households and Population**				
农村住户数(万户)	Rural Households (10000 households)	180.48	180.19	174.84	175.29
#农业生产户数	Agricultural Produeing	59.6	59.07	58.44	57.29
农村居委会住户数	Neighborhoood Committees				
农村社区居委会住户数	Rural community neighborhood committees	5.64	5.66	3.99	3.32
外来住户数	Household from Other Places	40.6	40.62	38.29	41.87
农村人口(万人)	Rural Population (10000 persons)	475.78	475.77	462.97	497.11
#农村居委会住户人口数	Neighborhoood Committees				
农村社区居委会住户人口数	Neighbourhood Committees of community	13.85	14.48	10.04	8.13
外来人口数	Population from Other Places	112.18	110.34	104.73	143.13
农村社会基础设施	**Social Basic Facilities in Rural Areas**				
自来水受益村数(个)	Villages with Tap Water (unit)	2577	2558	2557	2552
通汽车村数(个)	Villages with Bus Services (unit)	2577	2558	2557	2552
通电话村数(个)	Villages with Telephone Communication (unit)	2578	2559	2558	2553
通宽带村数(个)	Villages with Broadband Access (unit)			2544	2547

注：2012 年起，年报填报通宽带村数，不再填报通电村数，以下表同。

Note：Since 2012，annuat report began to fill in the broadband village number，no longer fill electricity villiage number，the same as the following table.

表 6－2　各县(市)、区农村基本情况(2013)
Basic Statistics on Rural Areas by Region

指标	Indicators	全市 Total	市区 Urban District	海曙 Haishu
农村基层组织	**Rural Grass Roots Units**			
乡镇政府(个)	Township and Town Governments(unit)	88	24	
乡政府(个)	Township Governments	11	2	
镇政府(个)	Town Governments	77	22	
农村街道办事处(个)	Subdistrict Offices(unit)	39	17	
农村居民委员会(个)	Neighbourhood Committees(unit)			
农村社区居委会(个)	Neighbourhood Committees of Community(unit)	32	10	
村民委员会(个)	Villages Committees(unit)	2555	784	
村民小组(万个)	Villages Groups(10000 units)	3.15	0.75	
农村住户数、人口	Households and Population			
农村住户数(万户)	Rural Households (10000 households)	175.29	60.22	
＃农业生产户数	Agricultural Produeing	57.29	12.53	
农村居委会住户数	Neighborhoood Committees			
村社区居委会住户数	Neighbourhood Committees of Community	3.32	1.16	
外来住户数	Household from Other Places	41.87	19.42	
农村人口(万人)	Rural Population (10000 persons)	497.11	153.23	
＃农村居委会住户人口数	Neighborhoood Committees			
农村社区居委会住户人口数	Neighbourhood Committees of Community	8.13	2.76	
外来人口数	Population from Other Places	143.13	53.41	
农村社会基础设施	**Social Basic Facilities in Rural Areas**			
自来水受益村数(个)	Villages with Tap Water (unit)	2552	782	
通汽车村数 (个)	Villages with Bus Services (unit)	2552	782	
通电话村数 (个)	Villages with Telephone Communication (unit)	2553	782	
通宽带村数(个)	Villages with Broadband Access (unit)	2547	779	

各区 by Districts					余姚 Yuyao	慈溪 Cixi	奉化 Fenghua	象山 Xiangshan	宁海 Ninghai
江东 Jiangdong	江北 Jiangbei	北仑 Beilun	镇海 Zhenhai	鄞州 Yinzhou					
	1	3	2	18	15	14	6	15	14
		1		1	1			5	3
	1	2	2	17	14	14	6	10	11
	3	5	3	6	6	4	5	3	4
		2	3	5	4	9	1		8
	93	203	62	426	265	297	356	490	363
	0.09	0.16	0.11	0.39	0.39	0.71	0.46	0.42	0.42
	5.01	12.56	10.17	32.48	24.98	45.42	14.87	12.94	16.86
	0.66	3.17	1.38	7.32	12.18	10.44	6.64	6.57	8.93
		0.04	0.33	0.78	0.33	0.76	0.10		0.98
	1.38	3.49	5.23	9.33	2.96	12.98	3.13	0.89	2.48
	13.19	31.92	24.55	83.57	95.13	119.56	40.06	39.84	49.29
		0.08	0.70	1.98	0.87	1.62	0.27		2.60
	5.54	9.92	11.74	26.22	33.01	38.09	8.83	2.53	7.25
	91	203	62	426	265	297	355	490	363
	91	203	62	426	265	297	355	490	363
	91	203	62	426	265	297	356	490	363
	91	200	62	426	264	297	356	488	363

表 6－3　各县(市)、区农村劳动力资源情况(2013)
Basic Statistics on Rural Laborers by Region

指标	Indicators	全市 Total	市区 Urban District	海曙 Haishu
农村劳动力资源总数	**Total Rural Laborers**	**341.21**	**102.36**	
其中:劳动年龄内的人口数	Number of Population in Working Age	308.44	91.95	
按性别分:	Grouped by Sex			
男劳动力资源数	Male	177.91	53.59	
女劳动力资源数	Female	163.30	48.77	
农村实有劳动力合计	Rural Laborers	312.07	92.60	
#外出劳动力	Laborers Going Outside	39.33	12.17	
#出省的劳动力	Going to Other Province	8.33	1.17	
按性别分	Grouped by Sex			
男劳动力	Male	163.02	48.38	
女劳动力	Female	149.05	44.22	
按部门分	Grouped by Sector			
农、林、牧、渔业	Farming, Forestry, Animal Husbandry & Fishery	53.28	10.57	
农业	Farming	42.71	9.21	
林业	Forestry	3.05	0.52	
牧业	Animal Husbandry	2.35	0.36	
渔业	Fishery	5.17	0.48	
工业	Industry	174.80	54.32	
建筑业	Construction	19.80	5.02	
其他行业从业人员	Other Industries	64.19	22.69	
附报:外来劳动力	**Labor from Other Places**	**138.21**	**56.53**	

单位：万人(10000 persons)

各区 by Districts									
江东 Jiangdong	江北 Jiangbei	北仑 Beilun	镇海 Zhenhai	鄞州 Yinzhou	余姚 Yuyao	慈溪 Cixi	奉化 Fenghua	象山 Xiangshan	宁海 Ninghai
	8.17	**23.28**	**17.18**	**53.73**	**59.89**	**84.90**	**30.84**	**27.88**	**35.34**
	6.82	20.50	15.31	49.32	56.99	77.08	25.44	25.42	31.56
	4.28	11.88	8.97	28.46	30.53	43.91	16.20	14.98	18.70
	3.89	11.40	8.21	25.27	29.36	40.99	14.64	12.90	16.64
	7.24	20.10	15.51	49.75	57.19	78.27	27.16	25.06	31.79
	0.83	2.75	1.84	6.75	4.57	4.45	3.13	6.68	8.33
	0.05	0.45	0.11	0.56	0.73	1.50	0.37	1.90	2.66
	3.77	9.99	8.18	26.44	29.32	40.69	14.22	13.50	16.91
	3.47	10.11	7.33	23.31	27.87	37.58	12.94	11.56	14.88
	0.63	2.61	1.20	6.13	8.23	10.03	6.81	9.33	8.31
	0.49	2.43	1.06	5.23	6.48	8.99	5.25	6.63	6.15
	0.05	0.04	0.04	0.39	1.00	0.19	0.54	0.38	0.42
	0.08	0.02	0.07	0.19	0.46	0.25	0.29	0.44	0.55
	0.01	0.12	0.03	0.32	0.29	0.60	0.73	1.88	1.19
	4.13	10.49	7.78	31.92	38.04	47.28	14.53	5.97	14.66
	0.30	1.03	1.72	1.97	3.05	4.32	1.36	3.47	2.58
	2.18	5.97	4.81	9.73	7.87	16.64	4.46	6.29	6.24
	5.19	**10.89**	**10.76**	**29.69**	**21.66**	**42.71**	**5.89**	**3.24**	**8.18**

表 6－4 历年农村劳动力按三次产业分的构成情况
Composition of Rural Labor Force by Three Industries Over the Years

单位：万人(10000 persons)

年份 Year	乡村实有劳动力 Rural Laborers	按三次产业分 Group by Three Industries					
		第一产业 Primary Industry		第二产业 Secondary Industry		第三产业 Tertiary Industry	
		人数 Population	比重% Proportion	人数 Population	比重% Proportion	人数 Population	比重% Proportion
1978	195.42						
1979	196.47						
1980	197.16						
1981	197.91						
1982	201.95						
1983	211.75						
1984	225.96						
1985	234.79	131.71	56.10	80.37	34.23	22.71	9.67
1986	240.88	130.51	54.18	85.73	35.59	24.64	10.23
1987	246.55	131.22	53.22	90.79	36.82	24.54	9.96
1988	250.35	132.86	53.07	90.64	36.21	26.85	10.72
1989	252.37	138.57	54.91	85.19	33.76	28.61	11.33
1990	254.12	142.33	56.01	81.83	32.20	29.96	11.79
1991	256.36	141.80	55.31	83.49	32.57	31.07	12.12
1992	260.65	141.29	54.21	82.79	31.76	36.57	14.03
1993	261.89	132.39	50.55	87.99	33.60	41.51	15.85
1994	263.13	126.79	48.19	89.13	33.87	47.21	17.94
1995	260.40	116.99	44.93	91.08	34.98	52.33	20.09
1996	260.37	115.02	44.18	93.06	35.74	52.29	20.08
1997	259.99	110.34	42.44	93.18	35.84	56.47	21.72
1998	259.23	109.77	42.35	91.96	35.47	57.50	22.18
1999	257.77	105.86	41.07	93.36	36.22	58.55	22.71
2000	257.44	99.83	38.78	97.90	38.03	59.71	23.19
2001	266.14	95.70	35.96	107.68	40.46	62.76	23.58
2002	270.04	92.29	34.17	114.46	42.39	63.29	23.44
2003	290.30	87.04	29.98	135.08	46.53	68.18	23.49
2004	306.15	78.32	25.58	153.53	50.15	74.30	24.27
2005	324.92	75.27	23.17	167.12	51.43	82.53	25.40
2006	320.85	69.14	21.55	170.56	53.16	81.15	25.29
2007	317.16	65.44	20.63	180.86	57.03	70.86	22.34
2008	305.56	64.14	21.00	173.42	56.75	68.00	22.25
2009	304.12	62.29	20.48	173.83	57.16	68.00	22.36
2010	306.32	59.17	19.32	177.28	57.87	69.87	22.81
2011	306.36	58.25	19.01	181.24	59.16	66.87	21.83
2012	293.79	55.31	18.83	175.83	59.85	62.65	21.32
2013	312.07	53.28	17.08	194.60	62.36	64.19	20.57

表 6－5 历年农林牧渔业总产值 Gross Output Value of Farming, Forestry, Animal Husbandry and Fishery Over the Years

单位：亿元(100 million yuan)

年份 Year	农林牧渔业总产值 Gross Output Value	其中 Of Which				
		农业 Farming	林业 Forestry	牧业 Animal Husbandry	渔业 Fishery	服务业 Services
1978	8.83					
1979	10.93					
1980	11.70					
1981	11.07					
1982	14.79					
1983	14.81					
1984	19.68					
1985	21.89	15.40	0.83	3.53	2.13	
1986	24.31	16.85	0.93	4.26	2.27	
1987	28.99	19.47	1.13	5.71	2.68	
1988	36.23	23.41	1.28	7.53	4.01	
1989	40.98	27.37	1.52	8.31	3.78	
1990	40.68	26.94	1.30	8.30	4.14	
1991	45.86	29.35	1.74	8.42	6.35	
1992	51.47	31.51	1.57	9.59	8.80	
1993	69.89	40.29	2.40	11.75	15.45	
1994	96.40	51.60	3.00	17.26	24.54	
1995	123.95	67.22	4.18	20.71	31.84	
1996	138.65	75.77	3.92	22.85	36.11	
1997	129.44	67.19	4.22	21.65	36.38	
1998	136.36	71.92	4.09	20.53	39.82	
1999	142.82	73.04	4.34	20.16	45.28	
2000	148.37	71.57	4.59	20.45	51.76	
2001	156.43	74.31	5.14	22.21	54.77	
2002	163.31	73.65	4.92	24.25	60.49	
2003	173.75	77.42	5.03	26.03	63.10	2.17
2004	193.13	86.94	5.01	29.61	69.18	2.39
2005	207.40	91.14	5.31	32.93	75.31	2.71
2006	207.93	97.14	6.01	32.20	68.97	3.60
2007	236.96	107.22	6.77	46.27	72.67	4.02
2008	262.44	119.31	7.32	48.29	83.27	4.25
2009	286.78	134.64	8.85	47.87	90.82	4.60
2010	339.59	167.51	9.83	51.74	105.62	4.89
2010	339.59	167.51	9.83	51.74	105.62	4.89
2011	397.93	191.64	10.86	62.54	127.68	5.21
2012	419.81	201.19	11.43	64.70	136.73	5.76
2013	428.72	202.28	11.64	60.54	148.29	5.96

注：本表按现行价格计算，2006 及 2007 年数据已根据农普数据进行调整

Note: Note: Data in this table are calculated at current prices. Data of the year 2006 & 2007 has been amended according to the last census of agriculture

表 6－6　各县(市)、区农林牧渔业总产值(2013)
Gross Output Value of Farming, Forestry, Animal Husbandry and Fishery by Region

指标	Indicators	全市 Total	市区 Urban District	海曙 Haishu
合计	**Gross Output Value**	**4287181**	**897906**	
农业产值	**Farming**	**2022774**	**623841**	
#副产品产值	By—products	7448	1881	
粮食作物	Grain	280973	71049	
谷物	Cereal	191106	62141	
豆类	Beans	41051	4740	
薯类	Tubers	48816	4168	
油料	Oil Plants	26750	2174	
棉花	Cotton	13762	223	
麻类	Fiber Crops			
甘蔗	Sugarcane	7940	2335	
药材类	Crude Drugs	29413	23110	
蔬菜	Vegetables	612131	196347	
食用菌	Edible Mushroom	3265	9	
花卉园艺	Flower & Horticulture	301148	108948	
茶、桑、水果、坚果	Tea, Mulberry & Fruits	709048	185556	
其他	Others	38344	34090	
林业产值	**Forestry**	**116442**	**25116**	
人造林木生长	Artificial Forestry	12194	5226	
林产品	Forest Products	71899	8531	
竹木采运	Cut Lumbering	26041	9910	
采集野生作物	Wild Plant Collected	6308	1449	
牧业产值	**Animal Husbandry**	**605389**	**141700**	
牲畜	Livestock Raising	390299	95528	
家禽饲养	Poultry Raising	83393	15826	
活的畜禽产品	Livestock Products	91433	24863	
捕猎野兽野禽	Hunting Wild Beast and Wild Fowl	3829	173	
其他动物饲养	Other Animals Raising	36435	5310	
渔业产值	**Fishery**	**1482936**	**87849**	
海水产品	Seawater Aquatic Products	1282520	49525	
淡水产品	Freshwater Aquatic Products	200416	38324	
农林牧渔服务业	**Services**	**59640**	**19400**	

注：本表按当年价格计算。
Note: Data in this table are calculated at current prices

单位：万元(10000 yuan)

各区 by Districts									
江东 Jiangdong	江北 Jiangbei	北仑 Beilun	镇海 Zhenhai	鄞州 Yinzhou	余姚 Yuyao	慈溪 Cixi	奉化 Fenghua	象山 Xiangshan	宁海 Ninghai
3769	**90313**	**112748**	**111594**	**579482**	**615399**	**717931**	**460621**	**1056953**	**538371**
	52580	**89246**	**79207**	**402808**	**400145**	**450591**	**190288**	**197764**	**160145**
	440	76	331	1034	916	2051	612	844	1144
	7293	3123	6606	54027	54124	45242	24140	36570	49848
	6772	506	5443	49420	40915	19307	19007	27937	21799
	197	938	817	2788	5454	23145	898	2949	3865
	324	1679	346	1819	7755	2790	4235	5684	24184
	102	208	37	1827	7170	12119	806	1939	2542
		117	3	103	3294	7154		108	2983
	43	7	197	2088	315	903	32	4157	198
		400		22710	1859	3800	78	382	184
	15305	14629	28728	137685	139993	182073	7867	55925	29926
		9			583	173	2500		
	5510	47714	27616	28108	58952	25804	80647	21762	5035
	21963	22635	12622	128336	133762	170599	73019	76734	69378
	2364	404	3398	27924	93	2724	1199	187	51
	3509	**1656**	**2236**	**17715**	**30486**	**4377**	**30754**	**9754**	**15955**
	359	723	296	3848	2093	237	1132	3058	448
	1932	540	368	5691	24641	1915	23695	2326	10791
	1218	392	569	7731	3662	2186	5680	206	4397
		1	1003	445	90	39	247	4164	319
3769	**22184**	**12761**	**25704**	**77282**	**121784**	**97920**	**84057**	**80716**	**79212**
3769	11158	9381	13247	57973	70340	66128	59118	53162	46023
	2852	1366	3668	7940	31843	6753	4845	10972	13154
	8118	812	5574	10359	8277	11745	19587	9432	17529
				173	33		12	3608	3
	56	1202	3215	837	11291	13294	495	3542	2503
	10945	**6160**	**1655**	**69089**	**57715**	**147477**	**150398**	**758814**	**280683**
	9936	4658	624	34307	7959	80764	146698	726087	271487
	1009	1502	1031	34782	49756	66713	3700	32727	9196
	1095	**2925**	**2792**	**12588**	**5269**	**17566**	**5124**	**9905**	**2376**

表 6－7 部分年份农林牧渔业分项产值
Gross Output Value of Farming, Forestry, Animal Husbandry and Fishery by Branch in Partial Years

单位：万元（10000 yuan）

指标	Indicators	2009	2010	2011	2012	2013
合计	**Gross Output Value**	**2867805**	**3395923**	**3979320**	**4198058**	**4287181**
农业产值	**Farming**	**1346351**	**1675123**	**1916397**	**2011924**	**2022774**
#副产品产值	By－products	6804	7127	7968	7806	7448
粮食作物	Grain	209857	241746	280624	281189	280973
谷物	Cereal	142258	167853	197813	200171	191106
豆类	Beans	30482	31790	39763	36593	41051
薯类	Tubers	37117	42103	43048	44425	48816
油料	Oil Plants	21826	23455	24580	26516	26750
棉花	Cotton	10570	17832	17253	16410	13762
麻类	Fiber Crops					
甘蔗	Sugarcane	9772	9392	10113	7514	7940
药材类	Crude Drugs	10116	12356	24220	25897	29413
蔬菜	Vegetables	420859	547737	607582	631964	612131
食用菌	Edible Mushroom	618	556	612	722	3265
花卉园艺	Flower & Horticulture	187262	239054	274437	297568	301148
茶、桑、果	Tea, Mulberry & Fruits	447409	559431	643140	687225	709048
其他	Others	24370	23564	33836	36919	38344
林业产值	**Forestry**	**88522**	**98252**	**108564**	**114301**	**116442**
人造林木生长	Artificial Forestry	8217	8349	11441	11383	12194
林产品	Forest Products	58721	62801	69674	72556	71899
村及村以下竹木采伐	Cut Lumbering	21584	24660	24509	26069	26041
采集野生作物	Wild Plant Collected	3692	2442	2940	4293	6308
牧业产值	**Animal Husbandry**	**478671**	**517412**	**625444**	**646977**	**605389**
牲畜	Livestock Raising	261299	293829	385045	414026	390299
家禽饲养	Poultry Raising	85012	90666	104780	101292	83393
活的畜禽产品	Livestock Products	89915	94687	102513	96978	91433
捕猎野兽野禽	Hunting Wild Beast and Wild Fowl	748	592	552	1151	3829
其他动物饲养	Other Animals Raising	4697	37638	32554	33530	36435
渔业产值	**Fishery**	**908243**	**1056250**	**1276779**	**1367257**	**1482936**
海水产品	Seawater Aquatic Products	785820	901585	1095365	1179800	1282520
淡水产品	Freshwater Aquatic Products	122423	154665	181414	187457	200416
农林牧渔服务业	**Services**	**46018**	**48886**	**52136**	**57599**	**59640**

注：本表按当年价格计算。

Note: Data in this table are calculated at current prices.

表 6－8 各地农林牧渔业中间消耗(2013)
Intermediate Consumption of Farming, Forestry, Animal Husbandry and Fishery by Region

单位:万元(10000 yuan)

地区	Region	中间消耗 Intermediate Consumption	其中 of Which 农业 Farming	林业 Forestry	牧业 Animal Husbandry	渔业 Fishery	服务业 Services
全市	**Total**	**1530045**	**518609**	**40049**	**336569**	**611763**	**23055**
市区	Urban Area	286012	165514	4963	65574	43121	6840
海曙	Haishu						
江东	Jiangdong	1206			1206		
江北	Jiangbei	30261	12922	932	10937	5093	377
北仑	Beilun	31639	16760	468	8741	4834	836
镇海	Zhenhai	44518	28319	1372	12864	993	970
鄞州	Yinzhou	178388	107513	2191	31826	32201	4657
县市	Rural Area						
余姚	Yuyao	213853	96595	9198	89547	16543	1970
慈溪	Cixi	225899	120066	2259	49785	46764	7025
奉化	Fenghua	177602	42567	14729	37372	80874	2060
象山	Xiangshan	479256	51686	5607	43817	373937	4209
宁海	Ninghai	147423	42181	3293	50474	50524	951

表 6—9 农林牧渔业增加值(2013)
Value Added of Farming, Forestry, Animal Husbandry and Fishery

单位:万元(10000 yuan)

指标	Indicators	总产值 Gross Output Value	其中 of Which		增加值率(%) Value—adding Rate
			中间消耗 Depreciation	增加值 Value—added	
总计	**Total**	**4287181**	**1530045**	**2757136**	**64.31**
农业	Farming	2022774	518609	1504165	74.36
林业	Forestry	116442	40049	76393	65.61
牧业	Animal Husbandry	605389	336569	268820	44.40
渔业	Fishery	1482936	611763	871173	58.75
服务业	Services	59640	23055	36585	61.34

表 6—10 各县(市)农林牧渔业增加值(2013)
Value Added of Farming, Forestry, Animal Husbandry and Fishery by Region

单位:万元(10000 yuan)

地区	Region	增加值 Value—added	其中 of Which				
			农业 Farming	林业 Forestry	牧业 Animal Husbandry	渔业 Fishery	服务业 Services
全市	**Total**	**2757136**	**1504165**	**76393**	**268820**	**871173**	**36585**
市区	Urban Area	611894	458327	20153	76126	44728	12560
余姚	Yuyao	401546	303550	21288	32237	41172	3299
慈溪	Cixi	492032	330525	2118	48135	100713	10541
奉化	Fenghua	283019	147721	16025	46685	69524	3064
象山	Xiangshan	577697	146078	4147	36899	384877	5696
宁海	Ninghai	390948	117964	12662	28738	230159	1425

表 6－11 历年主要农作物播种面积及产量
Sown Areas and Yield of Major Farm Crops Over the Years

单位：面积：千公顷 Sown：1000 hectares
产量：万吨 Yield：10000 tons

年份 Year	农作物播种面积 Sown Area	其中 of Which							
		粮食 Grain		棉花 Cotton		油料 Oil Plants		蔬菜 Vegetables	
		面积 Area	产量 Yield	面积 Area	产量 Yield	面积 Area	产量 Yield	面积 Area	产量 Yield
1978	638.43	422.61	180.51						
1979	638.61	420.13	196.36						
1980	625.37	413.95	171.60						
1981	622.19	396.91	153.88						
1982	626.41	402.19	191.11						
1983	624.95	410.17	166.30	51.88	4.79	40.21	5.97		
1984	616.76	410.39	213.70	51.36	6.98	32.96	5.99		
1985	612.90	380.39	188.52	48.13	3.91	44.45	7.99	34.57	143.97
1986	596.50	361.81	188.65	41.39	3.66	48.70	8.41	36.09	158.75
1987	595.54	372.05	185.23	34.27	2.95	45.09	7.77	42.89	166.61
1988	580.01	369.58	189.98	34.65	1.80	46.70	8.47	41.01	161.74
1989	579.97	360.69	183.84	31.30	2.07	49.44	7.55	47.79	151.00
1990	591.03	368.77	189.06	34.55	3.34	52.51	9.50	48.79	135.64
1991	587.53	372.02	205.63	33.84	3.84	52.08	9.19	44.58	135.36
1992	572.68	357.66	181.62	33.03	2.59	49.15	8.62	46.82	126.89
1993	522.02	317.08	175.44	27.37	2.36	32.28	6.13	52.73	152.20
1994	504.73	308.04	172.51	26.93	2.07	30.17	4.84	56.37	162.65
1995	512.08	316.57	172.76	27.59	2.48	40.29	7.34	50.04	144.62
1996	519.48	318.99	190.30	27.14	2.73	40.37	8.00	54.20	164.26
1997	502.21	316.44	173.73	24.19	1.53	35.27	6.81	51.86	158.10
1998	510.73	317.76	180.39	25.81	2.69	34.21	5.05	58.01	174.67
1999	504.82	308.98	173.67	14.75	1.59	36.16	7.37	69.73	207.62
2000	445.90	246.79	132.51	9.69	1.05	32.58	6.59	82.16	243.70
2001	406.64	200.16	112.17	10.20	1.18	27.28	5.59	99.25	299.22
2002	386.85	172.34	94.89	6.85	0.80	24.51	4.76	104.71	291.67
2003	348.64	136.73	75.61	6.55	0.76	19.98	4.21	98.86	275.04
2004	338.09	145.12	83.73	6.53	0.74	17.67	4.04	91.80	286.76
2005	332.53	145.27	80.12	6.77	0.72	17.71	4.01	93.36	274.86
2006	317.17	141.01	81.30	6.21	0.73	14.91	3.62	88.75	264.73
2007	314.67	134.98	74.77	6.11	0.69	14.47	3.52	94.03	266.00
2008	330.07	153.80	88.42	6.45	0.75	14.21	3.55	89.49	272.92
2009	321.72	148.14	86.32	6.53	0.75	17.52	4.33	86.76	274.42
2010	318.56	151.14	87.13	6.73	0.77	16.82	4.10	83.59	265.73
2011	314.28	150.95	90.14	6.48	0.82	15.05	3.78	82.13	269.09
2012	309.45	148.53	86.57	5.98	0.71	14.70	3.67	80.73	261.20
2013	307.91	148.57	81.25	5.32	0.61	14.22	3.58	80.05	248.79

注：2006 年数据已根据农普数据进行调整。从 2008 年年报开始，马铃薯作为粮食，不算蔬菜

Note：Data of the year 2006 has been amended according to the last census of agriculture. Potato is classified as food，not vegetable from 2008.

表 6－12 各县(市)、区农作物播种面积和产量(2013)
Total Sown Area and Yield of Major Farm Crops by Region

指标	Indicators	全市 Total	市区 Urban District	海曙 Haishu
农作物播种面积总计	**Sown Area of Farm Crops**	**307913**	**81925**	
粮食作物播种面积	**Sown Area of Grain**	**148574**	**37481**	
总产量	**Total Yield of Grain**	**812458**	**229579**	
谷物面积	Sown Area of Cereal	103781	31548	
总产量	Yield of Cereal	649823	203225	
稻谷面积	Sown Area of Rice	85248	28879	
总产量	Yield of Rice	567860	190096	
#早稻面积	Sown Area of Early Rice	15638	6926	
总产量	Yield of Early Rice	101023	45675	
晚稻及单季稻	Sown Area of Late Rice & Single Season Rice	69610	21953	
总产量	Yield of Late Rice & Single Season Rice	466837	144421	
小麦面积	Sown Area of Wheat	8358	1092	
总产量	Yield of Wheat	33870	4286	
大麦面积	Sown Area of Barley	685	165	
总产量	Yield of Barley	2438	593	
豆类面积	Sown Area of Beans	30792	3287	
总产量	Yield of Beans	90015	12501	
蕃薯面积	Sown Area of Tubers	14001	2646	
总产量	Yield of Tubers	72620	13853	
油料播种面积	**Sown Area of Oil Plants**	**14219**	**1229**	
总产量	**Yield of Oil Plants**	**35798**	**3827**	
油菜籽面积	Sown Area of Rapeseeds	9961	627	
总产量	Yield of Rapeseeds	22732	1437	
花生面积	Sown Area of Peanuts	3570	571	
总产量	Yield of Peanuts	11795	2329	
芝麻面积	Sown Area of Sesame	688	31	

单位：公顷，吨(hectare ton)

各区 by Districts									
江东 Jiangdong	江北 Jiangbei	北仑 Beilun	镇海 Zhenhai	鄞州 Yinzhou	余姚 Yuyao	慈溪 Cixi	奉化 Fenghua	象山 Xiangshan	宁海 Ninghai
	8207	**6731**	**10229**	**56758**	**62122**	**80933**	**22515**	**31291**	**29127**
	4336	**1612**	**3973**	**27560**	**32797**	**29833**	**11713**	**17479**	**19271**
	26566	**6475**	**25456**	**171082**	**176038**	**126121**	**72065**	**108335**	**100320**
	3897	395	3083	24173	27013	11792	9866	11028	12534
	25000	2011	22050	154164	152739	67916	66015	82019	77909
	3719	164	2834	22162	21752	6235	9127	10010	9245
	24142	1064	20620	144270	125655	43934	63453	78603	66119
	824	8	808	5286	6244	225	1046	861	336
	5556	49	5389	34681	38821	1482	6672	6105	2268
	2895	156	2026	16876	15508	6010	8081	9149	8909
	18586	1015	15231	109589	86834	42452	56781	72498	63851
	28	2	36	1026	2857	1697	266	275	2171
	106	9	132	4039	13620	6150	932	939	7943
	47		4	114	21	218	35	136	110
	179		14	400	89	715	129	511	401
	197	730	610	1750	3718	16703	796	2980	3308
	616	1869	2224	7792	12565	49383	1666	7186	6714
	242	487	280	1637	2066	1338	1051	3471	3429
	950	2595	1182	9126	10734	8822	4384	19130	15697
	116	**115**	**49**	**949**	**3105**	**6815**	**353**	**1229**	**1488**
	226	**350**	**117**	**3134**	**8042**	**17033**	**762**	**3232**	**2902**
	115	69	30	413	2665	4917	96	734	922
	224	173	64	976	6329	12070	138	1187	1571
	1	41	17	512	378	1417	245	457	502
	2	168	49	2110	1577	4056	604	1976	1253
		5	2	24	62	481	12	38	64

表 6－12 续表 Continued

指标	Indicators	全市 Total	市区 Urban District	海曙 Haishu
总产量	Yield of Sesame	1271	61	
棉花(皮棉)播种面积	Sown Area of Cotton	5322	85	
棉花(皮棉)总产量	Yield of Cotton	6072	138	
麻类播种面积	Sown Area of Fiber Crops			
麻类总产量	Yield of Fiber Crops			
甘蔗播种面积	Sown Area of Sugarcane	681	215	
甘蔗总产量	Yield of Sugarcane	39483	14350	
药材类播种面积	Sown Area of Medicinal Material	1437	693	
药材类总产量	Yield of Medicinal Material	5399	3072	
蔬菜类播种面积	Sown Area of Vegetables	80051	19646	
蔬菜类总产量	Yield of Vegetables	2487857	589929	
食用菌产量	Edible Mushroom	3934	10	
果用瓜播种面积	**Sown Area of Melon as Fruits**	**20128**	**5617**	
总产量	**Yield of Melon as Fruits**	**577568**	**189135**	
西瓜播种面积	Sown Area of Watermelon	14140	4246	
总产量	Yield of Watermelon	453342	157365	
草莓面积	Sown Area of Strawberry	1427	360	
总产量	Yield of Strawberry	24920	7556	
花卉苗木播种面积	**Sown Area of Flowers and Plants Nursery Stock**	**23010**	**8041**	
花卉面积	Sown Area of Flowers	9587	3797	
苗木面积	Sown Area of Plants Nursery Stock	13019	4181	
盆栽类园艺(万盆)	Potted Horticulture(10000 units)	191	135	
其他农作物播种面积	**Sown Area of Other Farm Crops**	**14491**	**8918**	
绿肥面积	Sown Area of Green Manure	3964	2069	
席草面积	Sown Area of Rush	5278	4547	
总产量	Yield of Rush	46874	41310	

单位:公顷,吨(hectare ton)

各区 by Districts									
江东 Jiangdong	江北 Jiangbei	北仑 Beilun	镇海 Zhenhai	鄞州 Yinzhou	余姚 Yuyao	慈溪 Cixi	奉化 Fenghua	象山 Xiangshan	宁海 Ninghai
		9	4	48	136	907	20	69	78
		37	4	44	1060	3009		80	1088
		82	5	51	1118	3515		80	1221
	5	1	15	194	63	123	12	229	39
	364	40	894	13052	3897	7856	303	11860	1217
	3	4		686	166	498	31	39	10
		3		3069	540	1486	82	186	33
	2290	1554	3293	12509	17032	27703	2522	8685	4463
	63324	34125	85129	407351	751441	786236	44153	197203	118895
		10			751	173	3000		
	283	**409**	**793**	**4132**	**2029**	**7827**	**804**	**1953**	**1898**
	8315	**9358**	**19717**	**151745**	**73593**	**180146**	**18061**	**51890**	**64743**
	226	319	425	3276	1451	5211	530	1344	1358
	6956	7649	13222	129538	55442	136760	13475	40265	50035
	18	23	129	190	128	497	222	138	82
	432	461	2697	3966	2555	6874	3797	2455	1683
	917	**2993**	**1538**	**2593**	**4640**	**2954**	**5617**	**1044**	**714**
	169	2164	503	961	3732	837	804	375	42
	740	827	1007	1607	849	2052	4596	669	672
	65	22	20	27	34	4	17	2	
	257	**6**	**564**	**8091**	**1230**	**2171**	**1463**	**553**	**156**
	182	4	309	1574	615	8	748	377	147
				4547	57		674		
				41310	654		4910		

表 6－13　各县(市)、区农业机械拥有量(2013 年末)
Possession of Agricultural Machinery by Region (End of 2013)

指标	单位	Indicators	Unit	全市 Total	市区 Urban District	海曙 Haishu
农业机械总动力	千瓦	Total Power of AgriculturalMachinery	kw	3236960	679974	128
耕作机械		Cultivation Machinery				
耕作机械动力合计	台	Mechanical Power of Cultivation	unit	25237	7804	6
	千瓦		kw	296265	80640	54
大中型拖拉机	台	Large and Medium Sized Tractors	unti	2772	554	
	千瓦		kw	104139	19463	
农用小型拖拉机	台	Mini—tractors for Agriculture	unit	15935	3555	2
	千瓦		kw	147121	36051	18
收获机械		Harvest Machinery				
收获机械动力合计	台	Mechanical Power of Harvesting	unit	2993	901	7
	千瓦		kw	94866	28161	25
联合收割机	台	Combine Harvesters	unit	2627	724	1
	千瓦		kw	79537	22068	15
谷物烘干机	台	Cereal Dryer	unit	737	238	
植保机械		Plant Protection Machinery				
植保机械动力合计	台	Mechanical Power of Plant Protection	unit	32685	2074	
	千瓦		kw	55404	4392	
机动喷雾(粉)器	架	Motorized Sprayer	unit	29282	1976	
	千瓦		kw	48422	3769	
排灌机械		Drainage & Irrigation Machinery				
排灌机械动力	台	Mechanical Power of Drainage and Irrigation	unit	76764	16874	2
	千瓦		kw	303857	74724	28
农用水泵	台	Water Pump for Agricultural Use	unit	63224	16436	2
农副产品加工机械		Processing Machinery of Agricultural Products				
农副产品加工机械动力合计	台	Mechanical Power of Farm Sideline Products Manufacturing	unit	17093	4122	1
	千瓦		kw	128681	25830	10
运输机械		Transport Machinery				
运输机械动力	台	Mechanical Power of Transportation	unit	36094	6205	
	千瓦		kw	706853	147823	
农用运输车	辆	Vehicles for Agricultural Use	unit	17423	2344	
	千瓦		kw	316981	74457	
运输型拖拉机	辆	Transport Tractors	unit	17412	3706	
	千瓦		kw	346028	65418	
其他农用机械		Other Mechanical				
其他农业机械动力合计	台	Other Mechanical Power	unit	35263	13478	10
	千瓦		kw	344344	119261	3

注：本表数据来自宁波市农业机械服务总站。

Note：Date in this table are obtained from Agricultural Machinery General Servise Station of Ningbo.

各区 by Districts									
江东 Jiangdong	江北 Jiangbei	北仑 Beilun	镇海 Zhenhai	鄞州 Yinzhou	余姚 Yuyao	慈溪 Cixi	奉化 Fenghua	象山 Xiangshan	宁海 Ninghai
288	49122	174349	64208	391879	634088	447474	293013	879095	303316
	630	1966	625	4577	4908	5916	3143	1689	1777
	7445	11364	7480	54297	69331	67136	34381	24033	20744
	170	44	51	289	927	610	234	282	165
	3940	1785	2076	11662	36033	22611	8409	9911	7712
	228	145	187	2993	3458	4209	2592	1001	1120
	2020	1417	2029	30567	29395	37767	24353	9405	10150
	186	9	50	649	733	338	350	431	240
	3559	265	2530	21782	22916	10626	8848	13049	11266
	180	9	50	484	701	333	323	354	192
	3375	265	2530	15883	21951	10410	7167	11981	5960
	22	13	41	162	186	81	75	73	84
	383	527	253	911	2391	17906	411	4701	5202
	716	902	626	2148	5308	25669	1249	8586	10200
	380	527	253	816	840	17712	350	3204	5200
	710	902	621	1536	3363	24739	1044	5417	10090
	1261	5672	1680	8259	20809	9519	8964	11468	9130
	10804	20252	7052	35508	89850	43943	33774	28696	32870
	1235	5536	1429	8234	13475	6400	8909	10754	7250
	286	362	210	3263	6288	2277	1766	1147	1493
	3313	2586	1217	18704	41407	19952	16138	11014	14340
21	202	1930	371	3681	9109	8190	3195	3421	5974
288	3933	38075	6274	99253	156086	122303	86031	97592	97018
		897		1447	5668	5283	1534	144	2450
		20385		54072	82281	63637	52681	5785	38140
21	202	927	371	2185	3369	2862	1589	2892	2994
288	3933	16170	6274	38753	69600	53262	32210	72238	53300
	714	730	903	11121	6139	5910	3545	4911	1280
	1985	22302	3879	91092	94339	65064	22015	23642	20023

表 6－14 各县(市)、区灌溉和水利情况(2013)
Irrigation and Water Conservancy Facilities of Farmland by Region

指标	单位	Indicators	Unit	全市 Total	市区 Urban District	海曙 Haishu
水库年末累计	座	Total Number of Reservoirs at the Year－end	set	421	98	
总库容量	万立方米	Total Capacity of Reservoirs at the Year－end	10000 cu. m	186279	54531	
＃大型水库	座	Large－sized Reservoirs	set	6	2	
总库容	万立方米	Capacity	10000 cu. m	78396	23180	
中型水库	座	Medium－sized Reservoirs	set	26	7	
总库容	万立方米	Capacity	10000 cu. m	71207	20984	
小型水库	座	Small－sized Reservoirs	set	389	89	
总库容	万立方米	Capacity	10000 cu. m	36676	10367	
水电站数量	座	Hydropower Station	set	102	13	
泵站数量	处	Pumping Station	unit	5304	108	4
灌溉面积总计	千公顷	Total Irrigated Area	1000 hectares	198.59	56.39	
有效灌溉面积	千公顷	Effective Irrigated Area	1000 hectares	183.38	52.89	
有效实灌面积	千公顷	Effective Fact Irrigated Area	1000 hectares	180.50	50.01	
旱涝保收面积	千公顷	Farmland Area of Stable Yields Despite Drought or Excessive Rain	1000 hectares	109.54	31.71	
节水灌溉面积	千公顷	Water－saving Irrigation Area	1000 hectares	82.13	28.22	
除涝面积	千公顷	Drainage Area	1000 hectares	61.28	19.48	
水土流失综合治理面积	千公顷	Area of Soil Erosion under Control	1000 hectares	170.88	38.65	
水闸座数	座	Sluice	set	1693	375	8
堤防长度	公里	Total Length of Dikes	km	1791.97	631.14	9.57
全部供水工程总供水量	万立方米	Annually Water Supply of Water Conservancy	10000 cu. m	176744	49024	
＃区域内农业供水	万立方米	Water Supply for Agriculture	10000 cu. m	57277	12268	
区域内工业供水	万立方米	Water Supply for Industry	10000 cu. m	44087	25175	
区域内城镇生活用水	万立方米	Water Supply for Urban life	10000 cu. m	22524	8046	

注：本表数据来自宁波市水利局。

Note: Data in this tables are obtained from Ningbo Municipal Bureau of Water Conservancy.

各区 by Districts									
江东 Jiangdong	江北 Jiangbei	北仑 Beilun	镇海 Zhenhai	鄞州 Yinzhou	余姚 Yuyao	慈溪 Cixi	奉化 Fenghua	象山 Xiangshan	宁海 Ninghai
	5	33	6	54	58	23	92	81	69
	2168	4383	4602	43378	26943	13910	31512	16654	42729
				2	1		2		1
				23180	12272		26104		16840
		1	1	5	3	4		6	6
		1474	2300	17210	9421	8612		9557	22633
	5	32	5	47	54	19	90	75	62
	2168	2909	2302	2988	5250	5298	5408	7097	3256
				13	76	3			10
2	33	30	13	26	4086	71	4	1016	19
	6.83	9.56	7.07	32.93	38.58	40.01	20.88	20.35	22.38
	6.20	8.36	6.42	31.91	36.73	38.99	20.40	16.46	17.91
	6.20	8.36	4.10	31.35	36.73	38.99	20.40	16.46	17.91
	3.15	4.01	1.50	23.05	30.41	0.00	22.00	15.30	10.12
	7.11	0.49	0.25	20.37	10.00	12.59	3.26	11.96	16.10
	3.50	9.56	6.42		7.97			18.22	15.61
	3.08	14.15	1.77	19.65	11.50	8.60	60.46	47.05	4.62
7	98	91	41	130	458	160	119	359	222
9.76	45.85	129.04	155.28	281.64	211.36	40.55	102.90	263.39	542.63
	9	2652	3420	42943	34843	19224	24382	10749	38522
		525	2005	9738	14861	9500	8035	3710	8903
	8	1221	930	23016	5381	3778	4111	2511	3130
	1	668		7377	2112	4180	2072	4243	1871

表 6－15　各县(市)、区林业生产情况(2013)
Basic Statistics on Forestry by Region

指标	Indicators	全市 Total	海曙 Haishu	江北 Jiangbei
营林情况（公顷）	**Afforestation (hectare)**			
造林面积合计(公顷)	Total Afforestation Area(hectare)	2558		151
按方式分	By Way of Afforestation			
当年人工造林面积	Area of Afforest artificially in this Year	2558		151
按用途分	By Use of Afforestation			
经济林	Economic Forest	737		
防护林	Shelter Forest	1718		151
迹地更新面积	Area of Forest Updating	375		
封山育林面积	Area of Afforestation in Enclosed Mountain	151048		3635
零星(四旁)植树（万株）	Planting Trees Piecemeal(10000 trees)	167		3
育苗面积(公顷)	Area of Growing Seedings(hectare)	20826		374
未成林抚育作业面积	Unpaired Forest Tending Operations Area	1990		
成林抚育面积	Area of Grown Forest Cultivated			
其中：中、幼龄林抚育面积	In,Young Forest Tending Area	12491		267
低产林改造面积	Area of Transform Low Yield Forest	374		
抚育改造出材量（立方米）	Output of Transform and Foster (Cubic Meter)			
主要林产品产量(吨)	**Output of Major Forest Products (ton)**			
笋罐头	Bamboo Can			
板栗	Chestnut	1405		
竹笋干	Dried Bamboo Shoots	13604		470
竹壳	Shell of Bamboo	250		
白果	Gingko	152		

注：本表数据来自宁波市林业局。

Note:Data in this tables are obtained from Ningbo Municipal Bureau of Forestry.

各县(市)、区 by Region								
北 仑 Beilun	镇海 Zhenhai	大榭 Daxie	鄞州 Yinzhou	余姚 Yuyao	慈溪 Cixi	奉化 Fenghua	象山 Xiangshan	宁海 Ninghai
121	80	2	601	337	375	208	415	268
121	80	2	601	337	375	208	415	268
				35	289	141	90	182
121	80		601	302	86	52	325	
			51	75		60	100	79
667		2	18569	1333		41217	36800	48825
5	2		10	26	15	13	51	41
4009	243		1972	3837	2258	7103	730	80
218		121		151			1500	
721	33	70	2000	1796	802	2000	2000	2667
33		30		78		200		33
13			50	620		180	42	500
187	104		1366	2500	759	4792	396	2970
							250	
			2			150		

表 6－16　各县(市)、区茶叶和水果生产情况(2013)
Basic Statistics on Tea and Fruits Production by Region

指标	Indicators	全市 Total	市区 Urban District	海曙 Haishu	江东 Jiangdong
茶叶生产	**Tea**				
茶园总面积(公顷)	**Tea Field Area(hectare)**	**11699**	**2877**		
本年新增	New—added in This Year	132	48		
本年采摘	Pluck in This Year	10018	2466		
茶叶总产量(吨)	**Output of Tea (ton)**	**15277**	**5619**		
春茶	Spring Tea	8806	2999		
夏茶	Summer Tea	4287	1611		
秋茶	Autumn Tea	2184	1009		
水果生产	**Fruits**				
果园面积合计(公顷)	**Area of Orchards(hectare)**	**47281**	**6763**		
柑桔园	Citrus	10973	1692		
梨园	Pears	2710	762		
桃园	Peaches	3912	386		
杨梅园	Red Bayberry	17851	1464		
枇杷园	Loquat	2142	68		
柿子园	Persimmon	286	68		
葡萄园	Grapery	5682	1702		
弥猴桃园	Kiwi Fruit	428	25		
其他果园	Others	3297	596		
水果总产量(吨)	**Output of Fruits (ton)**	**1284490**	**329369**		
柑桔	Citrus	250939	44140		
柑	Mandarin Orange	15929	5509		
桔	Mandarin	229792	34901		
橙	Orange	1179	186		
柚	Shaddock	1143	648		
梨	Pears	77879	24642		
桃子	Peaches	64829	5944		
杨梅	Red Bayberry	128715	12240		
枇杷	Loquat	7089	479		
柿子	Persimmon	2982	934		
葡萄	Grapes	150304	44121		
弥猴桃	Kiwi Fruit	1849	193		
果用瓜	Melon Used as Fruits	577568	189135		
其他	Others	22336	7541		

各区 by Districts								
江北 Jiangbei	北仑 Beilun	镇海 Zhenhai	鄞州 Yinzhou	余姚 Yuyao	慈溪 Cixi	奉化 Fenghua	象山 Xiangshan	宁海 Ninghai
242	**493**	**75**	**2067**	**3957**	**276**	**917**	**1084**	**2588**
3			45	7	17	49		11
230	401	75	1760	3821	263	650	774	2044
102	**588**	**130**	**4799**	**4267**	**147**	**1321**	**1269**	**2654**
65	399	60	2475	2470	138	690	595	1914
32	131	30	1418	1247	5	389	512	523
5	58	40	906	550	4	242	162	217
1321	**1275**	**973**	**3194**	**7689**	**8992**	**3989**	**11916**	**7932**
107	531	285	769	96	214	633	5937	2401
311	73	30	348	762	491	49	248	398
34	55	14	283	200	351	2064	301	610
247	334	179	704	5020	4597	655	3760	2355
2	4	8	54	4	48	12	1077	933
6	17	1	44	104	22	15	33	44
578	234	281	609	787	2612	157	329	95
9	4		12	37	27	48	46	245
27	23	175	371	679	630	356	185	851
38743	**33061**	**30971**	**226594**	**187537**	**324946**	**78978**	**204942**	**158718**
2721	13311	3256	24852	2478	5161	10463	121876	66821
191	1207	960	3151	269	3165	38	6700	248
2516	11950	1734	18701	1719	1990	10102	114550	66530
14	70		102	1	6	320	624	42
	84	562	2	489		3	2	1
11733	1215	1026	10668	25487	18735	668	4098	4249
561	724	194	4465	4031	10132	37853	2180	4689
1746	3166	480	6848	43442	42008	5172	12289	13564
11	46	36	386	31	595	100	4517	1367
74	220	39	601	1190	380	142	239	97
13386	4944	5563	20228	30897	64432	2808	6774	1272
9	19		165	98	207	128	219	1004
8315	9358	19717	151745	73593	180146	18061	51890	64743
187	58	660	6636	6290	3150	3583	860	912

表 6—17 各县(市)、区畜牧业生产情况(2013)
Basic Statistics on Animal Husbandry By Region

指标	Indicators	全市 Total	市区 Urban District	
				海曙 Haishu
生猪 (万只)	**Hogs (10000 heads)**			
年末存栏头数(含未断奶小猪)	Being Raised at Year—end	122.14	24.43	
#能繁殖的母猪	Reproducable	11.14	2.42	
年内肥猪出栏头数	Slaughtered Fattened Hogs	178.64	45.53	
全年饲养量	Number of Hogs Raised	300.78	69.95	
牛(头)	**Cattles & Buffaloes(head)**			
年末存栏头数	Being Raised at Year—end	17456	5456	
#良种及改良种乳牛	Milch Cows of Fine Breed and Improved Varieties	7320	3929	
年内出栏头数	Slaughtered Cattles & Buffaloes of the Year	8182	2438	
羊(万只)	**Sheep & Goat(10000 heads)**			
年末存栏只数	**Being Raised at Year—end**	9.44	0.98	
年内出栏只数	**Slaughtered Sheep & Goat of the Year**	10.76	1.10	
家禽 (万只)	**Poultry(10000 heads)**			
年末存栏只数	Being Raised at Year—end	1263.38	252.96	
年内出栏只数	Slaughtered Poultry of the Year	2305.93	520.51	
兔 (万只)	**Rabbits (10000 heads)**			
年末存栏只数	Being Raised at Year—end	43.11	9.94	
年内出栏只数	Slaughtered Rabbits	65.81	20.86	
养蜂年末箱数(箱)	**Number of Beehives(box)**	**83917**	**2408**	
畜禽产品产量 (吨)	**Output of Livestock Production(ton)**			
肉类产量	Output of Meat	195034	45905	
猪肉	Pork	152263	35953	
牛肉	Beef	1355	410	
羊肉	Mutton	1770	190	
兔肉	Rabbits Meat	38205	8950	
禽肉	Poultry Meat	1245	402	
其他	Others	198		
禽蛋产量	Poultry Eggs	75894	20295	
蜂蜜产量	Honey	6390	175	
蜂皇浆产量(公斤)	Royal Jelly(kg)	274001	8193	
牛奶产量 (吨)	Milk (ton)	21064	13778	
兔毛产量	Rabbit Wool	114	5	

各区 by Districts									
江东 Jiangdong	江北 Jiangbei	北仑 Beilun	镇海 Zhenhai	鄞州 Yinzhou	余姚 Yuyao	慈溪 Cixi	奉化 Fenghua	象山 Xiangshan	宁海 Ninghai
1.01	4.28	1.19	2.54	15.41	22.56	23.34	19.35	14.71	17.75
0.14	0.52	0.14	0.09	1.53	2.01	1.92	1.84	1.35	1.60
2.03	5.64	4.70	5.89	27.27	32.15	35.37	24.97	18.69	21.93
3.04	9.92	5.88	8.43	42.68	54.71	58.72	44.32	33.40	39.68
	2851	408	550	1647	2148	1032	1721	748	6351
	2749		370	810	1515	524	372		980
	480	367	240	1351	703	292	1624	575	2550
	0.06	0.23	0.13	0.56	1.62	2.65	1.16	1.87	1.16
	0.04	0.20	0.14	0.72	2.27	3.73	1.00	1.86	0.80
	76.23	11.89	55.30	109.54	268.23	165.71	170.61	148.15	257.72
	123.73	34.58	190.90	171.30	689.16	252.66	172.71	182.73	488.16
	2.48	0.84	6.29	0.33	11.18	21.11	0.02	0.80	0.06
	2.55	1.04	16.74	0.53	18.61	22.61	1.08	2.60	0.05
	140	**528**	**733**	**1007**	**8236**	**47707**	**4011**	**4869**	**16686**
1812	6841	4670	8805	23777	42875	34645	25312	20291	26006
1812	4637	3988	5011	20505	27261	28939	22479	16649	20982
	75	63	41	231	147	49	244	85	420
	13	36	33	108	426	589	150	297	118
	2053	563	3410	2924	14539	4629	2417	3185	4485
	63	20	310	9	359	414	22	47	1
					143	27		28	
	5009	826	5690	8770	7231	9701	16988	7869	13810
	3	12	87	73	872	4048	198	104	993
	620	2500	1356	3717	27837	202089	10821	5945	19116
	9548		710	3520	3622	2100	964		600
		1	3	1	39	70			

表 6－18　各县(市)、区水产品产量及养殖面积(2013)
Output and Area of Artificially Cultured of Aquatic Production by Region

指标	Indicators	全市 Total	市区		
			海曙 Haishu	江东 Jiangdong	江北 Jiangbei
水产品总产量	**Total Aquatic Products**	**992050**			**10675**
海水产品产量	**Seawater Aquatic Products**	**908400**			**9574**
按生产性质分	By Production Character				
海洋捕捞	Catching in Ocean	607476			3765
鱼类	Fish	475247			3765
甲壳类	Shrimps. Prawns and Crabs	68701			
贝类	Shell－Fish	8968			
其他类	Others	11196			
海水养殖	Seawater Aquiculture	281930			
鱼类	Fish	10877			
甲壳类	Shrimps. Prawns and Crabs	41715			
贝类	Shell－Fish	220172			
其他类	Others	1481			
远洋渔业	Pelagic Fishery	18994			5809
淡水产品产量	**Freshwater Aquatic Products**	**83650**			**1101**
按生产性质分	By Production Character				
淡水捕捞	Catching in Freshwater	10503			600
淡水养殖	Freshwater Aquiculture	73147			501
按类别分	By Category				
鱼类	Fish	43572			416
甲壳类	Shrimps. Prawns and Crabs	25036			50
贝类	Shell－Fish	730			15
其他类	Others	3809			20
海水养殖面积(公顷)	**Seawater Aquiculture Area(ha)**	**35961**			
淡水养殖面积(公顷)	**Freshwater Aquiculture Area(ha)**	**23636**			**486**

注：本表数据来自宁波市海洋渔业局。
Data in this tables are obtained from Ningbo Municipal Bureau of Ocean and Fishery.

单位：吨(ton)

Urban Districts			余姚 Yuyao	慈溪 Cixi	奉化 Fenghua	象山 Xiangshan	宁海 Ninghai
北仑 Beilun	镇海 Zhenhai	鄞州 Yinzhou					
2748	**724**	**19785**	**27189**	**51154**	**143341**	**576785**	**150064**
2031	**76**	**8138**	**1855**	**26044**	**140375**	**566071**	**144651**
1625	76	3148	1748	4540	134138	449106	9185
1080	58	650	643	1009	114530	351340	2027
539	8	108	537	946	4134	59032	3397
	2		442	2417	764	2153	3190
	8	2085	55	168	7955	925	
406		4990	107	21504	6237	113220	135466
			23	2183	1278	5249	2144
223		2476	84	6242	975	15788	15927
183		2413		12989	2158	85034	117395
				90	76	1315	
						3745	
717	**648**	**11647**	**25334**	**25110**	**2966**	**10714**	**5413**
469	104	3505	2668	2045	886		226
248	544	8142	22666	23065	2080	10714	5187
225	531	7149	16031	13189	879	2539	2613
21	10	574	3165	9562	1060	8020	2574
	3	163	344	112	93		
2		256	3126	202	48	155	
244		**1020**	**30**	**6993**	**1650**	**10832**	**15192**
334	**464**	**4065**	**5507**	**6418**	**1606**	**2670**	**2086**

表 6—19　各县(市)、区农村能源和农业物资消耗情况(2013)
Consumption of Energy and Agriculture Materials in Rural Areas by Region

指标	Indicators	全市 Total	市区 Urban District	海曙 Haishu
农村用电量（万千瓦小时）	**Electricity Consumed for Rural (10000 kwh)**	**1852634**	**589793**	
农用化肥施用量	**Agricultural Consumption of Chemical Fertilizers**			
按实物量计算	Calculated by Fact Use	360579	109084	
氮肥	Nitrogenous Fertilizer	161567	40597	
磷肥	Phosphate Fertilizer	71978	27105	
钾肥	Potash Fertilizer	28216	14957	
复合肥	Compound Fertilizer	98818	26425	
按折纯法计算	Calculated by Pure Consumption	112886	29025	
氮肥	Nitrogenous Fertilizer	50240	8927	
磷肥	Phosphate Fertilizer	15197	5067	
钾肥	Potash Fertilizer	8630	4153	
复合肥	Compound Fertilizer	38819	10878	
农用塑料薄膜使用量	**Plastic Film Use for Agriculture**	**11071**	**2388**	
#地膜使用量	Use of Plastic Film	4772	1242	
地膜覆盖面积（公顷）	Overcast Area of Plastic Film (hectate)	24263	8687	
农用柴油	**Consumption of Diesel Oil**	**339997**	**10948**	
农药使用量	**Consumption of Pesticide**	**7614**	**1649**	

单位：吨(ton)

各区 by Districts									
江东 Jiangdong	江北 Jiangbei	北仑 Beilun	镇海 Zhenhai	鄞州 Yinzhou	余姚 Yuyao	慈溪 Cixi	奉化 Fenghua	象山 Xiangshan	宁海 Ninghai
18	**16779**	**37994**	**76085**	**458917**	**257017**	**724552**	**120580**	**57642**	**103050**
	20503	6832	3546	78203	41786	95171	56845	29750	27943
	7290	1466	1071	30770	20659	36713	29841	18400	15357
	4501	1633	1064	19907	3322	23516	9226	4680	4129
	2399	448	515	11595	288	6905	4185	1210	671
	6313	3285	896	15931	17517	28037	13593	5460	7786
	4904	2948	1217	19956	13451	25810	20796	12421	11383
	1745	356	364	6462	4750	10280	12107	7728	6448
	913	390	180	3584	597	4703	1661	1685	1484
	719	231	303	2900	73	2417	1047	605	335
	1527	1971	370	7010	8031	8410	5981	2403	3116
	327	**142**	**277**	**1642**	**257**	**5458**	**538**	**1350**	**1080**
	127	47	113	955	80	2083	272	830	265
	955	210	594	6928	525	8210	1878	2597	2366
10	**242**	**4572**	**2313**	**3811**	**9023**	**8898**	**109771**	**196882**	**4475**
	112	**165**	**468**	**904**	**2353**	**1016**	**506**	**1090**	**1000**

主要统计指标解释

【农林牧渔业总产值】 指以货币表现的农、林、牧、渔业全部产品的总量。它反映一定时期内农业生产总规模和总成果。

农林牧渔业的统计范围是：

⑴ 农业 包括种植业和其他农业。

⑵ 林业 包括林木的载培(不包括茶园、桑园和果园的栽培、管理和收获等活动)、林产品的采集和村及村以下合作经济和农户的竹木采伐。

⑶ 牧业 包括除渔业养殖以外的一切动物饲养和放牧以及野生动物的捕猎和饲养。

⑷ 渔业 包括水生动物和海藻类植物的养殖和捕捞。

农林牧渔业总产值的计算方法通常是按农林牧渔产品及其副产品的产量分别乘以各自单位产品价格求得，少数生产周期长，当年没有产品或产品产量不易统计，则采用间接方法匡算其产值，然后将四业产品产值相加即为农林牧渔业总产值。

1957年以前的农业总产值包括了厩肥和农名自给性手工业(如农民自制衣服、鞋、袜，自己从事粮食加工等)。1958年以后的农业总产值，林业中增加了村以及村以下的竹木采伐产值；牧业取消了厩肥产值；副业中取消了农民自给性手工业产值，增加了村以及村以下的工业产值；渔业中增加了海洋捕捞产品产值。1980年及以后的农业总产值，在副业中增加了农民家庭兼营工业商品部分的产值。从1984年起村以及村以下半工业产值划归工业。从1993年起，取消副业，将野生动物的捕猎划入牧业。2010年起野生植物采集从农业划入林业，坚果从林业划入农业。

【粮食产量】 指全社会的产量。包括国有经济经营的、集体统一经营的和农民家庭经营的粮食产量，还包括工矿企业办的农场和其他生产单位的产量。粮食除包括稻、小麦、玉米、高粱、谷子及其他杂粮外，还包括薯类和豆类。其产量计算方法，豆类按去豆荚后的干豆计算；薯类(番薯和马铃薯，不包括芋头和木薯)1963年以前按每4公斤鲜薯折1公斤粮食计算，从1964年开始及以后改为按5公斤鲜薯折1公斤粮食计算。其他粮食一律按脱粒后的原粮计算。2008年起马铃薯从蔬菜中划出5折1后作为粮食统计。

【油料产量】 指全部油料作物的生产量。包括花生、油菜籽、芝麻、向日葵籽、胡麻籽(亚麻籽)和其他油料。不包括大豆，也不包括木本油料和野生油料。花生以带壳干花生计算。

【水产品产量】 指人工养殖的水产品和天然生长的水产品的捕捞量。包括海水的鱼类、虾蟹类、贝类和藻类以及内陆水域的鱼类、虾蟹类和贝类，不包括淡水生植物。

【猪、牛、羊肉产量】 指当年出栏并已屠宰后除去头蹄下水后带骨肉(即胴体重)的重量。

【农作物播种面积】 指实际播种或移植有农作物的面积。凡是实际种植有农作物的面积，不论种植在耕地上还是种植在非耕地上，均包括在农作物播种面积中，同时还包括因遭灾而重新改种和补种的农作物面积。

【农用化肥施用量】 指本年内实际用于农业生产的化肥数量。包括氮肥、磷肥、钾肥和复合肥。化肥施用量要求按折纯量计算数量。折纯法化肥施用量是把氮肥、磷肥和钾肥分别按含氮、含五氧化二磷、含氧化钾的百分之一百成份折算后的数量。复合肥按其所含主要成分折算。

【农业机械总动力】 指主要用于农、林、牧、渔业的各种动力机械的动力总和。包括耕作机械、排灌机械、收获机械、农产品加工机械、运输机械、植物保护机械、牧业机械、林业机械、渔业机械和其他农业机械[内燃机按引擎马力折成瓦(特)计算，电动机按功率折成瓦(特)计算]。不包括专门用于乡、镇、村、组办工业、基本建设、非农业运输、科学试验和教学等非农业生产方面用的动力机械与作业机械。

Explanatory Notes on Main Statistical Indicators

【Gross Output Value of Farming, Forestry, Animal Husbandry and Fishery】 refers to the total volume of products of farming, forestry, animal husbandry and fishery in value terms, which reflects the total scale and total result of agricultural production during a given period of time.

The statistical coverage of farming, forestry, animal husbandry and fishery is as follows:

(1) Farming includes cultivation of farm crops and other agricultural activities.

(2) Forestry refers to planting trees of various kinds (excluding tea plantations, mulberry fields and orchards), gathering of the forest products, and cutting and felling of bamboo and trees by villages and other cooperative organizations under villages.

(3) Animal Husbandry refers to raising and grazing of all animals except fishery and aquaculture, and hunting and raising of wild animals.

(4) Fishery refers to cultivation and catching of fish and other aquatic animals and cultivation and collection of seaweed and other aquatic plants.

Gross output value of farming, forestry, animal husbandry and fishery is obtained by first multiplying the output of each product by its price, resulting in the output of each single item. For a small number of products, animal output of which is not available or difficult to get due to the long production/growing process involved, the output value is estimated through an indirect approach. The sum of output value of all products of farming, forestry, animal husbandry and fishery is then equal to their gross output value.

Prior to 1957, China's gross agricultural output value included barnyard manure and handicraft products for self—consumption (clothes, shoes, stockings, and initial grain processing undertaken by peasants). Since 1958, cutting and felling of bamboo and trees by villages and other cooperative organizations under villages have been included in forestry. ; value of barnyard manure has been excluded from animal husbandry; self—consumed handicrafts have been excluded from sideline occupations, while the output value of industries run by villages and cooperative organizations under village has been included in sideline occupations and the out put value of fish catches by motor fishing boats has been added to fishery. Since 1980, the value of handicraft products made for sale by individual in the households has been added to sideline occupations. Since 1984, industries run by villages and cooperatives organizations under villagers have been included in the sector of industry. Since 1993, the subdivision of sideline occupations has been canceled, and the hunting of wild animals has been classified into animal husbandry, Since 1993, the subdivision of sideline occupations has been canceled, and the hunting of wild animals has been classified into animal husbandry. Since 2010, collection of wild plants has been classified from agriculture into forestry, nuts from forestry into agriculture. .

【Grain Yield】 refers to the yield in the whole country including grains produced by state farms, collective units, industrial enterprises and mines. Grain includes rice, wheat, corn, sorghum, millet and other miscellaneous grains as well as tubers and beans. Output of beans refers to dry beans without pods. The output of tubers (potatoes, do not including taros and cassava) was converted into that of grain at the ratio 4:1,I. e. Four kilograms of fresh tubers was equivalent to one kilogram of grain up to 1963. Since 1964 the ratio for conversion has been 5:1. Output of all other grains refers to husked grain. Since 2008, potato has been classified from vegetables into food crops at the ratio 5:1.

【Yield of Oil—bearing Crops】 refers to the total yield of oil bearing crops of various kinds, including peanuts, (dry, in shell) rapeseeds, sesame, sunflower seeds, flax seeds, and other oil bearing crops. Soybeans, oil bearing woody plants, and wild oil—bearing crops are not included.

【Output of Aquatic Products】 refers to catches of both artificially cultured and naturally grown aquatic products, including fish, shrimps, crabs and shellfish in sea and inland water as well as seaweed. Freshwater plants are not included.

【Output of Pork, Beef, and Mutton】 refers to the meat of slaughtered hogs, cattle, sheep and goats with head, feet, and offal taken away.

【Sown Area of Crops】 refers to area of land sown or transplanted with crops regardless of being in cultivated area or non cultivated area. Area of land re sown due to natural disasters is also included, every sown hectare is calculated.

【Consumption of Chemical Fertilizers in Agriculture】 refers to the quantity of chemical fertilizers applied in agriculture in the year, including nitrogenous fertilizer, phosphate fertilizer ,potash fertilizer and compound fertilizer. The consumption of chemical fertilizers is required in calculation to convert the gross weight into weight containing 100% effective component(e. g. 100% nitrogen content in nitrogenous fertilizer, 100% phosphorous pentoxide contents in phosphate fertilizer, 100% potassium oxide contents in potash fertilizer). Compound fertilizer is converted with its major component.

【Total Power of Farm Machinery】 refers to total mechanical power of machinery used in farming, forestry, animal husbandry, and fishery, including ploughing, irrigation and drainage, harvesting, transport, plant protection, stock breeding, forestry and fishery. The power of internal combustion engines is required to convert horsepower into watts and the power of electric motors is required to be converted into watts. Machinery employed for non agricultural purposes, such as the machines used in township run and village run industry, construction, non agricultural transport, scientific experiments and teaching, is excluded.

CHAPTER 7

NINGBO 2014 Statistical YearBook

第七篇 工业、能源消费和电力

INDUSTRY, ENERGY CONSUMPTION AND ELECTRICITY

工业、能源消费和电力
Industry, Energy Consumption and Electricity

主要统计指标
Major Statistics Indicators

2013年规模以上工业企业数	Number of Industrial Enterprises Above The Set Scale	7167	家	unit
比上年增长	Increase Over Last Year	5.3	%	
2013年规模以上工业总产值	Output Value of Industrial Enterprises Above The Set Scale	130100892	万元	10000 yuan
比上年增长	Increase Over Last Year	7.0	%	
2013年规模以上工业销售产值	Gross Industrial Products Sales of Industrial Enterprises Above The Set Scale	125914244	万元	10000 yuan
比上年增长	Increase Over Last Year	6.8	%	
2013年规模以上工业实现利税	Total Profits and Taxes of Industrial Enterprises Above The Set Scale	13159389	万元	10000 yuan
比上年增长	Increase Over Last Year	18.2	%	
2013年规模以上工业实现利润	Total Profits of Industrial Enterprises Above The Set Scale	7016804	万元	10000 yuan
比上年增长	Increase Over Last Year	26.8	%	
2013年规模以上应交增值税	Value—added Taxes Payable of Industrial Enterprises Above The Set Scale	3376861	万元	10000 yuan
比上年增长	Increase Over Last Year	12.3	%	

表 7—1 部分年份规模以上工业企业单位数
Number of Industrial Enterprises Designated Size in Partial Years

单位:个(unit)

指标	Indicators	2009	2010	2011	2012	2013
工业企业单位数	**Number of Industrial Enterprises**	**12059**	**12492**	**6616**	**6804**	**7167**
按轻重工业分	**By Light and Heavy Industry**					
轻工业	Light Industry	5313	5392	2792	2801	2939
重工业	Heavy Industry	6746	7100	3824	4003	4228
按注册登记类型分	**By Registered Type**					
国有企业	State—owned Enterprises	36	36	32	36	17
集体企业	Collective—owned Enterprises	90	80	26	23	15
股份合作企业	Share Cooperative Enterprises	152	59	18	25	21
联营企业	Joint—owned	7	6	2	1	
有限责任公司	Limited Liability Corporations	915	886	540	546	590
股份有限公司	Share—holding Corporations Ltd.	140	140	101	109	123
私营企业	Private Enterprises	7643	8325	3715	3958	4401
港、澳、台商投资公司	Hongkong, Macao and Taiwan Funded	1536	1529	1163	1118	1066
外商投资企业公司	Enterprises with Foreign Investment	1490	1431	1019	983	930
在总计中:亏损企业	Of the Total: Loss Making Enterprises	1836	1377	826	1034	1230
在总计中:国有及国有控股	Of the Total: State—owned and State—holding	103	99	91	97	100
按规模分	By Enterprises Size					
大型企业	Large—Sized	28	35	108	107	109
中型企业	Medium—Sized	900	1014	1086	1005	998
小型企业	Small—Sized	11131	11443	5352	5539	5893

注:2011 年起,规模以上工业企业为年主营业务收入 2000 万元及以上的企业,下表同。

Note: From 2011, Industrial enterprises above designated size are those with annual revenue from principal business over 20 million yuan. The others table are the same.

表7—2 部分年份规模以上工业企业总产值
Gross Output Value of Industrial Enterprises Above Designated Size in Partial Years

单位:万元(10000 yuan)

指标	Indicators	2009	2010	2011	2012	2013
工业总产值	**Gross Industrial Output Value**	**82728469**	**108535474**	**120447699**	**121550760**	**130100892**
按轻重工业分	**By Light and Heavy Industry**					
轻工业	Light Industry	27927737	34112854	34683454	34049449	36404426
重工业	Heavy Industry	54800732	74422621	85764245	87501311	93696465
按注册登记类型分	**By Registered Type**					
国有企业	State—owned Enterprises	5803085	7193904	8013730	8547018	6304640
集体企业	Collective—owned Enterprises	175097	193152	170815	111059	76561
股份合作企业	Share Cooperative Enterprises	597211	163059	106743	137049	91655
联营企业	Joint—owned	20919	20762	11779	9128	
有限责任公司	Limited Liability Corporations	8161975	11145328	12189111	12142989	17136831
股份有限公司	Share—holding Corporations Ltd.	9730314	13630949	17468406	17252477	19191004
私营企业	Private Enterprises	23084430	31749621	31028632	32872411	37126091
港、澳、台商投资公司	Hongkong,Macao and Taiwan Funded	18902072	24131396	29448789	28862744	29547796
外商投资企业公司	Enterprises with Foreign Investment	15881040	20307304	22009694	21553507	20604783
在总计中:亏损企业	Of the Total:Loss Making Enterprises	9972888	5055244	10908447	13314051	12879241
在总计中:国有及国有控股	Of the Total:State—owned and State—holding	18245477	24426588	31162756	30369003	32757503
按规模分	**By Enterprises Size**					
大型企业	Large—Sized	14772479	21449940	38131433	40247278	42694441
中型企业	Medium—Sized	30988021	40851033	39522112	36402444	39503925
小型企业	Small—Sized	36967970	46234502	42444047	43739373	46430882

注:工业总产值按现行价格计算。

Note:Gross industrial output value are calculated at current prices.

表 7—3 部分年份规模以上工业企业销售产值
Sales Value of Industrial Enterprises Above Designated Size in Partial Years

单位：万元(10000 yuan)

指标	Indicators	2009	2010	2011	2012	2013
工业销售产值	**Gross Industrial Products Sales**	**80492735**	**105629245**	**117898629**	**117880641**	**125914244**
按轻重工业分	**By Light and Heavy Industry**					
轻工业	Light Industry	27109132	33032063	33639832	33104213	35404606
重工业	Heavy Industry	53383603	72597182	84258797	84776428	90509638
按注册登记类型分	**By Registered Type**					
国有企业	State—owned Enterprises	5800116	7189224	8017179	8536128	6292237
集体企业	Collective—owned Enterprises	171398	187285	165908	111743	73095
股份合作企业	Share Cooperative Enterprises	582031	160539	102713	131655	88018
联营企业	Joint—owned	20767	20716	11688	9125	
有限责任公司	Limited Liability Corporations	7895091	10887393	11969274	11928565	16867818
股份有限公司	Share—holding Corporations Ltd.	9687753	13387235	17376222	16889319	18057626
私营企业	Private Enterprises	22234379	30779754	29950680	31394168	35742934
港、澳、台商投资公司	Hongkong, Macao and Taiwan Funded	18275721	23226285	28642232	28044561	28934977
外商投资企业公司	Enterprises with Foreign Investment	15462333	19790814	21662734	20772067	19836017
在总计中：亏损企业	Of the Total: Loss Making Enterprises	9717038	4896009	10657194	13013311	12605094
在总计中：国有及国有控股	Of the Total: State—owned and State—holding	18054011	24149681	31299012	30125079	31813141
按规模分	**By Enterprises Size**					
大型企业	Large—Sized	14575048	20807766	37600731	38897059	41044813
中型企业	Medium—Sized	29984116	39727953	38561314	35321924	38237444
小型企业	Small—Sized	35933571	45093526	41391137	42512942	45162152

注：工业销售产值按现行价格计算。

Note: Sales value of industrial products are calculated at current prices.

表 7—4 规模以下工业企业及个体工业单位主要经济指标(2013)
Main Economic Indicators of Industrial Enterprises Below Designated Size and Private and Individuals

指标	单位	Indicators	Unit	总计 Total
总计		**Total**		
企业(单位)数	个	Number of Enterprises(unit)	unit	118367
期末从业人员	人	Total Employees at Year—end	person	1558893
工业总产值	万元	Gross Industrial Output Value	10000 yuan	36486163
资产总计	万元	Total Asset	10000 yuan	2970620
企业主要经济指标		**Main Economic Indicators of Enterprises**		
企业数	个	Number of Enterprises(unit)	unit	40 839
期末从业人员	人	Total Employees at Year—end	person	914429
工业总产值	万元	Gross Industrial Output Value	10000 yuan	21480174
主营业务收入	万元	Prime Operating Revenue	10000 yuan	21267499
#出口产品销售收入	万元	Export Sales Revenue	10000 yuan	3837221
主营业务成本	万元	Operating Costs	10000 yuan	17075825
税金总额	万元	Total Taxes	10000 yuan	1110259
#所得税	万元	Income Taxes	10000 yuan	182674
营业利润	万元	Business Profits	10 000 yuan	1011660
应付职工薪酬	万元	Employee Compensation Payable	10000 yuan	2924701
本年折旧	万元	Depreciation	10000 yuan	766184
资产总计	万元	Total Asset	10000 yuan	23212862
负债合计	万元	Total Liabilities	10000 yuan	12627064
固定资产原值	万元	Actual Value of Fixed Assets	10000 yuan	8625121
固定资产净值	万元	Net Fixed Assets	10000 yuan	5565589
应收帐款	万元	Accounts Receivable	10000 yuan	4495855
利息支出	万元	Interest Expense	10000 yuan	341444
#银行借款利息	万元	Interest on Bank Borrowings	10000 yuan	320149
民间借款利息	万元	Civil Borrowing Interest	10000 yuan	21296
期末剩余订单额	万元	Final Remaining Orders	10000 yuan	1006100
生产能力(设备)利用率	%	Capacity Utilization	%	80. 13
个体工业主要经济指标		**Main Economic Indicators of Individuals**		
单位数	个	The Number of Units	unit	77528
期末从业人员	人	Total Employees at Year—end	person	644464
营业收入	万元	Operating Revenue	10000 yuan	14857415
生产支出	万元	Production Expenditure	10000 yuan	11003610
应付职工薪酬	万元	Employee Compensation Payable	10000 yuan	2023906
资产总计	万元	Total Asset	10000 yuan	6654538

表7—5 历年工业企业主要经济指标
Main Economic Indicators of Industrial Enterprises Over the Years

单位:亿元 万人(100 million yuan, 10000 persons)

年份 Year	总产值(当年价) Gross Industrial Output Value (current prices)	固定资产原值 Original Value of Fixed Assets	固定资产净值 Net Value of Fixed Assets	主营业务收入 Prime Operating Revenue	利税总额 Total Profits and Taxes	利润总额 Total Profits	全部从业人员年平均人数 Annual Average Employees
1978	15.79	7.07			4.29	2.59	
1979	18.11	8.25	6.28	18.71	4.73	2.86	
1980	23.73	9.59	7.35	24.89	6.17	3.93	
1981	29.67	11.38	8.76	30.05	6.94	4.26	
1982	29.99	13.53	10.49	32.36	7.99	4.86	
1983	35.23	15.84	12.17	38.98	9.07	5.57	
1984	50.93	21.09	16.67	54.57	11.30	6.53	
1985	68.63	32.55	26.43	76.16	14.62	7.65	65.48
1986	81.96	38.43	30.49	86.67	15.86	7.94	68.69
1987	102.16	52.61	41.79	110.96	18.54	9.92	71.29
1988	132.17	62.81	48.85	147.85	23.24	12.00	72.06
1989	159.41	74.80	56.60	162.81	23.64	11.47	69.05
1990	200.00	89.31	64.39	167.35	20.99	8.21	67.71
1991	261.62	107.17	79.45	218.15	25.27	11.79	72.02
1992	341.42	128.57	95.03	282.90	31.65	14.82	73.15
1993	491.07	192.06	147.38	430.65	45.15	22.68	73.94
1994	642.18	276.98	225.18	480.46	53.56	26.06	71.53
1995	837.80	357.05	281.28	664.70	62.61	29.46	66.08
1996	843.48	407.73	312.70	722.15	66.57	28.63	64.60
1997	842.62	496.05	374.92	747.51	78.60	33.32	55.88
1998	940.59	567.09	423.50	835.24	88.00	37.52	50.78
1999	1062.29	668.71	490.07	985.32	118.65	61.21	52.38
2000	1427.70	829.69	601.93	1350.52	163.26	88.11	58.42
2001	1629.66	926.49	648.50	1538.70	213.72	115.95	66.90
2002	2000.16	1058.90	727.01	1945.02	267.09	152.34	77.22
2003	2630.29	1251.24	854.79	2604.90	322.01	189.30	91.96
2004	3815.04	1602.75	1113.37	3660.69	417.63	241.31	128.94
2005	4890.97	1926.51	1337.30	4698.16	446.13	262.36	140.82
2006	6187.91	2469.35	1755.66	5930.59	525.65	312.63	159.64
2007	7789.01	2886.87	2013.56	7456.24	639.83	387.31	174.24
2008	8746.36	3422.49	2363.23	8283.18	489.32	221.25	178.59
2009	8272.85	3908.81	2633.33	7824.88	867.35	462.11	168.67
2010	10853.55	4431.40	2920.36	10396.63	1160.55	657.77	181.09
2011	12044.77	4543.83		11803.24	1193.21	631.66	152.25
2012	12155.08	4792.65		11795.98	1112.86	553.21	147.06
2013	13010.09	5092.25		12594.24	1315.94	701.68	147.50

注:1997年以前为乡及乡以上独立核算工业企业。1998年及以后为规模以上工业企业。

Note: Data in this table refer to all industrial enterprises with annual revenue from principal business over 5 million yuan, before 1997 to enterprises with independent accounting at townships and above level.

表 7—6 全市及各县(市)、区规模以上工业企业总产值(现行价格、2013)
Gross Output Value of Industrial Enterprises Above Designated Size by Region (at Current Price)

指标	Indicators	全市 Toal	市区 Urban District	海曙 Haishu
工业总产值	**Gross Industrial Output Value**	**130100892**	**85985775**	**3574819**
按轻重工业分	**Grouped by Light and Heavy Industry**			
轻工业	Light Industry	36404426	19408094	283578
重工业	Heavy Industry	93696465	66577681	3291241
按注册登记类型分	**Grouped by Registered Type**			
国有企业	State—owned Enterprises	6304640	4818753	3038039
集体企业	Collective—owned Enterpriese	76561	43788	
股份合作企业	Share Cooperative Enterprises	91655	59588	
有限责任公司	Limited Liability Corporations	17136831	12133667	396446
股份有限公司	Share—holding Corporations Ltd.	19191004	16625310	21741
私营企业	Private Enterprises	37126092	14613462	22818
港澳台商投资企业	Hong Kong. Macao & Taiwan Funded	29547796	22524844	88931
外商投资企业	Foreign Funded Enterprises	20604783	15147304	6844
在总计中:亏损企业	Of the Total:Loss Making Enterprises	12879241	8485270	34030
在总计中:国有及国有控股	Of the Total:State—owned and State—holding	32757503	28996612	3201406
按规模分	**Grouped by Enterprises Size**			
大型企业	Large—Sized	42694441	34145426	3129771
中型企业	Medium—Sized	39503925	24052351	271709
小型企业	Small—Sized	46430882	26688347	167934
按工业行业分	**Grouped by Sector**			
非金属矿采选业	Non—metallic Mining Industry	16159	16159	
农副食品加工业	Farm and Sideline Products Processing	1585472	690889	
食品制造业	Food Manufacturing	940694	227998	19986
酒、饮料和精制茶制造业	Wine, Beverages and Refined Tea Manufacturing	318242	178196	9864
烟草制品业	Tobacco Manufacturing	1271879	1271879	
纺织业	Textile Industry	3595186	2353384	59762
纺织服装、服饰业	Clothing, Apparel Industry	6283818	4742986	77298
皮革、毛皮、羽毛及其制品和制鞋业	Leather, Fur, Feather and Its Products and Footwear Industry	129981	71820	

单位:万元(10000 yuan)

各区 by Districts					余姚 Yuyao	慈溪 Cixi	奉化 Fenghua	象山 Xiangshan	宁海 Ninghai
江东 Jiangdong	江北 Jiangbei	北仑 Beilun	镇海 Zhenhai	鄞州 Yinzhou					
1945351	**4380318**	**29098911**	**24073789**	**21623686**	**12376426**	**17448888**	**3692926**	**4823726**	**5773151**
1475007	684844	4298058	1852739	10359251	4382482	7456007	1337531	1623997	2196316
470343	3695474	24800853	22221050	11264436	7993944	9992881	2355395	3199729	3576835
1280457		14994		485263	443388	581238	157861	149434	153967
		5656	22258	15873	22219	4052			6503
1509	24438	5748	3289	17011	2631	7348		22089	
211264	1423654	5343297	2052052	2565152	1138554	1148320	191547	999043	1525701
13327	880540	231778	13673612	1621212	1179810	617090		464510	304283
127704	1006958	1384945	2671617	9113353	5399626	10147160	1936428	2090918	2938498
299549	493040	12712327	2907066	5804654	2575701	2591024	959266	439907	457053
11541	551687	9390162	2737062	1998946	1614497	2352657	447823	657826	384676
33087	653974	4550882	1986672	1009747	1344817	1795766	484480	279105	489804
1392804	103640	8320129	15373976	575900	731177	596025	182348	829866	1421476
1384225	814112	10588445	14048108	4043434	1521898	3909553	729904	529628	1858033
326622	1995209	9726522	4129721	7081217	4512093	6263191	1066344	1996953	1612993
225692	1546626	8586243	5267650	10273059	6285469	7025545	1871060	2274472	2285989
		11350		4809					
3917	41270	425662		204583	319002	170417	75638	313176	16350
	44096	73898	32719	57300	522611	19565	38561	69425	62533
	3557	119687		45088	60918		42554	13424	23151
1271879									
	141111	717647	575841	848947	386612	549266	64122	153012	88789
73027	74333	1282671	66299	3113133	40481	119365	476764	811551	92672
1168		10137	17755	42759	12334	19152	16454		10221

表 7－6 续表 Continued

指标	Indicators	全市 Toal	市区 Urban District	海曙 Haishu
木材加工及木、竹、藤、棕、草制品业	Timber Processing, Bamboo, Rattan, Cane Palm, and Straw Products	122502	77288	
家具制造业	Furniture Manufacturing	854288	510835	
造纸及纸制品业	Paper－making and Paper Products Manufacturing	1564516	1077411	
印刷和记录媒介复制业	Printing and Record Duplicating	805730	626636	5575
文教、工美、体育和娱乐用品制造业	Culture, Art, Sports and Recreation Supplies Manufacturing	2871440	1417797	
石油加工、炼焦和核燃料加工业	Petroleum Processing, Coking & Nuclear Fuel Processing	16121204	16105080	
化学原料和化学制品制造业	Raw Chemical Materials and Chemical Products	14312832	12626667	
医药制造业	Medicines Manufacturing	547527	395082	7840
化学纤维制造业	Chemical Fiber Manufacturing	1615917	289505	
橡胶和塑料制品业	Rubber and Plastic Products Industry	3600196	1663769	6166
非金属矿物制品业	Nonmetal Mineral Products	2154774	1187677	
黑色金属冶炼和压延加工业	Smelting and Pressing of Ferrous Metals	5403571	3938895	
有色金属冶炼和压延加工业	Smelting and Pressing of Nonferrous Metals	5760873	3212282	2198
金属制品业	Metal Products Manufacturing	3669225	2190324	4445
通用设备制造业	General Purpose Equipment Manufacturing	7174537	3929410	10988
专用设备制造业	Special Purpose Equipment Manufacturing	3944789	2591983	6394
汽车制造业	Automobile Manufacturing	7507808	4009020	23022
铁路、船舶、航空航天和其他运输设备制造业	Railroad, Marine, Aviation and Other Transport Equipment Manufacturing	1547134	507752	
电气机械和器材制造业	Electric Equipment and Machinery Manufacturing	15384629	5560653	74669
计算机、通信和其他电子设备制造业	Computer, Communications and Other Electronic Equipment Manufacturing	8086193	6381519	63024
仪器仪表制造业	Instrument Manufacturing	1727600	784042	7586
其他制造业	Other Manufacturing	480132	161731	
废弃资源综合利用业	Waste Comprehensive Utilization of Resources Industry	760996	743542	
金属制品、机械和设备修理业	Metal Products, Machinery and Equipment Repair Industry	59709	12338	
电力、热力的生产和供应业	Production and Supply Electric Power and Thermal Power	8973106	5667063	3032635
燃气生产和供应业	Production and Supply Gas	661059	623725	163367
水的生产和供应业	Production and Supply Tap Water	247176	140437	

单位:万元(10000 yuan)

各区 by Districts					余姚 Yuyao	慈溪 Cixi	奉化 Fenghua	象山 Xiangshan	宁海 Ninghai
江东 Jiangdong	江北 Jiangbei	北仑 Beilun	镇海 Zhenhai	鄞州 Yinzhou					
		3492		73796	22744	1191	21279		
2360	51161	87879	11443	349456	240759	51706	17226	16879	16883
	6871	540050	16773	511140	96720	226814	45925	19519	98126
2015	9190	63276	46003	500578	83791	54047	20587	18231	2437
7210	138154	345631	70170	847576	143465	440126	51103	16730	802219
		2589799	13504683	10598			9415	6709	
	133342	7328747	4179576	946884	499643	956091	87651	51313	91468
	17069	34677	100315	225663	18040	52945	49210	12897	19355
		71698	195806	22002	173084	1096595	9793	44934	2007
3634	105939	317073	177066	1049683	768150	586053	166266	85396	330563
	193063	299134	158377	537103	399246	187104	48740	178677	153331
8608	46462	2709130	397252	709135	587657	418671	269913	141162	47273
38656	1716303	124186	502022	711733	931061	1216331	175931	17469	207799
27806	132743	704218	268528	1030532	504066	560387	176685	35761	202002
30650	241061	827397	1067898	1649524	683476	1265103	500039	394461	402049
37687	122701	1393081	386919	616615	658830	231805	34156	198880	229136
5482	361416	1703021	123200	1676575	277645	1873912	128482	720764	497985
8578		303005	66327	95646	41609	363494	394434	219165	20680
3456	441433	1208775	500700	2906067	2868140	5202482	308825	543413	901116
305306	141476	3732897	306320	1687431	835532	524299	226942	19571	98331
	184340	70392	12437	465491	493077	381722	29128		39632
	25462		25008	105873	56243	208003	33946		20210
		5787	729197	8558		13269		4186	
1565			10774				3841	35544	7986
		1540133	512242	555249	614248	595354	162985	670164	1263291
		454383		5975	7893	26032			3409
112347	7764		12138	8188	29352	37588	6333	11319	22148

表 7—7 全市及各县(市)、区规模以上工业企业销售产值(2013)
Sales Value of Industrial Enterprises Above Designated Size by Region

指标	Indicators	全市 Toal	市区 Urban District	海曙 Haishu
工业销售产值	**Gross Industrial Products Sales**	**125914244**	**83891848**	**3560649**
按轻重工业分	**Grouped by Light and Heavy Industry**			
轻工业	Light Industry	35404606	19167244	269803
重工业	Heavy Industry	90509638	64724603	3290846
按注册登记类型分	**Grouped by Registered Type**			
国有企业	State—owned Enterprises	6292237	4806350	3038039
集体企业	Collective—owned Enterpriese	73095	41562	
股份合作企业	Share Cooperative Enterprises	88018	55918	
有限责任公司	Limited Liability Corporations	16867818	11987273	386168
股份有限公司	Share—holding Corporations Ltd.	18057626	15624741	20526
私营企业	Private Enterprises	35742934	14306386	21744
港澳台商投资企业	Hong Kong,Macao & Taiwan Funded	28934977	22073263	87275
外商投资企业	Foreign Funded Enterprises	19836017	14977295	6897
在总计中:亏损企业	Of the Total:Loss Making Enterprises	12605094	8385142	34338
在总计中:国有及国有控股	Of the Total:State—owned and State—holding	31813141	28066493	3201406
按规模分	**Grouped by Enterprises Size**			
大型企业	Large—Sized	41044813	32932538	3119127
中型企业	Medium—Sized	38237444	23558404	271638
小型企业	Small—Sized	45162152	26301070	164479
按工业行业分	**Grouped by Sector**			
非金属矿采选业	Non—metallic Mining Industry	15612	15612	
农副食品加工业	Farm and Sideline Products Processing	1539821	694085	
食品制造业	Food Manufacturing	884913	225621	20003
酒、饮料和精制茶制造业	Wine, Beverages and Refined Tea Manufacturing	318645	179292	8731
烟草制品业	Tobacco Manufacturing	1259476	1259476	
纺织业	Textile Industry	3467500	2252930	50906
纺织服装、服饰业	Clothing, Apparel Industry	6176371	4708714	77345
皮革、毛皮、羽毛及其制品和制鞋业	Leather, Fur, Feather and Its Products and Footwear Industry	128158	70985	

单位:万元(10000 yuan)

各区 by Districts					余姚 Yuyao	慈溪 Cixi	奉化 Fenghua	象山 Xiangshan	宁海 Ninghai
江东 Jiangdong	江北 Jiangbei	北仑 Beilun	镇海 Zhenhai	鄞州 Yinzhou					
1875711	**4289725**	**28818112**	**22979355**	**21127117**	**11915634**	**16342671**	**3706948**	**4560992**	**5496152**
1463172	685789	4306104	1766494	10226393	4251576	7109093	1285319	1530966	2060408
412539	3603936	24512008	21212861	10900724	7664058	9233578	2421629	3030026	3435743
1268376		14679		485255	443388	581238	157861	149434	153967
		5656	20559	15347	21278	4052			6203
1509	21707	5844	3289	15730	2416	7214		22470	
209922	1404328	5334696	2016527	2496162	1100982	1220764	184586	988791	1516564
12488	878192	226517	12783651	1527698	1146314	592581		412007	281983
131157	986479	1385969	2629280	8872022	5156591	9700918	1852080	1962657	2764301
240644	494038	12491012	2791097	5763360	2502852	2457023	1078133	412099	411606
11615	504982	9343735	2728119	1949321	1541813	1778881	434288	613534	359063
32541	654432	4498116	1968679	992844	1298449	1727454	471186	271181	451682
1380723	100704	8290076	14491889	573279	731177	594913	182100	815677	1422781
1371822	817190	10419862	13082370	3986657	1511343	3433981	846338	476819	1843795
264869	1922605	9681321	4042048	6868890	4277207	6006336	1028477	1870566	1496455
229963	1525045	8516618	5224051	10051353	6071029	6653158	1806933	2190306	2139657
		11297		4315					
3922	38150	440029		196137	307672	157744	72201	291920	16199
	45391	72038	33035	55155	501583	19343	35002	55261	48104
	3557	121799		45205	60381		42287	13289	23396
1259476									
	148177	716247	506685	821942	405733	516795	62298	144211	85533
73672	74449	1264678	63797	3097209	39683	110752	460340	770681	86201
1139		10593	17735	41519	12121	18820	16309		9923

表 7—7 续表 Continued

指标	Indicators	全市 Toal	市区 Urban District	海曙 Haishu
木材加工及木、竹、藤、棕、草制品业	Timber Processing, Bamboo, Rattan, Cane Palm, and Straw Products	118128	74518	
家具制造业	Furniture Manufacturing	830131	506067	
造纸及纸制品业	Paper—making and Paper Products Manufacturing	1533401	1077794	
印刷和记录媒介复制业	Printing and Record Duplicating	780876	605866	5423
文教、工美、体育和娱乐用品制造业	Culture, Art, Sports and Recreation Supplies Manufacturing	2832719	1421050	
石油加工、炼焦和核燃料加工业	Petroleum Processing, Coking & Nuclear Fuel Processing	15220474	15203779	
化学原料和化学制品制造业	Raw Chemical Materials and Chemical Products	14158341	12529442	
医药制造业	Medicines Manufacturing	515719	380374	7333
化学纤维制造业	Chemical Fiber Manufacturing	1532415	290363	
橡胶和塑料制品业	Rubber and Plastic Products Industry	3513659	1673899	6969
非金属矿物制品业	Nonmetal Mineral Products	2139008	1182731	
黑色金属冶炼和压延加工业	Smelting and Pressing of Ferrous Metals	5258835	3839674	
有色金属冶炼和压延加工业	Smelting and Pressing of Nonferrous Metals	5587376	3159436	2047
金属制品业	Metal Products Manufacturing	3551777	2160250	4514
通用设备制造业	General Purpose Equipment Manufacturing	6892444	3797475	10963
专用设备制造业	Special Purpose Equipment Manufacturing	3754773	2475939	5698
汽车制造业	Automobile Manufacturing	6833913	3824398	23122
铁路、船舶、航空航天和其他运输设备制造业	Railroad, Marine, Aviation and Other Transport Equipment Manufacturing	1616270	498182	
电气机械和器材制造业	Electric Equipment and Machinery Manufacturing	14858160	5498859	72639
计算机、通信和其他电子设备制造业	Computer, Communications and Other Electronic Equipment Manufacturing	7798574	6187723	62058
仪器仪表制造业	Instrument Manufacturing	1642759	756985	6898
其他制造业	Other Manufacturing	465504	161132	
废弃资源综合利用业	Waste Comprehensive Utilization of Resources Industry	753153	736810	
金属制品、机械和设备修理业	Metal Products, Machinery and Equipment Repair Industry	59247	12292	
电力、热力的生产和供应业	Production and Supply Electric Power and Thermal Power	8969456	5665936	3032635
燃气生产和供应业	Production and Supply Gas	659566	623725	163367
水的生产和供应业	Production and Supply Tap Water	247072	140437	

单位:万元(10000 yuan)

各区 by Districts					余姚 Yuyao	慈溪 Cixi	奉化 Fenghua	象山 Xiangshan	宁海 Ninghai
江东 Jiangdong	江北 Jiangbei	北仑 Beilun	镇海 Zhenhai	鄞州 Yinzhou					
		3395		71123	21691	1381	20538		
2360	50710	88426	11380	344690	225305	49877	16631	15800	16450
	6566	537177	16415	515097	94815	215390	45645	18897	80860
2003	9136	62768	45809	480726	81897	51564	21018	18094	2437
7200	137410	374538	69592	823256	139669	423436	47691	15724	785149
		2577196	12615997	10585			9277	7418	
	131876	7309694	4123770	928018	477891	932493	85836	50961	81719
	16700	32766	89860	223035	17214	43615	46080	11818	16618
		72582	196250	21531	168608	1017652	9766	43983	2044
3532	107021	346409	175623	1030138	745319	535801	158151	84496	315993
	189769	301247	163293	528422	393797	184959	48113	174843	154565
11617	46370	2651962	377390	684028	576241	406657	254742	136227	45295
38651	1698964	118556	499791	684488	855799	1178486	177612	16795	199248
31455	131382	687945	269620	1015875	481593	529711	171831	32266	176126
30160	235857	806185	1058011	1561742	651088	1196187	481150	383774	382771
37161	124519	1303244	380344	597094	625653	222992	30912	191529	207748
5705	309997	1662637	120047	1600725	267170	1463433	123535	674509	480867
8900		296474	67230	91383	40648	367668	519504	169944	20325
3409	430808	1204392	475659	2891391	2750076	4995351	296985	499096	817792
241484	140942	3674589	304148	1633240	796297	484635	220020	19571	90329
	178681	68894	12361	449219	473393	349054	27977		35350
	25530		27512	103086	54244	198992	32755		18380
		5842	722460	8508		12758		3585	
1519			10774				3425	35544	7986
		1540133	512630	554073	612808	594996	162985	669439	1263291
		454383		5975	7893	24539			3409
112347	7764		12138	8188	29352	37588	6333	11319	22044

表 7—8　全市规模以上工业企业主要经济指标(2013)
Main Economic Indicators of Industrial Enterprises Above Designated Size

指标	Indicators	企业个数(个) Number of Enterprises (unit)	#亏损企业 Loss Making
总计	**Total**	**7167**	**1230**
按轻重工业分	**Grouped by Light and Heavy Industry**		
轻工业	Light Industry	2939	574
重工业	Heavy Industry	4228	656
按注册登记类型分	**Grouped by Registered Type**		
国有企业	State—owned Enterprises	17	
集体企业	Collective—owned Enterpriese	15	1
股份合作企业	Share Cooperative Enterprises	21	2
有限责任公司	Limited Liability Corporations	590	90
股份有限公司	Share—holding Corporations Ltd.	123	18
私营企业	Private Enterprises	4401	643
港澳台商投资企业	Hong Kong, Macao & Taiwan Funded	1066	246
外商投资企业	Foreign Funded Enterprises	930	230
在总计中:亏损企业	Of the Total: Loss Making Enterprises	1230	1230
在总计中:国有及国有控股	Of the Total: State—owned and State—holding	100	13
按规模分	**Grouped by Enterprises Size**		
大型企业	Large—Sized	109	7
中型企业	Medium—Sized	998	127
小型企业	Small—Sized	5893	1044
按工业行业分	**Grouped by Sector**		
非金属矿采选业	Non—metallic Mining Industry	3	
农副食品加工业	Farm and Sideline Products Processing	84	11
食品制造业	Food Manufacturing	48	11
酒、饮料和精制茶制造业	Wine, Beverages and Refined Tea Manufacturing	22	4
烟草制品业	Tobacco Manufacturing	1	
纺织业	Textile Industry	295	60
纺织服装、服饰业	Clothing, Apparel Industry	572	128
皮革、毛皮、羽毛及其制品和制鞋业	Leather, Fur, Feather and Its Products and Footwear Industry	30	4

单位:万元(10000 yuan)

工业总产值(现价) Gross Industrial Output Value (Current Prices)	工业销售产值 Value of Industrial Products Sales	＃出口交货值 Value of Export Products	资产合计 Total Asset	流动资产小计 Current Assets	固定资产小计 Total Fixed Assets	固定资产原价 Original Value of Fixed Assets
130100892	**125914244**	**28075640**	**114401358**	**68701412**	**32200934**	**50922498**
36404426	35404606	13515032	38763362	25021915	8252174	13024586
93696465	90509638	14560608	75637996	43679497	23948760	37897912
6304640	6292237	28044	3286107	1201940	1626161	3162751
76561	73095	1101	94559	66171	24757	37079
91655	88018	19077	82799	63790	16278	34691
17136831	16867818	1745681	19482322	9216072	8031821	12808628
19191004	18057626	814929	11328753	6010768	3675004	5305142
37126092	35742934	9217226	34293491	23105735	7135475	10488669
29547796	28934977	7539053	28608880	18367071	6570652	10532803
20604783	19836017	8710528	17207224	10657748	5116745	8545202
12879241	12605094	3208880	15503687	9367056	4553398	6670542
32757503	31813141	299422	19106800	6883187	10748508	18234187
42694441	41044813	8485705	31269095	16788943	10484670	16881945
39503925	38237444	9299561	35750536	21692714	9305618	14530502
46430882	45162152	10174742	45769403	29338413	11933370	18537030
16159	15612		52195	39707	5999	8165
1585472	1539821	450868	1576722	977323	343428	509033
940694	884913	337024	827265	478081	227355	288319
318242	318645	103060	402734	231547	128206	227714
1271879	1259476	27246	1207357	847398	167511	327685
3595186	3467500	778638	4177617	2830156	903012	1623776
6283818	6176371	2961362	6168301	4182806	997803	1569475
129981	128158	65512	140698	98791	27567	41888

表 7—8 续 1 Continued

指标	Indicators	企业个数（个）Number of Enterprises (unit)	#亏损企业 Loss Making
木材加工及木、竹、藤、棕、草制品业	Timber Processing, Bamboo, Rattan, Cane Palm, and Straw Products	26	6
家具制造业	Furniture Manufacturing	99	29
造纸及纸制品业	Paper—making and Paper Products Manufacturing	83	23
印刷和记录媒介复制业	Printing and Record Duplicating	90	14
文教、工美、体育和娱乐用品制造业	Culture, Art, Sports and Recreation Supplies Manufacturing	252	53
石油加工、炼焦和核燃料加工业	Petroleum Processing, Coking & Nuclear Fuel Processing	12	1
化学原料和化学制品制造业	Raw Chemical Materials and Chemical Products	234	42
医药制造业	Medicines Manufacturing	36	7
化学纤维制造业	Chemical Fiber Manufacturing	72	22
橡胶和塑料制品业	Rubber and Plastic Products Industry	460	83
非金属矿物制品业	Nonmetal Mineral Products	183	21
黑色金属冶炼和压延加工业	Smelting and Pressing of Ferrous Metals	223	37
有色金属冶炼和压延加工业	Smelting and Pressing of Nonferrous Metals	197	46
金属制品业	Metal Products Manufacturing	502	88
通用设备制造业	General Purpose Equipment Manufacturing	856	122
专用设备制造业	Special Purpose Equipment Manufacturing	389	57
汽车制造业	Automobile Manufacturing	436	44
铁路、船舶、航空航天和其他运输设备制造业	Railroad, Marine, Aviation and Other Transport Equipment Manufacturing	98	22
电气机械和器材制造业	Electric Equipment and Machinery Manufacturing	1159	154
计算机、通信和其他电子设备制造业	Computer, Communications and Other Electronic Equipment Manufacturing	352	60
仪器仪表制造业	Instrument Manufacturing	158	19
其他制造业	Other Manufacturing	64	11
废弃资源综合利用业	Waste Comprehensive Utilization of Resources Industry	58	42
金属制品、机械和设备修理业	Metal Products, Machinery and Equipment Repair Industry	6	1
电力、热力的生产和供应业	Production and Supply Electric Power and Thermal Power	40	
燃气生产和供应业	Production and Supply Gas	7	2
水的生产和供应业	Production and Supply Tap Water	20	6

单位：万元(10000 yuan)

工业总产值(现价) Gross Industrial Output Value (Current Prices)	工业销售产值 Value of Industrial Products Sales	#出口交货值 Value of Export Products	资产合计 Total Asset	流动资产小计 Current Assets	固定资产小计 Total Fixed Assets	固定资产原价 Original Value of Fixed Assets
122502	118128	70110	111149	78649	25165	47477
854288	830131	407549	928640	680325	183092	249657
1564516	1533401	353048	3226423	1656637	776976	1490723
805730	780876	228842	983036	598658	222804	390570
2871440	2832719	1331198	2518616	1642356	546364	812673
16121204	15220474	16095	4566428	2126732	2325621	3517623
14312832	14158341	836148	12289201	6306908	4769955	6463254
547527	515719	88499	601392	347665	163960	221207
1615917	1532415	160658	1672667	1189407	364400	596276
3600196	3513659	1179989	3460202	2204485	832018	1286264
2154774	2139008	79798	2282083	1587298	486446	833369
5403571	5258835	290014	4762142	2407392	1959352	3175579
5760873	5587376	272257	3265594	2258666	607388	889980
3669225	3551777	1591421	3479911	2373479	750875	1143932
7174537	6892444	2142193	7475205	4951274	1725251	2735193
3944789	3754773	1044195	4654797	3189858	966009	1489630
7507808	6833913	1027081	7803575	5006451	1490469	2078680
1547134	1616270	928818	2061062	1341689	523096	755619
15384629	14858160	5770939	14861818	10007869	2906705	4020667
8086193	7798574	4885088	6595294	4548399	1235335	2428273
1727600	1642759	412859	2468940	1625030	395199	561793
480132	465504	234336	483063	338241	98869	162052
760996	753153		359970	330700	14332	24416
59709	59247	799	116868	68812	45857	61085
8973106	8969456		6581429	1198209	4969805	9480700
661059	659566		629416	345952	190294	194379
247176	247072		1609549	604464	824420	1215372

表 7—8 续 2 Continued

指标	Indicators	本年折旧 Depreciation in This Year	负债小计 Total Liabilities
总计	**Total**	**3104457**	**70363253**
按轻重工业分	**Grouped by Light and Heavy Industry**		
轻工业	Light Industry	805935	24643391
重工业	Heavy Industry	2298522	45719862
按注册登记类型分	**Grouped by Registered Type**		
国有企业	State—owned Enterprises	155185	1652099
集体企业	Collective—owned Enterpriese	1800	54596
股份合作企业	Share Cooperative Enterprises	2693	52930
有限责任公司	Limited Liability Corporations	710643	12314635
股份有限公司	Share—holding Corporations Ltd.	305433	5784987
私营企业	Private Enterprises	748737	24976038
港澳台商投资企业	Hong Kong,Macao & Taiwan Funded	632129	15993737
外商投资企业	Foreign Funded Enterprises	574278	9521908
在总计中:亏损企业	Of the Total:Loss Making Enterprises	426001	12133395
在总计中:国有及国有控股	Of the Total:State—owned and State—holding	961334	10618154
按规模分	**Grouped by Enterprises Size**		
大型企业	Large—Sized	940505	17320405
中型企业	Medium—Sized	894837	22025153
小型企业	Small—Sized	1223020	29874060
按工业行业分	**Grouped by Sector**		
非金属矿采选业	Non—metallic Mining Industry	612	36497
农副食品加工业	Farm and Sideline Products Processing	27809	956208
食品制造业	Food Manufacturing	13652	505726
酒、饮料和精制茶制造业	Wine, Beverages and Refined Tea Manufacturing	10045	290423
烟草制品业	Tobacco Manufacturing	24261	212759
纺织业	Textile Industry	106292	2229199
纺织服装、服饰业	Clothing, Apparel Industry	90031	3506053
皮革、毛皮、羽毛及其制品和制鞋业	Leather, Fur, Feather and Its Products and Footwear Industry	2590	102297

单位:万元(10000 yuan)

所有者权益 Creditors' Equity	实收资本 Paid—in Capital	主营业务收入 Prime Operating Revenue	主营业务成本 Operating Costs	主营业务税金及附加 Tax and Extra Charge	销售费用 Sales Expenses	管理费用 Administrative Expenses	财务费用 Finance Charge
43967216	**23485487**	**125942442**	**107850090**	**2745051**	**2452781**	**5661627**	**1631842**
14032217	6686241	35234889	29163308	995410	1143302	1961468	668443
29934999	16799245	90707552	78686782	1749640	1309479	3700158	963399
1627925	110655	6111006	4949536	835120	49380	112776	6260
39963	10049	74172	61459	521	318	7814	739
29869	8570	89865	75278	692	1643	7494	1079
7207665	4185599	16964366	14181165	83184	266266	749325	283775
5543191	3088550	18189724	15322347	1203135	178787	476315	121287
9246042	4086451	35812683	30665326	165239	896631	2107838	746120
12588594	6656740	28775140	24864487	387552	632031	1273120	291411
7679067	5338026	19904161	17711315	69424	427609	925916	181158
3377713	3915751	12806982	12179071	33704	252900	656667	361448
8482563	5588460	31571938	26196679	2366378	133202	586581	171193
14003876	6777360	40328608	33696421	2097156	669372	1246641	223832
13713163	7049882	38582402	33343914	435987	809675	1880422	541722
15842152	9373445	45516704	39437416	205865	960431	2466992	834651
15698	20850	15463	11232	749		1016	680
611735	250620	1577683	1422850	3880	41408	51102	21290
321539	108771	895811	742117	2912	26920	35187	25007
112312	126815	312732	247212	15106	19175	16582	2863
994598	34160	1311953	246650	828627	40865	58593	—1969
1949874	872840	3551729	3086050	17417	60756	182014	53685
2635952	1055477	6083048	5121958	35893	255636	323196	72022
31884	23606	126888	111867	776	3681	8883	3310

表 7－8 续 3 Continued

指标	Indicators	本年折旧 Depreciation in this Year	负债小计 Total Liabilities
木材加工及木、竹、藤、棕、草制品业	Timber Processing, Bamboo, Rattan, Cane Palm, and Straw Products	2444	82247
家具制造业	Furniture Manufacturing	16715	742155
造纸及纸制品业	Paper－making and Paper Products Manufacturing	68854	2003225
印刷和记录媒介复制业	Printing and Record Duplicating	28649	556816
文教、工美、体育和娱乐用品制造业	Culture, Art, Sports and Recreation Supplies Manufacturing	49375	1579659
石油加工、炼焦和核燃料加工业	Petroleum Processing, Coking & Nuclear Fuel Processing	203131	2315727
化学原料和化学制品制造业	Raw Chemical Materials and Chemical Products	423372	7752616
医药制造业	Medicines Manufacturing	13799	286481
化学纤维制造业	Chemical Fiber Manufacturing	42720	1368890
橡胶和塑料制品业	Rubber and Plastic Products Industry	88145	2257070
非金属矿物制品业	Nonmetal Mineral Products	56762	1618326
黑色金属冶炼和压延加工业	Smelting and Pressing of Ferrous Metals	181620	3712944
有色金属冶炼和压延加工业	Smelting and Pressing of Nonferrous Metals	60172	2084142
金属制品业	Metal Products Manufacturing	77803	2340756
通用设备制造业	General Purpose Equipment Manufacturing	194684	4547059
专用设备制造业	Special Purpose Equipment Manufacturing	104715	2530304
汽车制造业	Automobile Manufacturing	151758	4357806
铁路、船舶、航空航天和其他运输设备制造业	Railroad, Marine, Aviation and Other Transport Equipment Manufacturing	42955	1515547
电气机械和器材制造业	Electric Equipment and Machinery Manufacturing	271903	10178384
计算机、通信和其他电子设备制造业	Computer, Communications and Other Electronic Equipment Manufacturing	173895	3749834
仪器仪表制造业	Instrument Manufacturing	36248	1067974
其他制造业	Other Manufacturing	10349	361626
废弃资源综合利用业	Waste Comprehensive Utilization of Resources Industry	2399	361530
金属制品、机械和设备修理业	Metal Products, Machinery and Equipment Repair Industry	2109	57587
电力、热力的生产和供应业	Production and Supply Electric Power and Thermal Power	449452	3619288
燃气生产和供应业	Production and Supply Gas	11261	346149
水的生产和供应业	Production and Supply Tap Water	63879	1129950

单位:万元(10000 yuan)

所有者权益 Creditors' Equity	实收资本 Paid-in Capital	主营业务收入 Prime Operating Revenue	主营业务成本 Operating Costs	主营业务税金及附加 Tax and Extra Charge	销售费用 Sales Expenses	管理费用 Administrative Expenses	财务费用 Finance Charge
28902	17780	118321	101722	935	2795	6111	3029
186482	193674	839840	710722	3778	36726	51944	25446
1221754	1024858	1386926	1162537	3603	50852	65970	50763
426120	101363	760541	651718	3043	13071	39556	13908
928147	480407	2838497	2404054	12230	98708	169407	50985
2250701	2129881	15258289	12925321	1476169	24145	172265	16734
4528788	2961338	14460055	13211754	28395	189220	405610	116728
291002	132051	516116	361696	3216	43772	49235	10356
305082	312608	1506338	1397974	3519	12609	35632	45823
1202848	535790	3572110	3006027	16509	108839	225734	69616
667217	363964	2121544	1817601	12205	53583	87135	41693
1047402	1349206	5429918	5055856	14614	33984	167055	58310
1181357	584645	5610648	5315775	8158	31874	143867	47560
1131777	562740	3593489	3078855	19046	86447	220764	78559
2919016	1229387	6884172	5582091	38482	212886	537696	122794
2120334	899840	3811665	2964650	20981	153433	344094	52430
3438039	1461830	6784748	5392281	33198	150775	499913	78471
545311	348209	1283564	1120891	6703	22314	86542	35918
4725283	1987763	14856685	12661088	60590	449877	934329	289912
2851292	1501744	7809538	6999361	21265	116413	375585	71478
1399259	486220	1654368	1254562	9803	65915	149285	20395
118172	83232	482107	409678	2469	16454	31481	11651
1136	63660	802946	809285	819	4150	17414	4668
53198	49150	66572	53730	531	927	6864	16
2962141	1491726	8723192	7609547	37030	8588	131454	114392
283267	313980	660680	635422	625	3507	8741	171
479599	325304	234268	165957	1772	12480	21374	23145

表 7—8 续 4 Continued

指标	Indicators	营业利润 Business Profits	利润总额 Total Profits	#应交所得税 Income Tax Payable
总计	**Total**	**6643090**	**7016804**	**1300072**
按轻重工业分	**Grouped by Light and Heavy Industry**			
轻工业	Light Industry	1675024	1766042	340048
重工业	Heavy Industry	4968066	5250762	960024
按注册登记类型分	**Grouped by Registered Type**			
国有企业	State—owned Enterprises	419556	412563	36253
集体企业	Collective—owned Enterpriese	4580	4529	1075
股份合作企业	Share Cooperative Enterprises	3760	3876	463
有限责任公司	Limited Liability Corporations	1613070	1693970	332694
股份有限公司	Share—holding Corporations Ltd.	1030997	1079697	195816
私营企业	Private Enterprises	1347233	1449063	279327
港澳台商投资企业	Hong Kong，Macao & Taiwan Funded	1538424	1644371	308246
外商投资企业	Foreign Funded Enterprises	684674	727992	145991
在总计中：亏损企业	Of the Total：Loss Making Enterprises	—628509	—633989	1652
在总计中：国有及国有控股	Of the Total：State—owned and State—holding	2451410	2500343	492384
按规模分	**Grouped by Enterprises Size**			
大型企业	Large—Sized	2960015	3109452	517204
中型企业	Medium—Sized	1762189	1866507	343304
小型企业	Small—Sized	1888062	1990565	428594
按工业行业分	**Grouped by Sector**			
非金属矿采选业	Non—metallic Mining Industry	1784	1963	38
农副食品加工业	Farm and Sideline Products Processing	46243	59632	8613
食品制造业	Food Manufacturing	64464	65351	1618
酒、饮料和精制茶制造业	Wine，Beverages and Refined Tea Manufacturing	14404	12734	32879
烟草制品业	Tobacco Manufacturing	150406	143629	32879
纺织业	Textile Industry	200351	223984	48557
纺织服装、服饰业	Clothing，Apparel Industry	402880	404983	78916
皮革、毛皮、羽毛及其制品和制鞋业	Leather，Fur，Feather and Its Products and Footwear Industry	—1383	14421	485

单位:万元(10000 yuan)

亏损企业 亏损总额 Total Loss	利税总额 Total Profits and Taxes	本年应付 职工薪酬 Employee Compensation Payable the Year	本年应交 增值税 Value－added Taxes Payable the Year	本年 进项税额 Withholdings on VAT the Year	本年 销项税额 Substituted Money on VAT the Year	全部从业人员 年平均人数(人) Annual Average Employees (person)
633989	**13159389**	**7138651**	**3376861**	**15404180**	**16144648**	**1475040**
196882	3750841	2981785	987942	4367425	4036386	681719
437106	9408548	4156866	2388919	11036755	12108261	793321
	1487234	88856	230470	440938	567983	11904
394	7913	8670	2841	8765	10357	1359
357	7981	10276	3412	10038	12241	2544
52282	2364801	818160	587123	2186328	2672523	129733
7284	2746789	389231	463859	2521187	2904009	57452
210254	2554756	2904222	937741	4574006	4481682	680149
142051	2861042	1637985	828524	3456008	3597996	337056
221367	1127025	1277633	321972	2204183	1894215	253881
633989	－398537	901406	200818	1646904	1470938	208491
21120	6198877	516350	1322927	3578291	4769356	43648
19381	6290342	1466877	1074772	4668431	5305210	262388
168165	3418555	2482772	1108071	4836097	4831328	505109
417071	3353726	3117156	1153577	5736402	5831673	703712
	4020	946	1308	1470	2778	220
1922	90659	64531	27146	156248	140940	15488
6517	88327	46538	20064	85899	67288	13098
171	41205	19708	13348	44430	49558	3698
	1140516	23408	168227	190859	356860	1083
20929	340908	291370	99458	466190	490948	66225
26055	615620	746713	174542	720058	685225	173244
2256	18059	17735	2816	12297	12733	4865

表 7—8 续 5 Continued

指标	Indicators	营业利润 Business Profits	利润总额 Total Profits	应交所得税 Income Tax Payable
木材加工及木、竹、藤、棕、草制品业	Timber Processing, Bamboo, Rattan, Cane Palm, and Straw Products	3704	3850	559
家具制造业	Furniture Manufacturing	13965	14904	6048
造纸及纸制品业	Paper—making and Paper Products Manufacturing	62738	61930	14809
印刷和记录媒介复制业	Printing and Record Duplicating	44332	47916	10021
文教、工美、体育和娱乐用品制造业	Culture, Art, Sports and Recreation Supplies Manufacturing	122233	128899	17486
石油加工、炼焦和核燃料加工业	Petroleum Processing, Coking & Nuclear Fuel Processing	666866	697720	169687
化学原料和化学制品制造业	Raw Chemical Materials and Chemical Products	574043	602058	120570
医药制造业	Medicines Manufacturing	52633	53430	7197
化学纤维制造业	Chemical Fiber Manufacturing	13983	15327	5740
橡胶和塑料制品业	Rubber and Plastic Products Industry	160092	161655	31922
非金属矿物制品业	Nonmetal Mineral Products	115793	128173	25298
黑色金属冶炼和压延加工业	Smelting and Pressing of Ferrous Metals	104144	112687	15405
有色金属冶炼和压延加工业	Smelting and Pressing of Nonferrous Metals	86966	99259	16592
金属制品业	Metal Products Manufacturing	121350	128082	33646
通用设备制造业	General Purpose Equipment Manufacturing	409328	427825	79212
专用设备制造业	Special Purpose Equipment Manufacturing	312909	328519	53775
汽车制造业	Automobile Manufacturing	699568	768742	102978
铁路、船舶、航空航天和其他运输设备制造业	Railroad, Marine, Aviation and Other Transport Equipment Manufacturing	27537	29002	5259
电气机械和器材制造业	Electric Equipment and Machinery Manufacturing	609897	667088	117071
计算机、通信和其他电子设备制造业	Computer, Communications and Other Electronic Equipment Manufacturing	291923	319633	46636
仪器仪表制造业	Instrument Manufacturing	154890	165542	25432
其他制造业	Other Manufacturing	10985	11992	2583
废弃资源综合利用业	Waste Comprehensive Utilization of Resources Industry	—31675	—22925	560
金属制品、机械和设备修理业	Metal Products, Machinery and Equipment Repair Industry	4642	4532	929
电力、热力的生产和供应业	Production and Supply Electric Power and Thermal Power	1098256	1098322	198700
燃气生产和供应业	Production and Supply Gas	15630	14198	4811
水的生产和供应业	Production and Supply Tap Water	17211	21751	5124

单位:万元(10000 yuan)

亏损企业亏损总额 Total Loss	利税总额 Total Profits and Taxes	本年应付职工薪酬 Employee Compensation Payable the Year	本年应交增值税 Value-added Taxes Payable the Year	本年进项税额 Withholdings on VAT the Year	本年销项税额 Substituted Money on VAT the Year	全部从业人员年平均人数(人) Annual Average Employees (person)
604	7774	12140	2989	12623	10140	2916
13713	35356	89773	16668	99759	74775	20096
8801	89815	73441	24045	223276	204371	14512
916	67178	60512	16218	98108	86764	14203
16500	201393	268863	60118	336828	256839	64515
2592	2819434	141749	645545	1934907	2577552	7808
144508	856825	283756	226236	2055035	2195651	36688
2822	76971	39549	20325	47951	62497	6387
21172	48055	44816	29188	207195	215803	10323
31193	289374	300235	110799	456768	413404	72627
8565	241263	99441	100778	136439	194089	19935
33865	219055	202151	91611	795478	845811	35076
16089	160867	140716	53214	888635	917845	28673
20630	232220	337250	84557	427530	343756	75577
40115	667885	648427	201007	868415	857373	138017
13390	462814	347320	112916	469960	490747	64681
11319	1017562	534826	215413	968663	1015046	95273
14660	64471	107104	28691	146968	124691	23779
72837	1072348	1213103	337063	1908595	1625438	266113
48325	422652	538282	81573	556853	503279	122345
6934	228312	162403	52858	204219	223913	36626
3161	23489	60757	8997	55263	43072	14041
30293	−17795	22710	4311	133360	126519	6000
16	7341	14225	2278	1562	3627	1908
	1470440	151446	326031	666573	887901	13931
5476	18774	10767	3845	24266	27456	1006
7643	36204	21942	12681	1501	9961	4063

表7—9 各县(市)、区规模以上工业企业主要财务指标(2013) Main Financial Indicators of Industrial Enterprises Above Designated Size by Region

指标	Indicators	全市 Toal	市区 Urban District	海曙 Haishu
企业单位数(个)	Number of Enterprises(unit)	7167	3379	31
#亏损企业	Deficits Enterprises	1230	654	6
工业总产值(现价)	Gross Industrial Output Value(Current Prices)	130100892	85985775	3574819
工业销售产值	Value of Industrial Products Sales	125914244	83891848	3560649
#出口交货值	Value of Export Products	28075640	16242036	147836
资产合计	Total Asset	114401358	69396406	1981304
流动资产小计	Current Assets	68701412	40082195	586908
固定资产小计	Total Fixed Assets	32200934	20836797	990860
本年折旧	Depreciation in this year	3104457	2017077	73854
负债合计	Total Liabilities	70363253	39553445	1518954
流动负债小计	Current Liabilities	63898286	35568194	878865
所有者权益合计	Total Owner' Equity	43967216	29765545	462042
#实收资本	Paid—in Capital	23485487	16838763	231411
主营业务收入	Prime Operating Revenue	125942442	84440119	3365907
主营业务成本	Operating Costs	107850090	72826529	3260491
主营业务税金及附加	Tax and Extra Charge	2745051	2550973	2756
销售费用	Sales Expenses	2452781	1446852	31355
管理费用	Administrative Expenses	5661627	3233862	38998
#税金	Tax	226314	126023	1090
财务费用	Finance charge	1631842	695361	6614
#利息支出	Interest Exchange	1867026	892754	9272
营业利润	Business Profits	6643090	4567118	298420
利润总额	Total Profits	7016804	4842992	297726
应交所得税	Income Tax Payable	1300072	912957	8368
亏损企业亏损总额	Total Loss	633989	444411	789
利税总额	Total Profits and Taxes	13159389	9603986	325518
本年应付职工薪酬	Employee Compensation Payable in this Year	7138651	3985198	50880
本年应交增值税	Value—added Taxes Payable in this Year	3376861	2191453	16249
本年进项税额	Withholdings on VAT in this Year	15404180	10127536	76772
本年销项税额	Substituted Money on VAT in this Year	16144648	11104864	86362
全部从业人员年平均人数(人)	Annual Average Employees(person)	1475040	750205	12736

单位:万元(10000 yuan)

各区 by Districts					余姚 Yuyao	慈溪 Cixi	奉化 Fenghua	象山 Xiangshan	宁海 Ninghai
江东 Jiangdong	江北 Jiangbei	北仑 Beilun	镇海 Zhenhai	鄞州 Yinzhou					
51	293	663	575	1689	1184	1268	437	430	469
12	77	173	185	184	164	163	82	76	91
1945351	4380318	29098911	24073789	21623686	12376426	17448888	3692926	4823726	5773151
1875711	4289725	28818112	22979355	21127117	11915634	16342671	3706948	4560992	5496152
201591	785217	7312533	1694187	5708499	3412433	4461648	1485251	1124648	1349625
2483101	4288936	26095341	13870703	18924495	11956878	16707810	3815300	6124571	6400393
1419593	2641499	14326696	7787160	12281236	8198005	10981768	2479009	3476454	3483982
602774	990441	9097025	5099636	3685184	2695659	3504954	1024418	1886380	2252727
65948	91172	875638	483834	391462	268100	396708	101395	145160	176016
910334	2535524	13717703	8630204	11186050	8476867	11491910	2744423	3960498	4136108
727979	2311435	12533494	7764611	10412461	7910045	10769159	2687966	3288663	3674260
1572767	1748705	12341782	5244035	7698465	3474042	5191126	1070666	2212780	2253058
331895	853743	7947956	3946379	3120721	1680593	2311146	587427	1046138	1021421
1925925	4435089	29040312	23450091	20972989	11895625	16046908	3510517	4609019	5440254
773293	3884091	25709141	20334080	17822091	10170916	13711989	2984765	3857460	4298432
831575	17223	373093	1221955	99160	48330	62436	25493	22326	35493
60511	99428	412378	206810	598875	267620	406898	78721	110690	142000
101672	268025	943917	640103	1148721	688854	911493	261782	227597	338038
4106	8814	48292	23990	36388	31589	40380	8039	8581	11702
11870	54099	131478	196165	268366	258286	312722	86024	126401	153049
16228	60500	266397	208898	304418	265628	337828	81334	125505	163978
218703	146509	1613307	938491	1279107	505149	685061	90070	294288	501404
220911	178147	1765157	968429	1332701	517936	740702	98403	305552	511219
36549	34136	344088	249088	227076	87775	107981	21269	60337	109754
2275	33691	172277	149201	63933	48305	78921	21567	16447	24337
1231878	283954	3000516	2734785	1922703	847625	1241305	212394	486643	767436
71511	295575	1327839	653965	1482120	821520	1219863	368764	328367	414939
179359	88367	861986	536908	489154	280827	437471	88143	158627	220342
263881	669387	3138622	3325996	2506187	1393958	2199457	394671	687739	600820
416531	677831	3461843	3747927	2578254	1291209	2105754	363666	623815	655339
11115	57427	236686	102892	311468	201802	272419	86354	70726	93534

表 7—10 各县(市)、区国有控股工业企业主要财务指标(2013)
Main Financial Indicators of State Holding Shares Industrial Enterprises by Region

指标	Indicators	全市 Toal	市区 Urban District	海曙 Haishu
企业单位数(个)	Number of Enterprises(unit)	100	67	4
#亏损企业	Deficits Enterprises	13	7	
工业总产值(现价)	Gross Industrial Output Value(Current Prices)	32757503	28996612	3201406
工业销售产值	Value of Industrial Products Sales	31813141	28066493	3201406
#出口交货值	Value of Export Products	299422	267690	
资产合计	Total Asset	19106800	14740202	1374855
流动资产小计	Total Current Assets	6883187	5526090	163964
固定资产原价	Original Value of Fixed Assets	18234187	14021857	1920466
#累计折旧	Accumulative Depreciation	8474433	6868450	1000937
负债合计	Total Liabilities	10618154	8020745	1170383
流动负债小计	Current Liabilities	8230526	6650988	567124
所有者权益合计	Total Owners' Equity	8482563	6719457	204471
#实收资本	Paid—in Capital	5588460	4735790	165309
主营业务收入	Prime Operating Revenue	31571938	27803251	2943531
主营业务成本	Operating Costs	26196679	23131946	2913989
主营业务税金及附加	Tax and Extra Charge	2366378	2342274	491
销售费用	Sales Expenses	133202	107383	4094
管理费用	Administrative Expenses	586581	468326	7152
财务费用	Finance Charge	171193	79691	—433
营业利润	Business Profits	2451410	2000516	271909
利润总额	Total Profits	2500343	2043312	269380
亏损企业亏损总额	Total Loss	21120	16317	
本年应付职工薪酬	Employee Compensation Payable in this Year	516350	408374	11355
本年应交增值税	Value—added Taxes Payable in this Year	1322927	1125994	4088
本年进项税额	Withholdings on VAT in this Year	3578291	3103964	21405
本年销项税额	Substituted Money on VAT in this Year	4769356	4193346	25438
全部从业人员年平均人数(人)	Annual Average Employees(person)	43648	29572	4012

单位：万元(10000 yuan)

各区 by Districts					余姚 Yuyao	慈溪 Cixi	奉化 Fenghua	象山 Xiangshan	宁海 Ninghai
江东 Jiangdong	江北 Jiangbei	北仑 Beilun	镇海 Zhenhai	鄞州 Yinzhou					
3	5	22	21	10	9	4	5	7	8
	1	2	2	1	2		1	2	1
1392804	103640	8320129	15373976	575900	731177	596025	182348	829866	1421476
1380723	100704	8290076	14491889	573279	731177	594913	182100	815677	1422781
27246	1498	195665	43212	70			2795	28937	
1761708	207463	5824066	5289452	240251	968298	385888	166003	1054992	1791417
908672	74321	2213719	2108722	46253	529617	116460	67469	263137	380415
981120	141390	5985976	4659162	291801	545105	367261	144019	1257853	1898093
440615	40111	2946967	2304453	124911	246719	151959	103319	508771	595215
558005	154216	3414067	2606370	85388	658052	173403	78519	658392	1029043
379276	60337	3083297	2478967	71624	502973	80926	71501	291920	632218
1203704	53247	2409999	2683081	154863	310246	212485	87483	390518	762374
224257	31463	1811689	2461641	29432	144391	26738	35472	246700	399368
1424031	100708	8253349	14483674	569506	730437	598409	183959	848435	1407448
336273	75716	6949403	12273726	554587	673334	565766	154704	673253	997676
829454	564	316145	1193645	1936	3185	2177	858	5274	12609
45439	3758	26502	26616	974	5287	2870	3217	4907	9539
66985	15001	159259	212496	6397	21813	15929	21640	9782	49091
6065	5282	30833	36239	1515	12977	5285	1632	26153	45455
156676	948	795890	770180	5377	26372	7903	2120	124876	289622
153553	2577	832357	775955	9145	30678	8347	2167	125552	290287
	4255	4699	6674	420	2558		100	733	1412
33192	11995	150209	186577	13270	21769	9736	10958	31253	34260
174313	4509	522678	405271	13997	30036	19696	8135	47568	91497
191607	13272	827833	2033120	13087	95065	87419	5304	160461	126078
362955	16869	1331807	2435239	16261	123665	103932	7224	130456	210733
2855	1459	9571	10184	1301	2499	1872	1344	4320	4041

表 7－11　各县(市)、区规模以上私营工业企业主要财务指标(2013)
Main Financial Indicators of Private Industrial Enterprises Above Designated Size by Region

指标	Indicators	全市 Toal	市区 Urban District	海曙 Haishu
企业单位数(个)	Number of Enterprises(unit)	4401	1766	6
＃亏损企业	Deficits Enterprises	643	285	1
工业总产值(现价)	Gross Industrial Output Value(Current Prices)	37126092	14613462	22818
工业销售产值	Value of Industrial Products Sales	35742934	14306386	21744
＃出口交货值	Value of Export Products	9217226	3262672	2277
资产合计	Total Asset	34293491	12712818	30734
流动资产小计	Total Current Assets	23105735	8610060	16508
固定资产原价	Original Value of Fixed Assets	10488669	3961495	17097
＃累计折旧	Accumulative Depreciation	3924271	1467045	4005
负债合计	Total Liabilities	24976038	8901202	26620
流动负债小计	Current Liabilities	23602086	8342215	25411
所有者权益合计	Total Owners' Equity	9246042	3768969	4114
＃实收资本	Paid－in Capital	4086451	1560528	1350
主营业务收入	Prime Operating Revenue	35812683	14622980	22180
主营业务成本	Operating Costs	30665326	12585461	19119
主营业务税金及附加	Tax and Extra Charge	165239	69952	50
销售费用	Sales Expenses	896631	326270	405
管理费用	Administrative Expenses	2107838	851417	1798
财务费用	Finance Charge	746120	252277	608
营业利润	Business Profits	1347233	575939	186
利润总额	Total Profits	1449063	637932	501
亏损企业亏损总额	Total Loss	210254	116204	148
本年应付职工薪酬	Employee Compensation Payable in this Year	2904222	1108728	2871
本年应交增值税	Value－added Taxes Payable in this Year	937741	359313	697
本年进项税额	Withholdings on VAT in this Year	4574006	1881437	3446
本年销项税额	Substituted Money on VAT in this Year	4481682	1864227	3391
全部从业人员年平均人数(人)	Annual Average Employees(person)	680149	248996	734

单位:万元(10000 yuan)

各区 by Districts					余姚 Yuyao	慈溪 Cixi	奉化 Fenghua	象山 Xiangshan	宁海 Ninghai
江东 Jiangdong	江北 Jiangbei	北仑 Beilun	镇海 Zhenhai	鄞州 Yinzhou					
24	149	204	281	1082	744	934	326	304	327
7	43	41	94	95	85	102	58	55	58
127704	1006958	1384945	2671617	9113353	5399626	10147160	1936428	2090918	2938498
131157	986479	1385969	2629280	8872022	5156591	9700918	1852080	1962657	2764301
28767	227067	325383	460747	2172858	1306874	2939661	429644	569470	708906
139262	1132880	1646812	2446250	7080061	4740436	9716747	1928820	2342222	2852449
123891	708052	1057014	1719342	4830469	3293595	6414076	1300228	1516928	1970849
24288	389316	605834	773749	2090856	1487610	2899440	643518	673215	823391
11875	137926	217946	286192	792367	532633	1149332	237959	212993	324308
105832	807909	1126963	1916214	4783508	3630163	7292325	1434246	1602898	2115205
104937	759412	992281	1772024	4572988	3473163	6837004	1392943	1489034	2067727
33430	324113	485747	534771	2284244	1108193	2412784	494364	735417	726316
14195	163724	244507	300361	793773	476191	1090821	274179	390933	293800
131701	1008568	1453549	2869109	8867728	5152988	9483710	1843704	1965065	2744237
114940	824333	1247388	2631055	7526467	4428029	8155969	1563154	1669745	2262968
554	5233	9060	9862	44111	20908	38090	11260	9412	15617
4644	39054	36120	50614	189512	114766	264268	50958	50495	89874
9537	82696	103848	138401	497907	296719	533496	134256	110610	181341
2495	21614	33233	57448	132988	110822	209379	50706	51232	71704
−247	42951	30825	−7226	486207	186730	317996	44083	79307	143177
565	52769	53097	11291	494108	188387	337402	49356	86072	149915
1973	7979	17345	61632	26286	18369	35353	15003	9901	15425
13303	98195	145726	177716	649477	383347	782059	222611	154251	253226
1828	28682	59482	42906	221637	119080	257719	54688	59445	87496
18831	122534	205641	402810	1092916	613304	1293579	231737	236429	317521
17284	123996	172493	384019	1128503	585980	1211026	239837	257218	323394
2881	22320	31973	41318	145782	96723	182617	54434	37121	60258

表 7－12 各县(市)、区规模以上大中型工业企业主要财务指标(2013) Main Financial Indicators of Large and Medium Size Industrial Enterprises Above Designated Size by Region

指标	Indicators	全市 Toal	市区 Urban District	海曙 Haishu
企业单位数(个)	Number of Enterprises(unit)	1107	546	10
#亏损企业	Deficits Enterprises	134	77	1
工业总产值(现价)	Gross Industrial Output Value(Current Prices)	82198367	58197777	3401480
工业销售产值	Value of Industrial Products Sales	79282257	56490941	3390765
#出口交货值	Value of Export Products	17785267	10890580	99348
资产合计	Total Asset	67019631	43169074	1657291
流动资产小计	Total Current Assets	38481657	24122098	369856
固定资产原价	Original Value of Fixed Assets	31412447	21866012	1951100
#累计折旧	Accumulative Depreciation	13341256	9767697	1007642
负债合计	Total Liabilities	39345558	23909949	1382977
流动负债小计	Current Liabilities	35287251	21404064	750395
所有者权益合计	Total Owners' Equity	27717039	19257866	274314
#实收资本	Paid－in Capital	13827242	10462529	196503
主营业务收入	Prime Operating Revenue	78911011	56439246	3186487
主营业务成本	Operating Costs	67040335	48322086	3113829
主营业务税金及附加	Tax and Extra Charge	2533143	2429940	1626
销售费用	Sales Expenses	1479048	927043	21383
管理费用	Administrative Expenses	3127063	1841665	22074
财务费用	Finance Charge	765554	319800	6608
营业利润	Business Profits	4722204	3273114	279886
利润总额	Total Profits	4975959	3445737	277512
亏损企业亏损总额	Total Loss	187546	128046	44
本年应付职工薪酬	Employee Compensation Payable in this Year	3949648	2351928	36694
本年应交增值税	Value－added Taxes Payable in this Year	2182843	1512832	11250
本年进项税额	Withholdings on VAT in this Year	9504528	6574055	52605
本年销项税额	Substituted money on VAT in this Year	10136538	7404610	59624
全部从业人员年平均人数(人)	Annual Average Employees(person)	767497	419103	9944

单位:万元(10000 yuan)

各区 by Districts					余姚 Yuyao	慈溪 Cixi	奉化 Fenghua	象山 Xiangshan	宁海 Ninghai
江东 Jiangdong	江北 Jiangbei	北仑 Beilun	镇海 Zhenhai	鄞州 Yinzhou					
9	46	149	74	242	151	222	74	50	64
	5	27	15	26	15	25	11	1	5
1710847	2809321	20314967	18177828	11124651	6033990	10172744	1796249	2526581	3471026
1636691	2739795	20101183	17124419	10855547	5788549	9440317	1874815	2347385	3340250
165852	386800	6147511	837094	2968057	1722758	2849992	1048052	636030	637854
1917322	2136340	17229092	8938921	10304602	5173381	9453039	2026900	3272207	3925031
1044941	1321446	9567643	4885435	6371642	3489985	6035789	1267354	1709496	1856935
1013671	687067	9497365	5104148	3248876	1706051	2888552	835128	1772639	2344065
458542	241608	4143071	2309696	1466917	660605	1150641	321187	668135	772991
664811	1095772	9320002	5181223	5657509	3418205	6050717	1493973	2103104	2369610
483598	1020349	8518784	4828271	5271486	3208150	5668119	1468961	1564269	1973688
1252512	1040569	7908922	3756597	4647094	1753221	3399201	532927	1218403	1555420
248486	474819	4777571	2799536	1764704	751475	1277945	246120	497505	591668
1682107	2802147	20168054	17228959	10717377	5821341	9237040	1689218	2397933	3326234
563918	2519801	17877918	14715530	8989313	5029477	7769108	1417080	1934205	2568379
830440	8139	339023	1108875	49050	20539	34144	14977	11967	21577
52674	52269	235231	114838	427274	114817	260475	35454	63753	77506
78906	135753	601612	367495	587816	309383	549537	136483	107620	182375
7155	14264	61831	93913	119235	105431	144412	41383	68303	86224
167721	91830	1127824	798804	767451	267128	496822	53484	219724	411932
164777	109222	1247032	804362	801898	281151	544988	58667	226631	418785
	4306	45826	39346	21438	10162	35891	11418	125	1904
50709	146725	946808	349622	763956	355240	702087	175277	159819	205298
174810	44210	619580	404847	250158	123131	261431	35573	99143	150733
230314	469191	2002180	2437879	1304189	690721	1304460	162199	415372	357722
382402	477631	2248509	2839901	1331305	624139	1233401	126953	331609	415826
6793	26211	170015	46383	150064	85091	148834	40324	31231	42914

表 7—13 各县(市)、区规模以上外商和港澳台投资工业企业主要财务指标(2013) Main Financial Indicators of Foreign Funded and Hongkong, Macao, Taiwan Funded Industrial Enterprises Above Designated Size by Region

指标	Indicators	全市 Toal	市区 Urban District	
				海曙 Haishu
企业单位数(个)	Number of Enterprises(unit)	1996	1189	9
#亏损企业	Deficits Enterprises	476	303	2
工业总产值(现价)	Gross Industrial Output Value(Current Prices)	50152579	37672148	95775
工业销售产值	Value of Industrial Products Sales	48770994	37050558	94172
#出口交货值	Value of Export Products	16249581	11612986	61077
资产合计	Total Asset	45816104	33052892	58864
流动资产小计	Total Current Assets	29024819	20149362	47215
固定资产原价	Original Value of Fixed Assets	19078005	15043280	21472
#累计折旧	Accumulative Depreciation	8146690	6511184	12786
负债合计	Total Liabilities	25515644	17267573	27826
流动负债小计	Current Liabilities	23623721	15770651	27764
所有者权益合计	Total Owners' Equity	20267661	15769031	31038
#实收资本	Paid—in Capital	11994766	9396789	16763
主营业务收入	Prime Operating Revenue	48679301	37267001	95406
主营业务成本	Operating Costs	42575802	32927744	78462
主营业务税金及附加	Tax and Extra Charge	456976	405031	902
销售费用	Sales Expenses	1059640	801700	2150
管理费用	Administrative Expenses	2199036	1477765	8500
财务费用	Finance Charge	472569	247981	938
营业利润	Business Profits	2223098	1695934	4767
利润总额	Total Profits	2372363	1816067	5062
亏损企业亏损总额	Total Loss	363418	277492	265
本年应付职工薪酬	Employee Compensation Payable in this Year	2915618	2008632	14427
本年应交增值税	Value—added Taxes Payable in this Year	1150496	878864	3594
本年进项税额	Withholdings on VAT in this Year	5660191	4177362	10347
本年销项税额	Substituted money on VAT in this Year	5492211	4258731	12293
全部从业人员年平均人数(人)	Annual Average Employees(person)	590937	383369	3046

单位:万元(10000 yuan)

各区 by Districts					余姚 Yuyao	慈溪 Cixi	奉化 Fenghua	象山 Xiangshan	宁海 Ninghai
江东 Jiangdong	江北 Jiangbei	北仑 Beilun	镇海 Zhenhai	鄞州 Yinzhou					
11	94	396	207	439	313	219	83	87	105
3	22	121	74	74	65	45	18	17	28
311090	1044727	22102488	5644128	7803600	4190199	4943681	1407090	1097732	841729
252260	999020	21834746	5519216	7712681	4044664	4367047	1512421	1025633	770670
108921	382840	6838324	1136544	2785622	1687892	1113231	997636	405320	432517
182514	1358721	18807641	4431788	7166388	4193504	4785789	1540962	1314344	928613
152903	877143	10963046	2757675	4767297	3034816	3283431	988041	921005	648163
39030	433065	9415701	2069138	2642666	1365619	1289006	725457	351538	303106
21921	149799	4033756	887339	1228008	582614	492635	274599	161290	124368
125314	748187	9195412	2506099	4050328	2860762	2864372	1069941	832492	620505
122997	696897	8497476	2222157	3676507	2689759	2722964	1064878	767347	608123
57200	606685	9610477	1925867	3105184	1327960	1908283	471021	483515	307851
30912	291616	6127493	1080701	1557021	861486	975764	268000	288664	204064
255027	1053718	22061280	5645043	7496934	4018694	4295835	1320233	1037160	740379
224962	850882	19920354	5024694	6265189	3431296	3642540	1125817	846964	601440
898	6527	337089	18273	38795	14479	15404	12553	5219	4290
6686	31812	339015	101502	296768	94716	83090	20457	33839	25839
13829	86158	678455	216921	419191	257257	229889	94355	73696	66074
1060	17218	61609	64214	86237	76215	66587	28702	28047	25037
10463	76554	819647	256172	507615	158452	250022	43451	55017	20222
10582	86403	928243	255726	506891	152740	279986	45446	56754	21371
278	10341	147705	69795	31674	26072	41102	5764	5686	7302
14091	102886	1001210	232283	590108	308297	292805	115985	105908	83992
703	23119	576591	103475	162500	86012	107572	21546	34319	22182
37687	135155	2265466	770957	885840	492224	577918	135304	189571	87812
22554	119172	2409629	773707	863382	392982	560379	94601	122489	63028
2941	20101	186231	40195	121918	79112	60013	25686	22220	20537

表 7—14 部分年份工业主要产品产量 Output of Major Industrial Products in Partial Years

主要工业产品	单位	Major Industrial Products	Unit	2010	2011	2012	2013
大米	万吨	Rice	10000 tons	9.56	8.36	8.19	6.87
配合饲料	万吨	Formulated Feed	10000 tons	21.47	25.41	25.51	28.91
食用植物油	万吨	Edible Vegetable Oil	10000 tons	25.48	25.78	16.88	12.64
水产加工品	万吨	Processed Aquatic Products	10000 tons	26.60	39.84	27.76	24.98
罐头	万吨	Canned Food	10000 tons	19.92	16.43	15.00	17.00
味精	万吨	Monosodium Glutamate	10000 tons	1.11			
啤酒	千万升	Beer	ten million liters	45.79	48.39	48.82	48.59
软饮料	万吨	Soft Beverage	10000 tons	25.77	17.03	6.94	4.70
瓶(罐)装饮用水	万吨	Bottled Drinking Water	10000 tons	8.50			
精制茶	万吨	Refine Tea	10000 tons	5.36	5.14	2.64	6.19
卷烟	亿支	Cigarette	100 million	359.28	372.49	394.92	380.61
纱	万吨	Yarn	10000 tons	26.30	29.86	44.82	41.32
布	万米	Cloth	10000 m	44946	38045	35380	33486
印染布	万米	Printing and Dyeing Cloth	10000 m	77592	90652	57673	50980
帘子布	万吨	Curtain Cloth	10000 tons	3.99	3.37	2.67	4.06
绒线(毛线)	吨	Knitting Wool	ton	2310	6488	5381	5905
呢绒	万米	Wool Fabric	10000 m	4347	2143	3284	1162
服装	万件	Garment	10000 units	155067	111977	113948	114648
梭织服装	万件	Shuttle Woven Garment	10000 units	19842	15792	15141	14252
#西服及西服套装	万件	Western—style Clothes	10000 units	2764	2291	1693	1524.71
衬衫	万件	Shirt	10000 units	8696	6029	6378	5881.44
羽绒服装	万件	Eiderdown Garment	10000 units	312.57	622.74	26.76	36.50
针织服装	万件	Knitting Garment	10000 units	135224	96185	98807	100397
机制纸及纸板	万吨	Paper—making and Paperboard	10000 tons	182.38	208.23	221.81	224.77
纸制品	万吨	Paper Products	10000 tons	118.67	86.91	84.21	83.10
原油加工量	万吨	Crude Oil Processed	10000 tons	2084.66	2717.43	2506.12	2688.75
汽油	万吨	Gasoline	10000 tons	283.03	295.53	264.08	279.64
煤油	万吨	Kerosene	10000 tons	154.56	162.89	156.23	208.97
柴油	万吨	DieselOil	10000 tons	750.62	742.00	679.24	686.55
石油沥青	万吨	Asphalt	10000 tons	281.58	277.43	263.53	322.32
液化石油气	万吨	Liquefied Petroleum Gas	10000 tons	109.47	110.37	96.40	106.22
硫酸(折 100%)	万吨	Sulphuric Acid(100%)	10000 tons	9.16	10.27	9.65	10.22
盐酸(含量 31%以上)	万吨	Hydrochloric Acid (above31%percent)	10000 tons	15.15	16.90	8.98	15.81
烧碱(折 100%)	万吨	CausticSoda(100%)	10000 tons	34.28	46.10	55.37	59.64
合成氨	万吨	SyntheticAmmonia	10000 tons	6.01	4.04	7.24	7.48
农用化肥(折纯)	万吨	ChemicalFertilizers	10000 tons	6.11	1.17	1.28	1.51

7－14 续表 Continued

主要工业产品	单位	Major Industrial Products	Unit	2010	2011	2012	2013
氮肥(折含 N100%)	万吨	NitrogenousFertilizer(100%)	10000 tons	6.11	1.17	1.28	1.51
尿素	万吨	Urea	10000 tons	4.87			
化学农药	吨	ChemicalPesticide	ton	5865.14	4912.54	2796.50	2364.15
纯苯	万吨	PureBenzene	10000 tons	29.07	41.05	37.92	39.90
建筑涂料	吨	BuildingDope	ton	2711.58			
染料	吨	Dye	ton	11092.40			
塑料树脂及共聚物	万吨	Plastic Resinand Copolyment	10000 tons	333.10	369.13	315.56	372.43
化学原料药	吨	Chemical Raw Medicine	ton	2094.03	2647.62	2104.77	1545.61
塑料制品	万吨	Plastic Products	10000 tons	112.41	88.77	92.00	76.89
水泥	万吨	Cement	10000 tons	1092.62	1303.81	1289.44	1598.53
粗钢	万吨	Rural Steel	10000 tons	433.05	471.37	456.77	486.09
成品钢材	万吨	Rolled－steel Final Products	10000 tons	662.04	762.50	830.16	882.20
铜	万吨	Copper	10000 tons	4.19	5.61	6.79	4.80
铜加工材	万吨	Copper Material	10000 tons	64.30	51.67	61.51	75.28
铝材	万吨	Aluminium	10000 tons	29.89	25.57	18.89	21.97
液压元件	万件	Hydraulic Pressure Elements	10000 units	5947.99	6363.74	7000.93	6439.14
气动元件	万件	Pneumatic Element	10000 units	6375.25	7311.24	6857.91	7217.65
粉末冶金制品	万吨	Powder Metallurgy Products	10000 tons	3.41	3.30	3.35	3.75
大中型拖拉机	台	Lager and Medium－sized Tractor	unit	36616	45990	28262	39069
汽车	辆	Motor Vechicle	unit	145660	170754	128942	129125
轿车	辆	Car	unit	145593	170754	128942	129125
摩托车	万辆	Motorcycles	10000 units	10.40	7.67	9.12	9.37
自行车	万辆	Bicycles	10000 units	343.64	403.39	371.76	384.23
民用钢质船舶	载重吨	Civil Steel Ship	DWT	897467	1032565	650674	359228
交流电动机	万千瓦	Alternating Current Motor	10000 kw	276.32	103.64	80.69	47.25
变压器	万千伏安	Transformer	10000 kev	1613.23	1829.46	1797.18	1543.74
电力电缆	万公里	Power Cable	10000 km	26.38	33.00	126.50	64.69
自动化仪表系统	万套	Instrument and Meter for Automation	10000 units	72.60			
原电池(折一号电池)	万只	Primary Cellsand Batterices	10000 units	441809	459965	437644	440383
家用洗衣机	万台	Household Washing Machine	10000 units	1360.46	1337.46	1483.26	1397.18
吸尘器	万台	Dust Catcher	10000 units	1027.39	1282.17	1109.28	1249.51
电风扇	万台	Electric Fan	10000 units	541.18	595.76	632.10	601.12
房间空气调节器	万台	Home Air Conditioner	10000 units	418.53	380.56	414.03	429.81
排油烟机	万台	Range Hoods	10000 units	109.39	62.81	145.98	191.48
移动电话机	万部	Mobile Phone	10000 units	393.97	233.14	253.12	586.44
光学仪器	万台	Optical Instrument	10000 units	273.24	280.48	336.85	368.17
发电量	亿千瓦小时	Generating Capacity	100 million kwh	844.59	952.48	887.22	948.17

表 7—15 各县(市)、区规模以上工业企业主要经济效益指标(2013)
Main Indicators on Ecnomic Benefit of Industrial Enterprises Above Designated Size by Region

指标	单位	Indicators	Unit	全市 Toal	市区 Urban District
产销率	%	Proportion of Products Sold	%	96.78	97.56
资产负债率	%	Assets Liability Ratio	%	61.51	57.00
成本费用利润率	%	Ratio of Profits to Industrial Cost	%	5.97	6.19
每百元固定资产原值实现利税	元	Pre—tax Profits Per 100 Yuan Original Value of Fixed Assets	yuan	25.84	27.99
每百元主营业务收入实现利税	元	Pre—tax Profits Per 100 Yuan Main Business	yuan	10.45	11.37
流动比率	%	Ratio of Circulating Funds to Current Liabilities	%	1.08	1.13
速动比率	%	Ratio of Quickassets to Current Liabilities	%	0.83	0.85
企业亏损面	%	Ratio of Number of Deficit Enterprises to Total Enterprises Number	%	17.16	19.35
亏损率	%	Losing Rate	%	8.29	8.41
出口交货值占工业销售产值比重	%	Ratio of Exports Products Value to Industrial Sales Value	%	22.30	19.36
利润总额占利税比重	%	Ratio of Total Profits to Total Pre—tax	%	53.32	50.43
存货周转次数	次	Number of Times of Turnover of Inventories	times	6.78	7.39

各区 by Districts						余姚 Yuyao	慈溪 Cixi	奉化 Fenghua	象山 Xiangshan	宁海 Ninghai
海曙 Haishu	江东 Jiangdong	江北 Jiangbei	北仑 Beilun	镇海 Zhenhai	鄞州 Yinzhou					
99.60	96.42	97.93	99.04	95.45	97.70	96.28	93.66	100.38	94.55	95.20
76.66	36.66	59.12	52.57	62.22	59.11	70.90	68.78	71.93	64.67	64.62
8.92	23.32	4.14	6.49	4.53	6.72	4.55	4.83	2.88	7.07	10.37
16.12	112.25	19.96	19.51	35.14	31.92	21.27	23.87	13.70	18.35	23.84
9.67	63.96	6.40	10.33	11.66	9.17	7.13	7.74	6.05	10.56	14.11
0.67	1.95	1.14	1.14	1.00	1.18	1.04	1.02	0.92	1.06	0.95
0.57	1.03	0.85	0.89	0.70	0.93	0.85	0.79	0.73	0.80	0.75
19.35	23.53	26.28	26.09	32.17	10.89	13.85	12.85	18.76	17.67	19.40
0.26	1.02	15.90	8.89	13.35	4.58	8.53	9.63	17.98	5.11	4.54
4.15	10.75	18.30	25.37	7.37	27.02	28.64	27.30	40.07	24.66	24.56
91.46	17.93	62.74	58.83	35.41	69.31	61.10	59.67	46.33	62.79	66.61
36.69	1.15	5.68	7.97	8.57	6.94	6.85	5.58	5.70	4.64	5.77

表 7－16 各县(市)、区规模以上工业企业综合能耗及产值能耗(2013)
Comprehensive Energy Consumption of Industrial Enterprises Above Designated Size by Region

指标	Indicators	全市 Toal	市区 Urban District
综合能耗(吨标准煤)	**Final Energy Consumption(Ton of SCE)**	**32735148**	**22679797**
黑色金属矿采选业	Ferrous Metals Mining and Dressing	9	9
非金属矿采选业	Non－metallic Mining industry	138	138
农副食品加工业	Farm and Sideline Products Processing	85643	43210
食品制造业	Food Manufacturing	95798	131964
酒、饮料和精制茶制造业	Wine, Beverages and Refined Tea Manufacturing	55586	42408
烟草制品业	Tobacco Manufacturing	11830	11830
纺织业	Textile Industry	667350	389324
纺织服装、服饰业	Clothing, Apparel Industry	113980	73193
皮革、毛皮、羽毛及其制品和制鞋业	Leather, Fur, Feather and Its Products and Footwear Industry	5843	3449
木材加工及木、竹、藤、棕、草制品业	Timber Processing,Bamboo,Rattan,Cane Palm,and Straw Products	8453	4637
家具制造业	Furniture Manufacturing	23333	14932
造纸及纸制品业	Paper－making and Paper Products Manufacturing	821736	720897
印刷和记录媒介复制业	Printing and Record Duplicating	15258.4	10773.22
文教、工美、体育和娱乐用品制造业	Culture, Art, Sports and Recreation Supplies Manufacturing	59348	28985
石油加工、炼焦和核燃料加工业	Petroleum Processing. Coking & Nuclear Fuel Processing	6505415	6504304
化学原料和化学制品制造业	Raw Chemical Materials and Chemical Products	2923232	2768679
医药制造业	Medicines Manufacturing	31506	20946
化学纤维制造业	Chemical Fiber Manufacturing	287342	111227
橡胶和塑料制品业	Rubber and Plastic Products Industry	186720	85693
非金属矿物制品业	Nonmetal Mineral Products	385786	161874
黑色金属冶炼和压延加工业	Smelting and Pressing of Ferrous Metals	3033173	2836273
有色金属冶炼和压延加工业	Smelting and Pressing of Nonferrous Metals	236522	121767
金属制品业	Metal Products Manufacturing	194318	115954
通用设备制造业	General Purpose Equipment Manufacturing	221269	115457
专用设备制造业	Special Purpose Equipment Manufacturing	97800	61793
汽车制造业	Automobile Manufacturing	218597	141348
铁路、船舶、航空航天和其他运输设备制造业	Railroad, Marine, Aviation and Other Transport Equipment Manufacturing	52007	25356
电气机械和器材制造业	Electric Equipment and Machinery Manufacturing	294832	86495
计算机、通信和其他电子设备制造业	Computer, Communications and Other Electronic Equipment Manufacturing	130753	105915
仪器仪表制造业	Instrument Manufacturing	29256	8183
其他制造业	Other Manufacturing	19591	5034
废弃资源综合利用业	Waste Comprehensive Utilization of Resources Industry	5201	4530
金属制品、机械和设备修理业	Metal Products, Machinery and Equipment Repair Industry	1249	25
电力、热力的生产和供应业	Production and Supply Electric Power and Thermal Power	15896697	8028861
燃气生产和供应业	Production and Supply Gas	5705	5534
水的生产和供应业	Production and Supply Tap Water	1387	7568

各区 by Districts						余姚 Yuyao	慈溪 Cixi	奉化 Fenghua	象山 Xiangshan	宁海 Ninghai
海曙 Haishu	江东 Jiangdong	江北 Jiangbei	北仑 Beilun	镇海 Zhenhai	鄞州 Yinzhou					
91866	**25629**	**158942**	**11707527**	**9451029**	**1155505**	**1045811**	**938001**	**207891**	**2785903**	**5077745**
			9							
					138					
	1026	458	34461	64	7158	7447	12163	4867	17185	772
249		2612	4089	3526	2721	71010	1222	3608	4320	2443
1403		2	31685	1846	7471	764		7007	236	5171
	11830									
211		5030	248067	53567	80543	94058	90125	5143	82252	6447
1383	712	1081	24723	1000	43600	780	1985	18111	12782	7109
	182		769	856	16423	290	531	247		1326
				29	4608	654	650	2513		
	257	858	2551	109	10857	5081	1353	189	752	1026
		1461	387359	10435	321188	9840	43989	7489	15193	24328
354	29	265	2501	81	7543	2721	642	923		199
	8	3011	10778	1567	13562	3585	9629	855	634	15660
			167816	6335658	830			1049	61	
		3237	1512222	1225996	25056	45593	91764	5963	3099	8133
56		174	2959	13401	4003	653	5126	2333	1307	1142
			41065	69376	787	17212	155378	788	2719	17
445	130	6064	40763	13693	23411	47470	30830	6922	3153	12652
		11210	39388	74642	36635	139556	12890	6131	25568	39767
2	498	13630	2656419	42365	117358	76842	63214	44072	7805	4967
99	973	54888	14879	27636	21395	30472	61909	8521	611	13242
221	148	7311	32418	33796	41549	28528	25720	9497	1965	12654
119	240	4853	20148	53306	35418	24024	48703	19173	3372	10541
164	466	1821	36701	7660	14626	18782	5326	488	4698	6713
454	112	21309	60110	4462	53879	7459	32466	4152	15594	17578
	355		20487	2074	2172	1157	9873	11603	3468	551
1293	237	9417	16912	9259	40466	54584	113903	11230	6530	22091
899	3805	5963	48918	5726	35344	8542	11769	2494	357	1675
34		2088	604	169	4284	13755	4910	1258		1150
		1379		535	3065	2176	8682	3266		433
			1235	3112	183		652		19	
	20			5				77	1145	1
83965			6242474	1453120	193820	331317	89244	17790	2569953	4859532
513			5018		2	9	161			
	4603	817		1958	190	1429	3191	135	1123	427

表 7—16 续表 Continued

指标	Indicators	全市 Toal	市区 Urban District
产值能耗(吨标煤/万元)	**Energy Consumption of Output Value(Ton of SCE/10000 yuan)**	**0.2558**	**0.2673**
黑色金属矿采选业	Ferrous Metals Mining and Dressing		
非金属框采选业	Non—metallic Mining Industry	0.0613	0.0613
农副食品加工业	Farm and Sideline Products Processing	0.0552	0.0654
食品制造业	Food Manufacturing	0.1023	0.0601
酒、饮料和精制茶制造业	Wine, Beverages and Refined Tea Manufacturing	0.1760	0.2371
烟草制品业	Tobacco Manufacturing	0.0093	0.0093
纺织业	Textile Industry	0.1898	0.1688
纺织服装、服饰业	Clothing, Apparel Industry	0.0190	0.0162
皮革、毛皮、羽毛及其制品和制鞋业	Leather, Fur, Feather and Its Products and Footwear Industry	0.0445	0.0471
木材加工及木、竹、藤、棕、草制品业	Timber Processing,Bamboo,Rattan,Cane Palm,and Straw Products	0.0686	0.0621
家具制造业	Furniture Manufacturing	0.0287	0.0305
造纸及纸制品业	Paper—making and Paper Products Manufacturing	0.4870	0.6323
印刷和记录媒介复制业	Printing and Record Duplicating	0.0235	0.0197
文教、工美、体育和娱乐用品制造业	Culture, Art, Sports and Recreation Supplies Manufacturing	0.0233	0.0217
石油加工、炼焦和核燃料加工业	Petroleum Processing. Coking & Nuclear Fuel Processing	0.4035	0.4039
化学原料和化学制品制造业	Raw Chemical Materials and Chemical Products	0.2079	0.2201
医药制造业	Medicines Manufacturing	0.0585	0.0534
化学纤维制造业	Chemical Fiber Manufacturing	0.1679	0.4775
橡胶和塑料制品业	Rubber and Plastic Products Industry	0.0534	0.0528
非金属矿物制品业	Nonmetal Mineral Products	0.1871	0.1425
黑色金属冶炼和压延加工业	Smelting and Pressing of Ferrous Metals	0.5421	0.7218
有色金属冶炼和压延加工业	Smelting and Pressing of Nonferrous Metals	0.0420	0.0386
金属制品业	Metal Products Manufacturing	0.0537	0.0533
通用设备制造业	General Purpose Equipment Manufacturing	0.0305	0.0288
专用设备制造业	Special Purpose Equipment Manufacturing	0.0259	0.0251
汽车制造业	Automobile Manufacturing	0.0304	0.0355
铁路、船舶、航空航天和其他运输设备制造业	Railroad, Marine, Aviation and Other Transport Equipment Manufacturing	0.0322	0.0501
电气机械和器材制造业	Electric Equipment and Machinery Manufacturing	0.0197	0.0157
计算机、通信和其他电子设备制造业	Computer, Communications and Other Electronic Equipment Manufacturing	0.0170	0.0175
仪器仪表制造业	Instrument Manufacturing	0.0167	0.0111
其他制造业	Other Manufacturing	0.0409	0.0279
废弃资源综合利用业	Waste Comprehensive Utilization of Resources Industry	0.0067	0.0060
金属制品、机械和设备修理业	Metal Products, Machinery and Equipment Repair Industry	0.0209	0.0020
电力、热力的生产和供应业	Production and Supply Electric Power and Thermal Power	1.7545	1.3953
燃气生产和供应业	Production and Supply Gas	0.0088	0.0089
水的生产和供应业	Production and Supply Tap Water	0.0568	0.0539

各区 by Districts						余姚 Yuyao	慈溪 Cixi	奉化 Fenghua	象山 Xiangshan	宁海 Ninghai
海曙 Haishu	江东 Jiangdong	江北 Jiangbei	北仑 Beilun	镇海 Zhenhai	鄞州 Yinzhou					
0.0257	**0.0131**	**0.0379**	**0.4050**	**0.3957**	**0.0549**	**0.0865**	**0.0551**	**0.0577**	**0.5915**	**0.8975**
					0.0613					
	0.2618	0.0143	0.0832	0.0563	0.0369	0.0231	0.0714	0.0649	0.0555	0.0558
0.0125		0.0592	0.0602	0.0948	0.0540	0.1359	0.0624	0.0960	0.0582	0.0391
0.1423		0.0007	0.2647	2.9013	0.1657	0.0126		0.1769	0.0176	0.2234
	0.0093									
0.0035		0.0336	0.3494	0.0964	0.0980	0.2438	0.1653	0.1139	0.5663	0.0736
0.0179	0.0092	0.0153	0.0198	0.0142	0.0150	0.0209	0.0167	0.0373	0.0170	0.0766
	0.1557		0.0760	0.0442	0.0386	0.0236	0.0279	0.0150		0.1297
				0.0183	0.0631	0.0287	0.0882	0.1355		
	0.1089	0.0171	0.0268	0.0183	0.0331	0.0221	0.0314	0.0132	0.0446	0.0608
		0.2126	0.7113	0.2413	0.5916	0.0799	0.1777	0.1631	0.3928	0.2648
0.0646	0.0143	0.0288	0.0453	0.0183	0.0161	0.0469	0.0271	0.0498		0.0816
	0.0166	0.0311	0.0319	0.0309	0.0161	0.0326	0.0320	0.0174	0.0379	0.0212
			0.0648	0.4691	0.0784			0.1114	0.0092	
		0.0268	0.2062	0.2952	0.0269	0.0921	0.1195	0.0710	0.0604	0.0929
0.0081		0.0102	0.0818	0.1336	0.0179	0.0362	0.0968	0.0512	0.1201	0.0590
			0.5717	0.4987	0.0358	0.0994	0.1256	0.0369	0.0605	0.0084
0.0722	0.0226	0.0546	0.1399	0.0817	0.0229	0.0617	0.0539	0.0489	0.0373	0.0413
		0.0570	0.1348	0.4647	0.0753	0.3607	0.0814	0.1229	0.1430	0.2601
0.0053	0.0578	0.2743	0.9805	0.1077	0.1677	0.1271	0.1037	0.1676	0.0552	0.1051
0.0451	0.0246	0.0323	0.1317	0.0555	0.0313	0.0335	0.0518	0.0502	0.0350	0.0693
0.0497	0.0045	0.0555	0.0458	0.1296	0.0406	0.0623	0.0456	0.0595	0.0561	0.0561
0.0103	0.0078	0.0233	0.0237	0.0515	0.0199	0.0340	0.0397	0.0375	0.0089	0.0258
0.0257	0.0124	0.0167	0.0276	0.0203	0.0255	0.0287	0.0249	0.0157	0.0236	0.0315
0.0196	0.0205	0.0622	0.0351	0.0376	0.0326	0.0305	0.0196	0.0351	0.0222	0.0353
	0.0414		0.0677	0.0320	0.0227	0.0267	0.0231	0.0289	0.0161	0.0236
0.0173	0.0140	0.0229	0.0141	0.0186	0.0139	0.0198	0.0227	0.0371	0.0121	0.0244
0.0142	0.0129	0.0412	0.0132	0.0191	0.0253	0.0105	0.0222	0.0115	0.0210	0.0207
0.0045		0.0132	0.0098	0.0188	0.0093	0.0287	0.0106	0.0432		0.0288
		0.0483		0.0132	0.0290	0.0424	0.0446	0.1039		0.0204
			0.2134	0.0042	0.0214		0.0491		0.0040	
	0.0126			0.0005				0.0201	0.0322	0.0002
0.0277			4.0509	2.8628	0.2995	0.5372	0.1499	0.1100	3.8390	3.8467
0.0031			0.0110		0.0004	0.0012	0.0091			
	0.0410	0.1053		0.1612	0.0232	0.0532	0.0850	0.0213	0.0992	0.0196

表7—17 各县(市)、区千吨以上工业综合能源消费量(2013)
Comprehensive Energy Consumption of Industrial Enterprises Above One Thousand Tons

指标	Indicators	全市 Toal	市区 Urban District
综合能源消费量总计(吨标准煤)	**Final energycomprehensive consumption per million (Tons of standard coal)**	**31088864**	**21759959**
黑色金属矿采选业	Ferrous Metals Mining and Dressing		
农副食品加工业	Farm and Sideline ProductsProcessing	57139	37043
食品制造业	Food Manufacturing	84566	8026
酒、饮料和精制茶制造业	Wine, Beverages and Refined TeaManufacturing	52556	40523
烟草制品业	Tobacco Manufacturing	11830	11830
纺织业	Textile Industry	594516	359411
纺织服装、服饰业	Clothing, Apparel Industry	50637	35700
皮革、毛皮、羽毛及其制品和制鞋业	Leather, Fur, Feather and ItsProducts and Footwear Industry	924	
木材加工及木、竹、藤、棕、草制品业	TimberProcessing,Bamboo,Rattan,Cane Palm, and StrawProducts	3199	519
家具制造业	Furniture Manufacturing	7473	7473
造纸及纸制品业	Paper—making and Paper ProductsManufacturing	793590	714763
印刷和记录媒介复制业	Printing and Record Duplicating	4331	3288
文教、工美、体育和娱乐用品制造业	Culture, Art, Sports and RecreationSupplies Manufacturing	21944	10797
石油加工、炼焦和核燃料加工业	Petroleum Processing. Coking &Nuclear Fuel Processing	6503670	6502621
化学原料和化学制品制造业	RawChemical Materials and Chemical Products	2577621	2436576
医药制造业	Medicines Manufacturing	23854	16620
化学纤维制造业	Chemical Fiber Manufacturing	260474	110441
橡胶和塑料制品业	Rubber and Plastic ProductsIndustry	73786	46302
非金属矿物制品业	Nonmetal Mineral Products	328348	129557
黑色金属冶炼和压延加工业	Smelting and Pressing of Ferrous Metals	2968423	2808426
有色金属冶炼和压延加工业	Smeltingand Pressing of Nonferrous Metals	181659	104828
金属制品业	Metal Products Manufacturing	108575	71011
通用设备制造业	General Purpose EquipmentManufacturing	70014	36746
专用设备制造业	Special Purpose EquipmentManufacturing	26343	22820
汽车制造业	Automobile Manufacturing	134348	87608
铁路、船舶、航空航天和其他运输设备制造业	Railroad,Marine, Aviation and Other Transport EquipmentManufacturing	32856	18769
电气机械和器材制造业	Electric Equipment and MachineryManufacturing	123531	35620
计算机、通信和其他电子设备制造业	Computer, Communications and OtherElectronic Equipment Manufacturing	70080	63400
仪器仪表制造业	Instrument Manufacturing	5541	837
其他制造业	Other Manufacturing	9500	3781
废弃资源综合利用业	Waste Comprehensive Utilization ofResources Industry	1235	1235
金属制品、机械和设备修理业	Metal Products, Machinery andEquipment Repair Industry	1145	
电力、热力的生产和供应业	Productionand Supply Electric Power and Thermal Power	15896591	8028785
燃气生产和供应业	Production and Supply Gas		
水的生产和供应业	Production and Supply Tap Water	8569	4603

各区 by Districts						余姚 Yuyao	慈溪 Cixi	奉化 Fenghua	象山 Xiangshan	宁海 Ninghai
海曙 Haishu	江东 Jiangdong	江北 Jiangbei	北仑 Beilun	镇海 Zhenhai	鄞州 Yinzhou					
85029	**19782**	**103073**	**11539917**	**9060040**	**876606**	**838531**	**669152**	**119412**	**2712671**	**4989140**
	1026		33229		2789	4937	7608	4261	3290	
		1865	3689	2473		70893	894		3158	1594
			31664	1846	7014			7007		5026
	11830									
		1155	241945	47546	67665	87156	73203	2740	67889	4118
			20622		15078			2173	5989	6774
										924
					519		591	2089		
					7473					
			385319	10340	319104	5202	33670	4445	15013	20496
			1765		1522	1043				
			5127		5669		4373			6775
			167080	6335541				1049		
		1477	1491268	924606	17303	42092	89009	2675	2082	5186
			1187	12754	2679		5126	2108		
			41065	69376		15449	132462		2122	
		2216	26723	5853	10586	13636	10943	1056	1186	664
		4952	32188	68500	23918	131915	3549	3822	20863	38643
		13002	2652825	40651	95940	66080	53376	30806	5845	3890
		54620	8703	22763	17642	26262	38586	5529		6454
		4902	22065	24943	19100	12742	14622	5969		4231
			1572	29423	5751	7592	15416	7658		2602
			20146	2673		2408			1115	
		11665	42199	2198	31546	1498	23387	1347	10124	10385
			17748	276	745		3656	10430		
1094		3484	7271	2284	16084	9400	60298	4343	2896	10973
	2323	2381	40823	2876	11412	2983	2825			872
					837	4704				
		1354			2427		3602	2117		
			1235							
									1145	
83935			6242456	1453119	193794	331317	89214	17790	2569953	4859532
	4603					1222	2744			

表 7—18 各县(市)、区千吨以上工业万元产值综合能耗(2013)
Comprehensive Energy Consumption of Industrial Enterprises Above One Thousand Tons

指标	Indicators	全市 Toal	市区 Urban District
万元产值综合能耗总计(吨标准煤)	**Final energycomprehensive consumption per million (Tons of standard coal)**	**0.3996**	**0.3761**
黑色金属矿采选业	Ferrous Metals Mining and Dressing	0.0000	
农副食品加工业	Farm and Sideline ProductsProcessing	0.0695	0.0961
食品制造业	Food Manufacturing	0.1229	0.0828
酒、饮料和精制茶制造业	Wine, Beverages and Refined TeaManufacturing	0.2689	0.2991
烟草制品业	Tobacco Manufacturing	0.0093	0.0093
纺织业	Textile Industry	0.2796	0.2545
纺织服装、服饰业	Clothing, Apparel Industry	0.0229	0.0183
皮革、毛皮、羽毛及其制品和制鞋业	Leather, Fur, Feather and ItsProducts and Footwear Industry	0.1178	
木材加工及木、竹、藤、棕、草制品业	TimberProcessing,Bamboo,Rattan,Cane Palm,and StrawProducts	0.2088	0.0763
家具制造业	Furniture Manufacturing	0.0578	0.0578
造纸及纸制品业	Paper—making and Paper ProductsManufacturing	0.5970	0.6802
印刷和记录媒介复制业	Printing and Record Duplicating	0.0260	0.0218
文教、工美、体育和娱乐用品制造业	Culture, Art, Sports and RecreationSupplies Manufacturing	0.0284	0.0604
石油加工、炼焦和核燃料加工业	Petroleum Processing. Coking &Nuclear Fuel Processing	0.4062	0.4064
化学原料和化学制品制造业	RawChemical Materials and Chemical Products	0.2139	0.2239
医药制造业	Medicines Manufacturing	0.1282	0.1839
化学纤维制造业	Chemical Fiber Manufacturing	0.1784	0.5236
橡胶和塑料制品业	Rubber and Plastic ProductsIndustry	0.0693	0.0651
非金属矿物制品业	Nonmetal Mineral Products	0.3225	0.2582
黑色金属冶炼和压延加工业	Smelting and Pressing of Ferrous Metals	0.6443	0.8244
有色金属冶炼和压延加工业	Smeltingand Pressing of Nonferrous Metals	0.0423	0.0383
金属制品业	Metal Products Manufacturing	0.0939	0.0819
通用设备制造业	General Purpose EquipmentManufacturing	0.0667	0.0729
专用设备制造业	Special Purpose EquipmentManufacturing	0.0279	0.0272
汽车制造业	Automobile Manufacturing	0.0341	0.0458
铁路、船舶、航空航天和其他运输设备制造业	Railroad,Marine, Aviation and Other Transport EquipmentManufacturing	0.0447	0.0652
电气机械和器材制造业	Electric Equipment and MachineryManufacturing	0.0234	0.0176
计算机、通信和其他电子设备制造业	Computer, Communications and OtherElectronic Equipment Manufacturing	0.0150	0.0156
仪器仪表制造业	Instrument Manufacturing	0.0216	0.0049
其他制造业	Other Manufacturing	0.0559	0.0479
废弃资源综合利用业	Waste Comprehensive Utilization ofResources Industry	0.2134	0.2134
金属制品、机械和设备修理业	Metal Products, Machinery andEquipment Repair Industry	0.0322	
电力、热力的生产和供应业	Productionand Supply Electric Power and Thermal Power	1.7718	1.4153
燃气生产和供应业	Production and Supply Gas		
水的生产和供应业	Production and Supply Tap Water	0.0551	0.0410

各区 by Districts						余姚 Yuyao	慈溪 Cixi	奉化 Fenghua	象山 Xiangshan	宁海 Ninghai
海曙 Haishu	江东 Jiangdong	江北 Jiangbei	北仑 Beilun	镇海 Zhenhai	鄞州 Yinzhou					
0.0277	**0.0125**	**0.0485**	**0.4963**	**0.4558**	**0.1175**	**0.1653**	**0.0778**	**0.0916**	**1.3649**	**1.6707**
	0.2618		0.0907		0.1863	0.0210	0.0968	0.0998	0.0411	
		0.1519	0.0605	0.1046		0.1404	0.1955		0.0615	0.0524
			0.2959	2.9013	0.2520			0.1769		0.2463
	0.0093									
		0.1322	0.3738	0.0941	0.2737	0.3579	0.2314	0.1468	0.6933	0.1085
			0.0185		0.0180			0.0184	0.0902	0.0900
										0.1178
					0.0763		0.4962	0.2853		
					0.0578					
			0.7625	0.3023	0.6242	0.1007	0.2616	0.3070	0.5004	0.3815
			0.2229		0.0107	0.0661				
			0.0554		0.0659		0.0354			0.0144
			0.0667	0.4695				0.1114		
		0.1608	0.2075	0.2785	0.0517	0.1023	0.1337	0.0693	0.0670	0.2476
			0.2158	0.1852	0.1672		0.0968	0.0494		
			0.5717	0.4987		0.0954	0.1266		0.0518	
		0.0465	0.2130	0.1129	0.0225	0.1100	0.0650	0.0903	0.0380	0.0365
		0.1748	0.1635	0.7763	0.1269	0.5446	0.2229	0.3302	0.1550	0.3452
		0.2871	1.0004	0.1497	0.1846	0.1474	0.1059	0.1649	0.1440	0.1844
		0.0323	0.1798	0.0557	0.0328	0.0348	0.0560	0.0817		0.1440
		0.1535	0.0515	0.2046	0.0671	0.2263	0.0761	0.3052		0.1927
			0.0548	0.0749	0.0696	0.0604	0.0630	0.0843		0.0307
			0.0281	0.0222		0.0259			0.0881	
		0.0892	0.0430	0.0588	0.0412	0.1076	0.0188	0.0282	0.0222	0.0402
			0.0691	0.0173	0.0495		0.0449	0.0286		
0.0172		0.0637	0.0209	0.0157	0.0140	0.0231	0.0270	0.7182	0.0138	0.0270
	0.0117	0.0577	0.0120	0.0186	0.0496	0.0064	0.0279			0.0224
					0.0049	0.0546				
		0.0577			0.0438		0.0412	0.5836		
			0.2134							
									0.0322	
0.0279			4.0896	3.0258	0.3057	0.5372	0.1517	0.1100	3.8390	3.8467
	0.0410					0.1276	0.0819			

表 7－19 按工业行业分组的主要能源消费量(2013)
Comprehensive Energy Consumption by Industrial Sector

指标	Indicators	能源合计 吨标准煤 Total Ton of SCE	原煤 Raw Coal	焦炭 Coke
按工业行业分	**Grouped bySector**	**91990904**	**42345720**	**1748747**
黑色金属矿采选业	Ferrous MetalsMining and Dressing	19		
农副食品加工业	Farm and Sideline Products Processing	88089	34904	
食品制造业	Food Manufacturing	97206	17313	
酒、饮料和精制茶制造业	Wine, Beverages and Refined Tea Manufacturing	55933	16661	
烟草制品业	Tobacco Manufacturing	12376		
纺织业	Textile Industry	686870	221062	
纺织服装、服饰业	Clothing, Apparel Industry	121474	39236	3
皮革、毛皮、羽毛及其制品和制鞋业	Leather, Fur, Feather and Its Products and Footwear Industry	6228	3351	
木材加工及木、竹、藤、棕、草制品业	TimberProcessing,Bamboo,Rattan,Cane Palm, and Straw Products	8799	6556	
家具制造业	Furniture Manufacturing	25355	2884	146
造纸及纸制品业	Paper－making and Paper Products Manufacturing	976062	1030048	
印刷和记录媒介复制业	Printing and RecordDuplicating	16900	2360	30
文教、工美、体育和娱乐用品制造业	Culture, Art, Sports and Recreation Supplies Manufacturing	64726	8428	225
石油加工、炼焦和核燃料加工业	Petroleum Processing. Coking & Nuclear Fuel Processing	49902912	2057671	
化学原料和化学制品制造业	RawChemical Materials and Chemical Products	2961407	1072707	
医药制造业	Medicines Manufacturing	33178	6266	
化学纤维制造业	Chemical Fiber Manufacturing	289067	50582	
橡胶和塑料制品业	Rubber and Plastic Products Industry	193975	21649	
非金属矿物制品业	Nonmetal MineralProducts	407625	213204	823
黑色金属冶炼和压延加工业	Smelting andPressing of Ferrous Metals	5630684	915439	1739623
有色金属冶炼和压延加工业	Smeltingand Pressing of Nonferrous Metals	241143	44512	1462
金属制品业	Metal Products Manufacturing	204364	27201	424
通用设备制造业	General Purpose Equipment Manufacturing	235826	9256	1109
专用设备制造业	Special Purpose Equipment Manufacturing	105253	2871	153
汽车制造业	Automobile Manufacturing	227495	8773	729
铁路、船舶、航空航天和其他运输设备制造业	Railroad, Marine, Aviation and Other Transport Equipment Manufacturing	65357	3404	199
电气机械和器材制造业	Electric Equipment and Machinery Manufacturing	323156	19931	3812
计算机、通信和其他电子设备制造业	Computer, Communications andOther Electronic Equipment Manufacturing	145905	3674	
仪器仪表制造业	Instrument Manufacturing	32490	554	3
其他制造业	Other Manufacturing	21526	794	
废弃资源综合利用业	Waste Comprehensive Utilization of Resources Industry	5604	132	
金属制品、机械和设备修理业	Metal Products, Machinery and Equipment Repair Industry	1476		6
电力、热力的生产和供应业	Productionand Supply Electric Power and Thermal Power	28782279	36504299	
燃气生产和供应业	Production and SupplyGas	5858		
水的生产和供应业	Production and SupplyTap Water	14148		

单位：吨(ton)

原油 Crude Oil	汽油 Gasoline	煤油 Kerosene	柴油 Diesel Oil	燃料油 Fuel Oil	液化石油气 LPG	其他油制品 Other Petroleum Products	热力 百万千焦 Heat million kilo—joule	电力 万千瓦时 Electricity 10000 kwh
26887536	**63521**	**7459**	**140069**	**296805**	**370088**	**3047581**	**48081835**	**3540718**
	6		1					7
	514		1551	1689	94		809156	18855
	464		777		75		355602	22274
	160		277		24		919549	9108
	44		2160				152033	2702
49	1899		2217	15	1087	51	7553250	145250
	4811	6	4429		40	8	946474	36114
	188		164		5	1	16037	2247
	178	54	317					2320
	821		1033		2	5	5289	13079
	820	13	4558	1057	18		1462271	149716
	828	4	685		183		4993	8546
	1831	99	1841	161	862	272	119655	34227
26887478	64		3567	239395	324258	2951265	1117573	278511
	3411	72	7316	38415	23735	37354	27544895	610565
	378		410	56	18		481784	8136
	278		449		3	106	3682464	87000
	3417	22	3703	312	505	643	332221	106822
	1161	18	35238	4061	1247	48632	246900	90905
	1249	30	3616	72	6365	32	398644	361562
	1075	149	5061	7432	1856	287	86490	112987
	3704	396	7353	465	1901	593	791575	96638
3	8442	5771	9494	404	986	3803	18364	144185
	5312	72	5871	389	262	1271	29715	54845
2	4361	75	6248	1275	98	551	285462	109191
	812	177	8110	709	1451	879	113215	28877
4	9672	297	12909	123	2324	1435	128063	205633
	3298	24	3004	22	471	328	299306	95761
	1284	180	1389	25	27	64		22093
	609		1481	77	1996		60326	9842
	232		1908		193			1610
	127	1	296					693
	1681		2438	649	3		120529	654766
	144		99					4445
	247		42		1			11160

表 7－20 各县(市)、区规模以上工业企业等价综合能源消费量(2013)
Equivalent Comprehensive Energy Consumption of Industrial Enterprises Above Designated Size by Region

指标	Indicators	全市 Toal	市区 Urban District	海曙 Haishu
综合能源消费量总计(吨标准煤)	**Final energycomprehensive consumption per million (Tons of standard coal)**	**23802452**	**18757096**	**229750**
黑色金属矿采选业	Ferrous Metals Mining and Dressing	33	33	
非金属矿业采选业	Non－Metallic Mining Industry	226	226	
农副食品加工业	Farm and Sideline ProductsProcessing	124499	58073	
食品制造业	Food Manufacturing	140218	20283	368
酒、饮料和精制茶制造业	Wine, Beverages and Refined TeaManufacturing	73520	56086	1573
烟草制品业	Tobacco Manufacturing	17593	17593	
纺织业	Textile Industry	953961	540157	453
纺织服装、服饰业	Clothing, Apparel Industry	191210	128567	2315
皮革、毛皮、羽毛及其制品和制鞋业	Leather, Fur, Feather and ItsProducts and Footwear Industry	10567	6223	
木材加工及木、竹、藤、棕、草制品业	TimberProcessing, Bamboo, Rattan, Cane Palm, and StrawProducts	13279	7497	
家具制造业	Furniture Manufacturing	50610	32765	
造纸及纸制品业	Paper－making and Paper ProductsManufacturing	895881	760778	
印刷和记录媒介复制业	Printing and Record Duplicating	33403	24607	619
文教、工美、体育和娱乐用品制造业	Culture, Art, Sports and RecreationSupplies Manufacturing	130818	61461	
石油加工、炼焦和核燃料加工业	Petroleum Processing. Coking &Nuclear Fuel Processing	6493469	6492273	
化学原料和化学制品制造业	RawChemical Materials and Chemical Products	4113472	3875862	
医药制造业	Medicines Manufacturing	48889	30861	113
化学纤维制造业	Chemical Fiber Manufacturing	457064	129606	
橡胶和塑料制品业	Rubber and Plastic ProductsIndustry	400249	173764	1163
非金属矿物制品业	Nonmetal Mineral Products	560944	222392	
黑色金属冶炼和压延加工业	Smelting and Pressing of Ferrous Metals	3560971	3176640	6
有色金属冶炼和压延加工业	Smeltingand Pressing of Nonferrous Metals	459321	242869	255
金属制品业	Metal Products Manufacturing	390971	231317	581
通用设备制造业	General Purpose EquipmentManufacturing	514248	269831	306
专用设备制造业	Special Purpose EquipmentManufacturing	211159	127365	328
汽车制造业	Automobile Manufacturing	438342	269693	1171
铁路、船舶、航空航天和其他运输设备制造业	Railroad, Marine, Aviation and Other Transport EquipmentManufacturing	121119	52244	
电气机械和器材制造业	Electric Equipment and MachineryManufacturing	720234	207838	3336
计算机、通信和其他电子设备制造业	Computer, Communications and OtherElectronic Equipment Manufacturing	330818	266094	2230
仪器仪表制造业	Instrument Manufacturing	75152	20664	79
其他制造业	Other Manufacturing	40532	12424	
废弃资源综合利用业	Waste Comprehensive Utilization ofResources Industry	8712	7029	
金属制品、机械和设备修理业	Metal Products, Machinery andEquipment Repair Industry	2815	79	
电力、热力的生产和供应业	Productionand Supply Electric Power and Thermal Power	2168016	1200476	213423
燃气生产和供应业	Production and Supply Gas	14442	14166	1434
水的生产和供应业	Production and Supply Tap Water	35698	19263	

各区 by Districts					余姚 Yuyao	慈溪 Cixi	奉化 Fenghua	象山 Xiangshan	宁海 Ninghai
江东 Jiangdong	江北 Jiangbei	北仑 Beilun	镇海 Zhenhai	鄞州 Yinzhou					
48368	**317992**	**7467220**	**8905241**	**1703529**	**1432804**	**1804310**	**398649**	**579274**	**830319**
		33							
				226					
1199	1074	43612	169	11875	12492	19770	7091	25845	1227
	3846	5730	6163	4176	104365	2156	4595	5623	3197
	6	41850	2417	10241	1447		9193	298	6495
17593									
	11841	326203	78785	119860	133756	154323	8860	100022	16843
1281	2785	37769	2349	80314	1432	4619	24895	22952	8746
453		1618	1578	2574	539	1109	640		2057
			88	7409	1595	1051	3136		
311	2306	5870	276	23386	11006	3616	509	1258	1456
	1955	403168	14410	340721	13502	59282	9735	20691	31893
68	714	4124	225	18858	4875	1951	1680		291
19	6029	23867	3563	27834	8796	21601	2285	1655	35020
		176862	6314455	957			1126	71	
	6028	2185571	1632156	47920	75720	135260	8988	5023	12618
	555	4790	18127	6605	1689	8433	4106	1906	1894
		46313	81743	1550	33619	284750	2051	6994	44
334	13243	77334	26920	51778	109212	65182	16551	7567	27974
	16571	71465	86516	47840	181963	20895	9588	56382	69726
1051	21288	2827089	104376	207236	159995	119774	83222	13146	8195
1336	109954	27458	48697	50853	60140	119376	17297	1147	18491
424	16510	67890	58581	85989	54885	56672	21143	3961	22994
602	11352	47691	120600	85888	56801	114287	44988	6609	21731
957	4883	75989	14370	30087	40754	15372	1257	9877	16534
256	38492	112792	9360	104843	16441	67860	9669	34722	39957
740		42723	3492	4625	2385	24640	34083	7008	759
576	21855	40663	22999	96517	132347	292132	21280	15152	51485
9555	15504	129702	13939	82424	21002	32459	6607	879	3777
	5641	1217	431	10700	34211	14995	3348		1934
	3456		1022	7804	5422	17133	4682		871
		1497	5067	464		1634		49	
65			14				202	2531	4
		623604	227306	131410	148635	135392	35407	225099	423007
		12726		6	50	226			
11548	2105		5050	561	3731	8362	437	2807	1098

表 7－21 全市规模以上工业企业能源购、消、存情况(2013)
Purchases, Sales and Inventory of Energy of Industrial Enterprises Above the Set Scale

指标	单位	Indicators	Unit	年初库存 Stock (Year－head)	购进量 Purchases 实物量 Material Amount	购进量 Purchases 金额(千元) Value (1000 yuan)	消费量合计 Consumption
原煤	吨	Raw Coal	ton	1974142	41815592	25288974	42345720
洗精煤	吨	Clenedcoal	ton	134867	1450726	2090330	1457108
煤制品	吨	Coal Products	ton	2227	342319	208213	340293
焦炭	吨	Coke	ton	59420	655069	1330352	1748747
天然气(气态)	万立方米	Natural Gas (Gas)	10000 Cubic Meters		150710	4755213	150710
液化天然气(液态)	吨	Liquefied Natural Gas (Liquid)	ton	285	5237	34482	5390
原油	吨	Crude Oil	ton	770060	26993725	145958611	26887536
汽油	吨	Gasoline	ton	726	62559	536081	63521
煤油	吨	Kerosene	ton	902	7458	58559	7459
柴油	吨	Diesel Oil	ton	5269	135539	1046475	140069
燃料油	吨	Fuel Oil	ton	9111	90103	347114	296805
液化石油气	吨	Liquefied Petroleum Gas	ton	1250	46265	314543	370088
炼厂干气	吨	Refinery Dry Gas	ton		1704	6979	1221334
石油焦	吨	Petroleum Coke	ton				585582
其他石油制品	吨	Other Petroleum Products	ton	28044	558410	1860551	3047581
热力	百万千焦	Heat	million kilo－joule		47655153	3095514	48081835
电力	万千瓦时	Electricity	10000 kwh		2629756	20049275	3540718
余热余压	百万千焦	Residual Heat and Pressure	million kilo－joule		104939	3419	9237512
能源合计	吨标准煤	Total	Ton of SCE				91990904

工业生产消费 Consumptiop of Industrial Production	非工业生产消费 Consumptiop of Non－Industrial Production	年末库存 Stock (Year－end)	能源转出量 Energy Producing	能源投入 Energy Input	火力发电 Generation of Electric Power by Thermal Power	供热 Heat Supply	炼油投入 Input of Oil Refining
42340558	5162	1524386		38280461	34708330	3520352	
1457108		128485		1361888			
340178	114	4263					
1748736	11	37221	1071662				
150344	366			116627	114158	2469	
5373	16	117		164	148	16	
26887482	54	862748		26887478			26887478
24579	38942	288	2796404				
7438	20	856	2089726				
109111	30959	4177	6865499	429	420	9	
296793	13	9701	831757	236905		13	236892
368169	1918	644	1062207	320119			320119
1221334		1	1221380	202323		2671	199652
585582			1173329	427794	330385	97409	
3047483	97	28250	8983182	213000			213000
47506487	575348		68420201				
3498230	42488		9434829				
9237512				2846901	2846901		
91804636	186268		57899811	74349747	27417745	2578977	43022245

表 7—22 全市及各县(市)全社会用电量(2013)
Total Electricity Consumption by Region

指标	Indicators	全市 Total	为上年(%) The Preceding Year=100(%)
总计	**Total**	**5593943**	**108.81**
全行业用电量	**Electricity Consumption for Non—Living Electricity**	**4932666**	**108.46**
农林牧渔业	Farming,Forestry,Animal Husbandry,Fishery	33422	116.36
＃排灌	Irrigation and Drainage	9238	113.48
①农业	Farming	8472	120.16
②林业	Forestry	421	108.72
③畜牧业	Animal Husbandary	4835	105.16
④渔业	Fishery	7144	127.32
⑤其他	Others	12550	113.29
工业	Industry	4149789	107.90
轻工业	Light Industry	1303187	104.87
重工业	Heavy Industry	2846603	109.35
建筑业	Construction	81823	103.42
交通运输、仓储和邮政业	Transportation,Storage and Post	85227	133.33
交通运输	Transportation	71865	137.75
仓储业	Warehousing Industry	11562	116.24
邮政	Post	1801	99.60
信息传输、计算机服务和软件业	Information Transmission,Computer Service and Software	29839	112.55
商业、住宿和饮食业	Trade,Hotel and Catering Trade	230736	107.55
金融、房地产、商务及居民服务业	Financial, Real Estate, Business and Resident Service	134362	119.00
公共事业及管理组织	Public Service and Management Organizations	187467	106.43
城乡居民生活用电量	**Electricity Consumption for Urban and Rural Residents**	**661277**	**111.49**
城市	Urban Residents	334887	111.02
乡村	Rural Residents	326389	111.97

单位:万千瓦时(10000 kwh)

市区 Urban District	#鄞州 Yinzhou	余姚 Yuyao	慈溪 Cixi	奉化 Fenghua	象山 Xiangshan	宁海 Ninghai
3081224	**765887**	**707855**	**1105005**	**261108**	**186261**	**252490**
2760838	**651812**	**625684**	**976156**	**219811**	**145227**	**204950**
11300	7046	4727	7073	2370	4651	3301
2468	1585	2304	916	734	2129	686
4663	2312	368	1385	838	740	477
147	66	26	47	90	24	87
821	408	1321	1319	418	460	495
1128	1012	562	2761	202	1158	1333
4540	3249	2450	1559	822	2269	909
2262718	534155	549954	869631	185471	106522	175492
531645	196009	205798	413650	44533	45673	61887
1731073	338146	344157	455980	140938	60849	113605
45273	15403	9431	16713	2762	4234	3409
68551	4474	8000	1460	5417	774	1024
56494	3310	7646	1102	5176	578	869
10922	719	161	185	184	61	49
1136	445	193	174	57	135	106
17638	4914	3065	3863	1852	1546	1875
142275	28649	24267	28657	10646	13889	11002
102403	27991	7937	15612	3323	2830	2257
110678	29182	18304	33146	7969	10780	6589
320387	**114076**	**82171**	**128849**	**41297**	**41034**	**47539**
220452	55987	24830	34036	17088	20495	17987
99935	58089	57341	94813	24209	20539	29552

表 7—23 历年全社会用电量 Total Electricity Consumption Over Years

年份 Year	总计 Total	比上年增长 Growth Rate over Preceding Year(%)	全行业用电 总计 Total	全行业用电 农业 Agriculture	全行业用电 工业 Industry
1978	70905				43704
1979	89023	25.6			56404
1980	106695	19.9			66886
1981	119606	12.1			72878
1982	129011	7.9			78879
1983	147338	14.2			91251
1984	164071	11.4			93618
1985	185167	12.9			98512
1986	223048	20.5			123033
1987	253457	13.6			140978
1988	279914	10.4			148756
1989	285460	2.0			218247
1990	314858	10.3	271855	16657	233766
1991	365090	16.0	315484	17682	273333
1992	421441	15.4	363939	18601	316558
1993	482578	14.5	416063	18680	359972
1994	552044	14.4	467366	20325	400080
1995	619447	12.2	517935	21262	439498
1996	670281	8.2	551953	22039	457688
1997	718416	7.2	595479	21339	496127
1998	799300	11.3	667837	20470	560624
1999	914936	14.5	778181	21063	664623
2000	1134811	24.0	983475	25777	840125
2001	1266535	11.6	1107317	30111	943788
2002	1520751	20.1	1333570	26115	1146566
2003	1890027	24.3	1651392	22305	1416625
2004	2189528	15.8	1967731	20410	1703126
2005	2684887	22.6	2421555	19142	2110735
2006	3135530	16.8	2833457	17176	2490873
2007	3671231	17.1	3321752	19856	2934498
2008	3849407	4.9	3453560	20562	3027597
2009	4002520	4.0	3577500	21990	3101523
2010	4590431	14.7	4092098	24240	3542660
2011	5053017	10.1	4517125	27067	3886156
2012	5140915	1.7	4547780	28724	3845918
2013	5593943	8.8	4932666	33422	4149789

单位:万千瓦时(10000 kwh)

Production Consumption				生活用电 Living Consumption		
其中 of Which					其中 of Which	
轻工业 Light Industry	重工业 Heavy Industry	建筑业 Construction	第三产业 Tertiary Industry	总计 Total	城市 Urban	农村 Rural
				4325		
				4835		
				5355		
				6315		
				6734		
				7500		
				9313		
				12603		
				17662		
				22881		
				29510		
				33088		
103301	130465	3770	21432	43003	11926	31077
122714	150619	3179	24469	49606	13406	36200
146272	170286	3898	28780	57502	15499	42003
171383	188589	5870	37412	66515	18972	47543
186145	213935	8016	46961	84678	26002	58677
209890	229608	9855	57175	101512	31626	69886
209606	248082	13586	72226	118328	40536	77792
240220	255907	12132	78013	122937	43257	79680
262246	298378	10589	86743	131463	48670	82793
305906	358717	9745	92495	136755	50740	86015
394760	445365	12559	117573	151336	59557	91779
402840	540948	14234	133418	159218	65054	94164
483275	663292	15523	160889	187188	74294	112886
574100	842525	21672	212462	238635	95616	143019
647516	1055610	31570	244195	221797	105639	116158
775922	1334813	34520	257158	263332	135827	127505
897750	1593123	36255	289154	302073	152348	149725
1013214	1921284	42460	324937	349479	174873	174606
1016912	2010684	44590	360812	395847	198536	197311
1045023	2056500	52322	401664	425020	216319	208701
1182101	2360559	62833	462365	498333	249932	248401
1260629	2625527	74231	529671	535891	271889	264003
1242699	2603219	79121	594017	593135	301647	291489
1303187	2846603	81823	667632	661277	334887	326389

表 7—24　2013 年主营业务收入前 20 位的工业企业
The Top 20 Enterprises on Annual Revenue from Principal Business in 2013

序号 No.	企业名称 Name of Enterprises	注册类型 Registered Type
1	中国石油化工股份有限公司镇海炼化分公司 Sinopec Zhenhai Refining & Chemical Co. ,Ltd.	股份有限公司 Share—holding Corporations Ltd.
2	中海石油宁波大榭石化有限公司 CNOOC Petrochemical Ningbo Daxie Co. ,Ltd.	与港澳台商合资经营 Equity Joint Ventures with HongKong,Macao &Taiwan
3	宁波群志光电有限公司 Ningbo Qunzhi Photoelectric Co. ,Ltd.	外资企业 Enterprises with Foreign Investment
4	浙江逸盛石化有限公司 Zhejiang Yisheng Petrochemical Co. ,Ltd.	与港澳台商合资经营 Equity Joint Ventures with HongKong,Macao & Taiwan
5	宁波钢铁有限公司 Ningbo Steel Co. ,Ltd.	其他有限责任公司 Other Limited Liability Corporations
6	宁波卷烟厂 Ningbo Cigarette Factory	国有企业 State—owned Enterprises
7	万华化学(宁波)有限公司 Wanhua Chemical (ningbo) Co. ,Ltd	其他有限责任公司 Other Limited Liability Corporations
8	浙江国华浙能发电有限公司 Zhejiang Guohua Zheneng Power Generation Co. ,Ltd.	其他有限责任公司 Other Limited Liability Corporations
9	宁波乐金甬兴化工有限公司 Ningbo LG Yongxing Chemical Industry Co. ,Ltd.	中外合资经营 Chinese—foreign Equity Joint Ventures Enterprises
10	宁波镇海炼化利安德化学有限公司 Ningbo ZRCC Lyondell Chemical Co. ,Ltd.	与港澳台商合作经营 Co—operative Business Operation with HongKong,Macao & Taiwan
11	宁波申洲针织有限公司 Ningbo Shenzhou Weaving Co. ,Ltd.	港澳台商独资 HongKong,Macao & Taiwan Funded Sole
12	宁波宝新不锈钢有限公司 Ningbo Baoxin Stainless Steel Co. ,Ltd.	中外合资经营 Chinese—foreign Equity Joint Ventures Enterprises
13	宁波奥克斯空调有限公司 Ningbo Aux Air—condition Co. ,Ltd.	其他有限责任公司 Other Limited Liability Corporations
14	台化兴业(宁波)有限公司 Taihua Xingye (Ningbo) Co. ,Ltd.	外资企业 Enterprises with Foreign Investment
15	宁波金田铜业(集团)股份有限公司 Ningbo Jintian Copper Group Co,. Ltd.	股份有限公司 Share—holding Corporations Ltd.
16	宁波市江北大创铜线有限公司 Ningbo Jiangbei Dachuang Copper Wire Co. ,Ltd.	其他有限责任公司 Other Limited Liability Corporations
17	宁波群友光电有限公司 Ningbo Qunyou Photoelectric Co. ,Ltd.	外资企业 Enterprises with Foreign Investment
18	宁波远景汽车零部件有限公司 Ningbo Vision Auto Parts Co. ,Ltd.	中外合资经营 Chinese—foreign Equity Joint Ventures Enterprises
19	宁波富德能源有限公司 Ningbo Fund Energy Co. ,Ltd.	其他有限责任公司 Other Limited Liability Corporations
20	宁波科元塑胶有限公司 Ningbo Keyuan Plastic co. ,Ltd.	港澳台商独资 HongKong,Macao & Taiwan Funded Sole

主要统计指标解释

【工业总产值】 是以货币形式表现的，工业企业在一定时期内生产的工业最终产品或提供工业性劳务活动的总价值量。它是反映一定时期内工业生产总规模和总水平的指标。

工业总产值包括：本期生产的成品价值、对外加工费收入和在制品半成品期末期初差额价值三部分。

【工业销售产值】 是以货币形式表现的，工业企业在一定时期内销售的本企业生产的工业产品或提供工业性劳务活动的价值总量。它是反映一定时期内工业企业产品销售总规模和总水平的重要指标。

【工业增加值】 是指工业企业在报告期内以货币形式表现的工业生产活动的最终成果，是企业全部生产活动的总成果扣除了在生产过程中消耗或转换的物质产品和劳务价值后的余额，是企业生产过程中新增加的价值。

【固定资产原价】 固定资产原值指企业在建造、购置、安装、改建、扩建、技术改造某项固定资产时所支出的全部货币总额。它一般包括买价、包装费、运杂费和安装费等。

【流动资产】 流动资产是指可以在一年或者超过一年的一个生产周期内变现或者耗用的资产，包括现金及各种存款、短期投资、应收及预付货款、存货等。

【主营业务收入】 指企业在销售商品(不一定是本企业生产)、提供劳务及让渡资产使用权等日常活动中所产生的收入

【主营业务成本】 指企业在销售商品、提供劳务及让渡资产使用权等日常活动而发生的实际成本。

【主营业务税金及附加】 指企业日常活动应负担的税金及附加，包括营业税、消费税、城市维护建设税、资源税、土地增值税和教育费附加等。

【利润总额】 指企业在生产经营过程中各种收入扣除各种耗费后的盈余，反映企业在报告期内实现的亏盈总额，包括营业利润、补贴收入、投资净收益和营业外收支净额。

【利税总额】 指企业利润总额、主营业务税金及附加和本年应交增值税之和。

【资产总计】 指企业拥有或控制的能以货币计量的经济资源，包括各种财产、债权和其他权利。资产按其流动性(即资产的变现能力和支付能力)划分为：流动资产、长期投资、固定资产、无形资产、递延资产和其他资产。

【负债合计】 指企业所承担的能以货币计量，将以资产或劳务偿付的债务，偿还形式包括货币、资产或提供劳务。负债一般按偿还期长短分为流动负债和长期负债。

【所有者权益】 指企业投资人对企业净资产的所有权。企业净资产等于企业全部资产减去全部负债后的余额，其中包括投资者对企业的最初投入，以及资本公积金、盈余公积金和未分配利润，对股份制企业即为股东权益。

【实收资本】 指投资者按照企业章程，或合同、协议的约定，实际投入企业的资本。企业实收资本按照投资主体划分为国家资本、集体资本、法人资本、个人资本、港澳台资本和外商资本六种。根据"资产负债表"中的"实收资本"项填列。实收资本中如有以外币形式投入的资本，需折合成人民币形式填写。

【综合能源消费量】 指一定时期、一定地域内工业企业在工业生产活动中实际消费的各种能源的总和净值。计算综合能源消费量时，需要先将使用的各种能源折算成标准燃料后再进行计算。

Explanatory Notes on Main Statistical Indicators

【Gross Industrial Output Value】 is in a form of currency. Total value of end—products or industrial services activities industrial enterprises provide in the period. It reflects the total achievements and overall scale of industrial production during a given period.

It includes the value of the finished products in a given period, the value of industrial services rendered to other units and the changes in the value of the semi finished products and products in process between the beginning and closing of the period.

【Industrial Sales Output Value】 is in a form of currency. Is the total volume of industrial products sold in value terms of an industrial enterprise and Industrial services activities, which reflects the total achievements and overall sales scale of industrial production during a given period.

【Value Added of Industry】 refers to the final results of industrial production in money terms during the reporting period. Is the total business results of all production activities deducted consumption in the production process and converted the value of material goods and services. Is the production process to increase the value of new.

【Original Value of Fixed Assets】 refers to the original value of all fixed assets owned by industrial enterprises, calculated at the cost paid at the time of purchase, installation, reconstruction, expansion, and technical innovation and transformation of the said assets, which includes expenses on purchase, package, transportation, and installation, etc.

【Liquid Assets】 is assets that can be turned into cash or consumed in more than one year or in a year, including cash and deposits, short—term investments, accounts receivable and prepaid inventories.

【Main Business Income】 refers to the enterprises in selling products (not necessarily in this enterprises'production), providing services and transferring assets, daily activities such as the right to the revenue that generated.

【Main Business Cost】 refers to the actual incurred costs the enterprises sell products, provide services, transfer assets, and other daily activities.

【Main Business Taxes and Surcharges】 refers to taxes and surcharges in the enterprises'daily production activities, including sales tax, consumption tax, urban maintenance and construction tax, resource tax, land tax and education surcharge, etc.

【Total Profits】 refers to the Surplus an enterprise products in the process of production and business activities after deducting all cost, reflecting the company's profit and loss during the reporting period, including operating profit, subsidy income, net investment income and the net non—operating income and expenditure.

【Total Profits and Taxes】 refer to total corporate profits taxes, business taxes and surcharges, and the sum of VAT of this year.

【Total Assets】 refer to all assets which are owned or controlled by enterprises, including circulating assets, long—term investment, fixed assets, intangible assets and deferred assets, other long—term assets, and defertaxes, etc. The summation of above items is equal to total assets shown in the balance sheets of the enterprises. (1) Circulating assets (working capital) refer to assets which can be cashed in or spent or consumed in an operating cycle of one year or over one year, including cash, all kinds of deposits, short term investment, receivables, advance payment, stock,etc. (2) Fixed assets refer to the net value of fixed assets, clearance of fixed assets, project under construction, fixed assets losses in suspense. These are corporations' fund holdings. (3) Intangible assets refer to the assets without material form used by enterprises over a long time, such as patents, non—patent technologies, trade marks, copyright, land use right, business reputation, etc

【Total Liabilities】 refer to the debts that enterprises are responsible for repayment, including liquid liabilities, long term liabilities and deferred taxes, etc. Total liabilities correspond to the summation item of liabilities shown in the balance sheets of the enterprises. Liabilities include short term loans and long—term loans.

【Creditors' Equity】 refers to equity investment in an enterprise net assets of the enterprise ownership. Net assets equal total assets minus total liabilities of business the balance, including the investor's initial investment in the enterprise, and capital reserve, surplus reserve and undistributed profits of the joint—stock company is the shareholders' equity.

【Paid—in capital】 refers to the investors in accordance with corporate charter, or contract, to the agreement, the actual capital invested enterprises. Business investment in paid—in capital in accordance with the main division of the state capital, collective capital, corporate capital, personal capital, Hong Kong, Macao, Taiwan capital and foreign capital six. Filled according to the " paid—up capital" items in the "balance sheet". Paid—up capital in any foreign currency in the form of capital investment required to fill out the form converted into RMB.

【Comprehensive Energy Consumption】 in a certain period, certain areas of industrial enterprises in the industrial production activities in the actual consumption of energy is the sum of net. Calculation of comprehensive energy consumption, need to be used in a variety of energy conversion to standard fuel after calculation.

CHAPTER 8

NINGBO 2014 Statistical YearBook

第八篇

固定资产投资和建筑业

INVESTMENT IN FIXED ASSETS AND CONSTRUCTION

固定资产投资和建筑业
Investment Fixed Assets and Construction

主要统计指标
Major Statistics Indicators

2013年固定资产投资额	Value of Investment Fixed Assets	3422.95	亿元	10000 yuan
比上年增长	Increase Over Last Year	18.0	%	
2013年房地产开发投资额	Value of Investment in Real Estate Development	1123.14	亿元	10000 yuan
比上年增长	Increase Over Last Year	27.0	%	
2013年房屋竣工面积	Floor Space of Building Completed	8674803	平方米	sq. m
比上年增长	Increase Over Last Year	3.3	%	
2013年商品房销售面积	Floor Space of Commercial Building Sold	7300878	平方米	sq. m
比上年增长	Increase Over Last Year	23.7	%	
2013年商品房实际销售额	Sales Volume of Commercial Buildings	8104011	万元	10000 yuan
比上年增长	Increase Over Last Year	22.2	%	
2013年商品房待售面积	Floor Space of Sale Building	4914547	平方米	sq. m
比上年增长	Increase Over Last Year	104.8	%	
2013年建筑业总产值	Gross Output Value of Construction	31354555	万元	10000 yuan
比上年增长	Increase Over Last Year	25	%	

表 8−1 历年固定资产投资情况
Invesment in Fixed Assets Over the Years

单位:亿元(100 million yuan)

年份 Year	总计 Total	其中 of Which			
		限额以上项目投资 Above Designated Size	工业投资 Industrial Investment	基础设施投资 Infrastructure Investment	房地产开发投资 Real Estate Development
1978	5.02				
1979	5.79				
1980	6.50				
1981	6.39				
1982	8.57				
1983	7.69				
1984	10.95				
1985	18.08				
1986	22.01				
1987	29.46				
1988	35.81				
1989	32.79				
1990	39.28				2.49
1991	51.42				3.00
1992	76.25				7.36
1993	129.27				25.44
1994	184.60				50.46
1995	264.19				71.59
1996	309.97				65.90
1997	300.57				51.92
1998	309.81				43.87
1999	318.93				46.54
2000	360.75				59.71
2001	470.28				87.08
2002	601.27				125.97
2003	740.92	556.66			184.26
2004	1026.64	782.38			244.26
2005	1268.55	1009.05			259.50
2006	1413.00	1099.42			313.58
2007	1486.54	1153.65			332.89
2008	1610.86	1303.11			307.75
2009	1860.45	1485.93	709.45	620.32	374.51
2010	2034.99	1477.72	619.01	610.87	557.27
2011	2385.50	1630.56	668.36	697.25	754.94
2012	2901.42	2017.07	817.24	845.71	884.35
2013	3422.95	2299.81	1061.90	846.70	1123.14

注:自 2003 年以后总计数为限额以上固定资产投资口径(即限额以上项目投资与房地产开发投资之和)

Note:The norm of the total count of fixed asset investment excessing the quota since 2003. That is the sum of real estate development investments and projects investments excessing the quota.

表 8－2　各县(市)固定资产投资完成情况(2013)
Investment in Fixed Assets by Region

指标	Indicators	全市 Total
固定资产投资完成额(按经营地)	**Total(By Place of Business)**	**34229529**
固定资产投资完成额(按建设地)	**Total(By Place of Building)**	**34229529**
限额以上项目投资	**Investment in Fixed Assets Above Designed Size**	**22998128**
按国民经济行业分	By Sector	
农林牧渔业	Framing,Forestry,Animal Husbandry and Fishery	211682
采矿业	Mining and Quarrying	20821
制造业	Manufacuring	9556611
电力、燃气及水的生产和供应业	Electric Power,Gas and Water Production and Supply	1041521
建筑业	Construction	43355
批发和零售业	Wholesale and Retail Trade	425185
交通运输、仓储和邮政业	Transportation,Storage and Post	2889340
住宿和餐饮业	Hotel and Catering Services	417379
信息传输、软件和信息技术服务业	Information Transmission, Software and Information Technology Services	67447
金融业	Financial Industries	139596
房地产业	Real Estate Industries	2855845
租赁和商务服务业	Leasing and Business Service Industries	390855
科学研究和技术服务业	Scientific Research and Technical Services	138798
水利、环境和公共设施管理业	Water Conservancy,Environment and Public Facility Management	3384559
居民服务、修理和其他服务业	Residents Service,Repair and Other Services	34945
教育	Education	468835
卫生和社会工作	Health and Social Work	244640
文化、体育和娱乐业	Culture,Sports and Entertainment	468602
公共管理、社会保障和社会组织	Public Management,Social Security and Social Organization	198112
房地产开发投资完成额(按经营地)	**Real Estate Development(By Place of Business)**	**11231401**
#住宅	Residential Buildings	6423263
房地产开发投资完成额(按建设地)	**Real Estate Development(By Place of Building)**	**11231401**
#住宅	Residential Buildings	6423263
城镇项目投资	**Investment in Fixed Assets in Town**	**15947207**
农村非农户投资	**Investment about Rural non Farm Households**	**7050921**

注:本表按2011年修订的国民经济行业标准统计。

Note:Statistics in this table are classified as the national economic category that was modified in 2011.

单位:万元(10000 yuan)

市区 Urban Disctict	#鄞州 Yinzhou	余姚 Yuyao	慈溪 Cixi	奉化 Fenghua	象山 Xiangshan	宁海 Ninghai
19405549	**5021491**	**4399391**	**5429495**	**1539766**	**1602311**	**1853017**
19320211	**5050840**	**4400581**	**5449750**	**1540246**	**1611571**	**1907170**
12632500	**3061880**	**3070234**	**3700561**	**1004026**	**1084846**	**1505961**
17849	7352	29448	42537	51355	47498	22995
16030	16030			1646		3145
4645568	1482244	1663934	2169040	276741	348019	453309
712229	103156	109684	13319	32848	77543	95898
40685	2060	370		2300		
212643	39685	43380	27240	22870	66491	52561
2029941	265146	202202	288648	163349	73450	131750
150818	86451	118121	53953	9460	60215	24812
59883	3650				4400	3164
94927	5075	8001	35825		843	
1535121	560368	422763	495553	123465	34964	243979
188308	19436	48984	57081	35696	28531	32255
96437	8248	8488	17720	12830	880	2443
1977457	294964	271980	307485	220063	247022	360552
19712	1	4488	7405		3100	240
286181	91055	39537	87633	14745	9723	31016
127669	21072	36583	36306	2821	16036	25225
324625	25455	21374	59087	20404	26975	16137
96417	30432	40897	1729	13433	39156	6480
6773049	**1959611**	**1329157**	**1728934**	**535740**	**517465**	**347056**
3629464	1167343	715269	1068426	393939	375530	240635
6687711	**1988960**	**1330347**	**1749189**	**536220**	**526725**	**401209**
3577483	1193453	716459	1084328	389331	381180	274482
9964559	**1565726**	**1455976**	**2385007**	**651813**	**517333**	**972519**
2667941	**1496154**	**1614258**	**1315554**	**352213**	**567513**	**533442**

表 8-3 部分年份分产业固定资产投资完成额
Fixed Assets Investment by Industry in Partial Years

单位:万元(10000 yuan)

指标	Indicators	2009	2010	2011	2012	2013
总计	**Total**	**20042179**	**21932830**	**23855072**	**29014258**	**34229529**
第一产业	Primary Industry	143785	113543	183918	270188	211682
第二产业	Secondary Industry	7767319	6975776	6683611	8198682	10662308
第三产业	Tertiary Industry	27665713	14843511	16987543	20545388	23355539
限额以上项目投资	**Investment in Fixed Assets Above Designed Size**	**14859345**	**14777197**	**16305624**	**20170744**	**22998128**
第一产业	Primary Industry	129961	104237	183918	270188	211682
第二产业	Secondary Industry	7166679	6312915	6683611	8198682	10662308
第三产业	Tertiary Industry	7562705	8360045	9438095	11701874	12124138
城镇限额以下投资	**Investment in Fixed Assets Below Designed Size in Town**	**170049**	**168730**			
第一产业	Primary Industry	3818	294			
第二产业	Secondary Industry	100696	103551			
第三产业	Tertiary Industry	65535	64885			
农村非农户限额以下投资	**Investment in Fixed Assets about Non-peasant Households & Below Designed Size in Rural Area**	**632431**	**667306**			
第一产业	Primary Industry	10006	9012			
第二产业	Secondary Industry	499944	559310			
第三产业	Tertiary Industry	122481	98984			
房地产开发	**Real Estate Development**	**3745119**	**5572683**	**7549448**	**8843514**	**11231404**
#住宅建设	Residential Buildings	2376419	3231195	4168184	5156454	6423263
农村私人固定资产投资	**Private Investment in Rural Areas**	**635235**	**746914**			

表 8—4 部分年份城镇以上新增固定资产及房屋建筑面积 Newly Increase Fixed Assets and Floor Space of Buildings Above City and Town Level in Partial Years

单位：万元，万平方米(10000 yuan，10000 sq. m)

年份	本年新增固定资产额 Newly Increase Fixed Assets in This Year	房屋施工面积 Floor Space of Buliding Under Construction	#住宅 Residential Buildings	房屋竣工面积 Floor Space of Buildings Completed	#住宅 Residential Buildings
1990	179769	308.76	137.73	180.48	77.30
1991	289108	362.09	175.07	182.28	88.11
1992	253780	518.29	254.60	209.38	91.38
1993	516881	906.08	501.36	383.28	224.91
1994	908056	1205.39	615.30	528.40	285.92
1995	1007217	1386.64	760.99	515.02	312.26
1996	1433274	1395.46	681.71	579.60	332.59
1997	1758309	1264.97	543.00	442.76	232.08
1998	1685871	1156.62	467.16	506.87	232.26
1999	1915400	1050.10	519.91	499.65	233.31
2000	2464806	1208.39	681.38	446.70	227.64
2001	2776661	1626.01	886.08	622.64	341.45
2002	2382537	2342.77	1132.48	745.33	365.88
2003	3292041	3401.43	1744.41	971.04	550.02
2004	3603854	4062.61	2225.05	996.97	546.09
2005	5708349	4600.43	2225.51	1562.32	680.51
2006	7321849	4542.09	2186.55	1427.87	671.66
2007	7166189	5715.13	2190.54	1452.22	535.06
2008	7523565	6505.64	2447.55	1746.09	712.79
2009	11797353	6741.74	2352.59	1669.41	500.54
2010	9781355	7679.59	2741.93	1486.97	470.94
2011	12296942	9792.22	3532.76	2232.56	672.49
2012	10643686	10925.24	4037.87	2025.64	615.75
2013	18423979	12227.39	4422.44	2558.33	666.48

表 8—5　城镇以上固定资产投资完成情况(2013) Investment in Fixed Assets of City and Town Level and Above

指标	Indicators	计划总投资 Total Investment of Project	累计完成投资 Accumulative Finish Total Investment
总计	**Total**	**59425031**	**40548529**
按登记类型	**By Registered Type**		
内资	Domestic—investment Enterprises	50635387	33970844
国有	State—owned	32645032	22288370
港澳台投资	Hongkong,Macao and Taiwan Funded	3862943	2572108
外资	Foreign Funded Enterprises	4922662	4002395
按隶属关系	**By Subordination**		
中央	Central	2477403	2073800
地方	Local	56947628	38474729
按建筑性质	**By type of Construction**		
#新建	New Construction	35073325	23630904
扩建	Expansion	15594129	10844865
改建	Reconstruction	3534337	2410936
按国民经济行业分组	**By Sector**		
农林牧渔业	Framing,Forestry,Animal Husbandry and Fishery	831880	550791
采矿业	Mining and Quarrying	1998	1646
制造业	Manufacuring	17231876	11329904
电力、燃气及水的生产和供应业	Electric Power,Gas and Water Production and Supply	2475095	1864093
建筑业	Construction	706953	773141
批发和零售业	Wholesale and Retail Trade	666304	492178
交通运输、仓储和邮政业	Transportation,Storage and Post	12531067	9566107
住宿和餐饮业	Hotel and Catering Services	1072958	788476
信息传输、软件和信息技术服务业	Information Transmission,Software and Information Technology Services	138993	128596
金融业	Financial Industries	561852	274365
房地产业	Real Estate Industries	8264072	4995991
租赁和商务服务业	Leasing and Business Service Industries	598256	417818
科学研究和技术服务业	Scientific Research and Technical Services	334640	225930
水利、环境和公共设施管理业	Water Conservancy,Environment and Public Facility Management	10755426	6916838
居民服务、修理和其他服务业	Residents Service,Repair and Other Services	76385	31540
教育	Education	887060	641839
卫生和社会工作	Health and Social Work	741235	375078
文化、体育和娱乐业	Culture,Sports and Entertainment	1033752	817528
公共管理、社会保障和社会组织	Public Management,Social Security and Social Organization	515229	356670

注:本表按 2011 年修订的国民经济行业标准统计。

Note:Statistics in this table are classified as the national economic category that was modified in 2011.

单位:万元(10000 yuan)

本年完成投资 Investment Completed of the Year	按构成分 by Composition					本年新增固定资产 Newly Increased Fixed Assets of the Year	本年房屋施工面积(平方米) Floor Space Under Construction (sq. m)	本年房屋竣工面积(平方米) Floor Space Completed (sq. m)
	建筑工程 Construction	安装工程 Installation	设备工器具购置 Purchase of Equipment and Instruments	其他费用 Others	#土地购置费 Purchase of Land			
15947207	**9058625**	**984366**	**2535697**	**3368519**	**1677714**	**14003811**	**53934302**	**16908498**
13615438	7894482	786386	1830594	3103976	1513873	11124217	42888729	12049009
7736160	5171341	380102	230382	1954335	883778	6665910	18230031	4138242
1247695	677168	101646	301564	167317	104588	660917	4445097	1510821
1081757	485486	96304	403539	96428	58461	2216587	6581638	3330999
363148	104961	126620	69209	62358	2586	1123661	357473	25284
15584059	8953664	857746	2466488	3306161	1675128	12880150	53576829	16883214
7908261	5025244	552027	535511	1795479	988093	7851371	29302000	8554978
4840637	2707041	264048	718939	1150609	433868	3781449	17561806	5467052
919695	662043	27571	68352	161729	101679	614186	983584	441914
123747	106447	4246	10856	2198		229708	16239	16039
1646			1646			1646		
5458089	2393010	433075	1918147	713857	477871	5106274	23595399	9414980
653576	297381	149552	121914	84729	6115	450468	369851	53606
36804	17628			19176	1050	17985	58804	
220771	147873	14507	3486	54905	48186	166320	1279674	443007
2448100	1571738	162828	270519	443015	90778	3429877	1847388	587862
267731	135764	46075	22932	62960	49009	348693	1084859	457973
67447	16742	11540	38000	1165	360	56555	154613	45233
126967	97217	9070	2388	18292	15341	43240	560196	3000
1942496	1394004	54313	14993	479186	320827	1291916	16500789	3768874
277917	138177	5031	99404	35305	31222	143731	728568	79326
123771	82232	3980	9143	28416	18669	87137	625304	216907
3067341	1864522	36302	1642	1164875	442597	1792551	2158388	317870
21632	12809	301	282	8240	7984	3000	63960	8732
384327	264055	12052	3209	105011	72429	247705	1879341	676447
191094	130876	20112	4456	35650	16634	75176	1174662	179258
376890	264180	6436	10372	95902	72773	408067	914683	412313
156861	123970	14946	2308	15637	5869	103762	921584	227071

表 8－6 各县(市)城镇以上固定资产投资主要指标(2013)
Main Indicators of Investment in Fixed Assets of City and Town Level and Above by Region

指标	Indicators	全市 Total
计划总投资	**Total Investment of Plan**	**59425031**
本年完成投资	**Finished Investment of This Year**	**15947207**
按经济注册类型分	**By Registration Status**	
国有经济	State—Owned Units	7736160
集体经济	Collective—owned Units	191237
其他有限责任公司	Share—holding Corporation Units	2494453
股份有限公司	Other Limited Liability Corporations	457394
港澳台投资经济	HongKong,Macao and Taiwan Funded	1247695
外商投资经济	Foreign Funded	1081757
按隶属关系分	**By Administrative Relationship**	
中央	Central	363148
省	Province	84923
省辖市	Municipalities	2132136
县(市)、区	Counties and Districts	5776578
其他	Others	7590422
按建设性质分	**By Type of Construction**	
新建	New Construction	7908261
扩建	Expansion	4840637
改建	Reconstruction	919695
按构成分	**By Use of Funds**	
建筑工程	Construction	9058625
安装工程	Installation	984366
设备工器具购置	Purchase of Equipment and Instruments	2535697
其他费用	Others	3368519
按国民经济行业分	**By Sector**	
农林牧渔业	Framing,Forestry,Animal Husbandry and Fishery	123747
采矿业	Mining and Quarrying	1646
制造业	Manufacuring	5458089
电力、燃气及水的生产和供应业	Electric Power,Gas and Water Production and Supply	653576

注:①本表按 2011 年修订的国民经济行业标准统计。②从 2012 年开始国家预算内资金改为国家预算资金,以下表同。

①Statistics in this table are classified as the national economic category that was modified in 2011. ②The state on budget funds have been change into state budget funds since 2012,same as the following tables.

单位:万元(10000 yuan)

市区 Urban District	#鄞州 Yinzhou	余姚 Yuyao	慈溪 Cixi	奉化 Fenghua	象山 Xiangshan	宁海 Ninghai
39565064	**5390929**	**3792625**	**7415394**	**2890387**	**1993695**	**3767866**
9964559	**1565726**	**1455976**	**2385007**	**651813**	**517333**	**972519**
4860218	569560	581583	733681	381735	352097	826846
173015	130984	430	11500	3330		2962
1276371	225126	7824	1044777	11800	40717	112964
241459	43257	190808	25127			
880928	73650	219872	108338	32107		6450
931150	118428	31403	98131	9743	6291	5039
356848	25698				6300	
84923						
2060422	33362	1200	35727	34787		
2925971	575165	639706	638965	308207	369125	894604
4536395	931501	815070	1710315	308819	141908	77915
5378325	793709	279334	1465485	358723	358982	67412
2786972	345687	541132	365417	211427	43751	891938
564254	196461	183625	58142	22921	77584	13169
4996676	886120	978670	1602823	416709	415275	648472
723685	64427	58711	131102	21533	9583	39752
1788570	240556	165309	480245	61715	22286	17572
2455628	374623	253286	170837	151856	70189	266723
9664		201	27364	31611	34244	20663
				1646		
3355778	659961	655367	1127641	208282	25773	85248
477319	85555	56167	11467	23209	18591	66823

表 8－6 续表 Continued

指标	Indicators	全市 Total
建筑业	Construction	36804
批发和零售业	Wholesale and Retail Trade	220771
交通运输、仓储和邮政业	Transportation,Storage and Post	2448100
住宿和餐饮业	Hotel and Catering Services	267731
信息传输、软件和信息技术服务业	Information Transmission ,Software and Information Technology Services	67447
金融业	Financial Industries	126967
房地产业	Real Estate Industries	1942496
租赁和商务服务业	Leasing and Business Service Industries	277917
科学研究和技术服务业	The Scientific Research and Technical Services	123771
水利、环境和公共设施管理业	Water Conservancy,Environment and Public Facility Management	3067341
居民服务、修理和其他服务业	Residents Service,Repair and Other Services	21632
教育	Education	384327
卫生和社会工作	Health and Social Work	191094
文化、体育和娱乐业	Culture,Sports and Entertainment	376890
公共管理、社会保障和社会组织	Public Management,Social Security and Social Organization	156861
本年新增固定资产	**Newly Increased Fixed Assets in This Year**	**14003811**
按资金来源分	**By Source of Funds**	
＃国家预算资金	State Budget	1730012
国内贷款	Domestic Loans	2654528
利用外资	Foreign Investment	678476
自筹资金	Fund Raising	10113689
房屋建筑面积(平方米)	**Floor Space of Buildings (sq. m)**	
施工面积	Floor Space of Buildings Under Construction	53934302
＃住宅	Residential Buildings	7945027
竣工面积	Floor Space of Buildings Completed	16908498
＃住宅	Residential Buildings	2039723
本年竣工房屋价值(万元)	Value of Building Completed(10000 yuan)	3637162
＃住宅	Residential Buildings	567048

单位:万元(10000 yuan)

市区 Urban District	#鄞州 Yinzhou	余姚 Yuyao	慈溪 Cixi	奉化 Fenghua	象山 Xiangshan	宁海 Ninghai
34504				2300		
110757	8947	8684	20000	18678	53750	8902
1789809	39273	145668	230684	98453	53786	129700
121309	82618	43865	53953	2952	42300	3352
59883	3650				4400	3164
89942	3430	1200	35825			
1070935	289246	255349	346137	37322	5000	227753
157766	19436		57080	35696	27375	
85148	8248	8488	17720	9092	880	2443
1858691	251454	216687	295125	152513	194296	350029
13477		750	7405			
256331	64075	9035	70832	11911	5402	30816
95108	17282	22250	34247	1191	15083	23215
291624	11741		49527	11771	8427	15541
86514	20810	32265		5186	28026	4870
10466403	**929642**	**926887**	**1327379**	**554794**	**424058**	**304290**
1191761	143269	10741	368405	25027	98266	35812
2145379	298767	28568	91139	80443	93262	215737
678276	44944			200		
5363204	968160	1322443	2061682	507317	297603	561440
27120302	7582016	4696234	11820755	3435798	1683487	5177726
5186706	1478351	797271	462010	687166	75247	736627
9614472	1588657	1946469	3769912	993334	229104	355207
1377139	229183	349267	137201	142573	13977	19566
2270174	343275	337025	733819	146814	77971	71359
413632	40827	73508	47022	25454	4000	3432

表 8－7 全市房地产企业开发投资情况(2013)
Develop and Investment of Enterprises for Real Estate Development

指标	Indicators	总计 Total	按控股情况分 国有 State－owned	集体 Colloective－owned
计划总投资	**Total Investment of Plan**	**45269290**	**6571704**	**638438**
本年完成投资	**Investment Made of the Year**	**11231401**	**1574406**	**179845**
土地购置费	Purchase of Land	3170393	341316	29697
配套工程投资	Ancillary Works	156574	20747	25489
按构成分	**By Composition**			
建筑工程	Construction	5918024	968517	95731
安装工程	Installation	766030	98497	29078
设备工器具购置	Purchase of Equipment and Instruments	170895	22500	5622
其他费用	Others	4376452	484892	49414
按工程用途分	**By Purpose**			
住宅	Residential Buildings	6423263	900568	104869
办公楼	Office Buildings	958136	170948	12811
商业营业用房	Buildings for Commercial Business	1530845	102779	17346
其他	Others	2319157	400111	44819
本年新增固定资产	Newly Increased Fixed Assets in the Year	4420168	496739	93010
待开发土地面积(平方米)	Land Space Needed Development (sq. m)	2811807	327596	212886
本年购置土地面积(平方米)	Land Space Purchased in the Year (sq. m)	2399161	102788	80901
本年土地成交价款	Actual Land Price of the Year	1999116	232806	17001

单位:平方米,万元(sq. m,10000 yuan)

By Holding Status			按隶属关系分 By Administrative Relationship				
私人 Private	港澳台商 Hongkong, Macao&Taiwan Funded	外商 Foreign Funds	一级 Firstl Class	二级 Secend Class	三级 Third Class	四级 Fourth Class	其他 Others
28891837	**2851981**	**3184286**	**3999496**	**3077251**	**15537951**	**1692116**	**20962476**
6857889	**969300**	**833507**	**772802**	**885921**	**3929426**	**423721**	**5219531**
2129495	327198	154798	178462	256872	893421	88876	1752762
95368	4315	952	35711	10908	63719	4865	41371
3208251	500641	598915	382960	467397	2195695	258650	2613322
532185	38665	40417	70428	35338	356063	35417	268784
113400	4058	18141	21149	12415	49202	6902	81227
3004053	425936	176034	298265	370771	1328466	122752	2256198
4058898	511203	451648	446473	565566	2405193	270814	2735217
598950	70366	32462	42438	40265	316709	16465	542259
835549	183312	285090	62239	92558	370067	47398	958583
1364492	204419	64307	221652	187532	837457	89044	983472
3331618	163931	228606	503857	543656	1546458	106245	1719952
1418462	213956	107013	119126	59020	1040111	85852	1507698
1498108	31259	424920	150385	61502	600498	86040	1500736
1114965	22194	445098	119205	37216	280898	19793	1542004

表8－8 全市房地产企业房屋施工及竣工情况(2013)
Buildings Construction and The Completed of Enterprises for Real Estate Development

指标	Indicators	总计 Total	按控股情况分	
			国有 State－owned	集体 Colloective－owned
房屋施工面积	**Floor Space of Buildings Under Consrtuction**	**68339592**	**5235292**	**4996298**
1.住宅	Residential Buildings	36279381	3500828	3104286
2.办公楼	Office Buildings	6014659	135893	290772
3.商业营业用房	Buildings for Commercial Business	9123412	280676	568389
4.其他	Others	16922140	1317895	1032851
本年新开工房屋施工面积	**Floor Space of Newly Started of The Year**	**18372030**	**715790**	**1047183**
1.住宅	Residential Buildings	10030984	392581	621283
2.办公楼	Office Buildings	1226758	48206	39778
3.商业营业用房	Buildings for Commercial Business	2943532	45186	149946
4.其他	Others	4170756	229817	236176
房屋竣工面积	**Floor Space of Buildings Completed**	**8674803**	**724649**	**985074**
#不可销售面积	Floor Space for Connot	2062332	165324	212741
1.住宅	Residential Buildings	4625109	405373	542001
2.办公楼	Office Buildings	863832		149063
3.商业营业用房	Buildings for Commercial Business	1025513	114156	114205
4.其他	Others	2160349	205120	179805
商品住宅竣工套数(套)	**Completed Residencial House (flat)**	**40741**	**2581**	**5110**
竣工房屋价值	**Value of Buildings Completed(10000 yuan)**	**3405651**	**377860**	**441044**
1.住宅	ResidentialBuildings	1769616	206105	252962
2.办公楼	Office Buildings	385615		54809
3.商业营业用房	Buildings for Commercial Business	445873	62966	41612
4.其他	Others	804547	108789	91661
出租房屋面积	**Floor Space of Lease House**	**616154**	**3563**	**129260**
1.住宅	Residential Buildings	3106		3106
2.办公楼	Office Buildings	75348		
3.商业营业用房	Buildings for Commercial Business	529640	2163	126154
4.其他	Others	8060	1400	
待售面积	**Floor Space of Vacant Building**	**4914547**	**453012**	**507592**
1.住宅	Residential Buildings	2251719	206038	208955
2.办公楼	Office Buildings	567619	325	76402
3.商业营业用房	Buildings for Commercial Business	1341650	122668	111827
4.其他	Others	753559	123981	110408

单位:平方米,万元(sq. m,10000 yuan)

By Holding Status			按隶属关系分 By Administrative Relationship				
私人 Private	港澳台商 Hongkong, Macao&Taiwan Funded	外商 Foreign Funds	一级 Firstl Class	二级 Secend Class	三级 Third Class	四级 Fourth Class	其他 Others
26482078	**2907386**	**28718538**	**5235292**	**4996298**	**26482078**	**2907386**	**28718538**
14636372	1757762	13280133	3500828	3104286	14636372	1757762	13280133
2343476	150276	3094242	135893	290772	2343476	150276	3094242
2573897	263974	5436476	280676	568389	2573897	263974	5436476
6928333	735374	6907687	1317895	1032851	6928333	735374	6907687
5723511	**349769**	**10535777**	**715790**	**1047183**	**5723511**	**349769**	**10535777**
3482985	233899	5300236	392581	621283	3482985	233899	5300236
287866	19909	830999	48206	39778	287866	19909	830999
639315	10513	2098572	45186	149946	639315	10513	2098572
1313345	85448	2305970	229817	236176	1313345	85448	2305970
3363012	**272886**	**3329182**	**724649**	**985074**	**3363012**	**272886**	**3329182**
844247	36634	803386	165324	212741	844247	36634	803386
1932981	165227	1579527	405373	542001	1932981	165227	1579527
259957	15801	439011		149063	259957	15801	439011
268183	40530	488439	114156	114205	268183	40530	488439
901891	51328	822205	205120	179805	901891	51328	822205
16581	**1504**	**14965**	**2581**	**5110**	**16581**	**1504**	**14965**
1165849	**79927**	**1340971**	**377860**	**441044**	**1165849**	**79927**	**1340971**
653878	48910	607761	206105	252962	653878	48910	607761
105720	4318	220768		54809	105720	4318	220768
102215	11761	227319	62966	41612	102215	11761	227319
304036	14938	285123	108789	91661	304036	14938	285123
406395	**1262**	**75674**	**3563**	**129260**	**406395**	**1262**	**75674**
				3106			
52357		22991			52357		22991
353838	1262	46223	2163	126154	353838	1262	46223
200		6460	1400		200		6460
2296780	**223521**	**1433642**	**453012**	**507592**	**2296780**	**223521**	**1433642**
1024635	163856	648235	206038	208955	1024635	163856	648235
309233	1234	180425	325	76402	309233	1234	180425
672706	24992	409457	122668	111827	672706	24992	409457
290206	33439	195525	123981	110408	290206	33439	195525

表 8－9 全市房地产企业房屋销售情况(2013)
Building Sale Situation of Enterprises for Real Estate Development

指标	Indicators	总计 Total	按控股情况分	
			国有 State－owned	集体 Colloective－owned
商品房销售面积	**Floor Space of Building Sold**	**7300878**	**1033558**	**151254**
1. 住宅	Residential Buildings	5819535	913028	128567
2. 办公楼	Office Buildings	495874	15567	6417
3. 商业营业用房	Buildings for Commercial Business	557051	33240	2561
4. 其他	Others	428418	71723	13709
现房销售面积	Floor Space of Completed Building	1349260	299641	108498
1. 住宅	Residential Buildings	872731	245729	95361
2. 办公楼	Office Buildings	116822	5249	
3. 商业营业用房	Buildings for Commercial Business	142860	4866	1985
4. 其他	Others	216847	43797	11152
期房销售面积	Floor Space of Forward Delivery Building	5951618	733917	42756
1. 住宅	Rèsidential Buildings	4946804	667299	33206
2. 办公楼	Office Buildings	379052	10318	6417
3. 商业营业用房	Buildings for Commercial Business	414191	28374	576
4. 其他	Others	211571	27926	2557
商品房销售额	**Sales Volume of Commercial Buildings**	**8104011**	**1020640**	**92130**
1. 住宅	Residential Buildings	6637387	929876	76359
2. 办公楼	Office Buildings	483513	22582	9646
3. 商业营业用房	Buildings for Commercial Business	764926	44013	3292
4. 其他	Others	218185	24169	2833
现房销售额	Sales Volume of Completed Building	1181748	168744	41863
1. 住宅	Residential Buildings	821281	140975	38258
2. 办公楼	Office Buildings	127809	11271	
3. 商业营业用房	Buildings for Commercial Business	146759	2148	2544
4. 其他	Others	85899	14350	1061
期房销售额	Sales Volume of Forward Delivery Building	6922263	851896	50267
1. 住宅	Residential Buildings	5816106	788901	38101
2. 办公楼	Office Buildings	355704	11311	9646
3. 商业营业用房	Buildings for Commercial Business	618167	41865	748
4. 其他	Others	132286	9819	1772

单位:平方米,万元(sq. m,10000 yuan)

By Holding Status			按隶属关系分 By Administrative Relationship				
私人 Private	港澳台商 Hongkong, Macao&Taiwan Funded	外商 Foreign Funds	一级 Firstl Class	二级 Secend Class	三级 Third Class	四级 Fourth Class	其他 Others
4483642	**497436**	**413253**	**513857**	**476625**	**2776622**	**353288**	**3180486**
3441598	443599	331998	443978	322694	2244048	287996	2520819
419284	18358	14244	931	54112	185679	10400	244752
345474	23318	58934	26233	63016	185882	29232	252688
277286	12161	8077	42715	36803	161013	25660	162227
833468	38913	16166	116493	75705	515142	21054	620866
484553	28365	14199	83010	32082	342393	15581	399665
98287	4950	53	931	19476	51101		45314
109676	3348	1531	11886	9289	47689	2428	71568
140952	2250	383	20666	14858	73959	3045	104319
3650174	458523	397087	397364	400920	2261480	332234	2559620
2957045	415234	317799	360968	290612	1901655	272415	2121154
320997	13408	14191		34636	134578	10400	199438
235798	19970	57403	14347	53727	138193	26804	181120
136334	9911	7694	22049	21945	87054	22615	57908
5088837	**624393**	**499531**	**717405**	**575463**	**2849735**	**301490**	**3659918**
4111404	553982	423591	657157	404632	2232391	240113	3103094
391148	23835	15466	559	52031	219565	5598	205760
435842	35972	55309	34278	91325	321337	42787	275199
150443	10604	5165	25411	27475	76442	12992	75865
865736	43237	28889	144625	69192	415324	14473	538134
575218	33796	27506	124354	35395	268303	11719	381510
105383	3393	22	559	14323	70928		41999
121714	4657	1159	10878	12543	51325	1672	70341
63421	1391	202	8834	6931	24768	1082	44284
4223101	581156	470642	572780	506271	2434411	287017	3121784
3536186	520186	396085	532803	369237	1964088	228394	2721584
285765	20442	15444		37708	148637	5598	163761
314128	31315	54150	23400	78782	270012	41115	204858
87022	9213	4963	16577	20544	51674	11910	31581

表 8—10　全市房地产企业经营情况(2013)
Main Economy Indicators of Real Estate Development

指标	Indicators	总计 Total	按控股情况分	
			国有 State—owned	集体 Colloective—owned
本年资金来源合计	**Total Capital Source in This Year**	**16070991**	**1841090**	**213965**
上年末结余资金	Balance at End of Previous Year	2160698	321746	14423
本年资金来源小计	Subtotal Capital of This Year	13910293	1519344	199542
1. 国内贷款	Domestic Loans	3148780	604393	46000
2. 利用外资	Foreign Investment	269922		
3. 自筹资金	Self—Financed Capital	5468753	598563	104604
4. 其他资金来源	Others	5022838	316388	48938
本年各项应付款合计	Total Account Payable This Year	2700230	315166	55676
年末资产负债情况	**Assets and Liabilities of Year—end**			
资产总计	Total Assets	573241851	131018786	6820604
#本年固定资产折旧	Depreciation of Fixed Assets in This Year	954019	88900	4556
负债总计	Total Liabilities	424086721	94673130	5550610
所有者权益合计	Creditors' Equity	149155130	36345656	1269994
实收资本合计	Total Capital Hold	127675839	16947674	23336819
损益情况	**Expenditureznd Income**			
主营业务收入	Prime Operating Revenue	81338014	6389021	1419238
土地转让收入	Land Transferred	64109	21038	
商品房屋销售收入	Commercial Buildings Sold	77148451	5876552	1401774
房屋出租收入	Buildings Leased	1057179	108906	1042
其他收入	Others	3068275	382525	16422
主营业务成本	Prime Operating Costs	57001090	4283138	1414620
主营业务税金及附加	Sales Taxes and Extra Charges	9225878	646787	110008
主营业务利润	Prime Operating Profits	15111046	1459096	—105390
销售费用	Sales Expenses	2124518	127294	14238
管理费用	Manage Expenses	3846360	458142	51769
财务费用	Finance Expenses	1859105	275697	27540
营业利润	Business Profits	10366851	1042325	—198136
利润总额	Total Profits	11388887	1234661	—201375
应付职工薪酬	Employee Compensation Payable	1663315	220536	23872

单位:万元(10000 yuan)

By Holding Status			按隶属关系分 By Administrative Relationship				
私人 Private	港澳台商 Hongkong, Macao&Taiwan Funded	外商 Foreign Funds	一级 Firstl Class	二级 Secend Class	三级 Third Class	四级 Fourth Class	其他 Others
10229794	**1151135**	**1375838**	**1125323**	**1185061**	**5504310**	**651475**	**7604822**
1301993	310265	71869	89460	94807	864280	57925	1054226
8927801	840870	1303969	1035863	1090254	4640030	593550	6550596
2042937	90371	117200	273466	307187	1192823	61574	1313730
	8899	261023					269922
3746307	242418	557470	325091	403707	1422588	216441	3100926
3138557	499182	368276	437306	379360	2024619	315535	1866018
1531706	245852	162765	106129	102978	1213813	98225	1179085
331074007	37702635	29537845	67987825	53343165	207673642	16608969	227628250
604401	72550	58749	68419	194029	413142	40258	238171
256162863	21066860	18729373	47544992	44028540	156149127	13815265	162548797
74911144	16635775	10808472	20442833	9314625	51524515	2793704	65079453
57136255	14441930	9296752	7108356	4643808	29310324	4121657	82491694
55431029	9677769	2170555	9906732	6436330	28878934	2262397	33853621
43071						43071	21038
52209694	9624222	2056500	9823860	6158215	25775438	2207204	33183734
611496	52109	108647	41368	207229	549972	7432	251178
2566768	1438	5408	41504	70886	2553524	4690	397671
38597240	7076767	1502530	5646148	4337526	20272873	1735006	25009537
6885001	728384	222618	1554594	830880	3068675	197714	3574015
9948788	1872618	445407	2705990	1267924	5537386	329677	5270069
1480241	188038	98656	129793	163432	800743	80147	950403
2688904	242395	145201	460720	494927	1515321	194727	1180665
1278015	33939	55629	275168	395629	748608	48336	391364
7012862	1477909	157136	3888770	495681	3029280	45720	2907400
7904055	1476292	150962	4576012	531390	3003233	29947	3248305
1024535	137406	100984	202691	165671	613880	74560	606513

表 8－11　各县(市)、区房地产企业开发投资情况(2013)
Develop and Investment of Enterprises for Real Estate Development

指标名称	Indicators	全市 Total	市区 Urban Disctict
计划总投资	**Total Investment of Plan**	**45269290**	**28885098**
本年完成投资	**Investment Made of the Year**	**11231401**	**6773049**
土地购置费	Purchase of Land	3170393	2108966
配套工程投资	Ancillary Works	156574	125987
按构成分	**By Composition**		
建筑工程	Construction	5918024	3430570
安装工程	Installation	766030	466429
设备工器具购置	Purchase of Equipment and Instruments	170895	90227
其他费用	Others	4376452	2785823
按工程用途分	**By Purpose**		
住宅	Residential Buildings	6423263	3629464
办公楼	Office Buildings	958136	887704
商业营业用房	Buildings for Commercial Business	1530845	788024
其他	Others	2319157	1467857
本年新增固定资产	Newly Increased Fixed Assets in the Year	4420168	3434778
待开发土地面积	Land Space Needed Development (sq. m)	2811807	1829858
本年购置土地面积	Land Space Purchased in the Year (sq. m)	2399161	1659375
本年土地成交价款	Actual Land Price of the Year	1999116	1693417
本年资金来源合计	**Total Funding Sources**	**16070991**	**10030050**
上年末结余资金	At the End of the Balance of Funds	2160698	1536826
本年资金来源小计	Total Fund Source of the Year	13910293	8493224
1. 国内贷款	1. Domestic Loans	3148780	1916628
2. 利用外资	2. Use of Foreign Capital	269922	269922
3. 自筹资金	3. Self－Financing	5468753	3433722
4. 其他资金来源	4. Other Sources	5022838	2872952
本年各项应付款合计	**The Total Payment of the Year**	**2700230**	**1464608**

注：本表房地产开发投资按建设地统计，表 8－12、8－13 同。

Note: Real Estate development investment is recorded by region in this table, as well as table 8－12. 8－13

单位：平方米，万元(sq. m,10000 yuan)

海曙区 Haishu	江东区 Jiangdong	江北区 Jiangbei	北仑区 Beilun	镇海区 Zhenhai	鄞州区 Yinzhou	余姚 Yuyao	慈溪 Cixi	奉化 Fenghua	象山 Xiangshan	宁海 Ninghai
1945945	4160281	3347885	4079035	4619827	8678178	4562787	6771971	2003987	1853483	1191964
432428	**827096**	**848391**	**1143884**	**1037298**	**1959611**	**1329157**	**1728934**	**535740**	**517465**	**347056**
146436	357815	427335	144936	252573	580552	380836	245334	218701	158202	58354
25047	4734	16855	27298	22042	15346	13849	8000	462	7306	970
182462	315592	311653	803664	603965	995119	676076	1171171	221357	292752	126098
47749	27676	19486	102221	67816	153020	103237	105286	35774	20005	35299
13896	14210	851	6707	8587	39141	40909	34285	1121	4253	100
188321	469618	516401	231292	356930	772331	508935	418192	277488	200455	185559
181956	271499	447768	629636	706104	1167343	715269	1068426	393939	375530	240635
116299	178908	77368	114012	89619	200793	18798	31184	2368	8492	9590
27685	102712	89022	172482	73137	282141	288423	339375	40642	44065	30316
106488	273977	234233	227754	168438	309334	306667	289949	98791	89378	66515
316291	162214	297946	491570	761168	1195069	272246	311875	190813	203195	7261
103774	174970	437269	100981	65408	934961	122978	478600	83000	288025	9346
54300	95056	201887	103091	108499	1039168	152998	441527	15000	96566	33695
60000	154427	463942	48590	51758	880459	66231	176707	1800	39773	21188
579829	**1142745**	**1214114**	**1453492**	**1231733**	**3747225**	**1775462**	**2482633**	**713272**	**648964**	**420610**
133749	392716	251263	115164	110638	363874	251054	208098	145395	9485	9840
446080	750029	962851	1338328	1121095	3383351	1524408	2274535	567877	639479	410770
46819	188283	110760	401899	212856	880611	355224	353874	193015	160140	169899
		23	8899		261000					
105155	304763	623738	484083	541632	1168991	506445	900298	168411	293709	166168
294106	256983	228330	443447	366607	1072749	662739	1020363	206451	185630	74703
114283	**80360**	**68744**	**267381**	**276438**	**541450**	**348187**	**570667**	**72295**	**134640**	**109833**

表 8－12　各县(市)、区房地产企业房屋施工及竣工情况(2013) Buildings Construction and The Completed of Enterprises for Real Estate Development

指标名称	Indicators	全市 Total	市区 Urban Disctict
房屋施工面积	**Floor Space of Buildings Under Consrtuction**	**68339592**	**40998118**
1. 住宅	Residential Buildings	36279381	19973451
2. 办公楼	Office Buildings	6014659	5502443
3. 商业营业用房	Buildings for Commercial Business	9123412	5263294
4. 其他	Others	16922140	10258930
本年新开工房屋施工面积	**Floor Space of Newly Started of The Year**	**18372030**	**11415681**
1. 住宅	Residential Buildings	10030984	6023714
2. 办公楼	Office Buildings	1226758	1118019
3. 商业营业用房	Buildings for Commercial Business	2943532	1478144
4. 其他	Others	4170756	2795804
房屋竣工面积	**Floor Space of Buildings Completed**	**8674803**	**6672394**
＃不可销售面积	Floor Space for Connot	2062332	1647299
1. 住宅	Residential Buildings	4625109	3571489
2. 办公楼	Office Buildings	863832	802715
3. 商业营业用房	Buildings for Commercial Business	1025513	698660
4. 其他	Others	2160349	1599530
商品住宅竣工套数(套)	**Completed Residencial House (flat)**	**40741**	**32819**
竣工房屋价值(万元)	**Value of Buildings Completed(10000 yuan)**	**3405651**	**2638317**
1. 住宅	Residential Buildings	1769616	1404295
2. 办公楼	Office Buildings	385615	357288
3. 商业营业用房	Buildings for Commercial Business	445873	302885
4. 其他	Others	804547	573849
出租房屋面积	**Floor Space of Lease House**	**616154**	**599961**
1. 住宅	Residential Buildings	3106	3106
2. 办公楼	Office Buildings	75348	75348
3. 商业营业用房	Buildings for Commercial Business	529640	513647
4. 其他	Others	8060	7860
空置面积	**Floor Space of Vacant Building**	**4914547**	**3107640**
1. 住宅	Residential Buildings	2251719	1043521
2. 办公楼	Office Buildings	567619	501810
3. 商业营业用房	Buildings for Commercial Business	1341650	996374
4. 其他	Others	753559	565935

单位：平方米，万元(sq. m，10000 yuan)

海曙区 Haishu	江东区 Jiangdong	江北区 Jiangbei	北仑区 Beilun	镇海区 Zhenhai	鄞州区 Yinzhou	余姚 Yuyao	慈溪 Cixi	奉化 Fenghua	象山 Xiangshan	宁海 Ninghai
2324059	**4461359**	**3597140**	**8344438**	**8026581**	**10949321**	**7183232**	**11034710**	**3549159**	**3212900**	**2361473**
1122220	1378599	1697191	4265442	4958654	5355296	3982741	6142838	2460190	2181082	1539079
440569	829940	530362	885497	616652	1448985	59134	325233	148	66370	61331
204682	797872	382102	1067335	669641	1686993	1349525	1759472	376219	191827	183075
556588	1454948	987485	2126164	1781634	2458047	1791832	2807167	712602	773621	577988
411327	**1096594**	**1421034**	**1040746**	**2703237**	**3507714**	**1234947**	**3454475**	**698363**	**871892**	**696672**
180605	472147	720178	266688	1805447	2394757	613836	1913124	354186	642324	483800
94593	166475	145543	78336	102821	206806	22593	85049	50	1047	
37221	130447	143210	343075	104097	358986	255936	960902	98860	74702	74988
98908	327525	412103	352647	690872	547165	342582	495400	245267	153819	137884
507795	**238304**	**609129**	**1192732**	**1721078**	**1911878**	**587628**	**628050**	**408661**	**378070**	
170658	64319	258208	213817	484550	318595	70430	104098	179873	60632	
274366	112791	296695	721090	1036109	953748	314722	294449	190654	253795	
110161	37961	50162	102436	120355	278960	366	60751			
18850	18844	95807	155221	156354	203056	95153	112599	109110	9991	
104418	68708	166465	213985	408260	476114	177387	160251	108897	114284	
3224	**904**	**2858**	**6612**	**10586**	**7185**	**1718**	**2368**	**1704**	**2132**	
251380	**130779**	**249693**	**443693**	**560018**	**810787**	**223994**	**290171**	**128666**	**124503**	
162403	64514	97107	242880	310215	444828	96794	123777	60563	84187	
33116	12714	29715	50095	83750	118749	55	28272			
10575	12374	49031	86378	57132	68838	50477	55901	34517	2093	
45286	41177	73840	64340	108921	178372	76668	82221	33586	38223	
12622	**198895**	**7658**	**8862**	**2252**	**349071**	**16193**				
	3106									
6260	41192	739			7009					
6362	148281	5375	8862	2252	342062	15993				
	6316	1544				200				
324513	**462526**	**224572**	**576596**	**406950**	**1001671**	**600880**	**719544**	**178650**	**178766**	**129067**
46895	92048	98231	284996	194512	301161	321944	523671	157588	143864	61131
54263	152394	22199	109666	11592	126743	1712	61777		2320	
150855	113920	45683	103215	126520	446661	209621	86743	8448	24268	16196
72500	104164	58459	78719	74326	127106	67603	47353	12614	8314	51740

表 8—13 各县(市)、区房地产企业房屋销售情况(2013)
Building Sale Situation of Enterprises for Real Estate Development

指标名称	Indicators	宁波市 Total	市区 Urban Disctict
商品房销售面积	**Floor Space of Building Sold**	**7300878**	**4388162**
1. 住宅	Residential Buildings	5819535	3376455
2. 办公楼	Office Buildings	495874	450370
3. 商业营业用房	Buildings for Commercial Business	557051	275033
4. 其他	Others	428418	286304
现房销售面积	Floor Space of Completed Building	1349260	1137159
1. 住宅	Residential Buildings	872731	699252
2. 办公楼	Office Buildings	116822	115265
3. 商业营业用房	Buildings for Commercial Business	142860	121606
4. 其他	Others	216847	201036
期房销售面积	Floor Space of Forward Delivery Building	5951618	3251003
1. 住宅	Residential Buildings	4946804	2677203
2. 办公楼	Office Buildings	379052	335105
3. 商业营业用房	Buildings for Commercial Business	414191	153427
4. 其他	Others	211571	85268
商品房销售额	**Sales Volume of Commercial Buildings**	**8104011**	**5179821**
1. 住宅	Residential Buildings	6637387	4292213
2. 办公楼	Office Buildings	483513	443772
3. 商业营业用房	Buildings for Commercial Business	764926	306948
4. 其他	Others	218185	136888
现房销售额	Sales Volume of Completed Building	1181748	974812
1. 住宅	Residential Buildings	821281	652703
2. 办公楼	Office Buildings	127809	126528
3. 商业营业用房	Buildings for Commercial Business	146759	115173
4. 其他	Others	85899	80408
期房销售额	Sales Volume of Forward Delivery Building	6922263	4205009
1. 住宅	Residential Buildings	5816106	3639510
2. 办公楼	Office Buildings	355704	317244
3. 商业营业用房	Buildings for Commercial Business	618167	191775
4. 其他	Others	132286	56480

单位：平方米，万元(sq. m，10000 yuan)

海曙区 Haishu	江东区 Jiangdong	江北区 Jiangbei	北仑区 Beilun	镇海区 Zhenhai	鄞州区 Yinzhou	余姚 Yuyao	慈溪 Cixi	奉化 Fenghua	象山 Xiangshan	宁海 Ninghai
396282	**265488**	**387399**	**983784**	**768634**	**1368503**	**792100**	**1258289**	**213133**	**287345**	**361849**
277105	219218	357140	786225	591385	1022385	613537	1081780	192852	271786	283125
63588	25250	5452	55538	34779	200634	10400	14785		6698	13621
18981	9610	6904	93364	54630	72170	131409	107753	11224	5731	25901
36608	11410	17903	48657	87840	73314	36754	53971	9057	3130	39202
109418	39327	83926	303324	354520	232460	84369	28179	21758	48991	28804
41094	31388	68473	202305	223704	126965	73155	22433	19439	41881	16571
34417	2211	2468	23963	8075	43807		53		1504	
4873	1857	699	40098	47434	20067	7576	5084	1829	2730	4035
29034	3871	12286	36958	75307	41621	3638	609	490	2876	8198
286864	226161	303473	680460	414114	1136043	707731	1230110	191375	238354	333045
236011	187830	288667	583920	367681	895420	540382	1059347	173413	229905	266554
29171	23039	2984	31575	26704	156827	10400	14732		5194	13621
14108	7753	6205	53266	7196	52103	123833	102669	9395	3001	21866
7574	7539	5617	11699	12533	31693	33116	53362	8567	254	31004
588186	**525318**	**598255**	**788758**	**593136**	**1805678**	**918333**	**1193812**	**213916**	**303643**	**294486**
449558	459646	557424	679375	491143	1464935	629785	989081	195368	283737	247203
73481	34705	8601	39990	22540	200352	5598	14512		6010	13621
47538	23243	19420	52397	54461	90192	253734	153622	14717	12211	23694
17609	7724	12810	16996	24992	50199	29216	36597	3831	1685	9968
131730	50063	146857	167964	169722	295190	57373	60459	17404	51246	20454
69139	42369	132360	103676	108416	189217	47829	46718	14349	41882	17800
35379	3072	3593	20811	3838	59585		22		1259	
14261	2718	1204	31936	37417	23040	7892	13317	2867	6575	935
12951	1904	9700	11541	20051	23348	1652	402	188	1530	1719
456456	475255	451398	620794	423414	1510488	860960	1133353	196512	252397	274032
380419	417277	425064	575699	382727	1275718	581956	942363	181019	241855	229403
38102	31633	5008	19179	18702	140767	5598	14490		4751	13621
33277	20525	18216	20461	17044	67152	245842	140305	11850	5636	22759
4658	5820	3110	5455	4941	26851	27564	36195	3643	155	8249

表 8—14 各县(市)农村非农户固定资产投资主要指标(2013)
Main Indicators of Investment in Fixed Assets of Non—peasant Households in Rural Area by Region

指标	Indicators	全市 Total
本年完成投资	**Finished Investment of This Year**	**7050921**
按国民经济行业分	**By Sector**	
农林牧渔业	Framing,Forestry,Animal Husbandry and Fishery	87935
采矿业	Mining and Quarrying	19175
制造业	Manufacuring	4098522
电力、燃气及水的生产和供应业	Electric Power,Gas and Water Production and Supply	387945
建筑业	Construction	6551
批发和零售业	Wholesale and Retail Trade	204414
交通运输、仓储和邮政业	Transportation,Storage and Post	441240
住宿和餐饮业	Hotel and Catering Services	149648
信息传输、软件和信息技术服务业	Information Transmission ,Software and Information Technology Services	
金融业	Financial Industries	12629
房地产业	Real Estate Industries	913349
租赁和商务服务业	Leasing and Business Service Industries	112938
科学研究和技术服务业	The Scientific Research and Technical Services	15027
水利、环境和公共设施管理业	Water Conservancy,Environment and Public Facility Management	317218
居民服务、修理和其他服务业	Residents Service,Repair and Other Services	13313
教育	Education	84508
卫生和社会工作	Health and Social Work	53546
文化、体育和娱乐业	Culture,Sports and Entertainment	91712
公共管理、社会保障和社会组织	Public Management,Social Security and Social Organization	41251

注:本表按2011年修订的国民经济行业标准统计。

Note:Statistics in this table are classified as the national economic category that was modified in 2011.

单位:万元(10000 yuan)

市区 Urban Disctict	# 鄞州 Yinzhou	余姚 Yuyao	慈溪 Cixi	奉化 Fenghua	象山 Xiangshan	宁海 Ninghai
2667941	**1496154**	**1614258**	**1315554**	**352213**	**567513**	**533442**
8185	7352	29247	15173	19744	13254	2332
16030	16030					3145
1289790	822283	1008567	1041399	68459	322246	368061
234910	17601	53517	1852	9639	58952	29075
6181	2060	370				
101886	30738	34696	7240	4192	12741	43659
240132	225873	56534	57964	64896	19664	2050
29509	3833	74256		6508	17915	21460
4985	1645	6801			843	
464186	271122	167414	149416	86143	29964	16226
30542		48984	1		1156	32255
11289				3738		
118766	43510	55293	12360	67550	52726	10523
6235	1	3738			3100	240
29850	26980	30502	16801	2834	4321	200
32561	3790	14333	2059	1630	953	2010
33001	13714	21374	9560	8633	18548	596
9903	9622	8632	1729	8247	11130	1610

表 8－15 部分年份城镇以上固定资产投资主要指标 Main Indicators of Investment in Fixed Assets of City and Town Level and Above in Partial Years

单位：万元(10000 yuan)

指标	Indicators	2009	2010	2011	2012	2013
计划总投资	**Total Investment of Plan**	**43943918**	**44888914**	**47604813**	**53339541**	**59425031**
累计完成投资	**Accumulative Finished Investment**	**28390303**	**28253456**	**29262704**	**33757190**	**40548529**
本年完成投资	**Finished Investment of This Year**	**11740560**	**11182943**	**12129369**	**14592260**	**15947207**
按经济注册类型分	**By Registration Status**					
国有经济	State－Owned Units	5425442	5804442	6119819	7536985	7736160
集体经济	Collective－owned Units	68312	95167	123743	197593	191237
股份有限公司	Share－holdingCorporation Units	1290064	362382	1372970	2001386	2494453
其他有限责任公司	Other Limited Liability Corporations	1097525	1037261	332185	312382	457394
外商投资经济	Foreign Investment	970546	991368	593015	775985	1247659
港澳台投资经济	HongKong，Macao and Taiwan Funded	683459	492546	1098615	776115	1081757
其他经济	Others	2205212	2399777			
按隶属关系分	**By Administrative Relationship**					
中央	Central Government			504730	570359	363148
省	Province			91767	98111	84923
省辖市	Municipalities			2679433	2806848	2132136
县(市)、区	Counties and Districts			3456025	4884449	5776578
其他	Others			5397414	6232493	7590422
按建设性质分	**By Type of Construction**					
新建	New Construction	6004342	5532359	6171252	7532996	7908261
扩建	Expansion	3148747	2783093	3419622	3975993	4840637
改建	Reconstruction	853728	1005946	763358	1073554	919695
其他	Others	1733743	1861545			
按构成分	**By Use of Funds**					
建筑工程	Construction	5635210	6031102	6828481	8244176	9058625
安装工程	Installation	1116482	753456	845852	877726	984366
设备工器具购置	Purchase of Equipment and Instruments	2386819	2077616	1928683	2215934	2535697
其他费用	Others	2466574	2320769	2526353	3254424	3368519
按资金来源分	**By Source of Funds**					
＃国家预算资金	State Budget	569611	593052	733398	1292692	1730012
国内贷款	Domestic Loans	1980857	2574096	2572961	2838994	2654528
利用外资	Foreign Investment	536241	556315	556010	542222	678476
自筹资金	Self－Financed Capital	8275184	6684896	7382210	8942861	10113689

表 8－16 部分年份建筑业生产经营及主要财务指标 Basic Statistics and Main Financial Indicators of Construction Enterprises in Partial Years

单位：万元(10000 yuan)

指标	Indicators	2010	2011	2012	2013
企业个数(家)	**Number of Enterprises (unit)**	**753**	**844**	**922**	**976**
建筑业总产值	**Gross Output Value of Construction**	**14250727**	**19333581**	**25091179**	**31354555**
1.建筑工程	Construction	12423675	17219536	22149575	27745638
2.安装工程	Installation	1430114	1585508	2205438	2699734
3.其他	Building Repair and Maintenance	396938	528536	736167	909183
竣工产值	Output Value of Buildings Completed	9609406	10890263	13418936	18465941
房屋建筑施工面积(万平方米)	Floor Space of Buildings Under Construction (10000 sq. m)	14288582	18161	22343	25043
房屋建筑竣工面积(万平方米)	Floor Space of Buildings Completed (10000 sq. m)	4586	5180	6058	7842
年末自有机械设备总台数(台)	Number of Machinery and Equipment (year－end) (set)	115541	111675	113171	122951
年末自有机械设备总功率(万千瓦)	Total Power of Machinery and Equipment (10000kw)	161.66	200.62	203.23	235.32
年末自有机械设备净值	Net Value of Machinery and Equipment	481635	5804214	660815	684957
计算劳动生产率的年平均人数(万人)	Average Employed Persons by Calculatied Labor Productivity (10000 persons)	72.10	76.96	89.04	98.76
年末资产负债	**Asset and Liabilities at Year－end**				
流动资产	Circulating Assets	7853800	9910592	1243742	14077843
固定资产小计	Fixed Assets	1008050	1138322	1326727	1415679
固定资产原价	Original Value of Fixed Assets	1252919	1556294	1786162	1933304
本年折旧	Depreciation in This Year	119301	91618	136199	126002
资产总计	Total Assets	9721438	12127310	15082502	16867867
流动负债	Liquid Liabilities	6028401	7538632	9396904	9803478
长期负债	Long－term Liabilities	233647			
所有者权益	Creditors' Equity	3459391	4184209	5191820	5954929
损益及分配	**Expenditure, Income and Distribution**				
工程结算收入	Revenue of Project Settlement Accounts	11922883	14577208	17996050	22766196
工程结算成本	Costs of Project Settlement Accounts	10620358	12957730	15973781	20254742
工程结算税金及附加	Taxes and Extra Charges on Project Settlement Accounts	382964	463273	588015	739751
工程结算利润	Profits of Project Settlement Accounts	886895	1116603	1386848	1771703
工资、福利费	**Wages and Welfare Expenses**				
本年应付工资总额	Total Wages Payable in this Year	1 899023			
本年应付福利费总额	Total Welfare Expenses Payable in this Year	86161			
建筑业增加值	**Value－added of Construction**	**3035482**			

表 8-17 建筑业企业生产情况(2013)
Basic Statistics on Production of Construction Enterprises

指标	Indicators	企业个数(家) Number of Enterprises (unit)	建筑业总产值 Gross Output Value of Construction	在外省完成的产值 Output Value of Other Province
总计	**Total**	**976**	**31354555**	**12645934**
按登记注册类型分组	**By Registered Type**			
内资企业	Domestic Funded Enterprises	972	31296894	12645425
国有企业	State-owned Enterprises	6	87973	1334
集体企业	Collective-oened Enterprises	5	9491	
股份合作企业	Share-holding Cooperative Enterprises	2	162994	15000
有限责任公司	Limited Liability Corporations	91	3293513	895586
股份有限公司	Share-holding Corporations Ltd.	17	7367143	5528371
私营企业	Private Enterprises	851	20375781	6205134
港、澳、台商投资企业	HongKong,Macro and Taiwan Funded	2	46389	509
外商投资企业	Enterprises with Foreign Investment	2	11273	
按建筑业行业分组	**By Sector**			
房屋和土木工程建筑业	Building and Civil Engineering	588	28711542	12137285
房屋工程建筑	Building	333	21563937	9103492
土木工程建筑	Civil Engineering	255	7147605	3033793
建筑安装业	Construction Installation	148	1209586	248229
建筑装饰业	Construction Decoration	192	995961	88832
其他建筑业	Other Construction	48	437467	171589
按控股情况分组	**By Holding Status**			
国有控股	State-holding	38	2394429	617306
集体控股	Collective-holding	21	638102	45130
私人控股	Private-holding	913	28282813	11978335
港澳台控股	Hong Kong, Macao and Taiwan Holdings			
外商控股	Foreign-holding			
按企业资质等级分组	**By Qualification Criteria**			
施工总承包	Construc General Contractor	528	28524447	12009068
特级	Special Class	5	6499947	3858121
一级	First Class	90	15005590	6858715
二级	Second Class	136	4230015	1017538
三级	Third Class	297	2788895	274694
专业承包	fxSpecial General Contractor	448	2830109	636867
一级	First Class	53	1648812	475971
二级	Second Class	117	633703	117096
三级	Third Class	278	547594	43801

单位:万元(10000 yuan)

建筑业总产值按构成分			承包工程完成产值 Gross Output Value of Contract Project			竣工产值 Output Value of Buildings Completed
1.建筑工程 Construction	2.安装工程 Installation	3.其他 Others	1.直接从建设单位承揽工程 Contract Project from Construction Unit Directly	其中 of Which 自行完成 Finish by Oneself	2.从建设单位以外承揽工程 Contract Project Outside Construction Unit	
27745638	**2699734**	**909183**	**30604657**	**30283293**	**1071263**	**18465941**
27701076	2689002	906817	30546996	30225632	1071263	18460216
85556	2416		80193	80193	7780	42485
6584	2908		9491	9491		6440
162994			162927	162927	68	43539
2587443	506847	199224	3311850	3182972	110541	1829635
6279340	756107	331696	7304603	7168715	198428	5235491
18579159	1420724	375897	19677932	19621334	754447	11302628
44023		2366	46389	46389		313
540	10733		11273	11273		5412
26373653	1645506	692383	28209419	28004842	706700	17085578
19974883	1117054	472000	21306213	21139645	424291	12753145
6398771	528452	220382	6903206	6865197	282408	4332433
219612	822462	167511	1000517	897660	311926	605671
843778	128146	24037	989584	982129	13832	633844
308595	103020	25252	405137	398662	38805	140849
1934649	307259	152522	2282250	2224175	170254	1040460
330326	293120	14656	708853	638102		469658
25449331	2094326	739156	27579209	27386672	896141	16934250
26136445	1640337	747665	28100379	27855913	668533	16741190
5804039	532451	163458	6499947	6405921	94026	4150667
13965895	677097	362598	14809135	14679791	325798	7871807
3932224	162662	135130	4131470	4112572	117443	2702734
2434288	268128	86479	2659827	2657629	131266	2015982
1609193	1059397	161519	2504277	2427379	402729	1724751
1033028	528458	87327	1431137	1387582	261230	880822
326222	273075	34406	575643	552422	81281	452483
249944	257864	39786	497498	487375	60219	391446

表 8—17 续表 Continued

指标	Indicators	房屋建筑施工面积（平方米）Floor Space Under Construction (sq. m)	其中 of Which #本年新开工 Newly Operating Projects in this Year	#投标承包面积 Floor Space of Biding System
总计	**Total**	**250432688**	**95110411**	**184109063**
按登记注册类型分组	**By Registered Type**			
内资企业	Domestic Funded Enterprises	250432688	95110411	184109063
国有企业	State—owned Enterprises			
集体企业	Collective—oened Enterprises			
股份合作企业	Share—holding Cooperative Enterprises	1157152	489810	1157152
有限责任公司	Limited Liability Corporations	12236514	4541439	9315260
股份有限公司	Share—holding Corporations Ltd.	76909069	20728948	62368338
私营企业	Private Enterprises	160129953	69350214	111268313
港、澳、台商投资企业	HongKong,Macro and Taiwan Funded			
外商投资企业	Enterprises with Foreign Investment			
按建筑业行业分组	**By Sector**			
房屋和土木工程建筑业	Building and Civil Engineering	247972122	93975073	183226216
房屋工程建筑	Building	237122926	89722151	174898919
土木工程建筑	Civil Engineering	10849196	4252922	8327297
建筑安装业	Construction Installation	952866	443147	478835
建筑装饰业	Construction Decoration	328940	137482	61673
其他建筑业	Other Construction	1178760	554709	342339
按控股情况分组	**By Holding Status**			
国有控股	State—holding	6546916	1838011	6004094
集体控股	Collective—holding	3452223	1287798	3413599
私人控股	Private—holding	239960692	91709849	174691370
港澳台控股	Hongkong,Macao&Taiwan—holding			
外商控股	Foreign—holding			
按企业资质等级分组	**By Qualification Criteria**			
施工总承包	Construc General Contractor	241190989	90298215	182317695
特级	Special Grade	76583955	19326049	63632065
一级	First Grade	116924013	46205644	96598532
二级	Second Grade	29286597	15345049	14717400
三级	Third Grade	18396424	9421473	7369698
专业承包	Special General Contractor	9241699	4812196	1791368
一级	First Grade	6301074	3123063	1453158
二级	Second Grade	2107694	1493539	328210
三级	Third Grade	832931	195594	10000

房屋建筑竣工面积（平方米）Floor Space Completed (sq. m)	竣工房屋价值 Value of Completed Building	年末自有机械设备总台数（台）Number of Machinery and Equipment (year—end)(set)	年末自有机械设备总功率（千瓦）Total Power of Machinery and Equipment (kw)	年末自有机械设备净值（万元）Net Value of Machinery and Equipment (10000yuan)	年末人数（人）Employed Persons at Year—end (person)	计算劳动生产率的年平均人员（人）Average Employed Persons by Calculatied Labor Productivity (person)
78418953	**126398832**	**122951**	**2353190**	**6849569**	**1091521**	**987587**
78418953	126398832	122848	2344074	6826053	1090329	986556
		468	14085	9349	3651	3309
		60	1730	5555	580	494
176869	429505	3125	9015	18551	3071	3065
3745406	7288498	13836	345496	1452839	67844	60627
23853720	44543678	12117	282334	628201	192306	202066
50642958	74137151	93242	1691414	4711558	822877	716995
		12	8520	22447	822	725
		91	596	1069	370	306
77484770	125325834	100371	2096450	6253494	990692	900495
73076762	117565348	77775	1221118	3006109	769159	688645
4408008	7760486	22596	875332	3247385	221533	211850
555100	498784	11798	142873	303238	40148	37624
261153	322070	8407	61257	145354	44371	33923
117930	252144	2375	52610	147483	16310	15545
1915310	4536957	7828	200399	1078550	32031	31864
380789	714437	5893	53841	135325	19937	18117
75831527	120972372	108621	2090914	5600766	1038877	936540
73095910	123146987	98685	2031685	5648436	983065	894262
19246700	39396076	8979	133885	270556	165230	158265
32466529	57628179	45714	906932	2866940	478515	463372
13068173	16549582	25412	504731	1357172	218101	166502
8314508	9573150	18580	486137	1153768	121219	106123
5323043	3251845	24266	321505	1201133	108456	93325
3319619	2102283	9826	129974	362181	63530	51157
1534043	780494	7912	76710	346829	25864	22993
469381	369068	6528	114821	492123	19062	19175

表 8—18 建筑业企业财务情况(2013)
Main Financial Indicators of Construction Enterprises

指标	Indicators	年末资产负债 资产合计 Total Assets	流动资产合计 Circulating Assets	固定资产合计 Fixed Assets
总计	**Total**	**16867867**	**14077843**	**1415679**
按登记注册类型分组	**By Registered Type**			
内资企业	Domestic Funded Enterprises	16812594	14028207	1413113
国有企业	State—owned Enterprises	237662	215224	8642
集体企业	Collective—oened Enterprises	15045	13204	1841
股份合作企业	Share—holding Cooperative Enterprises	33316	30213	1865
有限责任公司	Limited Liability Corporations	2717135	2213789	298107
股份有限公司	Share—holding Corporations Ltd.	3698607	3155117	121982
私营企业	Private Enterprises	10110829	8400660	980676
港、澳、台商投资企业	HongKong,Macro and Taiwan Funded	45771	40403	2305
商投资企业	Enterprises with Foreign Investment	9503	9233	262
按建筑业行业分组	**By Sector**			
房屋和土木工程建筑业	Building and Civil Engineering	14633680	12249327	1199266
房屋工程建筑	Building	9609223	8255008	645948
土木工程建筑	Civil Engineering	5024457	3994320	553318
建筑安装业	Construction Installation	1320921	1068818	127193
建筑装饰业	Construction Decoration	616351	529587	55814
其他建筑业	Other Construction	296916	230111	33406
按控股情况分组	**By Holding Status**			
国有控股	State—holding	2215585	1861218	223992
集体控股	Collective—holding	519508	455400	31963
私人控股	Private—holding	14083930	11722363	1151715
港澳台控股	Hong Kong, Macao and Taiwan Holdings			
外商控股	Foreign—holding			
按企业资质等级分组	**By Qualification Criteria**			
施工总承包	Construc General Contractor	14516993	12229162	1127141
特级	Special Class	3050824	2687310	85891
一级	First Class	6993608	5838207	513734
二级	Second Class	2450695	2027046	284056
三级	Third Class	2021866	1676599	243460
专业承包	Special General Contractor	2350874	1848681	288538
一级	First Class	967333	811170	88253
二级	Second Class	584676	410868	79257
三级	Third Class	798866	626644	121029

单位：万元(10000 yuan)

Total Assets and Liabilities at Year－end			损益及分配 Expenditure, Income and Distribution		
#本年折旧 Depreciation in this year	负债合计 Current Liabilities	所有者权益 Creditors' Equity	工程结算收入 Revenue of Project Settlement Accounts	工程结算成本 Costs of Project Settlement Accounts	工程结算税金及附加 Taxes and Extra Charges on Project Settlement Accounts
126002	**10901988**	**5954929**	**22766196**	**20254742**	**739751**
123778	10856344	5945300	22709509	20203786	737810
273	200505	37157	79369	72773	2044
33	10162	4432	14133	11671	548
197	17981	15335	99020	92342	3375
25921	1957898	759237	3215433	2863154	75663
11597	2723766	974840	4143913	3776364	130856
85758	5946032	4154298	15157642	13387482	525325
2169	39070	6701	50248	46032	1736
55	6574	2929	6439	4924	205
103575	9484138	5142205	20005613	17894275	668957
48024	6205108	3401006	14567855	13163184	493757
55551	3279030	1741199	5437758	4731091	175201
12697	881447	436888	1535172	1325357	29395
6534	354918	260406	816662	684656	27282
3197	181485	115431	408750	350454	14117
21195	1656859	558727	2455593	2217093	50979
3640	404371	114686	584581	521599	17640
100247	8803211	5270220	19706837	17500541	670862
92258	9360419	5149688	20305917	18170377	668183
6200	2248699	802126	4222399	3904291	131261
45697	4456899	2536710	10395371	9246990	336836
17408	1412772	1034814	3332944	2973155	114910
22953	1242050	776039	2355204	2045942	85176
33745	1541569	805242	2460279	2084365	71567
11177	648750	318583	1322705	1166249	34596
8274	337153	247524	557087	451703	17883
14294	555667	239135	580488	466413	19089

表 8—18 续表 Continued

		损益及分配	
		工程结算利润 Profits of Project Settlement Accounts	其他业务利润 Other Profits from Business
总计	**Total**	**1771704**	**39782**
按登记注册类型分组	**By Registered Type**		
内资企业	Domestic Funded Enterprises	1767913	39781
国有企业	State—owned Enterprises	4552	433
集体企业	Collective—oened Enterprises	1914	52
股份合作企业	Share—holding Cooperative Enterprises	3303	310
有限责任公司	Limited Liability Corporations	276616	18390
股份有限公司	Share—holding Corporations Ltd.	236694	10440
私营企业	Private Enterprises	1244835	10157
港、澳、台商投资企业	HongKong,Macro and Taiwan Funded	2480	
外商投资企业	Enterprises with Foreign Investment	1311	1
按建筑业行业中类分组	**By Sector**		
房屋和土木工程建筑业	Building and Civil Engineering	1442381	31226
房屋工程建筑	Building	910914	15482
土木工程建筑	Civil Engineering	531467	15744
建筑安装业	Construction Installation	180420	2674
建筑装饰业	Construction Decoration	104724	4187
其他建筑业	Other Construction	44179	1696
按控股情况分组	**By Holding Status**		
国有控股	State—holding	187521	3095
集体控股	Collective—holding	45342	12885
私人控股	Private—holding	1535434	23689
港澳台控股	Hong Kong, Macao and Taiwan Holdings		
外商控股	Foreign—holding		
按企业资质等级分组	**By Qualification Criteria**		
施工总承包	Construc General Contractor	1467357	30045
特级	Special Grade	186847	5889
一级	First Grade	811545	11135
二级	Second Grade	244879	12253
三级	Third Grade	224086	769
专业承包	Special General Contractor	304347	9737
一级	First Grade	121860	2833
二级	Second Grade	87502	2410
三级	Third Grade	94986	4495

单位:万元(10000 yuan)

Expenditure, Incomeand Distribution				应付职工薪酬 Employee Compensation Payable
管理费用 Management Expense	财务费用 Financial Expense	营业利润 Operating Profits	利润总额 Total Profits	
539386	**175150**	**1016516**	**1015926**	**4583326**
536653	174600	1016008	1015420	4578236
3929	−9	984	940	10853
1297	−54	678	623	2657
1290	−602	2902	3023	31092
102975	9348	169591	171877	673369
58303	44654	142401	144707	1142404
368860	121262	699451	694249	2717860
1994	459	27	26	2861
739	91	481	481	2229
398225	156681	857150	853930	4107796
215779	107912	576722	567872	3101768
182446	48769	280427	286058	1006029
78535	7229	90673	92528	258014
41248	7648	49733	50319	148627
21378	3592	18960	19149	68889
71809	3182	108616	110629	429167
29717	−1053	27006	27429	201374
436122	171934	880453	877446	3948085
404145	144156	893390	888091	4126891
49544	19913	114843	114908	907069
205420	90815	510285	515158	2063037
68250	19762	158182	148921	652931
80930	13667	110081	109104	503853
135242	30994	123126	127835	456436
49442	17026	52020	52626	275678
36429	6833	38924	41362	98538
49372	7135	32181	33848	82220

表 8－19　新增生产能力或效益(2013)
Newly Increase Production Capacity or Benefit

指标	单位	Indicators	Unit	本年新增 Added at this Year
粗钢	万吨/年	Crude Steels	10000 tons/year	3.6
钢材	万吨/年	Steels	10000 tons/year	75.1
其中:电解锌	吨/年	Electrolytic Zinc	tones/year	15000
铝加工材	吨/年	Alumina	tones/year	70000
铜加工材	吨/年	Copper	tones/year	275010.06
风力发电	万千瓦	Wind Power	10000 kw	3
输电线路长度(11 万伏及以上)	公里	Length of Transmission Lines (110,000 Volts and Above)	kilometer	659.42
水泥	万吨/年	Cement	10000 tons/year	130
平板玻璃	万重量箱/年	Plate Grass	10000 weightboxes/year	1.8
塑料树脂及共聚物	吨/年	Plastic Resin and Copolymer	tons/year	32500
轮胎外胎	万条/年	Tire	10000 units/year	20
轿车制造	辆/年	Car	units/year	50000
化学纤维	吨/年	Chemical Fiber	tons/year	347900
#合成纤维	吨/年	#Synthetic Fiber	tons/year	1200
粘胶纤维	吨/年	Viscose Fiber	tons/year	8000
棉纺锭	锭	Cotton Spindles	Spindles	170000
白酒	万吨/年	White Spirit	10000 tons/year	0.01
其他酒	万吨/年	Other Wine	10000 tons/year	10.8
家用电冰箱	万台/年	Household Refrigerators	10000 units/year	151
家用洗衣机	万台/年	Household Washing Machines	10000 units/year	40
房间空气调节器	万台/年	Room Air Conditioners	10000 units/year	50
新建公路	公里	New Highway	kilometer	163.79
#一级公路	公里	First Standard Road	kilometer	45.15
二级公路	公里	Second Standard Road	kilometer	36.88
改建公路	公里	Road Reconstruction	kilometer	269.29
#一级公路	公里	First Standard Road	kilometer	25.36
二级公路	公里	Second Standard Road	kilometer	12
新建独立公路桥梁	延长米	New Highway Bridge	meter	26.3
新建独立公路桥梁	座	New Highway Bridge	units	1
新建独立公路隧道	延长米	New Highway Tunnel	meter	1385
新建独立公路隧道	处	New Highway Tunnel	units	1
新(扩)建公路客、货运站	个	New (Expanding) Existing Road Passenger and Freight Station	units	2
新(扩)建公路客、货运站	平方米	New (Expanding) Existing Road Passenger and Freight Station	square meters	36307
城市自来水供水能力	万吨/日	Tap Water Supply Capacity	10000 tons/day	1
城市污水处理能力	万吨/日	Urban Sewage Treatment Capacity	10000 tons/day	18.31

表 8－20 本年完成建筑业总产值前 20 位企业(2013) The Top 20 Enterprises of Completed Total Output Value for Construction Industry

企业名称 Name of Enterprises	资质等级 Grade of Natural Endowments
龙元建设集团股份有限公司 Longyuan Construction Group Co. ,Ltd.	房屋建筑工程施工总承包特级 Whole Contract To Project of Building Construction by Special Grade
宏润建设集团股份有限公司 Hongrun Construction Group Co. ,Ltd.	市政工程施工总承包壹级 Whole Contract To Municipal Engineering Construction by First Grade
华丰建设股份有限公司 Ningbo Huafeng Construction Group Co. ,Ltd.	房屋建筑工程施工总承包特级 Whole Contract To Project of Building Construction by Special Grade
宁波建工集团有限公司 Ningbo Construction And Industry Group Co. , Ltd.	房屋建筑工程施工总承包特级 Whole Contract To Project of Building Construction by Special Grade
浙江省二建建设集团有限公司 Zhejiang No. 2 Construction Group Co. ,Ltd.	房屋建筑工程施工总承包特级 Whole Contract To Project of Building Construction by Special Grade
中达建设集团股份有限公司 Zhongda Construction Group Co. ,Ltd.	房屋建筑工程施工总承包特级 Whole Contract To Project of Building Construction by Special Grade
浙江欣捷建设有限公司 Zhe Jiang Xinjie Construction Co. ,Ltd.	房屋建筑工程施工总承包壹级 Whole Contract To Project of Building Construction by First Grade
宁波市建设集团股份有限公司 Ningbo Construction Group Co. ,Ltd.	房屋建筑工程施工总承包壹级 Whole Contract To Project of Building Construction by First Grade
浙江建安实业集团股份有限公司 Zhejiang Jian'an Industry Group Ltd.	房屋建筑工程施工总承包壹级 Whole Contract To Project of Building Construction by First Grade
浙江沈氏建设有限公司 Zhejiang Shen Construction Co. ,Ltd.	房屋建筑工程施工总承包壹级 Whole Contract To Project of Building Construction by First Grade
华锦建设股份有限公司 Huajing Construction Co. ,Ltd.	房屋建筑工程施工总承包壹级 Whole Contract To Project of Building Construction by First Grade
浙江天元建设(集团)股份有限公司 Zhejiang Tianyuan (Group) Co. ,Ltd.	房屋建筑工程施工总承包壹级 Whole Contract To Project of Building Construction by First Grade
大荣建设有限公司 Darong Construction Engineering Co. ,Ltd.	房屋建筑工程施工总承包壹级 Whole Contract To Project of Building Construction by First Grade
海达建设集团有限公司 Haida Construction Group Co. ,Ltd.	房屋建筑工程施工总承包壹级 Whole Contract To Project of Building Construction by First Grade
华恒建设集团有限公司 Huaheng Construction Group Co. ,Ltd.	房屋建筑工程施工总承包壹级 Whole Contract To Project of Building Construction by First Grade
浙江万华建设有限公司 Zhejiang Wanhua Construction Co. ,Ltd.	房屋建筑工程施工总承包壹级 Whole Contract To Project of Building Construction by First Grade
浙江新中源建设有限公司 Zhejiang New Zhongyuan Construction Co. ,Ltd.	房屋建筑工程施工总承包壹级 Whole Contract To Project of Building Construction by First Grade
宁波市市政设施景观建设有限公司 Ningbo municipal facilities Landscape Construction Co. ,Ltd.	市政工程施工总承包壹级 Whole Contract To Municipal Engineering Construction by First Grade
中交上航局航道建设有限公司 SDC Waterway Construction Co. ,Ltd.	港口与航道工程施工总承包壹级 Whole Constract To Port and Waterway Construction by First Grade
宁波住宅建设集团股份有限公司 Ningbo Residential Construction Group Co. ,Ltd.	房屋建筑工程施工总承包壹级 Whole Contract To Project of Building Construction by First Grade
博宏恒基集团有限公司 Bohohk Group Co. ,Ltd	房屋建筑工程施工总承包壹级 Whole Contract To Project of Building Construction by First Grade

表 8－21　1、2 级资质等级房地产开发经营企业(2013)
Enterprises for Real Estate Developing & Managing with Certificate in First, Second Grade of Natural Endowments

企业名称	Name of Enterprises	资质等级 Grade of Natural Endowments
宁波房地产股份有限公司	Ningbo Real Estate Co.,Ltd.	1
宁波永和建设开发股份有限公司	Ningbo Yonghe Construction Development Co.,Ltd.	1
宁波中房置业股份有限公司	Ningbo Zhongfang Real Estate Co.,Ltd.	1
仑江集团有限公司	Lun Jiang Group Co.,Ltd.	1
镇海石化工程有限责任公司	Zhenhai Petrochemical Engineering Co.,Ltd.	1
宁波东方建设开发有限公司	Ningbo Dongfang Construction Development Co.,Ltd.	1
宁波市五环房地产开发有限公司	Ningbo Wuhuan Estate Co.,Ltd.	1
宁波市甬佳房地产开发有限公司	Ningbo Yongjia Real Estate Developing Co.,Ltd.	1
宁波市交通房地产有限公司	Ningbo Jiaotong Real Estate Co.,Ltd.	1
宁波华泰股份有限公司	Ningbo Huatai Co.,Ltd.	1
雅戈尔置业控股有限公司	Youngor (Ningbo) Real Estate Co.,Ltd.	1
宁波银亿房地产开发有限公司	Ningbo Yingyi Real Estate Developing Co.,Ltd.	1
宁波宁兴房地产开发集团有限公司	Ningbo Ningxing Real Estate Developing Co.,Ltd.	1
宁波和锦房地产开发有限公司	Ningbo HejinReal Estate Development Co.,Ltd.	1
宁波舜大房地产开发有限公司	Ningbo Shunda Real Estate Developing Co.,Ltd.	1
荣安集团股份有限公司	Rongan Group Co.,Ltd.	1
宁波联合建设开发有限公司	Ningbo Lianhe Construction Developing Co.,Ltd.	1
宁波奥克斯置业有限公司	Ningbo Aux Ltd.	1
余姚市房地产开发经营有限公司	Yuyao Real Estate Developing Co.,Ltd.	1
宁波市镇海新城南区开发建设投资有限公司	Ningbo Zhenhai New South District Construction Investment Development Co.,Ltd.	1
宁波开投置业有限公司	Ningbo Kaituo Properties Co.,Ltd.	2
浙江广天建昌房地产股份有限公司	Zhejiang Guangtian Jianchang Real Estate Co.,Ltd.	2
宁波信达中建置业有限公司	Ningbo Xinda Zhongjian Real Estate Co.,Ltd.	2
宁波华丰建设房产有限责任公司	Ningbo Huafeng Construction Real Estate Ltd.	2
宁波经济技术开发区房地产总公司	Ningbo Economic and Technological Development Zone Real Estate Corporation	2
宁波市江东东城房屋开发公司	Ningbo Jiangdong Dongcheng House Development Ltd.	2
宁波市北仑区房地产建设开发有限公司	Ningbo Beilun Real Estate Construction Development Corp.	2
宁波新隆房地产股份有限公司	Ningbo Xinlong Real Estate Co.,Ltd.	2
宁波甬城房地产有限公司	Ningbo Yongcheng Real Estate Co.,Ltd.	2
宁波富豪房地产开发有限公司	Ningbo Fuhao Real Estate Developing Co.,Ltd.	2
宁波华龙投资建设开发有限公司	Niingbo Hualong Investment Construction and Development Co.,Ltd.	2
慈溪市住宅经营有限责任公司	Cixi House Managing Corp.	2
浙江兴润置业投资有限公司	Zhejiang Xingrun Real Estate Co.,Ltd.	2
宁波滕头房地产开发有限公司	Ningbo Tengtou Real Estate Development Co.,Ltd.	2
象山房地产开发有限公司	Xiangshan Real Estate Developing Co.,Ltd.	2
象山县地产房产开发总公司	Xiangshan Real Estate Developing Corporation	2
宁波富邦房地产开发有限公司	Ningbo Fontune Real Estate Development Co.,Ltd.	2
中信大榭房地产公司	CITIC Daxie Real Estate Company	2
宁波市镇海区住房发展投资有限公司	Ningbo Zhenhai House Developing & Investment Co,. Ltd.	2
象山金淼房地产发展有限公司	Xiangshan Jinmiao Real Estate Development Co.,Ltd.	2
宁波太平洋土地建设有限公司	Ningbo Pacific Land Construction Co.,Ltd.	2
宁波市拓展房地产开发有限公司	Ningbo Tuozhan Real Estate Developing Co.,Ltd.	2
慈溪新城房地产发展有限公司	Cixi Xincheng Real Estate Development Co.,Ltd.	2

表 8—21 续表 Continued

企业名称	Name of Enterprises	资质等级 Grade of Natural Endowments
浙江太平洋房产开发有限公司	Zhejiang Pacific Real Estate Developing Co. ,Ltd.	2
宁波金峰房地产开发有限公司慈溪分公司	Ningbo Cixi Jinfeng Branch Real Estate Development Co. ,Ltd.	2
宁波维科置业有限公司	Ningbo Veken Real Estate Co. ,Ltd.	2
余姚市赛格特经济技术开发有限公司	Yuyao Saigete Economic & Technology Developing Co. ,Ltd.	2
浙江山水房地产开发有限公司	Zhejiang landscape Real Estate Development Co. ,Ltd.	2
宁波振兴房地产开发有限公司	Ningbo Revitalization Real Estate Co. ,Ltd.	2
宁波舜龙房地产开发有限公司	Ningbo Sunlong Real Estate Development Co. ,Ltd.	2
奉化市城市建设投资有限公司	Fenghua City Constuction Co. ,Ltd.	2
宁波市镇海茗园房地产开发有限公司	Ningbo Zhenhai Mingyuan Real Estate Co. ,Ltd.	2
余姚市东方房产有限公司	Yuyao Dongfang Real Estate Co. ,Ltd.	2
宁波市镇海华鑫房地产开发有限公司	Ningbo Zhenhai Huaxin Real Estate Developing Co. ,Ltd.	2
慈溪市大通房地产开发有限公司	Cixi Datong Real Estate Developing Co. ,Ltd.	2
宁波宁盛置业有限公司	Ningbo Ningsheng Real Estate Co. ,Ltd.	2
余姚市万里房地产开发有限公司	Yuyao Wanli Real Estate Developing Co. ,Ltd.	2
宁波中宇房地产有限公司	Ningbo Zhongyu Real Estate Co. ,Ltd.	2
慈溪市飞龙房地产开发有限公司	Cixi Feilong Real Estate Developing Co. ,Ltd.	2
慈溪市环驰房地产开发有限公司	Cixi Huanchi Real Estate Developing Ltd.	2
慈溪中星房地产开发有限公司	Cixi Zhongxing Real Estate Developing Ltd.	2
宁波市恒和房地产开发有限公司	Ningbo Henghe Real Estate Development Co. ,Ltd.	2
宁波金沃房地产开发有限公司	Ningbo Jinwo Real Estate Development Co. ,Ltd.	2
宁波新恒德置业有限公司	Ningbo Xinhengde Ltd.	2
象山县万象房屋开发有限公司	Xiangshan Wanxiang Real Estate Developing Ltd.	2
宁波万基房地产开发有限公司	Ningbo Wanji Real Estate Developing Ltd.	2
余姚市久丰房地产开发有限公司	Yuyao Jiufeng Real Estate Developing Ltd.	2
宁海县和兴房地产开发有限公司	Ninghai Hexing Real Estate Developing Ltd.	2
象山华丰房地产有限责任公司	Xiangshan Huafeng Real Estate Co. ,Ltd.	2
宁波大丰房地产开发有限责任公司	Ningbo Dafeng Real Estate Co. ,Ltd.	2
宁波香格房地产开发有限公司	Ningbo Xiangge Real Estate Co. ,Ltd.	2
象山宏润房地产有限公司	Xiangshan Hongrong Real Estate Co. ,Ltd.	2
浙江华茂置业发展有限公司	Zhejiang Huanmao Real Estate Development Co. ,Ltd.	2
宁波市北仑华信置业有限公司	Ningbo Beilun Huaxin Properties Ltd.	2
宁波美华实业有限公司	Ningbo Meihua Industrial Co. ,Ltd.	2
宁波百隆房地产有限公司	Ningbo Bailong Real Estate Co. ,Ltd.	2
宁波申洲置业有限公司	Ningbo Shenzhou Properties Ltd.	2
宁波康园房地产开发有限公司	Ningbo Kangyuan Real Estate Development Co. ,Ltd.	2
宁波华垠房地产开发有限公司	Ningbo Huayin Real Estate Development Co. ,Ltd.	2
宁波前程房地产有限公司	Ningbo Future Real Estate Co. ,Ltd.	2
宁波金峰房地产开发有限公司	Ningbo Jinfeng Real Estate Development Co. ,Ltd.	2
宁波得力房地产有限公司	Ningbo Deli Real Estate Co. ,Ltd.	2
余姚市舜泉房地产开发有限公司	Yuyao Shunquan Real Estate Developing Co. ,Ltd.	2
宁波沧海控股集团有限公司	Ningbo Sea Holding Group Co. ,Ltd.	2
宁波和协拓展置业有限公司	Ningbo Hexie Real Estate Development Co. ,Ltd.	2
慈溪市城市发展有限公司房地产分公司	Cixi City Developing Ltd.	2

主要统计指标解释

【全社会固定资产投资】 固定资产投资是社会固定资产再生产的主要手段。通过建造和购置固定资产的活动,国民经济不断采用先进技术装备,建立新兴部门,进一步调整经济结构和生产力的地区分布,增强经济实力,为改善人民物质文化生活创造物质条件。这对我国的社会主义现代化建设具有重要意义。

固定资产投资额是以货币表现的建造和购置固定资产活动的工作量,它是反映固定资产投资规模、速度、比例关系和使用方向的综合性指标。全社会固定资产投资按经济类型可分为国有、集体、个体、联营、股份制、外商、港澳台商、其他等。按照管理渠道,全社会固定资产投资总额分为基本建设、更新改造、房地产开发投资和其他固定资产投资四个部分。

【房地产开发投资】 指房地产开发公司、商品房建设公司及其他房地产开发法人单位和附属于其他法人单位实际从事房地产开发或经营的活动单位统一开发的包括统代建、拆迁还建的住宅、厂房、仓库、饭店、宾馆、度假村、写字楼、办公楼等房屋建筑物和配套的服务设施,土地开发工程(如道路、给水、排水、供电、供热、通讯、平整场地等基础设施工程)的投资;不包括单纯的土地交易活动。

【农村非农户投资】 农村非农户建造和购置固定资产投资计划固定资本形成总额在500万元以上的项目,农村非农户包括以下二大类:

第一类为企业单位,分成(1)集体企业,包括集体直接经营及集体所有租赁给个人的企业;(2)股份合作企业;(3)联营企业;(4)有限责任公司(5)股份有限公司;(6)私营企业(7)与港澳台商合资、合作企业;(8)中外合资、合作企业;(9)其他企业。

联营和合资企业按其是否由农村集体与个人相对控股或绝对控股,或由农村集体、个人实际管理来确定是否纳入农村固定资产投资统计范围,其投资额按实际发生额全额统计;个体工商户外雇从业人员8人以上(含8人)的按企业统计。

第二类为乡镇行政事业单位及社会群众团体。

【新增固定资产】指通过投资活动所形成的新的固定资产价值。包括已经建成投入生产或交付使用的工程价值和达到固定资产标准的设备、工具、器具的价值及有关应摊入的费用。它是以价值形式表示的固定资产投资成果的综合性指标,可以综合反映不同时期、不同部门、不同地区的固定资产投资成果。

【新增生产能力(或工程效益)】指通过固定资产投资活动而增加的设计能力或工程效益,它是用实物形态表示的固定资产投资的成果。新增生产能力的计算,是以能独立发挥生产能力或工程效益的单项工程(或项目)为对象。当单项工程(或项目)建成,经有关部门鉴定合格,正式移交投入生产,即可计算新增生产能力。

新增生产能力或工程效益有以下几种表现形式:

⑴以建设项目或单项工程建成后的年产能力表示,如煤炭开采、石油开采等。

⑵以建设项目或单项工程建成后处理原料的能力表示,如选矿工程的年处理矿石能力、洗煤厂年洗原煤能力等。

⑶以新增的主要设备数量或容量表示,如棉纺锭锭数、发电机组容量等。

⑷以建筑物容积、容量、面积或长度表示,如水库容量、铁路公路里程等。

新增生产能力的数量一般按设计能力计算。设计能力是指设计文件中规定的在正常情况下能够达到的生产能力,而不论投产后的实际产量如何。以设备数量、建筑物容积、面积、长度等表示的新增生产能力或工程效益,则按建成的实际数量计算。

【建筑业统计单位】 指从事房屋、构筑物建造和设备安装活动的法人企业。建筑业法人企业应同时具备的条件是:①依法成立,有自己的名称、组织机构和场所,能够承担民事责任;②独立拥有和使用资产,承担负债,有权与其他单位签订合同;③独立核算盈亏,能够编制资产负债表。

【建筑业总产值(即自行完成施工产值)】 指建筑业企业或附属施工单位自行完成的按工程进度计算的建筑安装生产总值。施工产值包括:

①建筑工程产值:指列入建筑工程预算内的各种工程价值。

②设备安装工程产值:指设备安装工程价值。

③房屋、构筑物修理产值:指房屋、构筑物修理所完成的价值,但不包括被修理房屋、构筑物本身的价值和生产设备的修理价值。

④非标准设备制造产值:指加工制造没有定型的、非标准的生产设备的加工费和原材料价值,不论是现场还是附属加工厂为本单位承建工程制造的非标准设备的价值,都应计算产值。

【房屋建筑施工面积】 指报告期内施工的全部房屋建筑面积。包括本期新开工的面积、上期跨入本期继续施工的房屋面积、上期停缓建在本期恢复施工的房屋面积、本期竣工的房屋面积及本期施工后又停缓建的房屋面积。

【房屋建筑竣工面积】 指在报告期内房屋建筑按照设计要求已全部完工,达到住人和使用条件,经验收鉴定合格,正式移交使用单位的建筑面积。

【自有机械设备年末总台数】 指归本企业(或单位)所有,属于本企业固定资产的生产性机械设备年末总台数。包括施工机械、生产设备、运输设备以及其他设备。

【自有机械设备年末总功率】 指本企业(或单位)自有施工机械、生产设备、运输设备以及其他设备等列为在册固定资产的生产性机械设备年末总功率,按设定能力或查定能力计算。包括机械本身的动力和为该机械服务的单独动力设备,如电动机等。计算单位用千瓦,动力换算可按1马力=0.735千瓦折合成千瓦数。电焊机、变压器、锅炉不计算动力。

【工程结算收入】 指企业(或单位)按工程的分部分项自行完成的建筑产品价值并已与甲方在报告期内办理结算手续的工程价款收入,以及向甲方收取的除工程价款以外的按规定列作营业收入的各种款项,如临时设施费、劳动保险费、施工机械调迁费等以及向甲方收取的各种索赔款。

【工程结算利润】 指已结算工程实现的利润。如为亏损以"－"号表示。其计算公式为:

工程结算利润＝工程结算收入－工程结算成本－工程结算税金及附加

Explanatory Notes on Main Statistical Indicators

【Total Investment in Fixed Assets in the Whole Country】 Investment in fixed assets is the essential means for social reproduction of fixed assets. By means of construction and purchase of fixed assets, more advanced technologies and equipment are adopted in the national economy, and new sectors are established, which promote the adjustment of economic structure and the regional distribution of productive forces and enhance the economic strengths so as to provide the material conditions for improving people's livelihood. This is significant for speeding up the drive of socialist modernization in China.

Amount of investment in fixed assets refers to the volume of activities in construction and purchases of fixed assets in monetary terms. It is a comprehensive indicator which shows the size, pace, proportional relations and use orientation of the investment in fixed assets. Total investment in fixed assets in the whole country includes, by registration type of ownership, the investment by the state—owned units, collective units, individuals, joint ownership units, share—holding units, as well as investment by businessmen from foreign countries and from Hong Kong, Macao and Taiwan, and by other units. According to China 's current management system, the investment in fixed assets in the whole country is classified into the following four parts: investment in capital construction, investment in innovation, investment in real estates development and other investment in fixed assets.

【Investment in Real Estate Development】 It includes the investment by the real estate development companies, commercial buildings construction companies and other real estate development units of various types of ownership in the construction of house buildings, such as residential buildings, factory buildings, warehouses, hotels, guesthouses, holiday villages, office buildings, and the complementary service facilities and land development projects, such as roads, water supply, water drainage, power supply, heating, telecommunications, land leveling and other projects of infrastructure. It excludes the activities in simple land transactions.

【Individual Investment in Rural Areas】 The individual investment in the rural areas includes the investment in house construction and purchase of productive fixed assets by the individuals in the rural areas.

【non—agricultural investment in rural areas】 refers to the project which the estimated total investment amount of its fixed assets built or bought by the non—agriculture units in rural areas is over 5 million yuan. The non—agricultural units include two kinds as below:

I. enterprises. 1. Collective Co. (including companies both directly managed by collective leadership and rent to the private), 2. Stock—hoiding cooperation, 3. Joint Ownership Enterprises, 4. Limited liability Corporations, 5. Share—holding corporations Ltd. , 6. Private enterprises, 7. Joint ventures or Cooperative Operation with Hong kong, Macao and Taiwan, 8. Foreign joint ventures or Cooperative Operation Enterprises, 9. other Enterprises

whether the associated companies and the joint ventures should be considered as the rural fixed assets depends on whether they are actually possessed or managed by rural communities or privates. Their investment amounts refer to the capital which had been actually invested into the enterprises. Private businesses which employ 8 or more workers should be considered as enterprises in statistics

II. public undertakings and public communities in rural areas.

【Newly Increased Fixed Assets】 refer to the newly increased value of fixed assets through investment, including the value of projects completed and put into production, the value of equipment, tools, and vessels considered as fixed assets, as well as the relevant expenses as investment in fixed assets . This is a comprehensive indicator of investment in fixed assets, reflecting the achievements of investment in fixed assets in different periods, different sect ors, and different regions.

【Newly Increased Production Capacity】 refers to the increase of designed capacity and project efficiency through investment in fixed assets, which reflects the accomplishment of investment in fixed assets in kind. The calculation of newly increased production capacity is based on individual project which operates independently and efficiently. When an individual project is completed and checked and accepted and put into production, it is counted as newly increased production capacity.

The newly increased production capacity and project efficiency are usually expressed in one of the following forms:

(1) annual production capacity, such as extraction of coal and petroleum;

(2) raw material processing capacity, such as ore dressing capacity of ore dressing projects, the dressing capacity of a coal

washery;

(3)number or capacity of major equipment increased, such as the number of cotton spindles increased and the capacity of generating sets increased;

(4)physical measures of construction, such as volume, capacity, area, and length, for instance, the capacity of reservoirs, the length of railways or highways.

Newly increased production capacity in terms of quantity is calculated in designed capacity in general, which refers to the production capacity of a project under normal conditions designed in construction documents regardless of the actual output.

【Statistical units in construction industries】 refers to the legal enterprises which build architectures or install equipments. The legal enterprises should meet all the demands as follows, 1. being formed legally with own name, organizational structure and working place. Can fully bear civil responsibilities. 2. possessing and using its own assets independently, which means it should be able to incur liabilities and has right to make contracts with other enterprises. 3. should be an independent accounting unit which can draw balance sheet.

【Gross Output Value of Construction(Output Value of Projects Under Construction)】 refers to total of construction products, expressed in money terms,completed by construction and installation enterprises during a given period of time. It includes:

(1)Output value of construction projects, that is the value of projects covered by the project budgets;

(2)Output value of installation projects, that is the value of the installation of equipment,(excluding the value of the equipment to be installed);

(3)Output value of repair of buildings and structures, that is the value created through the repairs of buildings or structures, but does not include the value of buildings or structures being repaired and the value of the repair of production equipment;

(4)Output value of manufactured non—standard equipment, that is the value of no-standard production equipment(including raw materials and manufacturing cost)made for the construction project, and the equipment manufactured by subsidiary workshops.

【Floor Space under Construction】 refers to total floor space of all buildings under construction during the reference period, including floor space of newly started buildings during the reference period, floor space of construction extended from the previous period to the current period, floor space of construction suspended during the previous period and resumed in the current period, floor space of construction completed in the current period, and floor space of construction started and then suspended in the current period.

【Floor Space of Buildings Completed】 refers to the floor space of buildings completed in the reference period, which have come up to the designed standards and have been put into use.

【Total Number of Machinery and Equipment Owned by the Construction Enterprises】 refers to the number of machines and equipment owned by the enterprises (or units, and listed as the fixed assets of the enterprises(or units) by the end of the year, including machinery and equipment for construction, production and transportation.

【Total Power of Machinery and Equipment Owned by the Construction Enterprises】 refer to the total power of machinery and equipment owned by the enterprises(or units), and listed as the fixed assets of the enterprises (or units) by the end of the year, including machinery and equipment for construction, production and transportation. The power of the machinery is calculated on basis of the designed or verified capacity, covering the power of the machinery/equipment and the separate power equipment serving the machinery/equipment (such as electric motors), but excluding welders, transformers and boilers. The unit use for the calculation of power is kilowatt, with horsepower converted to kilowatt by 1horsepower=0. 735 kilowatt.

【Income from Settlement of Projects】 refers to the income received by the construction enterprise/unit from the completed portion of the project through settlement procedures with the contracted during the reference period, and other charges to the contracted as operational costs, such as facility fee, labor insurance premium, moving cost of construction unit, as well as various types of claims to the contracted.

【Profit from Settlement of Projects】 refers to profit realized through settled projects. It is calculated with the following formula:

Profit from Settlement of Projects=Income from Settlement of projects—Settled Cost—Settled Taxes and Other Cost.

CHAPTER 9

NINGBO 2014 Statistical YearBook

第九篇

港口、交通、运输、邮电

PORT, TRANSPORTATION, POST AND TELECOMMUNICATION SERVICE

港口、交通、运输、邮电
Port, Transportations, Post and Telecommunications

主要统计指标
Major Statistics Indicators

2013年全社会客运量	Total Passenger Traffic	24793	万人	10000 persons
比上年增长	Increase Over Last Year	−11.62	%	
2013年全社会货运量	Total Freight Traffic	35409	万吨	10000 tons
比上年增长	Increase Over Last Year	8.57	%	
2013年港口货物吞吐量	Cargo Handled at Ports	49592	万吨	10000 tons
比上年增长	Increase Over Last Year	9.47	%	
2013年集装箱吞吐量	Container Handled at Ports	1677	万标箱	10000 TEU
比上年增长	Increase Over Last Year	7.03	%	
2013移动电话用户	Number of Mobile Telephone Subscribers	1088.00	万户	10000 subcribers
比上年增长	Increase Over Last Year	5.7	%	
2013年固定电话用户	Number of Local Telephone Subscribers	298.00	万户	10000 subcribers
比上年增长	Increase Over Last Year	3.2	%	

表 9—1 历年港口、交通、邮电基本情况
Basic Statistics on Port,Transportation and Telecommunications Over the Years

年份 Year	港口货物吞吐量（万吨）Cargo at Throughput Ports (10000 tons)	集装箱吞吐量（万标箱）Container Throughput (10000 TEU)	货运量（万吨）Freight Traffic (10000 tons)	客运量（万人）Passenger Traffic (10000 persons)	固定电话用户（万户）Number of Local Telephone Subscribers (10000 subscribers)
1978	214		1385	2966	1.07
1979	236		1430	3369	1.19
1980	326		1562	4156	1.36
1981	349		1496	4654	1.53
1982	371		1617	5192	1.71
1983	483		1641	5652	1.86
1984	597		1810	6026	2.22
1985	1040		2015	6527	2.60
1986	1797		3204	7373	2.91
1987	1940		3745	7473	3.55
1988	2002		5408	7277	4.64
1989	2209		4570	7686	5.37
1990	2554	2.2	4763	7378	6.19
1991	3390	3.6	5070	8757	8.05
1992	4367	5.3	6492	9773	12.22
1993	5321	7.9	7583	11224	18.59
1994	5850	12.5	8711	17776	27.86
1995	6853	16.0	9577	19705	41.78
1996	7638	20.2	10460	21152	53.33
1997	8220	25.7	10547	21719	67.75
1998	8707	35.3	10317	21736	83.74
1999	9660	60.1	10344	22211	104.13
2000	11547	90.2	10819	22736	130.15
2001	12852	121.3	11283	23225	163.21
2002	15398	185.9	12429	23752	203.58
2003	18543	277.2	13919	24938	242.00
2004	22586	400.5	16026	27291	296.72
2005	26881	520.8	17664	28412	339.41
2006	30969	706.8	22238	29146	345.08
2007	34519	935.0	24363	30693	334.98
2008	36185	1084.6	27508	32250	338.24
2009	38385	1042.3	29028	33791	301.41
2010	41217	1300.4	30553	33911	317.39
2011	43339	1451.2	31228	28745	312.45
2012	45303	1567.1	32616	28053	308.00
2013	49592	1677.4	35409	24793	298.00

表 9－2 港口吞吐情况(2013)
Basic Statistics On Cargo at Ports Throughput

单位:万吨(10000 tons)

指标	Indicators	吞吐量 Capacity		其中 of Which			
				出口量 Export		进口量 Import	
		总计 Total	外贸 Foreign Trade	合计 Total	外贸 Foreign Trade	合计 Total	外贸 Foreign Trade
货物吞吐量	**Cargo at Throughput Ports**	**49592**	**27628**	**18361**	**9514**	**31231**	**18114**
#转口货物	Cargo of Transfer	10700	5089	5350	6	5350	5083
货物分类	**Type of Cargo**						
煤炭及制品	Coal And Its Products	7926	1341	941		6984	1341
石油及制品	Petroleum And Its Products	8090	5215	1936	166	6154	5050
金属矿石	Metal Ores	8929	5385	3530		5399	5385
钢铁	Steel and Iron	1078	99	130	27	948	73
矿建材料	Mineral Building Materials	1994		508		1486	
水泥	Cement	803		152		652	
木材	Timber	25	13	1		25	13
非金属矿石	Nonmetal Ores	466	1	11	1	455	
化肥及农药	Chemical Fertilizers and Pesticides	9	5	5	5	3	
盐	Salt	114	76	2		112	76
粮食	Grain	177	135	19		158	135
机械设备	Machinery Equipment	5	3	3	2	2	2
化工原料及制品	Industrial Chemicals And Its Products	1339	847	172	10	1167	838
轻工、医药	Products of Leight Industry and Medicine	44	14	4		40	14
农林牧渔业产品	Products of Farming, Forestry, Animal Husbandry And Fishery	14	7	3		11	6
其他	Others	18567	14486	10944	9304	7623	5182
旅客吞吐量(万人次)	**Number of Passenger In－And Out (10000 person. times)**	**158.56**		**79.89**		**78.66**	

表 9－3　港口国际集装箱吞吐量(2013)
International Container Throughput at Ports

航线	Shipping Lines	箱数(箱) Number of Container	重量(吨) Weigh(ton)	
			合计 Total	货重 Weigh of Cargo
总计	**Total**	**16773709**	**170496874**	**135734556**
国际航线合计	International Lines	14161616	133195888	103954351
非洲合计	Africa	690181	6808229	5378593
亚洲合计	Asia	6227677	62378472	49480923
欧洲合计	Europe	2924244	27605924	21596813
北美洲合计	North America	2952509	24965265	18954863
南美洲合计	South America	775132	6188094	4548833
大洋洲及太平洋岛屿合计	Oceania	391252	3156200	2313604
世界其他	Others	200621	2093704	1680722
内支线合计	Total of Domestic Sub－Line	1092527	13931514	11654963
天津	Tianjin	2260	46287	41584
大连	Dalian	19626	225290	185837
上海	Shanghai	16326	218264	185133
江苏	Jiangsu			
浙江	Zhejiang			
福建	Fujian			
山东	Shandong			
中国其他	Others	176640	2419626	2045946
国内航线合计	Total of Domestic Lines	1519567	23369472	20125242

表 9—4 历年客运量
Passenger Traffic Over the Years

单位:万人(10000 persons)

年份 Year	合计 Total	其中 of Which			
		铁路 Railway	公路 Highway	水路 Waterway	航空 Civil Aviation
1978	2966	105	2311	550	
1979	3369	122	2692	555	
1980	4156	317	3241	598	
1981	4654	351	3714	598	
1982	5192	366	4277	549	
1983	5652	411	4737	504	
1984	6026	480	5073	473	
1985	6527	502	5575	450	
1986	7373	482	6472	418	1.2
1987	7473	497	6536	438	2
1988	7277	536	6339	399	3.1
1989	7686	527	6790	366	3.2
1990	7378	462	6611	299	6
1991	8757	445	8006	295	11
1992	9773	414	9076	268	14
1993	11224	435	10523	245	21
1994	17776	486	16993	265	32
1995	19705	506	18870	283	45
1996	21152	405	20432	262	53
1997	21719	342	21101	222	55
1998	21736	300	21199	182	55
1999	22211	278	21734	146	53
2000	22736	288	22255	133	59.7
2001	23225	349	22700	115	61
2002	23752	393	23160	135	64
2003	24938	438	24320	115	65
2004	27291	567	26510	119	95
2005	28412	607	27570	113	122
2006	29146	745	28120	121	160
2007	30693	842	29541	130	180
2008	32250	1770	30130	152	198
2009	33791	1700	31545	142	403
2010	33911	1012	32340	107	452
2011	28745	2186	25960	97	501
2012	28053	1119	26285	123	527
2013	24793	1273	22850	124	546

注:2011 年,客运量为营业性客运量。

Note: In 2011, passenger volume is a business volume of passenger.

表 9—5 历年货运量
Freight Traffic Over the Years

单位：万吨(10000 tons)

年份 Year	合计 Total	其中 of Which 铁路 Railway	公路 Highway	水路 Waterway	航空(吨) Civil Aviation(ton)	管道 Pipeline
1978	1385	45	625	715		
1979	1430	67	681	682		
1980	1562	167	709	686		
1981	1496	170	714	612		
1982	1617	186	788	643		
1983	1641	217	810	614		
1984	1810	234	883	693		
1985	2015	284	955	776		
1986	3204	310	1910	984	237	
1987	3745	337	2576	832	371	
1988	5408	380	4196	832	567	
1989	4570	398	3443	729	500	
1990	4763	355	3800	608	800	
1991	5070	302	4143	625	1600	
1992	6492	429	5328	710	2200	25
1993	7583	428	6255	868	3262	32
1994	8711	455	7113	1112	4000	31
1995	9577	527	7843	1173	4900	34
1996	10460	573	8509	1233	5200	44
1997	10547	551	8612	1314	5400	41
1998	9952	569	8195	1143	6900	44
1999	10344	609	8154	1534	9000	46
2000	10819	682	8219	1829	11000	88
2001	11283	725	8300	2156	10000	101
2002	12429	980	8630	2716	12500	102
2003	13919	1158	9070	3568	13812	122
2004	16026	1210	9890	4734	18725	190
2005	17664	1207	10480	5619	23450	356
2006	22238	1238	11725	7349	23505	1924
2007	24363	1274	12889	8706	23608	1492
2008	27508	2171	13550	9993	24549	1792
2009	29028	2377	15594	11050	68700	1774
2010	30553	2060	16220	12265	81200	2109
2011	34385	2960	15280	13771	90000	2366
2012	32616	1924	16570	14113	90800	2443
2013	35409	2168	17790	15441	94900	2641

表 9－6 历年全社会旅客周转量和货物周转量 Total Turnover Volume of Passengers and Turnover Volume of Freight Traffic Over the Years

单位：万人公里，万吨公里(10000 tons－km，10000 persons－km)

年份 Year	旅客周转量 Turnover Volume of Passengers			货物周转量 Turnover Volume of Freight Traffic			
	总计 Total	其中 of Which		总计 Total	其中 of Which		
		公路 Highway	水路 Waterway		公路 Highway	水路 Waterway	管道 Pipeline
1985	147863	135273	12590	132890	34369	98521	
1986	176321	163351	12970	219594	86541	133053	
1987	182877	168280	14597	294320	130907	163413	
1988	191911	176853	15058	271187	89321	181865	
1989	193779	180061	13718	319319	135845	183474	
1990	202868	190057	12811	308099	134299	173800	
1991	229727	215573	14154	438528	187032	251496	
1992	270125	258068	12057	608363	242989	365157	217
1993	324919	314471	10448	777570	262057	515229	284
1994	623257	610761	12496	1243892	448457	795435	
1995	699514	685120	14394	1450892	495929	954674	289
1996	735912	721653	14259	1742582	523495	1218722	365
1997	755941	740381	15560	1853782	533382	1320018	382
1998	752757	741848	10909	1887113	491380	1395325	408
1999	771393	764287	7106	2311376	481555	1829381	440
2000	800193	794858	5335	2367484	482518	1884241	723
2001	822326	818704	3622	2727939	492170	2231435	4335
2002	870546	867830	2716	3342614	521700	2844927	5517
2003	921901	919900	2001	4559749	553005	4002654	4090
2004	992957	990870	2087	5545297	608310	4932308	4679
2005	1042307	1040410	1897	7478890	644800	6806210	27880
2006	1060134	1058100	2034	10361127	719114	8696860	945153
2007	1213443	1211162	2281	11298162	812007	9775967	710188
2008	1235559	1232691	2868	12470705	856713	10745112	868880
2009	1245586	1242710	2876	13216223	1351300	10999544	865379
2010	1362007	1360600	1407	15753422	2465250	13288172	997675
2011	1383064	1382100	963	20903442	2815110	16884961	1203371
2012	1431814	1430930	884	20710458	3025860	17684598	1232617
2013	1242765	1242030	735	22307108	3254460	19052648	1351735

表 9—7 公路运输工具拥有量(2013)
Number of Means of Transportation Through Highway

指标	单位	Indicators	Unit	营业性 Business	
				合计 Total	个体 Individual
总计	**辆**	**Total**	**unit**	**97905**	**41769**
汽车	辆	Automobile	unit	97905	41769
载客汽车	辆	Buses And Cars	unit	4169	
	客位		seat	130510	
#大型	辆	Large—Sized	unit	1852	
	客位		seat	87275	
中型	辆	Middle—Sized	unit	2155	
	客位		seat	42127	
载货汽车	辆	Trucks	unit	97905	41769
	吨位		ton	762757	112572
①普通载货汽车	辆	Ordinary Trucks	unit	62824	41001
	吨位		ton	236726	104091
#大型	辆	Large—Space	unit	14255	6237
	吨位		ton	175762	62602
重型	辆	Heavy	unit	10140	4150
	吨位		ton	151643	51056
中型	辆	Middle	unit	1417	698
	吨位		ton	5003	2476
②专用载货汽车	辆	Trucks for Special Purpose	unit	13293	36
	吨位		ton	403154	970
#集装箱车	辆	Container Trucks	unit	11557	4
	TEU		TEU	23342	8

表 9—8 水路运输工具拥有量(2013)
Number of Means of Transportation Through Waterway

指标	单位	Indicators	Unit	总计 Total	其中 of Which		
					内河 Freshwater	沿海 Coastal	远洋 Ocean
总计	**艘**	**Total**	**unit**	**683**	**51**	**626**	
机动船	**艘**	**Motor Vessels**	**unit**	**677**	**51**	**620**	**6**
净载重量	吨位	Dead Weight	ton	5789114	7159	5440303	341652
载客量	客位	Passenger Capacity	seat	4507	3068	1439	
标准箱位	TEU	Standard Container Space	TEU	7320		6896	424
功率	千瓦	Power	kw	1195759	6592	1139411	49756
机动船按类别分		**Group by Type on Motor Vessels**					
客船	艘	Passenger Ships	unit	40	28	12	
载客量	客位	Passenger Capacity	seat	2528	1568	960	
功率	千瓦	Power	kw	8422	3035	5387	
客货船	艘	Passenger—cargo Vessels	unit	9	3	6	
净载重量	吨位	Dead Weight	ton		434		
载客量	客位	Passenger Capacity	seat	1979	1500	479	
功率	千瓦	Power	kw	2574	506	2068	
货船	艘	Cargo Ships	unit	627	20	601	6
净载重量	吨位	Dead Weight	ton	5789114	7159	5440303	341652
标准箱位	TEU	Standard Container Space	TEU	7320		6896	424
功率	千瓦	Power	kw	1184028	3051	1131221	49756
#①油船	艘	Tanker	unit	126		126	
净载重量	吨位	Dead Weight	ton	434158		434158	
功率	千瓦	Power	kw	142592		142592	
②集装箱船	艘	Container Ships	unit	12		11	1
净载重量	吨位	Dead Weight	ton	114104		106281	7823
标准箱位	TEU	Standard Container Space	TEU	7320		6896	424
功率	千瓦	Power	kw	55592		50886	4706
拖船	艘	Tugboats	unit	1		1	
功率	千瓦	Power	kw	735		735	
驳船	艘	Barges	unit	6		6	
净载重量	吨位	Dead Weight	ton	11954		11954	

表9—9 部分年份运输线路里程长度
Length of Transportation Routes in Partial Years

单位:公里(km)

指标	Indicators	2009	2010	2011	2012	2013
公路总里程	**Overal Length For Highway**	**9884**	**9884**	**10439**	**10661**	**10892**
按技术等级分:	**Divided by Grade**					
①等级公路	Highway Grade	9272	9272	9881	10102	10350
高速公路	Express Way	370	370	416	463	496
一级公路	Highway Grade 1	769	769	945	960	1059
二级公路	Highway Grade 2	876	876	784	813	775
三级公路	Highway Grade 3	1492	1492	1551	1550	1533
四级公路	Highway Grade 4	5597	5764	6026	6173	6355
准四级公路	Near Highway Grade 4	167		159	143	132
②等外公路	Highway Without Grade	612	612	559	559	542
按路面等级分	**Divided by Road Surface**					
高级路面	High Grade Road Surface	8985	8985	9736	10003	10298
次高级路面	Sub—High Grade Road Surface	453	453	395	380	361
中级路面	Medium Grade Road Surface	446	446	309	278	233
低级路面	Lower Grade Road Surface					
按行政等级分	**Divided by Adminitrative Level**					
国道	State Way	453	453	497	497	497
省道	Province Way	718	718	724	771	804
县道	County Way	2671	2671	2819	2844	2885
乡道	Township Way	2137	2137	2186	2188	2189
专用道	Special Use Way	84	84	56	56	56
村道公路里程	Village Way	3821	3821	4158	4306	4462
内河通航里程	**Length of Navigable Inland Waterways**	**927**	**927**	**927**	**927**	**927**

表 9－10　历年电信业主要指标
Main Indicators of Telecommunications Services Over the Years

年份 Year	固定电话用户 （万户） Number of Local Telephone Subscribers (10000 subcribers)	#农话 Rural Telephone Subscribers	移动电话 （万户） Number of Subscribers of Mobile Telephone (10000 subscribers)	国际互联网用户 （户） User of International Computer Network (user)
1978	1.07	0.49		
1979	1.19	0.53		
1980	1.36	0.58		
1981	1.53	0.64		
1982	1.71	0.70		
1983	1.86	0.76		
1984	2.22	0.89		
1985	2.60	1.05		
1986	2.91	1.14		
1987	3.55	1.35		
1988	4.64	1.68		
1989	5.37	1.92		
1990	6.19	2.15		
1991	8.05	2.88		
1992	12.22	4.92	0.14	
1993	18.59	7.49	0.80	
1994	27.86	11.60	1.92	
1995	41.78	17.80	4.71	
1996	53.33	23.10	9.05	
1997	67.75	31.14	16.44	
1998	83.74	41.40	25.72	4248
1999	104.13	54.39	56.75	37334
2000	130.15	72.69	117.92	70928
2001	163.21	90.13	195.65	93208
2002	203.58	91.52	256.86	104293
2003	242.00	107.20	379.31	835674
2004	296.72	94.79	421.00	1040127
2005	339.41		467.10	1705300
2006	345.08		514.70	908123
2007	334.98		757.70	1737851
2008	338.24		821.58	1027689
2009	301.41		866.87	1360000
2010	317.39		845.50	1720000
2011	312.45		1029.46	1900000
2012	308.00		1088.00	2360500
2013	298.00		1228.00	2500000

注：2006 年起，国际互联网用户统计口径有变化。

Note：From 2006，international Internet user's statistical method will change .

表 9—11 部分年份邮政业务情况
Basic Statistics on Post Services in Partial Years

指标	单位	Indicators	unit	2010	2011	2012	2013
邮政局、所数	处	Number of Post Offices	unit	318	279	280	280
#在农村的	处	Rural Area	unit	235	193	193	194
邮路总长度(单程)	公里	Lengh of Postal Routes	km	4496	5019	5071	9604
农村投递路线	公里	Rural Delivery Routwes	km	27682	27977	27062	27233
邮政业务总量	万元	Business volume of Post Services	10000 yuan	93257	88746	76125	87977
函件	万件	Number of Letters	10000 pcs	12960.00	12520.80	11842.25	10451.32
#国际函件	万件	International Letters	10000 pcs	20.00	43.20	131.91	265.36
国内函件	万件	Domestic Letters	10000 pcs	12940.00	12477.60	4915.03	10185.96
集邮业务	万枚	Philately	10000 pcs	2090.00	2281.00	2260.46	2700.32
报纸期发份数	万份	Newspaper Issued	10000 copies	76.5	91.33	91.84	135.06
杂志期发份数	万份	Magazine Issued	10000 copies	59.3	62.09	57.59	65.58
订销报纸累计份数	万份	Number of Newspaper Circulation	10000 copies	24532.00	25881.00	28653.80	33991.76
订销杂志累计份数	万份	Number of Magazine Circulation	10000 copies	595.00	656.00	702.80	1224.47

表 9—12 各县(市)邮政业务基本情况(2013)
Basic Statistics on Post Services by Region

指标	单位	Indicators	unit	全市 Total	市区 Urban Districts	余姚 Yuyao	慈溪 Cixi
邮政局、所数	处	Number of Post Offices	unit	280	126	43	34
#在农村的	处	Rural Area	unit	194	78	29	26
邮路总长度(单程)	公里	Lengh of Postal Routes	km	9604	7241	811	632
农村投递路线	公里	Rural Delivery Routwes	km	27233	9321	5266	5673
邮政业务总量	万元	Business volume of Post Services	10000 yuan	87977	46804	10340	17784
函件	万件	Number of Letters	10000 pcs	10451.32	4772	1238.03	3157.84
国际函件	万件	International Letters	10000 pcs	265.36	237	8.13	17.64
国内函件	万件	Domestic Letters	10000 pcs	10185.96	4534	1229.91	3140.19
集邮业务	万枚	Philately	10000 pcs	2700	2250	98	82
报纸期发份数	万份	Newspaper Issued	10000 copies	135	69	15	26
杂志期发份数	万份	Magazine Issued	10000 copies	66	42	4	7
订销报纸累计份数	万份	Number of Newspaper Circulation	10000 copies	33992	16051	4975	6626
订销杂志累计份数	万份	Number of Magazine Circulation	10000 copies	1224	775	67	133

表 9—12 续表 Continued

指标	单位	Indicators	unit	奉化 Fenghua	象山 Xiangshan	宁海 Ninghai
邮政局、所数	处	Number of Post Offices	unit	28	33	16
#在农村的	处	Rural Area	unit	19	29	13
邮路总长度(单程)	公里	Lengh of Postal Routes	km	346	357	217
农村投递路线	公里	Rural Delivery Routwes	km	2690	1789	2494
邮政业务总量	万元	Business volume of Post Services	10000 yuan	5240	3079	4731
函件	万件	Number of Letters	10000 pcs	587.81	268.22	427.82
国际函件	万件	International Letters	10000 pcs	1.23	0.73	0.47
国内函件	万件	Domestic Letters	10000 pcs	586.58	267.49	427.35
集邮业务	万枚	Philately	10000 pcs	42	48	180
报纸期发份数	万份	Newspaper Issued	10000 copies	9	8	8
杂志期发份数	万份	Magazine Issued	10000 copies	3	7	3
订销报纸累计份数	万份	Number of Newspaper Circulation	10000 copies	2328	2008	2005
订销杂志累计份数	万份	Number of Magazine Circulation	10000 copies	72	97	81

主要统计指标解释

【公路里程】 指在一定时期内实际达到《公路工程技术标 JTJ01－88》规定的等级公路，并经公路主管部门正式验收交付使用的公路里程数。其计算单位为：公里。它包括大中城市的郊区公路以及通过小城镇街道部分的公路里程，也包括桥梁、渡口的长度，但不包括大中城市的街道、厂矿、林区生产用道和农业生产用道的里程。两条或多条公路共同经由同一路段，只计算一次，不得重复计算里程长度。公路里程是反映公路建设发展规模的重要指标，也是计算运输网密度等指标的基础资料。

【货(客)运量】 指在一定时期内，各种运输工具实际运送的货物(旅客)数量。是反映运输业为国民经济和人民生活服务的数量指标，也是制定和检查运输生产计划，研究运输发展规模和速度的重要指标。货运按吨计算，客运按人计算。货物不论运输距离长短，货物类别，均按实际重量统计；旅客不论行程远近或票价多少，均按一人一次作为客运量统计。半价票、小孩票也按一人统计。

【货物(旅客)周转量】 指在一定时期内，由各种运输工具运送的货物(旅客)数量与其相应运输距离的乘积之总和，是反映运输业生产总成果的重要指标，也是编制和检查运输生产计划，计算运输效率、劳动生产率以及核算运输单位成本的主要基础资料。通常以吨公里和人公里为计算单位。计算货物周转量通常按发出站与到达站之间的最短距离，也就是计费距离计算。

【港口货物吞吐量】 指由水运进出港区范围，并经过装卸的货物数量，包括邮件及办理托运手续的行李、包裹以及补给运输船舶的燃、物料和淡水。其计量单位为吨。货物吞吐量的货种分类及其主要流向流量，反映了港口在国内外物资交流和对外贸易运输中的地位和作用。吞吐量可以分为进口、出口，又可以分为国内贸易和对外贸易。

【邮电业务总量】 指以货币表现的邮电部门用于传递信息和提供其他邮电服务的总数量。它综合反映了一定时期邮电工作的总成果，是研究邮电业务量构成和发展趋势的重要指标。根据邮电管理体制不同，分为中央国营业务总量和地方国营业务总量。它用各种邮电分类业务量，如函件件数、电报份数、长话张数、市内电话和农村电话的年均户数、订销报刊累计份数等，分别乘以相应的平均单价(不变价)，加总后再加上出租电路和设备的收入、代用户维护电话交换机和线路等设备的收入、其他业务收入求得。

Explanatory Notes on Main Statistical Indicators

【Length of Highways】 refers to the length of highways which are built in conformity with the grades specified by the highway engineering standard formulated by the Ministry of Communications, and have been formally checked and accepted by the departments of highways and put into use. The length of highways includes that of the suburb highways at large and medium-sized cities, highways passing through streets at small cities and towns, and also the length of bridges and ferries. It does not include the length of streets in big and medium-sized cities and highways built for the production purpose at factories, mines, forest areas and agricultural areas, If two or more highways go the same section of the way, the length of the section is only calculated for once and no duplication is allowed. The length of highways is an important indicator to show the development of the highway construction and to provide essential information to calculate the transport network density.

【Freight(Passenger) Traffic】 refers to the volume of freight (passenger) transported with various means. Freight transport is calculated in to ns and passenger traffic is calculated in the number of persons. Despite the type of freight and traveling distance, the freight transport is calculated by the principle that one person can be counted only once in one travel. The passenger who travel with a half price ticket or a child ticket is also calculated as one person. The freight (passenger) traffic provides a quantitative measure to show how the transport industry serves the national economy and people, and is also an important indicator for planning the transport industry and for studying the development scale and speed of the transport industry.

【Freight Ton—kilometers(Passenger—kilometers)】 refers to the sum of the products of the volume of transported cargo(passengers) multiplying by the transport distance, usually using ton-kilometer and passenger-kilometer as units for measurement. Normally, the shortest distance between the departure station and the destination station(i. e. , the payable distance) is the basis to calculate the freight ton—kilometers. This is an important indicator to show the total results of the transport industry, to prepare and examine the transport plan and to measure the efficiency, the labor productivity and the unit cost of transport.

【Volume of Freight Handled】 refers to the volume of cargo passing in and out the harbor area of the major coastal ports and having been loaded and unloaded. The volume includes that of the coastal matters, registered luggage and fuels, materials and fresh water as supplies of the ships. The volume of freight dandled maybe classified as import, export, or as domestic trade and foreign trade. The volume of freight handled by type of cargo and by main flow direction reflects he position and function of the ports in the inflow of Chinese and foreign commodities and in the transportation of foreign trade.

【Business Volume of Post and Telecommunications】 refers to the total amount of the information delivered and other post and telecommunications services provided by the post and telecommunications departments for the customers. It is derived by first multiplying the business volume of different types, such as number of letters, telegrams, long distance calls, city and rural telephone subscribers and accumulated number of newspapers and journals subscribed and sold, etc. by their respective average unit price (fixed price) and then adding these products together: plus the income from maintenance of telephone exchanges and lines, and the income from other business operations. The business volume of post and telecommunications indicates the total achievements made by the post and telecommunications department during a given period of time in a comprehensive way, and is an important indicator to study the composition and development of the post and telecommunications business.

CHAPTER 10

NINGBO 2014 Statistical YearBook

第十篇

国内贸易、餐饮业

DOMESTIC TRADE AND CATERING TRADE

国内贸易、餐饮
Domestic Trade and Catering Trade

主要统计指标
Major Statistics Indicators

				总计 Total	比上年增长(%) Increase Over Last Year(%)
2013年社会消费品零售总额	万元	Total Retail Sales of Consumer Goods	10000 yuan	26357078	13.2
#批发零售贸易业	万元	Wholesale and Retail Sale	10000 yuan	24048524	13.7
住宿及餐饮业	万元	Hoteling and Catering Trade	10000 yuan	2308553	8.2
限额以上批发业主要指标		Main Indicators of Wholesales Trade Above Designated Size			
企业数	个	Number of Enterprises	unit	2259	17.5
从业人员数	人	Number of Employees	person	76296	6.7
销售总额	万元	Total Sales Value	10000 yuan	83839731	19.0
资产总计	万元	Total Assets	10000 yuan	32871550	40.2
利润总额	万元	Total Profits	10000 yuan	913833	60.8
限额以上零售业主要指标		Main Indicators of Retail Trade Above Designated Size			
企业数	个	Number of Enterprises	unit	676	13.2
从业人员数	人	Number of Employees	person	65814	3.6
销售总额	万元	Total Sales Value	10000 yuan	11684331	12.4
资产总计	万元	Total Assets	10000 yuan	5702514	24.2
利润总额	万元	Total Profits	10000 yuan	179839	243.4
2013年住宿餐饮业从业人员数	人	Number of Employees in Catering Trade and Hoteling	person	45288	−16.6
2013年个体工商户数	户	Number of Individual Industry and Commerce	Households	369798	2.7
2013年私营企业数	个	Number of Private Enterprises	unit	173875	12.7

表 10—1 历年社会消费品零售总额
Total Retail Sales of Consumer Goods Over the Years

单位:万元(10000 yuan)

年份 Year	全市 Total	其中 of Which	
		市区 Urban District	县(市)合计 Total County
1978	70663	26175	44488
1979	87628	32386	55242
1980	111793	40368	71425
1981	130182	47157	83025
1982	139809	50056	89753
1983	156913	55343	101570
1984	187876	66573	121303
1985	253306	99210	154096
1986	304587	117850	186737
1987	354706	133444	221262
1988	490453	191994	298459
1989	528158	215768	312390
1990	549750	232255	317495
1991	633841	273167	360674
1992	794007	335769	458238
1993	1182147	522124	660023
1994	1634110	666060	968050
1995	2268195	919410	1348785
1996	2591764	1011445	1580319
1997	2885811	1154527	1731284
1998	3133608	1211018	1922590
1999	3457632	1321484	2136148
2000	3892920	1459537	2433383
2001	4141801		
2002	4628655		
2003	5215347		
2004	6667809		
2005	7621595	3625494	3996101
2006	8879552	4209769	4669783
2007	10450094	4922829	5527266
2008	12532605	5869060	6663545
2009	14344121	7633573	6710548
2010	17045103	6962526	10082577
2011	20188617	10891450	9297167
2012	23292590	12458556	10834033
2013	26357078	14077290	12279788

表 10－2 部分年份分行业社会消费品零售总额
Total Retail Sales of Consumer Goods by Sector in Partial Years

单位：万元(10000 yuan)

年份 Year	社会消费品零售总额 Total Retail Sales of Consumer Goods	# 市的零售额 City	按行业分 Grouped by Sector		
			批发和零售贸易业 Wholesale and Retail Sale Trades	住宿及餐饮业 Hoteling and Catering Trade	其他 Others
1990	549750				
1991	633841				
1992	794007				
1993	1182147				
1994	1634110				
1995	2268195	1320420	1628556	125442	514198
1996	2591764	1555917	1929652	159592	502520
1997	2885811	1703928	2104330	199683	581798
1998	3133608	1792796	2356047	187135	590426
1999	3457632	2018154	2599967	276889	580776
2000	3892920	2247696	2965818	378127	548975
2001	4141801	2401013	3124797	442042	574962
2002	4628655	2737749	3442080	570221	616354
2003	5215347	3084765	4434412	672047	108888
2004	6667809	3947129	5845803	771788	50218
2005	7621595	4696200	6667717	917878	36000
2006	8879552	5470496	7862357	1012258	4937
2007	10450094	6428170	9289383	1158312	2400
2008	12532605	7839658	11124980	1405045	2580
2009	14344121	9207400	12776963	1564398	2760
2010	17045103	12737090	15461677	1583426	
2011	20188617	13674900	18343579	1845038	
2012	23292590	19549110	21159838	2132752	
2013	26357078	22135123	24048524	2308553	

注：①2004 年以前，住宿及餐饮业统计数据仅包含餐饮业。②2005—2008 年零售额数据根据第二次经济普查结果做出调整。③2010 年零售额的计算方法根据报表制度有所调整。

Note：①Hoteing and catering trade statistics only include the catering trade，before 2004. ②2005—2008 Retail sales data of the year 2005—2008 according had been adjusted to the results of the second economic census. ③Calculation of retail sales in 2010 had been adjusted according to the reporting system.

表 10－3 零售业零售业态(2013)
Status of Retail Sale

指标	Indicators	法人单位数（个） Number of Corporation (unit)	销售合计（万元） Total Sale (10000 yuan)	其中 of Witch	
				批发 Wholesale	零售 Retail
零售企业合计	**Total Retail Sale Enterprise**	**676**	**11684331**	**1239873**	**10444457**
按经营方式分：	**Grouped by Management Method**				
独立店	Sole Shop	581	8312978	701289	7611689
连锁商店总店	Chain General Shop	28	1602933	200134	1402799
连锁商店分店	Chain Shop	22	1284183	291825	992358
其他	Others	45	484236	46625	437611
按零售业态分：	**Grouped by Retail Sale Line**				
百货商店	Department Store	36	1094884	130267	964617
超级市场	Super Market	38	1572951	176024	1396927
专业(专卖)店	Special (Special Sale) Shop	559	8658690	871269	7787421
其他	Others	43	357806	62313	295493

表 10－4 部分年份批发零售贸易及住宿餐饮业总额
Total Sales of Wholesale, Retail Sale and Hotel Catering Trade in Partial Years

单位:万元(10000 yuan)

指标	Indicators	2009	2010	2011	2012	2013
批发零售贸易业合计	**Wholesale and Retail Trade**					
销售总额	**Total Sale Value**	**54330930**	**75065955**	**93937682**	**106107789**	**122063824**
批发额	Wholesale	41413925	59901950	76303606	85747965	92998179
零售额	Retail Sale	12917005	15164006	17634076	20359824	29065645
1. 限额以上	Above Designated Size					
批发额	WholeSale	30095749	48594953	64989031	70289363	83074297
零售额	Retail Sale	6491536	8536179	10545544	10969875	14243145
2. 限额以下	Under Designated Size					
批发额	Wholesale	11318176	11306997	11314575	15458602	9923882
零售额	Retail Sale	6425469	6627827	7088532	9389949	14822501
住宿餐饮业合计	**Hotel and Catering Service**					
营业总收入	**Total Service Income**	**1787002**	**1998337**	**2516281**	**3089844**	**3613778**
#零售额	Retail Sale	1564398	1583426	1723695	1956446	2206169
1. 限额以上	Above Designated Size					
营业总收入	Total Service Income	708616	882009	1068003	1109732	1152603
#零售额	Retail Sale	486012	608977	757017	806779	836445
2. 限额以下	Under Designated Size					
营业总收入	Total Service Income	1078386	1116328	1448278	1980112	2461175
#零售额	Retail Sale	1078386	974449	966678	1149668	1369724

注:销售额及营业额均仅含产业单位数据。

Note: Total sales and turnover include data of industrial units.

表 10－5 限额以上批发贸易业单位数和从业人员数(2013)
Number of Units and Employees of Wholesale Trade Above Designated Size

单位:个、人(unit,person)

指标	Indicators	法人企业数 Number of Corporations	从业人数 Number of Employees
批发业合计	**Wholesale Trade**	**2259**	**76296**
#国有及国有控股	State－owned and State－holding	66	5064
按注册类型分	**Grouped by Registration Type**		
内资企业	Domestic Funded Enterprises	2191	71233
国有企业	State－Owned Enterprises	4	356
集体企业	Collective－Owned Enterprises	2	31
股份合作企业	Share Cooperative Enterprises	1	20
联营企业	Joint－owned Enterprises		
有限责任公司	Limited Liability Corporations	334	17236
股份有限公司	Share－holding Corporations Ltd.	31	2929
私营企业	Private Enterprises	1817	50654
港、澳、台商投资企业	Hongkong,Macao and Taiwan Funded	35	3219
外商投资企业	Foreign Funded	33	1844
按行业分	**Grouped by Sector**		
农畜产品批发	Agricultural and Livestock Products	15	771
食品、饮料及烟草制品批发	Food,Beverages and Tobaccos	109	6423
#烟草制品批发	Tobacco	2	343
纺织、服装及日用品批发	Textile,Garments and Daily Consumer Articles	486	30571
#服装批发	Garments	162	8107
家用电器批发	Household Appliances	49	12378
文化、体育用品及器材批发	Culture,Sports Appliances and Equipments	108	4104
医药及医疗器材批发	Medicines and Medical Appliance	43	2927
矿产品、建材及化工产品批发	Mineral Products,Building Materials,Chemical Products	1098	18193
#石油及制品批发	Petroleum and Related Products	139	3923
金属及金属矿批发	Metal and Metallic Ore	442	5613
机械设备、五金交电及电子产品批发	Machine Equipments, Hardware, Electric Appliances, Electronic Equipment	324	11850
#汽车、摩托车及零配件批发	Motor Vehicles,Motorcycles and Parts	48	1689
其他批发	Others	76	1457

表 10—6 限额以上零售贸易业单位数和从业人员数(2013)
Number of Units and Employees of Retail Trade Above Designated Size

单位:个、人(unit,person)

指标	Indicators	法人企业数 Number of Corporations	从业人数 Number of Employees
零售业总计	**Total**	**676**	**65814**
♯国有及国有控股	State—owned and State—holding	62	6204
按注册类型分	**Grouped by Registration Type**		
内资企业	Domestic Funded Enterprises	638	52766
国有企业	State—Owned Enterprises	9	677
集体企业	Collective—Owned Enterprises	9	119
股份合作企业	Share Cooperative Enterprises	2	118
联营企业	Joint—owned Enterprises	2	27
有限责任公司	Limited Liability Corporations	154	14564
股份有限公司	Share—holding Corporations Ltd.	14	8618
私营企业	Private Enterprises	441	28537
港、澳、台商投资企业	Hongkong,Macao and Taiwan Funded	21	4145
外商投资企业	Foreign Funded	17	8903
按行业分	**Grouped by Sector**		
综合零售	Comprehensive Retail	71	27017
百货零售	General Merchandise	32	5965
超级市场零售	Super Market	32	20258
食品、饮料及烟草制品专门零售	Food,Beverages and Tobaccos	24	1356
纺织、服装及日用品专门零售	Textile,Garments and Articles for Daily Use	53	6527
♯服装零售	Garments	29	5007
文化、体育用品及器材专门零售	Culture,Sports Appliances and Equipments	34	1974
♯图书零售	Books	12	963
医药及医疗器材专门零售	Medicines and Medical Appliance	28	2871
汽车、摩托车、燃料及零配件专门零售	Automobile,Motorcycles,Fuels and Parts	351	20608
♯汽车零售	Motor Vehicles	248	17134
家用电器及电子产品专门零售	Household Appliances and Electronic Products	71	4247
♯家用电器零售	Household Appliances	32	2621
通信设备零售	Communication Equipment	10	734
五金、家具及室内装修材料专门零售	Hardware,Furniture and Decoration Materials	15	511
无店铺及其他零售	Non—shop and Others	29	703

表 10－7 限额以上批发贸易业购进、销售、库存总额(2013)
Total Purchases, Sale and Inventory of Wholesale Trade Above Designated Size

指标	Indicators	购进总额 Total Purchases	进口 Imports
批发业	**Wholesale Trade**	**75317546**	**8044525**
#国有及国有控股	State－owned and State－holding	8355285	440856
按注册类型分	**Grouped by Registration Type**		
内资企业	Domestic Funded Enterprises	70947899	7720972
国有企业	State－Owned Enterprises	1055800	
集体企业	Collective－Owned Enterprises	37659	13752
股份合作企业	Share Cooperative Enterprises	9426	
联营企业	Joint－owned Enterprises		
有限责任公司	Limited Liability Corporations	22788554	1855998
股份有限公司	Share－holding Corporations Ltd.	5423992	1441382
私营企业	Private Enterprises	41626714	4409840
港、澳、台商投资企业	Hongkong, Macao and Taiwan Funded	1809975	283045
外商投资企业	Foreign Funded	2559672	40508
按行业分	**Grouped by Sector**		
农畜产品批发	Wholesale of Agricultural and Livestock Products	252000	51986
食品、饮料及烟草制品批发	Wholesale of Food, Beverages and Tobaccos	3063382	35709
#烟草制品批发	Tobacco	1016083	
纺织、服装及日用品批发	Wholesale of Textile, Garments and Daily Consumer Articles	9744975	734799
#服装批发	Garments	3063013	112005
家用电器批发	Household Appliances	1381810	105548
文化、体育用品及器材批发	Wholesale of Culture, Sports Appliances and Equipments	1824150	85212
医药及医疗器材批发	Wholesale of Medicines and Medical Appliance	1031822	174016
矿产品、建材及化工产品批发	Mineral Products, Building Materials and Chemical Products	52632647	6276398
#石油及制品批发	Petroleum and Related Products	7277235	100681
金属及金属矿批发	Metal and Metallic Ore	20729511	2482624
机械设备、五金交电及电子产品批发	Machine Equipments, Hardware, Electric Appliances, Electronic Equipment	5508669	370643
#汽车、摩托车及零配件批发	Motor Vehicles, Motorcycles and Parts	681073	31565
其他批发	Others	1259902	315761

单位:万元(10000 yuan)

销售总额 Total Sales	其中 of Which 批发 Wholesale	出口 Exports	零售 Retail Sale	年末库存总额 Inventory (year—end)
83839731	**81254992**	**13424742**	**2584738**	**3905204**
10508105	9105641	736858	1402464	408970
79159859	76645650	13090695	2514209	3764529
1420869	1417831	10146	3039	44471
40297	39861	20830	435	4743
9426	9426			
23755587	23443905	4059187	311682	848538
8235236	6912990	1239296	1322246	250078
45692303	44815498	7761236	876805	2616689
2082207	2043152	162926	39055	114932
2597665	2566190	171120	31474	25743
251868	201798	17478	50069	46504
3634010	3497696	247267	136313	184192
1379998	1379724		274	44192
10781837	10614723	6190696	167114	1067030
3355363	3300347	2081359	55016	139989
1660188	1567609	595258	92579	44660
1950393	1941101	694286	9292	84763
1209369	973352	23593	236017	123154
58849269	56998563	2636287	1850706	2080520
9220375	8563904	34529	656471	186628
24101401	24022749	1321460	78653	985575
5827382	5696491	3377523	130891	223847
712605	645017	261862	67589	13902
1335604	1331267	237613	4337	95194

表 10－8 限额以上零售贸易业购进、销售、库存总额(2013)
Total Purchases,Sale and Inventory of Retail Trade Above Designated Size

指标	Indicators	购进总额 Total Purchases	进口 Imports
零售业合计	**Retail Trade**	**10752392**	**449040**
＃国有及国有控股	State－owned and State－holding	2003699	65994
按注册类型分	**Grouped by Registration Type**		
内资企业	Domestic Funded Enterprises	8387349	232644
国有企业	State－Owned Enterprises	53004	
集体企业	Collective－Owned Enterprises	36819	
股份合作企业	Share Cooperative Enterprises	10268	
联营企业	Joint－owned Enterprises	10100	
有限责任公司	Limited Liability Corporations	2632513	117241
股份有限公司	Share－holding Corporations Ltd.	1250497	
私营企业	Private Enterprises	4365360	115403
港、澳、台商投资企业	Hongkong,Macao and Taiwan Funded	853149	45871
外商投资企业	Foreign Funded	1511894	170525
按行业分	**Grouped by Sector**		
综合零售	General Retail	2492342	3725
百货零售	General Merchandise	1025093	3725
超级市场零售	Super Market	1428383	
食品、饮料及烟草制品专门零售	Retail of Food,Beverages and Tobaccos	94615	
纺织、服装及日用品专门零售	Retail of Textile,Garments and Daily Use Articles	508887	2695
＃服装零售	Garments	295569	2462
文化、体育用品及器材专门零售	Retail of Culture,Sports Appliances and Equipments	205080	
＃图书零售	Books	60234	
医药及医疗器材专门零售	Retail of Medicines and Medical Appliance	714099	
汽车、摩托车、燃料及零配件专门零售	Retail of Motor Vehicles,Motorcycles,Fuels and Parts	6102429	442119
＃汽车零售	Motor Vehicles	4728934	442119
家用电器及电子产品专门零售	Retail of Household Appliances and Electronic Products	495800	
＃家用电器零售	Household Appliances	326617	
通信设备零售	Communication Equipment	72516	
五金、家具及室内装修材料专门零售	Retail of Hardware,Furniture and Decoration Materials	60116	500
无店铺及其他零售	Non－shop and Other Retail	79023	

单位:万元(10000 yuan)

销售总额 Total Sales	其中:of Which			年末库存总额 Inventory (year—end)
	批发 Wholesale	出口 Exports	零售 Retail Sale	
11684331	**1239873**	**1764**	**10444457**	**1449704**
2100714	490496		1610218	93026
8962438	743325	1764	8219113	995697
58764			58764	10780
39094	692		38402	2740
10499			10499	1052
10703			10703	178
2743685	119263	1521	2624422	281434
1309504	322131		987373	134479
4759521	297223	243	4462298	559331
1111309	167564		943744	271497
1610585	328985		1281600	182509
2665197	314086		2351112	298745
1071132	130267		940865	66220
1555588	176024		1379565	230164
105895	17916		87979	13885
762255	181457	243	580799	317378
536873	155634		381238	261207
218683	28109		190575	59454
65094			65094	19847
746919	97185		649734	75221
6521241	518237	1521	6003004	607887
5084465	198047		4886417	585102
514352	48263		466089	43968
333159	14935		318225	27104
76234	19320		56913	6690
67714	27782		39932	25017
82074	6840		75234	8151

表 10－9 限额以上批发贸易业主要财务指标(2013) Main Financial Indicators of Wholesale Trade Above Designated Size

指标	Indicators	年末资产负债		
		流动资产合计 Current Funds	＃存货 Inventories	固定资产原价 Original Value of Fixed Assets
批发业合计	**Wholesale Trade**	**29920684**	**2841872**	**1559777**
＃国有控股	State－holding	2344945	373116	272797
按注册类型分	**Grouped by Registration Type**			
内资企业	Domestic Funded Enterprises	28155722	2729808	1492322
国有企业	State－Owned Enterprises	558971	66152	67573
集体企业	Collective－Owned Enterprises	14178	102	417
股份合作企业	Share Cooperative Enterprises	1218		196
联营企业	Joint－owned Enterprises			
有限责任公司	Limited Liability Corporations	7352247	808974	311183
股份有限公司	Share－holding Corporations Ltd.	1545056	245016	158066
私营企业	Private Enterprises	18683373	1609412	954665
港、澳、台商投资企业	Hongkong, Macao and Taiwan Funded	896052	78813	41924
外商投资企业	Foreign Funded	868910	33251	25531
按行业分	**Grouped by Sector**			
农畜产品批发	Agricultural and Livestock Products	130387	58236	32366
食品、饮料及烟草制品批发	Food, Beverages and Tobaccos	1692858	201233	154281
＃烟草制品批发	Tobacco	557246	65951	65738
纺织、服装及日用品批发	Textile, Garments and Daily Consumer Articles	8113604	323383	491300
＃服装批发	Garments	1272926	133014	90486
文化、体育用品及器材批发	Culture, Sports Appliances and Equipments	690788	71685	41011
医药及医疗器材批发	Medicines and Medical Appliance	623246	97437	51712
矿产品、建材及化工产品批发	Mineral Products, Building Materials, Chemical Products	15776164	1793299	584902
＃石油及制品批发	Petroleum and Related Products	1743104	182250	200211
金属及金属矿批发	Metal and Metallic Ore	7096093	897607	187192
机械设备、五金交电及电子产品批发	Machine Equipments, Hardware, Electric Appliances, Electronic Equipment	2424011	219799	150658
＃汽车、摩托车及零配件批发	Motor Vehicles, Motorcycles and Parts	355295	22864	17216
家用电器批发	Household Appliances	665284	42921	18109
其他批发	Others	309896	58589	45590

单位:万元(10000 yuan)

Total Assets and Liabilities at the Year—end				损益与分配 Profit,Loss and Distribution	
本年折旧 Depreciation in this year	资产合计 Total Asset	负债合计 Total Liabilities	所有者权益 Creditors' Equity	主营业务收入 Major Business Revenue	主营业务成本 Major Business Costs
159936	**32871550**	**27522032**	**5349518**	**77539627**	**74581191**
14596	2905030	1696138	1208892	9267163	8731271
156072	30968975	26327507	4641467	73056033	70486443
4199	626275	17116	609160	1215893	896103
6	14691	10507	4184	37680	35261
31	1320	800	520	8056	7678
18264	8357418	6981178	1376241	21913411	21220727
8436	1933193	1649578	283616	7552114	7413662
125130	20035209	17668050	2367159	42323066	40907271
2471	1001595	678965	322630	1939470	1737656
1393	900980	515559	385421	2544124	2357091
1256	211273	171128	40145	242575	236504
9556	1939120	1108344	830776	2933610	2438486
4128	623686	16628	607058	1179485	861209
87505	8610800	7763347	847454	10357318	9619515
6724	1486091	1285491	200600	3206380	2992097
3234	759473	594599	164874	1869598	1761659
3043	715143	525266	189876	1062233	893933
39673	17353279	14729802	2623477	54126215	53049020
10901	2148441	1707710	440730	8091131	7922482
12250	7706295	6457129	1249166	22543534	22054258
12216	2703149	2170126	533023	5664155	5351499
1389	375285	330782	44502	709438	678584
1478	690697	600554	90142	1519179	1275966
2853	412777	312528	100249	908081	864349

表 10—9 续表 Continued

指标	Indicators	损益与分配	
		主营业务税金及附加 Tax and Extra Charge	管理费用 Management Cost
批发业合计	**Wholesale Trade**	**124286**	**633528**
＃国有控股	State—holding	77936	96077
按注册类型分	**Grouped by Registration Type**		
内资企业	Domestic Funded Enterprises	119433	578166
国有企业	State—Owned Enterprises	72048	39913
集体企业	Collective—Owned Enterprises	4	226
股份合作企业	Share Cooperative Enterprises	8	88
联营企业	Joint—owned Enterprises		
有限责任公司	Limited Liability Corporations	13552	142353
股份有限公司	Share—holding Corporations Ltd.	2774	32583
私营企业	Private Enterprises	31014	362993
港、澳、台商投资企业	Hongkong, Macao and Taiwan Funded	4052	41251
外商投资企业	Foreign Funded	801	14110
按行业分	**Grouped by Sector**		
农畜产品批发	Agricultural and Livestock Products	111	5675
食品、饮料及烟草制品批发	Food, Beverages and Tobaccos	76964	78926
＃烟草制品批发	Tobacco	72028	39835
纺织、服装及日用品批发	Textile, Garments and Daily Consumer Articles	9604	163792
＃服装批发	Garments	2346	62838
文化、体育用品及器材批发	Culture, Sports Appliances and Equipments	1332	29182
医药及医疗器材批发	Medicines and Medical Appliance	3770	37793
矿产品、建材及化工产品批发	Mineral Products, Building Materials, Chemical Products	26454	208109
＃石油及制品批发	Petroleum and Related Products	5066	36845
金属及金属矿批发	Metal and Metallic Ore	9832	67724
机械设备、五金交电及电子产品批发	Machine Equipments, Hardware, Electric Appliances, Electronic Equipment	4121	97260
＃汽车、摩托车及零配件批发	Motor Vehicles, Motorcycles and Parts	723	8588
家用电器批发	Household Appliances	3664	21642
其他批发	Others	1735	9181

单位:万元(10000 yuan)

Profit,Loss and Distribution			工资福利与税金 Wages,Welfare and Tax in this Year	
财务费用 Financial Expenses	营业利润 Business Profits	利润总额 Total Profits	本年应付 职工薪酬总额 Total Employee Compensation Payable	本年应交 增值税总额 Total Value－added Taxes Payable
297795	**646992**	**913833**	**566891**	**353473**
－3517	285018	377238	95757	78308
284474	444602	715524	525466	319725
－15065	210335	196399	36617	50406
528	147	135	142	
9	24	16	273	65
46496	111992	180837	133110	90337
7496	19756	115019	44090	33542
245010	102331	223087	311216	145032
8561	56015	60313	26904	29897
4760	146376	137996	14522	3852
11527	－12174	－195	4970	14638
－797	217691	223273	69819	96773
－15129	210020	196136	36191	50206
54032	68753	86457	193954	54038
26020	23245	32935	57954	9082
11390	15311	19311	24982	5814
4430	60541	69018	19394	27235
176204	245920	360579	157760	121922
17310	46675	52148	42181	28621
83854	212218	224258	46162	39028
29472	39617	133464	88779	20686
4201	1073	1578	10048	3631
4035	10802	13077	65992	31013
10047	10263	20821	4985	12266

表 10－10 限额以上零售贸易业主要财务指标(2013)
Main Financial Indicators of Retail Trade Above Designated Size

指标	Indicators	年末资产负债		
		流动资产合计 Current Funds	＃存货 Inventories	固定资产原价 Original Value of Fixed Assets
零售业总计	**Total**	**3709704**	**984724**	**1127013**
＃国有控股	State－holding	397252	75886	112959
按注册类型分	**Grouped by Registration Type**			
内资企业	Domestic Funded Enterprises	3221159	827700	770606
国有企业	State－Owned Enterprises	43846	6196	12229
集体企业	Collective－Owned Enterprises	5757	2974	1957
股份合作企业	Share Cooperative Enterprises	2434	899	904
联营企业	Joint－owned Enterprises	1267	178	521
有限责任公司	Limited Liability Corporations	910089	224263	230351
股份有限公司	Share－holding Corporations Ltd.	560535	83985	146661
私营企业	Private Enterprises	1670339	488425	377887
港、澳、台商投资企业	Hongkong,Macao and Taiwan Funded	289558	76550	136472
外商投资企业	Foreign Funded	198987	80474	219935
按行业分	**Grouped by Sector**			
综合零售	Comprehensive Retail	1030248	150609	586898
＃百货零售	General Merchandise	456878	35747	279794
超级市场零售	Super Market	564973	112716	303891
食品、饮料及烟草制品专门零售	Food,Beverages and Tobaccos	74449	12373	14172
纺织、服装及日用品专门零售	Textile,Garments and Articles for Daily Use	392834	156846	30838
文化、体育用品及器材专门零售	Culture,Sports Appliances and Equipments	115603	42131	25661
医药及医疗器材专门零售	Medicines and Medical Appliance	248403	68823	28392
汽车、摩托车、燃料及零配件专门零售	Automobile,Motorcycles,Fuels and Parts	1583650	478782	353181
＃汽车零售	Motor Vehicles	1461851	461679	314515
家用电器及电子产品专门零售	Household Appliances and Electronic Products	180382	42903	18555
五金、家具及室内装修材料专门零售	Hardware,Furniture and Decoration Materials	27604	9092	59048
无店铺及其他零售	Non－shop and Others	56529	23165	10268
按经营方式分组	**Grouped by Management Method**			
＃独立商店	Sole Shop	2768720	757924	671034
连锁商店总店	Chain General Shop	591288	125509	288489
连锁商店分店	Chain Shop	186140	51090	18223
按零售业态分组	**Grouped by Retail Sale Line**			
＃百货商店	Department Store	466840	40259	279760
超级市场	Super Market	466840	40259	279760
专业店	Special Shop	1399752	400249	269189
专卖店	Special Sale Shop	1081202	356803	197595
便利店	Convenience Shop	21891	3793	2952

单位:万元(10000 yuan)

Total Assets and Liabilities at the Year—end				损益与分配 Profit,Loss and Distribution	
本年折旧 Depreciation in this year	资产合计 Total Asset	负债合计 Total Liabilities	所有者权益 Creditors' Equity	主营业务收入 Major Business Revenue	主营业务成本 Major Business Costs
67362	**5702514**	**4045026**	**1657488**	**9433375**	**8487371**
4688	783185	318030	465156	1166720	1039643
47154	4574904	3286575	1288329	7910010	7160555
601	59703	42925	16778	51387	42091
107	7723	3354	4369	35382	33694
92	3020	2499	521	9390	8711
47	2389	443	1946	9148	8586
15003	1353875	932388	421487	2359283	2111240
3846	946191	432535	513656	1166735	1054048
27452	2174117	1847312	326805	4247561	3872627
9435	676518	400921	275597	871701	740723
10774	451092	357530	93562	651665	586093
29972	2018144	1249118	769026	2307784	1989420
12014	1113074	567481	545593	893633	737542
17770	894581	671181	223401	1380880	1223960
919	101928	69645	32283	96606	84532
487	687991	418635	269356	573222	396101
1496	142287	96558	45729	187827	158261
1355	285201	213611	71590	629578	580905
30305	2104713	1701920	402793	5054859	4762670
28104	1907044	1595056	311987	4504009	4249080
1586	196230	156930	39300	441669	388761
690	95640	88836	6803	62848	56019
553	70381	49773	20609	78982	70703
44083	4238360	2999804	1238557	7247169	6630636
16214	891202	619373	271829	1367308	1209265
1749	226992	182178	44814	407122	312040
11965	1112923	578271	534653	913779	754940
18119	913030	677767	235264	1395951	1236530
19147	1791351	1357895	433456	3950822	3622692
18452	1411690	1135635	276054	2853500	2607930
253	24852	21800	3052	44456	38393

表 10—10 续表 Continued

指标	Indicators	损益与分配	
		主营业务税金及附加 Tax and Extra Charge	管理费用 Management Cost
零售业总计	**Total**	**35476**	**307609**
＃国有控股	State—holding	5758	28898
按注册类型分	**Grouped by Registration Type**		
内资企业	Domestic Funded Enterprises	27274	244223
国有企业	State—Owned Enterprises	199	3366
集体企业	Collective—Owned Enterprises	50	603
股份合作企业	Share Cooperative Enterprises	16	219
联营企业	Joint—owned Enterprises	14	158
有限责任公司	Limited Liability Corporations	11461	72668
股份有限公司	Share—holding Corporations Ltd.	5280	27816
私营企业	Private Enterprises	10238	139365
港、澳、台商投资企业	Hongkong,Macao and Taiwan Funded	5076	42406
外商投资企业	Foreign Funded	3125	20981
按行业分	**Grouped by Sector**		
综合零售	Comprehensive Retail	17219	116993
＃百货零售	General Merchandise	11602	71645
超级市场零售	Super Market	5502	42287
食品、饮料及烟草制品专门零售	Food,Beverages and Tobaccos	246	4760
纺织、服装及日用品专门零售	Textile,Garments and Articles for Daily Use	4427	34701
文化、体育用品及器材专门零售	Culture,Sports Appliances and Equipments	2897	8097
医药及医疗器材专门零售	Medicines and Medical Appliance	877	15152
汽车、摩托车、燃料及零配件专门零售	Automobile,Motorcycles,Fuels and Parts	7855	104096
＃汽车零售	Motor Vehicles	6921	97174
家用电器及电子产品专门零售	Household Appliances and Electronic Products	1455	13583
五金、家具及室内装修材料专门零售	Hardware,Furniture and Decoration Materials	154	7542
无店铺及其他零售	Non—shop and Others	346	2687
按经营方式分组	**Grouped by Management Method**		
＃独立商店	Sole Shop	25753	207112
连锁商店总店	Chain General Shop	5935	60380
连锁商店分店	Chain Shop	1659	14663
按零售业态分组	**Grouped by Retail Sale Line**		
＃百货商店	Department Store	11892	73722
超级市场	Super Market	11892	73722
专业店	Special Shop	8886	90379
专卖店	Special Sale Shop	6816	77989
便利店	Convenience Shop	123	2504

单位:万元(10000 yuan)

Profit,Loss and Distribution			工资福利与税金 Wages,Welfare and Tax in this Year	
财务费用 Financial Expenses	营业利润 Business Profits	利润总额 Total Profits	本年应付职工薪酬总额 Total Employee Compensation Payable	本年应交增值税总额 Total Value-added Taxes Payable
84790	**154530**	**179839**	**354166**	**113055**
2542	59222	60475	38486	12644
71822	76719	98869	283841	90485
-183	349	622	5650	1164
80	242	303	597	221
121	77	67	165	84
	288	283	96	64
17922	41313	49030	85644	31116
6392	42635	46539	45096	13287
47479	-9427	781	146283	44549
9545	92705	94157	36498	17463
3423	-14894	-13188	33827	5107
13362	38239	53598	134990	28183
12527	33619	42133	48479	13060
639	5805	12023	83512	14659
974	168	768	5567	985
9152	103975	107636	42904	25930
778	895	1541	13963	4828
4760	11044	11665	17645	7138
50824	6693	12809	112918	37569
49167	-12486	-6572	104037	33152
2467	732	-755	20447	7470
2390	-10539	-10519	3076	264
84	3324	3096	2657	688
79234	134473	144817	221079	79069
4061	12859	23902	84614	15682
111	6767	8399	32274	11525
12732	31318	40233	49731	13493
12732	31318	40233	84372	14778
30360	49328	53414	116234	39875
32212	-720	4463	87510	37204
118	-1566	-1033	4336	542

表 10—11 限额以上批发零售贸易业主要商品分类销售额(2013)
Sales of Wholesale and Retail Trade Above Designated Size by Category of Commodities

单位:万元(10000 yuan)

类别	Category	合计	批发 Wholesale	零售 Retail
食品、饮料、烟酒类	Food, Beverage, Tabacco and Liquor	4630050	3337766	1292284
#粮油类	Grain and Oil	2702370	1671554	1030815
饮料类	Beverage	294381	150485	143896
烟酒类	Tabacco and Liquor	1633300	1515727	117573
服装鞋帽、针、纺织品类	Garments, Shoes, Hats Knitwear and Textile	5759398	4606148	1153250
#服装类	Garments	3598799	2716621	882178
鞋帽类	Shoes, Hats	452675	309062	143613
针、纺织品类	Knitwear and Textile	1707924	1580465	127459
化妆品类	Cosmetics	171120	79749	91371
金银珠宝类	Jewelry	471415	181607	289809
日用品类	Articles for Daily Use	3173270	2854657	318613
五金、电料类	Hardware and Electrical Appliances	1182703	1142096	40608
体育、娱乐用品类	Recreation and Sports Articles	141342	126278	15064
书报杂志类	Books and Newspapers	65299	2916	62383
电子出版物及音像制品类	Electronic Publications and Audio—video Products	2052		2052
家用电器和音像器材类	Household Appliances and Audio—video Equipments	2105365	1593882	511483
中西药品类	Medicines	1465197	643730	821467
文化办公用品类	Culture and Office Articles	1416515	1244784	171731
家具类	Furnitures	281774	135754	146020
通讯器材类	Telecommunication Appliances	654165	478291	175874
煤炭及制品类	Coal and Coal Products	5505232	5501236	3996
木材及制品类	Timber and Timber Products	298445	292539	5906
石油及制品类	Petroleum and Products	11457690	9811093	1646597
化工材料及制品类	Chemical Materials and Products	15888826	15888826	
金属材料类	Metal Materials	23088486	23088486	
建筑及装潢材料类	Materials for Construction and Decoration	614727	527624	87102
机电产品及设备类	Mechanical and Electrical Equipments	1962148	1956419	5729
汽车类	Automobile	5711648	668861	5042786
种子饲料类	Seeds and Forage	70446	70446	
棉麻土畜类	Cotton and Flax Products	73709	73709	

表 10－12 住宿餐饮业单位数和从业人员数(2013) Number of Units and Employees of Catering Trade and Hotel

单位：个、人(unit,person)

指标	Indicators	法人企业数 Number of Corporations	从业人数 Number of Employees
总计	**Total**	**469**	**45288**
住宿业	**Hotel**	**197**	**24312**
＃国有及国有控股	State－owned and State－holding	22	2933
按登记注册类型分组	Grouped by Registration Type		
内资企业	Domestic Funded Enterprises	184	21211
国有企业	State－Owned Enterprises	7	787
集体企业	Collective－Owned Enterprises	5	528
股份合作企业	Share Cooperative Enterprises		
有限责任公司	Limited Liability Corporations	37	6727
股份有限公司	Share－holding Corporations Ltd.	7	1697
私营企业	Private Enterprises	128	11472
港、澳、台商投资企业	Hongkong,Macao and Taiwan Funded	7	2128
外商投资企业	Foreign Funded	6	973
按行业分	Grouped by Sector		
旅游饭店	Tour Hotel	121	19104
一般旅馆	Common Hotel	72	5017
餐饮业	**Catering Trade**	**272**	**20976**
＃国有及国有控股	State－owned and State－holding	4	578
按登记注册类型分组	Grouped by Registration Type		
内资企业	Domestic Funded Enterprises	264	20188
国有企业	State－Owned Enterprises	2	102
集体企业	Collective－Owned Enterprises		
股份合作企业	Share Cooperative Enterprises		
有限责任公司	Limited Liability Corporations	26	3565
股份有限公司	Share－holding Corporations Ltd.	2	235
私营企业	Private Enterprises	232	16220
港、澳、台商投资企业	Hongkong,Macao and Taiwan Funded	8	788
外商投资企业	Foreign Funded		
按行业分	Grouped by Sector		
正餐服务业	Dinner Services	253	19442
快餐服务业	Snack Services	9	916
饮料及冷饮服务业	Beverage Services		
其他餐饮服务业	Others	10	618

表 10—13 星级住宿业和限额以上餐饮业经营情况(2013)
Main Operation Indicators of Catering Trade and Star—rated Hotel

指标	Indicators	营业额 Business Revenue	其中 客房收入 Room Rate Revenue	餐费收入 Catering Revenue
总计	**Total**	**763579**	**208246**	**484468**
住宿业	**Hotel**	**423798**	**171152**	**199110**
#国有及国有控股	State—owned and State—holding	45169	15463	23282
按登记注册类型分组	Grouped by Registration Type			
内资企业	Domestic Funded Enterprises	348762	145083	156374
国有企业	State—Owned Enterprises	8265	3469	3844
集体企业	Collective—Owned Enterprises	7023	2239	4065
股份合作企业	Share Cooperative Enterprises			
有限责任公司	Limited Liability Corporations	113129	41123	52118
股份有限公司	Share—holding Corporations Ltd.	32760	11732	12655
私营企业	Private Enterprises	187586	86520	83693
港、澳、台商投资企业	Hongkong,Macao and Taiwan Funded	61418	19457	36935
外商投资企业	Foreign Funded	13618	6613	5801
按行业分	Grouped by Sector			
旅游饭店	Tour Hotel	346323	124245	176084
一般旅馆	Common Hotel	75211	45157	22819
餐饮业	**Catering Trade**	**339781**	**37094**	**285358**
#国有及国有控股	State—owned and State—holding	5367	782	4583
按登记注册类型分组	Grouped by Registration Type			
内资企业	Domestic Funded Enterprises	328157	35010	276857
国有企业	State—Owned Enterprises	1327	211	1116
集体企业	Collective—Owned Enterprises			
股份合作企业	Share Cooperative Enterprises			
有限责任公司	Limited Liability Corporations	59535	8271	46414
股份有限公司	Share—holding Corporations Ltd.	3662	693	2849
私营企业	Private Enterprises	263244	25634	226288
港、澳、台商投资企业	Hongkong,Macao and Taiwan Funded	11624	2084	8501
外商投资企业	Foreign Funded			
按行业分	Grouped by Sector			
正餐服务业	Dinner Services	311301	37094	258421
快餐服务业	Snack Services	16051		15287
饮料及冷饮服务业	Beverage Services			
其他餐饮服务业	Others	12430		11650

单位:万元

of Which		年末餐饮营业面积（平方米）Business Area of Catering in the Year—end (sq. m)	年末拥有床位数（个）Hold Beds in the Year—end (bed)	年末拥有餐位数（位）Hold Seat of Catering in the Year—end (unit)
商品销售收入 Commodity Sales Revenue	其他收入 Others			
12555	**58309**	**955129**	**56285**	**194865**
7708	**45828**	**394830**	**46782**	**80261**
881	5544	45521	4816	8949
7330	39975	360620	42676	72784
2	950	5760	1613	2080
6	714	7733	1018	2300
2346	17543	118947	9982	22183
3309	5064	16989	3094	5664
1668	15705	211191	26969	40557
352	4674	20254	2662	4001
25	1178	13956	1444	3476
6437	39557	316911	30362	65379
1266	5970	76539	15719	14554
4848	**12482**	**560299**	**9503**	**114604**
	2	6167	482	798
4741	11549	541655	9118	111329
		2540	82	400
3051	1799	76173	2018	15041
	119	4995	210	1312
1690	9631	453947	6783	94126
106	933	18644	385	3275
4132	11654	538478	9503	103850
	764	12885		7441
715	64	8936		3313

表 10－14 部分年份限额以上批发零售贸易业主要财务指标
Main Financial Indicators of Wholesale and Retail Trade Above Designated Size of Partial Years

单位：亿元(100 million yuan)

指标	Indicators	2009	2010	2011	2012	2013
主营业务收入	Prime Operating Revenue	3261.5	5170.2	6758.0	7279.6	8697.3
主营业务成本	Operating Costs	3065.8	4891.9	6429.2	6941.9	8306.9
主营业务税金及附加	Tax and Extra Charge	6.8	10.8	12.0	12.9	15.9
其他业务利润	Profits from Other Business	12.6	17.7	19.2	17.7	18.7
管理费用	Management Cost	46.2	59.3	72.3	80.3	94.1
财务费用	Financial Expenses	12.9	21.6	34.7	40.1	38.3
利润总额	Total Profits	58.3	69.5	82.9	62.1	109.4
资产总计	Total Assets	1370.8	1879.3	2449.2	2804.4	3857.4
＃流动资产	Current Assets	1151.0	1617.4	2140.6	2433.7	3363.0
＃存货	Inventory	190.6	274.3	342.2	338.1	382.7
负债合计	Total Liabilities	1061.9	1497.7	1987.6	2299.2	3156.7
所有者权益合计	Total Owner's Equities	308.8	381.6	461.6	505.2	700.7
应付职工薪酬	Employee Compensation Payable			63.8	76.6	92.1

表 10－15 部分年份星级住宿业及限额以上餐饮业主要财务指标
Main Financial Indicators of Catering Trade Above Designated Size and Star－rated Hotel in Partial Years

单位：亿元(100 million yuan)

指标	Indicators	2009	2010	2011	2012	2013
主营业务收入	Prime Operating Revenue	53.3	73.7	83.1	86.7	75.4
主营业务成本	Operating Costs	21.9	30.1	35.0	35.7	30.7
营业费用	Business Expenses	16.5	21.5	23.7	27.3	26.8
主营业务税金及附加	Tax and Associate Charge	2.9	4.1	4.6	4.7	4.2
管理费用	Management Cost	13.1	16.8	18.8	19.9	19.7
＃税金	Taxes	0.4	0.8	0.7	0.7	0.6
财务费用	Financial Expenses	2.2	3.5	4.8	5.2	4.8
利润总额	Total Profits	－1.0	－0.5	－2.0	－3.8	－7.2
资产总计	Total Assets	118.7	149.3	182.1	186.9	187.1
＃流动资产	Current Assets	36.9	54.7	72.3	76.7	72.6
负债合计	Total Liabilities	85.9	112.5	142.9	151.7	160.6
所有者权益合计	Total Owner's Equities	32.8	36.9	39.1	35.2	26.5
应付职工薪酬	Employee Compensation Payable			16.2	18.8	20.4

表 10－16 亿元以上商品交易市场成交情况(2013)
Basic Statistics of Commodity Exchange Market with Total Sale Over 100 million Yuan

单位:万元(10000 yuan)

指标	Indicators	摊位个数(个) Number of Stalls (unit)	总成交额 Transaction Volume
总计	**Total**	**70281**	**27314444**
食品、饮料、烟酒类	Food, Beverage, Tabacco and Liquor	37413	5492641
食品类	Foodstuff	36538	5240125
#粮油类	Grain and Oil	979	451778
肉禽蛋类	Meat. Poultry and Egg	3042	685967
水产品类	Aquatic Product	21605	1977700
蔬菜类	Garden Stuff	8256	1354967
干鲜果品类	Dry Fruit and Fresh Fruit	1857	589775
饮料类	Beverage	251	104342
烟酒类	Tabacco and Liquor	624	148174
服装鞋帽、针、纺织品类	Garments, Shoes, Hats Knitwear and Textile	8068	1479186
服装类	Garments	5161	779177
鞋帽类	Shoes, Hats	1058	344114
针、纺织品类	Knitwear and Textile	1849	355895
化妆品类	Cosmetics	162	30272
日用品类	Articles for Daily Use	2751	380156
五金、电料类	Hardware and Electrical Appliances	2217	348968
体育、娱乐用品类	Recreation and Sports Articles	135	10315
书报杂志类	Books and Newspapers	5	16
电子出版物及音像制品类	Electronic Publications and Audio－video Products		
家用电器和音像器材类	Household Appliances and Audio－video Equipments	203	35085
中西药品类	Medicines		
文化办公用品类	Culture and Office Articles	1490	191607
家具类	Furnitures	1872	299469
通讯器材类	Telecommunication Appliances		
煤炭及制品类	Coal and Products	69	1909445
木材及制品类	Timber and Timber Products	805	167789
石油及制品类	Petroleum and Products	46	1126516
化工材料及制品类	Chemical Materials and Products	3423	7306448
金属材料类	Metal Materials	3712	5654935
建筑及装潢材料类	Materials for Construction and Decoration	4005	1071525
机电产品及设备类	Mechanical and Electrical Equipments	145	58481
汽车类	Automobile	994	656385
种子饲料类	Seed and Feedstuff	147	45123
棉麻类	Cotton and Flax Products		
其他类	Others	2495	1046914

表 10—17 个体工商业情况(2013)

Basic Statistics of Individual Industry and Commerce

指标	Indicators	全市期末实有 Total at the End of this Year	其中 of Which 本期开业 Openning for this Term	城镇 Districts
户数(户)	**Number of Households(unit)**	**369798**	**73966**	**171195**
农、林、牧、渔业	Farming. Forestry. Animal Husbandry and Fishery	3808	1510	1133
采矿业	Mining and Quarrying Industry	51		15
制造业	Manufacturing Industry	77723	13004	15033
电力、燃气及水的生产和供应业	Electric Power,Gas and Water Production and Supply	27	2	8
建筑业	Construction	1926	319	930
交通运输业、仓储和邮政业	Transportation and Warehousing	27968	6086	13748
信息传输、计算机服务和软件业	Information Transmission, Computer Service and Software Industries	334	85	205
批发和零售业	Wholesale and Retail Trade	202504	39714	107844
住宿和餐饮业	Hotel and Catering Trade	18960	5199	10443
房地产业	Real Estate Industries	1141	245	881
租赁和商务服务业	Leasing and Business Service Industries	4215	1045	2918
居民服务和其它服务业	Resident Service and Other Service Industries	27411	5916	15901
卫生、社会保障和社会福利业	Health Care,Social Security and Social Welfare	434	37	296
文化、体育和娱乐业	Culture,Sports and Entertainment	1932	558	1016
其它行业	Others	1364	246	824
从业人员(人)	Emplyment Personnel(person)	748996	146151	357583
农、林、牧、渔业	Farming. Forestry. Animal Husbandry and Fishery	11972	4953	3649
采矿业	Mining and Quarrying Industry	217		69
制造业	Manufacturing Industry	248861	41071	79901
电力、燃气及水的生产和供应业	Electric Power,Gas and Water Production and Supply	50	2	13
建筑业	Construction	6666	1232	3313
交通运输业、仓储和邮政业	Transportation and Warehousing	32901	7020	16523
信息传输、计算机服务和软件业	Information Transmission, Computer Service and Software Industries	553	171	365

注:本表数据来自于宁波市工商行政管理局。

Note:Data in this table are obtained from Ningbo Administration for Industry & Commerce.

表 10－17 续表 Continued

指标	Indicators	全市期末实有 Total at The End of This Year	其中 of Which 本期开业 Openning for This Term	其中 of Which 城镇 Districts
批发和零售业	Wholesale and Retail Trade	320214	59729	172479
住宿和餐饮业	Hotel and Catering Trade	51872	14607	32668
房地产业	Real Estate Industries	2157	565	1698
租赁和商务服务业	Leasing and Business Service Industries	8116	2098	5775
居民服务和其它服务业	Resident Service and Other Service Industries	56316	12658	35557
卫生、社会保障和社会福利业	Health Care, Social Security and Social Welfare	934	86	644
文化、体育和娱乐业	Culture, Sports and Entertainment	5523	1374	3192
其它行业	Others	2644	585	1737
注册资金(万元)	Registered Capital (10000 Yuan)	2203368	609862	1119469
农、林、牧、渔业	Farming. Forestry. Animal Husbandry and Fishery	154481	76479	52692
采矿业	Mining and Quarrying Industry	2326		527
制造业	Manufacturing Industry	653436	132591	183312
电力、燃气及水的生产和供应业	Electric Power, Gas and Water Production and Supply	227	10	41
建筑业	Construction	24282	5737	10560
交通运输业、仓储和邮政业	Transportation and Warehousing	145985	32041	70646
信息传输、计算机服务和软件业	Information Transmission, Computer Service and Software Industries	1443	459	908
批发和零售业	Wholesale and Retail Trade	829096	258306	534229
住宿和餐饮业	Hotel and Catering Trade	187124	48705	128526
房地产业	Real Estate Industries	4360	1504	3529
租赁和商务服务业	Leasing and Business Service Industries	30560	8446	21027
居民服务和其它服务业	Resident Service and Other Service Industries	122795	34976	79908
卫生、社会保障和社会福利业	Health Care, Social Security and Social Welfare	10245	676	6784
文化、体育和娱乐业	Culture, Sports and Entertainment	29800	7691	21715
其它行业	Others	7207	2241	5056

表 10—18 私营企业基本情况(2013)
Basic Statistics on Private Enterprises

指标	Indicators	全市期末实有 Total at the End of this Year	其中 of Which 本期开业 Openning for this Term	城镇 Districts
户数(户)	**Number of Households(unit)**	**173875**	**29495**	**103679**
农、林、牧、渔业	Farming. Forestry. Animal Husbandry and Fishery	2408	833	694
采矿业	Mining and Quarrying Industry	92	4	27
制造业	Manufacturing Industry	72732	8143	28585
电力、燃气及水的生产和供应业	Electric Power, Gas and Water Production and Supply	136	13	49
建筑业	Construction	7119	1306	5005
交通运输业、仓储和邮政业	Transportation and Warehousing	4393	621	3120
信息传输、计算机服务和软件业	Information Transmission, Computer Service and Software Industries	3321	578	2734
批发和零售业	Wholesale and Retail Trade	52172	10825	39639
住宿和餐饮业	Hotel and Catering Trade	2120	493	1534
房地产业	Real Estate Industries	2747	449	1841
租赁和商务服务业	Leasing and Business Service Industries	13623	3376	11081
居民服务和其它服务业	Resident Service and Other Service Industries	3232	751	2407
卫生、社会保障和社会福利业	Health Care, Social Security and Social Welfare	183	25	122
文化、体育和娱乐业	Culture, Sports and Entertainment	1334	365	1072
其它行业	Others	8263	1713	5769
从业人员(人)	Emplyment Personnel(person)	2243946	311755	1329412
农、林、牧、渔业	Farming. Forestry. Animal Husbandry and Fishery	22347	7593	7056
采矿业	Mining and Quarrying Industry	1184	34	338
制造业	Manufacturing Industry	1192568	87675	528706
电力、燃气及水的生产和供应业	Electric Power, Gas and Water Production and Supply	1280	148	523
建筑业	Construction	79511	13496	54938
交通运输业、仓储和邮政业	Transportation and Warehousing	47441	6367	35487
信息传输、计算机服务和软件业	Information Transmission, Computer Service and Software Industries	33346	5889	27302

注:本表数据来自于宁波市工商行政管理局。
Note: Data in this table are obtained from Ningbo Administration for Industry & Commerce.

表 10－18 续表 Continued

指标	Indicators	全市期末实有 Total at the End of this Year	其中 of Which	
			本期开业 Openning for this Term	城镇 Districts
批发和零售业	Wholesale and Retail Trade	507103	99774	407243
住宿和餐饮业	Hotel and Catering Trade	38799	19448	17616
房地产业	Real Estate Industries	29351	4568	20304
租赁和商务服务业	Leasing and Business Service Industries	150880	36424	126304
居民服务和其它服务业	Resident Service and Other Service Industries	30945	6492	24637
卫生、社会保障和社会福利业	Health Care, Social Security and Social Welfare	1752	175	1166
文化、体育和娱乐业	Culture, Sports and Entertainment	14249	3629	11077
其它行业	Others	93190	20043	66715
注册资金(万元)	Registered Capital (10000 Yuan)	53539702	11288068	40581489
农、林、牧、渔业	Farming, Forestrym, Animal Husbandry and Fishery	401809	160626	182752
采矿业	Mining and Quarrying Industry	17626	321	7713
制造业	Manufacturing Industry	12161517	801441	5425635
电力、燃气及水的生产和供应业	Electric Power, Gas and Water Production and Supply	89783	5382	51463
建筑业	Construction	3333061	263911	2567177
交通运输业、仓储和邮政业	Transportation and Warehousing	1604010	345368	1372999
信息传输、计算机服务和软件业	Information Transmission, Computer Service and Software Industries	449744	99079	397132
批发和零售业	Wholesale and Retail Trade	8412152	1122114	6968980
住宿和餐饮业	Hotel and Catering Trade	262278	28188	190830
房地产业	Real Estate Industries	5285031	550968	3898273
租赁和商务服务业	Leasing and Business Service Industries	18225529	7428042	17060272
居民服务和其它服务业	Resident Service and Other Service Industries	249406	44798	208579
卫生、社会保障和社会福利业	Health Care, Social Security and Social Welfare	19957	1977	16496
文化、体育和娱乐业	Culture, Sports and Entertainment	209193	57120	181245
其它行业	Others	2818606	378733	2051943

表10—19 限额以上服务业企业主要经济指标
Main Economic Indicators of Service enterprises Above Designated Size

指标	Indicators	企业数 Number of Enterprises	#亏损企业 Loss—making Enterprises	从业人员数 Number of Employees	资产总计 Total Asset
总计	Total	6485	1997	676894	307540999
#国有控股企业	State—holding Enterprises	580	138	149668	173936101
按注册类型分	Grouped by Registration Type				
内资企业	Domestic Funded Enterprises	6239	1915	628679	294974311
国有企业	State—Owned Enterprises	152	35	33333	31831765
集体企业	Collective—Owned Enterprises	75	11	3894	162974
股份合作企业	Share Cooperative Enterprises	23	3	7512	19194673
联营企业	Limited Liability Corporations	6	0	350	25811
有限责任公司	Share—holding Corporations Ltd.	1094	304	149759	37628943
股份有限公司	Private Enterprises	193	64	76079	175051678
私营企业	Private enterprises	4647	1490	354362	30920974
其他企业	Other enterprises	49	8	3390	157492
港澳台商投资企业	Hongkong,Macao and Taiwan Funded	134	42	30302	7618002
外商投资企业	Foreign—invested enterprises	112	40	17913	4948687
按行业分	Grouped by Sector				
批发和零售业	Wholesale and retail trade	2929	924	142110	38574064
交通运输、仓储和邮政业	Transport, storage and postal service	1040	277	96589	12486178
住宿和餐饮业	Accommodation and catering industry	467	267	45288	1870948
信息传输、计算机服务和软件业	Information transmission, computer services and software industry	199	70	18116	2779703
金融业	Financial sector	184	55	66290	221893810
房地产业	Real Estate industry	193	61	44585	1370475
租赁和商务服务业	Rental and business services sector	728	190	208858	25360787
科学研究、技术服务与地质勘查业	Scientific research, technical services and geological prospecting industry	317	31	24140	975811
水利、环境和公共设施管理业	Irrigation works,environment and public facilities management	76	25	7368	1226421
居民服务和其他服务业	Resident and other services	183	48	9519	208151
教育	Education	53	7	4275	89703
卫生和社会福利业	Hygiene and social welfare	36	11	3542	150360
文化、体育与娱乐业	Civilization, sports and entertainment industry	80	31	6214	554590
公共管理、社会保障与社会组织	Public management,,The social security and social organization				

注：房地产业不包括房地产开发经营，限上服务企业包含了批发和零售业、住宿和餐饮业。

Note: Real Estate excludes Real estate development and management, Wholesale, retail, accommodation and catering are included above designated size.

单位:个、万元(unit,10000 yuan)

负债合计 Total Liabilities	所有者权益合计 Crediters' Equity	营业收入 Business Revernue	营业成本 Business Costs	营业税金及附加 Tax and Extra Charge	三项费用 Three Costs	应付职工薪酬 Employee Compensation Payable	营业利润 Business Profits	利润总额 Total Profits
272258019	**35282981**	**121426880**	**107626552**	**1011032**	**8470962**	**4911349**	**4745608**	**5358349**
156154680	17781422	28092696	22379697	600748	2440855	1695520	2773307	3001670
265780467	29193844	112886811	100259779	972828	7720942	4579804	4168894	4757306
29543515	2288250	4154400	2739810	174898	405633	363177	843875	819461
93354	69620	138099	104953	2284	23541	19482	7819	8302
17371617	1823056	1153941	535056	30304	242887	146424	346228	332899
8856	16956	18728	16204	62	1057	4380	1402	1394
25869819	11759125	30399910	27770761	126116	1847808	1056190	671151	938096
167564614	7487064	23039481	18476704	483579	2232457	1073260	2015181	2177845
25262540	5658434	53884447	50559900	154007	2944812	1898140	265954	461696
66152	91340	97804	56391	1579	22747	18751	17284	17612
2995925	4622076	3564894	2913834	23828	478724	213805	291587	318041
3481627	1467060	4975176	4452939	14376	271296	117740	285127	283002
31567058	7007005	87234680	83142393	161683	3292621	921057	801522	1093672
7346055	5140123	8640741	7536150	35294	670230	704080	431589	521995
1605912	265036	768825	307756	41920	512280	203693	−93186	−72728
662668	2117035	1665322	764789	43567	446970	175934	399577	426566
213695582	8198228	17586549	11918622	602821	2265520	1146060	2795181	2785382
964270	406205	357450	201519	20196	135430	177722	593	15859
14648007	10712780	3555894	2820360	73858	690168	1144687	205552	346828
443579	532232	828318	463353	15260	200247	229647	151693	168819
916073	310347	194775	116876	4485	67082	44719	5826	8232
126544	81608	208507	155438	3203	40772	40785	9067	19718
38439	51264	82851	39149	3213	23379	31698	17117	17261
62782	87578	101314	40809	638	51963	27558	8385	8339
181051	373539	201655	119337	4888	74294	63710	12693	18406

表 10－20　批发业销售收入前 20 位企业(2013)
The Top 20 Enterprises of Wholesales Trade at Sales Revenue

排名 No.	企业名称	Name of Corporation	所在区域	Location
1	浙江前程石化股份有限公司	Zhejiang Future Petrochemical Co.,Ltd.	高新区	Gaoxin
2	宁波恒逸贸易有限公司	Ningbo Hengyi Trading Co.,Ltd.	北仑区	Beilun
3	宁波神化化学品经营有限责任公司	Ningbo Sunhu Chem Products Co.,Ltd.	江东区	Jiangdong
4	远大物产集团有限公司	Grand Group Corporation	北仑区	Beilun
5	中基宁波集团股份有限公司	China－Base Ningbo Foreign Trade Co.,Ltd.	鄞州区	Yinzhou
6	中国石油化工股份有限公司浙江宁波石油分公司	Ningbo Branch of Sinopec	海曙区	Haishu
7	宁波保税区首德贸易有限公司	Ningbo bonded area Shoude Trade Co.,Ltd.	北仑区	Beilun
8	浙江省烟草公司宁波市公司	Ningbo branch of Zhejiang Tobacco	江东区	Jiangdong
9	远大石化有限公司	Ningbo Yuanda Petrochemical Co.,Ltd.	高新区	Gaoxin
10	宁波君安物产有限公司	Ningbo Junan Resources Co.,Ltd.	江东区	Jiangdong
11	中国石化化工销售有限公司宁波经营部	Sinopec Chemical Sales Co.,Ltd. Operating the Department of Ningbo	高新区	Gaoxin
12	宁波杉杉物产有限公司	Ningbo Shanshan Resources Co.,Ltd.	鄞州区	Yinzhou
13	中航国际钢铁贸易有限公司	AVIC international steel trade Co.,Ltd.	北仑区	Beilun
14	浙江生水实业有限公司	Zhejiang Water Industry Co.,Ltd.	高新区	Gaoxin
15	宁波山煤华泰贸易有限公司	Ningbo Mountain Coal Trading Co.,Ltd.	北仑区	Beilun
16	宁波沙洲贸易有限公司	Ningbo Shazhou Trading Co.,Ltd.	北仑区	Beilun
17	日出实业集团有限公司	Pict Sunrise Group Corporation	鄞州区	Yinzhou
18	宁波银亿进出口有限公司	Ningbo Yinyi Import and Export Co.,Ltd.	海曙区	Haishu
19	宁波展杰磁性材料有限公司	Ningbo Zhanjie Magnetic Materials Co.,Ltd.	慈溪市	Cixi
20	宁波久东贸易有限公司	Ningbo Jiudong Trading Co.,Ltd.	海曙区	Haishu

表 10－21　零售业销售收入前 20 位企业(2013)
The Top 20 Enterprises of Retail Trade at Sales Revenue

排名 No.	企业名称	Name of Corporation	所在区域	Location
1	中石化碧辟(浙江)石油有限公司宁波分公司	BP Sinopec (Zhejiang) Petroleum Co.,Ltd. Ningbo Branch	海曙区	Haishu
2	三江购物俱乐部股份有限公司	Ningbo Sanjiang Shopping Mall Co.,Ltd.	海曙区	Haishu
3	宁波医药股份有限公司	Ningbo Pharmaceutical Co.,Ltd.	海曙区	Haishu
4	浙江华润慈客隆超市有限公司	Zhejiang Cikelong Shopping Mall Ltd.	慈溪市	Cixi
5	宁波太平鸟时尚服饰股份有限公司	Ningbo Peace Bird fashion clothing Co.,Ltd.	海曙区	Haishu
6	浙江华联商厦有限公司	Zhejiang Hualian Trade Co.,Ltd.	余姚市	Yuyao
7	哈工大首创科技股份有限公司	Hit Shouchuang Polytron Technologies Inc	海曙区	Haishu
8	宁波捷骏汽车销售服务有限公司	Ningbo Junjie Auto Sales & Service Co.,Ltd.	江东区	Jiangdong
9	宁波欧尚超市有限公司	Ningbo Auchan Supermarket Co.,Ltd.	海曙区	Haishu
10	浙江大生医药有限公司	Zhejiang Tai Sang Medicine Co.,Ltd.	北仑区	Beilun
11	宁波太平鸟风尚男装有限公司	Ningbo Peace Bird fashion men's clothing Co.,Ltd.	高新区	Gaoxin
12	宁波宝恒汽车销售服务有限公司	Ningbo Baoheng Auto Sale & Service Co.,Ltd.	鄞州区	Yinzhou
13	宁波市北仑加贝购物俱乐部(普通合伙)	Ningbo beilun Jiabei Shopping Mall	北仑区	Beilun
14	宁波中基汽车销售服务有限公司	Ningbo Zhongji Car Sales Services Co.,Ltd.	鄞州区	Yinzhou
15	宁波润达汽车销售服务有限公司	Ningbo Runda Auto Sale & Service Co.,Ltd.	江北区	Jiangbei
16	宁波丰颐汽车销售有限公司	Ningbo FengYi Automobile Sales Co.,Ltd.	鄞州区	Yinzhou
17	银泰百货宁波海曙有限公司	Intime Department Store Co.,Ltd. Ningbo Haishu	海曙区	Haishu
18	宁波天华汽车销售服务有限公司	Ningbo Tianhua Automobile Sales Co.,Ltd.	镇海区	Zhenhai
19	宁波之星汽车维修服务有限公司	Ningbo Star Auto Services Co.,Ltd.	鄞州区	Yinzhou
20	宁波新江厦连锁超市有限公司	Ningbo New Jiangxia Supermarket Chains Co.,Ltd.	鄞州区	Yinzhou

表 10－22 星级住宿业营业收入前 20 位企业(2013)
The Top 20 Enterprises of Hotelat Business Revenue

排名 No.	企业名称	Name of Corporation	所在区域	Location
1	香格里拉大酒店(宁波)有限公司	Shangri－La Hotel (Ningbo) Co. ,Ltd.	江东区	Jiangdong
2	宁波东港波特曼大酒店有限公司	Portman Plaza Hotel Ningbo	江东区	Jiangdong
3	宁波南苑集团股份有限公司	Ningbo Nanyuan Group Co. ,Ltd.	海曙区	Haishu
4	宁波华侨饭店有限公司	Ningbo Howard Johnson Hotel Co. ,Ltd.	海曙区	Haishu
5	宁波太平洋大酒店有限公司	Ningbo Pacific Hotel Co. ,Ltd.	余姚市	Yuyao
6	慈溪市杭州湾大酒店有限公司	Cixi Hangzhou Gulf Hotel Co. ,Ltd.	慈溪市	Cixi
7	宁波开元大酒店有限公司	Ningbo Kaiyuan Hotel Co. ,Ltd.	江东区	Jiangdong
8	宁波市凯洲实业有限公司	Ningbo Kai Zhou Industrial Co. ,Ltd.	海曙区	Haishu
9	宁波开元名都大酒店有限公司	Ningbo Kaiyuan Mingdu Grand Hotel Co. ,Ltd.	鄞州区	Yinzhou
10	宁波万达置业有限公司万达索菲特大饭店	Sofitel Wanda Ningbo Wanda Hotel Properties Co. ,Ltd.	鄞州区	Yinzhou
11	宁波新晶都酒店有限公司	Holiyacht Crystal Hotel	江东区	Jiangdong
12	宁波九龙湖开元华城度假村有限公司	Ningbo Kaiyuan Huacity Jiulong Lake Co. ,Ltd.	镇海区	Zhenhai
13	余姚宾馆有限责任公司	Yuyao Hotel Co. ,Ltd.	余姚市	Yuyao
14	宁波南苑商务旅店连锁股份有限公司	Ningbo Nanyuan Business Hotel Chain Co. ,Ltd.	鄞州区	Yinzhou
15	宁波市鄞州天港禧悦酒店管理有限公司	Ningbo Yinzhou Tiangangxiyue Inn Management Co. ,Ltd.	鄞州区	Yinzhou
16	浙江三碧酒店股份有限公司	Zhejiang 3－B Hotel	江北区	Jiangbei
17	余姚中塑石浦大酒店有限公司	Zhongsu Shipu Hotel	余姚市	Yuyao
18	宁波凯利大酒店有限公司	Ningbo Kaili Hotel Co. ,Ltd.	江北区	Jiangbei
19	慈溪市金色港湾旅业有限公司	Cixi Golden Harbour Tourism Co. ,Ltd.	慈溪市	Cixi
20	余姚辰茂河姆渡宾馆有限公司	Yuyao Excemon Hemudu Hotel	余姚市	Yuyao

表 10－23 餐饮业营业收入前 20 位企业(2013)
The Top 20 Enterprises of Catering Trade at Business Revenue

排名 No.	企业名称	Name of Corporation	所在区域	Location
1	宁波南苑环球酒店管理有限公司	Nanyuan International Hotel Management Co. ,Ltd.	鄞州区	Yinzhou
2	宁波市来必堡餐饮管理有限公司	Ningbo Laibi Fort Restaurant Management Co. ,Ltd.	海曙区	Haishu
3	宁海金海开元名都大酒店有限公司	Ninghai Jinhai Hotel Management Co. ,Ltd.	宁海县	Ninghai
4	宁波外婆家餐饮有限公司	My Grandmother's Home in Ningbo Catering Co. ,Ltd.	海曙区	Haishu
5	浙江向阳渔港集团股份有限公司	Zhejiang Xiangyang Port Group Co. ,Ltd.	江东区	Jiangdong
6	宁波和丰花园酒店有限公司	Ningbo Hefeng Garden Hotel Co. ,Ltd.	江东区	Jiangdong
7	宁波恒元大酒店有限公司	Ningbo Hengyuan Hotel Co. ,Ltd.	慈溪市	Cixi
8	宁波银苑大酒店有限公司	Ningbo Yinyuan Restaurant Co. ,Ltd.	鄞州区	Yinzhou
9	余姚阳明温泉山庄实业有限公司	Yuyao Yangming Hot Spring Resort	余姚市	Yuyao
10	宁波海底捞餐饮管理有限公司	Ningbo Haidilao Restaurant Management Co. ,Ltd.	海曙区	Haishu
11	宁波市江东天港禧悦酒店管理有限公司	Ningbo Jiangdong Sky Harbor Jubilee Paradise Hotel Management Co. ,Ltd.	江东区	Jiangdong
12	宁波石浦酒店管理发展有限公司	Ningbo Shipu Restaurant Management Development Co. ,Ltd.	鄞州区	Yinzhou
13	宁波四季永逸大饭店有限公司	Luotuo Forever Peace Hotel	镇海区	Zhenhai
14	宁波东方明珠娱乐有限公司	Ningbo Oriental Pearl Amusement Co. ,Ltd.	江东区	Jiangdong
15	象山飞扬餐饮管理有限公司	Xiangshan Feiyang Catering Management Co. ,Ltd.	象山县	Xiangshan
16	宁海世贸中心大酒店有限公司	World Trade Center Hotel	宁海县	Ninghai
17	余姚雍和宫大酒店有限公司	Yuyao Yonghogong Restaurant Co. ,Ltd.	余姚市	Yuyao
18	宁波杭州湾新区世纪金源大饭店有限公司	Ningbo Hangzhou Bay Empark Hotel	慈溪市	Cixi
19	浙江竹林人家餐饮有限公司	Zhejiang Bamboo Country Food Co. ,Ltd.	海曙区	Haishu
20	宁波汉唐餐饮管理有限公司	Ningbo Hantang Restaurant Management Co. ,Ltd.	海曙区	Haishu

表 10－24　年成交额前 20 位的交易市场(2013)
The Top 20 Commodity Exchange Market with Transaction Volume

排名 No.	企业名称	Name of Corporation	所在区域	Location
1	余姚市中国塑料城	China Plastic Exchange Market (Yuyao)	余姚市	Yuyao
2	宁波市镇海煤炭交易市场有限公司	Ningbo Zhenhai Coal Exchange Co. ,Ltd.	镇海区	Zhenhai
3	宁波镇海液体化工产品交易市场	Ningbo Zhenhai Liquid Chemical Products Market	镇海区	Zhenhai
4	宁波镇海大宗生产资料交易中心	Ningbo Zhenhai Mass Production Trading Center	镇海区	Zhenhai
5	宁波华东物资城	East China Material Market of Ningbo	江东区	Jiangdong
6	宁波市镇海厚恒物资城	Ningbo Zhenhai Houheng Material City	镇海区	Zhenhai
7	浙江长三角石油化工发展有限公司	Zhejiang Changsanjiao Petroleum Chemical Industry Co. ,Ltd.	慈溪市	Cixi
8	慈溪市农副产品批发市场	Cixi Wholesale Market of Farm & Sideline Products	溪市	Cixi
9	余姚市模板市场	Yuyao MasterPlate Market	余姚市	Yuyao
10	宁波轻纺城	Ningbo Light Textile Market	鄞州区	Yinzhou
11	余姚市农副产品批发市场	Yuyao Wholesale Market of Farm & Sideline Products	余姚市	Yuyao
12	慈溪市工业品批发市场	Cixi Wholesale Market of Industrial Products	慈溪市	Cixi
13	宁波鄞州新时代钢材市场	Ningbo Yinzhou New Times Steel Market	鄞州区	Yinzhou
14	浙江象山水产城实业有限公司	Zhejiang Xiangshan Aquatic Product City Industrial Co. ,Ltd.	象山县	Xiangshan
15	宁波市江东水产批发市场	Ningbo Jiangdong aquatic products wholesale market	江东区	Jiangdong
16	宁波华东物资城王家弄市场	Wangjia Long Market of East China Material Market	鄞州区	Yinzhou
17	宁波江北华东物资城浙甬市场开发有限公司	Ningbo Jiangbei East China Material City Zhejiang Ningbo market development Co. Ltd.	江北区	Jiangbei
18	慈溪市周巷副食品批发市场	Cixi Zhouxiang Wholesale Market of Subsidiary Food	慈溪市	Cixi
19	宁波万国商城	Ningbo Wanguo Commodity Market	鄞州区	Yinzhou
20	慈溪市胜山服装布料市场	Cixi Shenshan Garment and Cloth Market	慈溪市	Cixi

主要统计指标解释

【社会消费品零售额】 指各种经济类型的批发零售贸易业、餐饮业、制造业和其他行业对城乡居民和社会集团的消费品零售额。这个指标反映通过各种商品流通渠道向居民和社会集团供应的生活消费品来满足他们生活需要，是研究人民生活，社会消费品购买力、货币流通等问题的重要指标。社会消费品零售额包括:(1)售给城乡居民作为生活用的商品和修建房屋用的建筑材料;(2)售给社会集团的各种办公用品和公用消费品(3)售给 机关、团体、学校、部队、企业、事业单位的职工食堂和旅店(招待所)附设专门供本店旅客食用，不对外营业的食堂的各种食品、燃料;企业、单位和国营农场直接售给本单位职工和职工食堂的自已生产的产品;(4)售给部队干部、战士生活用的粮食、副食品、衣着品、日用品、燃料;(5)售给来华的外国人、华侨、港澳(台)同胞的消费品;(6)居民自费购买的中、西药品、中药材及医疗用品;(7)报社、出版社直接售给居民和社会集团的报纸、图书、杂志、集邮公司出售的新、旧纪念邮票、特种邮票、首日封、集邮册、集邮工具等;(8)旧货寄售商店自购、自销部分的商品;(9)煤气公司、液化石油气站售给居民和社会集团的煤气灶具和罐装液化石油气;(10)农民售给非农业居民和社会集团的商品。不包括售给国民经济各部门企业、事业单位(包括国有经济的农场)生产经营用的各种原材料、燃料、设备、工具等和售给批发零售贸易业、餐饮业作为转卖用的商品、旧货寄售商店受托寄售卖出的商品、服务业的营业收入、邮局出售邮票的收入、自来水、电力、煤气生产(供应)单位的产品供应收入，也不包括农民之间的商品销售。

【限额以上批发企业】 指年销售额在2000万元及以上，并且年末从业人员在20人及以上的批发贸易企业。

【限额以上零售企业】 指年销售额在500万元及以上，并且年末从业人员在60人及以上的零售企业。

【限额以上餐饮企业】 指年销售额在200万元及以上，并且年末从业人员在40人及以上的餐饮企业。

【批发零售贸易业商品购、销、存总额】 指以各种经济类型的批发、零售贸易业(不包括个体)为总体的商品购、销、存。

【商品购进总额】 指从本企业(单位)以外的单位和个人购进(包括从国外直接进口)作为转卖或加工后转卖的商品。这个指标反映批发零售贸易业从国内、国外市场上购进商品的总量。商品购进总额包括:(1)从工农业生产者购进的商品;(2)从出版社、报社的出版发行部门购进的图书、杂志和报纸;(3)从各种经济类型的批发零售贸易企业(单位)购进的商品;(4)从其他单位购进的商品，如从机关、团体、企业单位购进的剩余物资，从餐饮业、服务业购进的商品，从海关、市场管理部门购进的缉私和没收的商品，从居民收购的废旧商品等;(5)从国(境)外直接进口的商品。不包括企业(单位)为自身经营用，和未通过买卖行为而收入的商品以及销售退回、商品升溢等。

【商品销售总额】 指对本企业(单位)以外的单位和个人出售(包括对国(境)外直接出口)的商品。这个指标反映批发零售贸易业在国内市场上销售商品以及出口商品的总量。商品销售总额包括:(1)售给城乡居民和社会集团消费用的商品;(2)售给工业、农业、建筑业、运输邮电业、批发零售贸易业、餐饮业、服务业等作为生产、经营使用的商品;(3)售给批发零售贸易业作为转卖或加工后转卖的商品;(4)对国(境)外直接出口的商品。不包括:出售本企业(单位)自用的废旧包装用品，未通过买卖行为付出的商品，经本单位介绍，由买卖双方直接结算，本单位只收取手续费的业务，购货退出的商品以及商品损耗和损失等。

Explanatory Notes on Main Statistical Indicators

【Total Retail Sales of Consumer Goods】 refer to the sum of retail sales of consumer goods by the establishments in wholesale trade, retail sale trade, catering trade, manufacturing industry and other industries of different types of ownership, to urban and rural residents and social groups. This indicator is used to show the supply of consumer goods through various channels to households and institutions to meet their demands, and is therefore very important for the study of the issues on people's livelihood, on the purchasing power of consumer goods and on the circulation of money. The retail sales of consumer goods include: (1)commodities sold to urban and rural residents for residential use and building materials sold to them for the construction or repair of houses;(2)food and fuels sold to canteens of institutions, enterprises, schools, military units and to canteens of hotels and hostels that only serve their guests, and commodities produced by enterprises, institutions or state farms and sold directly to their employees or their canteens; (3)grain and non—staple food, clothing, daily articles and fuels sold to military personnel; (4)consumer goods sold to foreigners, overseas Chinese, and Chinese compatriots from Taiwan, Hong Kong and Macao during their stay in the mainland of China; (5)Chinese an d western medicines, herbs and medical facilities purchased by residents; (6) newspapers, books and magazines directly sold to residents and social groups by publishers, new and old commemorative stamps, special stamps, first day covers, stamp albums and other stamp collection articles sold by stamp companies; (7)consumer goods purchased and then sold by second—hand shops; (8)stoves and other heating facilities and liquified gas sold by gas companies to households and institutions; (9)commodities sold by farmers to non—agricultural residents and social groups. Excluded under this heading are: raw materials, fuels, equipment, tools sold to enterprises, institutions and state farms for production purpose; commodities sold to trade establishments for re—selling; commissioned sales at second—hand shops; operational income of urban public utilities; stamps sold at post offices; income of water, power, gas production and supply establishments from the supply of their products; and sales of commodities among farmers.

【Enterprises of Over—norm Wholesale Volume】 refers to wholesale trade enterprises that register an annual sales volume of over 20 million yuan RMB and a total year-end staff of more than 20.

【Enterprises of Over—norm Retail Sales Volume】 refers to those that register an annual sales volume of over 5 million yuan RMB and a total year—end staff of more than 60.

【Catering Enterprises of Over—norm Sales Volume】 refers to those that register an annual sales volume of over 2 million yuan RMB and a total year—end staff of more than 40.

【Purchase, Sales and Stock of Commodities by Wholesale and Retail Trade】 refer to the purchase, sales and stock of commodities by wholesale and retail establishments of different ownership(excluding individual sellers).

【Total Purchases of Commodities】 refer to the purchases of commodities by the establishments from other establishments or individuals (including direct import from abroad) for the purpose of re—selling, either with or without further processing of the commodities purchased. This indicator is used to show the total value of purchases of commodities by wholesale and retail establishments from domestic and overseas markets. The total purchases include: (1)agricultural and industrial products purchased from producers; (2)books, magazines and newspapers purchased from distribution departments of the publishers; (3) commodities purchased from wholesale and retail establishments; (4)commodities purchased from other units, such as surplus materials purchased from government agencies, enterprises or institutions, commodities purchased from catering and service establishments, confiscated goods purchased from customs authorities or market management agencies, second—hand goods and wastes purchased from residents; and (5)commodities directly imported from abroad. Excluded are commodities purchased by establishments(units)for use in their own business operation, commodities obtained without buying or selling procedures, rejected commodities, etc.

【Total Sales of Commodities】 refer to selling of commodities by the establishments to other establishments and individuals(including direct export) . This indicator is used to show the total value of sales of commodities at domestic markets and export. The total sales include: (1)commodities sold to urban and rural residents and social groups for their consumption; (2)commodities so ld to establishments in industry, agriculture, construction, transportation, post and telecommunications, wholesale and retail trades, catering trade and public utility for their production and operation; (3)commodities sold to wholesale an d retail establishments for re—selling, with or without further processing; and (4)commodities for direct export to other countries. Excluded are selling of waste packaging materials used by the establishments(units) themselves, commodities transferred without buying or selling procedures, commission income from brokerage in transactions whose settlement is directly handled by buyers and sellers , rejected commodities in the purchase, loss in commodities, etc.

CHAPTER 11

NINGBO 2014

Statistical YearBook

第十一篇

对外经济、旅游

FOREIGN TRADE AND TOURISM

对外经济、旅游
Foreign Trade and Tourism

主要统计指标
Major Statistics Indicators

2013 年自营进出口总额	Total Direct Import and Export	10032895	万美元	USD 10000
比上年增长	Increase Over Last Year	3.9	%	
2013 年自营出口总额	Total Exports	6571020	万美元	USD 10000
比上年增长	Increase Over Last Year	7.0	%	
2013 年自营进口总额	Total Imports	3461875	万美元	USD 10000
比上年增长	Increase Over Last Year	−1.4	%	
2013 年新签合同数	Number of Projects of Signed Contracts	442	个	unit
比上年增长	Increase Over Last Year	1.1	%	
2013 年实际利用外资金额	Value of Foreign Captial Actually Used	327483	万美元	USD 10000
比上年增长	Increase Over Last Year	14.8	%	
2013 年接待境外旅游者人数	Number of Received Oversea Tourists	1273439	人	person
比上年增长	Increase Over Last Year	9.6	%	
2013 年旅游创汇收入	Foreign Exchange Earnings	79656	万美元	USD 10000
比上年增长	Increase Over Last Year	8.5	%	
2013 年国内旅游总收入	Earning From Domestic Tourism	904.2	亿元	100 million yuan
比上年增长	Increase Over Last Year	10.6	%	

表 11－1 历年对外经济贸易基本情况
Basic Statistics on Foreign Economy and Trade Over the Years

单位：万美元(USD 10000)

年份 Year	外商直接投资情况 Foreign Direct Investments			自营进出口 Direct Import and Export		口岸进出口 Import and Export of Port	
	新批项目数(个) Number of Projects(unit)	合同利用外资 Foreign Capital Signed Agreements	实际利用外资 Foreign Capital Actually Used	进出口 Total	#出口 Exports	进出口 Total	#出口 Exports
1980	1	5	5				
1981							
1982						14917	10963
1983						17683	12173
1984	8	850	21			26336	16102
1985	11	682	359	1029	389	45474	23521
1986	7	447	500	2079	540	54690	34432
1987	13	4341	429	2061	791	52493	29999
1988	62	4002	689	14766	11458	78717	39155
1989	64	6295	1758	22024	18005	110175	53615
1990	89	5624	2197	29840	27962	125527	63253
1991	184	17460	2680	57339	47532	219638	87101
1992	636	156725	11497	99072	78389	260387	101699
1993	1015	107152	34455	169434	110824	328871	120138
1994	680	77149	35812	251462	174992	375919	168340
1995	496	114630	39909	385335	226825	521501	232789
1996	322	87838	50162	418573	233003	586140	252248
1997	260	45849	55408	460896	293332	663807	311848
1998	281	51198	50329	421237	296386	610109	339904
1999	364	65660	52035	500898	347721	774194	411200
2000	550	95151	62186	754065	516781	1372547	703357
2001	806	195519	87446	889202	624500	1613794	869768
2002	1017	320024	124696	1227343	816304	2145755	1232723
2003	1209	344382	172727	1880962	1207398	3394193	1888206
2004	1081	413633	210322	2611222	1668967	5157576	2664100
2005	873	421015	231079	3349427	2223256	6749471	3614462
2006	1034	442746	243018	4221188	2877052	8649306	4958297
2007	854	450107	250518	5649909	3825509	11176033	6744103
2008	528	412339	253789	6784036	4632638	14018503	8371436
2009	403	342362	220541	6081252	3865068	11692277	7317493
2010	495	404608	232336	8290424	5196745	16134445	10052342
2011	411	501463	280929	9818682	6083159	20044269	12375307
2012	437	531276	285252	9657269	6144526	19757789	12419370
2013	442	582029	327483	10032895	6571020	21190173	13397419

注：2003 年起，利用外资统计口径有变动。

Note: From 2003, the Statstistical Standard which will utilize the foreign capitals have changed.

表 11-2 按企业性质分的进出口总值(2013)
Total Value of Imports and Exports by Registered Type of Enterprises

单位:万美元(USD 10000)

企业性质	Grouped by Registered Type	进出口 Imports and Exports		其中 of Which 出口 Exports		其中 of Which 进口 Imports	
		贸易额 Value	增长率(%) Rate of Increase	贸易额 Value	增长率(%) Rate of Increase	贸易额 Value	增长率(%) Rate of Increase
合计	**Total**	**10032895**	**3.9**	**6571020**	**7.0**	**3461875**	**-1.4**
国营企业	State-Owned Enterprises	788143	-7.0	490941	-14.0	297203	7.4
三资企业	Foreign Funded Enterprises	3829994	0.3	2185373	1.5	1644620	-1.3
#外合作企业	Cooperative Operation Enterprises	36786	3.7	20872	-8.6	15914	25.8
外合资企业	Joint Venture Enterprises	1517622	1.8	948625	4.4	568997	-2.4
外商独资企业	Foreign-funded Sole Enterprises	2275585	-0.8	1215876	-0.5	1059709	-1.0
集体企业	Collective Owned Enterprises	422747	-36.7	267806	-26.6	154941	-48.8
私营企业	Private Enterprises	4980118	15.5	3617573	18.8	1362545	7.7
个体工商户	Individual Enterprises	10508	28.4	8729	19.5	1778	102.3

注:本表至 11-5 表数据来自宁波海关。

Note:Data from Tables 11-2 to 11-5 are obtained from Ningbo Customs.

表 11-3 按贸易方式分的进出口总值(2013)
Total Value of Imports and Exports by Trade Property

单位:万美元(USD 10000)

企业性质	Grouped by Registered Type	进出口 Imports and Exports		其中 of Which 出口 Exports		其中 of Which 进口 Imports	
		贸易额 Value	增长率(%) Rate of Increase	贸易额 Value	增长率(%) Rate of Increase	贸易额 Value	增长率(%) Rate of Increase
总额	**Total**	**10032895**	**3.9**	**6571020**	**7.0**	**3461875**	**-1.4**
一般贸易	General Trade	7808089	6.0	5320065	8.3	2488024	1.5
进料加工贸易	Processing by Supplied Material	1550239	-1.7	986808	-0.3	563432	-4.1
来料加工装配贸易	Processing by Import Material	183466	-15.9	116182	-4.5	67285	-30.3
外商投资企业作为投资进口的设备、物品	Imports of Foreign-invested Enterprises As Investment in Equipment&Goods	39003	74.8			39003	74.8
保税仓库进出境货物	Import & Export Commodities in Protective Tariff Zone	282209	-6.0	102593	7.1	179616	-12.2
保税区仓储转口货物	Transit Goods in Protective Tariff Zone	149805	-9.6	30837	40.8	118969	-17.3
其他	Others	19011	218.9	14535	453.6	4475	34.2

表 11—4　分洲别及主要国家(地区)的进出口总值(2013)
Total Value of Exports and Imports by Continent and Country

单位:万美元(USD 10000)

地区 Region	进出口 Imports and Exports		其中 of Which			
			出口 Exports		进口 Imports	
	贸易额 Value	增长率(%) Rate of Increase	贸易额 Value	增长率(%) Rate of Increase	贸易额 Value	增长率(%) Rate of Increase
合计 Total	**10032895**	**3.9**	**6571020**	**7.0**	**3461875**	**−1.4**
亚洲 Asia	4127425	2.5	2046316	8.3	2081109	−2.7
#东盟 The Aaaociation of Southeast Asian Nations	825737	6.1	445526	9.9	380211	2.0
中国香港 Hongkong,China	265047	17.1	250228	19.5	14819	−13.1
日本 Japan	702525	−3.7	366841	1.5	335685	−8.8
韩国 Republic of Korea	432383	−12.3	180941	−1.3	251442	−18.8
中国台湾 Taiwan,China	808042	0.2	88673	3.5	719368	−0.2
非洲 Africa	442000	15.1	358853	13.7	83147	21.8
欧洲 Europe	2391205	4.2	1976168	6.8	415037	−6.4
#欧盟 European Free Trade Association	2020534	5.3	1666829	6.3	353704	0.9
南美洲 South America	786217	−8.9	572066	1.1	214151	−27.9
北美洲 North America	1780733	5.9	1406621	6.5	374112	3.8
#美国 USA	1568552	4.3	1275558	6.0	292994	−2.7
大洋洲 Oceania	505259	24.6	210997	4.9	294262	43.9

表 11—5 部分年份按各大洲分的进出口分类表
Total of Exports and Imports by Continent in Partial Years

单位:万美元(USD 10000)

指标	Indicators	2009	2010	2011	2012	2013
进出口总额	**Total Value**	**6081275**	**8290424**	**9818682**	**9657269**	**10032895**
亚洲	Asia	2591883	3351962	4032006	4028317	4114668
非洲	Africa	230491	299694	383281	383516	442000
欧洲	Europe	1596394	2211169	2521035	2295008	2403962
#欧盟	European Union	1366552	1881681	2086243	1911695	2020533
南美洲	South America	457860	716580	877477	863475	786217
北美洲	North America	970730	1362281	1620770	1681639	1780733
大洋洲	Oceania	233907	348612	384033	405258	505259
出口	**Export**	**3865073**	**5196745**	**6083159**	**6144526**	**6571020**
亚洲	Asia	1265819	1561718	1860362	1889581	2033716
非洲	Africa	194823	239464	298086	315709	358853
欧洲	Europe	1263197	1755764	2009977	1851381	1988768
#欧盟	European Union	1145332	1560351	1721005	1561309	1666829
南美洲	South America	264997	419562	534138	565966	572066
北美洲	North America	746262	1034205	1192375	1320751	1406621
大洋洲	Oceania	129975	186032	188220	201138	210997
进口	**Import**	**2216202**	**3093679**	**3735523**	**3512743**	**3461875**
亚洲	Asia	1326064	1790244	2171644	2138736	2080952
非洲	Africa	35668	60230	85195	67807	83147
欧洲	Europe	333197	455404	511058	443627	415194
#欧盟	European Union	221220	321330	365238	350386	353704
南美洲	South America	192864	297019	343339	297509	214151
北美洲	North America	224468	328076	428396	360887	374112
大洋洲	Oceania	103932	162580	195813	204120	294262

表 11－6　按投资方式分的利用外资基本情况(2013)
Utilization of Foreign Capital by Investment Way

单位:万美元(USD 10000)

指标	Indicators	项目数(个) Projects (unit)	合同利用外资 Foreign Capital Contracted	实际利用外资 Foreign Capital Actually Used
总计	**Total**	**442**	**582029**	**327483**
对外借款	**Foreign Loans**			
外国政府贷款	Foreign Government Loans			
国际金融组织贷款	Loans from International Financial Organization			
外国银行商业贷款	Commercial Loans from Foreign Banks			
其他	Others			
外商直接投资	**Foreign Direct Investment**	**442**	**582029**	**327483**
合资经营	Joint Venture Enterprises	160	101402	72235
合作经营	Cooperative Operation Enterprises	2	63	103
独资企业	Foreign－funded Sole Enterprises	278	476770	250433
外商投资股份制	Share－system Enterprises	2	3794	4712
外商其他投资	**Other Foreign Investment**			

注:本表至 11－9 表数据来自宁波市对外贸易经济合作局。

Note:Data from Tables 11－6 to 11－9 are obtained from Ningbo Municipal Bureau of Foreign Trade & Economic Cooperation.

表 11－7　部分年份按投资方式分的利用外资基本情况
Utilization of Foreign Capital by Investment Way in Partial Years

单位:万美元 (USD 10000)

指标	Indicators	2009	2010	2011	2012	2013
合同利用外资	**Foreign Capital Contracted**	**342362**	**404608**	**501463**	**531276**	**582029**
对外借款	Foreign Loans					
外商直接投资	Foreign Direct Investment	342362	404608	501463	531276	582029
合资经营	Joint Venture Enterprises	29327	87743	129624	79038	101402
合作经营	Cooperative Operation Enterprises	5133	3674	2573	345	63
独资企业	Foreign－funded Sole Enterprises	307297	308159	367406	443435	476770
实际利用外资	**Actual Used Foreign Capital**	**220541**	**232336**	**280929**	**285252**	**327483**
对外借款	Foreign Loans					
外商直接投资	Foreign Direct Investment	220541	232336	280929	285252	327483
合资经营	Joint Venture Enterprises	50987	80959	61695	70949	72235
合作经营	Cooperative Operation Enterprises	20	29	664	560	103
独资企业	Foreign－funded Sole Enterprises	159241	150768	215230	208879	250433

表 11—8 部分年份按行业分外商直接投资情况
Foreign Direct Investments by Sectors in Partial Years

指标	Indicators
总计	**Total**
农、林、牧、渔业	Farming, Forestry, Animal Housbandry and Fishery
＃农业	Farming
制造业	Manufacturing
＃纺织业	Textile Industry
纺织服装、鞋、帽制造业	Textile Clothing. Shoes. Cap Manufacturing
文教体育用品制造业	Cultural. Educational and Sports Goods Manufacturing
化学原料及化学制品制造业	Raw Chemical Materials and Chemical Products
塑料制品业	Plastic Products
金属制品业	Metal Products
通用设备制造业	General Equipment Manufacturing
专用设备制造业	Special Equipment Manufacturing
交通运输设备制造业	Transport Equipment Manufacturing
电气机械及器材制造业	Electric Equipment and Machinery Manufacturing
通信设备、计算机及其他电子设备制造业	Communication Equipment. Computer and Other Electronic Equipment Manufacturing
仪器仪表及文化、办公用机械制造业	Instruments. Meters. Cultural and Office Machinery
电力、燃气及水的生产和供应业	Electricity, Gas and Water Production and Supply
建筑业	Construction
交通运输、仓储和邮政业	Transport, Storage and Post
批发和零售贸易业	Wholesale and Retail Sale Trade
餐饮业	Catering Service
房地产业	Real Estate Management
居民服务和其他服务业	Resident Services and Other Services Industries
其他行业	Other Sectors

单位:万美元(USD 1000)

新批项目数(个) Number of Newly Projects(unit)			合同利用外资 Foreign Capital Signed Agreements			实际利用外资 Foreign Investment Actually Used		
2011	2012	2013	2011	2012	2013	2011	2012	2013
411	**437**	**442**	**501463**	**531276**	**582029**	**280929**	**285252**	**327483**
2	4	4	2533	127	3642	8699	171	1077
1	4	4	134	73	2638	3445	171	77
201	208	161	321371	315277	249095	117915	127785	136456
2	1	2	2606	−1606	11947	2553	2046	1974
6	7	2	19690	7968	2967	10381	7149	1920
2	1	1	3424	2783	2221	1195	1145	678
6	8	3	31517	30511	26050	16365	25140	29253
10	16	19	7339	17063	33221	6030	6160	3206
7	17	7	12425	21207	11682	5432	5886	5823
28	31	26	39406	50142	18763	12019	12595	10858
18	15	18	17863	6833	23631	4487	3915	17931
33	32	27	41681	39833	28880	14904	12218	9256
34	31	26	41613	47935	37030	10128	5221	10071
31	19	19	46745	40094	26890	14229	10654	21826
5	6	1	6006	8977	7446	3111	4579	7509
	4	1	72	3353	1932	1307	1786	283
2	5	2	410	13294	3102		1993	4427
3	3	4	1238	4077	15095	1767	2759	29353
145	144	177	56491	70049	92571	26638	52233	31710
5	4	3	1485	−51	355	279	31	12
8	8	16	86574	82198	164978	90198	68947	94204
	1		43	4		1200		
	1			4				

表 11－9 部分年份按国别(地区)分的外商直接投资情况
Foreign Direct Investment by Country and Territory in Partial Years

国别、地区	Country, Region	新批项目数(个) New Projects(unit)		
		2011	2012	2013
总计	**Total**	**411**	**437**	**442**
香港	Hongkong, China	183	151	197
台湾省	Taiwan, China	33	44	20
日本	Japan	20	17	10
韩国	Korea Rep	6	12	20
印度尼西亚	Indonesia	1	2	1
新加坡	Singapore	12	13	14
文莱	Brunei	2	1	1
马来西亚	Malaysia	3	5	3
泰国	Thailand			
阿拉伯联合酋长国	United Arab Emirates		1	2
毛里求斯	Mauritius	1	1	1
英国	United Kingdom	4	6	5
德国	Germany	17	15	9
法国	France	7	6	10
意大利	Italy	15	7	7
荷兰	Netherlands	4	7	3
比利时	Belgium	1	1	0
西班牙	Spain	5	2	5
瑞典	Sweden	3	6	3
瑞士	Switzerland	2	1	1
俄罗斯	Russia	1	2	3
巴哈马	The Bahamas			
巴西	Brazil	2	1	2
开曼群岛	Cayman Islands	4	3	2
乌拉圭	Uruguay			
英属维尔京群岛	British Virgin Islands	9	19	15
加拿大	Canada	2	9	11
美国	United States	29	35	46
澳大利亚	Australia	10	14	4
库克群岛	The Cook Islands			
新西兰	New Zealand	3	6	2
萨摩亚	Samoa	8	7	8

单位:万美元 (USD 10000)

合同利用外资 Foreign Investment Contracted			实际利用外资 Actual Utilization of Foreign Capital		
2010	2011	2012	2010	2011	2012
501463	**531276**	**582029**	**280929**	**285252**	**327483**
340526	317369	466585	181274	187026	225647
8913	37923	5551	1705	1719	489
7163	6089	14385	7698	5166	8147
5516	4195	8464	8339	2090	5076
598	109	2479	748	15	160
7233	20440	8871	4185	8148	8135
2853	−359	914		225	39
68	171	224	207	94	177
	15		7		15
−209	5	1034	11	9	526
−3251	−427	2700	3008	341	280
4564	5965	5524	809	745	360
7254	3682	419	869	878	1981
1772	10006	4591	291	1420	1293
8491	1343	1417	777	173	288
3096	205	258	602	2966	1
83	78	−64	194	41	118
3638	187	31	172	152	47
160	145	28	75	224	30
−1528	2487	11	521	2140	271
−612	8	41	3		
995	80	29	313	249	616
16185	7729	−27604	9817	5984	8480
		5			
9485	36884	23208	29004	22165	18724
−149	4174	4095	102	723	850
16158	5599	16633	2895	4219	1975
821	7730	1308	707	928	433
696	3509	13	116	114	158
13763	27024	9103	3622	10532	18433

表 11－10 部分年份旅游业简况 Basic Statistic on Tourism in Partial Years

指标		Indicators	Unit	2011	2012	2013
旅行社合计	（家）	International Travel Agencies	（unit）	332	364	302
＃出境旅行社	（家）	Outbound Travel Agencies	（unit）	13	18	18
国内入境旅行社	（家）	Domestic Inbound Travel Agencies	（unit）	246	267	284
旅游星级饭店	（家）	Star－rated Hotel	（unit）	190	170	160
国内旅游总人数	（万人次）	Number of Domestic Tourists	（10000 person－times）	5181	5748	6226
旅游总收入	（亿元）	Income of Tourism	（100 million yuan）	751.3	862.8	953.5
＃旅游创汇	（万美元）	Foreign Exchange Earnings	（USD 10000）	65472	73428	79656
国内旅游总收入	（亿元）	Domestic Tourism Receipts	（100 million yuan）	708.74	816.4	904.2

注：本表至 11－12 表数据来自宁波市旅游局。

Note：Dara from Tables 11－10 to 11－12 are obtained from Ningbo Municipal Bureau of Tourism.

表 11－11 部分年份国际旅游情况 Basic Statistic on International Tourism in Partial Years

指标	单位	Indicators	Unit	2011	2012	2013
接待过夜境外旅游者人数	**（人）**	**Number of Oversea Tourists Staying Overnight**	**（person）**	**1074157**	**1162088**	**1273439**
外国人		Foreigner		608899	631033	666231
台湾同胞		Compatriots from Taiwan，China		239832	282622	337725
香港同胞		Compatriots from Hongkong，China		170708	186801	196144
澳门同胞		Compatriots from Macao，China		61632	73339	
接待过夜境外旅游者人天数	**（人天）**	**Person－days of Oversea Tourists Staying Overnight**	**（person－day）**	**3097184**	**3275117**	**3546179**
外国人		Foreigner		1862334	1883598	1909898
台湾同胞		Compatriots from Taiwan，China		613188	705084	860814
香港同胞		Compatriots from Hongkong，China		454784	515853	547397
澳门同胞		Compatriots from Macao，China		166878	170582	228070

表 11—12 部分年份接待外国旅游者人数(按国别分)
Number of Foreign Tourists by Country in Partial Years

单位:人(person)

国家(地区)	Country	2009	2010	2011	2012	2013
总计	**Total**	**464598**	**538932**	**608899**	**631033**	**659392**
亚洲	Asia	226121	252894	264007	270656	262926
#日本	Japna	87695	96111	99371	80214	76916
韩国	Korea Rep	50542	56309	55243	56171	53939
印度尼西亚	Indonesia	9755	12161	11589	10555	9830
马来西亚	Malaysia	11354	14066	15383	14496	13269
新加坡	Singapore	15360	17817	18965	18751	17762
泰国	Thailand	6949	9250	12000	14210	15225
印度	India	11348	12579	15516	18003	18851
欧洲	Europe	115376	135517	164423	163241	194765
#英国	United Kingdom	16854	20245	27227	29019	35659
法国	France	15254	18481	21243	23166	26497
德国	Germany	16789	19574	26126	23524	29282
意大利	Italy	11207	14237	16236	14691	18323
俄罗斯	Russia	12889	16705	19771	7698	16243
美洲	America	74388	92254	113920	125750	312026
#美国	United States	49515	62230	80571	73084	79415
加拿大	Canada	12810	15870	19460	22416	24881
大洋洲	Oceania	27438	32746	37696	41096	37113
#澳大利亚	Australia	15215	18311	23033	24515	22704
非洲	Africa	8491	10372	11835	18431	21332
其他	Others	12784	15180	17018	11881	11230

表 11－13 宁波市前十名出口企业(2013)
The Top 10 Enterprises For Export in Ningbo

序号 No	企业名称	Name of Corporation	所在区域	Location
1	宁波申洲针织有限公司	Ningbo Shenzhou Shitong Weaving Group Co.,Ltd.	北仑区	Beilun
2	宁波群志光电有限公司	Ningbo Qunzhi Photoelectric Co.,Ltd.	北仑区	Beilun
3	宁波市慈溪进出口股份有限公司	Ningbo Cixi Import & Export Co.,Ltd.	慈溪市	Cixi
4	浙江造船有限公司	Zhejiang Shipbuilding Co.,Ltd.	奉化市	Fenghua
5	万华化学(宁波)能源贸易有限公司	Wanhua Chemical (Ningbo) Energy Trading Co.,Ltd.	北仑区	Beilun
6	浙江新景进出口有限公司	Zhejiang Xinjing Import & Export Co.,Ltd.	北仑区	Beilun
7	中基宁波集团股份有限公司	China－Base Ningbo Group Co.,Ltd.	鄞州区	Yinzhou
8	环球控股集团有限公司	Global Holding Group Co.,Ltd.	江东区	Jiangdong
9	宁波奥克斯进出口有限公司	Ningbo AUX Import & Export Co.,Ltd.	鄞州区	Yinzhou
10	宁波君安物产有限公司	Ningbo Jun An Resources Co.,Ltd.	江东区	Jiangdong

表 11－14 宁波市前十名进口企业(2013)
The Top 10 Enterprises For Import in Ningbo

序号 No	企业名称	Name of Corporation	所在区域	Location
1	宁波群志光电有限公司	Ningbo Qunzhi Photoelectric Co.,Ltd.	北仑区	Beilun
2	中基宁波集团股份有限公司	China－Base Ningbo Group Co.,Ltd.	鄞州区	Yinzhou
3	浙江逸盛石化有限公司	Zhejiang Yisheng Pertochemical Co.,Ltd.	北仑区	Beilun
4	宁波钢铁有限公司	Ningbo Steel Company Limited	北仑区	Beilun
5	宁波金田铜业(集团)股份有限公司	Ningbo Jintian Copper Group Co.,Ltd.	江北区	Jiangbei
6	宁波萍钢贸易有限公司	Ningbo Steel Company Limited	北仑区	Beilun
7	台化兴业(宁波)有限公司	Formosa Industrial (Ningbo) Co.,Ltd.	北仑区	Beilun
8	台化塑胶(宁波)有限公司	Formosa Plastics (Ningbo) Co.,Ltd.	北仑区	Beilun
9	台塑聚丙烯(宁波)有限公司	Formosa Polypropylene (Ningbo) Co.,Ltd.	北仑区	Beilun
10	宁波雅戈尔国际贸易运输有限公司	Ningbo Youngor International Trade and Transportation Co.,Ltd.	鄞州区	Yinzhou

主要统计指标解释

【进出口总额】 海关进出口总额是指实际进出我国国境的货物总金额。包括对外贸易实际进出口货物,来料加工装配进出口货物,国家间、联合国及国际组织无偿援助物资和赠送品,华侨、港澳台同胞和外籍华人捐赠品,租赁期满归承租人所有的租赁货物,进料加工进出口货物,边境地方贸易及边境地区小额贸易进出口货物(边民互市贸易除外),中外合资经营企业、中外合作经营企业、外商独资经营企业进出口货物和公用物品,到、离岸价格在规定限额以上的进出口货样和广告品(无商业价值、无使用价值和免费提供出口的除外),从保税仓库提取在中国境内销售的进口货物以及其他进出口货物。进出口总额用以观察一个国家在对外贸易方面的总规模。我国规定出口货物按离岸价格计算,进口货物按到岸价格计算。

【利用外资】 指我国各级政府、部门、企业和其他经济组织通过对外借款、吸收外商直接投资以及用其他方式筹措的境外现汇、设备、技术等。

【外商直接投资】 是指外国企业和经济组织或个人(包括华侨、港澳台胞以及 我国在境外注册的企业)按我国有关政策、法规,用现汇、实物、技术等在我国境内开办外 商独资企业、与我国境内的企业或经济组织共同举办中外合资经营企业、合作经营企业或作 合作开发资源的投资(包括外商投资收益的再投资)以及经政府有关部门批准的项目投资总 额内,企业从境外借入的资金。

【外商其他投资】 指除对外借款和外商直接投资以外的各种利用外资的形式。包括企业在境内外股票市场公开发行的以外币计价的股票(目前主要是在香港证券市场发行的 H 股和在境内证券市场发行的 B 股)发行价总额,国际租赁进口设备的应付款,补充贸易中外商提供的进口设备、技术、物料的价款,加工装配贸易中外商提供的进口设备、物料的价款。

【旅游人数】 包括入境国际旅游者人数、出境居民人数和国内旅游者人数。

⑴入境国际旅游者人数:指来中国参观、访问、旅行、探亲、访友、休养、考察、参加会议和从事经济、科技、文化、教育、宗教等活动的外国人、港澳和台湾同胞的人数。不包括外国在我国的常驻机构,如使领馆、通讯社、企业办事处的工作人员;来我国常住的外国专家、留学生以及在岸逗留不过夜人员。

⑵出境居民人数:指大陆居民因公务活动或私人事务短期出境的人数。公务活动出境居民人数包括在国际交通工具上的中国服务员工,因私出境居民人数不包括在国际交通工具上的中国服务员工。

⑶国内旅游者人数:指我国大陆居民和在我国常住 1 年以上的外国人、港澳台同胞离开常住地在境内其他地方的旅游设施内至少停留一夜,最长不超过 6 个月的人数。

【国际旅游(外汇)收入】 指入境旅游的外国人、华侨、港澳台同胞在中国大陆旅游过程中发生的一切旅游支出,对国家来说就是国际旅游(外汇)收入。

Explanatory Notes on Main Statistical Indicators

【Total Imports and Exports】 refer to the value of commodities imported into and exported from the boundary of China. They include the actual imports and exports through foreign trade, imported and exported goods under the processing and assembling trades and materials, supplies and gifts as aid given gratis between government and by the United Nations and other international organizations, and contributions denoted by overseas Chinese, compatriots in Hong Kong, Macao and Taiwan and Chinese with foreign citizenship, leasing commodities owned by tenants at the expiration of leasing period, the imported and exported commodities processed with imported materials, commodities trading, imported and exported small value trading goods in border areas (excluding mutual change goods), the imported and exported commodities and articles for public use of the Sino—foreign joint ventures, Sino—foreign cooperative enterprises and ventures exclusively with foreign own investment. They also included import and export of samples and advertising goods for those CIF or FOB value are beyond the permitted ceiling (excluding goods of no trading or no use value and free commodities for export), imported goods sold in China from bonded warehouse and other imported and exported goods. The indicator of total imports and exports at customs can be used to observe the total size of external trade in a country. In accordance with the stipulation of the Chinese government, imports are calculated at CIF, while exports are calculated at FOB.

FOB refer to Free on Board. CIF refer to Cost Insurance and Freight.

【Utilization of Foreign Capital】 refers to remittance, equipment and technology financed from abroad, by loans, foreign direct investment and other forms undertaken by the Chinese governments at all levels, by various departments, enterprises and other economic units.

【Direct Investment by Foreign Entrepreneurs】 refers to the investments inside China by foreign enterprises and economic organizations or individuals (including overseas Chinese, compatriots from Hong Kong and Macao, and Chinese enterprises registered abroad), following the relevant policies and laws of China, for the establishment of ventures exclusively with foreign own investment, Sino—foreign joint ventures and cooperative enterprises or for cooperative exploration of resources with enterprises or economic organizations in China. It includes the re—investment of the foreign entrepreneurs with the profits gained from the investment and the funds that enterprises borrow from abroad in the total investment of projects which are approved by the relevant department of the government.

【Other Overseas Investments】 refer to all kinds of investments except the foreign loan and the FDI. They include: the total value(in foreign currency) of the stocks of one enterprises distributed publicly both at home and abroad(now mainly refer to H. shares at HK bond market, and B. shares at China mainland bond market); the rent charges of the foreign equipments; the total value of Technology, raw material and foreign equipment provided by foreign investors in supplemental trades, and value of foreign raw material, equipment in the trade of assemble machining.

【tourists number】 is a sum of overseas tourists, local residents going abroad and domestic tourists.

overseas tourists number. Which refers to the number of foreigners and residents from Hongkong, Macao and Taiwan who come to China to go sightseeing, travel, visit relatives and friends, spend holidays, inspect, attend conferences and to do activities in economics, science, education, religious etc. Personnel as below are not taken into calculation, office workers in Chinese standing bodies at abroad, such as in embassies, news agencies, oversea offices of companies. Foreign experts and students living in China and foreigners who enter China only for voyage transferring are also not calculated.

number of local residents going abroad. Which refers to the number of mainland China residents who go abroad either for official business or for private affairs. Number of Chinese workers who serve in the international transportation vehicles are included in those who exit for official business, but not in those for private affairs.

domestic tourists. Which refers to the number of people who leave their living places to stay in the tourism facilities for at least one night but no more than 6 months, including mainland China residents, foreigners, residents from HK, Macao and TW who lived in China for more than one year.

【Foreign Exchange Earnings from International Tourism】 refer to the total expenditures of the foreigners, overseas Chinese, compatriots from HongKong, Macao and Taiwan in the process of their tourism in the mainland of China. Their expenditures mentioned above are foreign exchange earnings to China.

CHAPTER 12

NINGBO 2014 Statistical YearBook

第十二篇

文化、教育、卫生 体育、科学技术

CULTURE, EDUCATION, PUBLIC HEALTH AND SPORTS, SCIENCE & TECHNOLOGY

文化、教育、卫生、体育、科学技术
Culture, Education, Public Health, Sports and Science & Technology

主要统计指标
Major Statistics Indicators

2013 年群艺馆、文化馆	Number of Mass Art Center and Cultural Center	12	个	unit
2013 年公共图书馆	Number of Public Libraries	12	个	unit
2013 年电影观众人次	Number of Spectator	946.79	万人次	10000 person—times
2013 年各类学校数	Number of Various School	2252	所	unit
2013 年各类学校招生人数	Number of New Students Enrollment of Various Schools	271846	人	person
2013 年各类学校在校学生数	Number of Students Enrollment of Various Schools	1416047	人	person
2013 年各类学校毕业人数	Number of Graduates by Various Schools	316932	人	person
2013 年专任教师数	Number of Full—time Teacher	78176	人	person
2013 年高等学校在校生人数	Number of Students Enrollmentin Institutions of Higher Education	148954	人	person
2013 年医疗机构床位数	Number of Beds in Health Institutions	29356	张	bed
2013 年卫生技术人员数	Number of Medical Technical Personnel	51510	人	person
2013 年医生数	Number of Doctors	19949	人	person
2013 年参赛获奖数	Number of Obtain Awards by Athletic Competition	992	枚	unit
2013 年有线电视用户数	Number of User Terminal for Cable TV Station	244.85	万户	10000 users

表 12—1 部分年份文化事业单位、机构、人员及活动情况
Basic Statistics on Cultural Institutions and Personnel in Partial Years

指标	单位	Indicators	Unit	2009	2010	2011	2012	2013
艺术表演团体	**个**	**Art Performance Troupes**	**unit**	**6**	**5**	**5**	**5**	**4**
机构人员数	人	Persons of Institutions	persons	408	410	518	518	484
国内演出场次	场次	Internal Performances	times	1126	970	1200	1180	1016
国内观众人次	千人	Internal Spectator	1000 persons times	1217	1207	1111	1111	1013
艺术表演场所	**所**	**Art Performance Places**	**unit**	**4**	**7**	**7**	**6**	**5**
机构人员数	人	Persons of Institutions	persons	42	82	78	77	76
演出场次	场次	Performances	times1822	719	1430	1690	2300	5535
观众人次	千人	Spectator	1000 persons times	188	316	312	689	624
公共图书馆	**个**	**Public Libraries**	**unit**	**12**	**13**	**13**	**12**	**12**
机构人员数	人	Persons of Institutions	persons	287	343	345	345	361
总藏量	万册	Total Collections	10000 volumes	633	734	733	733	668
古籍	千册	Ancient Books	1000 volumes	170	113	166	166	141
图书	万册	Books	10000 volumes	374	483	458	448	601
群艺馆、文化馆	**个**	**Mass Art Center and Cultural Center**	**unit**	**12**	**12**	**12**	**12**	**12**
机构人员数	人	Persons of Institutions	persons	293	318	311	311	303
文化站	**个**	**Cultural Center**	**unit**	**148**	**148**	**149**	**149**	**147**
机构人员数	人	Persons of Institutions	persons	425	447	449	449	503
文物单位		**Historical Relic Protection Units**						
文物保护管理机构	个	Historical Relic Protection Institutions	unit	13	13	13	13	12
国家级文保单位	个	Historical Relic Protection Units of State Level	unit	22	22	22		
博物馆、纪念馆	个	Museums, Memorial Hall	unit	7	7	7	6	18
文物商店	个	Historical Relic	unit	1	1	1	1	1
电影放映单位		**Film Projecting Units**						
放映管理机构	个	Projecting Management Institutions	unit	11	11	7	11	11
电影院	个	Movie House	unit	31	15	23	33	49
放映队	个	Projecting Teams	unit	73	167	120	117	71
电影放映场次	万场	Projecting Performance	10000 times	9.50	14.60	16.90	2.89	43.28
电影观众人次	万人次	Spectator	10000 persons times	1634.20	1490.00	1112.97	860.70	946.79

注：本表至 12—4 表数据来自宁波市文化广电新闻出版局。
Note: Data from Tables 12—1 to 12—4 are obtained from Ningbo Bureau of Culture Radio & TV, Press and Publication.

表 12—2 各县(市)文化事业单位、机构、人员及活动情况(2013)
Basic Statistics of Cultural Institutions and Personnel by Region

指标	单位	Indicators	Unit	全市 Total
艺术表演团体	个	**Art Performance Troupes**	**unit**	**4**
机构人员数	人	Persons of Institutions	persons	484
国内演出场次	场次	Internal Performances	times	1016
国内观众人次	千人	Internal Spectator	1000 persons times	1013
艺术表演场所	所	**Art Performance Places**	**unit**	**5**
机构人员数	人	Persons of Institutions	persons	76
演出场次	场次	Performances	times	5535
观众人次	千人	Spectator	1000 persons times	624
公共图书馆	个	**Public Libraries**	**unit**	**12**
机构人员数	人	Persons of Institutions	persons	361
总藏量	万册	Total Collections	10000 volumes	668
古籍	千册	Ancient Books	1000 volumes	141
图书	万册	Books	10000 volumes	601
群艺馆.文化馆	个	**Mass Art Center and Cultural Center**	**unit**	**12**
机构人员数	人	Persons of Institutions	persons	303
文化站	个	**Cultural Center**	**unit**	**147**
机构人员数	人	Persons of Institutions	persons	503
文物单位		**Historical Relic Protection Units**		
文物保护管理机构	个	Historical Relic Protection Institutions	unit	12
国家级文保单位	个	Historical Relic Protection Units of State Level	unit	0
博物馆.纪念馆	个	Museums,Memorial Hall	unit	18
文物商店	个	Historical Relic	unit	1
电影放映单位		**Film Projecting Units**		
放映管理机构	个	Projecting Management Institutions	unit	11
电影院	个	Movie House	unit	49
放映队	个	Projecting Teams	unit	71
电影放映场次	万场	Projecting Performance	10000 times	43.28
电影观众人次	万人次	Spectator	10000 persons times	946.79

市区 Urban District	＃鄞州 Yinzhou	余姚市 Yuyao	慈溪市 Cixi	奉化市 Fenghua	象山县 Xiangshan	宁海县 Ninghai
1	**1**	**1**				**1**
277	32	111				64
399	137	270				210
360	127	206				320
2					**1**	**1**
35					20	3
512					4345	158
123					64	71
1	**1**	**1**	**1**	**1**	**1**	**1**
107	24	28	58	16	15	28
178	116	53	62	21	41	35
77		36	8	0	1	20
155	114	45	47	21	35	29
1	**1**	**1**	**1**	**1**	**1**	**1**
72	27	25	25	33	20	19
	23	**21**	**18**	**11**	**18**	**18**
	104	55	93	21	44	50
1	1	1	1	1	1	1
3		3	8		1	
1						
6	1	1	1	1	1	1
23	7	8	6	4	4	4
12	2	14	15	11	3	16
24.86	5.90	6.36	4.12	1.94	1.57	2.04
636.55	156.30	82.18	114.94	40.62	34.37	15.90

表 12—3 各县(市)广播电视基本情况(2013) Basic Statisits on Broadcasting and Television by Region

指标	单位	Indicators	Unit	全市 Total
广播电视机构		**Broadcasting and Television Institutions**		
电台	座	Broadcasting Station	set	9
电视台	座	Broadcasting and Relaying Stations	set	9
广播电视站	个	TV and Transfer Stations	set	111
全年播出公共节目时间		**Full—year Broadcasting & TV Hours**		
广播播音时间	小时	Broadcasting Hours	hour	91005
#制作节目播出时间	小时	Time of Self—Producting Programs	hour	74351
电视播出时间	小时	Hours Through TV Broadcasting	hour	90281
#制作节目播出时间	小时	Time of Self—Producting Programs	hour	28739
公共电视套数	**套**	**TV Channel**	**set**	**13**
公共广播套数	**套**	**Public Broadcasting Band**	**set**	**13**
发送功率		**Transfer Power**		
中波功率	千瓦	Middle—Wave Power	kw	41
调频功率	千瓦	Frequency Modulation Power	kw	85.1
电视功率	千瓦	TV Power	kw	33.60
有线电视用户数	**万户**	**Number of User Terminal of Cable TV Station**	**10000 users**	**244.9**

表 12—4 部分年份广播电视基本情况 Basic Statisits on Broadcasting and Television in Partial Years

指标	单位	Indicators	Unit	2011	2012	2013
广播电视机构		**Broadcasting and Television Institutions**				
电台	座	Broadcasting Station	set	9	1	9
电视台	座	Broadcasting and Relaying Stations	set	9	10	9
广播电视站	个	TV and Transfer Stations	set	104	111	111
全年播出公共节目时间		**Full—year Broadcasting & TV Hours**				
广播播音时间	小时	Broadcasting Hours	hour	91728	95936	91005
#制作节目播出时间	小时	Time of Self—Producting Programs	hour	71645	76905	74351
电视播出时间	小时	Hours Through TV Broadcasting	hour	85973	91210	90281
#制作节目播出时间	小时	Time of Self—Producting Programs	hour	21446	31949	28739
公共电视套数	**套**	**TV Channel**	**set**	**13**	**14**	**13**
公共广播套数	**套**	**Public Broadcasting Band**	**set**	**13**	**14**	**13**
有线电视用户数	**万户**	**Number of User Terminal of Cable TV Station**	**10000 users**	**218.70**	**227.873**	**244.85**

市区 Urban District	#鄞州 Yinzhou	余姚 Yuyao	慈溪 Cixi	奉化 Fenghua	象山 Xiangshan	宁海 Ninghai
4	1	1	1	1	1	1
4	1	1	1	1	1	1
43	20	19	19	9	13	8
57869	5859	8120	6387	6401	6205	6023
49706	4917	7149	4647	4302	3800	4747
55580	5121	5840	8760	6570	6961	6570
13826	1301	2000	5777	2600	1970	2566
8	**1**	**1**	**1**	**1**	**1**	**1**
8	**1**	**1**	**1**	**1**	**1**	**1**
41						
74.0	0.6	3.1	0.2	5.0	0.6	2.2
26.80	2.00	2.60	3.00	0.30	0.60	0.30
118.6	**46.3**	**29.5**	**42.2**	**15.5**	**18.3**	**20.8**

表 12—5 部分年份学生入、升学率 Percentage for Enrollment and Graduation of Students

单位.%

指标	Indicators	2009	2010	2011	2012	2013
小学学龄儿童入学率	Enrollment Rate for Children of School Age	100.00	100.00	100.00	100.00	100.00
小学毕业升学率	Graduation Rate for Pupils	100.00	100.00	100.00	100.00	99.99
初中毕业升学率	Graduation Rate for Students of Secondary School6	98.97	99.09	99.09	99.02	
升入普通高中	Rate of Enrolling Senior School	49.34	49.49	49.88	50.13	51.19
升入职业高中	Rate of Enrolling Vacational Senior School	49.36	49.49	49.21	48.96	47.83
升入中专技校	Rate of Entrolling Technical Secondary School					
高等教育毛入学率	Gross Enrollment Rate of Higher Education	49.00	50.00	55.00		

表 12－6 各县(市)各类学校数(2013)
Number of Various Schools by Region

项目	Item	全市 Total	市区 Urban District
各类学校数	**Number of Various School**		
(一)全日制学校	**Number of Full－time School**	**2095**	**855**
高等学校	Regular Institutions of Higher Education	14	14
#大专	Junior Colleges	6	6
初中	Regular Secondary Schools	216	87
高中	Senior Secondary Schools	81	39
职业中学	Vocational Secondary Schools	55	21
普通小学	Primary Schools	465	189
特殊教育学校	Special Education Schools	10	5
幼儿园	Kindergarten	1254	500
(二)成人学校数	**Number of School for Adult Education**	**157**	**34**
成人高校数	Number of Higher Education for Adult	2	2
成人中学	Secondary Education for Adult	155	32

注：本表至 12－8 表数据来自宁波市教育局。高等学校中包省属学校。

Note：Data from Tables 12－6 to 12－8 are obtained from Ningbo Municipal Bureau of Education. Regular institutions of higher education including the provincial school.

单位:所(unit)

#鄞州 Yinzhou	余姚市 Yuyao	慈溪市 Cixi	奉化市 Fenghua	象山县 Xiangshan	宁海县 Ninghai
319	**309**	**401**	**151**	**150**	**229**
31	39	34	17	21	18
13	10	14	5	6	7
9	9	7	5	7	6
84	83	87	29	26	51
1	1	1	1	1	1
181	167	258	94	89	146
22	**19**	**19**	**24**	**1**	**60**
		0			
22	19	19	24	1	60

表 12—7 各县(市)各类学校学生情况(2013)
Basic Statistics on Student of Various Schools by Region

项目	Item	全市 Total	市区 Urban District
各类学校招生人数	**New Students Enrollment of Various Schools**	**271846**	**156287**
研究生	Postgraduates	1412	1412
普通高校	Institutions of Higher Education	41534	41534
#大专	Junior Colleges	18744	18744
初中	Regular Secondary Schools	65395	29052
高中	Senior Secondary Schools	30565	13283
职业中学	Secondary Vacational Schools	25707	11599
普通小学	Primary Schools	84926	37178
特殊教育学校	Special Education Schools	132	54
成人高校	Higher Education for Adult	22175	22175
各类学校在校学生数	**Students Enrollment of Various Schools**	**1416047**	**706569**
研究生	Postgraduates	3929	3929
普通高校	Institutions of Higher Education	145025	145025
#大专	Junior Colleges	54582	54582
初中	Regular Secondary Schools	188972	84604
高中	Senior Secondary Schools	96940	40529
职业中学	Secondary Vacational Schools	78345	34679
普通小学	Primary Schools	486971	212512
特殊教育学校	Special Education Schools	916	461
成人高校	Higher Education for Adult	53320	53320
成人中学	Secondary Education for Adult	85724	2435
幼儿园在园人数	Persons of Kindergarten	275905	129075
各类学校毕业人数	**Graduates by Various Schools**	**316932**	**139195**
研究生	Postgraduates	911	911
普通高校	Institutions of Higher Education	36358	36358
#大专	Junior Colleges	18180	18180
初中	Regular Secondary Schools	60482	24634
高中	Senior Secondary Schools	34387	14274
职业中学	Secondary Vacational Schools	26502	12343
普通小学	Primary Schools	70889	30832
特殊教育学校	Special Education Schools	64	57
成人高校	Higher Education for Adult	19098	19098
成人中学	Secondary Education for Adult	68241	688

单位：人(person)

#鄞州 Yinzhou	余姚市 Yuyao	慈溪市 Cixi	奉化市 Fenghua	象山县 Xiangshan	宁海县 Ninghai
33795	**29294**	**37088**	**14222**	**15245**	**19710**
10588	9453	10782	4691	4891	6526
4203	4309	5704	2130	2452	2687
4013	3349	4491	1997	1772	2499
14970	12162	16089	5396	6110	7991
21	21	22	8	20	7
192507	**151033**	**278364**	**77085**	**90844**	**112152**
29906	26951	30815	13577	14251	18774
13406	13493	19708	7015	7590	8605
12913	10547	14218	6220	5650	7031
84153	68456	91841	32617	34629	46916
132	127	152	37	79	60
1750	1140	69319	2340	6462	4028
50247	30319	52311	15279	22183	26738
30957	**28217**	**90315**	**16405**	**21126**	**21674**
8312	9335	11260	4555	5128	5570
6695	4678	6875	2584	2468	3508
5040	3232	4192	2322	1960	2453
10883	10090	12791	5012	5184	6980
27				6	1
	882	55197	1932	6380	3162

表 12—8　各县(市)各类学校教职工情况(2013)
Basic Statistics on Teachers and Staff of Various Schools by Region

项目	Item	全市 Total	市区 Urban District
各类学校教职工人数	**Number of Teachers and Staff of Various Schools**	**103739**	**54042**
高等学校	Regular Institutions of Higher Education	10881	10881
#大专	Junior Colleges	2962	2962
普通中学	Regular Secondary Schools	29655	13186
职业中学	Secondary Vacational Schools	6461	2726
普通小学	Primary Schools	23768	10368
特殊教育学校	Special Education Schools	257	155
成人高校	Higher Education for Adult	657	657
成人中学	Secondary Education for Adult	897	255
幼儿园	Kindergarten	31163	15814
各类学校专任教师人数	**Number of Full—time Teachers of Various Schools**	**78176**	**40017**
普通高校	Institutions of Higher Education	7524	7524
#大专	Junior Colleges	1992	1992
初中	Regular Secondary Schools	14815	6566
高中	Senior Secondary Schools	8388	
职业中学	Secondary Vacational Schools	5714	
普通小学	Primary Schools	24025	10817
特殊教育学校	Special Education Schools	223	130
成人高校	Higher Education for Adult	472	472
#电大	Radio and TV Universities	344	344
成人中学	Secondary Education for Adult	721	168
幼儿园	Kindergarten	16294	8159
各类学校兼任教师人数	**Number of Part—time Teachers of Various Schools**	**2867**	**961**
普通中学	Regular Secondary Schools	113	80
职业中学	Secondary Vacational Schools	504	260
普通小学	Primary Schools	7	7
成人高校	Higher Education for Adult	471	471
成人中学	Secondary Education for Adult	1772	143

单位：人(person)

#鄞州 Yinzhou	余姚市 Yuyao	慈溪市 Cixi	奉化市 Fenghua	象山县 Xiangshan	宁海县 Ninghai
15188	**12401**	**16818**	**5694**	**6969**	**7815**
3731	4466	4958	2038	2914	2093
1162	830	1293	525	548	539
4136	3636	4723	1484	1269	2288
31	29	31	11	12	19
194	158	177	176	48	83
5934	3282	5636	1460	2178	2793
11735	**8768**	**13233**	**4707**	**5389**	**6062**
2144	2003	2738	1085	1198	1225
3978	3150	4665	1586	1658	2149
30	25	27	11	11	19
119	96	177	161	36	83
3089	1707	2919	821	1338	1350
202	**166**	**1338**	**154**	**47**	**201**
68	30				
74	74	78	20	31	41
60	62	1260	134	13	160

表 12—9 历年教职工数和在校学生数
Number of Teachers and Staff and Students Enrollment Over the Years

单位：万人(10000 persons)

年份 Year	在校教职工 Teachers and Staff	#教师 Teachers	在校学生 Students Enrollment 大学生 Higher Education	中学生 Secondary Schools	小学生 Primary Schools
1978	4.15	3.55	0.10	27.16	59.11
1979	4.01	3.53	0.21	23.04	57.85
1980	4.28	3.48	0.25	20.99	56.39
1981	4.13	3.23	0.20	19.36	52.02
1982	3.31	2.75	0.15	18.77	46.67
1983	3.72	3.06	0.16	19.48	41.71
1984	3.73	3.00	0.21	21.42	38.50
1985	3.94	3.16	0.27	23.47	36.43
1986	4.09	3.28	0.34	24.35	36.90
1987	4.21	3.34	0.39	23.48	36.41
1988	4.32	3.47	0.45	20.34	38.69
1989	4.45	3.56	0.49	18.75	41.84
1990	4.24	3.34	0.49	19.65	42.70
1991	4.34	3.39	0.48	22.01	41.62
1992	4.37	3.47	0.53	24.39	40.16
1993	4.59	3.61	0.66	25.03	40.40
1994	4.75	3.76	0.83	26.76	41.92
1995	5.00	4.01	0.98	28.93	41.29
1996	5.12	4.17	1.04	30.07	41.80
1997	5.27	4.32	1.15	29.93	43.14
1998	5.44	4.40	1.25	29.00	43.91
1999	6.16	4.81	1.68	25.12	43.36
2000	6.59	5.17	2.59	27.98	42.40
2001	6.86	5.12	4.34	29.60	42.24
2002	7.05	5.27	6.21	30.86	44.55
2003	7.46	5.61	7.99	30.99	45.26
2004	7.85	5.92	9.60	32.09	47.61
2005	8.59	6.46	11.12	40.25	47.60
2006	8.68	6.55	12.13	40.95	47.38
2007	9.09	6.84	12.76	41.12	47.15
2008	9.27	7.04	13.04	41.70	46.80
2009	9.13	7.42	13.75	41.42	45.03
2010	9.61	7.29	14.08	40.61	46.19
2011	9.82	7.70	14.14	39.13	47.61
2012	9.95	7.63	14.54	37.55	47.88
2013	10.37	7.82	14.90	36.43	48.70

注：在校教职工包括幼儿园。

Note: The number of teachers and staff include kinder—gardens

表 12—10　部分年份教育事业基本情况
Basic Statistics on Education in Partial Years

单位：人(person)

指标	Indicators	2008	2009	2010	2011	2012	2013
学校数(所)	**Number of Schools(unit)**						
高等学校	Institutions of Higher Education	15	15	14	14	14	14
中等专业学校	Specialized Secondary Schools	8					
普通中学	Regular Secondary Schools	310	306	301	299	299	297
职业中学	Vocational Secondary Schools	38	57	56	57	55	55
小学	Primary Schools	564	536	513	490	476	465
专任教师	**Number of Full—time Teachers**						
高等学校	Institutions of Higher Education	6829	6933	7146	9086	7374	7524
中等专业学校	Specialized Secondary Schools	1022					
普通中学	Regular Secondary Schools	22345	22718	22961	22897	23021	23203
职业中学	Vocational Secondary Schools	3146	4734	4955	5283	5519	5714
小学	Primary Schools	20864	21184	21577	22265	23139	24025
招生数	**New Student Enrollment**						
高等学校	Institutions of Higher Education	43574	42644	42806	43735	44001	42946
中等专业学校	Specialized Secondary Schools	2135					
普通中学	Regular Secondary Schools	116235	110570	107982	99456	98660	95960
职业中学	Vocational Secondary Schools	25039	30058	27781	28469	25569	25707
小学	Primary Schools	79383	74952	84725	87239	85933	84926
在校学生数	**Student Enrollment**						
高等学校	Institutions of Higher Education	130440	137495	140818	144424	145358	148954
中等专业学校	Specialized Secondary Schools	6324					
普通中学	Regular Secondary Schools	343449	332945	325407	308563	295203	285912
职业中学	Vocational Secondary Schools	73530	81293	80724	82783	80294	78345
小学	Primary Schools	467988	450322	461931	476085	478816	486971
毕业生数	**Number of Graduates**						
高等学校	Institutions of Higher Education	36268	37118	37733	38022	38226	37269
中等专业学校	Specialized Secondary Schools	3177					
普通中学	Regular Secondary Schools	101063	110130	105199	104584	99238	94869
职业中学	Vocational Secondary Schools	25865	26406	24835	24270	26908	26502
小学	Primary Schools	87163	79440	76536	69412	73173	70889

表 12—11 部分年份平均每一专任教师负担的学生数
The Ratio of Student Enrollment and Full—time Teachers in Partial Years

单位：人(person)

年份 Year	高等学校 Institutions of Higher Education	中等专业学校 Specialized Scendary Schools	普通中学 Regular Secondary Schools	职业中学 Vocational Secondary Schools	小学 Primary Schools
1994	8.9	15.9	19.9	16.1	25.7
1995	9.1	18.0	20.0	16.2	24.6
1996	9.7	23.5	19.7	14.6	24.2
1997	10.7	21.7	18.3	16.6	24.2
1998	11.3	22.4	17.4	17.2	24.7
1999	12.8	22.3	16.9	16.6	24.5
2000	11.3	24.1	17.7	16.2	23.9
2001	15.7	30.5	17.8	16.5	23.7
2002	17.6	26.1	17.8	17.5	24.4
2003	18.9	24.1	17.0	27.9	24.5
2004	17.0	20.4	16.6	26.5	24.7
2005	18.5	15.9	16.0	29.6	23.9
2006	18.7	9.4	16.0	28.0	23.5
2007	19.2	7.0	15.6	27.1	22.9
2008	19.1	6.2	15.4	23.4	22.4
2009	19.8		14.7	17.2	21.3
2010	19.7		14.2	16.3	21.4
2011	15.6		13.5	15.7	21.4
2012	19.7		12.8	14.6	20.7
2013	19.8		12.3	13.7	20.3

表 12—12 部分年份平均每万人口在校学生数
Student Enrollment Per 10000 Populations in Partial Years

单位：人(person)

年份 Year	大学生 University and College Students	中专学生 Specialized Scendary Schools Students	中学学生 Regular Secondary Schools Students	职业中学生 Vocational Secondary Schools Students	小学生 Primary Schools Schools
1994	15.8	30.5	458.0	53.4	801.1
1995	18.5	37.3	488.8	60.5	784.2
1996	19.7	47.5	511.7	57.6	791.4
1997	21.7	43.7	493.1	69.8	811.4
1998	23.3	47.7	463.0	79.7	821.9
1999	31.3	50.8	467.9	82.2	807.6
2000	48.0	46.5	518.4	81.6	785.6
2001	80.1	41.8	545.9	83.3	779.1
2002	113.9	35.3	566.5	93.5	817.8
2003	145.9	34.4	565.8	119.0	826.4
2004	174.3	32.3	582.5	134.6	864.2
2005	199.3	26.1	582.3	143.4	858.2
2006	215.2	17.8	595.6	137.6	848.1
2007	226.0	13.4	594.2	134.2	835.2
2008	229.6	11.1	604.6	129.4	823.8
2009	240.8		583.1	142.4	788.6
2010	245.3		566.8	140.6	804.6
2011	245.7		536.4	143.9	827.6
2012	251.9		650.7	139.1	829.8
2013	257.3		493.9	135.3	841.2

表 12－13 历年卫生事业主要指标
Basic Statistics on Health Care Over the Years

年份 Year	卫生机构数（个）Number of Health Institutions (unit)	＃医院 Hospitals	卫生机构床位（张）Number of Beds in Health Institutions (bed)	＃医院 Hospitals	卫生技术人员（万人）Number of Medical technical (10000 persons)	＃医生 Doctors
1978	949	400	5989	5549	0.93	0.36
1979	1013	398	6618	5871	0.99	0.36
1980	1032	397	6948	6368	1.06	0.38
1981	1077	394	7537	7015	1.13	0.44
1982	1100	400	8130	7230	1.19	0.48
1983	1107	396	8372	7525	1.24	0.50
1984	1117	396	8823	7954	1.28	0.53
1985	1123	311	9067	8250	1.30	0.54
1986	1181	320	9436	8605	1.34	0.56
1987	1199	327	9922	9057	1.41	0.60
1988	1259	330	10447	9629	1.46	0.73
1989	1293	331	11073	10067	1.53	0.74
1990	1301	344	11449	10522	1.58	0.75
1991	1313	345	11731	10816	1.66	0.76
1992	1270	303	12175	11259	1.69	0.78
1993	1262	300	12529	11633	1.70	0.80
1994	1257	345	12976	12090	1.76	0.84
1995	1257	345	13193	12316	1.74	0.87
1996	1123	297	13012	12299	1.78	0.88
1997	1678	296	13654	8849	1.83	0,92
1998	1407	296	13689	9481	1.86	0.91
1999	961	54	13795	9364	1.89	0.93
2000	929	56	14535	9968	1.92	0.95
2001	921	57	14393	10246	1.96	0.97
2002	1263	58	14653	10292	2.01	0.99
2003	1297	55	15279	10654	2.15	1.06
2004	1555	58	17053	12119	2.51	1.14
2005	1667	265	18458	17856	2.91	1.32
2006	1854	268	19711	19339	3.25	1.46
2007	2270	255	21000	20306	3.53	1.54
2008	2276	257	22155	21523	3.69	1.51
2009	2359	243	23475	22299	4.00	1.62
2010	2377	230	26097	24762	4.31	1.72
2011	4221	106	27127	23046	4.67	1.84
2012	4035	108	28290	24296	4.92	1.91
2013	4032	109	29356	25753	5.15	1.99

表 12－14　各县(市)卫生事业单位机构情况(2013)
Basic Statistics on Health Care Institutions by Region

指标	Indicators	全市 Total
卫生事业机构数	**Number of Health Care Intitiutions**	**4032**
1. 医院合计	Total Hospitals	109
综合医院	Comprehensive Hospitals	58
中医医院	Hospitals of Chinese Medicine	11
中西医结合医院	Combined Chinese and Western Medicine Hospital	2
专科医院	Specialized Hospitals	38
口腔医院	Oral and Dental Hospitals	5
眼科医院	Ophthalmology Hospitals	3
妇产(科)医院	Obstetrics and Gynecology Hospitals	4
精神病医院	Mental Hospitals	1
传染病医院	Infectious Disease Hospitals	6
皮肤病医院	Dermatology Hospital	1
骨科医院	Orthopedist Hospitals	4
康复医院	Healing Hospitals	3
其他专科医院	Others Specialized Hospitals	11
2. 社区卫生服务中心(站)	Community Sanitation Service Sites	557
社区卫生服务中心	Community Health Center	58
社区卫生服务站	Community Health Service Station	499
3. 卫生院	Local Hospitals	110
乡镇卫生院	Town and Township Local Hospitals	110
中心卫生院	Center Locale Hospitals	33
乡卫生院	Towhship Locale Hospitals	77
4. 村卫生室	Village Health Room	2099
5. 门诊部合计	Clinics	104
6. 诊所、卫生所、医务室	Special Clinics	984
7. 急救中心(站)	First－aid Centre(Stations)	13
8. 采供血机构	Blood Collecting and Supplying Organization	4
9. 妇幼保健院(所、站)	Maternity and Child Care Centers or Stations	11
10. 专科疾病防治院(所、站)	Specialized Prevention and Treatment Centers or Stations	8
11. 疾病预防控制中心	Center for Disease Control and Prevention	1
12. 卫生监督所(中心)	Health Supervision Centers(Center)	13
13. 医学科学研究机构	Research Institution of Medicine	3
14. 医学在职培训机构	Medical Institution of On－the－job Training	5
15. 其他卫生机构	Others Health Care Institutions	11

注：本表至 12－17 表数据来之宁波市卫生局。

Note: Data from Tables 12－14 to 12－17 are obtained from Ningbo Municipal Bureau of Health.

单位：个(unit)

市区 Urban District	#鄞州 Yinzhou	余姚 Yuyao	慈溪 Cixi	奉化 Fenghua	象山 Xiangshan	宁海 Ninghai
1609	**575**	**532**	**705**	**467**	**260**	**459**
67	12	7	16	8	6	5
33	7	5	11	4	3	2
5		1	1	1	2	1
2	1					
27	4	1	4	3	1	2
5	1					
2			1			
2			2			
1						
2		1	1	1	1	
1						
1				1		2
2	1			1		
11	2					
353	84	97	37	40		30
43	7	7	6	1		1
310	77	90	31	39		29
17	17	14	16	22	17	24
17	17	14	16	22	17	24
6	6	5	5	4	7	6
11	11	9	11	18	10	18
558	311	271	517	285	190	278
66	13	11	25		1	1
507	131	127	87	107	41	115
8	1	1	1	1	1	1
3	2		1			
6	1	1	1	1	1	1
4	1	1	1	1		1
1						
8	1	1	1	1	1	1
3						
1		1	1		1	1
7	1		1	1	1	1

表 12－15 各县(市)卫生事业人员、床位情况(2013) Number of Health Care Personnel and Beds by Region

指标	Indicators	全市 Total
从业人员总计(人)	**Total Employment(person)**	**61543**
卫生技术人员	Medical Technical Personnel	51510
医生数	Number of Doctors	19949
执业医师	Medical Practitioner	17257
执业助理医师	Assistant Medical Practitioner	2692
注册护士	Register Nurse	19668
药师(士)	Pharmacists	3398
技师(士)	Laboratory Technicians	2720
检验师	Laboratory Examiner	2091
其他	Others	5775
见习医师	Trainee Doctors	2299
其他技术人员	Other Technical Personnel	1911
管理人员	Manager	1928
工勤技能人员	Logistics Workers	4490
每千人拥有卫生技术人员	Number of Medical Technical Personnel Per 1000 Persons	8.88
每千人拥有医生	Number of Doctors Per 1000 Persons	3.44
每千人拥有注册护士	Number of R. N. Per 1000 Persons	3.39
卫生事业床位数(张)	**Number of Beds (bed)**	**29356**
医院床位	Beds of Hospitals	25753
社区卫生服务中心床位	Beds of Health Service Center of Communities	719
卫生院床位	Beds of Local Hospitals	2300
妇幼保健院(所、站)床位	Beds of Maternity and Child Care Centers	514
专科疾病防治院(所、站)床位	Beds of Specialized Prevention Stations	50
每千人拥有总床位	Total Beds of Per 1000 Persons	5.06
每千人拥有医院卫生院床位	Beds of Hospitals and Local Hospitals Per 1000 Persons	4.96

市区 Urban District	#鄞州 Yinzhou	余姚 Yuyao	慈溪 Cixi	奉化 Fenghua	象山 Xiangshan	宁海 Ninghai
34400	**8471**	**6398**	**9157**	**3718**	**3384**	**4486**
29154	7116	5279	7562	2962	2881	3672
11025	2772	2031	3030	1257	1180	1426
9997	2380	1688	2373	1065	981	1153
1028	392	343	657	192	199	273
11292	2488	2087	2815	1086	1098	1290
1905	530	344	508	198	232	211
1569	376	251	416	133	151	200
1221	308	192	310	104	123	141
3363	950	566	793	288	220	545
1124	309	293	347	179	123	233
965	232	141	348	172	80	205
1353	276	136	210	66	94	69
2586	760	524	624	272	148	336
12.81	8.47	6.32	7.25	6.12	5.30	5.93
4.84	3.30	2.43	2.90	2.60	2.17	2.30
4.96	2.96	2.50	2.70	2.25	2.02	2.08
17434	**3589**	**2601**	**3629**	**2204**	**1654**	**1834**
16450	3011	2203	2826	2018	1376	880
493	98	100	126			
480	480	298	419	136	258	709
11			208	50		245
			50			
7.66	4.27	3.11	3.48	4.56	3.04	2.96
7.66	4.27	3.11	3.23	4.45	3.00	2.57

表 12－16 各级医院工作情况(2013) Medical Treatment of Various Hospitals

指标	Indicators	门诊人次合计（万人次） Out－Patients （10000 person－times）
全市总计	**Total**	**8060**
1. 医院合计	Total Hospitals	3651
综合医院	Comprehensive Hospitals	2574
省辖市属医院	Urban Hospitals Administered by Province	602
#市第一医院	The No. 1 Hospital of Ningbo	181
市第二医院	The No. 2 Hospital of Ningbo	153
市第三医院	The No. 3 Hospital of Ningbo	108
市李惠利医院	Li Huili Hospital of Ningbo	140
市华慈医院	Hua Ci Hospital of Ningbo	20
中医医院	Hospitals of Chinese Medicine	574
#市中医院	Hospital of Chinese Medicine of Ningbo	106
中西医结合医院	Combined Chinese and Western Medicine Hospital	18
专科医院	Specialized Hospitals	485
口腔医院	Oral and Dental Hospitals	35
眼科医院	Ophthalmology Hospitals	49
妇产(科)医院	Obstetrics and Gynecology Hospitals	189
#市妇儿医院	Hospital for Maternity and Child of Ningbo	184
精神病医院	Mental Hospitals	84
#市康宁医院	Kangning Hospital of Ningbo	15
骨科医院	Orthopedist Hospitals	84
2. 社区卫生服务中心	Health Service Center of Communities	1499
3. 卫生院	Local Hospitals	1564
4. 门诊部	Policlinic	648
5. 村卫生室	Village Health Room	151
6. 诊所、卫生所、医务室	Clinic	352
7. 妇幼保健院(所、站)	Maternity and Child Care Centers or Stations	160
8. 专科疾病防治院(所、站)	Specialized Prevention and Treatment Centers or Stations	26

本年入院人数 (万人) Inpatients in this Year (10000 persons)	平均住院日 (天) Average Day In—patients (day)	本年出院人数 (万人) Discharged Patient in this Year (10000 persons)	期末实有病床数 (张) Factual Beds at the Year—end (bed)	平均开放病床数 (张) Average Openning Bed (bed)	病床使用率 (%) Occupancy of Hospital Beds (%)
89.0	**88.8**	**10.3**	**29356**	**28758**	**85.7**
81.9	81.7	10.4	25753	25297	90.4
63.7	63.6	9.5	18546	18250	90.9
19.9	19.8	10.0	5582	5491	98.5
5.3	5.3	10.5	1546	1529	100.2
6.1	6.0	10.3	1901	1833	92.7
3.3	3.3	9.7	835	833	105.5
5.2	5.2	9.2	1300	1296	100.2
6.3	6.3	11.4	2203	2189	89.6
1.4	1.4	15.6	600	598	100.3
0.1	0.1	8.6	120	120	28.1
11.7	11.7	15.2	4884	4738	90.6
			30	30	
0.8	0.8	5.7	192	191	68.2
4.8	4.8	8.0	1042	1039	100.6
4.7	4.7	8.0	982	979	106.2
1.1	1.1	72.4	1745	1666	98.5
0.4	0.4	48.3	520	519	101.6
3.8	3.8	10.5	1190	1140	95.2
0.8	0.8	14.1	719	670	49.1
3.7	3.7	9.7	2300	2227	44.0
			20		
2.6	2.6	6.0	514	519	82.5
			50	46	73.4

表 12—17　居民病伤死亡原因(2013)
Main 10 Diseases of Death in Urban Residents

指标	Indicators	死亡人数(人) 合计 Total
宁波市总计	**Total in Ningbo**	**36767**
十种死因合计	Main 10 Causes of Death	34606
1. 恶性肿瘤	Malignant Tumour	11900
2. 脑血管病	Cerebral Vascular Disease	6699
3. 呼吸系病	Respiratory Disease	5508
4. 心脏病	Cardiopathy	3644
5. 损伤和中毒	Trauma and Toxicosis	3409
6. 消化系统疾病	Digestive Disease	996
7. 内分泌等疾病	Internal System Disease	962
8. 神经系统疾病	Nervous system diseases	640
9. 传染病(不包括呼吸道结核)	Infectious Disease(Respiratory Tuberculosis not Included)	438
10. 精神障碍	Mental Disorder	410
市区总计	**Total in Urban Destricts**	**13110**
十种死因合计	Main 10 Causes of Death	12347
1. 恶性肿瘤	Malignant Tumour	4451
2. 脑血管病	Cerebral Vascular Disease	2240
3. 呼吸系病	Respiratory Disease	1943
4. 心脏病	Heart Disease	1255
5. 损伤和中毒	Injury and Poisoning	1154
6. 内分泌等疾病	Internal System Disease	475
7. 消化系统疾病	Digestive Disease	342
8. 神经系统疾病	Nervous system diseases	212
9. 泌尿系疾病	Urologic Diseases	143
10. 传染病(不包括呼吸道结核)	Infectious Disease(Respiratory Tuberculosis not Included)	132

Number of Death (person)		死因构成 (%) Composition of Death(%)	死亡专率(/10 万) Death Rate (per 0.1 million persons)		
男 Male	女 Female		合计 Total	男 Male	女 Female
20673	**16094**	**100.00**	**635.09**	**716.01**	**554.58**
19674	14932	94.12	597.76	681.41	514.54
7968	3932	32.37	205.55	275.97	135.49
3498	3201	18.22	115.71	121.15	110.30
2882	2626	14.98	95.14	99.82	90.49
1777	1867	9.91	62.94	61.55	64.33
1809	1600	9.27	58.88	62.65	55.13
583	413	2.71	17.20	20.19	14.23
428	534	2.62	16.62	14.82	18.40
283	357	1.74	11.05	9.80	12.30
276	162	1.19	7.57	9.56	5.58
170	240	1.12	7.08	5.89	8.27
7275	**5835**	**100.00**	**577.91**	**649.60**	**508.01**
6970	5377	94.18	544.27	622.37	468.13
2938	1513	33.95	196.21	262.34	131.72
1172	1068	17.09	98.74	104.65	92.98
1014	929	14.82	85.65	90.54	80.88
608	647	9.57	55.32	54.29	56.33
568	586	8.80	50.87	50.72	51.02
217	258	3.62	20.94	19.38	22.46
187	155	2.61	15.08	16.70	13.49
101	111	1.62	9.35	9.02	9.66
82	61	1.09	6.30	7.32	5.31
83	49	1.01	5.82	7.41	4.27

表 12－18　部分年份全市体育工作情况
Basic Statistics on Physical Culture Schools and Sports in Partial Years

指标	单位	Indicators	Uuit	2010	2011	2012	2013
各类体校情况		**Various Physical Culture and Sports School**					
体育运动学校数	个	Physical Education and Sports School	unit	1	1	1	1
在校学生数	人	Student Enrollment	person	770	720	810	750
专职教练员	人	Full－time Coaches	person	45	60	47	62
业余体校个数	个	Sparetime Sports Schools	unit	5	5	5	6
＃重点业余体校	个	Emphatic Sparetime Sports School	unit	5	5	5	5
业余体校在校学生数	人	Student Enrollment in Sparetime Sports Schools	person	830	840	910	1020
业余体校送入优秀运动队	人	Number of Persons from Sparetime Sports School Enrolling Excelent Sports Team	person	88	36	39	42
业余体校考入高等院校	人	Number of Persons Admitted to Institutions Higher Education from Sparetime Sports School	person	40	50	50	52
传统项目布局情况		**Distribution on Traditional Events**					
分布学校数	个	Number of Distributing Schools	unit	108	131	136	146
＃中学	个	Secondary Schools	unit	20	37	21	46
小学	个	Primary Schools	unit	88	94	125	100
市区新增健身设施	套	New built Health－care Facilities in Urban Districts	set	202			
传统项目活动情况		Statistics on Traditional Events					
参加活动学生人数	人	Number of Participants in Student	person	8600	19200	9620	20050
参加田径学生	人	Track and Field	person	4100	8000	4500	9000
参加游泳学生	人	Swimming	person	1000	2000	1100	1000
参加射击学生	人	Shoot	person	200	1000	220	200
参加蓝球学生	人	Basketball	person	500	2000	600	2000
参加排球学生	人	Volleyball	person	300	1600	400	1500
参加足球学生	人	Football	person	500	1600	1200	2000
参加乒乓排球学生	人	Pingpong	person	1000	2000	800	2350
参加羽毛球学生	人	Badminton	person	1000	1000	800	2000
游泳池情况(体育系统)		**Swimming Pool Managed by Physical Department**					
游泳池个数	个	Number of Swimming Pools	unit	5	11	6	17
＃室内游泳池	个	Indoor	unit	4	10	4	12
游泳池活动场次	场次	Number of Running Swimming Pool	times	10020	13000	11000	1530
＃室内游泳池	场次	Indoor	times	9500	10500	9500	497
参赛获奖数	**枚**	**Number of Obtain Awards by Athletic Competition**	**unit**	**651**	**963**	**593**	**992**
＃省级及以上金牌	枚	Gold Medals Won in Province Level Competitions	unit	230	383	173	389
＃省级及以上银牌	枚	Silver Medals Won in Province Level Competitions	unit	180.5	315	180	318
＃省级及以上铜牌	枚	Bronze Medals Won in Province Level Competitions	unit	240.5	265	240	285

表 12—19 部分年份科协系统活动情况
Basic Statistics on Science and Technology Associations in Partial Years

指标	Indicators	2010	2011	2012	2013
基本情况	**Basic Situation**				
科协机构数(个)	Insitutions of Science and Technology(unit)	89	90	91	92
直属单位	Organizations Attached to the Institutions		6	6	6
科技馆(科普活动中心)	S&T Museum(Activity Center of Popular Science)		8	8	4
活动情况	**Activity Situation**				
举办学术交流活动(次)	Number of Academic Exchange Activities		293	450	400
科普讲座次数(次)	Number of S&T Popularization Lectures(times)	1918	1317	5252	11320
宣讲活动受众人数(人)	Propaganda Lecture the Audience				1064499
播放科技广播、影视节目(次)	Radio and Television Programs about S&T				67320
编著科技图书(种)	Number of Editor S&T Books		50	104	45
举办青少年科技竞赛(次)	Number of Teenagers' S&T Competition		136	114	136
开展"讲、比"活动企业数(个)	Enterprise Number of S&T Competition Acitivities		149	275	149

注:本表和 12—21 表数据来自宁波市科协。

Note:a)Data in Tables 12—19 and 12—21 are obtained from Ningbo Associations for Science and Technology.

①S&T is a short form that means Scientific and Technological. The other table are the same.

表 12—20 部分年份市级以上科技成果鉴定、获奖、专利授权情况
Basic Statistics on Verification, Award—Winning and Patent Right of Above Municipal Level in Partial Years

单位:个(unit)

指标	Indicators	2009	2010	2011	2012	2013
科技成果登记	Scientific and Technological Enrollment of Results			428	457	510
科学技术奖	Scientific and Technological Awards	104	120	106	107	115
国家级	State Leve	6	4	1	1	3
省级	Province Level	22	24	26	26	32
市级	Municipal Level	76	92	79	80	80
授权专利数	Number of Patent Applications Approved	15824	25971	37342	59175	58406
#发明	Inventions	802	1209	1625	2065	2246
实用新型	Utility Models	5943	11230	12966	21407	28367
外观设计	Designs	9078	13532	22751	35703	27793

注:本表和 12—22 表数据来自宁波市科技局。

Note:Data in Tables 12—20 and 12—22 are obtained from Ningbo Municipal Bureau of Science and Technology.

表 12—21 科协系统情况(2013)
Basic Statistics on Science and Technology Associations

指标	单位	Indicators	Unit	市科协 S&T Associations of Ningbo Municipal	县(市)区科协 S&T Associations by Region	市级学(协)会 S&T Associations for Municipal Level
科协组织和机构		**Basic Situation**				
科协机构数	个	Institutions of Science and Technology	unit	1	11	80
直属单位	个	Organizations Attached to the Institutions	unit	3	3	
团体会员(学会、协会、研究会)	个	Group members (Academy, the Association, the Research Council)	unit	80	212	4069
企事业科协	个	Enterprise and Non—profit Organizations Institutions of S&T	unit	8	126	
科学普及活动		**Activity for Popular Science**				
举办科普讲座	次	Number of S&T Popularization Lectures	times	118	712	10490
播放科技广播、影视节目	次	Radio and Television Programs about S&T	times	23000	44320	
宣讲活动受众人数	人	Propaganda Lecture the Audience	person	15440	272010	777049
举办实用技术培训	次	Number of Practical Technology Training	times	829	2254	
青少年科技教育		**Teenagers S&T Education**				
举办青少年科技竞赛	次	Number of Teenagers' S&T Competition	times	10	126	
举办青少年科技夏(冬)令营	次	Number of Teenagers' S&T Summer (Winter) Camp	times		17	
举办青少年科技培训	人次	Number of Teenagers' S&T Training	person—time	4	212	
科普基础设施建设		**Infrastructure of Popular Science**				
科技馆(科普活动中心)	个	S&T Museum (Activity Center of Popular Science)	unit		4	
科普教育(示范)基地	个	S&T Education (Model) Base	unit	36	96	
科普画廊(活动站、中心室)	个	Gallery of Popular Science	unit		2918	
学术交流		**Academic Activities**				
举办学术交流活动	次	Number of Academic Exchange Activities	unit	29	39	332
编著科技图书	种	Number of Editor S&T Books	kind	7	19	19
接待或派往境外科技团组(人数)	个	Receive or Sent Foreign S&T Group	unit	117	118	587
科技活动和社会服务		**S&T Activities and Social services**				
开展"讲、比"活动企业数	个	Enterprise Number of S&T Competition Acitivities	unit		149	
院士工作站	个	Academician Workstation	unit	69	46	
表彰奖励科技工作者	人	Award of Scientific and Technical Workers	person	10	178	231
反映科技工作者建议	条	Number of S&T Workers' Proposal	piece	3	143	586
普网工程培训	人次	Universal Network Engineering Training	person—time	21199	21060	

表 12—22 各县(市)市级以上科技成果鉴定、获奖、专利情况(2013) Basic Statistics on Verification, Award—Winning and Patent Right of Above Municipal Level by Region

单位:个(unit)

指标	Indicators	全市 Total	市区 Urban District	鄞州 Yinzhou	余姚 Yuyao
科技成果登记	Scientific and Technological Enrollment of Results	510	390	45	11
科学技术奖	Science and Technology Awards	115	88	19	8
国家级	State Level	3			
省级	Province Level	32	26	5	1
市级	Municipal Level	80	62	14	7
授权专利数	Number of Patent Applications Approved	58406	28308	15131	12507
发明	Inventions	2246	1595	653	183
实用新型	Utility Models	28367	16328	7020	2075
外观设计	Designs	27793	10385	7458	10249

表 12—22 续表 Continued

单位:个(unit)

指标	Indicators	慈溪 Cixi	奉化 Fenghua	宁海 Ninghai	象山 Xiangshan
科技成果登记	Scientific and Technological Enrollment of Results	73	13	16	7
科学技术奖	Science and Technology Awards	4	1	4	7
国家级	State Level				
省级	Province Level		1	2	2
市级	Municipal Level	4		2	5
授权专利数	Number of Patent Applications Approved	11443	2198	1854	2096
发明	Inventions	282	63	46	77
实用新型	Utility Models	5487	1810	1744	923
外观设计	Designs	5674	325	64	1096

注:国家级科学技术奖包括参与完成项目。

Note: Science and Technology Awards at State Levelincluded Participating.

表 12—23 各县(市)计量标准质监情况(2013) Basic Statistics On Standard Measuring and Quality Supervising by Region

指标	单位	Indicators	Unit
计量验收情况		**Measuring Implements Test**	
已开展强制检定数	项	Measurement Implement Tested Compulsively	kind
开展强制检定种数	种	The Kind of Measurement Implement Tested Compulsively	kind
强制检定实际检出数	件	Actual Quantity Checked by Compulsively Examined Out	piece
计量仪器实际检出数	件	Actual Quantity Checked by Messurement Implement Tested	piece
质监情况		Quality Supervision	
国家监督抽查批次	批次	Batch of supervises and Check by Country	batch. time
#合格批次	批次	Regular Batch	batch. time
批次合格率	%	Ratio of Regular by Batch	%
省定期监督抽查企业数	个	Number of Enterpriese of Periodic Supervises and Check by Province	unit
省定期监督抽查批次	批次	Batch of Periodic supervises and Check by Province	batch. time
#合格批次	批次	Regular Batch	batch. time
批次合格率	%	Ratio of Regular by Batch	%
宁波市质量指数	%	Index of Product Quality about NingBo	%

注:本表数据来自宁波市质量技术监督局。

Note:Data in this table are obtained from Administration of Quality and Technology Supervision of Ningbo Municipality.

全市 Total	市区 Urban District	#鄞州 Yinzhou	余姚市 Yuyao	慈溪市 Cixi	奉化市 Fenghua	象山县 Xiangshan	宁海县 Ninghai
39	39	18	11	13	11	10	12
80	80	26	22	23	20	16	19
970672	582663	97193	82980	74741	85830	75421	69037
1230422	828899	91627	82388	87216	87392	71635	72892
367	139	75	31	174	10	1	12
323	122	65	29	153	8	1	10
0.88	0.88	0.87	0.94	0.88	0.80	1.00	0.83
1370	619	298	216	391	50	36	58
1527	698	348	225	427	67	50	60
1464	678	335	217	399	64	48	58
0.96	0.97	0.96	0.96	0.93	0.96	0.96	0.97
99.34	99.89	99.83	98.00	98.16	96.62	99.89	99.94

主要统计指标解释

【艺术表演团体】 指从事戏曲、音乐、舞蹈、杂技等专业艺术表演，有独立帐 户，实行单独核算的团体。不包括半工半艺、半农半艺和民间职业剧团。

【艺术表演观众人数(人次)】 指售票、包场演出或民族地区免费演出的艺术表演观众人次数。不包括彩排审查和内部观摩演出的观众人次数。

【电影放映单位】 指具有放映机器设备、固定或不固定的放映场所与专职或兼职的放映技术人员，经有关部门登记批准，经常为一定的观众对象放映电影的机构。包括经批准对外开放进行营业，并与电影发行放映管理机构分帐的专用放映单位和军委系统租片单位。

【普通高等学校】 指按照国家规定的设置标准和审批程序批准举办，通过国家统一招生考试，招收高中毕业生为主要培养对象，实施高等教育的全日制大学、独立设置的学院和高等专科学校、短期职业大学。

【成人高等学校】 指按照国家有关规定审批，招收通过全国成人高教统一招生 考试的具有高中毕业或同等学历的在职从业人员利用脱产、半脱产、业余或函授等多种形式 对其实施高等学历教育，培养高等教育专科或本科毕业水平的专门人才，修业年限、课程设 置和总学时数均按高等学历教育要求付诸实施的学校。包括广播电视大学、职工高等学校、农民高等学校、管理干部学院、教育学院、独立设置的函授学院等。

【小学学龄儿童入学率】 指调查范围内已入小学学习的学龄儿童占校内外学龄儿童总数(包括弱智儿童在内，但不包括盲聋哑儿童)的比重。计算公式为：

小学学龄儿童入学率＝已入学的小学学龄儿童数×100％

校内外小学学龄儿童总数

【医院】 指名称为医院，设有固定床位能收容病人住院并能为病人提供医疗、护理服务的医疗机构。包括县及县以上医院、农村乡卫生院、其他医院三部分。按所属性质分为卫生部门、工业及其他部门，集体经济单位三类。其中县及县以上医院按业务性质分为 综合医院和专科医院。

【卫生技术人员】 指卫生事业机构支付工资的全部固定职工和合同制职工中现任职务为卫生技术工作的专业人员。具体包括中医师、西医师、中西医结合高级医师、护师、中 药师、西药师、检验师、其他技师、中医士、西医士、护士、助产士、中药剂士、西药剂士 、检验士、其他技士、其他中医、护理员、中药剂员、西药剂员、检验员，其他初级卫生技术人员。

【医生】 指经卫生部门审查合格，从事医疗工作的专业人员。分为中医医生和西医医生。包括卫生技术人员中的中医师、西医师、中西结合高级医师、中医士、西医士和其他中医。

【专利申请数】 指当年单位向专利管理机关提出专利申请并被受理的件数。

Explanatory Notes on Main Statistical Indicators

【Art Troupe】 refers to the troupe which is engaged in drama, opera, music, dance, acrobatics or other art performance, opens independent accounts with banks and has self—supporting accounting system; excluding the troupes which h are engaged partly in industrial or agricultural activities, partly in art performance and the professional troupes organized by the people.

【Number of Sectors at Art Performance】 refers to the number of attendants at commercial shows completely booked shows or free shows given in minority national areas, and does not include the number of spectators at rehearsals for examination and initial shows for study.

【Film Projection Units】 refer to units with film projection equipment, full or part time projectionists, permanent or nonpermanent places, approved by related administrative departments to show films regularly for certain groups of audience, including those film projection units which have been approved to give commercial shows and run business with independent accounting system as well as those film-renting units of the military system.

【Regular Institutions of Higher Learning】 refer to educational establishments set up according to the government evaluation and approval procedures, enrolling graduates from senior secondary schools and providing higher education courses and training for senior professionals. They include full—time universities, colleges, high professional schools and short—term professional universities.

【Institutions of Higher Learning for Adults】 refer to educational establishments, set up in line with relevant rules approved by the government, enrolling staff and workers with senior secondary school or equivalent education, and providing higher education courses in many forms of full—time, part—time, spare—time, or correspondence for adults. Professionals thus trained receive a qualification equivalent to graduates studying regular courses at regular universities, colleges and professional colleges. Institutions of higher learning for adults include Radio and TV universities, schools of high education for staff and workers and peasants, colleges for management cadres, pedagogical colleges, independent correspondence colleges.

【Enrollment Rate of Primary School—age Children】 refers to the proportion of school—age children enrolled at schools to the total number of school—age both in and outside schools (including retarded children, but excluding blind, deaf and mute children). The formula is:

Enrollment Rate of Primary School—age Children=Total Primary School—age Children at Schools×100%

Total Primary School—age Children at and Outside Schools

【Hospitals】 refer to medical institutions named as "hospital" with permanent hospital beds, which are able to take in patients and provide them with medical and nursing services. Hospitals are classified into three categories : hospitals at or above the county—level, hospitals of rural townships, and other hospitals. According to their ownership, hospitals can be classified into three categories: hospitals under the public health departments, hospitals under industrial and other departments and collective—owned hospitals. Hospitals at or above county level are divided into comprehensive and specialized hospitals.

【Medical Technical Personnel】 refers to all permanent medical staff and workers employed by medical institutions, including doctors of Chinese and Western medicine, senior doctors who integrate traditional Chinese therapeutics with Western therapeutics in practice, senior nurses, pharmacists of Chinese and Western medicine, laboratory specialists, other specialists, paramedics of Chinese and Western medicine, nurses, midwives, druggists in Chinese and Western medicine, laboratory technicians, other technicians, other practitioners of Chinese medicine, nursing attendants, pharmacological workers of Chinese and Western medicine, laboratory workers, and other primary medical personnel.

【Doctors】 refer to qualified professional medical workers approved to practice by public health departments. They are classified into doctors of Chinese medicine, doctors of Western medicine, senior doctors who integrate traditional Chinese therapeutics with Western therapeutics in practice, paramedics of Chinese medicine and Western medicine, and other specialists of Chinese medicine.

【Applied Number of Patents】 refers to the number of patent applied by a unit to the patent office and then accepted in a reporting year.

CHAPTER 13

NINGBO 2014 Statistical YearBook

第十三篇 市政、环保、民政、政法及其他

CIVIL FACILITIES, ENVIRONMENT, CIVIL AFFAIRS, JUDICATURE AND OTHERS

市政、环保、民政、政法及其他
Civil Facilities, Environment, Social Welfare, Judicature and Others

主要统计指标
Major Statistics Indicators

2013 年人均日生活用水量	Per Capita Daily Consunption of Tap water for Resiential Use	229.91	升	liter
2013 年人均拥有道路面积	Per Capita Area of Paved Roads	20.54	平方米	sq. m
2013 年人均公园绿地面积	Per Capita Public Green Areas	11.25	平方米	sq. m
2013 年建成区绿化覆盖率	Coverage Rate of Green Area in Developed Area	38.23	%	
2013 年废水排放总量	Total Volume of Waste Water Discharged	57037	万吨	10000 tons
2013 年工业废气排放量	Volume of Industrial Waste Gas Emission	6217.88	亿标立米	100 million cu. m
2013 年环境噪声达标面积	Standardization Areas of Environment Noise	260.21	平方公里	sq. km
2013 年收养性福利单位床位数	Number of Beds in Socail Welfare－Units for Adopting	37934	张	bed
2013 年社会救济总人数	Number of Persons Receiving Relief	55235	人	person
2013 年末实有社团机构数	Factual Number of Social Organizations at The Year－end	2227	个	unit
2013 年基层工会数	Number of Trade Unions at Basic－Level	27293	个	unit
2013 年律师人数	Number of Lawyers	1733	人	person
2013 年办理公证事项	Number of Notarized Documents	83564	件	case
2013 年调解纠纷总件数	Number of Mediating Disputes	117549	件	case
2013 年交通事故数	Number of Traffic Accident	2791	件	case
2013 年档案馆数	Number of Archives	12	个	unit

表 13－1 部分年份市政公用事业基本情况
Basic Statistics on Municipal Public Utilities in Partial Years

指标	单位	Indicators	Unit	2010	2011	2012	2013
供水及供气		**Water Supply and Gas Supply**					
年供水总量	万吨	Annuall Volume of Tap Water Supply	10000 tons	65740	68617	70122	72619
#居民家庭用水量	万吨	Water Consumption for Residents Use	10000 tons	20928	22439	23130	23354
人均日生活用水量	升	Per Capita Daily Consumption of Tap Water for Residential Use	liter	232.56	240.31	239.49	229.91
用水普及率	%	Percentage of Population with Access to Tap Water	%	100.00	100.00	100.00	100.00
液化石油气供气总量	万吨	Total Volume of Liquefied Petroleum Gas	10000 tons	28.50	21.66	20.13	19.42
#家庭用量	万吨	For Residents Use	10000 tons	12.17	10.37	10.09	10.53
用液化气人口	万人	Population with Access Liquefied Petroleum Gas	10000 persons	205.79	193.81	202.46	163.94
燃气普及率	%	Percentage of Population with Access to Gas	%	100.00	100.00	100.00	100.00
市政设施		**Municipal Infra－strucutre**					
年末城市实有道路面积	万平方米	Area of Paved Roads(Year－end)	10000 sq. m	6445.3	6930.5	7124.6	7276.62
人均拥有道路面积	平方米	Per Capita Area of Paved Roads	sq. m	19.65	20.44	20.53	20.54
排水管道长度	公里	Length of Sewage Pipes	km	6265	6574.8	6907.4	7761.90
排水管道密度	公里/平方公里	Density of Sewage Pipes	km/sq. km	14.47	14.60	15.11	16.57
公共交通		**Public Traffic**					
年末实有公交营运车辆	标台	Number of Public Transportations Vehicles under Operation	unit	4842	5302.5	6143.9	7149
每万人拥有公共交通车辆	标台	Number of Public Transportations Vehicles Per 10000 Persons	unit	6.50	6.96	8.08	12.30
年末实有出租汽车数	辆	Operating Taxes at Year－end	unit	5442	5551	5834	6360
城市绿化		**Afforestation in Cities**					
园林绿地面积	公顷	Green Areas in Parks and Gardens	hectare	15780	16666	17107	17640
#公园绿地面积	公顷	Public Green Areas	hectare	3483	3662	3807	3986
人均公园绿地面积	平方米	Per Capita Public Green Areas	sq. m	10.62	10.80	10.97	11.25
建成区绿地率	%	Rate of Green Area in Developed Area	%	33.94	34.27	34.76	34.91
建成区绿化覆盖率	%	Coverage Rate of Green Area in Developed Area	%	37.52	37.82	38.21	38.23
环境卫生		**Environmental Sanitation**					
污水处理率	%	Percentage of Sewage Disposed	%	82.81	84.16	85.75	88.42
生活垃圾无害化处理率	%	Innocuous Disposal Rate of Living Garbage	%	100.00	100.00	100.00	100.00

注：2009 年开始，排水管道密度为建成区排水管道密度。

Note：Densitly of sewage pipes from 2009 refered to builting area.

表 13-2 各县(市)城市市政、公用事业情况(2013)
Basic Statistics on Civil Facilities and Public Utilities by Region

指标	单位	Indicators	Unit
城市面积		**City Areas**	
建成区面积	平方公里	Developed Areas	sq. km
城市建设用地面积	平方公里	land Areas of the Urban Construction	sq. km
居住用地面积	平方公里	For Residential Building Uses	sq. km
公共管理与公共设施面积	平方公里	For Public Management and Utilities Uses	sq. km
工业用地面积	平方公里	For Industry Uses	sq. km
供水及供气		**Water Supply and Gas Supply**	
年供水总量	万吨	Annuall Volume of Tap Water Supply	10000 tons
#居民家庭用水量	万吨	Water Consumption for Residents Use	10000 tons
人均日生活用水量	升	Per Capita Daily Consumption of Tap Water for Residential Use	liter
用水普及率	%	Percentage of Population with Access to Tap Water	%
液化石油气供气总量	吨	Total Volume of Liquefied Petroleum Gas	ton
#家庭用量	吨	For Residents Use	ton
用液化气人口	万人	Population with Access Liquefied Petroleum Gas	10000 persons
燃气普及率	%	Percentage of Population with Access to Gas	%
市政设施		**Municipal Infra-strucutre**	
年末城市实有道路面积	万平方米	Area of Paved Roads(Year-end)	10000 sq. m
人均拥有道路面积	平方米	Per Capita Area of Paved Roads	sq. m
排水管道长度	公里	Length of Sewage Pipes	km
建成区排水管道密度	公里/平方公里	Density of Drainpipes	km/sq. km
公共交通		**Public Traffic**	
年末实有公交营运车辆	标台	Number of Public Transportations Vehicles under Operation	unit
每万人拥有公共交通车辆	标台	Number of Public Transportations Vehicles Per 10000 Persons	unit
年末实有出租汽车数	辆	Operating Taxes at Year-end	unit
城市绿化		**Afforestation in Cities**	
园林绿地面积	公顷	Green Areas in Parks and Gardens	hectare
#公园绿地面积	公顷	Public Green Areas	hectare
人均公园绿地面积	平方米	Per Capita Public Green Areas	sq. m
建成区绿化覆盖面积	公顷	Coverage Area of Green Area in Developed Area	hectare
建成区绿地率	%	Rate of Green Area in Developed Area	%
建成区绿化覆盖率	%	Coverage Rate of Green Area in Developed Area	%
环境卫生		**Environmental Sanitation**	
污水处理率	%	Percentage of Sewage Disposed	%
城市生活垃圾无害化处理率	%	Innocuous Disposal Rate of Living Garbage	%

注:本表数据来自宁波市城乡建委。

Note:Data in this table are obtained from Ningbo Municipal Construction Committee.

全市 Total	市区 Urban District	余姚市 Yuyao	慈溪市 Cixi	奉化市 Fenghua	象山县 Xiangshan	宁海 Ninghai
468.39	294.95	49.24	43.30	18.75	28.45	33.70
543.44	346.82	47.04	41.25	34.43	36.02	37.88
141.76	76.17	14.00	19.55	11.04	9.95	11.05
47.79	30.38	3.79	2.91	2.30	6.09	2.32
185.46	128.30	12.90	8.87	11.49	10.03	13.87
72619	47309	4611	10156	3237	4135	3171
23354	14606	2103	2596	1487	1174	1388
229.91	286.35	145.02	177.24	161.17	158.15	242.38
100.00	100.00	100.00	100.00	100.00	100.00	100.00
194218.34	133322.96	4753.00	29179.00	6487.15	11954.05	8522.18
105255.01	54049.62	3451.00	27051.00	5618.00	8582.39	6503.00
163.94	21.52	27.88	41.52	33.25	23.80	15.97
100.00	100.00	100.00	100.00	100.00	100.00	100.00
7277	2869	1053	1715	422	727	491
20.54	15.74	23.55	33.14	12.69	30.54	26.60
7762	4492	719	1277	199	522	553
16.57	15.23	14.60	29.49	10.59	18.36	16.41
7149	5385	624	588	192	154	206
12.30	23.70	7.50	5.60	4.00	2.80	3.30
6360	4627	440	605	200	210	278
17640	10905	1761	1890	973	852	1259
3986	1927	459	673	400	284	243
11.25	10.58	10.27	13.01	12.03	11.93	13.16
17907	11290	1989	1722	762	787	1357
34.91	35.01	35.76	35.80	37.33	26.57	37.36
38.23	38.28	40.39	39.77	40.64	27.66	40.27
88.42	90.32	85.02	85.00	85.15	81.28	87.01
100.00	100.00	100.00	100.00	100.00	100.00	100.00

表 13－3 各县(市)环境保护基本情况(2013)
Basic Statistics on Environment Protection, Enviroment Sanitation by Region

指标	单位	Indicators	Unit
废水排放总量	**万吨**	**Volume of Waste Water Discharged**	**10000 tons**
工业废水排放总量	万吨	Industrial Waste Water Discharged	10000 tons
生活污水排放量	万吨	Discharged Amount of Living Sewage	10000 tons
化学需氧量(COD)排放量	**吨**	**Discharged Amount of Chemical oxygen demand (COD)**	**tons**
工业废水中化学需氧排放量	吨	Discharged Amount of COD in Industrial Waste Water	tons
工业用水总量	万吨	Water Consumption for Industrial Use	10000 tons
工业重复用水率	%	Rate of Water Utilized Repeatedly in Industry	%
废水治理设施数	套	Number of Administration Facility of Waste Water	unit
工业废气排放量	**亿标立米**	**Industrial Waste Gas Emission**	**100 million cu. m**
工业二氧化硫排放量	吨	Industrial Sulphur Dioxide Emission	ton
工业氮氧化物(NOx)排放量	吨	Industrial Nitrogen Oxide (NOx) Emissions	ton
工业烟尘排放量	吨	Soot Emission	ton
一般工业固体废物产生量	**万吨**	**Volume of Industrial Solid Wastes Produced**	**10000 tons**
一般工业固体废物综合利用量	万吨	Volume of General Industrial Solid Waste Utilized	10000 tons
一般工业固体废物处理量	万吨	Volume of General Industial Solid Waste Treated	10000 tons
一般工业固体废物倾倒丢弃量	吨	Volume of General Industrial Solid Wastes Dumped Discarded	ton
工业固体废物综合利用率	%	Rate of Industrial Solid Waste Utilized	%
工业固体废物处置利用率	%	Rate of Industrial Solid Waste Treated and Utilized	%
工业污染处理本年施工项目数	个	Number of Projects Treating Industrial Pollution	unit
建设项目"三同时"环保投资额	万元	Investment Amount of Construction Project " Three Simultaneous " of Environment Protection	10000 yuan
环境噪声达标面积	平方公里	Standardization Areas of Environment Noise	sq. km

注:本表数据来自宁波市环境保护局。工业"三废"统计范围为重点调查工业企业与非重点调查单位测算之和。

Note:a)Data in this table are obtained from Ningbo Environment Protection Bureau. b)Statistical Information of Waste Water,Waste Gas and Waste Residue Collected is calculated data that investigate industrial enterprise especially and non－investigate unit especially

全市 Total	市区 Urban Districts	#鄞州 Yinzhou	余姚 Yuyao	慈溪 Cixi	奉化 Fenghua	象山 Xiangshan	宁海 Ninghai
56197.00	31366.82	8168.35	6126.43	9044.60	2908.70	3635.44	3115.01
19666.24	12725.46	1879.93	1534.81	1827.96	1243.70	1714.32	620.00
36530.76	18641.36	6288.42	4591.63	7216.64	1665.00	1921.12	2495.02
63810.00	**27608.43**	**9345.93**	**9222.32**	**9122.96**	**4949.71**	**6453.63**	**5382.18**
19873.05	10511.34	1948.93	3449.50	2337.10	1169.90	1720.30	684.90
1068300.40	1036892.92	6274.09	2919.54	4822.69	1771.68	12057.82	9835.75
46.36	45.72	61.86	15.16	47.55	16.24	82.19	84.62
928	481	114	49	139	114	84	61
6486.95	**4242.83**	**94.78**	**262.37**	**123.81**	**15.47**	**724.67**	**1117.81**
134630	95849	4458	5268	8548	2393	7368	15204
212519	136806	2973	5497	3241	556	23976	42443
25275	14620	1751	2922	2240	545	2832	2115
1343.04	**987.68**	**16.16**	**12.77**	**21.18**	**5.90**	**127.01**	**188.50**
1236.87	903.12	13.46	12.55	11.66	5.84	116.20	187.49
63.68	42.07	3.16	0.22	9.52	0.06	10.81	1.01
90.06	88.96	81.47	91.29	53.78	86.12	91.35	99.38
96.81	95.69	99.92	100.00	99.97	100.00	100.00	100.00
81	49	4	18	7	7		
126530.90	68802.00	3456.00	13567.50	35679.50	784.80	4238.70	3458.40
260.21	151.82	17.93	24.35	31.05	9.09	23.90	20.00

表 13－4 各县(市)社会团体机构情况(2013)
Basic Statistics on Social Organizations and Unions by Region

指标	Indicators	全市 Total
上年准予登记社团机构数	Number of Social Organizations Authorized in Last Year	2159
年末实有社团机构数	Factual Number of Social Organizations at the Year－end	2227
年末实有民办非企业数	Factual Number of Civilian－run Non－enterprises at the Year－end	3161

注:本表至 13－8 表数据来自宁波市民政局。

Note:Data from Tables 13－4 to 13－8 are obtained from Ningbo Municipal Bureau of Civil Affairs.

表 13－5 各县(市)社会福利、优抚、救济工作情况(2013)
Basic Statistics on Social Welfare, Subsidy and Commiseration by Region

指标	单位	Indicators	Unit
收养人数	**人**	**Number of Adopted Persons**	**person**
优待情况		Favoured Treatment	
安置军转干部、士兵	人	Setting Military Cadres or Soldiers Transferred to Civilian Work	person
优待军属户数	户	Service men's Families	household
优待总金额	万元	Total Amount of Give Special Treatment	10000 yuan
抚恤、补助情况		**Special Pensions, Allowances and Relief**	
年末享受定补人数	人	Number of Persons Receiving Periodical Subsidies at the Year－end	person
＃在乡复员军人	人	Rural Demobilized Soldiers	person
＃在乡退伍军人	人	Rural Veteransn	person
伤残人员	人	Number of Wounded or Disabled Health	person
年末定期抚恤人数	人	Number of Persons Receiving Periodical Commiseration	person
＃烈士家属	人	Members of Revolutionary Martyr's Family	person

单位：个(unit)

市区 Urban District	#鄞州 Yinzhou	余姚 Yuyao	慈溪 Cixi	奉化 Fenghua	象山 Xiangshan	宁海 Ninghai
1192	172	196	280	158	168	165
1229	180	199	290	170	170	169
1470	376	354	616	193	189	339

全市 Total	市区 Urban District	#鄞州 Yinzhou	余姚 Yuyao	慈溪 Cixi	奉化 Fenghua	象山 Xiangshan	宁海 Ninghai
394	**74**	**21**	**67**	**89**	**45**	**61**	**58**
2581	896	400	418	507	243	222	295
4160	874	226	843	907	506	428	602
6298.30	2012.90	561.50	1250.40	1058.10	640.70	545.10	791.10
21791	6204	3027	2499	4468	2976	1663	3981
2843	1032	538	363	677	276	272	223
12881	2769	1443	1688	2061	2536	760	3067
2408	988	308	330	468	228	174	220
758	324	92	110	132	63	51	78
368	142	60	69	48	24	34	51

表 13－6 民政部门收养性福利优抚事业情况(2013) Basic Statistics on Adopting, Welfare & Special Pensions by Civil Administration Department

指标	单位	Indicators	Unit	全市 Total	其中 of Which	
					#市区 Urban District	光荣院 Homes for Disabled Veterans
收养性福利单位数	**个**	**Number of Adopting Socail Welfare Units**	**unit**	**22**	**16**	**2**
全部职工人数	**人**	**Total Numeber Staff and Workers**	**person**	**518**	**395**	**17**
#女性	人	Female	person	346	275	7
年末固定资产原值	**万元**	**Original Value of Fixed Assets at the Year－end**	**10000 yuan**	**14455**	**13263**	**95**
各院病床数	**张**	**Number of Beds in Each Hospital**	**bed**	**5049**	**3827**	**66**
年末在院人数	**人**	**In－patients at the Year－end**	**person**	**3062**	**2343**	**31**
#优抚人员	人	Adopting Persons for Enjoying Favoured Treatment	person	114	101	31
"三无"对象人员	人	Non Depending on, Non Ability to Labor and Non Income	person	615	509	
自费人员	人	Persons on Self－expense	person	2333	1733	
#老年人	人	Old People	person	2127	1515	31
青壮年人员	人	Young People	person	520	494	
少年儿童	人	Juvenile and Child	person	415	334	

表 13－6 续表 Continued

指标	单位	Indicators	Unit	其中 of Which		
				社会福利院 Social Welfare Homes	儿童福利院 Welfare Homes for Children	精神病福利院 Welfare Homes for Mental Patients
收养性福利单位数	**个**	**Number of Adopting Socail Welfare Units**	**unit**	**18**	**1**	**1**
全部职工人数	**人**	**Total Numeber Staff and Workers**	**person**	**430**	**24**	**47**
#女性	人	Female	person	298	19	22
年末固定资产原值	**万元**	Original Value of Fixed Assets at the Year－end	**10000** yuan	**7382**	**1549**	**5430**
各院病床数	张	Number of Beds in Each Hospital	bed	4319	304	360
年末在院人数	人	In－patients at the Year－end	person	2367	304	360
#优抚人员	人	Adopting Persons for Enjoying Favoured Treatment	person	23		60
"三无"对象人员	人	Non Depending on, Non Ability to Labor and Non Income	person	329	228	58
自费人员	人	Persons on Self－expense	person	2015	76	242
#老年人	人	Old People	person	1946		150
青壮年人员	人	Young People	person	315		205
少年儿童	人	Juvenile and Child	person	106	304	5

表 13－7 城乡居民最低生活保障情况(2013)
Basic Statistics on Receiving Lowest Cost－of－living in Urban and Rural Area

地区	Region	社会救济总人数(人) Number of Persons Receiving Relief (person)	城镇低保人数(人) Number of ①RLCU (person)	城镇低保家庭数(户) Households of RLCU ① (household)	城镇低保资金支出(万元) Expenditure for RLCU (10000 yuan)	农村低保人数(人) Number of RLCR② and Receiving Relief (person)	农村低保家庭数(户) Households of RLCR② (household)	农村救济资金支出(万元) Expenditure for RLCR② (10000 yuan)
宁波市	**Total**	**55235**	**8625**	**6211**	**4843.60**	**46610**	**31234**	**18072**
市区	Urban District	11487	5868	4209	3597.80	5619	3497	3405
#鄞州区	Yinzhou	4510	688	448	400.40	3822	2194	2301
余姚市	Yuyao	9493	804	605	412.90	8689	5055	3070
慈溪市	Cixi	8716	562	411	285.70	8154	5522	3678
奉化市	Fenghua	7688	605	438	239.00	7083	5364	2488
象山县	Xiangshan	8999	486	342	200.70	8513	5452	2665
宁海县	Ninghai	8852	300	206	107.50	8552	6344	2766

注:①RLCU 是城镇低保的缩写。
②RLCR 是农村低保的缩写
Note:①RLCU is the short form that means Receiving Lowest Cost－of－living in Urban Area.
②RLCR is the short form that means Receiving Lowest Cost－of－living in Rural Area.

表 13－8 社会收容遣送情况(2013)
Basic Statistics on Accepted and Relief

	遣送站情况 Repatriated Units			本年救助(人次) Relief Person in this Year (person－times)
	站数(个) Number of Units (unit)	年末职工人数(人) Number of Staff and Workers (person)	年末固定资产原值(万元) Original Value of Fixed Assets (10000 yuan)	
全市总计 Total	8	59	2172.90	6234

表 13－9 各县(市)妇联工会组织及活动情况(2013)
Basic Statistics on Women Federation and Trade Unions by Region

指标	单位	Indicators	Unit
妇联组织机构		**Women's Federation**	
市、县(市)区妇联	个	Women's Federation in Municipal, County and Urban District	unit
镇、乡(街道)妇联	个	Women's Federation in Township, Town (Subdistrict)	unit
基层妇代会	个	Basic－Level Women Congress	unit
机关事业单位妇委会	个	Women Commission of Agencies and Institutions	unit
团体会员	个	Group Member	unit
人员状况		**Cadre of Women's Federation**	
市、县(市)区级干部	人	Level of Municipal, County and Urban District	person
镇、乡(街道)级干部	人	Cadre in Township, Town(Subdistrict)	person
妇联工作情况		**Works of Women's Federation**	
双学双比及巾帼建功活动		Activity of Double Study And Double Compare, And Women Making Contribution	
参赛数	万人	Number of Participants	10000 persons
#女农民技术人员	人	Female Peasant Technician	person
先进女能手	人	Female Advanced Expert	person
巾帼建功先进个人	人	Advanced Women by Making Contribution	person
工会基本情况		**Trade Unions**	
1. 基层工会数	个	Number of Trade Unions at Basic－Level	unit
2. 工会专职干部人数	人	Number of Full－Time Cadres of Trade Unions	person
3. 建立工会单位全部职工	人	Total Staff And Workers of Establishing Trade Unions	person
#女职工	人	Female Staff And Workers	person
工会会员	人	Member of Trade Unions	person
#女会员	人	Female Member	person
4. 本年度职工提出合理化建议	件	Advanced Rationalization Proposals	case
本年度已实施合理化建议	件	Implement Rationalization Proposals	case
本年度已实施合理化建议产生的效益	万元	Economic Benefit Created by Rationalization Proposals	10000 yuan

注:本表数据来自宁波市总工会和宁波市妇联。

Note: Date in this table are obtained from Ningbo Federation of Trade Unions and Ningbo Women's Federation.

全市 Total	市区 Urban District	#鄞州 Yinzhou	余姚 Yuyao	慈溪 Cixi	奉化 Fenghua	象山 Xiangshan	宁海 Ninghai
12	7	1	1	1	1	1	1
148	61	23	22	18	11	18	18
6624	2550	1488	265	274	1579	1568	388
510	288	48	35	53	48	61	25
49	21	5	5	12	5	4	2
118	76	9	10	9	9	8	6
226	113	53	22	18	14	27	32
57.69	1.85	1.05	28.00	1.00	14.00	9.84	3.00
403	257	78	16	80	28		22
54	5	2	10	12		2	25
153	25	11	10	22		8	88
27293	14675	4764	3584	3334	1809	2255	1636
1210	509	105	278	162	66	117	78
3597283	1970094	628311	474555	486440	230404	232525	203265
1563648	862093	267084	233590	210469	91555	76102	89839
3488933	1913826	597093	450932	480555	218726	223526	199868
1534743	846054	257232	228404	208314	90134	73919	88918
74724	54679	67	12825	5634	337	514	735
38803	30674	28	4160	3062	246	336	325
65201.00	49690	44	10817	3329	385	600	380

表 13－10　各县(市)、区公务员及参照公务员管理的群团机关工作人员情况(2013)
Basic Statistics on Civil Servant and Employee Refer to Civil Servant in Government Organ by Region

单位:人(person)

指标	Indicators	合计 Total	其中:女 of which: Female	按行政级别分 By Administrations Level 省部级 Province Level	地厅司局级 Department/ Bureau Level	县处级 County Level	乡科级 Section Chief	科员及以下 Section and Below
全市	**Total**	**28114**	**6969**		**292**	**7198**	**16225**	**4399**
市直单位	Municipal Department	7125	1497		265	3637	2689	534
市区	Urban Districts	9319	2518		23	3388	5185	723
海曙区	Haishu	1098	331		4	391	599	104
江东区	Jiangdong	1016	298		5	404	553	54
江北区	Jiangbei	1260	353		5	455	710	90
镇海区	Zhenhai	1369	346		4	514	746	105
北仑区	Beilun	1835	452		2	630	1081	122
鄞州区	Yinhzou	2741	738		3	994	1496	248
县合计	**Total of County**	**11670**	**2954**		**4**	**173**	**8351**	**3142**
余姚	Yuyao	2717	702		1	38	1984	694
慈溪	Cixi	2861	768		2	40	2041	778
奉化	Fenghua	1963	500		1	34	1425	503
象山	Xiangshan	2096	523			32	1411	653
宁海	Ninghai	2033	461			29	1490	514

表 13－11 部分年份律师、公证工作基本情况
Basic Statistics on Lawyers and Notarization in Partial Years

指标	Indicators	2010	2011	2012	2013
律师工作情况	**Lawyers**				
律师事务所(个)	Number of Law Offices (unit)	113	121	128	129
个人律师事务所(个)	Personal Law Office(unit)		32	34	35
合伙制律师事务所(个)	Law Offices in Partnership(unit)	83	89	94	94
律师数(人)	Number of Lawyers (person)	1228	1390	1495	1733
#专职律师(人)	Full－time Lawyers (person)	1066	1302	1437	1556
聘请担任常年法律顾问单位(家)	Number of Units with Permanent Legal Advisors (unit)	4368	7079	5265	5378
民事案件代理(件)	Agent of Civil Cases (case)	17934	27819	20492	21673
经济案件代理(件)	Agent of Economic Cases (case)				
#索回赔数 (万元)	Debt and Indemnity Claimed (10000 yuan)				
刑事辩护和代理(件)	Agent of Criminal Defense (case)	3354	6003	3715	3920
非诉讼法律事务(件)	Agent of Non－Litigious Legal Affairs (case)	1614	1761	1495	1441
行政案件代理(件)	Agent of Administrative Action (case)	666	731	611	292
涉外及港澳台法律事务(件)	Legal Affairs With Foreign、HongKong、Macao、Taiwan(case)	27	24		4
解答法律文书(件)	Legal Advisory Services (case)	22023	5676	22518	21194
代写法律文书(件)	Legal Document Written on Behalf of Clients(case)	3296	4920	2688	3139
公证工作情况	**Notarization**				
公证处(个)	Notary Offices (unit)	11	11	11	11
#办理涉外公证(人)	Registered Foreign Affairs (person)	31	31	33	29
公证人员人数(人)	Notarial Personnel (person)	132	90	91	150
#公证员(人)	Notaries(person)	52	53	56	56
办理公证事项(件)	Notarized Documents (case)	65525	62851	60899	83564
国内经济公证(件)	Domestic Economic Affairs(case)	12941	10308	8567	8726
国内民事公证(件)	Domestic Civil Affairs(case)	32242	32020	27578	36467
涉外及港澳台公证(件)	Documents on Foreign、HongKong、Macao、Taiwan(case)	20342	20523	24664	38371
接待来访 (人次)	Reception (person－times)	42658	75693	5896	31580
处理来信 (件)	Treatment (case)	389	230	162	102

表 13－12　部分年份基层司法工作及人民调解情况
Basic Statistics on Basic－Level Judicial Work and People Mediation in Partial Years

指标	Indicators	2010	2011	2012	2013
基层法律服务	**Basic－Level Service for Legal Advice**				
司法助理员人数（人）	Number of Judicial Assistants (person)	790	268	397	968
专职司法助理员（人）	Full－Time Judicial Assistants(person)	527	268	291	660
兼职司法助理员（人）	Part－Time Judicial Assistants (person)	263		106	308
基层法律服务所（所）	**Basic－Level Service for Legal Advice (unit)**	**76**	**74**	**74**	**74**
配备工作人员（人）	Provide Staff (person)	502	497	463	517
代理讼诉事务（件）	Agent of Litigious Affairs (case)	9460	9380	10763	9958
代理非讼诉事务（件）	Agent of Non－Litigious Legal Affairs (case)	1824	966	1067	990
调解纠纷（件）	Mediating Disputes (case)	1867	320	3153	2369
协办公证（件）	Handling Document Jointly (case)				
见证（件）	Witness (case)				
担任法律顾问（件）	Taking Legal Advisors (case)	2229	2550	6348	4142
代写法律文书（件）	Legal Document Written on Behalf of Clients (case)		3127	965	649
解答法律咨询人次（人次）	Legal Advisory Services (person－times)	31817	3350	37307	60770
挽回经济损失（万元）	Economic Loss Avoided and Reclaimed (10000 yuan)	54866	41688	47232	12324
办理法律援助事务（件）	Handling Succorab leLegal Affairs (case)	1311	6038	545	15534
参与司法行政工作（人次）	Participating Judicial Administration (person－times)	433	247	124	
人民调解工作	**Peoples Mediation**				
人民调解委员会（个）	Peoples Mediation Committees (unit)	5213	4786	4793	4683
调解人员数（人）	Number of Mediators (person)	20701	18379	19251	18895
调解纠纷总件数（件）	Number of Mediating Disputes (case)	106291	127927	126447	117549
调解成功件数（件）	Number of Success (case)	104600	126154	124658	115624
婚姻、继承、赡养抚养（件）	Marrige, Rights of Inheritance, Supporting and Fostering (case)	6159	7722	7010	6151
房屋宅基地（件）	Ground of Building (case)	3729	4240	3542	2792
债务（件）	Debt (case)	2932	2876	3670	2088

注：本表数据来自宁波市司法局。

表 13—12 续表 Continued

指标	Indicators	2010	2011	2012	2013
生产经营（件）	Production & Management (case)	8644	1046	1665	1323
邻里关系（件）	Relation of Neighborhood (case)	18704	21291	18366	15473
赔偿（件）	Compensation (case)	49751	15842	12772	15441
其他调解（件）	Other Mediating (case)	12983	73137	79152	74281
调解纠纷成功率（%）	Rate of Mediating Success (%)	98.4	98.6	98.6	98.4
防止可能发生非正常死亡事件（件）	Avoiding Accident of Abnormal Deaths (case)	15	36	29	34
防止可能发生非正常死亡人次（人次）	Avoiding Accident Times of Abnormal Deaths (person—times)	15	55	36	34
安置帮教工作情况	**Placement and help and Educate**				
刑释人员数(当年)(人)	Number of Ex—Convict Personnel in this Year (person)	1936	2411	2667	3223
刑释人员数(五年内)(人)	Number of Ex—Convict Personnel in Current 5 Years (person)	11128	12296	12889	13421
解教人员数(当年)(人)	Number of Unchain Labor Reeducation in this Year(person)	289	170	118	128
刑释人员安置数(当年)(人)	Number of Placement of Ex—convict in this Year (person)	2051	2441	2662	3196
刑释人员帮教数(当年)(人)	Number of Help&Educate of Ex—convictin this Year(person)	2155	2523	2729	2653
重新犯罪人数(当年)(人)	Number of Re—criminal in this Year(person)	163	113	155	140
重新劳教人数(当年)(人)	Number of Again Labor Reeducation in this Year (person)	17	10	11	2
监狱，劳教工作	**Prison and Labor Reeducation**				
市属监狱（所）	Number of Prison (unit)	2	2	2	2
年内新收押罪犯(人)	Detain Criminal in this Year(person)	5483	3497	337	4249
年内刑满释放(人)	Ex—Convict Personnel in this Year(person)	3139	2693	2755	3833
市属劳教所(所)	Numbet of Labor Reeducation Unit (unit)	1	1	1	1
年内新收容劳教人员(人)	Newly Accept Labor Reeducation Personnel in this Year(person)	545	383	393	17
年内解除劳教(人)	Unchain Labor Reeducation (person)	662	541	387	370
年内新收容收教人员(人)	Newly Accept Take in Reeducation Personnel in this Year(person)	59	29	28	31
年内解除收教(人)	Unchain Labor Reeducation (person)	67	32	27	29

Note: Data in this table are obtained from Bureau of Justice of Ningbo Municipality.

表 13－13　二级人民法院收、结案情况(2013)
Cases Accepted & Settled by People's Court

单位:件(case)

指标	Indicators	上年留案 Retained in Last Year	全年新收案 New Accepted in this Year	办结案件数 Number of Cases Closed	年末未结案件 Retained Caseat Year－end
总计	**Total**	**10905**	**142684**	**142354**	**11235**
一审案件数	Number of First Trial Cases	7879	85219	85128	7970
刑事	Criminal Case	345	13013	13051	307
民商事	Civil & Economic Case	7497	71699	71564	7632
行政	Administrative Case	37	507	513	31
二审案件数	Number of Second Trial Case	350	4253	4278	325
刑事	Criminal Case	32	605	607	30
民事	Civil Case	147	2212	2182	177
经济	Economic Case	158	1261	1309	110
行政	Administrative Case	13	175	180	8
审判监督	Number of Cases Judged and Supervised	27	187	182	32
刑事	Criminal Case	2	60	49	13
民商事	Civil & Economic Case	25	127	133	19
行政	Administrative Case				
执行	Carry out Case	2616	44541	44295	2862
刑事案件(有财产部分)	Criminal Case (With Property)	60	987	991	56
民事	Civil Case	2328	32683	32380	2631
行政	Administrative Case		25	25	
行政非审查与执行	Administration No－examine and Carry Out	76	2617	2649	44
其他案件	Others Case	152	8229	8250	131
申诉申请再审	Appeal and Applying for Review	19	580	557	42
司法赔偿	Juridical Compensation		6	6	
减刑	Commutation		4376	4376	
假释	Parolee		625	625	

表 13－14 人民法院及检察院补充信息(2013)
Added Information of People's Court and Procurator's Offices

指标	单位	Indicators	unit	总计 Total
人民法院		**People's Court**		
办结申诉申请再审案件	件	Appeal and Applying for Review Closed	case	557
处理群众来信	件次	Deal with Letter from People	case－times	2528
群众来访人数	人次	People Come to Appeal for Help	person－times	3344
判决被告人	人	Adjudge defendant	person	17771
判处罪犯		Sentence Criminals	person	17769
宣告无罪	人	Declare Innocent	person	2
五年以上有期徒刑直到无期徒刑	人	Fixed－term Imprisonment of More than 5 years until Life Imprisonment	person	1388
不满五年有期徒刑	人	Fixed－term Imprisonment of Below 5 years	person	7189
缓刑	人	Probation	person	5103
免于刑事处分	人	Avoid Criminal Sanction	person	43
其他处理	人	Others	person	4046
#18－25周岁罪犯	人	Between 18 until 25 Years Old	person	3893
#少年犯	人	Juvenile Criminal	person	762
#女性犯罪	人	Female Criminal	person	37
一审民商案件中解决争议标的	万元	Solve Amount of Disputed Bid for Civil & Economic Case in First Instance	10000 yuan	3558137
执行案件中执结标的	万元	Carry out Amount of Money in Carry out Case	10000 yuan	1605409
办结经济犯罪	件	Closed Economic Criminal	case	1388
为国家，集体挽回经济损失	万元	Retrieve Economic Losses for State & Collective	10000 yuan	7824
办结申请公示催告和支付令的案	件	Closed Apply to Show the Demand Commonly & Indemnity	case	1159
标的	万元	Total Amount of Money	10000 yuan	190
检察机关		**Procurator's Offices**		
立案查处贪污贿赂犯罪	件	Cases Registered for Corruption and Bribery	case	185
立案查处贪污贿赂犯罪	人	Cases Registered for Corruption and Bribery	person	242
立案查处渎职侵权犯罪	件	Cases Registered for Abuse and Dereliction of Duty	case	37
立案查处渎职侵权犯罪	人	Cases Registered for Abuse and Dereliction of Duty	person	59
批捕各类犯罪嫌疑人	人	Approve to Arrest Crime Suspects	person	11000
起诉各类犯罪被告人	人	Accuse Crime Suspects	person	18041
受理群众来信来访	件	Accept Public Report, Accuse Crime and Visit	case	2363
举报	件	Reporting of the Offence	case	624
控告	件	Accuse	case	592
申诉	件	Appeal	case	47
提出民事行政抗诉	件	Submit Civil and Administrative Counterappeal.	case	13

表 13－15 各县(市)火灾情况(2013)
Basic Statistics on Fires by Region

指标	单位	Indicators	Unit	全市 Total
火灾起因情况		**Cause of Fire**		
放火	起	Arson	case	93
电器	起	Electric Appliances	case	1606
违章操作	起	Operation Against Rules	case	
生产作业	起	Production Operations	case	187
吸烟	起	Smoking	case	138
其他原因	起	Others	case	3055
重大火灾		**Heavy Fire**		
起火	起	Fire	case	
损失	万元	Losses	10000 yuan	
死亡	人	Deaths	person	
损失情况		**Situation of Losses**		
起数	起	Number	case	6949
死亡	人	Deaths	person	22
伤人	人	Injuries	person	44
损失	万元	Losses	10000 yuan	9005.38

市区 Urban District	#鄞州 Yinzhou	余姚 Yuyao	慈溪 Cixi	奉化 Fenghua	象山 Xiangshan	宁海 Ninghai
61	15	6	4	2	19	1
795	246	116	178	261	113	143
91	18	17	24	27	17	11
72	4	15	32	1	9	9
1616	727	679	656	15	250	39
3385	1250	1006	1143	597	463	355
11	3	2	4	3	1	1
31	15	4	8			1
5004.51	1216.86	1226.43	656.82	201.39	531.24	1384.99

表 13－16 交通事故情况(2013)
Basic Statistics on Traffic Accident

指标	Indicators	合计(Total)			
		事故次数(次) Number of Accident (case)	死亡人数(人) Deaths (person)	受伤人数(人) Injuries (person)	直接损失(万元) Direct Pecunlary Losses (10000 yuan)
总计	**Total**	**2791**	**655**	**2807**	**724.97**
机动车	Motor Vehicles	2425	590	2415	660.12
客运车辆	Passenger Vehicles	68	8	89	21.41
公共汽车	Buses	27	6	24	4.45
一般货运	General Cargos	413	163	329	124.19
企事业单位	Institutions and Enterprises	24	9	18	10.02
军队武警	Armed Forces	4		5	2.20
私用轿车	Individuals	881	138	901	240.98
其他	Others	600	160	568	159.77
摩托车	Motorcycles	347	85	431	82.66
拖拉机	Tractors	61	21	50	14.44
非机动车	Non－motor－driven Vehicles	354	59	385	60.29
其他及行人	Others and Pedestrians	12	6	7	5

城市(Urban)				农村(Rural)			
事故次数(次) Number of Accident (case)	死亡人数(人) Deaths (person)	受伤人数(人) Injuries (person)	直接损失(万元) Direct Pecunlary Losses (10000 yuan)	事故次数(次) Number of Accident (case)	死亡人数(人) Deaths (person)	受伤人数(人) Injuries (person)	直接损失(万元) Direct Pecunlary Losses (10000 yuan)
1149	**175**	**1206**	**238.10**	**1642**	**480**	**1601**	**486.87**
984	155	1024	215.85	1441	435	1391	444.27
37	2	44	11.35	31	6	45	10.06
17	5	13	2.04	10	1	11	2.41
116	37	94	33.85	297	126	235	90.34
5		6	2.00	19	9	12	8.02
2		2	2.10	2		3	0.10
444	48	461	83.65	437	90	440	157.33
222	41	218	43.27	378	119	350	116.50
129	18	176	34.25	218	67	255	48.41
12	4	10	3.34	49	17	40	11.10
159	17	179	19.97	195	42	206	40.32
6	3	3	2.3	6	3	4	2.17

表 13—17 全市档案人员及馆藏和编研情况(2013)
Conditions of Files Stored and Used in the Archives

指标	单位	Indicators	Unit	全市 Total	其中 of Which 市局馆 Municipal	市区合计 Urban District	县市合计 County
机构数	个	**Number of Institutions**	**unit**				
档案行政管理机构(档案馆)	个	Administrative Department of Archives	unit	12	1	6	5
现有工作人员数	人	Number of Staff and Workers	person				
档案行政管理机构(档案馆)	人	Administrative Department of Archives	person	178	39	60	79
馆藏档案		**Archives Stored**					
全宗	个	Whole Volume	unit	2639	440	865	1334
案卷	卷	Files	volume	1360575	229619	403817	727139
以件为保管单位档案	件	Archives Which Regard a Storage Unit by Files	pieces	412968	51835	218227	142906
录音、录象影片档案	盘	Records,Films on Videotape	copy	2752	564	734	1454
照片档案	张	Pictures	pieces	210344	30327	84282	95735
馆藏资料	册	Number of Material Stored	volume	103583	32450	38174	32959
档案馆总建筑面积	平方米	Floor Space of Archives	sq. m	38595	7900	16950	13745
档案库房建筑面积	平方米	Floor Space of Storerooms	sq. m	15302	3500	6954	4848
本年档案资料利用		Use of Material in This Year					
利用人次	人次	Number of Persons Using Material	times	41527	2758	13822	24947
利用档案	卷次	Number of Archives Used	volume	70574	10867	23334	36373
利用资料	册次	Number of Material Used	times	5799	3033	1981	785
利用档案	件次	Number of Archives Used	times	3446		1396	2050
本年编研档案资料内部参考	万字	**Compiling and Researching Material Restricted**	**10000 words**	**62**		**19**	**44**
本年编研档案资料公开出版物	万字	**Public Press Compiling and Researching Material**	**10000 words**	**639**	**457.8**	**135.6**	**45.6**

注:统计范围:市,县(市)区档案局,国家综合档案馆

Note:Statistical Limits are Archives of Each District and County

主要统计指标解释

【全年供水总量】 指公用自来水厂和自备水源的社会单位全年的供水总量,包括有效供水量及损失水量。

【城市人口用水普及率】 指城市用水的非农业人口数(不包括临时人口和流动人口)与城市非农业人口总数的比例。计算公式:

用水普及率=(城市用水的非农业人口数÷城市非农业人口数)×100%

【公共绿地】 指供游览休息的各种公园、动物园、植物园、陵园、以及花园、游园和供旅游休息用的林荫道绿地、广场绿地。不包括一般栽植的行道树及林荫道的面积。

【废水排放总量】 包括生产废水和生活污水。生产废水指企、事业单位在生产、科研过程中向外排放的所有排放口的废水量总和。生活污水指城镇居民区和企、事业单位职工集中居住区排放的污水量。

【工业废水排放量】 指经过企业厂区所有排放口排到企业外部的工业废水量 。包括生产废水、外排的直接冷却水、超标排放的矿井地下水和与工业废水混排的厂区生活污水,不包括外排的间接冷却水(清污不分流的间按冷却水应计算在内)。

【工业废水排放达标量】 指各项指标都达到国家或地方排放标准的外排工业废水量,包括未经处理外排达标的和经过处理后外排达标的和两部分。国家排放标准见 GB8978－88。

【工业废气排放量】 指企业厂区内燃料燃烧和生产工艺过程中产生的各种排入空气的含有污染物的气体的总量,以标准状态(273K,101325Pa)计。

【工业粉尘排放量】 指企业在生产工艺过程中排放的颗粒物重量。如钢铁企业的耐火材料粉尘、焦化企业的筛焦系统粉尘、烧结机的粉尘、石灰窑的粉尘、建材企业的水泥粉尘等。不包括电厂排入大气的烟尘。

【工业粉尘回收量】 指经生产工艺废气净化处理装置处理回收的粉尘和尘泥量(包括干法和湿法)。不包括电厂的烟尘。通常情况下:

工业粉尘产生量=工业粉尘排放量+工业粉尘回收量

【工业固体废物产生量】 指企业在生产过程中产生的固体状、半固体状和高浓度液体状废弃物的总量,包括危险废物、冶炼废渣、粉煤灰、炉渣、煤矸石、尾矿、放射性 废物和其他废物等;不包括矿山开采的剥离废石和掘进废石(煤矸石和呈酸性或碱性的废石 除外)。酸性或碱性废石是指采掘的废石其流经水、雨淋水的 pH 值小于 4 或 pH 值大于 10.5 者 。

【社会福利事业单位】 指集中收养社会孤老,残,幼的机构。包括由民政部门管理的社会福利院、儿童福利院、精神病人福利院和城镇集体办的福利院,以及农村集体举 办的敬老院。

Explanatory Notes on Main Statistical Indicators

【Annual Volume of Water Supply】 refers to the total volume of water supplied by the public water—works and those owned by individual enterprises and institutions during the whole year, including both the effective water supply and loss during the water supply.

【Percentage of Urban Population with Access to Tap Water】 refers to the ratio of urban non—agricultural population (excluding temporary and mobile population) with access to tap water to the total urban non—agricultural population. The formula is: Percentage of Population with Access to Tap Water=(Urban Non—agricultural Population with Access to Tap Water ÷ Urban Non—agricultural Population) 100%

【Public Green Area】 refers to green areas of various parks, zoos, botanical gardens, cemeteries, amusement parks, tree—flanked boulevards, green—land squares for tourism and relaxation. Area with trees planted along—side the streets and boulevards are excluded.

【Total Discharge of Sewage】 includes production sewage and domestic sewage. Production sewage refers to the total discharge by the enterprises and institutions in their production and scientific research. Domestic sewage refers to the discharge by urban and rural residential communities and the residential neighborhoods of the enterprise/institutions staff.

【Volume of Industrial Waste Water Discharged】 refers to the volume of industrial waste water discharged, through all outlets, to the outside of industrial enterprises, including waste water produced, direct cooling water, underground water from mines that does not meet the standard of discharge, and the domestic sewage mixed up with industrial waste water when discharged, but excluding discharged indirect—cooling water.

【Volume of Waste Water up to the Standard for Discharge】 refers to the volume of discharged industrial waste water that, with or without treatment, has come up to the national or local standards for discharge.

【Volume of Waste Gas Emission】 refers to waste gas emitted from burning of fuels and from production process in the area of the factory, and is measured by 10000 standard cubic metres each year under normal condition.

【Industrial Dust Discharged】 refers to the total weight of solid dust discharged by industrial enterprises in the production process, such as dust of refractory materials from iron plants, dust from coke—screening system or from sintering machines of coking plants, dust from lime kilns, cement dust from building material enterprises, etc. but excluding smoke and dust discharged by power plants.

【Volume of Recovery of Industrial Dust】 refers to the volume of dust and dirt recovered by production process purification devices, including both dry process and wet process, not the fly ash emitted into the air by power station. Generally, the formula goes:

Industrial Dust Produced=Industrial Dust Emitted + Industrial Dust Recovered

【Volume of Industrial Solid Wastes Produced】 refers to the total volume of solid, semi-solid or high concentration liquid residue produced by industrial enterprises in their production process, including dangerous wastes, residues from melting, slag, powdered coal ash, gangue, chemical residues, tailings, radioactive residues and other residues, but excluding stripped or dug stones in mining (except gangue and acid or alkali stones which are stones washed or soaked by water with a pH value smaller than 4 or larger than 10.5.)

【Social Welfare Institutions】 refer to institutions taking care of old people without children, handicapped people and orphans. They include social welfare institutions run by civil affairs departments, children's welfare institutions social welfare institutions for mental patients, and collective-owned old people's homes in tualareas.

CHAPTER 14

NINGBO 2014

Statistical YearBook

第十四篇

企业景气指数

PROSPERITY INDEX ON ENTERPRISES

企业景气
Prosperity on Enterprises

主要统计指标
Major Statistics Indicators

		第一季度 1st. Quarter	第二季度 2st. Quarter	第三季度 3st. Quarter	第四季度 4st. Quarter
企业家信心指数	Index of Confidence by Enterprisers				
指数	Index	122.6	114.5	125.7	118.2
即期	Demand	119.9	114.9	124.0	122.7
预期	Expectation	124.4	114.1	126.8	115.2
企业景气指数	Prosperity index of Enterprises				
指数	Index	130.8	122.6	127.9	122.1
即期	Demand	123.2	120.6	125.2	128.0
预期	Expectation	135.8	124.0	129.6	118.2
工业企业	Industrial Enterprises				
指数	Index	138.8	126.5	129.7	125.0
即期	Demand	129.2	125.2	128.9	135.9
预期	Expectation	145.1	127.4	130.3	117.7
建筑业企业	Construction Enterprises				
指数	Index	157.6	153.7	153.7	147.8
即期	Demand	148.8	146.3	146.3	153.7
预期	Expectation	163.4	158.5	158.5	143.9
交通运输、仓储和邮政业企业	Transport. Storage and Post Enterprises				
指数	Index	118.1	113.6	129.7	123.9
即期	Demand	106.5	109.7	125.8	125.8
预期	Expectation	125.8	116.1	132.3	122.6
批发和零售业企业	Wholesale and Retail Sale Enterprises				
指数	Index	119.2	114.2	122.1	109.6
即期	Demand	116.7	110.4	120.8	108.3
预期	Expectation	120.8	116.7	122.9	110.4
住宿和餐饮业企业	Hotels and Catering Trade Enterprises				
指数	Index	77.4	74.8	85.2	61.3
即期	Demand	58.1	71.0	67.7	61.3
预期	Expectation	90.3	77.4	96.8	61.3
房地产企业	Real Estate Enterprises				
指数	Index	103.2	98.4	111.1	115.1
即期	Demand	107.9	107.9	107.9	113.5
预期	Expectation	100.0	92.1	113.2	116.2
社会服务业企业	Social Services Enterprises				
指数	Index	130.5	129.0	126.5	126.3
即期	Demand	127.5	127.5	125.0	126.3
预期	Expectation	132.5	130.3	127.5	126.3
信息传输、计算机服务和软件业企业	Information Transmission, Computer Service and Software Enterprises				
指数	Index	136.8	133.7	137.4	142.6
即期	Demand	121.1	121.1	126.3	147.4
预期	Expectation	147.4	142.1	144.7	139.5

表 14－1 企业景气指数(2013) Prosperity Index of Enterprises

单位:点(point)

指标	Indicators	一季度 1st. Quarter	二季度 2st. Quarter	三季度 3st. Quarter	四季度 4st. Quarter
企业景气指数	**ProsperityIndexofEnterprises**				
指数	**Index**	**130.8**	**122.6**	**127.9**	**122.1**
即期	**Demand**	**123.2**	**120.6**	**125.2**	**128.0**
预期	**Expectation**	**135.8**	**124.0**	**129.6**	**118.2**
按登记注册类型分	**ByRegistrationStatus**				
国有企业	State－OwnedEnterprises				
指数	Index	151.7	140.0	141.7	133.1
即期	Demand	151.3	137.1	145.4	135.8
预期	Expectation	152.0	142.0	139.2	131.3
有限责任公司	LimitedLiabilityCorporations				
指数	Index	117.9	115.0	115.2	109.3
即期	Demand	112.2	115.7	116.6	118.7
预期	Expectation	121.7	114.5	114.3	103.1
股份有限公司	Share－holdingCorporationsLtd.				
指数	Index	125.3	120.8	128.5	125.3
即期	Demand	117.6	121.2	127.7	121.9
预期	Expectation	130.4	120.6	129.1	127.6
私营企业	PrivateEnterprises				
指数	Index	136.4	119.7	133.0	118.4
即期	Demand	124.4	108.0	124.7	119.8
预期	Expectation	144.3	127.5	138.6	117.5
港、澳、台商投资企业	Hongkong,MacaoandTaiwanFunded				
指数	Index	130.6	123.6	124.2	124.5
即期	Demand	111.3	121.5	121.1	125.7
预期	Expectation	143.4	125.1	126.2	123.6
外商投资企业	EnterpriseswithForeignInvestment				
指数	Index	135.1	113.4	104.8	101.4
即期	Demand	130.8	112.1	93.0	95.4
预期	Expectation	138.0	114.2	112.7	105.4
按行业分	**BySector**				
工业	Industry				
指数	Index	138.8	126.5	129.7	125.0
即期	Demand	129.2	125.2	128.9	135.9
预期	Expectation	145.1	127.4	130.3	117.7

表 14－1 续表 Continued　　单位：点（point）

指标	Indicators	一季度 1st. Quarter	二季度 2st. Quarter	三季度 3st. Quarter	四季度 4st. Quarter
建筑业	Construction				
指数	Index	157.6	153.7	153.7	147.8
即期	Demand	148.8	146.3	146.3	153.7
预期	Expectation	163.4	158.5	158.5	143.9
交通运输、仓储和邮政业	Transport,StorageandPost				
指数	Index	118.1	113.6	129.7	123.9
即期	Demand	106.5	109.7	125.8	125.8
预期	Expectation	125.8	116.1	132.3	122.6
批发和零售业	WholesaleandRetailSaleTrade				
指数	Index	119.2	114.2	122.1	109.6
即期	Demand	116.7	110.4	120.8	108.3
预期	Expectation	120.8	116.7	122.9	110.4
住宿和餐饮业	HotelsandCateringTrade				
指数	Index	77.4	74.8	85.2	61.3
即期	Demand	58.1	71.0	67.7	61.3
预期	Expectation	90.3	77.4	96.8	61.3
房地产业	RealEstate				
指数	Index	103.2	98.4	111.1	115.1
即期	Demand	107.9	107.9	107.9	113.5
预期	Expectation	100.0	92.1	113.2	116.2
社会服务业	SocialServices				
指数	Index	130.5	129.0	126.5	126.3
即期	Demand	127.5	127.5	125.0	126.3
预期	Expectation	132.5	130.0	127.5	126.3
信息传输、计算机服务和软件业	InformationTransmission,Computer Service and Software				
指数	Index	136.8	133.7	137.4	142.6
即期	Demand	121.1	121.1	126.3	147.4
预期	Expectation	147.4	142.1	144.7	139.5
按观察指标分	**BytheObservationIndex**				
盈利(亏损)变化	ChangesofProfit(Loss)	72.2	73.7	75.6	79.6
企业融资	CorporateFinance	87.6	85.3	88.5	85.1
用工计划	EmploymentPlan	114.9	104.6	107.2	106.1
固定资产投资	FixedAsset	92.5	94.9	94.7	90.7
人工成本	Labor Cost	83.1	84.1	82.5	84.0
物料成本	Material Cost	91.5	92.9	94.6	93.4

表 14－2　企业家信心指数(2013)
Index of Confidence on Macro Economy of Enterprisers

单位:点(point)

指标	Indicators	一季度 1st. Quarter	二季度 2st. Quarter	三季度 3st. Quarter	四季度 4st. Quarter
企业家信心指数	**Index of Confidence by Enterprisers**				
指数	**Index**	**122.6**	**114.5**	**125.7**	**118.2**
即期	**Demand**	**119.9**	**114.9**	**124.0**	**122.7**
预期	**Expectation**	**124.4**	**114.1**	**126.8**	**115.2**
按登记注册类型分	**By Registration Status**				
国有企业	State－Owned Enterprises				
指数	Index	151.1	132.7	124.2	127.7
即期	Demand	143.1	120.3	125.0	138.4
预期	Expectation	156.4	140.9	123.7	120.6
有限责任公司	Limited Liability Corporations				
指数	Index	117.2	104.5	111.6	106.0
即期	Demand	117.9	105.3	115.1	113.5
预期	Expectation	116.8	103.9	109.4	100.9
股份有限公司	Share－holding Corporations Ltd.				
指数	Index	125.4	108.6	132.1	118.4
即期	Demand	116.2	111.8	133.2	116.6
预期	Expectation	131.5	106.4	131.3	119.6
私营企业	Private Enterprises				
指数	Index	126.8	118.5	133.7	128.0
即期	Demand	118.2	108.9	123.8	137.4
预期	Expectation	132.5	124.9	140.3	121.7
港、澳、台商投资企业	Hongkong, Macao and Taiwan Funded				
指数	Index	126.1	122.2	119.7	117.3
即期	Demand	119.9	120.0	117.1	122.8
预期	Expectation	130.2	123.7	121.4	113.7
外商投资企业	Enterprises with Foreign Investment				
指数	Index	109.3	107.7	111.1	106.1
即期	Demand	108.1	107.1	108.5	108.8
预期	Expectation	110.2	108.1	112.7	104.3

表 14－2 续表 Continued

单位：点(point)

指标	Indicators	一季度 1st. Quarter	二季度 2st. Quarter	三季度 3st. Quarter	四季度 4st. Quarter
按行业分	**By Sector**				
工业	Industry				
指数	Index	127.4	119.9	124.6	119.2
即期	Demand	121.2	117.8	122.9	125.5
预期	Expectation	131.4	121.3	125.7	115.0
建筑业	Construction				
指数	Index	145.9	148.3	153.7	152.7
即期	Demand	148.8	143.9	153.7	151.2
预期	Expectation	143.9	151.2	153.7	153.7
交通运输、仓储和邮政业	Transport,Storage and Post				
指数	Index	107.7	101.3	132.3	121.9
即期	Demand	100.0	112.9	132.3	125.8
预期	Expectation	112.9	93.6	132.3	119.4
批发和零售业	Wholesale and Retail Sale Trade				
指数	Index	116.3	96.3	123.3	110.0
即期	Demand	125.0	100.0	120.8	112.5
预期	Expectation	110.4	93.8	125.0	108.3
住宿和餐饮业	Hotels and Catering Trade				
指数	Index	95.5	76.8	88.4	56.8
即期	Demand	83.9	80.7	61.3	64.5
预期	Expectation	103.2	74.2	106.5	51.6
房地产业	Real Estate				
指数	Index	91.6	90.5	108.4	94.1
即期	Demand	86.8	92.1	113.2	97.3
预期	Expectation	94.7	89.5	105.3	91.9
社会服务业	Social Services				
指数	Index	129.5	126.0	126.5	131.1
即期	Demand	125.0	127.5	125.0	134.2
预期	Expectation	132.5	125.0	127.5	129.0
信息传输、计算机服务和软件业	Information Transmission,Computer Serviceand Software				
指数	Index	140.0	138.4	141.1	140.5
即期	Demand	144.7	144.7	147.4	150.0
预期	Expectation	136.8	134.2	136.8	134.2

表 14－3　工业企业景气状况(2013)
Prosperity Index of Industrial Enterprises

单位:点(point)

指标	Indicators	一季度 1st. Quarter	二季度 2st. Quarter	三季度 3st. Quarter	四季度 4st. Quarter
企业景气指数	Prosperity Index of Enterprises				
总指数	Combined Index	138.8	126.5	129.7	125.0
即期	Demand	129.2	125.2	128.9	135.9
预期	Expectation	145.1	127.4	130.3	117.7
企业家信心指数	Index of Confidence by Enterprisers				
总指数	Combined Index	127.4	119.9	124.6	119.2
即期	Demand	121.2	117.8	122.9	125.5
预期	Expectation	131.4	121.3	125.7	115.0
产品订货量(与上季度比)	Production Order (Compared with the Previous Quarter)				
指数	Index	91.2	86.1	87.2	92.7
增加(%)	Increase(%)	7.1	5.2	5.1	9.6
持平(%)	Flat(%)	77.0	75.7	77.1	73.6
减少(%)	Decrease(%)	15.9	19.1	17.9	16.8
产品订货中的出口订货量	Export Orders				
指数	Index	92.0	91.3	90.8	93.6
增加(%)	Increase(%)	6.2	5.7	3.2	6.4
持平(%)	Flat(%)	79.7	80.0	84.4	80.9
减少(%)	Decrease(%)	14.2	14.4	12.4	12.7
产成品库存(本季度)	Stock of Finished Production				
指数	Index	102.2	104.8	100.9	102.3
增加(%)	Increase(%)	7.1	7.4	6.4	6.4
持平(%)	Flat(%)	88.1	90.0	88.1	89.6
减少(%)	Decrease(%)	4.9	2.6	5.5	4.1
企业融资(本季度)	Corporate Finance				
指数	Index	76.1	72.2	76.2	71.4
增加(%)	Increase(%)	6.2	4.4	8.3	6.4
持平(%)	Flat(%)	63.7	63.5	59.6	58.6
减少(%)	Decrease(%)	12.0	13.9	16.1	17.3
用工计划(下季度比本季度)	Employment Plan (Next Quarter than the Quarter)				
指数	Index	115.0	103.0	108.7	113.2
增加(%)	Increase(%)	24.8	18.3	20.6	25.9
持平(%)	Flat(%)	65.5	66.5	67.4	61.4
减少(%)	Decrease(%)	9.7	15.2	11.9	12.7
固定资产投资(下季度比本季度)	Fixed Asset (Next Quarter than the Quarter)				
指数	Index	87.2	94.4	94.5	85.5
增加(%)	Increase(%)	15.0	16.1	15.1	10.0
持平(%)	Flat(%)	57.1	62.2	64.2	65.5
减少(%)	Decrease(%)	27.9	21.7	20.6	24.6
企业盈利状况(本季度)	The Profitability of Enterprises				
指数	Index	69.5	73.9	73.9	78.6
增加(%)	Increase(%)	1.8	2.2	1.8	3.2
持平(%)	Flat(%)	65.9	69.6	70.2	72.3
减少(%)	Decrease(%)	32.3	28.3	28.0	24.6

表 14—4 建筑业企业景气状况(2013)
Prosperity Index of Construction Enterprises

单位:点(point)

指标	Indicators	一季度 1st. Quarter	二季度 2st. Quarter	三季度 3st. Quarter	四季度 4st. Quarter
企业景气指数	Prosperity Index of Enterprises				
总指数	Combined Index	157.6	153.7	153.7	147.8
即期	Demand	148.8	146.3	146.3	153.7
预期	Expectation	163.4	158.5	158.5	143.9
企业家信心指数	Index of Confidence by Enterprisers				
总指数	Combined Index	145.9	148.3	153.7	152.7
即期	Demand	148.8	143.9	153.7	151.2
预期	Expectation	143.9	151.2	153.7	153.7
工程合同(比去年同期)	Project Contract Signed (year—on—year)				
指数	Index	82.9	95.1	90.2	97.6
增加(%)	Increase(%)	7.3	9.8	7.3	14.6
持平(%)	Flat(%)	68.3	75.6	75.6	68.3
减少(%)	Decrease(%)	24.4	14.6	17.1	17.1
建筑工程量(比去年同期)	Project Quantity of Construction (year—on—year)				
指数	Index	119.5	119.5	136.6	122.0
增加(%)	Increase(%)	36.6	36.6	43.9	41.5
持平(%)	Flat(%)	46.3	46.3	48.8	39.0
减少(%)	Decrease(%)	17.1	17.1	7.3	19.5
新开工工程量(比去年同期)	New Construction Projects (year—on—year)				
指数	Index	95.1	109.8	92.7	100.0
增加(%)	Increase(%)	24.4	26.8	22.0	29.3
持平(%)	Flat(%)	46.3	56.1	48.8	41.5
减少(%)	Decrease(%)	29.3	17.1	29.3	29.3
建筑材料购进价格(比上季度)	Purchase Price of Building Materials (Compared with the Previous Quarter)				
指数	Index	82.9	95.1	82.9	73.2
下降(%)	Decline(%)	9.8	12.2	4.9	4.9
持平(%)	Flat(%)	63.4	70.7	73.2	63.4
上升(%)	Rise(%)	26.8	17.1	22.0	31.7

表 14—4 续表 Continued　　单位:点(point)

指标	Indicators	一季度 1st. Quarter	二季度 2st. Quarter	三季度 3st. Quarter	四季度 4st. Quarter
盈利(亏损)变化	Changes of Profit(Loss)				
指数	Index	70.7	82.9	82.9	87.8
好于正常水平(%)	Better than Normal Level(%)	0.0	0.0	2.4	7.3
正常水平(%)	Normal Level(%)	70.7	82.9	78.1	73.2
差于正常水平(%)	Worse than Normal Level(%)	29.3	17.1	19.5	19.5
企业融资	Corporate Finance				
指数	Index	95.1	92.7	100.0	97.6
容易(%)	Easy(%)	12.2	14.6	14.6	17.1
一般(%)	General(%)	70.7	63.4	70.7	63.4
困难(%)	Difficulties(%)	17.1	22.0	14.6	19.5
工程款拖欠(比上季度)	Arrears (Compared with the Previous Quarter)				
指数	Index	119.5	73.2	78.1	87.8
减少(%)	Decrease(%)	41.5	14.6	17.1	17.1
持平(%)	Flat(%)	36.6	43.9	43.9	53.7
增加(%)	Increase(%)	22.0	41.5	39.0	29.3
用工计划(下季度比本季度)	Employment Plan (Next Quarter than the Quarter)				
指数	Index	158.5	131.7	131.7	87.8
增加(%)	Increase(%)	61.0	39.0	41.5	19.5
持平(%)	Flat(%)	36.6	53.7	48.8	48.8
减少(%)	Decrease(%)	2.4	7.3	9.8	31.7
固定资产投资(下季度比本季度)	Fixed Asset (Next Quarter than the Quarter)				
指数	Index	114.6	104.9	95.1	102.4
增加(%)	Increase(%)	24.4	19.5	9.8	17.1
持平(%)	Flat(%)	65.9	65.9	75.6	68.3
减少(%)	Decrease(%)	9.8	14.6	14.6	14.6
人工成本(比上季度)	Labor Cost (Compared with the Previous Quarter)				
指数	Index	56.1	36.6	31.7	53.7
下降(%)	Decline(%)	2.4	0.0	0.0	0.0
持平(%)	Flat(%)	51.2	36.6	31.7	53.7
上升(%)	Rise(%)	46.3	63.4	68.3	46.3

表 14—5　交通运输、仓储和邮政业企业景气状况(2013)
Prosperity Index of Transport,Storage and Post Enterprises

单位:点(point)

指标	Indicators	一季度 1st. Quarter	二季度 2st. Quarter	三季度 3st. Quarter	四季度 4st. Quarter
企业景气指数	Prosperity Index of Enterprises				
总指数	Combined Index	118.1	113.6	129.7	123.9
即期	Demand	106.5	109.7	125.8	125.8
预期	Expectation	125.8	116.1	132.3	122.6
企业家信心指数	Index of Confidence by Enterprisers				
总指数	Combined Index	107.7	101.3	132.3	121.9
即期	Demand	100.0	112.9	132.3	125.8
预期	Expectation	112.9	93.6	132.3	119.4
业务预订(比上季度)	Business Book (Compared with the Previous Quarter)				
指数	Index	77.4	83.9	90.3	100.0
增加(%)	Increase(%)	0.0	6.5	6.5	16.1
持平(%)	Flat(%)	77.4	71.0	77.4	67.7
减少(%)	Decrease(%)	22.6	22.6	16.1	16.1
业务量(下季度比本季度)	Business Volume (Next Quarter than the Quarter)				
指数	Index	116.1	103.2	112.9	119.4
增加(%)	Increase(%)	35.5	29.0	35.5	41.9
持平(%)	Flat(%)	45.2	45.2	41.9	35.5
减少(%)	Decrease(%)	19.4	25.8	22.6	22.6
盈利(亏损)变化	Changes of Profit(Loss)				
指数	Index	61.3	67.7	80.7	96.8
好于正常水平(%)	Better than Normal Level(%)	6.5	3.2	3.2	6.5
正常水平(%)	Normal Level(%)	48.4	61.3	74.2	83.9
差于正常水平(%)	Worse than Normal Level(%)	45.2	35.5	22.6	9.7
企业融资	Corporate Finance				
指数	Index	87.1	87.1	96.8	96.8
容易(%)	Easy(%)	16.1	12.9	16.1	16.1
一般(%)	General(%)	54.8	61.3	64.5	64.5
困难(%)	Difficulties(%)	29.0	25.8	19.4	19.4
用工计划(下季度比本季度)	Employment Plan (Next Quarter than the Quarter)				
指数	Index	112.9	96.8	100.0	106.5
增加(%)	Increase(%)	16.1	12.9	12.9	19.4
持平(%)	Flat(%)	80.7	71.0	74.2	67.7
减少(%)	Decrease(%)	3.2	16.1	12.9	12.9
固定资产投资(下季度比本季度)	Fixed Asset (Next Quarter than the Quarter)				
指数	Index	100.0	83.9	90.3	93.6
增加(%)	Increase(%)	16.1	9.7	16.1	12.9
持平(%)	Flat(%)	67.7	64.5	58.1	67.7
减少(%)	Decrease(%)	16.1	25.8	25.8	19.4
人工成本(比上季度)	Labor Cost (Compared with the Previous Quarter)				
指数	Index	58.1	64.5	64.5	74.2
下降(%)	Decline(%)	3.2	9.7	6.5	3.2
持平(%)	Flat(%)	51.6	45.2	51.6	67.7
上升(%)	Rise(%)	45.2	45.2	41.9	29.0
场租成本(比上季度)	Pict Rental Cost (Compared with the Previous Quarter)				
指数	Index	58.1	67.7	83.9	83.9
下降(%)	Decline(%)	3.2	3.2	6.5	6.5
持平(%)	Flat(%)	51.6	61.3	71.0	71.0
上升(%)	Rise(%)	45.2	35.5	22.6	22.6

表 14－6　批发和零售业企业景气状况(2013)
Prosperity Index of Wholesale and Retail Sale Enterprises

单位:点(point)

指标	Indicators	一季度 1st. Quarter	二季度 2st. Quarter	三季度 3st. Quarter	四季度 4st. Quarter
企业景气指数	Prosperity Index of Enterprises				
总指数	Combined Index	119.2	114.2	122.1	109.6
即期	Demand	116.7	110.4	120.8	108.3
预期	Expectation	120.8	116.7	122.9	110.4
企业家信心指数	Index of Confidence by Enterprisers				
总指数	Combined Index	116.3	96.3	123.3	110.0
即期	Demand	125.0	100.0	120.8	112.5
预期	Expectation	110.4	93.8	125.0	108.3
购货合同	Purchase Contract				
指数	Index	83.3	77.1	83.3	85.4
增加(%)	Increase(%)	10.4	2.1	2.1	2.1
持平(%)	Flat(%)	62.5	72.9	79.2	81.3
减少(%)	Decrease(%)	27.1	25.0	18.8	16.7
商品销售(下季度比本季度)	Total Sales of Goods (Next Quarter than the Quarter)				
指数	Index	89.6	87.5	93.8	102.1
较多(%)	More(%)	27.1	27.1	22.9	33.3
一般(%)	General(%)	35.4	33.3	47.9	35.4
较少(%)	Less(%)	37.5	39.6	29.2	31.3
商品库存	Inventory of Goods				
指数	Index	81.3	81.3	81.3	85.4
低于正常水平(%)	Below the Normal Level (%)	6.3	4.2	6.3	6.3
正常水平(%)	Normal Level (%)	68.8	72.9	68.8	72.9
高于正常水平(%)	Higher than Normal Level (%)	25.0	22.9	25.0	20.8
盈利(亏损)变化	Changes of Profit(Loss)				
指数	Index	79.2	72.9	77.1	70.8
好于正常水平(%)	Better than Normal Level(%)	8.3	4.2	6.3	4.2
正常水平(%)	Normal Level(%)	62.5	64.6	64.6	62.5
差于正常水平(%)	Worse than Normal Level(%)	29.2	31.3	29.2	33.3

表 14—6 续表 Continued 单位:点(point)

指标	Indicators	一季度 1st. Quarter	二季度 2st. Quarter	三季度 3st. Quarter	四季度 4st. Quarter
企业融资	Corporate Finance				
指数	Index	106.3	114.6	114.6	112.5
容易(%)	Easy(%)	18.8	20.8	20.8	22.9
一般(%)	General(%)	68.8	72.9	72.9	66.7
困难(%)	Difficulties(%)	12.5	6.3	6.3	10.4
用工计划(下季度比本季度)	Employment Plan (Next Quarter than the Quarter)				
指数	Index	100.0	106.3	102.1	104.2
增加(%)	Increase(%)	8.3	12.5	10.4	14.6
持平(%)	Flat(%)	83.3	81.3	81.3	75.0
减少(%)	Decrease(%)	8.3	6.3	8.3	10.4
固定资产投资(下季度比本季度)	Fixed Asset (Next Quarter than the Quarter)				
指数	Index	91.7	97.9	93.8	93.8
增加(%)	Increase(%)	14.6	10.4	8.3	8.3
持平(%)	Flat(%)	62.5	77.1	77.1	77.1
减少(%)	Decrease(%)	22.9	12.5	14.6	14.6
人工成本(比上季度)	Labor Cost (Compared with the Previous Quarter)				
指数	Index	75.0	87.5	72.9	70.8
下降(%)	Decline(%)	8.3	12.5	8.3	6.3
持平(%)	Flat(%)	58.3	62.5	56.3	58.3
上升(%)	Rise(%)	33.3	25.0	35.4	35.4
场租成本(比上季度)	Rental Cost (Compared with the Previous Quarter)				
指数	Index	100.0	100.0	100.0	100.0
下降(%)	Decline(%)	0.0	0.0	0.0	0.0
持平(%)	Flat(%)	100.0	100.0	100.0	100.0
上升(%)	Rise(%)	0.0	0.0	0.0	0.0

表 14—7 住宿和餐饮业企业景气状况(2013)
Prosperity Index of Hotels and Catering Trade Enterprises

单位:点(point)

指标	Indicators	一季度 1st. Quarter	二季度 2st. Quarter	三季度 3st. Quarter	四季度 4st. Quarter
企业景气指数	Prosperity Index of Enterprises				
总指数	Combined Index	77.4	74.8	85.2	61.3
即期	Demand	58.1	71.0	67.7	61.3
预期	Expectation	90.3	77.4	96.8	61.3
企业家信心指数	Index of Confidence by Enterprisers				
总指数	Combined Index	95.5	76.8	88.4	56.8
即期	Demand	83.9	80.7	61.3	64.5
预期	Expectation	103.2	74.2	106.5	51.6
业务预订(比上季度)	Business Book (Compared with the Previous Quarter)				
指数	Index	32.3	22.6	32.3	35.5
增加(%)	Increase(%)	3.2	3.2	0.0	6.5
持平(%)	Flat(%)	25.8	16.1	32.3	22.6
减少(%)	Decrease(%)	71.0	80.7	67.7	71.0
业务量(比上季度)	Business Volume (Compared with the Previous Quarter)				
指数	Index	3.2	25.8	25.8	19.4
增加(%)	Increase(%)	0.0	9.7	3.2	3.2
持平(%)	Flat(%)	3.2	6.5	19.4	12.9
减少(%)	Decrease(%)	96.8	83.9	77.4	83.9
客房出租	Room Occupancy				
指数	Index	67.7	61.3	71.0	67.7
80%以上(%)	More than 80%	9.7	6.5	6.5	6.5
50—80%(%)	50—80%	48.4	48.4	58.1	54.8
50%以下(%)	Below than 50%	41.9	45.2	35.5	38.7
盈利(亏损)变化	Changes of Profit(Loss)				
指数	Index	29.0	19.4	25.8	38.7
好于正常水平(%)	Better than Normal Level(%)	3.2	0.0	0.0	6.5
正常水平(%)	Normal Level(%)	22.6	19.4	25.8	25.8
差于正常水平(%)	Worse than Normal Level(%)	74.2	80.7	74.2	67.7

表 14－7 续表 Continued

单位：点(point)

指标	Indicators	一季度 1st. Quarter	二季度 2st. Quarter	三季度 3st. Quarter	四季度 4st. Quarter
企业融资	Corporate Finance				
指数	Index	106.5	90.3	90.3	77.4
容易(%)	Easy(%)	22.6	6.5	9.7	9.7
一般(%)	General(%)	61.3	77.4	71.0	58.1
困难(%)	Difficulties(%)	16.1	16.1	19.4	32.3
用工计划(下季度比本季度)	Employment Plan (Next Quarter than the Quarter)				
指数	Index	80.7	87.1	106.5	103.2
增加(%)	Increase(%)	12.9	19.4	22.6	25.8
持平(%)	Flat(%)	54.8	48.4	61.3	51.6
减少(%)	Decrease(%)	32.3	32.3	16.1	22.6
固定资产投资(下季度比本季度)	Fixed Asset (Next Quarter than the Quarter)				
指数	Index	83.9	93.6	90.3	80.7
增加(%)	Increase(%)	9.7	16.1	19.4	16.1
持平(%)	Flat(%)	64.5	61.3	51.6	48.4
减少(%)	Decrease(%)	25.8	22.6	29.0	35.5
人工成本(比上季度)	Labor Cost (Compared with the Previous Quarter)				
指数	Index	51.6	74.2	77.4	61.3
下降(%)	Decline(%)	3.2	19.4	12.9	9.7
持平(%)	Flat(%)	45.2	35.5	51.6	41.9
上升(%)	Rise(%)	51.6	45.2	35.5	48.4
物料成本(比上季度)	Material Cost (Compared with the Previous Quarter)				
指数	Index	77.4	77.4	93.6	64.5
下降(%)	Decline(%)	12.9	12.9	19.4	9.7
持平(%)	Flat(%)	51.6	51.6	54.8	45.2
上升(%)	Rise(%)	35.5	35.5	25.8	45.2

表 14—8　房地产业企业景气状况(2013)
Prosperity Index of Real Estate Enterprises

单位:点(point)

指标	Indicators	一季度 1st. Quarter	二季度 2st. Quarter	三季度 3st. Quarter	四季度 4st. Quarter
企业景气指数	Prosperity Index of Enterprises				
总指数	Combined Index	103.2	98.4	111.1	115.1
即期	Demand	107.9	107.9	107.9	113.5
预期	Expectation	100.0	92.1	113.2	116.2
企业家信心指数	Index of Confidence by Enterprisers				
总指数	Combined Index	91.6	90.5	108.4	94.1
即期	Demand	86.8	92.1	113.2	97.3
预期	Expectation	94.7	89.5	105.3	91.9
土地购置(比上季度)	Acquisition of Land (Compared with the Previous Quarter)				
指数	Index	89.5	92.1	102.6	94.6
增加(%)	Increase(%)	7.9	5.3	13.2	5.4
持平(%)	Flat(%)	73.7	81.6	76.3	83.8
减少(%)	Decrease(%)	18.4	13.2	10.5	10.8
土地购置(下季度比本季度)	Acquisition of Land (Next Quarter than the Quarter)				
指数	Index	92.1	92.1	86.8	100.0
增加(%)	Increase(%)	10.5	2.6	5.3	5.4
持平(%)	Flat(%)	71.1	86.8	76.3	89.2
减少(%)	Decrease(%)	18.4	10.5	18.4	5.4
商品房预售(比上季度)	Commercial House Advance Sold (Compared with the Previous Quarter)				
指数	Index	84.2	86.8	84.2	97.3
增加(%)	Increase(%)	18.4	18.4	18.4	24.3
持平(%)	Flat(%)	47.4	50.0	47.4	48.7
减少(%)	Decrease(%)	34.2	31.6	34.2	27.0
商品房销售(包括预售)价格(比上季度)	Commercial Housing Sales (including Pre — sale) Price (Compared with the Previous Quarter)				
指数	Index	100.0	97.4	81.6	86.5
上升(%)	Rise(%)	5.3	5.3	2.6	2.7
持平(%)	Flat(%)	89.5	86.8	76.3	81.1
下降(%)	Decline(%)	5.3	7.9	21.1	16.2
商品房销售(包括预售)价格(下季度比本季度)	Commercial Housing Sales (including Pre — sale) Price (Next Quarter than the Quarter)				
指数	Index	94.7	97.4	100.0	94.6
上升(%)	Rise(%)	5.3	7.9	7.9	8.1
持平(%)	Flat(%)	84.2	81.6	84.2	78.4
下降(%)	Decline(%)	10.5	10.5	7.9	13.5

表 14—8 续表 Continued

单位:点(point)

指标	Indicators	一季度 1st. Quarter	二季度 2st. Quarter	三季度 3st. Quarter	四季度 4st. Quarter
待售商品房(上季度)	Commercial housing for sale (the Previous Quarter)				
指数	Index	150.0	144.7	147.4	135.1
增加(%)	Increase(%)	57.9	50.0	55.3	46.0
持平(%)	Flat(%)	34.2	44.7	36.8	43.2
减少(%)	Decrease(%)	7.9	5.3	7.9	10.8
盈利(亏损)变化	Changes of Profit(Loss)				
指数	Index	94.7	81.6	81.6	81.1
好于正常水平(%)	Better than Normal Level(%)	5.3	2.6	0.0	0.0
正常水平(%)	Normal Level(%)	84.2	76.3	81.6	81.1
差于正常水平(%)	Worse than Normal Level(%)	10.5	21.1	18.4	18.9
企业融资	Corporate Finance				
指数	Index	81.6	73.7	73.7	73.0
容易(%)	Easy(%)	5.3	0.0	5.3	2.7
一般(%)	General(%)	71.1	73.7	63.2	67.6
困难(%)	Difficulties(%)	23.7	26.3	31.6	29.7
用工计划(下季度比本季度)	Employment Plan (Next Quarter than the Quarter)				
指数	Index	107.9	94.7	92.1	97.3
增加(%)	Increase(%)	23.7	7.9	2.6	13.5
持平(%)	Flat(%)	60.5	79.0	86.8	70.3
减少(%)	Decrease(%)	15.8	13.2	10.5	16.2
固定资产投资(下季度比本季度)	Fixed Asset (Next Quarter than the Quarter)				
指数	Index	94.7	84.2	100.0	97.3
增加(%)	Increase(%)	15.8	18.4	18.4	16.2
持平(%)	Flat(%)	63.2	47.4	63.2	64.9
减少(%)	Decrease(%)	21.1	34.2	18.4	18.9
人工成本(比上季度)	Labor Cost (Compared with the Previous Quarter)				
指数	Index	81.6	76.3	76.3	78.4
下降(%)	Decline(%)	5.3	5.3	2.6	5.4
持平(%)	Flat(%)	71.1	65.8	71.1	67.6
上升(%)	Rise(%)	23.7	29.0	26.3	27.0
土地购置价格(比上季度)	Land Purchase Price (Compared with the Previous Quarter)				
指数	Index	86.8	89.5	92.1	97.3
下降(%)	Decline(%)	2.6	0.0	0.0	2.7
持平(%)	Flat(%)	81.6	89.5	92.1	91.9
上升(%)	Rise(%)	15.8	10.5	7.9	5.4

表 14—9 社会服务业企业景气状况(2013)
Prosperity Index of Social Services Enterprises

单位:点(point)

指标	Indicators	一季度 1st. Quarter	二季度 2st. Quarter	三季度 3st. Quarter	四季度 4st. Quarter
企业景气指数	Prosperity Index of Enterprises				
总指数	Combined Index	130.5	129.0	126.5	126.3
即期	Demand	127.5	127.5	125.0	126.3
预期	Expectation	132.5	130.0	127.5	126.3
企业家信心指数	Index of Confidence by Enterprisers				
总指数	Combined Index	129.5	126.0	126.5	131.1
即期	Demand	125.0	127.5	125.0	134.2
预期	Expectation	132.5	125.0	127.5	129.0
服务预订(比上季度)	Reservation Services (Compared with the Previous Quarter)				
指数	Index	97.5	100.0	92.5	92.1
增加(%)	Increase(%)	7.5	10.0	5.0	2.6
持平(%)	Flat(%)	82.5	80.0	82.5	86.8
减少(%)	Decrease(%)	10.0	10.0	12.5	10.5
业务量(比去年同期)	Business Volume(year—on—year)				
指数	Index	95.0	97.5	95.0	126.3
增加(%)	Increase(%)	17.5	22.5	20.0	39.5
持平(%)	Flat(%)	60.0	52.5	55.0	47.4
减少(%)	Decrease(%)	22.5	25.0	25.0	13.2
盈利(亏损)变化	Changes of Profit(Loss)				
指数	Index	90.0	87.5	90.0	97.4
好于正常水平(%)	Better than Normal Level(%)	7.5	10.0	7.5	13.2
正常水平(%)	Normal Level(%)	75.0	67.5	75.0	71.1
差于正常水平(%)	Worse than Normal Level(%)	17.5	22.5	17.5	15.8
企业融资	Corporate Finance				
指数	Index	115.0	105.0	107.5	107.9
容易(%)	Easy(%)	22.5	17.5	12.5	18.4
一般(%)	General(%)	70.0	70.0	82.5	71.1
困难(%)	Difficulties(%)	7.5	12.5	5.0	10.5
用工计划(下季度比本季度)	Employment Plan (Next Quarter than the Quarter)				
指数	Index	117.5	100.0	97.5	89.5
增加(%)	Increase(%)	20.0	17.5	7.5	2.6
持平(%)	Flat(%)	77.5	65.0	82.5	84.2
减少(%)	Decrease(%)	2.5	17.5	10.0	13.2
固定资产投资(下季度比本季度)	Fixed Asset (Next Quarter than the Quarter)				
指数	Index	100.0	102.5	102.5	107.9
增加(%)	Increase(%)	10.0	17.5	15.0	18.4
持平(%)	Flat(%)	80.0	67.5	72.5	71.1
减少(%)	Decrease(%)	10.0	15.0	12.5	10.5
人工成本(比上季度)	Labor Cost (Compared with the Previous Quarter)				
指数	Index	50.0	50.0	67.5	63.2
下降(%)	Decline(%)	2.5	2.5	5.0	5.3
持平(%)	Flat(%)	45.0	45.0	57.5	52.6
上升(%)	Rise(%)	52.5	52.5	37.5	42.1
物料成本(比上季度)	Material Cost (Compared with the Previous Quarter)				
指数	Index	70.0	57.5	80.0	81.6
下降(%)	Decline(%)	10.0	5.0	7.5	10.5
持平(%)	Flat(%)	50.0	47.5	65.0	60.5
上升(%)	Rise(%)	40.0	47.5	27.5	29.0

表 14—10　信息传输、计算机服务和软件业企业景气状况(2013)
Prosperity Index of Information Transmission,Computer Service and Software Enterprises

单位:点(point)

指标	Indicators	一季度 1st. Quarter	二季度 2st. Quarter	三季度 3st. Quarter	四季度 4st. Quarter
企业景气指数	Prosperity Index of Enterprises				
总指数	Combined Index	136.8	133.7	137.4	142.6
即期	Demand	121.1	121.1	126.3	147.4
预期	Expectation	147.4	142.1	144.7	139.5
企业家信心指数	Index of Confidence by Enterprisers				
总指数	Combined Index	140.0	138.4	141.1	140.5
即期	Demand	144.7	144.7	147.4	150.0
预期	Expectation	136.8	134.2	136.8	134.2
产品订货	Products Order				
指数	Index	79.0	92.1	94.7	105.3
较多(%)	More(%)	2.6	7.9	5.3	18.4
一般(%)	Flat(%)	73.7	76.3	84.2	68.4
较少(%)	Less(%)	23.7	15.8	10.5	13.2
营业收入(比去年同期)	Business Income(year—on—year)				
指数	Index	92.1	110.5	113.2	134.2
增加(%)	Increase(%)	26.3	39.5	42.1	55.3
持平(%)	Flat(%)	39.5	31.6	29.0	23.7
减少(%)	Decrease(%)	34.2	29.0	29.0	21.1
盈利(亏损)变化	Changes of Profit(Loss)				
指数	Index	68.4	73.7	76.3	89.5
好于正常水平(%)	Better than Normal Level(%)	0.0	7.9	2.6	18.4
正常水平(%)	Normal Level(%)	68.4	57.9	71.1	52.6
差于正常水平(%)	Worse than Normal Level(%)	31.6	34.2	26.3	29.0
企业融资	Corporate Finance				
指数	Index	107.9	107.9	100.0	97.4
容易(%)	Easy(%)	26.3	18.4	18.4	21.1
一般(%)	General(%)	55.3	71.1	63.2	55.3
困难(%)	Difficulties(%)	15.8	10.5	15.8	21.1
用工计划(下季度比本季度)	Employment Plan (Next Quarter than the Quarter)				
指数	Index	118.4	113.2	110.5	102.6
增加(%)	Increase(%)	26.3	29.0	21.1	15.8
持平(%)	Flat(%)	65.8	55.3	68.4	71.1
减少(%)	Decrease(%)	7.9	15.8	10.5	13.2
固定资产投资(下季度比本季度)	Fixed Asset (Next Quarter than the Quarter)				
指数	Index	94.7	100.0	89.5	81.6
增加(%)	Increase(%)	13.2	15.8	13.2	13.2
持平(%)	Flat(%)	68.4	68.4	63.2	55.3
减少(%)	Decrease(%)	18.4	15.8	23.7	31.6
人工成本(比上季度)	Labor Cost (Compared with the Previous Quarter)				
指数	Index	81.6	71.1	81.6	73.7
下降(%)	Decline(%)	13.2	5.3	7.9	2.6
持平(%)	Flat(%)	55.3	60.5	65.8	68.4
上升(%)	Rise(%)	31.6	34.2	26.3	29.0
物料成本(比上季度)	Material Cost (Compared with the Previous Quarter)				
指数	Index	63.2	68.4	57.9	60.5
下降(%)	Decline(%)	7.9	5.3	7.9	0.0
持平(%)	Flat(%)	47.4	57.9	42.1	60.5
上升(%)	Rise(%)	44.7	36.8	50.0	39.5

表 14—11　部分年份企业家信心指数
Index of Confidence on Macro Economy of Enterprisers in Recent Years

单位：点(point)

年份 year	一季度 1st. Quarter	二季度 2st. Quarter	三季度 3st. Quarter	四季度 4st. Quarter
1999	113.1	109.8	108.2	110.7
2000	131.5	133.7	127.3	133.2
2001	142.2	135.6	133.0	120.9
2002	136.5	138.0	146.0	145.1
2003	145.4	133.7	149.8	148.9
2004	148.3	141.1	139.7	133.4
2005	137.1	132.2	130.4	132.0
2006	138.3	130.7	132.8	139.4
2007	139.0	140.5	137.8	137.1
2008	123.4	109.6	106.7	88.8
2009	89.1	104.6	115.1	123.4
2010	137.3	135.0	138.2	140.1
2011	132.6	126.1	126.1	111.1
2012 指数	118.8	115.6	110.1	117.9
2012 即期	114.1	114.9	109.8	117.7
2012 预期	121.9	116.1	110.3	118.0
2013 指数	122.6	114.5	125.7	118.2
2013 即期	119.9	114.9	124.0	122.7
2013 预期	124.4	114.1	126.8	115.2

表 14—12　部分年份企业景气指数
Prosperity Index of Enterprises in Recent Years

单位：点(point)

年份 year	一季度 1st. Quarter	二季度 2st. Quarter	三季度 3st. Quarter	四季度 4st. Quarter
1999	124.5	119.3	117.3	118.2
2000	122.7	131.8	126.7	125.8
2001	12.9	128.1	124.5	127.3
2002	134.2	144.5	143.1	147.9
2003	144.3	131.8	140.7	153.4
2004	148.7	140.2	138.1	144.4
2005	136.5	135.3	136.1	143.8
2006	130.7	134.6	139.8	146.5
2007	136.9	145.8	137.0	137.5
2008	119.9	122.2	108.1	102.1
2009	98.4	114.1	124.5	126.4
2010	137.9	142.6	140.8	146.3
2011	135.5	134.1	133.8	132.8
2012 指数	126.5	126.0	120.6	123.7
2012 即期	117.0	123.9	116.3	125.9
2012 预期	132.8	127.4	123.5	122.1
2013 指数	130.8	122.6	127.9	122.1
2013 即期	123.2	120.6	125.2	128.0
2013 预期	135.8	124.0	129.6	118.2

主要统计指标解释

【企业家信心指数】 也称宏观经济景气指数。是根据企业决策者对企业外部市场经济环境与宏观政策的认识、看法、判断与预期(对"乐观"、"一般"、"不乐观"的选择)而编制的指数,反映企业决策者对国家宏观经济发展的信心和预期,是企业决策者对当前宏观经济状况及未来走势的一种感受、体验与期望。

【企业景气指数】 也称企业综合生产经营景气指数。是根据企业决策者对本企业当前生产经营情况的判断及未来企业生产经营状况的预期(对"良好"、"一般"、"不佳"的选择)而编制的指数,是企业决策者对企业生产经营现状及未来景气动向的一种综合评价和判断。

【景气指数】 又称景气度,是对企业景气调查中定性指标的定量描述,以直观地反映经济所处的状态。景气指数采用纯正数形式表示,以 100 为临界值,取值范围在 0—200 之间。当景气指数大于 100 点时,表明经济状况趋于上升或改善,处于景气状态;当景气指数小于 100 点时,表明经济状况趋于下降或恶化,处于不景气状态。

2012 年之后改变计算方法:

1. 计算方法改进说明:为更充分体现企业景气调查对经济形势的预判功能,从 2012 年一季度开始,企业景气指数的计算方法,改进为对当前形势的判断和对未来预期的综合,并赋予预期相对更高的权重。

2、指数计算方法:企业景气指数=0.4×即期企业景气指数+0.6×预期企业景气指数;即期企业景气指数=企业负责人对本季度本企业综合经营状况回答良好比重－回答不佳的比重＋100;预期企业景气指数=企业负责人对预计下季度本企业综合经营状况回答良好比重－回答不佳的比重＋100。

Explanatory Notes on Main Statistical Indicators

【Entrepreneur Confidence Index】 As well as Macroeconomic Business Cycle Index, which is indexed according to the entrepreneurs' opinions, consideration, estimations and expectations (choice of "optimistic", "general" and "miserable") on outer economic environment and macroeconomic policies, to reflect general confidence about the macroeconomic environment of entrepreneurs of the business deciders, and also to reflect the situation and trend of the macroeconomics. **【Enterprise Business Prosperity Index】** As well as Enterprise General Production and Management Business Cycle Index, which is indexed according to estimations and expectations (choice of "good", "general" and "bad") of general management of products at present and in the future, to reflect the enterprisers' evaluation and judgement of the production and management status comprehensively. **【The range of Business Prosperity Index is between 0—200】** As well as Booming Index, which uses the positive to reflect the status of economy directly. 100 is the critical value of Business Cycle Index (ranges from 0 to 200) which shows unobvious change of business cycle. 100—200 is the prosperous space interval, which shows ascending and improving economic status, closer to 200 more prosperous. 0—100 is the unprosperous space interval, which shows descending and deteriorating economic status, closer to 0 more unprosperous.

中国统计出版社最新图书简目

(仅供参考,以最后出书为准)

统计资料

综合类：中国统计年鉴 中国统计摘要 中国发展报告

国际资料类：国际统计年鉴 金砖国家联合统计手册 世界能源资源年鉴

区域资料类：中国区域经济统计年鉴 中国县域统计年鉴 中国城市统计年鉴 中国农村统计年鉴 中国地区经济监测报告

经贸与投资类：中国贸易外经统计年鉴 中国对外直接投资统计公报 中国商品交易市场统计年鉴 大中型批发零售和住宿餐饮企业统计年鉴 中国零售和餐饮连锁企业统计年鉴

住户与物价类：中国住户调查年鉴 中国价格统计年鉴 中国农产品价格调查年鉴 全国农产品成本收益资料汇编

资源与环境类：中国环境统计年鉴 中国能源统计年鉴

产业类：中国工业统计年鉴 中国建筑业统计年鉴 中国房地产统计年鉴 中国第三产业统计年鉴 中国证券期货统计年鉴

科技类：中国科技统计年鉴 中国高技术产业统计年鉴 工业企业科技活动资料

人口与就业类：中国劳动统计年鉴 中国人口和就业统计年鉴 中国人才资源统计报告

社会与文化类：中国社会统计年鉴 中国文化及相关产业统计年鉴

公共管理类：中国民政统计年鉴 中国民族统计年鉴 中国乡镇街道行政区域简册

省级综合统计年鉴系列

北京 天津 河北 山西 内蒙古 辽宁 吉林 黑龙江 上海 江苏 浙江 安徽 福建 江西 山东 河南 湖北 湖南 广东 广西 海南 重庆 四川 贵州 云南 西藏 陕西 甘肃 青海 宁夏 新疆 新疆生产建设兵团

市(县)级综合统计年鉴系列

天津滨海新区 石家庄 唐山 邯郸 太原 大同 阳泉 长治 晋城 朔州 晋中 运城 忻州 临汾 呼和浩特 鄂尔多斯 包头 沈阳 大连 长春 吉林市 四平 哈尔滨 黑龙江垦区 上海浦东新区 南京 无锡 徐州 常州 苏州 南通 连云港 淮安 盐城 扬州 镇江 泰州 宿迁 江阴 丹阳 杭州 宁波 温州 嘉兴 绍兴 金华 衢州 舟山 台州 丽水 合肥 福州 厦门 宁德 福州经济技术开发区 南昌 济南 青岛 郑州 洛阳 平顶山 三门峡 南阳 武汉 十堰 荆州 宜昌 荆门 咸宁 长沙 广州 深圳 惠州 东莞 南宁 柳州 桂林 来宾 海口 三亚 成都 贵阳 昆明 西安 兰州 庆阳 银川 乌鲁木齐 兵团一师 兵团十师

调查年鉴系列

山西 内蒙古 吉林 辽宁 上海 福建 湖北 广西 重庆 四川 云南 甘肃 宁夏 新疆 南宁 桂林

“十二五”规划教材

统计学（经济管理类专业本科适用，单薇 等） 抽样调查理论与方法（冯士雍 等）

贝叶斯统计（茆诗松 等） 统计学（黄良文 等） 试验设计（茆诗松 等）

统计学：从数据到结论（吴喜之） 医学统计学（于浩） 统计学（经济、管理类专业基础教材，张小斐）

概率论与数理统计三十三讲（魏振军） 概率论与数理统计三十三：学习指导与习题解答（魏振军）

非参数统计（吴喜之 等） 统计学：经济与管理中的数据分析（李慧云 等）

卫生管理统计学（新编医学院校基础课教材，尚磊） 医院统计学（新编医学院校基础课教材，徐天和 等）

社会统计学（蒋萍 等） 现代金融投资统计分析（李腊生 等）

国民经济核算初级教程（经济类、统计类、管理类专业适用，蒋萍 等）

重点图书

新中国65年 新编英汉汉英统计大词典 中华医学统计百科全书

挑大学选专业2014—考研择校指南 挑大学选专业2014—高考志愿填报指南